D1370517

The Dryden Press

Publications in Interpersonal Relations

GENERAL EDITOR

THEODORE M. NEWCOMB

UNIVERSITY OF MICHIGAN

RUTH L. MUNROE

SCHOOLS OF PSYCHOANALYTIC THOUGHT

An Exposition, Critique, and
Attempt at Integration

THE DRYDEN PRESS · PUBLISHERS

PREFACE

I AM A PSYCHOLOGIST, writing about psychoanalytic schools of thought for students, for fellow psychologists, for social workers, for social scientists in variety, for doctors whose work lies outside the realm of mental disorder, for laymen with the patience to follow a lengthy, semitechnical account of ideas they hear about frequently—and also for psychoanalysts who either want information about schools other than the one in which they are carefully trained or are curious as to what a psychologist does with the problem of integration.

Most readers know pretty well what is meant by the label "psychologist" today,* and may be interested in my special qualifications for writing about psychoanalysis. A few readers, however, may wish for a brief explanation of the difference between the two fields.

"Psychoanalysis"† began around 1890 as an offshoot of psychiatry—the branch of *medicine* concerned with mental illness. Many of its peculiarities as a scientific field are due to the fact that it was conceived and guided for forty years by a towering genius, Sigmund Freud. This fact goes far to explain the intransigent loyalties and rebellions within psychoanalysis which make a book such as this one necessary. The point of emphasis here, however, is the *medical* tradition behind Freud and almost all other analysts.‡ The medical

* I shall use the term in quotation marks occasionally throughout this book when I wish to refer to this special scientific discipline without tedious explanation. The quotation marks serve to *identify* a discipline to which I am proud to belong.

† I shall not use quotation marks for the major topic of this book beyond this initial exposition of its special place in psychological science.

‡ The schools reported in this book vary in the rigor of their requirements for medical training. Membership in the American Psychoanalytic Association (Freudian) requires the M.D. degree, a psychiatric residency, and several years of specialized analytic training: courses, a personal (didactic) analysis, analysis of patients under supervision (control) during which the candidate reports weekly to a senior analyst on the course of treatment with his (the junior analyst's) patient.

tradition rests upon care for the patient as an individual and upon understanding of the complex but identifiable *syndrome* of his disease (diagnosis and treatment). Doctors are homespun philosophers, as a rule, and medicine tends to rely for its progress more upon study of the individual case than upon a rigorous, formalized scientific methodology.

"Psychology" derives historically from philosophy. Around 1890, also, were established the first "psychological" laboratories effectively proclaiming that the human mind is subject to systematic empirical investigation. In most colleges these laboratories remained for many years a part of research and teaching under the official aegis of the department of philosophy. Full liberation is a matter of recent decades. Apart from the specialized training programs set up in the universities, there are still no schools for "psychologists," whereas most of the psychoanalytic schools of thought maintain separate "institutes." (In fact, psychoanalytic units in medical schools are of recent development.)

"Psychologists" now work in mental hospitals, engage in psychotherapy, and are active consultants in schools, in industry, in the armed forces, in almost every practical endeavor. I think one may still say, however, that our basic training emphasizes the original orientation. The Ph.D. program requires extensive familiarity with theoretical concepts and the tools of scientific inquiry developed in our field. Whatever his area of specialization, every "psychologist" is taught the principles of scientific method as applied in the laboratory, in statistical analysis of data with due care for the nature of their provenance, in "tests."

In America especially, "psychology" has perhaps at times become so infatuated with its methodologies as to apply them pedantically to the detriment of its essential aim—the understanding of people. Deliberate limitation of the *person* to such aspects of his behavior as we can study under scientifically controlled conditions makes it difficult to develop insights into trends and relationships among trends beyond our original hypothesis.

The psychoanalyst, dealing directly with patients, may be biased. Patients are atypical by definition. But patients are *people*. No other discipline has been *allowed* such close, continued study of the functioning person-as-a-whole. In many ways it may be easier to correct for the atypical quality of a "patient" group than for the selective limitation of behavior imposed by a standardized psychological test or the hypothesis which governs an experiment or controlled

---

One may sympathize with the feeling of analysts that a training so long and expensive, so vigilantly controlled by the professional association, entitles them to a certain preciousness about the label "psychoanalyst" and to some annoyance with people who pretend to understand psychoanalysis without this apprenticeship and the later experience as mature doctors.

observation with statistical check. The psychoanalyst is in an especially favored position for the study of *people*.

I think what bothers most of us outsiders who would like to use the formulations reached by psychoanalysts in their privileged study of the individual is the factor of *bias on the part of the observer*—the analyst himself in relation to the theoretical guide lines he uses in understanding, handling, and reporting the vividly individualized human material which makes up his working day. Reading this book about theories, we can relax into reasonable consideration. The *therapist* cannot pause for a detached theoretical review of all the possible interpretations of the bits of behavior presented moment by moment in the treatment session. Successful therapy is not scientific detachment. It is a creative experience between doctor and patient, no matter how "objective" or "nondirective" are the prescriptions for the doctor's approach. The difference between talking to a friend or a fakir (or to the sea and the mountains) and talking to an analyst lies precisely in the fact that the analyst does interpret the patient to himself on the basis of the broad understanding of human behavior which the analyst has learned in his training. For effective therapy, he must be prepared to handle the vagaries of his patients *as they arise* in relation to himself and to the patient's associates. At the present time such immediate understanding probably *must* be school-oriented in the sense of a secure frame of reference within which particular bits of behavior may be "placed" in quick evaluation of their deep meaning. The analyst needs a coherent theory, just as the surgeon needs a plan for a complex operation and cannot use small variations in technique unless he fully understands their relationship to his plan.

The "psychologist" (unless he happens also to be a psychoanalyst) is less directly involved in moment-by-moment experience with the patient at the deepest levels of personality function. Often familiar with the problems, data, and theories of psychoanalysis, he is more detached in his relationship to them. The philosophico-scientific tradition of his training may serve as a sort of critical balance wheel against the excesses of theories developed in such close relationship to the people whom the analyst is privileged to study in detail— his patients. This background may help him to discern major theoretical trends (significant similarities and differences among the various psychoanalytic schools) more effectively than the most broad-minded approach of a practicing analyst.

Something of this line of thought must have been in the mind of the director of The Dryden Press when he deliberately chose a "psychologist" to write a book about the various schools of psychoanalysis. He felt that a great many people of the kind described in my opening paragraph wanted to understand "psychoanalysis" as a serious scientific and therapeutic discipline—with help in forming an unbiased judgment among the clamorous, quarrelsomely different schools currently thought of as psychoanalytic. The experience of a "clinical psychologist" should be especially useful in providing information about the psychoanalytic schools, with a detachment and perspective one cannot expect from analysts who actively belong in one or another school. Moreover, he felt that an "outsider" could write better for fellow outsiders than any psychoanalyst who tried to be *fair* about the position of schools other than his own.

Among "psychologists," the director of the Press came to me because, he said, my name had been suggested repeatedly as a reputable member of the species who had had especially close contacts with psychoanalysis. I accepted his proposal to write the kind of book he described partly for the reasons he advanced but mainly because I had felt for years that I and many colleagues were borrowing ideas from psychoanalysis with a sort of patchwork eclecticism which we could not really defend. I selfishly welcomed the compulsion of writing a book as a means of forcing myself to think through concepts I was using every day as psychological technician, without the philosophico-scientific orientation to which I had been trained.

I felt, furthermore, that I was teaching a new crop of "psychologists" in a manner which did not support the old tradition in an overly narrow emphasis on methodology but which offered no replacement. I am indebted to many earnest young students who brought to my attention their utter bewilderment as to theoretical guide lines when a "test" (the Rorschach) is taught as a method requiring the clinical acumen of the examiner—without defining its clinical referents. The book here offered does not define the referents as neatly as the students might wish. I hope that possible referents to clinically oriented theories are well presented, and that my own comments continue the philosophico-scientific orientation described above as the essence of "psychology."

I should like to express appreciation of a publisher who has steadfastly encouraged the author of his choice in a book which was not only delayed far beyond the date initially proposed but which became much more voluminous than at first conceived. The book is still essentially an objective account of psychoanalytic schools of thought. Much time and space, however, have gone into a more serious attempt at an integrative approach than was originally planned.

If a book by a "psychologist" succeeds in preserving the flavor of psychoanalysis as a medical specialty, much of the credit belongs to my husband,

Dr. Bela Mittelmann—a psychoanalyst. He has patiently explained many obscure points of theory and has gently corrected tendencies toward a limited bookishness in reporting the analytic schools. He read most of the manuscript as it was being written, and he helped to clarify and crystallize the ideas which appear in this book. It is a measure of his stature that he has encouraged me to go my own way in writing, despite a tediously long gestation period for the book and my insistence on going off into problems which he considered secondary.

I shall explain in Chapter One the contribution, direct and indirect, of a great many other psychoanalysts and friends toward this book. The list of people who have devoted a substantial amount of time to reading parts of the manuscript with critical attention has become so long that it is impossible to express indebtedness in a differentiated way. The understanding editorship of Stanley Burnshaw, Theodore M. Newcomb, and David Klein has been invaluable. The secretarial contribution of Laura Malkenson has been enhanced by a professional knowledge of the field far beyond what one expects of a secretary. Dr. David Beres read all of the "Freudian" section with friendly care for accuracy of statement and with illuminating comment on emphasis. Dr. Peter Glauber performed the same herculean task for the "non-Freudian" section. (Although Dr. Glauber is now a "Freudian," his first contacts in the field were with Adler, and he has retained a sympathetic interest in the so-called dissident developments.) I am especially grateful to these men for the time-consuming work of following my presentation through many chapters with steady sentence-by-sentence critique. Consulted on the accuracy of my account of his own work, Dr. Abram Kardiner asked to see the entire manuscript. I am indebted to him for occasional sharpened statements throughout the book, although he "skimmed" much of it, instead of reading with the attention to detail so valuable in the reading of Dr. Beres and Dr. Glauber. I mention again the self-evident importance of reading by Dr. Bela Mittelmann.

I am indebted very specifically to Dr. David Rapaport for much of the background and formulation of my discussion of ego psychology in Chapter Three, as for many other ideas. The pages labeled ego psychology are essentially an adaptation of an outline he supplied, amplified by Dr. Heinz Hartmann with sympathy for the effort of a "psychologist" to make her own synthesis in this area.

I cannot mention by name the students and friends outside the profession whose comments have been used. Their name is legion, and their contribution valuable on many counts. Many professional psychoanalysts and "psychologists" have read piecemeal whatever parts of the book belonged in their special province. Since I cannot explain every contact with school experts in detail, I resort to a simple listing of the names of people whose comments on the manuscript have been extensively used. A few readers whose contribution was very important in early stages of writing have not seen later developments.*

For their helpful and sympathetic comment in specialized areas, I am grateful to Herbert Aptekar, Peter Blos, Lydia Burnshaw, Joseph Campbell, Alan Frank, Lawrence K. Frank, Mary Frank, Erich Fromm, Muriel Ivimey, Ernst Kris, Helen Lynd, Alexander Mintz, A. H. Maslow, Gardner Murphy, Lois Murphy, Molly Parkes, Clara Thompson, Ulrich Sonnemann, and Frances G. Wickes.

RUTH L. MUNROE

New York, N. Y.
June 1955

---

* Ernst Kris and Muriel Ivimey, especially. Several others did not see the manuscript in its last stages, but we have talked about it so often that I have no hesitation in assuming continuation or judicious modification of points made in early comment.

SYNOPTIC TABLE OF CONTENTS

(For full table of contents, see pages xiii to xvi)

CONTENTS

xiii

PART THREE

ADLER, HORNEY, FROMM, AND SULLIVAN

PART FOUR

JUNG AND RANK

PART FIVE

EPILOGUE

Part One

AN OVERVIEW

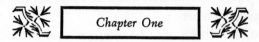

Chapter One

AN APPROACH TO PSYCHOANALYTIC THOUGHT

EACH OF THE SCHOOLS of psychoanalytic thought presented in this book is a theoretical system with an inner coherence of its own. In writing, I have tried to feel myself into each system as a whole, thinking for the nonce in the terms of its major premises and working through to its conclusions as if I were successively a Freudian, an Adlerian, a follower of Horney, Fromm, Sullivan, Jung, or Rank. My hope is that the writing is persuasive enough to invite the reader to a similar course, in contrast to the effort to judge each school at once according to its dicta concerning such isolated problems as he may consider of special interest.

For the inner coherence of a theoretical psychological system cannot be neglected if one is to understand its contribution. Its vocabulary and its interpretation of whole areas of human function, even the facts it reports, derive their dynamic significance from the context. Out of context, specific formulations have at best a sham convincingness often disapproved by the school itself; at worst they seem absurd or repellent. The tendency of people unfamiliar with the actual data of psychoanalysis, so largely drawn from observation of the unconscious under special conditions, is to select those aspects of all theories which most nearly approach their own conscious observations. The result is too often a patchwork eclecticism which misses the inner dynamics of all schools and fails to provide the meaningful hypotheses necessary for guidance, therapy, diagnosis, or research. No criticism or partial adoption of the views of any psychoanalytic school can be valid without a rather thorough grasp of its fundamental tenets.

Nevertheless, the schools must be compared and evaluated. Their several contributions must be used fruitfully and correctly by people whose field of specialization (psychology, social work, the social sciences, etc.) demands the valuable insights offered by psychoanalysis but precludes thorough immersion in its special methods of inquiry. Furthermore, each psychoanalytic school offers some insights peculiarly its own which, when considered in proper perspective, may prove of especial import to other disciplines.

To facilitate comparison and application to other fields, I have presented the schools according to a uniform broad outline of topics. This procedure entails certain difficulties which are avoided in the more usual technique of opening each account with the premises emphasized by the school discussed. One is sometimes forced to begin at the periphery, with topics relatively neglected by the system under consideration. In such cases a bald preliminary description of major tenets must be supplied if only to indicate why these topics have been neglected. As one attempts to explain the views of a writer on a set series of topics instead of allowing for a more organic development of his ideas, a certain amount of repetitiousness is inevitable. I feel, however, that the advantages of the outline outweigh the difficulties. One is less be-mused by the system-as-a-whole and can discern more clearly the broad areas of strength and weakness. Genuine parallels and differences among the schools stand out more sharply.

The outline is not very formidable; it is, in fact, hardly more than a common-sense grouping. I have deliberately phrased its topics in words which everybody knows but which are slightly strange in this context. What I hope to convey by them is a *neutral* orientation to the topic, asking the reader to lay aside, so far as he can, his prior convictions in order to listen—for a while— to the ideas of these analysts on topics of obvious importance.

THE TERMS OF THE ORGANISM

The first item of the outline is "The Terms of the Organism." It could be called "Biological Inheritance" or "Constitution" or "Human Nature," except that all these phrases have connotations that I should like to avoid.

The structure of any organism determines the nature of the basic demands it makes upon the environment and the extent and mode of its capacity to learn, to change itself or its surroundings. It sets certain terms which must be satisfied if life is to be maintained and within which adjustments can be made.

The human organism is a peculiarly flexible one as regards relations with the environment. Its flexibility is mediated by the complex development of the central nervous system; by a capacity for *symbolization* (concept formation) apparently much more elaborated than in any other species. Adjustments are made largely by means of the ability to interpret a situation from very small cues, *to compare cues before taking overt action*, whether remembered from experience or learned as cues—in short to think. This distinctively human capacity does not, however, imply a total revision of organismic structures developed over aeons of biological evolution. Like plants, we need oxygen. And our bodies are so similar to those of most mammals that medical procedures tried out successfully on guinea pigs usually work on humans as well.

What *are* the terms of the human organism? What are the demands it must make on the environment? What, that is, are its basic needs and goals? Granted that symbols of all kinds are crucially important for this animal with a big brain, how are they related to the structures he inherits as a living organism essentially similar to other animals?

It is a mistake to separate man's "animal" nature from his "spiritual" nature (or, more modestly, his symbolizing capacities) in a drastic manner as has been done by many religions, philosophies, and "scientific" theories. These two aspects of his nature belong together in any dynamic view of the functioning person. One cannot assign so and so much importance to "heredity" as against the measurable impact of "environment." One must be very cautious in describing "human nature" as different from animal nature, or as being the same in radically different societies with radically different types of symbolization.

Yet it is important to distinguish between those requirements of the person that are part of his being a human animal, so to speak, and those that proceed primarily from the cues he has learned—partly from his own experience, partly as the symbols hallowed in his society. The word *organism* is more dignified than "human animal" and more neutral in its connotations. I hope it conveys a sense of the continuity of man with all living creatures, without the flavor of primitive reactions often associated with the word "animal."

The word *terms* is intended to suggest a sense of the directions, conditions, and limits set by the organism in deliberate contrast to words which connote a set of specific inborn traits for "human nature." I quote from the

Oxford English Dictionary definition of *terms*: "Conditions or stipulations limiting what is to be granted or done . . . mutual relations between two parties."

THE TERMS OF THE MILIEU

The other party to the contract here considered is the world in which the organism lives. This landlord sets terms of his own without regard to the needs of his many tenants. Those who stay with him are either extremely compliant or work out complex agreements, among which the terms of man are the most brash. Man proposes to master his environment rather than adapt his body to it, to create a *human* world in which temperature is regulated by a thermostat instead of a furry skin, in which food comes so regularly and so neatly packaged that he is scarcely aware of the fact that the terms of his body require the unsportsmanlike killing of fellow animals on a grand scale. In general, man's needs as an organism, the terms he presents for tenancy on this planet, have become so confused with the terms he has imposed on his environment that it becomes difficult to say where one set of terms leaves off and the other begins. Nevertheless, the human organism must relate itself to the terms of its landlord, the world into which it is born. These terms are relatively fixed for each individual and must be studied in their own right.

Instead of calling the second item of the outline "The Terms of the Milieu," I might have called it "The Influence of the Environment." Perhaps the title should be limited to "Social Factors in Personality Development," since only passing mention is made of the effect of natural conditions, such as climate and disease, on human living. Our environment is essentially social, our own creation. I have preferred the word *milieu* as having less colorful connotations in psychological science than "environment." The word *terms* again has the connotation of limits or conditions less definitely set for the organism than is implied by the word "factors." Many aspects of our environment are determined by conditions beyond our control as individuals. But they do not necessarily affect our psychological reactions importantly or in the same way. I should like to get away from any notion of social conditions as directly "causing" specific variations in personality development, or as providing a series of "influences" which may be investigated as such and mechanically applied to human beings in complex relationship to a series of hereditary factors.

The essence of the heredity-environment problem is the dynamic interaction *between* the organism and its milieu from the moment of its existence.

No living action is possible without such interaction. Even plants grow differently under different conditions (terms) of weather and nourishment.

Once I transplanted what appeared to be a pretty "moss" from a sun-baked rock on a barren hillside to a more favorable spot in our rock garden, and I was annoyed when it turned into dull plants of everlasting, a foot tall. A botanist would, of course, have known at once the resources and limits of this "moss," its terms as an organism. It was environment that changed a "moss" to a flower, but only within its own nature. It could not possibly become a rose. I dolefully add that not all plants find the environment of our garden so encouraging to an effulgence of their organismic potential. The soil is often too poor or too rich, too dry or too wet, too alkaline or too acid, too sunny or too shaded to allow the lovely growth promised in the seed catalogues. We like the isolation of our summer place. So do the woodchucks. Their quite *external* depredations complicate the problem of intimate dynamic relations between organism and milieu in our garden, much as acts of God, wars, depressions, and the like complicate the problem in the human area—and with great variety in effect. Some plants become more luxuriant with woodchuck pruning. Others are so constituted that they do not flower that year if the main stalk is cut but start again another year from sound roots. Still others die forever.

This horticultural interlude is intended only as a very general analogy to human problems, which are, of course, much more complex. The familiar complexities of the garden may serve, however, as a corrective to the common tendency of people theorizing about people to separate constitutional and environmental factors with a foolish rigidity. People do not easily see themselves in their relation to their birth and experience with the flexible understanding they apply to plants and animals. Yet such understanding is urgently needed.

The difficulty does not lie wholly in the vanity of the human species considering itself, or in the bias bred in all of us by the special society within which we have lived. It is inherent in the nature of the human animal. All human beings are more alike in organismic structure than the varieties of plants which the gardener handles with care for their special nature. Yet individuals—and social groups—also present radical differences. The flexible learning process of the human animal is not so flexible that he can change his basic code of symbols overnight without reference to his organismic structure, but the significant cues for action he has developed in the course of living are of enormous importance.

In a book about psychoanalysis, it will not be possible to consider in detail the structure of societies, which to a very considerable extent sets the conditions (terms) for the experience of the individual. Social structures are human creations, essentially dependent on the psychological reactions of the individuals who make up "society." Societies also possess a certain autonomy of their own. No individual can buck his society without serious difficulties in his own life, whether he protests against its laws, its economic structure, or simply Mrs. Grundy. Moreover, he is profoundly influenced as an individual by the society within which he grows up and lives as an adult. The cues he learns from experience and the cues he is taught and the cues to which he must adapt himself are importantly conditioned by his society—in dynamic relation to his organismic needs.

For the most part psychoanalysts have been more interested in the individual than in the social conditions within which he grows and functions. Most analysts in actual practice take a milieu for granted. The milieu considered is the immediate family and the social factors which a particular patient actually has to cope with. Analysts, like other doctors, easily extend understanding of the patient to his life situation with more insight and tolerance than most laymen, but with no necessary special professional perspective toward "social factors."

The social *theorizing* of many analysts, including Freud himself, tends to emphasize the deep instinctual trends of individuals as expressed in social institutions and operating through them. No analyst has considered observation of such trends a *sufficient* explanation of specific events. A very large place is left for the influence of social, economic, and political factors which as "factors"—as durable institutions in their own right—work more or less independently of the psychological factor. Although the analyst disclaims special competence in evaluating the first three factors, he feels that he can contribute importantly toward understanding of the psychological factor. Stripped of its cautious preamble and elaboration, such theorizing often sounds as if the psychological factor were given major, if not exclusive importance in social theory.

Some analysts, including Freud himself, have tried to investigate the mechanisms whereby "society" influences the individual and vice versa. This seems to me the crux of the current problem of how the psychoanalytic contribution can be *used* in concrete understanding of social groups. The important question today is not so much the psychological factor *versus* social factors, or even *among* them in determining social trends, as it is the *between* relationship of organism to milieu, of the individual psyche to the conditions under which it grows and functions. I devote considerable attention to analysts who have addressed themselves specifically to the *psychosocial* problem (notably Kardiner, Roheim, Erikson, and Fromm). In reporting Freud's views, I have given more space to his analysis of *between* relationships than to his occasional summary statements concerning modern society as a whole.

My critical comment (set in the double-column format) will carry through an orientation toward a *psychosocial* statement of fundamental problems somewhat different from the position of the schools reported. I shall not offer "answers" to these problems. My hope is rather to suggest how questions may be formulated so as to use psychoanalytic data in fruitful conjunction with other modes of inquiry. Negative critique of psychoanalytic schools will often be addressed more to their failure to provide workable lines of empirical investigation along psychosocial lines than to difficulties in explaining the behavior of individuals in our own culture.

THE GENETIC PROCESS

The third item of my outline is called "The Genetic Process." It could be called "Child Psychology," except that the "child" is not the focus of interest in his own right. "The child" is discussed here as father to the man, with only incidental reference to childhood as such.

If personality is considered as essentially an emergent phenomenon, developing out of the relationship between the organism and its milieu, then the process of emergence becomes crucially important. *How* does personality develop? The early years must be of especial significance simply because they are the first and therefore may be expected in some measure to set the pattern for later learning. As the twig is bent, so the branch inclines. How firm is this early setting of pattern? Does it merely serve as a kind of orientation toward interpretation of later events or are some aspects of the infantile reactions preserved timelessly in the adult psyche by the mechanism of repression, as Freud supposed? Above all, what experiences are so important to the infant and young child as to influence profoundly the "set" of the emergent personality, or to occasion massive repression?

Everyone knows that all psychoanalysts stress the importance of the early years for personality development. Since I shall discuss this emphasis in the next chapter as one of the basic concepts of psychoanalysis, I shall not elaborate further here. The short space allotted to the genetic process in preliminary explanation is no measure of the space allotted in later exposition. On the contrary, I shall explain in a moment that I have chosen variations in interpretation of the genetic process for my major grouping of analytic schools—putting into Part II all those analysts who take the "sexual" (by Freud's definition) concerns of the child as especially determining in the growth process, in the development of personality; and putting into Parts III and IV those analysts who have emphasized "social" factors with more or less active repudiation of the special significance of "sexual" development.

THE DYNAMICS OF THE FUNCTIONING PERSONALITY

Up to this point, I have been able to translate the outline headings into familiar terms with little more difficulty than an effort to broaden concepts which the reader already knows under a more technical or a more popular label. I can think of no technical label for my fourth item more familiar than the title itself, but I can clarify my meaning by a popular question: What makes people tick?

Obviously the terms of the organism and the terms of the milieu and the way in which they come together emergently in the genetic process are crucial to the understanding of John Doe. But if we meet John, even on the analyst's couch, our concern is mainly with how he is making out as a person in his own life. Very probably he is what he is "because" his parents did not love him enough, or he was weaned too soon, or he was brought up in very bad circumstances, or something dreadful happened to him, or he married the wrong woman, or he got into the wrong job. Actually the "because" that I here follow with a lot of "or's" usually turns out to be followed by a lot of "and's." The important thing about John Doe is not so much his history, conveniently classified under scientific rubrics, but what he is actually doing with his life.

All psychoanalytic schools pay attention to these "or's" and "and's," plus many others, but their main concern is with John Doe as a functioning adult who—as a patient—presents very special problems of his own. I have already commented that psychoanalysis is essentially a medical specialty, and I shall point out occasionally that the analyst's emphasis on a specific line of thought may be related to the kind of patient that he mainly sees. Freud began with the study of "hysterics." Horney dealt mostly with the character neuroses of the upper middle class. These facts are not irrelevant to their theories.

Here I repeat the comment made in the preface—that the analyst deals with all the ramifications of "causes," of "and's and or's," *as they are operating in the complex unity of a person.* No other discipline enjoys the privilege of such minute study of the actual life process of many individuals, with so much leisure to *observe* the effect of external events on the reaction pattern of the person, or so much opportunity to *experiment* with varieties of therapeutic intervention within the safety of the long-term psychoanalytic relationship. (These rather cryptic remarks will be explained further—a little in Chapter

2 and in more detail in Chapters 7 and 12, which deal directly with psycho-analytic therapy.)

The analyst cannot effectively observe or experiment with the enormous wealth of material presented by the analysand (the patient on the couch) unless he possesses certain guide lines for understanding. He can modify them more flexibly than the "psychologist" who sets up a formal experiment de-signed to control some variables but necessarily ignoring those that are ir-relevant to the hypothesis he is testing. The psychoanalyst is not, of course, infallible. He *may* interpret the productions of the patient too much in terms of his own guide lines, or he *may* be so "neutral" in his approach that the patient is not helped out of the pathological web he has wrought but rather weaves the therapist into the complex pattern of his own life. The aim of psychoanalysis of any school, however, is defined as helping the patient toward a better integration of his own life *as a person*, in his special relations with his milieu.

In Chapters 6 and 11, then, labeled "Dynamics of the Functioning Per-sonality," I shall try to present the major guide lines developed by each school for understanding the complex patterns of individual behavior.

PATHOLOGY AND TREATMENT

Chapters 7 and 12 deal with the specifically medical aspects of psycho-analysis. The first part of each chapter, "Pathology," reports the dynamic interpretation offered by the analytic schools of the major syndromes of mental disease as classified by psychiatry. Although the account is brief and general, its thorough comprehension does require some background in abnormal psy-chology. Perhaps it will be of interest only to those readers whose work brings them into contact with the more severe forms of mental disorder.

The second part of each of these chapters presents the techniques and theories of psychoanalysis as a very special mode of treatment. Although the general subdivision of psychoanalytic schools adopted for this book is main-tained for these chapters, I hope that the reader will see the discussion of treatment in the two chapters as something of a unit. Variations in treatment procedures have often been starting points for radical variations in theoretical development among the schools. Yet in writing about them, I found that I would be endlessly repetitious if I attempted to present the dynamics of therapy separately for each school. Furthermore, my own observation and focused discussion with school experts revealed a flexibility in handling patients according to their special needs beyond the formalized rubrics for treatment that I could report in a few pages. A doctor treating a patient is not quite the same as a doctor abstracting from his treatment procedures those aspects which he considers sufficiently new, important, and generally applicable to justify a written report to his colleagues. He may not wish to have specific variations in treatment quoted in print, but he also objects to a definition of his work narrowed to the shibboleths of his school.

There is much more common ground among psychoanalytic schools as regards therapy than the outsider realizes as he listens to theories of treatment. Perhaps there is more common ground than the analysts themselves realize, since they have a tendency not to talk to one another informally once a serious rift in approach has occurred, and the patient who goes to an analyst of a different school after unsuccessful treatment is very often recriminative and unfair. The new analyst is usually aware of the mechanism, but it is difficult to be entirely objective when the patient's complaints correspond with the analyst's personal preconception of the limitations of the alien school. Further, the individual analyst may have handled a specific patient in a manner not characteristic of his school or of his own general approach to therapy.

It has seemed to me that there are important differences in *emphasis* among the schools. These I have tried to report, but my own emphasis has been on the extensive areas of overlap. I have not been bold enough to distill the essence of psychoanalytic therapy into a separate outline, as I tried to do for basic theoretical concepts in Chapter 2. The problem of treatment is essentially a medical problem, beyond the purview of the reflective outsider. My own efforts at critique are minimal in these chapters, and I suggest that the chapters be considered more as information about what happens on the analytic couch than as material for judgment by readers who do not understand the treatment requirements of different types of mental disorder.

THE SCHOOLS DISCUSSED

Many ideas are characteristic of psychoanalysis regardless of school variation. Indeed, many of the concepts I shall here discuss as "psychoanalysis" have origins and parallel developments relatively independent of psychoanalysis. In Chapter 2, I present the concepts and modes of procedure which seem to me fundamental to the discipline called psychoanalysis today without much regard for concomitant developments in other fields—a narrowness dictated by the special topic of this book.

The choice of psychoanalytic authors for relatively detailed reporting has been determined mainly by their direct influence on disciplines related to psychoanalysis. I have selected the analysts whom most of us in America think of as having established "schools." (For an English audience, Melanie Klein would require such reporting.) Many analysts (Abraham, Ferenczi, *et al.*) have had an influence on psychoanalytic thinking itself more profound than that of some of the analysts here discussed, but their influence on related disciplines has been indirect. People outside the field have scarcely heard their names, whereas the books of analysts here discussed have been widely read or have been followed by more or less literal "schools" associated with their name. They are the analysts that we outsiders have heard most about.

Short of detailed report, I have tried to give the reader some notion of the key ideas associated with a great many other analysts. Sometimes the report of these ideas runs to several pages, sometimes to fairly long footnotes, sometimes to passing mention in the text or in bibliographical reference. There is no substantial correlation between the importance of the author and the amount of space accorded him in this book. I have no yardstick of "importance" in an absolute sense, and I freely confess to overemphasis on some authors who have written extensively on problems which I feel ought to be discussed. Incidental quotations are often taken from articles I happen to have read while thinking about a special topic.

THEIR SETTING IN PSYCHOANALYSIS

I cannot here present anything like a history of psychoanalysis, but I can suggest the general background of the people who are dealt with in this book. Everybody knows that Alfred Adler, Carl Jung, and Otto Rank were part of the early psychoanalytic movement, although they soon established their own schools in outspoken rebellion against Freud. Their contemporaries mentioned in this book are Karl Abraham, Sandor Ferenczi, Wilhelm Reich, Wilhelm Stekel, Paul Federn, and Ernest Jones. Abraham is the Freudian figure behind Erich Fromm and Melanie Klein. Ferenczi's approach influenced the Sullivan approach, via Clara Thompson, and also the approach of Franz Alexander and the "Chicago" school. Reich and Stekel have small schools devoted to the master, but their major impact on psychoanalysis seems to have been through appreciation of important aspects of their work by other analysts before their theories were elaborated to "school" dimensions. Federn remained essentially a classical Freudian. He is discussed briefly for his special views on the ego. Jones is mentioned only for his remarkable work on the biography of Freud.

The English school to which Jones belongs is poorly represented in this book, because until recently it has had little direct impact on American psychoanalysis. Contemporary English psychoanalysis seems to have taken two directions, under the leadership of Melanie Klein and Freud's daughter, Anna Freud. It is interesting to note that both these women began their work as child analysts. Their position is described briefly, with little mention of the English analysts who have worked with them.

Contemporary American schools are still dominated by Europeans who came here as invited leaders before Hitler, or as welcome refugees after he made psychoanalysis impossible in Europe. Of the authors chosen for detailed reporting because of their familiarity to an American audience, only one (Sullivan) is American by birth. The great majority of authors reported or merely cited are of European origin. Yet, except for Freud and Jung and some of their contemporaries, most of these analysts have lived and worked in the United States so long that it is hard to think of them as foreigners. Adler and Rank spent long periods here, with direct influence on American thought. Karen Horney and Erich Fromm have lived here. Most of the analysts briefly quoted are American by adoption.

New York is the main center of American psychoanalysis, as regards both the number of practicing analysts and the number of schools of thought operating with some independence. The group founded by Horney is called the Society for the Advancement of Psychoanalysis and has its own "Institute" for training. The "Sullivan" group began in Washington and Baltimore and is sometimes informally called the Washington-Baltimore school. Frieda Fromm-Reichmann leads an important division in that area, but the William Alanson White Foundation (the formal name for this group) also maintains an important organization and a literal school (Institute) in New York. Fromm's major professional affiliations are with this psychoanalytic group, although his main impact has come through his books, lectures, and teaching in various places. Adlerian and Jungian groups in America are scattered (and comparatively small), but their greatest concentration seems also to be New York. Jungian groups are strong in England and, of course, in Switzerland under Jung's personal leadership. The Rankian group is strongest in Philadelphia but has important representation in New York.

The "Freudian" New York Psychoanalytic Society is by far the largest organization of analysts in the city. It too has its own "Institute" for training. In recent years many of the big medical schools have established psychoanalytic divisions with facilities for training students in psychoanalysis. The orientation is usually moderately classical or eclectic. At Columbia University, an important special influence has been the "adaptational approach," represented mainly by Sandor Rado, Abram Kardiner and their associates.

The "Chicago" school usually refers to Franz Alexander, Thomas French, and their associates, although the majority of analysts in that city are more or less classical in orientation. The same comment may be made about analysts in Washington and Baltimore, despite the informal labeling of Sullivan's group as the Washington-Baltimore school. Almost every large city now has a psychoanalytic society, usually fairly classical Freudian, frequently with some controversy.*

The largest organization of psychoanalysts in the United States is the American Psychoanalytic Association. It is affiliated, in turn, with the International Psychoanalytic Society. The membership of the American association numbers about 600; the international society has about 1200 members. The overwhelming majority of the members (in America all of the younger members) have the M.D. degree plus the special training in psychiatry and psychoanalysis described in the preface. This association is essentially Freudian, although it includes some organized groups with a left-wing orientation. Often the older leaders of what are now often called "splinter" groups are themselves members of the national association, but their trainees do not become members until the training program has been approved by the large group. The size of the national association should be considered in relation to the rigorous standards of membership maintained.

MAJOR SCHOOL CLASSIFICATION FOR THIS BOOK

For purposes of reporting, I have divided the schools described into two categories—roughly, those that accept the "libido theory" and those that reject it quite specifically, building up their theories almost *against* this Freudian concept. The division was chosen on rather practical grounds. This was the topic about which the analysts seemed to be quarreling in the most intransigeant manner and on which my fellow "psychologists" seemed to become most heated.

* Controversy in any group is not exclusively a matter of rational difference of opinion, nor are the theoretical issues precisely the same in every city. We cannot concern ourselves here with problems of interpersonal relationships among analysts or with the relationship of psychoanalysis to specific communities. A loose theoretical generalization seems permissible.

There seems to be a general tendency for "left-wing" analysts to emphasize problems of self-evaluation and interpersonal relations in contrast to the major Freudian emphasis on the libido theory, on the role of the instinctual drives of sex and aggression—how they are handled and how they interact. Analysts who maintain the latter emphasis are often called orthodox or conservative. Many of them justifiably resent the implication that they are slavish followers, unwilling to accept new ideas. Some of them, indeed, have made radical modifications in Freudian theory, while ardently defending the tenets of the libido theory. The adjective *classical* has been used throughout in this book as more descriptive than *orthodox* or *conservative* for analysts whose point of departure is Freud's theory of instincts.

It has served well for the moment, although the focus of controversy will probably change. There is currently a very large measure of overlap among psychoanalytic schools as regards what the Freudians have come to call ego psychology. But in my reading and in discussion with school experts, the fundamental problem that arises continually is *the role of infantile sexuality* in personality formation and in the unconscious dynamics of adult function. I have classified as "Freudian," occasionally with some arbitrariness, all those analysts who emphasize the specific importance of the sexual drives and the instinct of aggression. Kardiner and Alexander, among others, do not follow the libido theory in all its ramifications, but since they continue to stress the significance of the biological needs and modes of reaction which Freud called sexual or aggressive, they are described in this group. Freud himself is presented in detail according to the outline discussed above, the other authors only in so far as they have elaborated or modified Freud's position on one or another point. Freud and the "Freudians" take up Part II of the book.

Under the rubric "non-libido schools" I present Adler, Horney, Fromm, and Sullivan in some detail, following my outline of topics. Although they are grouped together in Part III, they are treated sufficiently discretely so that the reader may, if he prefers, read about each author sequentially. They are discussed together only in the chapter on the genetic process, since— by definition of the group—they all fail to describe the biological push of needs specific to infancy and childhood, and in the chapter on treatment, because there seems to be so much overlap in basic approach that this chapter is almost continuous with its counterpart in the "Freudian" section, with relatively minor discussion of differences among the schools.

More positively described, the contribution of these schools could be characterized by their emphasis on the "self" as the primary factor in psychodynamics, in contradistinction to the instinctual drives and their consolidation into structures (id, ego, superego) emphasized by Freudians. Yet Adler, Horney, Fromm, and Sullivan do not entirely agree on a definition of the "self" or its dynamics, and it would be ridiculous to suggest that the "Freudians" ignore the concept of the "self." The difference is a matter of emphasis— of the kind of dynamics considered fundamental—rather than an outright dichotomy. Perhaps one may say that the "Freudians" derive the sense of self from experience better defined, they think, in terms of instinctual needs, etc., as elaborated through experience, whereas the "non-libido schools" consider such needs as incidental to the primary needs of the human "self." At any rate, even after prolonged study of the analytic schools of thought, it seems to me that the libido–non-libido dichotomy is still the fundamental one—that it lies directly behind the overt rebellion of Adler and Horney and is implicit in the position taken by Fromm and Sullivan.

Two analysts familiar to the American concept of psychoanalytic schools—Jung and Rank—do not fit this libido–non-libido dichotomy. They also vigorously repudiate the libido theory, and perhaps their theories can also be called psychologies of the self, but their more differentiated contribution does not follow the division I found useful for the other authors. Although everyone knows their names and acknowledges their influence, and although some of their concepts have become part of a very general vocabulary, there is comparatively little interest in the detailed development of their theoretical systems among professional psychological groups in the United States today except, for Rank, in the area of social work. Writers, artists, and historians would tell a different story, especially for Jung. Since the orientation of this book is primarily clinical, however, it seemed better to present these two men briefly in a manner designed to bring out their distinctive emphasis instead of viewing them in the framework of my outline. Adler, the third member of the trio of early rebels, is given more discussion not because he is more important in himself but because his position is closer to major developments in America.

Although this book was designed to be read as a whole, the reader with less time at his disposal may prefer to merely read only the summaries on schools of little immediate interest to him. For the most part they are long and inclusive enough to serve as brief presentations of the school position. Occasionally I have been unwilling to chop into summary statements discussions in which my intent was to build up a *feeling* for analytic procedures or in which the argument of the analyst is so closely knit and already so compact in presentation that further summary seems to break a system into meaningless fragments. In such circumstances, I have taken the simple recourse of describing what was discussed in the chapter instead of summarizing. These descriptive statements serve to alert the reader to the topics necessarily neglected in summary review.

MY OWN BACKGROUND AND PROCEDURE IN WRITING

In the preface I introduced myself as a "psychologist" with an orientation toward psychoanalytic schools of thought conditioned by training in this related discipline rather than in the active practice of psychoanalytic therapy. The main material for my discussion of schools is, of course, the published work of analysts. Page references are supplied for many statements—I hope for all those in which my account goes beyond ideas familiar to the knowledgeable reader.

Even a report consisting entirely of direct quotations cannot, of course, avoid author bias in the selection of the quotations, especially when the report concerns the development of ideas still in process of growth. In this book I hope to convey something of the lively growth process in all analytic schools, not a frozen scheme laid down by an omniscient master. In reporting current usage and trends, I sometimes use the phrase "my impression." This is a frank acknowledgment of possible bias, but at times "my impression" has seemed more accurate than would-be objective reporting. To give the reader some means of evaluating "my impression," a brief description of my own background in psychoanalysis is in order.*

Although I write about psychoanalysis as a "psychologist" rather than as an active practitioner, it is with an unusual amount of inside knowledge of its actual operation. I cannot claim equal inside knowledge for all schools reported in this book, but I can claim some inside knowledge for most of them, and a respectful attitude toward clinically established approaches sometimes absent among "psychologists" whose contact with the schools is less direct or less varied.

In the actual writing of the book my procedure has been to read and listen and observe in each school, write the best account I could—and then submit the account to experts selected for their special acquaintance with the school. I have been very fortunate in the serious interest which acknowledged leaders brought to the reading of my exposition of the school theory they follow. Specific criticism was addressed, by my invitation, to any factual errors and to gross errors of emphasis or omission.

* I am a *clinical* "psychologist," specializing in diagnostic tests. My work has been partly in educational and other institutions, partly in private practice. I may say, however, that I have "done testing" for some fifty analysts of various schools. The testing has often involved a good deal of discussion with the analyst as to the nature of the patient's disorder and what should be done about it. In a way, therefore, I have been a professional collaborator, with professional privileges of confidence about the patient and about the concerns of the analyst.

At the age of twenty-two I married a young doctor, John Levy, shared some aspects of his special training in the handling of mental disorders, and in some ways collaborated in the treatment of patients and in writing. The book we wrote together in 1938, *The Happy Family*, is still widely used. Some years after his death (1938), I married Dr. Bela Mittelmann, an established analyst. I owe much to the direct influence of these two men. A perquisite of marriage relevant to this book has been the opportunity to listen in on the shop talk of analysts among themselves. The name of the patient is, of course, carefully concealed (analysts are almost fanatical on this point), but the patient's problem is discussed very freely, usually in close relationship to therapeutic procedures, sometimes in relation to school differences.

As part of my training as clinical psychologist as well as for personal reasons, I have been in analysis with a fairly classical Freudian and at another period with one of Horney's first lieutenants. To some extent, therefore, I can write from the patient's point of view—from direct experience of the analytic hour. Furthermore, although patients are discouraged from talking about their analyses, many of them do—especially to a psychoanalytically oriented friend. I have sometimes preferred the confidences of friends to printed materials as a source of illustrative examples. Printed examples are typically very long or else edited to bring out a point a little different from the one required at a particular point in my exposition.

I trust that the factual errors have been eliminated. Errors of emphasis and omission were more difficult to correct. The complaints were usually that I perpetuated narrow misunderstandings of the basic theory, with insufficient attention to modifying aspects in current use and clearly identifiable in the scripts of the school from the master on. Since my initial account was considered "unusually understanding for an outsider," revision in the direction of still broader insight into the *active* tenets of the school has led to a curious result. The few specialist readers who have read my account of schools other than their own seem to have two reactions: (1) My report of *their* school is good, so good that they become annoyed with me for not driving home the ideas they consider most important for any honest psychological science. If the report is this good, why can't it be still better—on their terms? (2) My account of the *other* schools is inaccurate, they say, because I read my own intelligence into them, with insufficient knowledge of their history and actual practice.

The first reaction is doubtless well taken. No outsider can hope to offer as vividly coherent an account of a living school as its active proponents wish, especially if the aim of writing is an unbiased survey of many such schools.

I object to the second reaction because the statements criticized as due to "my" intelligence are usually very careful rephrasings from important writings of the author reported, passed by the school experts or corrected in the direction of a still more "intelligent" presentation. (If I listened to the Jungian experts consulted, I would hardly mention the "inheritance" of a collective unconscious; if I listened to the Rankians, the birth trauma; to many Freudians, the libido theory as commonly understood, etc., etc.) The rather liberal presentation of the schools is definitely *not* a fancy of my own. It has been hammered out of reading, observation, and direct consultation on the manuscript with experts who backed up their comments with documentation—maybe not complete documentation but documentation that a reporting author cannot possibly ignore. It is the schools, not I, that have supplied the liberalizing intelligence of each presentation in some contrast to the narrow shibboleths by which they are often identified.

CRITIQUE AND INTEGRATION

This description of the background of the expository sections leads to further discussion of the second direction promised for the writing of this book—that is, a critical stance, an attempt at integration of the schools presented from the relatively detached point of view of a "clinical psychologist."

My main reason for undertaking the book was the opportunity to think through for myself the variety of concepts I encountered in professional contacts and used after a fashion myself. My own "thinks" loomed large, therefore, in the task of writing. I have tried hard to keep them separate from exposition by means of this introductory chapter, an epilogue, and a series of comments, plainly identified by double-column style throughout the book and appearing mainly at the end of each chapter. They are printed in a different format so that the reader may be kept constantly alerted to the fact that Munroe is talking for herself rather than for the school.

My comments are of two orders, often closely commingled. The first order represents the reflections of a "clinical psychologist" interested in the problems of patients, of normal people in our culture, of our culture itself, of empirical research. The point of departure is, of course, the views of the analytic school just presented. If my own remarks often seem predominantly negative or tangential, it is because I do not repeat ideas already carefully explained. I merely specify the ideas that seem to me valid as presented, and go on from there.

My aim in this order of comment has *not* been to convince readers of a concrete position of my own as a neatly finished substitute for the position of the analytic school reported. It has been rather to invite thought and inquiry in areas which, I feel, have been neglected by the school. Observations are introduced not so much to "prove" a specific theoretical point as to suggest new lines of research or new relationships among the typically analytic data and data gathered by other disciplines operating within a different framework of basic concepts and methods.

The second order of discussion is more abstract and formalistic. Perhaps it merits the term "philosophical." At any rate, I have borrowed many ideas from contemporary philosophers, notably from the semanticists and the logical positivists. As empirical scientists and practitioners, we are often too close to our major problems to get a broad view of them. We work out concepts and methods for the problems we see, the problems we work with and in some measure solve. But our very solutions put blinders on us. We continue to elaborate a theory that has worked successfully in many ways, fight for its tenets, and fail to develop a more inclusive theory which would integrate with our own observations the data accumulated by our opponents. We are caught in our own words and in scientific methodologies so firmly set that we tend to view with suspicion any formulations established in a different way.*

* This problem is well discussed by A. H. Maslow in the introduction to *Motivation and Personality*, Harper, 1954.

For me at least, a formalistic rephrasing of the basic problems of psychological science has been a means of integrating the schools reported here. Such formalistic ("philosophical") rephrasing must be very directly addressed to specific theories before it can become meaningful to the people who are doing the real work of science. The empirical scientist and the practicing analyst cannot pause long in experiment or treatment to reflect upon logical redefinition of their fundamental premises—not unless such redefinition is brought close to home.

TERMINOLOGY

In my effort to present a broad perspective toward the analytic theories, I have reluctantly introduced new terms of my own in a science overburdened with terms. I could find no other way of keeping my point of view vivid throughout a long book short of continual re-explanation of a complex position. With the possible exception of the *self-image* (a familiar term which I try to define with attention to its dynamics in a somewhat special way), the terms introduced are designed only for the purpose of keeping the reader aware of the general perspective. They are not intended as the permanent pillars of a new inclusive theory to be substituted for the theories reported but rather as a temporary rephrasing such as may help us envisage common problems within a common framework. Each school will undoubtedly keep to its own vocabulary for many years to come. Needless controversy may be diminished, however, and more flexible interchange of ideas encouraged if the problems are once seen in this abstract form.

A View of Systems. The phrase *a view of systems* will recur very often and will carry the full weight of the perspective I shall urge. The word *system* here does *not* mean primarily systematic schools of thought—the first meaning likely to occur to the reader of a book about theories. The coherent system of thought developed by a school is respect-worthy and must be understood in its systematic aspects. This was the note sounded in my opening paragraph. A theory, however, is a very special type of system, one that must be used with caution. It is indispensable for ordering the inchoate mass of observational data in such a manner that dynamic systems *intrinsic to the data* may be discerned and utilized. It is nevertheless a human conceptual scheme, and therefore fallible. Connections may be read into events which are not dynamically connected at all—the night air, for example, was long considered responsible for consumption, whereas fresh air, even at night, later became the main prescription for the tuberculous patient.

Or a system that is truly *intrinsic to the data* may be considered as "the" cause of events—even of events not very obviously connected. There are theorists, for example, who insist that tidal action is responsible for all fundamental change in coastal contours, who study the history of tides very carefully and dismiss as irrelevant evidence concerning winds and volcanic action. It is always possible to "prove" that the tide has an effect. But is it the most important factor on every coast? Isn't it equally important to study winds and volcanic action? Does a good theory have to be all-inclusive?

Reductionism. I shall use a special word for this kind of error—*reductionism*. Reductionism does not mean that a theory is *wrong*, like the attribution of tuberculosis to night air. It means that a perfectly sound idea is being applied too generally, with neglect or exclusion of concomitantly operating systems-of-events. This word of opprobrium falls upon all the psychoanalytic schools at one time or another and is limited to psychoanalysis only because this book is limited to psychoanalytic theories. It would apply equally well to many other theories in the life sciences.

Multidimensional. I shall also use a special word of praise—*multidimensional*.* The meaning is not unlike William James's when he titled a book *This Pluralistic Universe*. My clumsier term has the temporary merit of scientific usage, and it fits well with the "view of systems." It implies that data may be studied along many lines (dimensions), which are *then* related to one another. Integration must still take place, but not in the reductionist manner of reducing "everything" to a master principle. In this respect the advantage of "Freudian" theory lies in the room it gives for learning new things with some *separateness* rather than as variations on a single theme. This principle seems to me more important than whether instinctual drives or the sense of self should be considered as "the" basic principle for psychological theory.

Unfortunately the principle of multidimensionality in scientific theorizing has its dangers. The dimensions selected may not be the most important for continuing investigation, or those that most truly reveal the systematic relationships intrinsic to a specific problem. The major danger in theorizing here may be called *reification*. A dimension tentatively presented by the new theorizer of genius often becomes solidified in the minds of his followers and even in his own mind as a sort of *thing*. A concept which begins as a useful flexible description of emergent dynamic relationships among systems of intrinsic importance may later be thought of in too great separation as an

---

* The more common Freudian word is perhaps "overdetermination," to be discussed on pp. 54ff. This term is confusing to outsiders who do not immediately understand that *multiple* determination is usually implied rather than excessive reaction to a single determinant.

entity in itself. Examples may be drawn from the very theory whose merits were extolled in the preceding paragraph. Freud's "structural" concepts—id, ego, superego—were offered as *emergent* subdivisions whose origin and function was suggested with brilliant insight, especially if one considers the date of writing. There is little doubt, however, that these concepts often became so reified in later "Freudian" theory as to justify rebellious protest. One should not chop up the human psyche into theoretical chunks to be studied as such regardless of the *between* reactions among them as emergent systems in their emergent phase as well as later. In so far as Freudian multidimensionality has led to reification, I, too, shall protest. Indeed, psychological theory *needs* frequent refreshment of the basic idea of the human organism as essentially adaptive and creative, in contrast to *any rigid parceling-out of instinctual drives, psychic institutions, and the like.* Such refreshment, such emphasis on the free movement of the personality, has usually led, however, to the reductionism discussed above.

It would be gratifying to present a philosophical perspective which would tell the empirical scientist what to do with his data and how to plan his investigations. Yet such presentation is impossible. Sciences have not developed in a primarily logical fashion in the past, and there is little reason to suppose that their line of development will quickly change. A scientist is a person. In consequence of his own temperament and the orientation of his society, he is interested in some problems more than in others. Science follows and creates human needs within the "terms of the millieu," not in a rational vacuum. We cannot blueprint the needs of science on logical or even on social terms. A science cannot begin to answer questions of moment until it has means of investigation expediently related to the questions. A science usually develops in close relationship to its means, but it also develops means in relation to questions. Thus far scientific growth has involved a vividly *reciprocal* relationship between rather specific questions and rather specific means. I do not think this relationship can be abrogated—not over night, and not by the fiat of philosophers or research grants. At present, and probably for a long future, it seems intrinsic to the kind of thinking we call "scientific."

SCIENTIFIC TRUTH AS SYSTEM

Psychology has always tended to ape physics beyond what was quite appropriate to its own needs, and I do not wish to perpetuate the error of applying blindly the means and questions of physics to the systems important for psychological science. Nevertheless, it is the physicists who, with the philosophers, have taken the lead in redefining science as a matter of operating systems rather than of universal laws. In modern physics and chemistry the old concept of atoms and laws governing their behavior has given way to concepts of the structure of the atom. Hydrogen is no longer considered as an irreducible element, with chemical affinities to some other elements. It has become a special *structure* of "elements" which are not peculiar to hydrogen, but which seem intrinsically the same for all atoms. Gravitation has become a special instance of the systems observed by astronomers. The familiar laws of the physical sciences are not abrogated but are *explained as instances of events within systems.* Aspects of physics not readily comprehended by observable atomic and molecular structure are dealt with effectively by a "field" theory. Many electromagnetic phenomena, for example, cannot be analyzed into their "elements," not even with attention to their structural aspects. But they can be understood to the point of highly successful manipulation if they are considered as a "field."*

In my efforts to understand a little of the way modern physicists think, I was initially baffled by the statement that they cheerfully accepted two incompatible theories of the nature of light—one of their fundamental tools in conceptualization and in experimentation. One important set of data supported the wave theory, and valid predictions could be made on its assumptions. Other phenomena were better explained and predicted by the corpuscular theory. But surely, I thought, one must itch to know which is *right*; surely one cannot work comfortably with two theories one of which must be wrong. Finally I came to see that one could do exactly that if the theory is really envisaged as a provisional *systematization of events*, not as a provisional "truth." Perhaps the physicists have already solved the problem of the nature of light. The solution expected—and it is only the problem and expectation that warrant an illustration so far beyond our ken as psychologists—was not a decision in favor of either theory but rather a wider formulation which would include both.

The perspective I urge toward criticism of the analytic schools is somewhat similar. The problem should not be envisaged as a matter of decisive choice among the various theories considered as conceptual systems. The problem is rather to discern the areas of human function best explained by one or another school, best handled by one or another methodology in treatment or in research; and to develop a theoretical *perspective* which will explain the cogency of the particular ordering of observational data under one or

* I shall call such phenomena in the area of psychological science "relatively autonomous systems" in an effort to avoid overly direct analogy to physics, or too close an identification with the "field theories" of Kurt Lewin and Gardner Murphy. (I am obviously much indebted to both men.)

another school rubric as a valid *systematization*—without the reductionism of the usual "school" approach.

Too often this perspective (should I call it *operationalism?*) has led to efforts at careful definition and measurement in psychological science analogous to the methods of physics. Many of these efforts seem to me inappropriate to our essential task. The systems we deal with in psychology are of a different order, and must be studied in different ways. Almost by definition, the exact sciences deal with systems which are repeatable and measurable for the purpose of the investigation (the hypothesis). I shall refer to such systems as "tight."

Fairly tight systems are not unknown in the life sciences, but most of our significant problems are subject to scientific ordering only through recognition of *processes*. Our useful systematizations *should* be thought of as relatively "loose"—as *not* definable and measurable with anything like the precision of physics. Any organism has a *history* peculiar to itself which makes it intrinsically different from every other organism, unlike the atoms which resemble one another so closely that the physicist or chemist can cheerfully ignore variation up to the farthest reaches of quantum theory. By virtue of its especially great flexibility in learning, the human organism is especially variable as a unit that is observed. Its past experience is of crucial importance. Furthermore, it adapts itself creatively moment by moment to the current situation—not as a neatly definable entity, *homo sapiens,* but as an organized personality.

Psychological science *must,* I think, work with processes and trends, with "loose" systems. Exact definition and measurement are helpful tools for many aspects of our problem. For the most part, however, better understanding of a trend (a system) is more feasible and more useful and more *correct* than a finicking precision.

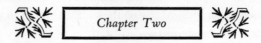

Chapter Two

BASIC CONCEPTS OF
PSYCHOANALYSIS

THIS CHAPTER, like the preceding one, postpones direct discussion of the various schools of psychoanalytic thought. Chapter 1 dealt with the mode of presentation adopted for the book as a whole and with the theoretical framework I shall use in my efforts at critique and integration. The present chapter is devoted to an exposition of concepts and lines of inquiry common to all the psychoanalytic schools. Take-off points for the development of the various schools will be briefly indicated, but I shall here do no more than suggest the general direction of differences to be presented in detail later.

The chapter is addressed primarily to the reader who knows very little about psychoanalysis, or whose knowledge has been mainly theoretical. It falls into two parts: the first deals with Freud's *underlying premises* as currently used by all analytic schools; the second, much longer, deals with the major concern of psychoanalysis—*unconscious processes*. I shall point out repeatedly that no psychoanalytic school thinks of the unconscious as an entity somehow set apart from the rest of the functioning personality. On the contrary, the unconscious is always viewed in intimate relationship to the needs and goals emphasized by the school. But theories differ as to its structural connections with conscious processes—that is, with the needs and goals of which

26

we are aware and with the development of logical thought. It is impossible to present an accurate picture of unconscious dynamics without a full presentation of each school theory.

It has seemed to me, however, that many arid disputes about the status of psychoanalysis as a science, and much incomprehension and bewilderment about the strange "evidence" adduced by psychoanalysts, might be avoided if outside critics had more understanding of how this "evidence" is obtained and used. Because of its complex nature, it is not easily controllable by the methodologies developed in "psychology." Since it deals with nonrational materials, it often sounds fanciful and random until one begins, with Freud, to see the consistencies in the language of the unconscious, until one sees how these slippery data are carefully checked and rechecked in the course of analytic work. I shall not deal in this book with the problem of methodology as such, but the lengthy discussion of the unconscious is intended as an explanation of the psychoanalytic method and is implicitly a defense of the right of psychoanalysts to call their method scientific.

UNDERLYING PREMISES

PSYCHOLOGICAL DETERMINISM

In a sense, the concept of determinism is as old as human thought, and as broad in scope. It ranges from very complex philosophical theories to the fatalism of the soldier who believes that he will be killed only by the bullet with his name on it. Determinism *vs.* free will, mechanism *vs.* vitalism, science *vs.* religion—these are the hoary controversies usually implied.

But this is not the sense in which the term is used in psychoanalysis. As a philosopher, Freud was primarily a scientist who believed fervently in the power of rational understanding, rooted in empirical observation. He was no more "deterministic" than any scientist. His primary motivation was to obtain deeper insight into "what makes people tick." His ultimate achievement was to bring new areas of the human psyche into the field of scientific investigation and to reorient such investigation toward the study of dynamic trends *within* the individual instead of universal laws applied *to* the individual.

A major aspect of Freud's approach was the tenet that none of human behavior is "accidental";* hence the emphasis on the word *determinism*. Earlier scientific psychologists were prepared to maintain, usually on the analogy of nineteenth-century physics, that our slightest action is determined by ultimate universal laws. But they attributed our actions to rational motives or instincts quite narrowly defined, to mechanical linkages by contiguity or similarity, or to chance—that is, to a multitude of "causes" acting independently. The small mistakes of everyday life, our reveries and dreams, the queer symptoms of the mentally diseased, were, to be sure, determined, but only as the flight of a feathered seed is determined by wind, gravity, its minute peculiarities in structure, and a host of other factors too transient for fruitful investigation. Over-all laws of association could be established; mental disorders could be usefully classified; dreaming could be explained as the reappearance of the past under certain physiological conditions with characteristic distortions of logical thinking. Unfortunately, the more carefully such laws and classifications were worked out, the further psychology traveled from common-sense usefulness.

Freud began his investigations as a doctor attempting to treat the bizarre symptoms of a mental disorder: hysteria. With Breuer (*Studies in Hysteria*, 1896), he observed that the peculiar behavior of a patient *made sense* in terms of an important episode in her past which she had forgotten. Of course, the patient was ill, but her illness appeared to consist precisely in re-enacting a fragment of the past (recoverable under hypnosis). Her specific symptom was not "accidental." In 1896 hysteria was a well-known phenomenon. Many efforts had been made to explain it and to trace its course. The old idea of the patient's being "possessed" had long been abandoned. The supreme importance of the new Breuer-Freud formulation lay in its insight into the meaningful *continuity of events* in the mental life of the individual. Hysteria was no longer considered as a strange pathological incursion but as the *exaggerated expression of psychological processes common to mankind*. Choice of symptom, which had previously seemed arbitrary, became a revelation of the specific psychic stresses of the patient.

With the observed "logic" of the hysterical symptom as his point of departure, Freud rapidly went on to show a similar "logic" in the unconsidered fragments of normal life: dreams and small mistakes.[1] Freud's psychological determinism very markedly reduced the areas that earlier psychologists considered unexplorable because they thought them to be ruled by chance—that is, by the independent action of so many transiently operating causes that the scientist cannot hope to measure and predict the outcome. Freud showed that

---

* *None* is too strong a word for most psychoanalysts, and Freud himself was not puristic in his attempts to interpret every fragment of behavior as unconsciously determined.

the queernesses of mental life not only have meaning but provide especially useful clues to underlying continuities in the personality which profoundly affect even the rational goals of the normal person. Such continuities help to explain the development of mankind's conscience, ideals, and thoughtfulness, as well as of the bizarre hysterical symptom.

THE ROLE OF THE UNCONSCIOUS

For Freud, the initial observations on hysteria raised fundamental questions. *How* were these continuities determined? Clearly the new psychological determinism operated outside of full consciousness. *The role of the unconscious* may be called the second basic concept in psychoanalysis. Obviously, the hysterical patient was not aware of the meaning of her behavior prior to therapeutic intervention. Yet she acted in many ways *as if* she remembered. The memory was not conscious, but it was certainly not dead. On the contrary, it played a very active role in determining her actions. Freud went on to a very careful study of the unconscious as such.*

MOTIVATION AND DYNAMICS

With only a promissory note about the unconscious, I come to a third basic concept, which can be labeled *motivation,* or, simply, *dynamics*. The concept is given heavy emphasis in all the theoretical schemes presented in this book and in most of modern psychology. Indeed, modern psychological determinism may be thought of as the organizing of behavior by the needs and aims—that is, the motivation—of the person. It was Freud among the analysts who took the all-important first step toward appreciation of the essentially *goal-directed* quality of human behavior as a matter of necessary and feasible inquiry. And it was psychoanalysis, broadly speaking, that contributed most largely (though not exclusively) toward making this formulation a commonplace in contemporary psychological science.

In describing Freudian doctrine specifically in later chapters, I shall begin from a contemporary point of view, with the clear purpose of presenting understandably ideas which Freudians *now* consider basic. I shall follow the same

---

* Every psychoanalyst deals with unconscious factors in one way or another. Although philosophers for a time objected on semantic grounds to applying the term "mental" to nonconscious phenomena, psychologists never boggled much at this point. Since Freud (and earlier), it has been possible to demonstrate quite conclusively that the unconscious acts "like a mind" in structuring behavior in a directed manner.

practice in presenting the other schools. Here I offer an oversimplified account of Freud's very first position. He corrected and elaborated it himself, but it shows with peculiar sharpness the leap Freud made toward effective grasp of the function of *goals* in human behavior. (The contrast is obvious both with the atomistic brass-instrument psychological science of his time and with the speculative approach of philosophers who emphasized "the will.")

Freud perceived not only that the strange symptoms of the hysteric were comprehensible as partial reinstatements of forgotten episodes but that they seemed to have a *purposiveness* of their own. He saw that the episodes had been forgotten for good reason: they were painful or dangerous to the conscious self. In one patient after another, the forgotten memories recovered during hypnosis or later through the technique of free association (see pp. 38-40) seemed to concern sexual events in early childhood. It seemed to Freud at first that the unconscious phenomena he was learning to see had as their purpose the fulfillment of a *wish*, apparently a sexual wish dating from infancy, which was intolerable to the adult personality. The wish was therefore *censored* and could strive for expression only in the disguised form of the symptom.

This statement is full of exaggerations, crudities, and errors of omission, even beyond those of Freud's first formulation. But it contains the nuclear principles of virtually the whole of modern dynamic psychology.

Let us first consider the *wish*. For a time Freud was as sophistical about discovering the underlying "wish" element as ever La Rochefoucauld or the hedonists were in identifying their special talismans, but Freud's "wish" very readily gave way to libidinal needs and instinctual needs, and, with little strain, to the abstract concept of goal-directedness—whatever one's definition of goal. The modern idea of goal-striving had other origins too, of course, but the orientation of looking for the underlying goal in any item of human behavior undeniably took on enormous impetus from the psychoanalyst's practical habit of looking for the aim of the item rather than for the "laws" governing its appearance. Breuer did not see the unconscious as *purposive;* rather he saw in unconscious processes a falling apart of purposiveness under conditions of stress or psychic weakness.* The goal-directed quality of the unconscious was a Freudian concept.

From the outset Freud saw that the nature of the unconscious purpose could be subjected to investigation. His emphasis on sexuality arose very clearly from observation of his patients, and his observations have been confirmed thousands of times. No psychoanalyst today doubts the importance of sexuality,

* *Cf.* Pierre Janet, a French psychiatrist contemporary with Freud, whose views have had some influence on American thought. See Elton Mayo, *Some Notes on the Psychology of Pierre Janet,* Harvard University Press, 1948.

especially infantile sexuality, in psychic life. Freud's destruction of the mythological age of innocence has been generally accepted. What is *not* accepted by
non-Freudian psychoanalysts, and still more heatedly denied by nonpsychoanalytic psychological schools, is Freud's idea of *the preponderant role played
by infantile sexuality* in the development of human goals. We shall pass over
this controversy for the present because it will be treated fully later, when the
schools are described in detail. The point here is that Freud, perhaps even
more clearly than his divergent followers, *tried* to find the basis of his theories
about goals in the actual productions of his patients and to base his theories on
observation. Perhaps he did not wholly succeed—certainly he did not succeed
completely, since no investigator can wholly escape the ingrained preconceptions of his own period. At the very least, however, Freud opened up for
investigation a new range of human motives with the paradigm that one may
try to discover underlying trends by looking at the data with as little bias as
possible.

Freud saw from the outset that "the unconscious," with its sexual wish,
was only part of the personality. Here again we encounter crossroads of development. Some investigators, notably Adler, leaped at once to the idea that
the whole of the personality is directly determined by unrecognized wishes, not
necessarily sexual. Adler saw in Freud's early formulations implications for the
understanding of character as well as of the neurotic symptom, for the determination of the psychology as well as the psychopathology of everyday life. He
extended the concept of purposiveness to the total adjustive process of living
(the life style, pp. 425f.) and tried to show how every act directly reflects the
central goal of the human personality: the goal of superiority. Adler thus
arrived at a radically holistic view of human nature whereby all behavior falls
into place in the wake of its goal as water takes a predictable form in the wake
of a ship. Any fragment of behavior could be interpreted by insight into the
specific goal of the individual (his path to superiority) and could be changed
automatically by persuading the person to change his goal. The later non-
libido psychoanalysts also emphasize the *immediate* structuring power of an
underlying need. For them also, the neurotic symptom or character trend must
be understood *directly* as the expression of the person's current need for security, for significance, or whatever. (Their views are more complex than Adler's,
as we shall see.)

Freud himself took a longer way around to an understanding of the goal-
directed quality of the total personality. The sexual wish, he observed, appeared to press for immediate gratification, regardless of consequences, and
was regularly opposed by *something*, which he at first called the *censor*,
lumping together all the social, moral, and rational forces behind the opposition. From the outset he assumed that these forces were also "instinctual,"

and later on he searched energetically to discover exactly where they came from, and how. During the 1920's he developed what he called the structural approach—an analysis of the process whereby the ego (mainly rational) and the superego (mainly moral) are crystallized out of the id* (primitive instinctual). *Once crystallized out,* these provinces of the mind tend, according to Freud, to function to a large extent independently and act readily in complex opposition to the id, from which they came.

The intricate story of instinctual development and function is, of course, reserved for the section on Freud. Here the point of emphasis is that Freud—in his structuring of the id, ego, and superego—erected quite specific *categories of human function,* a framework which Adler vehemently repudiated and which the other non-libido analysts tend to view with suspicion. The slavish devotion to these categories among some lesser Freudians today readily promotes sympathy with Adler's vehemence. Doubtless any rigid categorization of creatively interacting systems holds dangers for essentially pedantic minds.

It is no part of the purpose of this chapter to defend Freud's structural approach in its specificity. In a discussion of basic concepts, however, it is important to underline how Freud arrived at his "provinces of the mind" (institutions, spheres—various terms are used) in contrast to the older "faculties of the mind," so long the bulwark of psychological thought. It is not enough to say that Freud was more empirical. On the contrary, the older categories are much more obvious. We remember, we imagine, we feel, we will. The armchair psychologists concocted these faculties because they fitted quite well with experience thought of from a chair. Even today it is easier to get beginning psychology students to understand this kind of categorization from their own experience as they sit in class before the professor than to put them through the task of understanding the Freudian id, ego, and superego. Freud was more empirical—but with patients rather than with normal adults, and with a more penetrating empiricism. His was a sort of *laboratory* empiricism, dealing with active trends in the relative isolation dictated by their pathological exaggeration (*cf.* p. 306).

THE GENETIC APPROACH

Freud's categorization was genetic—a product of the experience of the growing child. *We may call the genetic approach the fourth basic concept*

---

* More precisely ego-id—a primary undifferentiated state. See Chapter 3 for discussion of this important aspect of Freudian theory.

accepted by all psychoanalytic schools. The old "faculties" were just there, somehow or other, as attributes of the human mind. They were either purely descriptive or dragged into an evolutionary scheme by speculative analogy. Freud dismissed them cheerfully—the more so because in his medical training he, unlike the professional psychologists of his time, had probably never encountered them vividly as a coordinated science. Freud set himself the task of explaining *how* and *why* people come to have moral and rational judgments, and *why* they care about their fellows. When he got around to it,* Freud naturally approached his study of the forces *opposing* expression of the sexual wish in the same empirical *developmental* fashion as his study of the sexual drives themselves. Freud's provinces of the mind grow out of the experience of the human organism in its milieu. The complex attributes of the adult are built out of his living; they are not simply *there* for identification.

Again there was a bifurcation or multifurcation in the later development of psychoanalytic theory. Psychoanalysts differ as to just *how* early experiences structure later personality trends and as to the specific role of the infantile unconscious. Adler and Horney tend to think of the problem mainly through a more careful interpretation of the old saw: as the twig is bent so the branch inclines. In their view, early experience sets the pattern for later expectations and later techniques of adaptation. Freudians, however, tend to think of a relatively separate history for the various aspects of development, of the actual freezing of some aims at the infantile level by the mechanism of repression, while other aims develop more or less in accordance with the requirements of the social milieu and are only *influenced by* the persistence of the repressed aims.

Only the basic concept is highlighted here: whatever psychological patterns one considers significant in the adult personality are the product of the *adaptive experience of the person*. The longitudinal patterning of human systems must be considered as well as, or even more carefully than, their cross-sectional structure. Prediction depends upon history, the line of new development being subtended from the past—obviously in creative interaction with the present.

Early childhood is the time when the malleable, adaptable, flexible human psyche takes on the essential directions it will pursue. Because the human infant is so unformed by nature, because these experiences are the first, the events of infancy have a psychological importance very naturally overlooked

---

* Freud states frequently that study of these matters was delayed by the need to clarify the totally new concept of unconscious sexual pressures.

by the adult philosopher in his study or the adult scientist among his instruments. More than any other single discipline, psychoanalysis drew attention to the overwhelming importance of this early period of life and offered new indications of what to look for in studying children.*

In partial summary of the dynamic aspects of Freud's contribution as followed up by every psychoanalytic school (and most of the other contemporary schools), we may note first a thoroughgoing concept of psychological determinism, valuable because it showed a way of interpreting both the queernesses and the sublimities of the human psyche by the scientific method of empirical examination and investigation. The goal-directed quality of human activity attained scientific status as a premise and as a focus of investigation—with recognition of hidden (unconscious) goals as a necessary part of any psychology, and with emphasis on early childhood as the period when the major directions of the personality are set. Differences among psychoanalytic schools in the working out of these basic concepts have been adumbrated. Their elaboration is the task of this book.

THE UNCONSCIOUS PROCESSES

THE PROMISSORY NOTE mentioned on page 29 is honored at this point. The following discussion is drawn mainly from Freud, but all psychoanalytic schools make constant use of the principles and procedures here presented. I will, so far as possible, arbitrarily eliminate considerations of deep psychological dynamics and confine discussion to the technical problem of *how* the operations of the unconscious can be observed and interpreted.

By definition the operations of the unconscious cannot be directly discovered by introspection. The person is not aware of his unconscious drives—

---

* Nonpsychoanalytic schools have probably thus far outstripped the analytic schools in direct observation and quasi-experimentation in the field of child psychology, and their efforts have often proceeded from quite different premises. Indeed, psychoanalysts have until recently shown a curious blindness to the careful studies of "child psychologists," and vice versa. Fruitful collaboration is just beginning. The psychoanalytic contribution to date has been to effect a shift in attitude toward the early years rather than the accumulation of *direct* information about them. Perhaps the outstanding success of the annual publication *The Psychoanalytic Study of the Child* may be seen as a harbinger of change. These volumes contain many empirical studies of childhood problems, conceived and executed within the framework of psychoanalytic thought.

a tautology of some value in view of the scientist's very frequent repudiation of psychoanalytic interpretations of motivation on the grounds of his inability, expressed sincerely and in all good will, to remember or feel any of the things attributed to him by psychoanalytic theory. This repudiation is profoundly true whether he is asked to remember his Oedipal attachments *à la* Freud or to feel the violent hostility which makes him extra tender *à la* Horney. The more deeply unconscious the motivation, psychoanalytically speaking, the more obvious it is that the person will *not* be aware of it. In fact—just to prevent such awareness, which would be experienced as threatening—defenses are often built up in the form of militantly *opposite* conscious attitudes.

Freud early distinguished between a *primary process,* whereby the instinctual drives manifest themselves psychologically—in ways to be described under the heading "Characteristics of Unconscious Thought Processes" (pp. 47-67)—and a *secondary process,* whereby these drives are ordered and controlled by rational thought and voluntary action.

> So far as we know [Freud writes], a psychic apparatus possessing only the primary process does not exist, and is to that extent a theoretical fiction; but this at least is a fact: that the primary processes are present in the apparatus from the beginning, while the secondary processes only take shape gradually, during the course of life, inhibiting and overlaying the primary. . . .[2]

Freud does *not* conceive of an "unconscious mind" as a separate, unchangeable entity somehow inhabiting our mortal flesh. The non-libido analysts would also find such a notion wholly unacceptable. It is mentioned here as a common misinterpretation of psychoanalytic doctrine, understandable because in all psychoanalytic literature conscious and unconscious processes are informally contrasted and goal-directedness is ascribed to each with some separateness—in fact, often with complete antagonism. The popular dichotomy, however, is far too simple.

Freud approaches the concept of *a* timeless unconscious most closely in his emphasis upon relatively focused infantile wishes which become *repressed* and continue in their initial direction the more insistently because they are cut off from normal integration with the emerging secondary processes. They may become elaborated as they attach to themselves the new materials and even the new partial integrations of ongoing experience. Thus, intricate patterns may be formed at the unconscious level which function to some extent as a dynamic unit and which combine in a variety of ways with the secondary processes as they take shape during the course of life. These various combinations of primary and secondary processes will be discussed in Chapter 6 under the heading "Defense Mechanisms of the Ego," after Freud's theory of instincts and the process of growth have been discussed. Only then shall we be in a position to understand the complex relationship between conscious and unconscious aspects of personality function.

Adler, and in less measure the other non-libido analysts, prefer to envisage the operations of the unconscious in a much more immediate relationship to problems which begin at birth and are continuously determining throughout life. Modes of coping with them initiated in infancy tend to persist as a life style or safety device in adult situations, where they are no longer appropriate. The underlying problems and the essential nature of the devices employed in attempts at solution are, of course, largely unconscious. The major difference from Freud's view of the unconscious lies in repudiation of the idea that the infantile problems are in any sense split off from the functioning personality as a whole, so as to function in any sense as partially separable dynamic units in the unconscious. Again, we shall postpone elaboration of this view to the homologous chapter on dynamics for these authors (Chap. 11), with my own comment and efforts at integration following the presentation of all the data.

We have noted that for all schools the unconscious is a process—or better, processes—conceived within a dynamic (motivational) theory of human behavior. It is *never* thought of as an isolated entity which can be studied independently of the total personality, according to its own peculiar laws. I insist upon the point with fervor, because the rest of this chapter will be devoted to just such study, *artificially* dissected from its proper context. My reason for the dissection seems sound: every psychoanalytic school today, and many non-psychoanalytic psychological approaches, constantly use within the constellation of their various dynamic theories the techniques and observations herewith presented. But people who have little direct acquaintance with psychoanalytic procedures often do not understand how the analyst arrives at his conclusions. On the contrary, people unfamiliar with analytic *techniques* tend to evaluate psychoanalytic theories on the basis of their own conscious experience, or to apply scientific checks inappropriately—just as people at one time repudiated theories of radioactivity and electromagnetism because they did not conform to the scientific tenets of the times. Science expands *partly* through the development of new techniques designed to explore new areas. Understanding critique of the new area (here the unconscious processes) depends *partly* on understanding the avenues of information available and something of the nature of the new area.

The purpose of this section is, therefore, mainly to *describe* (1) how information about unconscious processes may be obtained and (2) the characteristics of unconscious processes. Variants in phraseology are used without precision simply in the interest of avoiding stylistic monotony. "The unconscious" must not be considered to imply a distinctly separable entity. The phrase "thought processes" does not imply "thought" rigorously divorced from impulse or emotion. In a section aimed at description of processes which are essentially dynamic, it is not possible to eliminate dynamic concepts altogether, but the dynamic concepts have deliberately been kept vague and secondary. Interpretation has been offered only on terms acceptable to almost everyone, or has been only implied, with the recommendation that the reader carry it further himself with whatever dynamic insights he may have. The point here is merely to suggest *how* psychoanalytic interpretation is reached.

AVENUES OF INFORMATION

Freud grasped early the general principle that the unconscious reveals itself most readily when the rational goal-directedness of our usual activities is abated, either temporarily, as in the small errors and slips of everyday life and in sleep, or in major derangements. Inaccessible to direct observation, the unconscious can be studied through those fragments of behavior which the conscious mind dismisses as silly mistakes and accidents or rationalizes as having a different intent from the one actually operating. Of somewhat late development in Freudian theory, although emphasized from the outset by Adler, is the analysis of extensive systems of behavior (character trends, ostensible vocational goals, deeply held "rational" convictions and aspirations) for their unconscious directives. Thus, the *pattern of behavior* over large sectors of the life span as well as the out-of-key fragment reveals unconscious purpose.

Because inquiry into the unconscious came into scientific prominence via pathology, most of us fail to realize that perfectly normal goals are in large part unconsciously determined. No healthy person lives by a minute-to-minute ordering of his activities and feelings according to a conscious plan rationally determined and executed at all points. His life is mainly ordered unconsciously, as the poets have always known. So long as his unconscious goals are in harmonious relationship with his conscious aims and are pursued according to the canons of reasonableness approved by his society, they are very difficult to discern. Being out of key with consciousness is not a necessary attribute of the unconscious but merely isolates it for study—much as a single voice in a good chorus is hardly perceptible as such unless it is off pitch.

The following pages describe the various ways by which the analyst gains information about the unconscious. Discussion is focused on rather well-codified approaches available to the analyst in his office. They were developed and are still mainly used in therapy. I have, however, suggested extensions currently in use beyond the intimate doctor-patient contact, notably in psychoanalytically oriented study of the life history and in that branch of psychological testing currently known as the projective method.

FREE ASSOCIATION

Freud's early grasp of the general principle of studying the unconscious under conditions of relaxation of conscious control led to the development of a technique basic to psychoanalysis as a therapeutic method: *free association*. The patient is asked to try deliberately to relax his normal directedness of thinking and speak out everything that comes into his mind—good, bad, or utter twaddle. This request is not an invitation to the subject to confide his innermost thoughts, as many outsiders seem to believe. On the contrary, the analyst usually listens patiently to a confidential outpouring of unseemly thoughts and actions considered top secret, and then begins the real work of psychoanalysis. The patient finally just talks with no idea of revealing or concealing. (We shall see later that some types of patient find this "fundamental rule of psychoanalysis" extremely difficult.) Occasionally this technique leads to a concrete memory hitherto forgotten, the reinstatement of which has the dramatic consequences cited in the very early cases of cure through recovery of memories in hypnosis. Much more often the free associations cover mere fragments of past events from childhood or more recent years, bits of things read or heard, casual judgments, hopes, feelings, none of which is important in itself. Curiously enough, these unrelated bits and pieces which merely pop into the mind tend to show a theme of their own. They are not truly random but are guided by unconscious preoccupations.

Illustration is difficult because the free associations of any person are highly idiosyncratic, involving happenings and ideas peculiar to his own life, fleetingly alluded to in circumstances which reduce the task of ordered social communication to a minimum. The analyst, if he is to understand the allusions without constant interruption, must eventually became familiar with his patient's acquaintanceship back to the nursery, his literary, musical, and artistic affiliations, his ordinary quirks of phrase and thought. In view of the fact that the average analysis requires five hour-long sessions per week for one to three years, such familiarity with the details of the patient's life is not beyond the compass of the doctor's mind. It is difficult, however, to reproduce a convincing five minutes of free association in illustration without ten pages of annotation. The following is a telescoped reconstruction of a sequence described by an unusually cultured patient (a friend of the author). It is a useful example provided that the reader realizes that the usual analytic free associations contain a much higher proportion of inert ingredients.

The patient begins with a brief report of the previous day—a sort of routine in his analytic sessions. Nothing special: he had a conference with his boss about a going project. He didn't quite like the boss's policy, but it was not too bad and who was he, in the hierarchy of his institution, to contradict the boss? By now this was an old issue in the analysis: did he habitually give in too easily, or did he evaluate correctly the major contours of his job? In any event, the conference was just a conference like any other. He'd had a dream—something about an ironing board, but that was as far as he could go. Associations to ironing board? Well, we have one. "Matter of fact, my wife said our maid irons badly. She could iron my shirts better herself, but I don't think she could and I'm sure she wouldn't. Anyhow, my shirts look all right to me. I wish she wouldn't worry so much. I hope she doesn't fire that maid." The patient suddenly hums a bit from *Lohengrin* and has to hunt for the words on the request of the analyst. It is the passage where Lohengrin reveals his glorious origin. ("My father, Parsifal, wears his crown and I am his knight, Lohengrin.") Patient: "Now I think of that last report X [his boss] turned in. That was *my* work—only I can't say so. That ironing board—my mother was ironing. I jumped off the cupboard, wonderful jump, but I sort of used her behind as support—she was leaning over. She told father I had been disrespectful and he gave me a licking. I was awfully hurt. I hadn't even thought about her old behind—it was just a wonderful jump. Father would never let me explain. My sister says he was proud of me. He never acted that way. He was awfully strict. I wish he hadn't died when I was so young—we might have worked things out."

It is the task of the analyst to select from this material the themes most worthwhile to pursue at any given period. For us it is enough to observe that the *non sequiturs* of the patient's own job situation (where he did not *consciously* feel threatened), the ironing board, with his wife's attitude toward the maid's job, the enormous self-reassurance of the *Lohengrin* passage, and finally the resurgence of a childhood memory are all closely related.

The process is quite different from the rational consideration: "I am worried about my job, the boss is not such a hotshot as he thinks, and I am sorry for the maid because she seems to be in the same situation." Or perhaps, "My wife is as censorious and unjust as my mother," etc. (The reader will doubtless identify other themes of deeper importance.) On the contrary, the patient would honestly deny any such concerns, at least on the occasion of an ordinary job conference. Indeed, at the time the wife-maid sequence appears, the patient has not remembered the childhood episode and is not aware that he is making more than a passing comment on a trifling domestic incident consciously considered as being outside his own sphere of interest. Far from seeking consolation in the *Lohengrin* saga consciously, he does not even realize what he is humming until the analyst asks him.

This kind of thematically oriented *non sequitur* occurs daily, five times a week, in any successfully moving analysis. The orderliness of such random thought serves as evidence for the existence of a structuring power in the mind beyond the consciously directed mental process. For more than fifty years analysts have used the technique of free association as a very important avenue of information toward the unconscious problems of the patient—information rather easily shared with the patient himself as he too comes to recognize the underlying themes.

RESISTANCE

Thus far the impression may have been created that such free flow of unconscious material is of perfectly regular occurrence. One may even wonder why analysis takes so long when an intelligent patient could surely see from a dozen sessions the major contours of his unconscious life. The dynamic— and hence therapeutic—aspects of the problem will be considered later. At this point, we shall consider only the fact of *resistance*.

Consciously or unconsciously, the patient often does not see the underlying theme, apparently does not *want* to see it. He may *consciously*, without quite meaning to frustrate his expensive treatment, break off the train of associations when it approaches uncomfortable territory. For example, the patient just cited might so love his wife as to wish to keep their relationship free from the possible misunderstandings of the analyst, himself prejudging the relationship as essentially good and too sacred for prying inquiry. Thoughts concerning his wife may therefore not be reported, with good conscience. Or some ideas may be so offensive to his self-esteem that he does not speak them out. Or he may feel sure that the analyst will misconstrue their meaning. Or he himself may be convinced that they are entirely trivial. Sometimes the patient's judgment is correct, but at all points he *quite consciously* breaks the fundamental rule of psychoanalysis—to report everything. Such conscious resistance is of no theoretical interest for this chapter—except as special areas of conscious resistance may become indexes of an unconscious *pattern* (cf. pp. 43-44). The psychoanalyst's task in dealing with it is hardly different from that of the medical doctor whose patient deliberately conceals his symptoms or misrepresents his adherence to the doctor's prescription.

Freud early noted, and all psychoanalysts have confirmed, the fact of *unconscious resistance*. A highly intelligent patient may honestly fail to see connections obvious to a child. For example, our patient may stoutly maintain that the *Lohengrin* passage is a favorite of his because of the lovely music, and that his sudden humming had nothing to do with the words. The patient is sometimes correct in rejecting a particular tie-up suggested by the analyst (analysts are fallible like anyone else), but more often he is wrong, no matter how ingenious his "reasons" for criticism. The patient quoted has engaged in a successful professional life for years, on the basis of a carefully modulated evaluation of himself and his superiors. The sudden incursion of "my father Parsifal" and "I his knight" strikes him quite legitimately as absurd—and in so far as he has been unconsciously toning down his own demands for prestige out of unconscious fear, the interpretation is positively frightening. The *analyst* may see that the patient is actually demanding, unconsciously, an infantile absolute acceptance of his powers with fears which belong to his early relationship with his parents. (The dynamics of these statements will be discussed in later chapters.) It is in the highest degree unlikely that in the early stages of analysis the *patient* could effectively recognize as part of his own psyche attitudes at such variance with his whole attitude toward himself and his relations with other people. At any point at which the evidence is overwhelming, he may offer an intellectual acquiescence, but he will remain at first unconvinced as to the general operation in his own life of the trends so acknowledged. Thus, for a long time, the interpretation of every new instance is again resisted in the same manner.

This quasi-reasonable repudiation of the analyst's interpretation is only one of the manifestations of unconscious resistance—actually one of the most subtle and most difficult to disentangle from genuinely reasonable criticism.* Much more obvious is the sudden failure of the free-association sequence. The invitation to talk about anything at all sounds easy. Doubtless there is always something or other in our minds which should be reportable if we do not have to care what it is. Yet every analytic patient reports at times that his mind becomes a complete blank, or that it jumps about like a spoonful of water in hot grease, with so many burning droplets of ideas that any selection feels like a matter of arbitrary, *conscious* choice. The *Lohengrin* tune imposed itself, as

---

* In the chapters on treatment (7 and 12), I shall explain how analysts generally handle this problem in practice by a very sparing use of complex interpretations. Usually the analyst *leads the patient to formulate his own interpretations*—by interjecting a question, by suggesting a new juxtaposition of materials presented by the patient, often simply by repeating the patient's own words with slightly different emphasis.

it were, when the mind was left relaxed. But how to choose among a dozen pressing ideas which seem somehow simultaneously present when one tries to relax?

Psychoanalysts have observed over and over that such blockage of the associational stream typically occurs when topics are approached which the patient unconsciously does not want to have clarified. Each school has its own theories as to *why* such unconscious protectiveness sets in and as to what to do about it, but they all recognize its occurrence. In a way, this readily observable *stoppage* of the associational process is as convincing evidence for the unconscious as the phenomena (described above) that occur when it is moving freely. Provided that blockage does not continue too long, it can be as useful an avenue of information toward specific unconscious content as is free association. If one traces carefully where the breaks occur, one can discern quite clearly the items within the unconscious processes about which the patient is most anxious—that is, most coy, reserved, and protective.*

A great many other techniques may be employed by the patient's unconscious in resistance. We shall see later that some patients report the events of the day, dreams, childhood memories, in such a manner as to make them genuinely trifling—that is, with semiconscious control. The associations come freely enough, but only along a familiar track thoroughly sanctioned by the "censor" and hence dynamically insignificant. We may extend the concept of resistance in psychoanalysis somewhat beyond the handling of free association as an isolated technique. The patient may suddenly come late to appointments, forget appointments, make mistakes about payment or protest the amount he has to pay, criticize the analyst's office furnishings, quote derogatory remarks about him sometimes heard months earlier, and so forth. These small unpleasantnesses occur so regularly in any analysis as to be an expected part of the treatment and should be seen in broader context than resistance to a specific line of interpretation (see the discussion of transference, pp. 305-307). They tend to occur specifically, however, when the analysis threatens to uncover unconscious processes that the person cannot tolerate.

We have noted that things become unconscious for a reason important to the personality and are kept unconscious for a reason, and not through inadvertence or ignorance. Resistance, therefore, is an *active* process which serves to maintain the repression in opposition to the new forces, leading toward insight and release, brought into play by the analysis. It is especially

---

* We have here been discussing free association as it occurs in the analytic session. Many of the same phenomena can be observed in the association *test,* in which the subject is asked to respond to a stimulus word with the first word that comes to his mind. Here delays and complicated or peculiar responses also seem to indicate unconscious problems—which, of course, cannot be immediately followed up in detail as in the analytic session.

important in revealing the nature of the opposing forces. Many analysts nowadays feel that analyzing with the patient the precise nature of his resistances is quite as fruitful as overcoming them in the sense of allowing the repressed materials to appear.

THE DREAM

Next to free association and the related problem of resistance, the avenue of information about the unconscious most generally used in psychoanalysis is the *dream*. Analysts vary widely, even within their school affiliations and from patient to patient, in the amount of attention devoted to the dream in the therapeutic session. Interpretation varies somewhat with the theoretical orientation of the analyst, and there is some difference of opinion as to the role of the dream in the total psychic economy. But these variations within psychoanalysis are trivial in comparison with the overwhelming judgment of all analysts that the dream "has meaning" and is a very important source of information. The variations among analysts will be mentioned where they become appropriate. No further discussion of the dream is offered here because it will be used as a point of departure for our discussion of the characteristics of unconscious thought processes (pp. 49-54).

THE LIFE PATTERN

Study of the *life pattern* as a source of information about the unconscious was of comparatively late development in psychoanalysis except for the Adlerian school.* At the outset Freud was primarily interested in the neurotic symptom as a more or less isolated phenomenon. He observed in some patients an amazing recurrence of the same kind of disastrous "accidents" over an extended sector of the life span—a pattern which he called the *Schicksal*, or "fate," neurosis. These patients seemed pursued by a malign fate. Far from profiting by sad experience, Freud noted, they seemed compelled somehow to repeat the same mistake and unconsciously to call down the same misfortune upon their heads time after time. We shall see that this "repetition compulsion" was one of the observations which led Freud to the formulation of a *death instinct*, essentially destructive in its aim (see pp. 80-81).

Many Freudians and all of the non-libido analysts prefer a different ex-

---

* Freudian readers point out that insight into the life pattern is *inherent* in all of Freud's case studies. True, and I do not wish to insist on historical origins. Nevertheless, I feel that Adler was the one who first gave *explicit* recognition to the importance of the life pattern, and my own impression is that many classical Freudians still tend to consider it of relatively secondary significance.

planation of the same phenomenon, which seems actually more common than Freud at first suggested—indeed, in some measure, it appears to be a general characteristic of neurosis. The explanation preferred by the non-libido analysts (notably Horney) is that so long as the same unconscious problems persist, the neurotic naturally persists in trying to solve them in the neurotic manner characteristic for him. He is not aiming for repetitious disaster, even unconsciously (except as an unconscious need for punishment may be one of his problems). Repetitious disaster is merely an incidental consequence of his continued pursuit of unconscious aims which inevitably get him into trouble. An example familiar to the tabloids is that of the rich man who falls in love with one bleached blonde after another, with mounting alimony expenses. Most of us have had the experience of helping a friend through marital or job difficulties only to find that, through no apparent fault of his own, he encountered similar misfortune in the new situation, although it looked more promising and so different.

Adler pointed out long ago that careful consideration of the life story of an individual could show a kind of coherence attributable to the structuring power of his unconscious goals. Indeed, Adler relied more upon such analysis of the "life style" (see pp. 340-342) than upon the specialized techniques thus far described for information about the underlying trends of the patient. At the present time it is probably correct to say that every psychoanalyst of whatever school uses the *pattern* of the patient's behavior over his whole life span to understand and to demonstrate to the patient the nonrational directives of his personality. Emphasis upon this material varies from school to school, as I shall try to explain later.

The technique can be adapted readily to any workable dynamic theory with many different kinds of material. Blos and others[3] have been able to construct a reasonably accurate picture of the deeper personality trends of students without ever meeting them in the flesh, by analyzing specimens of their themes, drawings, etc., done in the ordinary course of school assignments, plus observation of their behavior by teachers and fellow students and such biographical materials as can be obtained in a normal friendly situation. Blos's theoretical framework is definitely Freudian, and his data are such as any classroom teacher could accumulate if he took the trouble to preserve the material produced in the workaday school routine. Psychoanalysts seldom get their hands on this kind of material and are rarely patient enough to put up with the practical difficulties of obtaining ingress to a normal group. Moreover, they seriously dislike working exclusively with such "superficial" materials for any purpose. They generally use the life pattern as an avenue of information *only in conjunction with* free association, dreams, and other resources available in the doctor-patient relationship. It is part of the analytic treatment, not a study in itself.

THE PROJECTIVE METHOD

Akin to the study of the pattern of the patient's life story and everyday behavior is the *projective method of psychological testing*,* which has come into prominence in America within the last ten to twenty years. (It was accepted much earlier in Europe.) It is interesting to note that the two major tests of this nature, the Rorschach and the Thematic Apperception Test, were developed by psychoanalytically oriented psychiatrists (Rorschach and Murray). Psychologists trained in carefully objective, standardized techniques of test construction initially viewed the new method with great suspicion; psychiatrists were unwilling to entrust it to psychologists who lacked training and experience with the kind of judgment required for insight into unconscious trends. Indeed, the tests can be used only by psychologists who understand the special principle on which they are based and who have sufficient background to apply it wisely.

Successful interpretation depends upon appreciation of the *pattern* of the subject's reaction to the test stimuli in infinite variety. No two subjects are exactly the same, as no two daisies are alike; no single test element carries a specific meaning. Rather crude (standardizable) indexes may be used for the identification of gross differences in personality, as a daisy may be readily distinguished from a rhododendron. Such differences are usually so apparent that special testing is unnecessary. The projective method becomes indispensable when a significant differentiation can be made only by examination of *patterns* too intricate for the objective measurement of single trends as prefigured in the well-constructed standardized test.† No one would confuse an elm leaf with a holly leaf, but we may well reflect upon the difficulties of differentiation by separate, isolated measures of length, breadth, serration, etc. Like judgment in the analytic hour, accurate interpretation of these complex, spontaneous test materials often depends upon appreciation of the direction and interaction of many small items, any one of which might be interpreted differently in a

* The test stimulus is made as unstructured, loose, ambiguous, "meaningless" as possible (ink-blots, vague pictures, half-heard sounds, drawings made with minimal directives, etc.), and the subject is asked to tell what it might mean or somehow to take focused action. The meaning and focus are thus introduced by the subject. His unguided choice provides the material used by the examiner in interpretation.

† These abbreviated statements about test construction are, I think, comprehensible to most of the "psychologists" who read this book. The point is dear to my heart because much of my own work in research, teaching, and private practice concerns the projective methods. It is not a *necessary* part of this book, however, and I suggest that any reader who does not understand the terms used here cheerfully disregard all my comments on psychological testing!

different context. Like the psychoanalyst, the examining psychologist must learn the language of the unconscious, but he applies it with special reference to the test stimuli.

It is the latter point which differentiates the test from the analytic situation. The analyst offers the patient virtually no specific reality problem and carefully adapts his provocative comment to the current needs of the patient. The test stimuli, however vaguely structured, have more definition—as established by the many subjects who have reacted to them. The essential test criterion of comparing an individual's performance with that of his peers is preserved. Thus, the subject who calls a certain ambiguous figure (Card 3 of the T.A.T.) a *woman* is objectively just as "correct" as the one who sees it as a *man,* but if the examiner knows that the majority of subjects unhesitatingly see this figure as masculine, he is alerted to something special about the subject who calls it a woman or remarks that its sex is not clear. Homosexual trends are one *possibility,* but the examiner will not proffer this explanation unless he finds that the subject deviates at other points as well in a manner characteristic for homosexual identifications. Perhaps the subject is generally a doubting Thomas; perhaps he has special reasons to think of women in shorts.

A doubting Thomas doubts almost all his test judgments. The doubting, overcritical attitude of some persons stands out against the more casual approach of the vast majority of subjects. Furthermore, since any construction the subject may make from the formless test materials involves tolerance of some inaccuracies, examination of the *pattern of criticism* becomes revealing. Again the tester has the advantage of knowing which inaccuracies are usually tolerated and is impressed when the subject strains at an inaccuracy most people consider a gnat and swallows a number of camels, sometimes of his own invention.

The response determined by an idiosyncratic experience of the subject usually sticks out *as such.* It may be dismissed as an incidental, unusable item. Occasionally it is so distinctive that the examiner can make a very sharp guess about the nature of the experience, especially if he knows the language of unconscious symbols. Such guesses may seem like black magic, and they are relatively rare in test interpretation. They are more than guesses only when the tester is so well acquainted with the test situation and with psychodynamics that he can appreciate the significance of the response which is idiosyncratic in the test setting.

SUMMARY

In partial summary we may say that free association, resistance, dreams, and the life pattern are used routinely by all psychoanalysts (with some variation) in their effort to understand the unconscious processes operating in their patients. The projective method of psychological testing was a relatively late development based on the same principles, with the added feature of enabling the interpreter to compare the "unconscious" response of one person with the "unconscious" response of his peers in the test situation.

In the chapters on therapy, a number of other avenues of information will be mentioned: memories recaptured under hypnosis or drugs; the influence of traumatic states, accidental or induced, on the emotionality of the patient and hence, often, on his accessibility to therapeutic intervention; his bodily reactions (motility, including but going beyond facial expression, vasomotor changes seen grossly as flushing or blanching, variations in timbre of voice or tempo of speech beyond what the words communicate). There are in addition a host of cues which psychiatrists are only beginning to order scientifically, although such cues may doubtless be perceived in any sensitive interpersonal contacts. These avenues of information are omitted from discussion here because at present they are merely lanes used by relatively few psychoanalysts. Probably they will never be accepted at the same level as the current verbalistic modes of expression for the excellent reason that the language of the body is less differentiated than speech. As the *adjunctive* value of these subsidiary avenues becomes clarified, one may prophesy developments far beyond their current status. For patients (or cultures) whose difficulties in verbal exchange are almost insuperable, they may become the main avenue of information. Their neglect here should be seen in historical perspective, and in the perspective of the major therapeutic aims of psychoanalysis.

CHARACTERISTICS OF
UNCONSCIOUS THOUGHT PROCESSES

Critics of psychoanalysis often complain not only that they cannot observe in themselves the motivations and feelings ascribed to the unconscious but that psychoanalysts resort to fantastically far-fetched arguments in support of their position. The rational man is not easily impressed by a pun offered in sober scientific proof or by the solemn statement that a particular item must be true because it is so vehemently denied. Yet if the reader has been able to follow with any sympathy the foregoing discussion of avenues of information about the unconscious, he has already demonstrated a measure of understanding of peculiar ("unconscious") modes of thought and behavior which nevertheless have a kind of coherence in their very peculiarity.

Freud was deeply interested in this peculiar coherence from the outset of his work with the unconscious. He describes himself with some justice as a man concentrated rather narrowly on scientific matters. He approached the scientific problem as a doctor concerned with finding a cure for hysteria, as a reflective man (he has been called the last of the great philosophers) concerned with universal meanings. Nevertheless, he found time during the early years to write four long books and numerous papers on trivial and peripheral matters: *The Interpretation of Dreams, The Psychopathology of Everyday Life, Wit and Its Relation to the Unconscious, Totem and Taboo*. During this same period he was writing *Three Contributions to a Theory of Sex* and other papers of definitely clinical or metapsychological nature. Why did a "narrowly scientific" man trouble himself with the small mishaps of trivial social situations, with jokes, with remote savages, at a time when interest in these matters among psychologists was far less common than it is today?

Freud's major purpose in these books was to clarify how the unconscious operates, not only in disease, but also in many aspects of normal living. His important dynamic concepts concerning the nature of instincts and the complex adjustive mechanisms of the personality as a whole are brought into the discussion only toward the end of each of these works. Through hundreds of pages Freud merely traces the regularities observable in the primary process, the techniques of expression characteristic of the unconscious. His observations have long been freely used by everyone who works with unconscious materials, no matter how divergent the motivational theory finally used in interpretation.

The Interpretation of Dreams (1900) is by far the most useful book in this series—and the most systematic. Chapter 7, "The Psychology of the Dream Processes," remains the most inclusive statement of the dynamics of thinking in Freud's work. Freud himself said of this book that it represented a discovery so great as to be given to a man to make only once in a lifetime. The discovery was not merely of the importance of the dream process, but actually of the orderliness and significance of all the irrational aspects of psychic life. It was the gift of a new language—the paving of a highroad into a wilderness whose very existence had been unknown to science.

I have chosen the dream as the point of departure for my exposition of the techniques of the unconscious partly because it was the focus of Freud's most systematic analysis but also because the reasons behind Freud's choice are still cogent. All analysts use the dream in therapy. We all dream, and the conditions of our dreaming are roughly similar throughout the world—*i.e.*, we are asleep, and for the nonce relieved of responsibility for direct action in a social world. Therefore, it is comparatively easy to understand the peculiarities of the dream as contrasted with consciously directed thought, regardless of special background and knowledge on the part of either the dreamer or the interpreter. Our special background always plays a role in our dreaming, as we shall see, but the essential language of the dream seems to be much more universally human than the language of our waking hours, which is always carefully adapted to the small daily requirements of our quite special role in our quite special social group.

THE ROLE OF DREAMING

The Interpretation of Dreams will be used, then, to present in some detail a description of the language of the unconscious, with the understanding that the dream is only one instance of processes readily observable elsewhere. At the risk of tedious protraction, I would like to preserve Freud's essential comments on the place of the dream in the total economy of mental life as a vivid illustration of the caution required in *any* interpretation of the unconscious. The primary process never appears as an isolated phenomenon. Indeed, we can see it only through characteristic distortions of the secondary process under certain conditions. There are always, of course, varying admixtures of stimuli and judgments proper to "rational" thought. When one is thirsty, it is not entirely rational to dream of a bubbling brook instead of getting up for a glass of water, but all the ingredients of common-sense response to a strong stimulus are present, and not even Freud finds this kind of dream very useful as an expression of perduring unconscious trends. In 1900 Freud was more concerned than need be reported here with theories of the dream proposed prior to his own discovery. He stated that he found little to *reject* in these theories beyond a dogmatic claim to all-sufficient explanation. What will be reported here (unfortunately too briefly for historical acknowledgment) are the outlines of Freud's placement of dream processes *of all sorts* within a dynamic psychology which relates primary and secondary modes of thought.

In sleep the conscious mind is *relatively* inactive, mainly because it is released from its reality-testing functions and from immediate responsibility for the execution of its decisions. The motorium is almost entirely excluded from participation in the psychic life, the sensorium drastically limited. Thus, the inward intellective and affective processes continuously operative have relatively free play without the usual corrective controls of immediate physical and social contacts. Consequently, as in free association, structuring by unconscious "wishes" (Freud) or "goals" (Adler) is much more obvious, once one learns to understand the curious language in which they find expression.

It should not be thought that the unconscious expresses its wishes or goals openly, even in sleep. Very few dreams show their meaning directly. Children's dreams may show such directedness before the psyche has become intricately organized. What Freud called "dreams of convenience"—as when we dream of a stream of refreshing water after a midnight snack of salty food, or when the intern awake most of the night on an emergency case reacts to the morning alarm clock with the dream that he has gone to the hospital on schedule, while still remaining cozily in bed—may also require no great subtlety of interpretation.

Somewhat akin to this very direct representation of a current reality need which penetrates sleep is the continuation or repetition of a waking process in sleep or near-sleep. Poincaré, for example, reports the correct solution of an abstruse mathematical problem during the night. The victim of traumatic neurosis often relives quite literally in his dreams the original shocking experience. But more often the dream process translates the cogent activity of the day into concrete "symbols" and provides only an illusory solution, if any. Mental labor may appear as the sawing of endless blocks of wood, and the dream solution of a fantastic gadget for getting through with the task more quickly does not prove practical when applied to the real, mental task.

From these "easy" symbolizations one may learn one of the important tricks of the dream process cited by many students of the dream even outside the psychoanalytic camp: the concretization of an abstract problem, usually in visual terms.[4]

An experience of my own in a hypnogogic state close to full dreaming may clarify this point. In bed, I was still planning a lecture on Freud to be delivered the next day; specifically, I was planning how to introduce the superego as the product of the child's relationship with the parents and the hostility of this differentiated part of the id to other infantile id demands. Suddenly I realized that I was no longer thinking abstractly. I was simply watching a well-groomed little boy walk upstairs between a nice-looking couple, while another little boy, of the gamin type, dodged about from room to room bent on mischief and occasionally making provocative gestures toward the child walking so decorously with his parents. The analogy to Freud's theory is not good enough to serve in a lecture and was by no means planned as such, but it is clear enough. The little scene is a pretty fair concretization of the abstract ideas with which my conscious mind was concerned at the moment of falling asleep.

Such dreams are comparatively rare in adults and perhaps occur mainly in the half-dream state, in which conscious preoccupations still dictate the contour of the dream. Much more typically, the dream is a highly complex amalgam of unconscious wishes and fears, goals and needs, repressed or carefully controlled during waking life, which find expression *along with* an even more primitive type of resistance than we have thus far discussed. Freud points out that *even in sleep direct expression of wishes is censored* because of the concomitant danger which such expression entails in the infantile unconscious.

Censorship, rooted in fear, is as sleepless as the wish. The rules of censorship change somewhat in sleep, but they are followed rigidly. In fact, if the patient dreams too nakedly, he scares himself into waking up. I remember a horror story on the radio in which a woman who had committed a secret crime could not sleep because a recurrent dream constantly took her to the brink of destruction and she awakened just in time. Her affectionate husband, on medical advice, slipped a soporific into her coffee, and at the appropriate point in her dream she died. This was horror fiction. So far as we know, people do not actually die in their sleep for any such reason—but unconscious fear, according to Freud, operates in a similar manner to waken the sleeper from what he conceives as mortal danger.

Most wishes are repressed (*i.e.*, become unconscious) originally because their fulfillment is considered dangerous by the same childish aspect of the mind which formulated them. The psychic processes continue by night as by day, and one function of the dream is to prevent "mental" excitation from building up to the point at which the only defense is to wake up. Thus, Freud considers a major biological function of the dream to be that of preserving sleep.

DREAM MATERIALS AND THE MEANING OF DREAMS

However bizarre at first glance, the dream *materials*, its sensorimotor ingredients and memories, are similar to those of waking life. This fact was recognized by scientific students of the dream long before Freud. Current bodily sensations and external stimuli undoubtedly contribute to its formation.

The often-cited "guillotine" dream of Maury[5] is too long to repeat here, but the reader may remember that a coherent drama almost as complex as *A Tale of Two Cities* was precipitated by a slight blow on the neck from which the dreamer awakened almost immediately. The reader is probably familiar with the involuntary muscle jerks which often follow unwonted strenuous physical exercise. For years my dream state produced a rationalization of this jerk as jouncing down a curb in a small wagon—an absurd bit which, under the proper physical conditions, would inject itself without adequate setting into almost any dream. Presumably this dream rationalization harks back to some real experience of affective importance which I have never been able to recover. Together with the long Maury dream, this item shows how the dream work may use *in quite different ways* a sensorimotor stimulus which breaks through the threshold of all-obliterating sleep.

For Freud (and most previous investigators), much more important than such stimuli was the residue of the day's activities. What one has just been doing or thinking tends to crop up in the dream, and many people still seem to feel that a dream has been *explained* when the elements have been identified as somehow present in recent recollection. Freud observed that the dream materials were very likely to come from *childhood* as well as from the quite recent past, with relatively sparse representation of conscious memories in between.

What impressed Freud was that the dream residue of events current in the life of the patient was so often apparently trivial. After a day filled with important happenings and thoughts, the dream often perversely selects some tiny observation, a phrase from someone's conversation, any trifling bit of nonsense. Freud points out that these fragments seem to gain access to the association process by virtue of their ability to evoke the energy belonging to childhood events, as the current mention of the ironing board in the dream described on page 39 derived its strength from the early incident.

Even important current attitudes seemed to Freud capable of appearing in the dream only as they related to infantile attitudes (with the possible exception of the repetitive dreams following severe shock). He substantiated his case by the analysis of hundreds of dreams in which a preliminary analysis of some subtlety, revealing current worries or semiconscious conflicts—such as, let us say, our patient's worry about his job and resentment toward his wife in the first aspect of the ironing-board dream—ultimately leads back to the infantile unconscious. Freud felt that the infantile unconscious provided the major dynamics of the dream, could be considered almost as its "cause." The non-libido analysts believe that the childhood material is brought in because it is part of the same unconscious attitude, and that it is *the deeply ingrained attitude* which structures the dream.

Usually the meaning of the dream emerges through the free associations of the patient to its elements. The analyst is often familiar enough with the patient's life to seize upon relationships among events not fully apparent to the patient. (Note the importance of the concept of *pattern*.) Connections may be plain to the analyst which are quite obscure to the patient. A brilliant *tour de force* of this nature is reported by Monroe Meyer. The patient could recall from his dream only the word "Lindbergh" and could produce no associations. He had come for treatment because of a depression. His attitude toward the analyst was challenging; his productions were extremely meager and flat. Although the patient was married, strong homosexual trends were apparent. He had mentioned with his customary detachment that his son had announced his engagement the previous day. The kidnapping of the Lindbergh baby happened to be front-page news at the moment. The analyst quietly asked: "Is your son's fiancée older than he?" The patient confirmed this fact with popeyed astonishment and was probably somewhat more amenable to psychoanalytic treatment thereafter. The analyst, of course, promptly explained his "magical" inference. How was the first news of the kidnapping likely to affect this patient unconsciously to the point of dreaming "Lindbergh"? The *analyst* here made the association between "cradle snatcher," as a term for an older woman marrying a younger man, and the front-page kidnapping; the *analyst* realized that the marriage of the son was likely to affect the patient profoundly.

The illustration is by no means typical of everyday practice, and it should be noted that the analyst introduced his interpretation with an innocent factual question easily dropped if the highly inferential guess had proved wrong. (With a challenging, detached patient a small, concrete demonstration of almost magical insight may be a useful device if employed very sparingly.) In the present context the "Lindbergh" dream is used to illustrate how a single word, clearly a residue from the day's newspaper, represents a highly complex and important psychological configuration, even when the connections are entirely obscure to the patient.

This point brings us now to a formal distinction accepted by all analysts: that between the *manifest dream content*—its actual materials as reported by the dreamer, whatever their origin—and the *latent dream thoughts* which reveal its unconscious meaning. Tracing the origin of the manifest dream materials no more explains the dream for the psychoanalyst than identifying the sounds of speech in the babbling infant explains language. Interpretation depends upon perception of the purposive process underlying the selection of materials. Why, out of all the day's residue was the trivial episode about the ironing board selected? Surely not on grounds of recency, frequency, or vividness, but intelligibly enough in terms of the unconscious themes of the patient's life as suggested also by his free associations. The dream is not thought of as a mysteriously inspired psychic event. What happens is merely that deeplying goals continuously operative are *differently* and *less drastically* modified by the secondary process during sleep, for the reasons mentioned at the outset of this discussion. Any of the examples used in this chapter show that the *latent dream thought* has a compelling organization beyond the bizarre manifest content of the dream. This organization usually follows unconscious themes. The skeptical reader may be referred to *The Interpretation of Dreams*, which presents a far more careful analysis of many more dreams.

Discerning the *latent* meaning of the dream requires special familiarity with the language of the unconscious and, almost always, supplementary materials, such as the patient's associations, or an intimate knowledge of the patient's experience and way of reacting. It requires a dynamic theoretical orientation—that is, a capacity to perceive patterns from a few disjointed fragments.

OVERDETERMINATION

One more general principle must be presented before we can come to the long-promised discussion of interpretation: *the principle of overdetermination*. Perhaps *multiple determination* would be a more descriptive term, but overdetermination is the one commonly used by Freudians.

Several different trends, conscious and unconscious, typically operate *simultaneously* to determine a given psychic event. The infantile unconscious, for example, could not gain access to the motorium or any kind of conscious expression unless it could seize upon some currently activated pathway. On the other hand, the current activation might not be sufficient for overt expression even in the dream without reinforcement from the persisting infantile layers. The principle need not be limited to current and infantile materials. Psychoanalysts generally accept the idea that the same event is determined in multiple ways at different levels of psychic function and that it can be interpreted with some coherence at any level.

The example of free association given on page 39 can serve to illustrate how a number of different themes appear together in the same time span. The principle of overdetermination is important enough to warrant a further example from everyday experience. Why does a boy enlist in the army? (1) His country has a cause to defend. (2) His friends are enlisting. (3) He does not know what else to do vocationally. (4) He is in difficulties with his girl or his parents. (5) He has glamorous illusions about the army. (6) He responded to the personal appeal of a recruiting officer, or maybe he got drunk, or both. One could continue to list at least a dozen familiar reasons, and it will surprise no one to hear that in a specific case they were *all* operating. We become uneasy only when someone maintains that men enlist *only* for the glory of their country, *only* on the rebound from a love affair, etc. Thus, there is no reason why a limited item should not participate in many systems of psychic events simultaneously and have a different underlying meaning as one looks successively to one system or another for its explanation. A hidebound analyst who insisted that a dream element means one thing and nothing else would be not unlike a recruiting officer who maintained that men enlist for one reason only—and as rare.

THE UNCONSCIOUS PROCESSES IN OPERATION

Alogic. We may now begin the description of the characteristics of unconscious processes. One characteristic of the unconscious which Freud noted especially was that *diametrically opposite meanings frequently stand side by side. Consciously,* our enlister may join the army to escape paternal authority and then find that the sergeant is even more authoritarian. *Consciously,* he feels he made a sad mistake, although his friends point out that the army is noted for its discipline. Very frequently the fact is that *unconsciously* he wanted *both* freedom and authority and that his enlistment was determined by both wishes simultaneously. The unconscious is not troubled by contradictions. It is completely *non*logical (as logic is considered in the secondary process), every aspect of the unconscious system demanding full and immediate gratification, regardless of the rest. Indeed, in the later discussion of dynamics we shall see that, regardless of whether one adopts Freud's concept of reaction formation or Horney's concept of the vicious circle or any of the other dynamic concepts, one comes to the conclusion that opposites are especially likely to appear together in the unconscious processes. The important characterization here, however, is the lack of consideration in the unconscious for those rules of thinking which the conscious mind takes for granted.

An important subdivision of this nonlogical quality of the primary process is its disregard for time. Freud emphasized the timeless quality of the affects and judgments attached to infantile events, which undergo repression and emerge again with pristine freshness, undulled by time, unstaled by custom. The non-libido analysts protest this concept of the freezing of infantile experience with later "return of the repressed." For them, as we shall see, there is a much more constant restructuring of the attitudes proceeding from infantile events in the course of later experience. But for them, too, the unconscious is, in a sense, timeless. Grief over the death of one's child may appear in the same dream sequence as the destruction of one's doll at the age of five, and the childhood event helps to explain the special flavor of the present event. By no analytic theory is mature grief to be simply equated with a broken doll, but in every analytic study of the unconscious, as in poetry, time as such plays a very small role—time as rationally demarcated, that is. Old events, old attitudes are as immediately present in the dream as things that happened yesterday. The time sequence of the dream (or of any other unconscious expression) does not follow a calendar. When the creative artist interweaves present and past in building up the mood or message of his creation, he uses a technique present in the unconscious processes of all of us, but he selects from the array of items those that are relevant to a particular mood and are more generally evocative.

The unconscious also disregards the exigencies of space. The dream transfers us from Europe to America without so much as a by-your-leave. Two objects may occupy the same space at the same time, or, rather, the same object often somehow *is* two things simultaneously, without even the brief temporal transformation of baby into pig as observed by Alice. Size relationships and plausibilities of locale are often neglected. A patient who had just undergone an abdominal operation fell into a morphine-induced sleep after reading a novel in which two young people were searching desperately for the tombstone of their mother. She awoke with the conviction that they would not find it because it was in her own stomach, and that she should get out of bed and let them know. Amusingly enough, she finally rationalized staying in bed on the ground that the tombstone in her stomach could not be the proper one because her operation had taken place after the publication of the book. The patent absurdity of the space relationship, not to mention the more complex incongruities, did not occur to her until the following day.

An early reader of this manuscript suggests the following example of such absurdities in waking life. "I have caught myself thinking somewhat similar nonsense on occasion, for a fraction of a second, before having time to discard it. Most recent: We sit in a diner, our baby on my lap. I hear a dish breaking behind the counter and wonder for a moment how our baby managed to break something that far away. Then I tell my wife the silly idea that had just occurred to me and we both laugh."

Spatial distortion is a common effect of some drugs and of some organic conditions (*e.g.*, encephalitis). Children—even though they are able to match shapes and sizes very competently on an intelligence test—not infrequently fear that they will slip down the drain when the water is going out of the bathtub, or that a huge animal will spring out of the toilet bowl. Such basic misconceptions are very common also in the thinking of adult psychotics—indeed, they may be used in the differential diagnosis between psychosis and severe neurosis. An extreme example is the woman who screamed with pain when she saw a trolley car a block away because it was "running over [her] stomach." Radical indifference to ordinary evaluations of time and space is by no means peculiar to the dream, nor is it of any great importance in dream interpretation. It is characteristic of any condition where conscious control is in abeyance. It belongs to the primary process.

Since many of the illustrations of unconscious processes given in this book will seem very close to ordinary ways of thought, it is well to recognize clearly the fundamental alogic of the unconscious connections as such and the absence of the most primitive attention to the requirements of external reality. Such recognition will prevent many unjustified criticisms of psychoanalytic interpretations as "far-fetched" or "impossible." The unconscious recognizes no impossibles. In so far as its associations are not guided by the *learned* processes of adaptation to everyday reality and the rules of thinking more or less elaborately developed in any culture (the secondary process), its conclusions can be more fantastic than any the adult mind can imagine. Only with a full understanding of this principle can we begin to read the cryptography of those partially rationalized fragments made available to us in dreams and other avenues of information.

Dramatization; Imagery; Use of Words. Ideas and affects are very often *dramatized*—that is, cast in loose narrative form with mainly *visual* imagery. The semi-dream cited on page 50, in which two little boys represented the dynamics of the id and the superego, can serve again as illustration of a process so general that most of us think of a dream as a story. Such dramatization, however, is not *necessary* to the dream, as in the very succinct dream statement quoted: "Lindbergh" (p. 53). Freud observed that a phrase remembered on waking as having been spoken (*i.e.,* definitely *heard* as such rather than loosely imagined in the dialogue of the story) very often carries special unconscious significance. The same is true of odd proper names, numbers—probably any vivid peculiarity in the typical dream process. I remember a long dream of my own in which my analyst took me on a yacht—a dream crowded with the problems and trends we had been discussing, expressed with very patent symbolism. The analyst put it through the usual paces with no great enthusiasm—whereas *I* thought it was a remarkably useful dream. Finally he asked: "What was the name of that yacht, again?" I repeated the name—*Newland,* which I accented like the word *England.* It was not until he remarked that this was the part of the dream he liked best that the obvious words *new land* struck me, and that it even occurred to me that the name of the yacht was unusual. Actually, it looked as though the dream story as a whole was merely a rehash in dream language of points already discussed in analysis and intellectually accepted, whereas the important item was the obviously unconscious shift away from a pessimistic absorption in the past to an incipient hopefulness. (See p. 59 for further discussion of this interpretation.)

The illustration points to another characteristic of most dreams: their *verbalistic* quality, with ambiguous use of word meanings. The dream is an arrant punster. The primary process has no such settled notions as the conscious mind about the proper realm of discourse of any word, or any great respect for its format. Reik[6] reports a dream in which the recurrent and apparently irrelevant auditory phrase "I am afraid of the dog" resisted all efforts at analysis along lines of canine associations but yielded at once to the transposition of dog into God. Although brought up in a strongly religious family, and himself strongly religious in early adolescence, the patient had later adopted a contemptuous atheism. The dream phrase made very good sense wherever it occurred once it was seen as a continuing fear of the Lord with deep unconscious roots, plus the later contempt.

Condensation. Dreams very often have a knack of *condensing* or telescoping complex ideas into a word, a phrase, a brief scene or story which would do credit to the greatest wit. Freud discusses this characteristic at length in *Wit and Its Relation to the Unconscious.* These attributes of the dream work (the unconscious) are just as strange to waking experience as the juxtapositions in space and time, which find their analogue in poetry. Indeed, poetry also constantly uses words in contexts that would be absurd or repellent if given full literal meaning. A teetotaller relishes Homer's phrase "the wine-dark sea," and no one is so besotted as to wish that the sea were actually made of wine. To be thoroughly literal, wine comes in a variety of colors, so one may well argue that the phrase has no sensible meaning at all. "Wine-dark" is more poetic than "purple" or "reddish" because of the inspiriting connotations of wine in human history, which go far beyond the dictionary definitions or even our personal experience with the drink. The adjective brings the ocean into the sphere of human feeling as vividly as Proteus rising from the sea or Triton blowing his wreathed horn in Wordsworth's sonnet.

The phrase "I am afraid of the dog" is not likely to strike the rest of us as either wit or poetry. But as an expression of three separate important trends in the patient's personality it is a marvel of condensation and telescoping. He is afraid of God; he conceals his fear; he is contemptuous. The setting of the phrase in the dream yields still further information about the origin and role of "God" in the patient's psyche.

Displacement, Devaluation, Substitution. Other very common mechanisms in the dream, and in other manifestations of the primary process, are the phenomena of *displacement, devaluation,* and *substitution.* Very often—indeed, typically—the real focus of the dream appears as a quite incidental element, and the apparent psychic intensity falls elsewhere. The major purpose of this lack of proper proportion, this *displacement* of affect, seems to be the familiar one of avoiding censorship. Appropriate feeling directly expressed would excite the dreamer to the waking point. The same intensity expressed about some sanctioned or trivial matter can be tolerated.

My dream about the yacht *Newland* is as good an illustration as I can think of for relatively pure displacement (usually some *substitution* is intrinsic to the process) and offers a good review of the process of censorship and re-sistance. The analyst fastened on this quite incidental item, and I failed to notice anything odd about the name at first, even when he singled it out for attention. A little more background is necessary to understand why a dream thought so agreeable should undergo censorship and arouse resistance. I had entered treatment in a state of mild depression following the death of a dearly loved person—with the typical symptoms described in this book on page 289. Anyone will recognize the formulation of the bereaved: life is empty; I can never be happy again; I cannot form new attachments; I cannot really care about anything. Mourning quite generally involves impulses of clamping down on renewed expansiveness—sporadic and transitory in most cases, very trouble-some to many of us. Thus it had actually been easier for me, as patient, to recognize a number of trends ordinarily censorable than to accept a growing optimistic, outgoing, energetic outlook. In the dream this feature was well concealed by its *triviality,* and the sense of well being was ascribed to trends which, to be sure, are generally considered censorable, but which had been given sanction during the treatment. (Not that they had been "cured." See Chaps. 7 and 12 for discussion of the to-and-fro activity of the unconscious during treatment.)

Akin to displacement in the pure sense is the technique of *devaluation*: the censorable situation is presented more or less directly, but the dreamer is quite casual about it (see mechanism of isolation, pp. 254f.). A rather prudish woman, for example, commented that her unconscious must be unusually free because she often dreamed of finding herself in her chemise, barefoot, or even naked on public occasions with no more than a feeling that her habiliments were in poor taste—whereas many people report feelings of severe shock in dreams involving nudity. A surgeon somewhat inclined to worry told of similar "casual" dreams in which, although the patient died under his knife, he was distressed only by some minor point of operating-room etiquette. He even came to worry about whether his dreams represented a genuine lack of human concern. He wondered whether his conscious worries about his patients were a mere disguise for neurotic compulsiveness.

The actual dynamics behind such dreams are too complex to discuss here, but it is safe to say that the woman is not "free" and the surgeon is not indifferent to the fate of his patients. Such dreams can occur only when the obvious meaning has been somehow devaluated for the time being. It is as if the dreamer said to himself, "Look here, these things are not really so dangerous; they don't matter to me a whit," and could thus allow quite open expression.

It is difficult to find illustrations for displacement and devaluation in pure form, because typically they appear through the further mechanism of *substitution*. The displacement is accomplished by substituting a different person or thing for the censorable object. An important dream thought is devaluated by translating it into some trivial circumstance, representing it by its opposite, and so on. A death wish toward the father may be represented by dreaming of his going on a journey; the analyst may be portrayed as a strange man whose only similarity to the analyst is a pointed beard; the envied scientific work of a colleague may appear as a pamphlet criticized by the father in the dreamer's childhood. A patient, after a bitter quarrel with his father about his future career, dreamed of visiting some queer, gigantic ruins. A mole scuttled out of the ground and laughed at him. (Like Hamlet's query to his father's ghost: "Dost work i' the ground so fast, old mole?") Almost any dream contains such substitutions and is subject to analysis only as the true object and attitude are clarified.

The substitution apparently takes place along the lines familiar to the old associationist psychology—by contiguity or similarity, provided these principles are broadly construed. Any aspect of an object or event can stand for the whole thing; any similarity will serve; any chance simultaneity of events, even in the remote past; even any opposite. The line of association may be concrete, highly abstract, or purely verbal. A neat illustration is given by Freud from one of his own dreams (though in a different connection). He had reacted resentfully to the criticism of an eminent scientific friend by a younger man; the same night he dreamed that Goethe attacked another young man of his acquaintance. Here there is an analogy with the eminence of Goethe, the substitution of another young man, and a reversal of the real situation which obviously supplied the material for the manifest dream content.

Such displacements and substitutions occur constantly in waking life as well. Probably many of our feelings of attraction or repulsion for new acquaintances are due to some quite incidental similarity to significant persons of our past whom we loved or hated, often a similarity of which we are quite unaware. We take an instant dislike to Mr. Smith because his hearty manner *unconsciously* reminds us of Uncle Henry, who so often embarrassed and disappointed us in our childhood. A friend who had almost consciously selected as husband a man who was temperamentally the exact opposite of a "hated" father came to realize in analysis that she was *also* powerfully drawn to him because he was in some ways physically *like* her father. She came to remember the exciting awareness of her father's unusually hairy arms when he fondled her as a child, and to recognize some of the excitement and terror of her relations with her husband as connected by displacement with this childhood experience—via the fact that her husband too is unusually hirsute. It would be a mistake to suggest that this woman's marital choice was dictated entirely or even primarily by this small physical likeness of husband and father. But one can understand how she might be powerfully attracted to her husband beyond the many aspects of congeniality with him and rebelliousness toward the father operating concurrently, and how difficulties in sexual relations might arise as the hairy husband reminded her *unconsciously* of the hairy father of her childhood.

Symbolization. One further characteristic of the primary unconscious processes must be mentioned: *the use of symbols.* In a broad sense, any *pars pro toto* may be considered a symbol, any item which *stands for* something else. The mole in the dream reported above is a symbol for the father. As a matter of fact, any word or gesture is a symbol. Exact sciences abound in symbols very carefully developed to stand for extremely complex experience and concepts. *In psychoanalytic parlance,* however, the word *symbol* usually refers to a representation of greater durability than the temporary substitution in a dream, more widely shared with other individuals, but without such rationally delimited universality as the scientific symbol. The word *dawn* for *beginning* is almost as universally understood as *x* for the unknown, but on a rough experiential basis. It does not belong to a codified notational system which can be lawfully manipulated as such. It derives from an experiential observation common to the entire race. However unprecise, its meaning is clear and can be applied "symbolically" in many situations in which the literal shift from night to day is irrelevant.

Psychoanalytic parlance *usually* requires a further consideration—that the quasi-universal meaning be *repressed.* Thus, "dawn" as a symbol has little interest for the psychoanalyst because its meaning is almost as overt and conventionalized as "beginning." The term *symbol* is reserved for the use of this mechanism in the primary process rather than in the conscious or preconscious. The symbols of everyday life and of science are often called *signs.* (This topic is developed further in the comment on Jung, Chap. 13.)

Freud observed that symbols of a more or less universal nature are employed by the dream or other unconscious manifestations, and that they must be interpreted as such apart from the particular associations and experiences of the individual. In *The Interpretation of Dreams,* he comments, with somewhat reluctant appreciation, on Stekel's elaborated development of this idea. Freud cites a number of dreams which can be interpreted adequately only by recognizing the symbolic meaning of many elements. Freud lists Stekel's observations with some emendations of his own. He points out that *sexual* symbols, as uncovered by the psychoanalyst, typically have primitive or censorable implications and are, therefore, not consciously recognized, as is our introductory example of the dawn. It is the *sexual* symbols and a few others related to universal interpersonal experience (mother, father, siblings, etc.) that are usually meant when the Freudian psychoanalyst speaks of *symbolism*. (Jung's view has important similarity with Freud's, but is not identical. Again, see Chap. 13.)

Freud's uneasiness in the matter lay in the temptation to *mis*apply symbol interpretation as a sort of sophisticated dream-book approach. In any given dream, an element *may* have this universal significance, or it may have the more idiosyncratic background already described. Or, by the principle of over-determination, it may have *both* implications. In either case, the symbol would be used by the dreamer along the purposive lines which Freud considered basic to sound psychological interpretation. Any routinized application of universal symbolic meanings would tend to destroy the dynamic approach to the understanding of the dream process which Freud correctly viewed as his major discovery.

The problem of such universal symbols will be discussed in some detail in the section on Jung, because he is the analyst who has carried the idea furthest. At the present time, all analysts work with it to some extent, and so do "psychologists" in their interpretation of projective test materials. Most "psychologists" are hesitant in its application, for the very good reasons suggested by Freud himself (and emphasized by Jung as well). Any sticklike object *may* be a symbolic phallus—or it may be a sticklike object of some quite special concern to the patient in a transitory manner or with particular nonphallic associations of long standing, or it may be something else. It seems overly cautious to blind oneself altogether to symbolic interpretations which enrich the reading of almost any product through which unconscious manifestations reveal themselves. In handling relatively brief samples of such manifestations, however, a high degree of caution is essential for discriminating use of this valuable avenue of information.

The Problem of Interpreting the Unconscious

In somewhat spotty and incomplete fashion, we have reviewed the techniques of the unconscious thought processes (the primary process) in contrast to the more ordered procedures of rational thinking (the secondary process).

The reader who has never worked with this kind of material may well wonder how interpretations of these processes can be made with anything like scientific accuracy when every element *may* mean exactly what it seems to mean, or its opposite, or something quite different, by virtue of highly idiosyncratic associations and quasi-universal symbols; when the sequential meaning may be reversed, condensed, telescoped, displaced, devalued; when the material means several different things at once; and when interpretation admittedly requires—and varies with—an underlying theoretical approach on the part of the interpreter. Skeptics have often said that sequential interpretation reflects *merely* the wildcat theoretical bias of the interpreter, and that a child, if asked for his untutored judgments, would chance upon the crazy notions of the analyst.

The latter half of this criticism tends to backfire. Actually, children and the insane very often *do* interpret unconscious materials very much along the lines suggested by the analysts, clearly without sophisticated theoretical bias. Since children and psychotics are much closer to the primary process in their natural living than the careful scientist, the observed truth in the skeptical wisecrack becomes an important independent confirmation. Young children and the insane are too biased by their own limited experience to serve as reliable interpreters for the whole range of unconscious phenomena that comes to the attention of the mature scientist. Nevertheless, their objective judgment of materials within their range, as well as their own spontaneous productions, tend to support Freud's conclusions from dreams, jokes, and the small mistakes of everyday life. "Savages" seem equally clever in "inventing" the ways of thought described by Freud.* Dreams of hypnotic subjects who are given the suggestion to dream about a topic unacceptable or disturbing to them in their waking state show distortion along the lines described by Freud.[7]

It should be noted that the psychoanalyst—or the psychologist interpreting materials from projective tests—gradually acquires from the actual experience of interpretation a *sense* for the unconscious processes that cannot be gained from merely reading about them. Reik, in *Listening with the Third Ear*, has described the semi-intuitive approach of the analyst. Not all analysts would agree entirely with so forthright a statement of the doctor's participation, but most of them recognize a measure of identification with the patient—a slipping into his unconscious patterns for the moment—as a valid part of sound interpretation. The analyst is, of course, in a position almost simultaneously to step outside the patient's pattern for purposes of rational review and understanding.

The danger that too personal a relationship with the patient may lead to uncritical distortion by the analyst's own (unconscious) attitudes is recognized

* An excellent analysis may be found in Heinz Werner's *Comparative Psychology of Mental Development*, Harper & Bros., 1940.

by Freudians and is discussed under the topic of "countertransference" on page 306. The problems of countertransference and of limitations in theoretical insight undoubtedly affect any interpretation. It would be a mistake to claim complete objectivity for work with such fluid data. Yet such "intuitiveness," controlled by careful training and experience with many kinds of patients, allows for a much sounder grasp of the unconscious process than rigid application of rules. The skilled analyst is rarely guilty of deductions from fragmentary data—unlike the amateur who recalls some of Freud's principles and catchy examples and then applies them rigorously.

Accuracy in the interpretation of elements with such slippery meanings is achieved mainly through the context or pattern within which they appear. Four kinds of check in common use may be mentioned:

(1) *The underlying trend is discernible through many types of material, derived from different sources.* It is impossible to illustrate this point by a brief example, because it requires complex analysis of independent sequences, each too involved for compact presentation. Any of Freud's longer analyses of dreams in *The Interpretation of Dreams* will show the curious reader how successive attention to the sources of different elements reveals a constant theme despite the diversity of the background.*

(2) *The latent dream thought or underlying unconscious trend observed in other materials has internal consistency, both as regards content and type of "thinking."*

(3) *It is consistent with what is already known about the patient in analysis.*

(4) *It leads readily to fruitful elaboration along lines consonant with the gradually emerging understanding of the patient.*

Clearly, all these points are concrete variations on the theme of interpretation via the *pattern* of the patient's productions. And in practice they are not easily separable. As a rule, the pattern is so plainly visible to the analyst that the introduction of any element atypical for the patient stands out prominently. It may be the harbinger of a much desired and carefully prepared change—like the yacht *Newland*. It may indicate retrogression, or it may merely suggest that the pattern envisaged at first was oversimplified, if not incorrect.

---

* The psychological tester may regard some aspects of his interpretation of a patient's Rorschach responses as intuitive to the point of fancifulness, but if the same trends appear in the patient's performance on the Thematic Apperception Test or other projective methods, the tester offers a much bolder statement than would be justified by the data available from any one of the tests. Within a single test, as within a single dream, the same trend may reveal itself in different ways which *for the subject* are independent of one another. Slight variations in the use of shading in the Rorschach, in the way movement is projected, in content, etc., often yield quite convincing evidence of a trend *when taken together*, although separately the variations are too slight to carry interpretive weight.

In the analytic situation, interpretation regularly includes modification and correction in the light of the total picture presented by the patient, past, present, and *future,* in the sense that a tentative hunch from any small bit of evidence may later be fully confirmed—or discarded. Thus, although the analyst is aided by training in such "principles" as have been briefly described here, his sense of confidence comes from his grasp of the on-going dynamics of the patient's psychic life, where information from different modalities and temporal sequences *together* form a reasonably reliable pattern.

In illustration, the dream about the mole laughing in the ruins may be reviewed from the angle of consistency in itself and in a wider view of the patient. The young man himself promptly gave the association to *Hamlet,* but the point of interest here is that the analyst would *expect* this association from an intellectual urbanite. By itself the mole might have other meanings, of course, referable either to the habits of the animal or to specific experiences with it. By the principle of overdetermination, it is even likely that several meanings are operating at once. But since the associations brought to light no special memories about moles for this patient, the *Hamlet* reference appeared to be the major determinant. One may fruitfully ask, however, why Hamlet addressed his revered father as an old mole, and why the line is so familiar to people of the patient's cultural background. There is more than a hint of universal symbolism here.

The mole laughs at the dreamer—distinctly un-mole-like behavior, distinctly appropriate to the father who had ridiculed the patient's cherished aspirations. Furthermore, moles are not usually associated with gigantic ruins. Yet how poetically consonant this metaphor for fallen ambitions is with the flavor of the *Hamlet* reference. The dream is no random linkage of chance experiences and ideas. One may note also the emphasis on *size*—the gigantic ruins; the tiny, subterranean mole. To the simple formulation "My father laughed at me and ruined my hopes" one may add the vastness of the hopes and the contempt for the father, with the curious backtwist that the mole is, after all, triumphant. The analyst may wonder whether the problem does not go deeper than a quarrel about work. The dream suggests also an evaluation of the self of quite heroic proportions, with an extreme sense of vulnerability; also, very ambivalent attitudes toward the father. The introduction of *Hamlet* into the structure of the dream work on the reality problem of the previous day suggests a possible identification with the melancholy Dane beyond this single reference, which might further clarify the deeper intention of the dream.

None of these elaborations would be a thoroughly defensible conclusion from the short dream taken by itself. When they fit the pattern of the patient's attitudes as earlier observed from other dreams and materials, the analyst feels increasingly sure of his interpretation. Many straws determine the direction of the wind with a good deal of certainty.

The reaction of the patient to the analyst's interpretative comment also helps to confirm or correct it. Mere acquiescence in its general plausibility, such as I hopefully expect from the reader, is of no great value in treatment. Of greater therapeutic importance is the patient's sense of revelation, accompanied by release of further confirmatory material, usually emotionally toned, when the interpretation hits home sharply. Or there may be unduly sharp resistance on some points, quite different in tone from the relatively neutral pros and cons the reader may adduce in intellectual consideration of somebody else's dream. This, too, may offer confirmation—where it fits a pattern. For example, the patient may bitterly protest the attitude of contempt for the father suggested by the mole. The *bitterness* of the protest—or it may be the amount of time devoted to it—will paradoxically confirm the truth of the interpretation—especially if the patient has repeatedly overreacted to interpretation along these lines.

No analyst would doubt that this dream refers, at least in part, to the father and to the vocational aspirations of the son. Every analyst would be impressed by the difference in size, by the reference to Hamlet, etc. The Adlerian would probably concentrate on the inflated goals of the son; the Freudian would probably want, eventually, to concentrate on the relationship of son to father in its Oedipal origins and meanings; and so through the other schools. It is at this point that the bias of the analyst's theoretical approach enters the picture. Very probably, a dozen analysts would give a dozen different interpretations, *if they could be persuaded to undertake interpretation of an isolated dream at all*—which is very unlikely in view of their insistence on the importance of seeing the dream and associations to it within the ongoing pattern of the patient's reactions in analysis as viewed from many angles. (Parenthetically, I remind the reader again that I have written at length about the dream only because it offers a relatively clear example of the characteristics of the unconscious processes, not because it is in any sense unique in this respect.)

Very likely, variations in interpretation would occur *mainly* along lines of the theories espoused by the different psychoanalytic schools, but undoubtedly some "Freudians" would be closer to some "non-libido" analysts, as here differentiated, than to what I may call *orthodox* Freud—that is, to points of view which Freud himself modified but which are sacrosanct to some of his early disciples and to some people trained under them. (I have used the adjective "classical" for Freudians who keep to Freud's major emphases in a more flexible manner.) There would be intraschool variation, due either to subdivisions within schools or to the special proclivities of the analyst as a person.

In Chapters 7 and 12, we shall consider how information about the unconscious processes is elicited during the analytic hour by the different psychoanalytic schools, and how it is used in treatment. I think it will become clear that, so far as the *patient* is concerned, the variations from school to school are more a matter of emphasis than of sharp contrast. In all schools, the analyst makes every effort *not* to impose a theoretical interpretation. In fact, overintellectualization is generally recognized as a hindrance in therapy. The problem is to help the patient become aware of aspects of attitudes and feelings that he has in one way or another shut off from the major flexibly integrative powers of his personality (very roughly, from "consciousness"). In their books and papers, psychoanalysts of different schools offer elaborate and contradictory interpretations. But in treating the patient, "interpretation" usually consists of no more than a pointed question (*e.g.*, my own analyst: "What was the name of that yacht?"), a pregnant silence, a striking parallel from the patient's own account of his action in other situations, etc., etc., with *occasionally* a brief, trenchant comment of a summarizing nature. Thus, in treatment it is mainly the *patient* who does the "theorizing," if he is so inclined, on the basis of quite fragmentary remarks from the analyst. He develops "insight" in his own way, not by applying textbook "rules."

The more I have studied carefully the theories of the various psychoanalytic schools, and the more I have inquired about what analysts really do in practice (listening to many sources, and at times myself offering the pointed questions, etc., like the properly trained interviewer, although much more informally), the more I have felt I understood why *all* psychoanalytic schools have so many successes—and all of them some failures. They all deal with *essentially* the same basic trends and patterns, regardless of their specific theoretical systematization, and they all *essentially* see their job as helping the patient to understand himself through the peculiar resources of the analytic session. The theoretical aura attached to a specific unconscious manifestation does not greatly affect the quality of the *patient's* insight, in a treatment designed to help the patient help himself. *Occasionally* the major problems of a patient are strongly focused about a point a special analytic school is not well equipped to understand. Such cases offer the spectacular examples of cure by one school after failure by another that are so often quoted in every camp. In my observation there is not so great a preponderance of spectacular cures by any one school as to constitute proof of the superiority of its special theory (see pp. 326*ff.*).

SUMMARY

FOUR BASIC CONCEPTS are accepted by all schools of psychoanalysis: psychological determinism, "the unconscious," goal-directedness, a genetic approach. By his observation of the structuring power of unconscious motives, Freud extended scientific ordering of data to aspects of human function that had previously been considered "accidental" or that had been wrongly attributed to limited rational or instinctual forces. By emphasis on the importance of early experience, he suggested a dynamic origin for attributes of the human psyche that had previously been considered descriptively and statically as faculties prefigured in the species.

The nature of the significant goals and the precise role of early experience are envisaged differently by the various analytic schools and will be discussed in later chapters.

The bulk of this chapter was devoted to a description of the avenues of information toward "the unconscious" available to the psychoanalyst, and to a discussion of its outstanding characteristics. The reader is again reminded that the term "the unconscious" has here been used very loosely. No school actually considers it a single entity, as this isolated use of the term may imply. Our discussion has involved an artificial separation of techniques from their underlying dynamics, justified only by the wish to acquaint the reader with a type of evidence unfamiliar to those who are not trained in the procedures of psychoanalysis.

[1] S. Freud, *The Interpretation of Dreams* and *Psychopathology of Everyday Life*, both in *The Basic Writings of Sigmund Freud*, Random House, Modern Library, 1938.

[2] ———, *The Interpretation of Dreams*, p. 536.

[3] P. Blos, *The Adolescent Personality*, Appleton-Century, 1941. L. B. Murphy and H. Ladd, *Emotional Factors in Learning*, Columbia University Press, 1944. I. E. Bender *et al.*, *Motivation and Visual Factors*, Dartmouth College Publications, 1942. R. L. Munroe, *Teaching the Individual*, Columbia University Press, 1942.

[4] H. Silberer, "Report on a Method of Eliciting Certain Symbolic Hallucination-Phenomena," in D. Rapaport (ed.), *Organization and Pathology of Thought*, Columbia University Press, 1951, pp. 195-207; "On Symbol-forma-

tion," *loc. cit.*, pp. 208-233.

[5] S. Freud, *The Interpretation of Dreams*, in *The Complete Psychological Works of Sigmund Freud*, London: Hogarth Press, 1953, IV, Chap. 1. (The edition of this work referred to throughout this book is the one contained in *The Basic Writings of Sigmund Freud*. In that edition, Chap. 1 is abridged and the dream referred to has been deleted, so that interested readers are referred to the Hogarth edition.)

[6] T. Reik, *Listening with the Third Ear*, Farrar, Straus & Co., 1948, p. 338.

[7] M. Nachmansohn, "Concerning Experimentally Produced Dreams," in D. Rapaport, *loc. cit.*, pp. 257-287. G. Roffenstein, "Experiments on Symbolization in Dreams," *loc. cit.*, pp. 249-256. K. Schroetter, "Experimental Dreams," *loc. cit.*, pp. 234-248.

Part Two

FREUD AND THE "FREUDIANS"

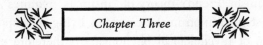

Chapter Three

THE TERMS OF THE ORGANISM

FREUD DISTINGUISHED with especial clarity between the biological structure of the organism and its adaptation to the demands of external reality. Indeed, the process of such adaptation is the keynote of Freudian doctrine. Personality development and symptom formation in disease are the resultants of the interplay between instinctual demands and reality demands. Human nature is not, for Freud, an ultimate which gradually unfolds in a vacuum; nor are pathological symptoms occurrences to be described merely as elements of a mysterious disease. Instead, as Freud was among the first to see, there is a dynamic relationship between the structure of the organism and its milieu, between what the person wants on a biological level and the expedients he is put to in order to satisfy his wants in a real world.

Although this dynamic relationship is fundamental to his entire approach, Freud concentrated for many years on certain aspects of the organism (libidinal development, the "id") with relative neglect of other aspects (ego and superego) whose significance he himself later came to appreciate and which have become the focus of investigation for many of his followers. Many aspects of ego and superego development are not part of biological inheritance but are dependent upon later learning in close relationship to environmental pressures. However, many aspects of this later learning are so regular in appearance—despite variations in their concrete form—as to be considered implicit in the terms of the organism. Freud's theory of "instincts" requires a report of their major lines of systematization in the course of living. His approach to significant classification of psychological phenomena is therefore presented in this chapter, as well as his theory of biological inheritance.

Freud not only made a brilliant first discovery and elaborated a new theoretical system but kept his system flexibly integrated with new observations throughout a long lifetime. He did this by virtue of quite radical changes, which were nevertheless carefully related to his previous formulations. The modifications retained the old summaries and explained their limitations and the means by which they might be integrated in a new perspective. Freud constantly tried to relate observational materials to "metapsychological" problems with all the zeal of a nineteenth-century philosopher-scientist for the formulation of universal laws—a zeal which perhaps hampered his theoretical efforts in a manner which I will discuss in critical comment but which also served to keep empirical data in close alignment with scientific generalizations.

Because of this continual process of change, it becomes extraordinarily difficult to present Freud's theory of the terms of the organism simply, briefly, and precisely. It changed repeatedly over the years, and Freud's final dichotomous instinct theory (Eros and Thanatos) is the one least generally acceptable to contemporary Freudians.* In writing this chapter I have relied mainly on the books Freud wrote for a more general public as fairly systematic presentations of his theoretical approach.† I must also include *The Problem of Anxiety* (*Hemmung, Symptom und Angst*, 1926), which was not intended for general reading but is crucial for an understanding of Freud's major shift in ideas between the publication of the *General Introduction* and the *New Introductory Lectures*. My account is historical only in the very gross sense of presenting the most important successive formulations, with a brief comment on why Freud felt the change was necessary.

A further section is added on "ego psychology," which begins with Freud and was partly acknowledged by him even as of developments which had gone somewhat beyond his own position. He could readily envisage the incorporation of this new material into his general framework, whereas he was generally unsympathetic toward all efforts, no matter how successful in limited areas,

* The reader may be referred to Bibring, "The Development and Problems of the Theory of the Instincts," *International Journal of Psycho-Analysis*, 1941, 22:102-131, for a brilliant analysis of the development of Freud's thinking about instincts.

† *A General Introduction to Psycho-Analysis* (1916), *New Introductory Lectures* (1932), and *An Outline of Psychoanalysis* (1940).

which approached the study of ego psychology with repudiation of this framework. Freud's basic theory not only allows for but even demands further study of what he himself called the neglected aspects of the personality.

THE NATURE OF INSTINCT

THE MOST VALUABLE feature of Freud's instinct theory I take to be his insistence upon the derivation of all "instincts"* from the bodily structure of the organism. Freud specifically repudiates the postulate of a "multitude of small occasional instincts," such as an instinct of self-assertiveness, of imitation, of play, and the like.[1] The variegated lists of instincts, so common in the psychological thinking of his day, give way to the concept of an energy which finds its source in a state of excitation in the body—i.e., a purely physiological phenomenon. The aim of the organism is to reduce the tensions arising either directly from internal bodily processes or from external events which have acquired stimulus value. Such a concept as McDougall's "instinct of self-assertiveness" implies an inborn concept of the self, however vague, in relation to others or to the outside world, whereas Freud's theory implies nothing beyond bodily structure.

Freud tried to show how the observable phenomena previously called "instincts" are derived with some regularity from the energy made available by states of excitation within the body. Further, Freud as a physician was deeply concerned with the strange irregularities exhibited by those deviant individuals, his patients. His search was for principles which would order the fantastic vagaries of the mentally ill along with the regularities of human nature.

Freud remarked that an "instinct" can be characterized as to three different aspects: its source, its aim, and its object.

> The *source* is a state of excitation within the body, and its aim is to remove that excitation; in the course of its path from its source to the attainment of its aim, the instinct becomes operative mentally. . . . The aim can be attained in the subject's own body but as a rule an external object is introduced in which the instinct attains its external aim; its internal aim is always a somatic modification which is experienced as satisfaction.[2]

* Freud's German word is *Trieb*, for which "drive" is perhaps a better translation than the more common "instinct." I shall use the words interchangeably. Hartmann and several other Freudians prefer to use the term *instinctual drives* consistently, but since the mass of Freudian literature uses the old term *instinct*, I have not thought it desirable to be puristic on this point.

As a rule, the object aspect of the instinct, its external aim, is the one most easily observed. It is also the least reliable, because it is established through experience and is relatively subject to modification. For example, one cannot properly call the sexual drive the "instinct of mating" by virtue of its *usual* object or external aim. In the majority of cases this object classification would be correct, but what about the homosexual or the confirmed bachelor Don Juan? Freud points to a community in biological *aim*—gratification of a specific organ system—but shows how the choice of an *object* grows out of experience. The choice of an object of the same sex follows the same developmental principles as mate-seeking, with special conditioning factors. In fact, "normal" object choice is shown to be the happy result of a very complex set of influences, not a matter of instinct.

Freud's distinction between object and aim becomes even more cogent if we apply it to a standard item of controversy: the profit motive. With what fervor is it maintained by many politicians that any social order which diminishes money reward goes against human nature! No reputable psychologist espouses the notion of a specific money-making instinct, and even the more broadly descriptive concept of an acquisitive instinct has disappeared from the textbooks. Yet eager pursuit of the dollar is a sharply empirical fact in contemporary America. Freud's emphasis on the *source* and *aim* of instincts as inherent in body structure allows for progressive understanding of the more constant biological roots of behavior. At the same time, the introduction of the *object* as a necessary component of instinct which derives from experience and *may be shifted or replaced* provides a useful theoretical framework for explaining the tenacity with which some concrete goals, such as money-making, may be pursued by an individual or a group, despite the fact that they are clearly not "human nature" in any universal sense.

Freud's formulation permits a dynamic view of instinct problems. Basically, the "instincts" are no more (and no less) than the tension systems presented by the organ systems of the body. Their aim is reduction of tension, which is experienced as gratification (pleasure). In so far as the body functions as a unit, the specific aims (gratification of a special organ system) may become fused, one may be substituted for another under some conditions, or some sort of coordination may be effected in the interests of the organism as a whole. Manifest behavior is not (in theory) neglected, but the concept of object as separate from aim offers a conceptual framework for considering the variabilities of behavior in relation to the biological constants which are thought of as the only true "instincts."

The energy proceeding from these states of excitation Freud called the libido. He writes: "The most prominent of the parts of the body from which this libido arises are described by the name of *erotogenic zones, though strictly* *speaking the whole body is an erotogenic zone* [my italics]."[3] In Chapter 6, on personality dynamics, I shall discuss Freud's view of the libido as a kind of energic quantum which may be thought of as initially moving rather freely from one object to another and also as becoming "bound" or "fixated" with greater or less permanence on specific objects. Since this concept is easily considered by many psychologists distastefully mystical and *non*physiological, I prefer to postpone presentation of its complex ramifications until the reader is more familiar with Freud's handling of the development and operation of instincts in a somewhat more conventional sense.[*]

EARLY FORMULATIONS

FREUD'S GROUPING OF INSTINCTS

Freud made certain tentative *groupings* of instincts within the broad concept of biological need. He initially offered two major categories—the ego instincts and the sexual instincts.[†] The former were conceived as subsidiary to the need for self-preservation; the latter, to the need for preservation of the race through reproduction. This dichotomy was familiar enough to the biological thinking of his time.

New to the point of scandal was Freud's analysis of the sexual instincts. Observation of his patients led him very early to the conclusion that the definition of sexuality should be broadened in several ways. First, not only the genitals but also other zones of the body, notably the mouth and the excretory organs, had a primary pleasure function which seemed closely akin to "sexual"

---

[*] I am also postponing discussion of the somatic source of the "energies" Freud saw as proceeding from the ego instincts in his early formulation and from the death instinct (aggression) in his later theory. Freud was not puristic about "somatic source," on the grounds that scientific knowledge of such sources (physiology) is very incomplete. At no stage of his thinking did he consider the sexual libido as wholly explanatory of human drives.

[†] Freud's paper on narcissism (1914) marked the beginning of a careful consideration of the relationship between sexual and ego instincts which led to several efforts at solution, culminating (in the 1920's) in the formulation of the Eros-Thanatos dichotomy, or, as many Freudians would prefer, in the recognition of an instinct of aggression as primary as the sexual instincts, plus a new "structural approach" to the problems of ego development.

This advance note of important change is introduced here to emphasize the fact that the instinct groupings discussed in the next few pages are not *now* part of Freudian doctrine. I present them in some detail because it seems to me that they had certain merits which were lost in Freud's later revision. In my critical comment I shall suggest a reconsideration of this early point of view, of course with important modification, including much of the later revision.

pleasure. Secondly, the pleasure function of the genital organs did not begin with puberty but in early childhood. The theory of infantile sexuality appeared very early in the Freudian scheme. It remains fundamental in the strictly Freudian school, and although other schools place less emphasis upon it, there can be no doubt that Freud's observations of the genesis of sexuality have carried the field. The age of innocence is gone for good. Thirdly, the sexual instincts, thus broadly defined, are mainsprings of action. By various processes which we shall consider in detail later, the infant's primitive longings for gratification in the organ systems described as "sexual" become the attitudes and actions of the adult. It should be emphasized that we are here dealing with Freud's early formulations, when the "ego instincts" were still left without elaboration or careful study in their own right.

The sexual instincts operate under what Freud called the *pleasure principle,* or the pleasure-pain principle. Reduction of tension in an organ system is experienced as pleasure. Again, there was nothing very novel in this basic formulation, even at the turn of the century. The emphasis on a quasi-physiological definition of pleasure aligns the Freudian position more closely with the sober concept of "homeostasis"* developed by physiologists than with the earlier hedonistic philosophies. The terms "sexuality" and "pleasure" so easily awaken associations of wine, women, and song that it is necessary to keep reminding ourselves of the almost too strictly scientific sense in which Freud used them and of his adherence to a purely biological criterion.

The really new and tremendously important feature of Freud's "pleasure principle" was his observation that the sexual instincts strive for pleasure or avoidance of pain first, last, and always in a very primitive and uncompromising manner. Listening to his patients under hypnosis, analyzing their dreams and their free associations, Freud was impressed by wishes (instinctual aims) that were sometimes brutal or indecent and very often childish or stupid. Of course, his patients did not act out their wishes—in fact, usually did not even know consciously of their existence. In their dreams and in the small accidents of everyday life, normal people, too, Freud found, betrayed such wishes.

With this observation, the pleasure principle became no longer merely a special phrase for a generally acceptable biological principle such as homeostasis. The observation led directly to the concept of the unconscious, as described in Chapter 2.

Observation showed that *typically* even the sophisticated adult, neurotic or normal, unconsciously wants and strives for gratification along the lines

---

* "Homeostasis" can be defined as a tendency to uniformity or stability in the normal body states of an organism.

prefigured in his biological structure. These wants are typically irrational, inexpedient, non-ethical and childish. Many people with insight have remarked that human behavior is not what it seems. The *Maxims* of La Rochefoucauld, for example, cleverly point to the guises assumed by an underlying self-interest. Freud brought to the fore the nature of the underlying wants, both their physiological origin and their characteristic irrationality.

Freud further asked, however, why his patients did not act upon the compelling influence of the underlying wish. Why were they so resistant to recognition that the wish was there? There must be some inner force, Freud argued, that opposes its expression and recognition. In the *General Introduction to Psycho-Analysis* (1916), he remarked ironically that "it is a real pleasure for once to be in agreement with the opponents of psychoanalysis" in declaring that sexuality is not "everything."[4] This opposing force he called the *censor,* which he at first felt represented mainly the ego instincts. This latter group he viewed as operating under a different principle: the *reality principle*.

Freud described the inevitable conflict between these two sets of instincts operating under two different principles. Although his own description of the instincts and their relation to these "principles" underwent radical change with the years, the basic idea of an *unconscious conflict resulting in compromise behavior* was one of his most profound contributions to the scientific study of human nature. We saw, in Chapter 2, that the importance of unconscious conflict is now generally accepted, although concepts of the elements of the conflict vary and understanding of the mechanisms used in compromise has become more refined. Freud was the first to formulate in workable terms the play of intrapsychic forces and to emphasize that their interplay is the very core of psychological dynamics. Any account of his theory of instincts must stress this cardinal point.

SEXUAL *vs.* EGO INSTINCTS

The crude dualism of Freud's early opposition of sexual and ego instincts—the pleasure principle and the reality principle—was resolved by Freud himself in a very interesting way in his earlier books.* He suggested that the dichotomy was itself a consequence of experience. Both sets of instincts start out with the

* Cf. *A General Introduction to Psycho-Analysis*, Liveright Publishing Corp., 1935, pp. 310*ff.* With the shift in evaluation of the instinct problem, Freud no longer needed this solution. I present it in some detail, however, because I shall refer to it in my critical comment in which I return, with modification, to a point of view rather close to this aspect of the early Freudian position.

same biologically determined craving for immediate satisfaction of bodily need, with little or no awareness of the role played by the outside world in supplying satisfaction. The infant is simply hungry. He wards off many noxious stimuli in an *almost* reflex manner. He simply wants oral pleasure.

Very early, however, the two sets of instincts take divergent courses. The "ego instincts" (early formulation), because of the more directly urgent character of their demands, quickly learn to conform to the exigencies of reality. If hunger is not satisfied, the individual perishes. Survival depends upon mastery of the external world—a mastery which paradoxically involves submission to *its* laws—*i.e.*, to the reality principle. Just because the realistic satisfaction of hunger need cannot be long postponed, the individual learns postponement in this area, learns to interpose the delay of expedient action between perception of the bodily need and its satisfaction.

The sexual instincts are, on the other hand, more malleable. The organism survives even if satisfaction is long postponed or actually denied. To a considerable extent, satisfaction may be obtained autoerotically, by a very limited mastery of one's own body, or by substitute activities in variety. Whereas hunger requires a relatively specific type of satisfaction (nourishing food), a great miscellany of objects can more or less adequately meet the requirements of the sexual instincts. The "object" component of the sexual instincts is much less specifically prescribed by biological structure.

In his early work, Freud was interested primarily in the concrete description of the sexual instincts and left the ego aspect of the dichotomy very unclear. The "ego instincts" were a sort of mixture of cognitive functions, personal ideals, self-protection, and moral or social restrictions. They had a vague integration in the idea of self-preservation as a biological necessity. Mostly, however, they were simply lumped together in the concept of the censor, and the emphasis lay on the interplay between the unconscious sexual wishes and the censor.

Delineation of the sexual instincts proceeded mainly along the lines of a developmental psychology, for the most part reconstructed from analysis of adult patients. Freud denominated as *partial* or *component instincts* of the sexual drive the libidinal energies proceeding from the erogenous (or erotogenic) zones of the body: oral, anal and urethral, and genital. At first he also included among the component instincts sadism (pleasure in cruelty), masochism (pleasure in being hurt), scoptophilia (pleasure in looking), and various other apparently universal trends. The term *component instincts* is still used, rather loosely, for the powerful special organizations of the sexual instincts. We shall see in a moment, however, that it was primarily the difficulty of coordinating the phenomena of sadism and masochism with instinctual components like the oral, anal, and genital libido which led Freud to a major revision of his early dichotomy between the sexual and the ego instincts.*

LATER FORMULATIONS

FREUD WAS NEVER wholly satisfied with his early grouping of instincts. The prominent phenomena of sadism and masochism could not be clearly aligned with either the "sexual" or the "ego" instincts, nor did the early theory adequately explain the extraordinary self-centeredness *and* altruism of human loves and hates. My description of Freud's early position is drawn mainly from the *General Introduction to Psycho-Analysis,* but at that time (1916) he was already posing new problems and groping toward new solutions in papers written for his colleagues. His paper "On Narcissism" (1914) is a milestone for Freudians. The titles of a few other specialized books and papers will show the trend of Freud's thinking more clearly than pages of exposition about this transitional period preceding the next semipopular summary, *New Introductory Lectures on Psycho-Analysis* (1932). He wrote about "Instincts and Their Vicissitudes," about *The Ego and the Id,* about *Group Psychology and the Analysis of the Ego,* about "Mourning and Melancholia" (formulation of the concept of the superego), about a theory *Beyond the Pleasure Principle,* about

---

* I hesitate to discuss the smaller component instincts—scoptophilia, motility, skin erotism, thermal reactions, etc.—which are rather vaguely mentioned in Freud's early writings, and which have been mostly lost sight of in the main trends of psychoanalysis. Scoptophilia has been retained in the sense of an inborn wish to look at objects of sexual importance to the child. A few Freudian analysts have attempted to integrate new observations on the primary role of the other small component instincts with Freud's later approach.

It is quite impossible for an outsider reporting on major trends in psychoanalysis to work out the historical relationship between Freud's early writings and a variety of observations on the component instincts by contemporary Freudians, presented in different theoretical contexts. With acknowledgment to some Freudians, I offer a personal summary. The smaller component instincts represent Freud's direct observations of human behavior before his major theoretical framework was fully established. They often seem to involve an undifferentiated mixture of ego and libido trends, which he later tried to resolve by the "structural" approach I shall report presently.

Some return to these early observations seems highly desirable as a corrective to excessive emphasis on the erogenous zones and the structural trichotomy of id, ego, and superego. The return requires the insights expressed in Freud's later formulations; it should not be merely a reiteration of ideas Freud dismissed as crude approximations. Freud himself never forgot the problems posed by such phenomena and repeatedly warned against considering the erogenous zones as the *sole* source of libidinal energy. "They are the ones we know most about."

The Problem of Anxiety (better described in the German title *Hemmung, Symptom und Angst*—literally, Inhibition, Symptom and Anxiety).

Bibring's article "The Development and Problems of the Theory of the Instincts" may be consulted by readers interested in the transitional phases of Freud's thinking about instincts. I shall here report only the conclusion Freud reached about 1920 (*Beyond the Pleasure Principle*) and retained in its essential outlines. He proposed a new dichotomy: Eros and Thanatos, the life and death instincts, libido and aggression. The clinical observations Freud cites were taken from traumatic neuroses, so plentiful in the war years, in which the patient endlessly relives the terrible event leading to his psychological disturbance; from the repetition compulsion—*i.e.*, the tendency of many patients to repeat the same disastrous mistakes; from the play of normal children, which is often repetitive and at times seems gratuitously cruel.

In this first general formulation of his new position, Freud called upon the science of biology for support of the idea that there is a tendency in all living things to revert to the inorganic state—*i.e.*, to die. This is an instance of a general formula "to the effect that instincts tend toward a return to an earlier state."[5] Since all living things arose out of the inanimate, the trend toward death may be considered inborn, a death instinct, *Thanatos*. The striving here is no longer for a "pleasurable" reduction of tension among organ systems which constantly build up new energies. The striving of the death instinct is toward absolute zero. Freud accepted for this process a term suggested by an early follower, Barbara Low: the Nirvana principle.

With this formulation the concept of the sexual instincts was broadened still further. *Eros* came to represent all the trends in the organism which seek to unify, bind together, preserve, and build up. The term *libido* was applied not only to the more obviously sexual instincts but to "the whole available energy of Eros . . . present in the as yet undifferentiated ego-id [the newborn organism] and [serving] to neutralize the destructive impulses which are simultaneously present."[6] Freud did not hesitate at this point to subsume the instincts of self-preservation and the reality principle under Eros, along with instincts leading to preservation of the species. Similarly, love of self and love of others (ego love and object love) belong in the same instinct grouping.[7]

There is no special term like libido for the energy of the death instinct* and Freud considered this instinct very difficult to study. So long as it operates internally, it remains "silent." "We only come across it after it has become diverted outward as an instinct of destruction."[8] The diversion outward seems

* *Mortido* and *destrudo* have been suggested as terms analogous to libido, but have not been widely adopted, probably because Thanatos, the destructive and aggressive instincts, does not have so readily identifiable a source in the body, or so predictable a course, as the libido. Nor have psychoanalysts agreed so generally upon the underlying theory regarding them.

to be mediated by the skeletal musculature—and in this manner the development of "aggression" becomes a normal and even necessary phenomenon. Otherwise it remains too far internalized and can lead only to self-destruction.

Normally there occurs a *fusion* of the death instinct and Eros—that is, the outwardly directed aggressiveness develops in close relationship to experiences of libidinal gratification, with a consequent increasing tenderness toward the object of love and constructive care for its preservation. Where such fusion fails to occur, the outwardly directed aggression may remain relatively unmodified or may not appear at all—as in the pitiful infants observed by Spitz (see pp. 185*ff*.), who simply die for want of any loving stimulus to turn their instincts toward the outside world. In later life *de*fusion may occur, resulting in aggression either toward the object or toward the self when the energy attached to the object (object cathexis) is for some reason withdrawn and the psychic drama becomes again internalized. (See Chap. 6 for further explanation of these terms and processes.)

Some portion of self-destructiveness remains permanently within, until it at length succeeds in doing the individual to death, not, perhaps, until his libido has been used up or has become fixated in some disadvantageous way.[9]

Detailed discussion of the libido has been postponed to Chapter 6—because I think the value of the concept can be fully grasped only when the reader is in a position to see it as a kind of working summary of component instincts closely related to specific bodily structures. The development and role of the component instincts (the genetic process) are discussed in Chapter 5. Unless viewed in this context, the libido sounds like a mysterious psychic energy, apparently at variance with the often repeated statement that Freud was insistent upon the somatic basis of all psychological phenomena.

Similarly, although the death instinct must be presented as an important part of Freud's theory of the terms of the organism, it cannot be adequately explained at this point. For most Freudians, the highly complex concept of the death instinct became an inborn *aggressivity* which requires consideration as such. The young child "naturally" destroys and takes pleasure in destruction. This urge is thought of not as merely a by-product of thwarted libido but as an instinctual trend in its own right which requires expression and may undergo repression in much the same manner as the sexual instincts. The idea that fusion and defusion with the sexual instincts may occur is generally accepted. Many Freudians consider "aggression" highly constructive as well as destructive and at times seem almost to equate it with the energetic effort characteristic of the healthy child to investigate and conquer the outside world. We shall return to this problem in the section on ego psychology.

THE ANATOMY OF THE MENTAL PERSONALITY*

DURING THE EARLY 1920's, Freud concerned himself especially with an aspect of psychodynamics which cross-cuts the problem of instinct: the "anatomy of the mental personality." His views have been generally accepted by Freudians and represent what is termed the *structural* approach. The three categories Freud isolated (id, ego, superego) do not represent inborn dynamic trends (instincts). On the contrary, they are thought of as "institutions" or provinces of the mind which become crystallized in the course of experience and thereafter function with some independence of one another, although they are, of course, constantly interactive. After the sixth year, or thereabouts, when the latest "institution," the superego, is formed,† Freudians find it essential to consider the functioning of the personality not only in terms of underlying instincts (the dynamic approach) but also in terms of the manner in which these "institutions" have developed and their dynamic relationship to one another. Although the "institutions" are not inborn, their appearance is so regular and necessary a part of human functioning, as Freud sees it, that they unquestionably belong in a chapter on the terms of the organism.

Related to this structural point of view is the *topographical* approach, which cross-cuts the total personality in terms of the various layers of *consciousness* observable. The perceptual conscious is what we are actually aware of at any given moment. This rather narrow field extends into the *preconscious,* or *foreconscious* (the terms are interchangeable), which includes the host of immediate perceptions and memories available to us if our attention requires them. As I write, I do not hear the street noises—but I *can* hear them all too plainly if my concentration flags, or if I focus upon some outside event. At the age of eighteen I spent a year in France, reading enormous quantities of French classical literature. It so happens that most of the people I have known since are totally uninterested in the French classics, and this reading

---

* The heading is taken from the title of the chapter in the *New Introductory Lectures* dealing with these problems. Although the phrase is not in general use today, Freud's own title seems the most descriptive for this complex topic.

† I do not mean, of course, that study of the functioning personality must be postponed until the sixth year. Quite the contrary. Differentiation begins at birth and is far advanced at the age of five. The major institutions, however, are not fully demarcated until about that age, according to Freud. *Cf.* p. 211 for a discussion of Melanie Klein's divergent view.

has remained a sort of island in my intellectual life. Yet to the astonishment of my husband—and myself—I can, when a rare occasion demands, suddenly discourse about Racine and Corneille. This memory is still available in my *foreconscious,* a little fogged by time, but quite easily shined up. Such knowledge, present and past, lies at the periphery of consciousness and requires only the green light of attention to come into full awareness. The process is quite different with the *unconscious.* Freud reserves this term for those aspects of our mental experience which we *cannot* bring to consciousness when the occasion demands because they are actively repressed or otherwise kept at a distance from full awareness.

In Freud's early formulation, sexual instincts were unconscious, the ego functions conscious or preconscious. The conflict between the conscious repressing forces and the instinctual forces striving for expression seemed relatively simple. Closer observation of the repressing forces soon revealed, however, that they were by no means entirely conscious. The dynamic systems of the personality (id, ego, superego) do not follow the simple line of cleavage suggested by our awareness but are all at least partly rooted in the unconscious. Freud presents a diagram of the relationships of the three provinces or institutions to one another and to consciousness (*pcpt-cs* refers to *perceptual-conscious*).*

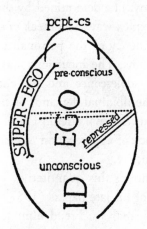

Before discussing the id, ego, and superego, I would like to call attention to two other *types of approach* implicit in Freud's writings, which are spoken of as relatively distinctive: the *genetic* and the *economic* approaches. All approaches are used in thorough description of an individual case, but understanding is clarified if the distinction is maintained. The *genetic* approach is oriented toward the actual fate of the instinctual drives and ego functions

* Reproduced from S. Freud, *New Introductory Lectures on Psycho-Analysis,* W. W. Norton & Co., 1933, p. 111.

during the period of basic personality formation. It includes consideration of their current function, unconscious as well as conscious. This approach, which will be discussed in Chapter 5 on the genetic process, is crucial in understanding why the ego and superego of the patient have taken the specific form observed. However, the doctor cannot proceed fruitfully in interpreting such matters to the patient until he sees how the patient has "institutionalized" his experience, as it were—how he has organized his approach to the problems of living (structural approach).

Further, the organization of trends and countertrends (instincts, sublimations, and defenses derived from experience) depends to a large extent on the *strength* of the separate trends, countertrends, and "institutions" active *at any given moment*. Consideration of the shifting internal balance of operating trends is called the *economic* approach. From the very beginning, and especially in his late papers, Freud himself stressed the importance of the *quantitative* distribution of energies for understanding of the individual case. *Qualitatively* there is no very great difference between normal and pathological conflicts, but Freud did *not* conclude that pathology is, therefore, a simple quantitative extension of "normal" conflict. The problem is rather that when any particular trend becomes excessively intensified, it may upset the person's entire equilibrium.

The *manner* of upset will be determined by the previous structure of the personality, in a highly complex way. The break or continued distortion occurs because of the over-all tendency of the personality to maintain itself despite *quantitatively* great incursions. The incursions may come from within, as exemplified by the crises of adolescence and the climacteric, in which bodily changes tend to increase the libidinal demands of the organism. Or the incursions may come from various external circumstances which impinge upon each person according to his mode of apperception, sometimes so heavily as to cause a drastic shift in his personality.

Freud constantly mentions this quantitative, *economic* aspect of personality function, and in one of his late papers (1937)[10] remarks that it has been underemphasized in psychoanalysis. Freud himself attempted no *codification* of this problem, and I shall not attempt to carry this line of argument further until it appears again in the discussion of pathology, Chapter 7.* There I shall try to show more concretely how it is related to the actual functioning of the individual.

* It occurs to me in rereading this chapter that perhaps the discussion of the terms of the milieu, Chapter 4, could also be considered as a problem in the *economic* approach to psychodynamics. When a culturally rather than a uniquely determined individual experience determines the quantitative distribution of energy (the economic approach), the problem is complicated in a manner which requires special consideration.

THE STRUCTURAL APPROACH

FREUD, AS WE HAVE SAID, isolated three major provinces of the mind: id, ego, and superego. Very roughly indeed, these terms may be indentified as the vital substratum of biologically determined impulse (id), adaptive mechanisms more or less oriented toward reality (ego), and, finally, conscience (superego). The id is always unconscious; the ego and superego are largely conscious, but by no means exclusively so (see diagram, p. 83). The censor of earlier theory is abandoned in favor of a developmental approach whereby the regulatory and idealizing or self-condemnatory aspects of the personality are examined in their own right. The provisional "opposing forces" to innate trends toward total expression of bodily demands (id) become more carefully differentiated as ego and superego, institutions which develop functionally out of the experience common to childhood. The original matrix in the newborn out of which these institutions develop is called the ego-id.

THE ID

The id remains the reservoir of instinctual needs which press toward immediate fulfillment. It is the major source of the drive energy, essentially somatic in origin, which Freud presents as the only valid assumption for psychology. Its relatively undifferentiated operation may be seen in the "primary process" (see pp. 54ff.), although, as Anna Freud points out with especial sharpness,[11] we can never learn about the id directly, but only through relatively primitive operations of the ego. This id includes all the component sexual instincts, the major somatic origin of which seems referable to the erotogenic zones: oral, anal, and genital. It also includes the instinct of aggression. Although almost all Freudians consider aggression as part of the id, it has no clearly somatic base and remains a controversial problem. I shall not carry description of the id further at this point because its delineation requires careful delineation of the genetic process. In a way, the whole of Chapter 5, which describes this process, may be seen as an elaboration of the concept of instinctual demands (id) as they meet the circumstances of living (adaptation).

THE EGO

The ego (as an "institution") is defined by Freud as the precipitate of the learning process of the individual in his encounter with the external world of people and things. It is not inborn, as the id is inborn. Rather, it is an achievement of living, and its major function is continued maintenance of the organism *vis-à-vis* the demands made upon it by "three harsh masters"—external reality, the id, and the superego (whose origin and demands we shall discuss presently). The functions of the ego are partly *synthetic* in that they operate to maintain the organism as a whole. Partly, they are directed toward more specific realistic adaptations as the child learns to relate external stimuli to his own needs.

Neither the id nor the superego is concerned with viable compromise. The id demands total fulfillment of biological impulses; the superego demands control up to the point of total suppression of many such impulses. The external world of reality makes still further demands, some of them relatively extraneous to the personality as the child learns to deal with the basic relationships prevailing in the world of *things,* some of them very close to the personality as the child learns about people and develops a model of his own self and of his social relationships from his early experience with people.

Freud's account of the *ego* is never very clear, although his isolation of this structural aspect of the personality may be held as one of his most brilliant achievements. One of his problems in describing the ego—a relatively simple problem—is semantic. Freud occasionally uses the word "ego" in referring to the totally undifferentiated organism, the "self" at its most primitive level, although his usage is usually more precise. Further, Freud's description of the dynamics of the ego is ambiguous. My reference to the "three harsh masters" is drawn from the *New Introductory Lectures* (1932), in which the structural approach is presented in semipopular manner as an established theoretical unit.* At this period, he felt that the ego had no energies of its own traceable to organic sources. All its dynamic powers were "borrowed" from the id and superego, and it maintained itself by "tricks" whereby the energies of these other provinces could be turned to the advantage of the ego. The quoted words are Freud's, and although I have selected picturesque terms, I have not done violence to Freud's position on the ego in 1932. The ego has no intrinsic dynamic power; it is the major integrative institution of the personality, and it maintains

---

* The structural approach began much earlier, of course. Indeed, its major outlines are stated in *The Ego and the Id* (1923).

itself by organizing dynamic trends, often in conflict with one another. *At the same time,* Freud writes that the hope of the world lies in the ego. "Where id was, there shall ego be."[12] In his technical writings, Freud was coming closer to sober recognition of the role of the ego in psychodynamics.

I shall not try to clarify Freud's views about the ego further at this point because they are the point of departure for new developments in post-Freudian psychoanalysis, so important as to warrant a long separate section in this chapter (see pp. 95-104). I should like to stress here his idea that the "self" we commonly talk about, and the clever way in which it handles the problems of living, is not equivalent to the total human organism. "Something" is interposed between direct biological impulse and its biological gratification—"something" that is more a matter of *organization* of experience than of instinctual drives per se. The concept of the ego as a developmental institution solves a host of problems which every school of psychology has found baffling in so far as it has tried to derive the dynamics of sophisticated adult behavior from the biological substratum—or, indeed, from any list of instincts, drives, trends, or units of behavior established by conditioning.

THE SUPEREGO

We come now to the third member of Freud's trichotomy: the superego. Originally, all the forces opposing free gratification of biological (mainly sexual) impulses were lumped together as the censor. Conscience was clearly one of these forces, and in the course of work with patients Freud came to study its operation more narrowly. He was struck by the fact that the machinations of conscience sometimes appear quite as irrational and compelling as the id impulses themselves, just as "queer" from the standpoint of reasonable adjustment, just as foreign to the plans of the ego. Patients suffering from a well-known psychiatric condition, *melancholia,* take to berating themselves cruelly for actions and trivial shortcomings to which they had previously paid little attention. They become, in fact, so preoccupied with self-condemnation that they are sometimes unable to carry on their ordinary responsibilities and must be protected against suicide. Yet after a time the terrific guilt abates, and they see themselves again as worthwhile human beings. The vehemence of this attack of the self upon the self required explanation.

Freud came to the conclusion that conscience was neither just an unanalyzable part of the censor nor a categorical imperative but a specific psychological development. As usual, he sought an answer in biological fact: the long period of helplessness in the human infant and his dependence upon his immediate family. Adler makes much of this point also, remarking that the helplessness of the child leads to feelings of inferiority and compensatory striving for power. Freud's concept is different—indeed, he views the feeling of inferiority as being essentially fear of the loss of love. According to Freud, the infant is at first amoral, with no internal inhibitions against pleasure-seeking impulses. The parents are the main source of satisfaction—and, simultaneously, the main restrictive influences. The little child fears direct punishment. Even more, he fears loss of love, the withdrawal of the satisfaction and protection so profoundly associated with the parents. At the outset, the child begins to conform to parental dictates because of "objective anxiety"—that is, the conditioned fear of the consequence of his actions.

Later on, however, especially during the period of the Oedipus complex, when the genital wish for the parent of the opposite sex presents a special problem, a new process sets in. *The child identifies with the parents.** Their commands, their image, become *introjected*—incorporated into the child's own psyche. We shall discuss this process in greater detail in Chapter 5, but we may here mention that studies of grief, submission to political authority, movie attendance, hero worship, etc., show quite clearly that the individual often may not so much love, admire, or expect return from the object of devotion as somehow *become* the object. Adolescents who relish gangster films or pore over screen-magazine accounts of the intimate life of stars do not usually expect any real contact with Humphrey Bogart or Ginger Rogers. Rarely do they consciously try to pattern themselves after these actors in any systematic manner, nor is the character portrayed on the screen taken as a conscious model to any great extent. But as they watch the movie they quite simply *are* the hero. They *identify* with him, or with whatever character portrayed in the movie best fits their own personality.

It is by this mechanism that the parental dictates become internalized. The child thus, in a manner of speaking, becomes the parent and follows the parental admonition as if it came entirely from himself. Freud does not deny the importance of later identifications in determining character, but he calls the later identifications "later editions of the parents." He remarks that these affect the ego only and have no influence on the superego, which is determined by the earliest parental images.[13]

Once formed, the superego tends to operate with all the force of the parental dictates *as the child understood them* at the period of major introjection. It functions directly with the energies of the "id." The superego is so organized as *often* to represent the exact opposite of the primitive wish. Love

---

* The general process of identification begins very early in infancy. In Chapter 5 the special character of identification at the Oedipal period will be discussed more fully.

for the parent may become fear of the parent, even hate. Although in a general way "conscience" works toward the "higher" things, it can become destructive and nonrealistic. It is an organized mode of operation, an institution, not a biological given.

EGO PSYCHOLOGY

IN FAIRLY RECENT YEARS an aspect of psychoanalysis previously somewhat neglected has come into prominence—namely, careful study of the ego as distinct from the innate drives of man with their somatic sources—(*i.e.,* from the sexual and aggressive instincts). For some analysts this emphasis has led to actual repudiation of Freud's views of instincts. Theories constructed on the basis of repudiation will be presented in Part III of this book. The present discussion is confined to Freud and to Freudians who have continued to accept the libido theory as basic. For these analysts—and they are greatly in the majority—ego psychology is integrated with the older view of instinctual drives.

We have seen that in the early 1920's Freud modified his position in two ways. One was the full recognition of aggression as instinctual in much the same way as sexuality rather than as part of the vaguely defined ego instincts. The other modification was the development of the structural approach, whereby the ego became a special institution of the mind established through the life experience of the person. The source of energy for the ego remained unclear, in contrast to that of the superego, which represented a transformation of libidinal and aggressive energies organized in a definable manner. Even in the *New Introductory Lectures* (1932), the ego appears *mainly* as a helpless mediator, whose superior knowledge of reality and control of the pathways of attention, memory, and action allow it a measure of expedient action, but only in the service of the id and the superego. The ego makes use of "tricks" which allow it to call upon one aspect of the personality to master another. The integrative function of the ego is stated, but it is not exploited either in the positive sense of aiding the personality toward unified function or in the negative, pathogenic sense emphasized by Horney (see p. 454) of excessive idealization of the self. Indeed, the force of the "ego ideal" emphasized by Freud in earlier writings (notably *Group Psychology and the Analysis of the Ego*, 1921) becomes subsidiary to the concept of the superego, which stands in a more immediate relationship to instinctual drives, as described in the foregoing pages.

Nevertheless, the development of the structural approach set the stage for the study of the ego as a kind of organization of biological givens rather than as a series of special ego instincts (cf. Sullivan's concept of the self dynamism, pp. 480ff.). This concept permits a much more flexible understanding of the endless variations in human behavior and a relatively simple ordering of their complexities, without the danger of reductionism.

Investigation of the ego by post-Freudians has taken two general directions, both of which have their origins in Freud's writings. One carries on the concept of the *mechanisms of defense*. The leader in this direction has been Anna Freud, whose small volume *The Ego and the Mechanisms of Defence* (1936) remains the clearest exposition of a point of view now very widely adopted among Freudians as indispensable to the work of analysis. The other direction has to do with clarification of the *secondary process*, the development of those aspects of the ego that seem to derive from maturation of the reality-adapted aspects of the organism (rational thought and action, perception, attention, memory, cognition, locomotion, and the like) and that may be considered conflict-free in essence, however intimately they are interwoven with drives (instincts) in the course of living. The leader in this direction may be considered Heinz Hartmann, although Kris, Loewenstein, Rapaport, and many others have been close collaborators or have developed parallel ideas. The first decisive publication presenting this point of view is perhaps Hartmann's article "Ich-Psychologie und Anpassungsproblem" (1939), translated, with some omissions, by Rapaport as "Ego Psychology and the Problem of Adaptation."*

DEFENSE MECHANISMS

The concept of *defense* appeared very early in Freud's writings (see especially "The Defence Neuro-Psychoses," 1894)[14] but was dropped for thirty years. During this period, Freud used the concept of repression to represent the means whereby instinctual drives were controlled. He also studied the nature of instincts and their relationship to one another and to objects more carefully than others had before him. With the development of the structural approach, however, and after observation of the different ways in which dif-

---

* In D. Rapaport, *Organization and Pathology of Thought*, Columbia University Press, 1951, pp. 362-396. For a list of further relevant works by these authors, see the bibliography at the end of this chapter.

ferent types of patients seemed to handle the same instinctual problems, Freud felt that it was desirable to return to the early formulation. In *The Problem of Anxiety* (1926) he writes,

> I now think that it confers a distinct advantage to readopt the old concept of defense if in doing so it is laid down that this shall be the general designation for all the techniques of which the ego makes use in the conflicts which potentially lead to neurosis, while repression is the term reserved for one particular method of defense, one which because of the direction that our investigations took was the first with which we became acquainted.[15]

In this book, Freud first developed the idea, which has since become standard, that anxiety is not the *result* of repression, as he had at first supposed, but is actually its *cause*. Although originally an inborn response to *present* danger, it comes, in the course of development, to function as a signal of *potential* danger, which the ego then tries to avoid. The pain of anxiety and the threat can be warded off in various ways, among which repression is only one. Naturally, one might wish that the individual would appreciate realistically the total situation confronting him: his inner wishes and their possibilities for fulfillment in the external world. Unfortunately, this kind of insight is impossible for the infant and the young child. What inevitably happens is that the *child's* ego forms its own concept of the dangers confronting it from without and from within and its own methods of handling them. These methods of handling conflict tend to become more or less firmly institutionalized as "mechanisms of defense."

Freud himself began the delineation of defense mechanisms, and Freudians had been aware of the complex disguises assumed by neurotic conflicts long before the present development of ego psychology. Nevertheless, psychoanalysis tended to concentrate its attention on the materials of the id and to envisage the task of therapy essentially in terms of the discovery and release of the repressed instinctual drives. It was Anna Freud who pointed out most cogently that the ego, too, has its archaic forms which are mainly unconscious and which are deeply involved in the transformations of drives actually operating in the personality. Moreover, the instinctual drives are subject to observation by analyst or patient only *via their representations in the ego,* and these are always more or less well organized in terms of the mechanisms of defense established by the ego.

It is comparatively easy to bring the buried materials of the id into consciousness. After all, by their very nature, the id materials strive toward expression. But their irruption into consciousness, either as impulses or as affects, immediately calls into play the defensive maneuvers of the ego, which again tend to distort them in a manner characteristic for the patient. The manner of distortion is not directly related to the type of impulse pressing toward expression; rather, it must be understood as determined by the general mode or modes the ego has adopted. These modes may be very deeply embedded in the personality as character traits (what Reich called the armorplating of character, *Charakterpanzerung*), or they may be relatively shifting as the individual ego selects now one defensive method, now another.[16]

Because a large part of Chapter 6, on personality dynamics, and some parts of Chapter 7, on pathology and treatment, will be devoted to the operation of the defense mechanisms, I shall not continue the discussion at this point. My purpose here is merely to indicate the new theoretical developments which relate the defense mechanisms to the basic structure of the personality. The ego is envisaged as a developing structure rather than as an instinctual given, but its dynamic role is not diminished by this shift in origin. On the contrary, the new formulation allows for a much more exact investigation of processes which Freud observed from the start as opposing the pressure of instinctual drives. Freud laid the groundwork for such investigation in the 1920's. Anna Freud posed the theoretical and practical problems involved in her detailed study in 1936. In 1937, Freud himself wrote a paper (*Analysis Terminable and Interminable*) which goes far toward integrating problems proceeding from id and ego in the task of analysis.[17] Analysis of the ego defenses has long since become a routine part of classical Freudian therapy; discussion of the defense operations of the ego has almost superseded discussion of "id" problems in the technical Freudian journals—although the majority of articles represent a fairly comfortable mixture.

It should be emphasized that concern with the ego has *not* replaced the libido theory for the Freudian schools. The castration complex, for example, seems as "nuclear" in Anna Freud's writings as in Freud's, although in the cases she describes it rarely appears as the direct explanation of the presenting symptoms. Aggressive behavior *may* be a manifestation of the aggressive instinct, but it also may be a device of the ego—as, for example, when a child identifies with an authority which he sees as aggressive (with or without justification) and in this manner merely "borrows" the aggression, as it were, from the external model as a defensive measure.[18]

Anna Freud cites as an example a shy, inhibited five-year-old boy who became fiercely aggressive when his analysis was about to touch on material connected with masturbation. He pretended to be a roaring lion, tried to strike people, carried a rod like Krampus (a devil who punishes naughty children), and laid about him with it at home and in the analyst's office. He even took to brandishing kitchen knives. Yet analysis showed that the aggression was not due to the lifting of his inhibition on some instinctual impulses. Rather, he feared that *he* would be roared at, slapped, beaten, and perhaps have his organ cut off in punishment for his sexual activities and fantasies. Anna Freud interprets the aggressive behavior *at this point of the analysis* in the following way. "He had introjected the aggression of the adults in whose eyes he felt guilty and, having exchanged the passive for the active part, he directed his own aggressive acts against those same people."[19] Once the child had actually communicated his forbidden behavior and thoughts to the analyst and his anxious expectation of punishment was reduced, the compulsive aggressive behavior disappeared.

In this example, Anna Freud does not mean to imply that the *ego* device of identification with the aggressor can be substituted for the id impulse in a general psychological theory. The little boy is not "cured" at this point in the analysis; indeed, he may be expected to show some sort of aggressive symptoms later, as instinctual impulses are genuinely released from inhibition. And identification with the aggressor should not be considered as the *only* device a child's ego may employ. There are many such devices (ego mechanisms), which may or may not become consolidated into the defense mechanisms of the adult personality. Nevertheless, the distinction between id impulses and ego devices must be maintained, and the predominant dynamics of the behavior patterns observed by the analyst must be considered. *Behavior* may be part of an ego mechanism *or* a manifestation of the id. It cannot be diagnosed simply as behavior, at a phenomenological level, but must be understood in its origins and current significance. For Anna Freud, the basic theory of instincts and their successive levels of organization in the early years of childhood is not greatly different from Freud's formulation.

Critical Comment

IN THIS conservatism, Anna Freud and the vast majority of analysts who call themselves Freudian differ from the analysts discussed in Part III of this book, and also from some schools that still remain within the fold of the Psychoanalytic Association—for example, Melanie Klein, who leads one branch of a sort of bifurcation in English psychoanalysis. (Anna Freud has lived in London since 1938, and leads another branch of psychoanalysis in England.) Klein's basic ideas will be presented briefly in Chapter 5, on the genetic process, and are mentioned here only because they represent a different view of the instinctual-maturational approach in its relations to the emerging structure of the personality. In a very different way, Kardiner, Rado, Fenichel, and others have challenged one or another aspect of Freud's instinct theory—indeed, debate on the death instinct and problems of aggression is quite general. On the whole, however, I think it is correct to state that, for most Freudians (and this means for the vast majority of practicing psychoanalysts), further investigation of the defense mechanisms of the ego, no matter how new and radical the findings may prove, is a quite natural development of Freud's position. Even if the tail ultimately is accepted as wagging the dog, it is still a tail. Ego defenses may come to play a larger and larger part in therapeutic analyses and in the interpretation of nonmorbid phenomena. For the Freudian this would not mean a repudiation or even a basic modification of the theory of instincts—as it did for Adler, Horney, and the other non-Freudian analysts—but rather a more careful study of how they operate via the ego.

It is not accidental that ego devices which approach the normal or even the ideal are still called "defenses." The term arises from pathology, from the fact that psychoanalysis has developed a general theory of human psychology based upon principles discovered largely through investigation of the distortions of mental illness. But the usage has deeper roots in Freud's basic theory of instincts—as Horney has pointed out with especial emphasis.[20] If man's inborn nature is to be considered as constituted primarily of his instinctual drives, and if, further, these drives are envisaged as blindly sexual and blindly aggressive—in any event, unacceptable for social living—then the outlook seems "pessimistic." We have already noted Freud's idea that the sexual drives are controlled mainly by anxiety (in the sense that anxiety triggers the defense mechanisms of the ego) and that the death instinct is prevented from fulfilling itself at once by being turned outward in complex fusion with the libido.

I have deliberately crammed into one paragraph all the Freudian terms which have been called nasty, cynical, and pessimistic. Horney and many other writers often quote these terms in a manner which implies a *value* judgment—as if Freud's theories called on the worst in man, and theirs on the best. This type of judgment is, I think, quite inappropriate. *In practice,* optimism about the possibility of curing the patient is much more a matter of the personality of the doctor and his breadth of vision than it is a matter of school theory. There are overoptimistic Freudians and overpessimistic analysts of other persuasions.

I hope the reader has already seen enough of the derivation and operation of Freudian concepts to understand that they really have nothing to do with value judgments. They are ways of formulating observational material in a dynamic manner in whatever terms were most meaningful at the time. If Freud had talked about synthetic versus conservative or disintegrative trends in the organism, variously related to its biological structures, nobody would accuse him of pessimism, cynicism, or nastiness. The chances are that nobody would have accused him of anything, for the excellent reason that nobody would have understood what he was talking about, or cared. Freud's formulations had tremendous impact partly because they dealt openly with very real human problems in a vocabulary familiar to all of us. Unfortunately, the use of value-laden terms in the nonvalue context of a scientific theory readily leads to precisely the confusion and inappropriate antagonism that Freud encountered. For people who ardently desire scientific appreciation of the creative, constructive potential of the human spirit, such words as "defense," "conflict," and "anxiety" for the mainsprings of action are quite as distasteful as "sexuality" and "aggression."

My main reason for making the foregoing comment is to introduce the second aspect of contemporary ego psychology in an altogether necessary atmosphere of *neutrality* as regards the humanistic value judgments the reader may very easily read into the distinctions to be drawn in the following pages. "Conflict-free" sounds much pleasanter than "defense." Yet it should be made very clear that Hartmann, whose position I now report, is in no way rescuing the dignity of the human psyche from the nasty, deterministic driven-ness of the Anna Freud position. In articles which would take us too far afield in this book (see bibliography), he undertakes to re-examine the formation of psychic structure, the theory of aggression (with Kris and Loewenstein), and problems of technique and attitudes toward normal development. All these articles accept and use the Freudian instinct theory. The changes Hartmann suggests are consistent rather than subversive, *modifying* the problem of how the instinctual drives function rather than repudiating the instinctual drives. With this cautionary introduction, I present Hartmann's handling of the second aspect of contemporary ego psychology: the careful examination of the primary and secondary processes.

THE AUTONOMOUS FUNCTIONS OF
THE EGO: HARTMANN

The classical Freudian position tends to assume that human behavior is derived from instinctual drives and that the independent function of the ego arises out of the necessary conflicts among drives within the organism and between these drives and reality. The ego, the emergent institution which orders the relations among drives and between drives and the outside world, is thought of as drive-connected. It "borrows" its drives and plays off one instinctual drive against another.

If instinctual demands could find immediate satisfaction through the environment, we should probably hear nothing about them. They would be "silent." It seems that a measure of frustration and conflict is the necessary condition for the development of such personality devices as the higher thought processes, ideals, and conscience (*cf.* the somewhat similar attitude of Fromm toward such problems). If he is to progress toward planning and detailed appreciation of the world around him, the infant must learn to tolerate *delay* in instinctual gratification; he must learn to give up one type of gratification in order to enjoy another. Experience must be synthesized in the interest of inner harmony and progressive mastery both of primitive instinctual needs and of the external environment.

Freud repeatedly writes of the ego functions (Hartmann calls them *apparatuses*)—the sensorium, motility, memory, imagination, and the like— whereby the ego accomplishes this necessary operation. Here again, the problem is more clearly stated in some of Freud's early works than later, when he was deeply preoccupied with the development of libido dynamics and the aggressive instinct. Chapter 7 of the *Interpretation of Dreams* (1900) remains the most comprehensive analysis of the functions that can be lumped together under the label *secondary process*. The series of "metapsychological papers" between 1911 and 1917 touches upon the problem, notably "Formulations Regarding the Two Principles in Mental Functioning" (1911),[21] in which Freud attempts to trace the origin and function of the reality principle in contrast to the pleasure principle. It seems clear that Freud considered the ego functions (apparatuses) as biological givens of the human organism, essentially under the control of the ego, but his conception of the problem remained relatively fluid and tentative.

Beginning with his important article "Ego Psychology and the Problem of Adaptation" (1939), Heinz Hartmann attacks the problem of ego psychology with especial vigor. His synthesis includes not only the new achievements of Freud's instinct theory, the structural approach, and the concept of defense, but also concepts from academic psychology. Hartmann urges that the initial matrix of psychic development be envisaged as not simply the id but the whole gamut of bodily structures, among which must be counted the *apparatuses* of the ego described above. These have a *primary autonomy*—that is, they function independently in their own right. They are the consequence of the evolution of the human species quite as definitely as the organ systems underlying the libidinal drives. The human being is born with a kind of pre-adaptedness to the average conditions of biological existence for this species, which includes the sensorimotor and regulatory apparatuses generally necessary for survival, as well as the vegetative systems. There is no special instinct of self-preservation—in fact, very little prefigured response to specific aspects of the environment such as one finds in many of the lower animals. "Yet on the average the whole ensemble of drives, ego-functions, ego-apparatuses, and the principles of regulation, as they meet the average expectable environmental conditions, do have survival value."[22]

The functioning of the ego apparatuses is initially, for Hartmann, therefore, conflict-free. Furthermore, their functioning seems to be subjectively experienced as a "pleasure" in its own right. Hartmann writes: "The pleasure possibilities of the apparatuses of the conflict-free ego-sphere seem to play a very significant role in the adaptation to the external world." The child spontaneously exercises his limbs and his sense organs, is attentive to objects, remembers, etc. All this is as much a part of his being as his spontaneous activity and pleasure in the erotogenic zones, at birth and during the period of maturation.

To some extent, these autonomous apparatuses develop integrations of their own.* But to some extent they become *instrumental* in the infant's han-

---

* For example, eye-hand coordination shows a sequential development so regular that age norms have been developed against which the maturational level of the individual infant may be studied. The work of Gesell, Bühler, and others may be considered in this connection.

dling of other aspects of his organismic needs—the instinctual drives. From the moment when the infant learns to anticipate the breast or bottle; to cease crying when it appears; to turn toward it adaptively; above all, to develop a hallucinatory image of the object in its absence; a new aspect of ego development has set in. Or we may say that, at the moment when the infant cries not purely as an expression of distress but with some notion, however crudely associative, of the cry as a preliminary of relief, the sensorimotor apparatus has begun to be drive-connected (cathected).* From this point on, the ego apparatuses become closely involved with the drives, although they retain a certain autonomy peculiar to themselves.

In this manner, patterns of behavior typically develop which have what Hartmann calls a *secondary autonomy*. The fragmentary, primitive connections of the ego apparatuses with the drive states become organized as complex integrated reaction patterns, organized in various ways.† In his drive-connected relations with his parents or other significant adults, the infant develops types of behavior which then become important in themselves. He walks not only for fun but also for the increment of adult love that his new accomplishment calls forth. He masters the art of eating tidily and maintaining bowel control not only by virtue of his greater capacity for coordination but also in order to avoid the pain of parental disfavor. New patterns of behavior are thus built up in close relation to his instinctual trends *and* to the attitude of the parents toward them. Behavior patterns so established tend to be per-

---

* Freud thought of the process whereby an external stimulus (object) comes to elicit an instinctual response as analogous to the manner in which a neutral physical object acquires an electrical charge and behaves as if it were itself an electrical force. This process is called cathecting. An object or even a complex reaction pattern may be cathected—*i.e.,* acquire "charge" from the original instinctual drive. This concept will be discussed further in Chapter 6.

† A succinct statement of Hartmann's view of "the mutual influences in the development of ego and id" may be found in a paper so entitled read before the Seventeenth Congress of the International Psycho-Analytical Association, Amsterdam, August 8, 1951, and discussed by Anna Freud at the same meeting. I quote from Anna Freud's discussion: "Ego interests, qualities and attitudes become independent of the instinctual tendencies, or the defense mechanisms against instinctual tendencies, from which they have arisen. . . . In Hartmann's words, 'reactive character formation, originating in defense against the drives, may gradually take over a host of other functions in the ego' and continue to exist long after its function as defense mechanism has ceased to be important" ("The Mutual Influences in the Development of Ego and Id: Introduction to the Discussion," *The Psychoanalytic Study of the Child,* Vol. VII, International Universities Press, 1952, pp. 48*f.*).

Anna Freud has a gift for clear statement. Her brief review of Hartmann's paper is the best short reference I can offer to take the reader beyond the present account. It should be remembered that Anna Freud was talking to a congress of psychoanalysts on a theoretical topic chosen because of its current importance to the advancement of psychoanalytic theory at a highly specialized level. Her discussion includes the views of other analysts who presented papers at the meeting, plus her own formulation of this basic problem. Following up this reference would give the reader a much more vivid sense of current feeling about ego problems among the analysts themselves than I can possibly convey. Furthermore, the reader may be tempted to read other articles in the same volume. This annual book publication is, to my mind, especially useful to the "outsider" in getting a feeling for how analysts go about their empirical studies and how they *use* the concepts I must present rather abstractly in this book.

petuated beyond the situation which gave rise to them and to become elaborated in their own right. Thus, the habit of cleanliness, with a fear of any break in careful control, develops a *secondary autonomy* extending far beyond the nursery. It is "neutralized."

It is not easy for a child to forego defecating as he pleases in favor of a regime set by his parents, to eat "properly" when he is very hungry or when he is so little hungry that he would like to experiment with all sorts of new manipulatory and social techniques. In even the best-regulated household, such situations are conflict-laden for the child. They require complex organizations of behavior, with varying relationships between the autonomously developing patterns of the ego apparatuses and the instinctual drives to which they are necessarily connected. Hartmann's point is that organizational units constantly arise in the course of development which then tend to function autonomously. They arise in intimate connection with drive states. Although they employ ego apparatuses which tend to develop autonomously in their own right (primary autonomy), they have a special organization important in its own right. Above all, Hartmann's point is that a drive state arising from *inner* tensions, as in the spontaneous development of the sexual instinctual drives, may "trigger" a complex ego organization in much the same way as an external stimulus. These ego organizations, however, may also be used as *units* in reactions which are essentially drive-connected.

The case of Nancy is instructive. Nancy's speech development was average up to the age of two and a half. Rather abruptly, this development paused, to the point where at four she was still using a language of her own, quite simple in form and intelligible only to people in constant association with her. Again rather abruptly, her speech then took on impetus, so that within a month she was chattering like any four-year-old. At the age of ten, she underwent a severe psychological crisis, one manifestation of which was a hysterical muteness lasting several hours. To her own terror, the little girl was unable to utter a word, despite an urgent wish to tell her mother about the event which precipitated the crisis, or to talk with a schoolmate who telephoned about an event in which Nancy was keenly interested.

This example demonstrates how an ego function (speech) which normally develops early as a pattern of essentially primary autonomy was interrupted in the developmental stage, probably because it became drive-connected *as an apparatus*. It then recovered its autonomy but underwent temporary eclipse again *as a unit*, clearly in response to renewed inner tension very probably similar in kind to the drive conflict operating in Nancy's babyhood. The nature of the conflict is irrelevant to the present discussion, which is concentrated on the manner whereby an autonomous ego function of great complexity may change its relationship to drives. In Freudian vocabulary, it may become drive-cathected, neutralized, and recathected by drives. The shifts may occur not only in response to external stimuli, but also in response to inner stimuli, with little appropriateness to the current external situation.

Organizations of *secondary* autonomy may have the same variable relationship to drives. For example, the child learns habits of tidiness in eating through his relationships with his parents—that is, in a highly drive-connected manner—typically with a greater or less degree of conflict as observed above. There is no primary autonomy for table manners as for the function of speech. As a rule, these habits become organized in their own right and normally expand in a "neutral" or "conflict-free" manner as the child learns to use a fork instead of a spoon and, finally, in a complex society, to use the right fork. However, once such an organization is instituted, it may be used *as such* in various ways. One way in which such an organization is used is for greater mastery of reality. Knowing the right fork may be an unfortunately trivial example of "mastery," but the reality value of this knowledge in many social situations is clear.

A second way is the expression of a drive conflict through the later pattern, as when the person under stress clings absurdly to the social rituals of good manners or, conversely, deliberately breaks them in a spirit of defiance.

A third way in which these organizations may be used is as *signals* of mounting inner tension. Small breaks and discomforts within the complex pattern alert the ego to *dangers from within,* so that new alignments of the defense maneuvers may be made far short of direct expression of instinctual drives, which might be devastating to the general maintenance of the personality. An example of this may be the adolescent's sudden finickiness about manners. In part this finickiness belongs to the conflict-free elaboration of ego patterns as the youngster learns the realistic importance of good manners in social adjustment, especially as regards the opposite sex. But any parent knows that this is not the whole story. Anna Freud points out (see p. 221) that the bodily pubertal changes increase the intensity of *all* the sexual drives, pregenital as well as genital. As drive tensions mount for physiological reasons, there is some danger that *all* the secondary ego structures may be swamped. In the light of these *inner* circumstances, the casual untidiness of the little boy becomes for the adolescent no longer mainly a realistic lack of attention to the continued preachments of his elders. It becomes, instead, a reminder of the untrammeled drives of infancy—with all the old conflicts. If these "reminders" are a small part of complex ego patterns rather securely related to the early drives, then the adolescent's slight squeamishness about table manners and the like may not only reflect the drive systems but may serve to reintegrate the secondarily developed ego patterns along new lines appropriate to new demands.

When the complex ego patterns of secondary autonomy have been developed in overly close relationship to the primary drive systems (*i.e.*, are highly cathected), when the little boy has not related his untidiness step by step with the demands of his parents and his compeers but has kept himself "clean" by parental admonitions too thoroughly introjected—then his slightest misstep or small fantasy may operate as a "signal" for reinstatement of the entire pattern of infantile conflict. Thus the "model child" frequently turns into a rebel or a neurotic in *apparent* response to a very small event.

Thus far I have discussed mainly the elaborations of instinctual needs in the development of ego patterns of secondary autonomy and have used only implicitly the concept of elaboration of what we may call counterneeds. The proper Freudian term is countercathexis—that is, the "charging" of attitudes opposed to direct gratification. Thus, when the infant refrains from a given action, he does so out of "fear"—in the infantile period, out of quite primitive "fears" of loss of love and, as more focused biological needs develop, of punishment. Specific impulses may be repressed, at times so completely that all one sees of them is what Anna Freud has called a "gap in the ego." Such repression is difficult to maintain. A much easier means of control is to engage actively in behavior which opposes the dangerous impulse. This process will be discussed in Chapter 6 as "reaction formation." The point here is that patterns built up *against* instinctual drives tend toward secondary autonomous elaboration just as do those more directly drive-connected.

One may see the process quite clearly in an early stage of infancy. The child reaches toward a forbidden object, then himself says, "No-no," and withdraws, or perhaps does something else quite vigorously. One little boy surveyed an open case of small *objets d'art* on a visit to his aunt. He regarded them with his hands clasped behind him and finally remarked, "What a lot of no-no's!" If one observes in this story the tightly clasped hands and realizes the difficulty of verbalizing the explanatory "no-no," the mechanism of "countercathexis" becomes apparent. The hands are moved by an impulse *opposed to* reaching. This opposing impulse may come to seem the main response to the stimulus, the positive impulse being quite submerged. If one considers the greater pressure of the sexual and aggressive instincts, and the much more emphatic "no-no's" connected with them, it is not at all surprising that behavior instituted in much the same manner as clasping the hands tightly to restrain an impulse to handle should become a very powerful force.

When the child's impulse is not adequately integrated with his maturing ego apparatuses, a quite primitive type of reaction pattern may remain in force —the pattern of the *primary process,* described in Chapter 2. Primitive meanings remain cogent for some objects. Modes of handling conflicts characteristic for the child may remain operative in adult life, either rather generally, as in the case of the "armor-plating of character," or as defense mechanisms against more specific threats, along the lines emphasized by Anna Freud.

The same personality, however, may develop in other areas in a much more freely elaborative manner on many levels of integration. The child learns some school subjects better than others, sometimes because he likes the teacher, sometimes with the zest of moderate competition, sometimes because of special opportunities for "interesting" experience of a relatively conflict-free nature, sometimes by virtue of constitutional giftedness in one or another ego apparatus. Outside school, in a similarly variegated way, he develops special skills with things, with other people, with his own body. All these more or less specialized substructures of the ego then stand ready for the wider organizations it institutes and keeps instituting throughout life.

Thus far I have presented the autonomous functions of the ego, primary and secondary, as a series of disconnected patterns which were once important to the person for many reasons. In my presentation they seem to be floating around in a psychological vacuum, rather vaguely caught up in motivations. This impression is the fault of an effort to highlight the special contributions of ego psychology toward analysis of the complex problems with which a psychology of maturity must deal. The concrete observable behavior of the adult cannot be interpreted directly as an expression of instinctual drives. It must be seen in relation to part-systems of diverse origin which come to function as more or less tight units, as "substructures."

Hartmann writes: "Differentiation progresses not only through the mastery of new demands and tasks by creating new apparatuses, but mainly by the latter taking over, on a higher level, functions which were originally carried out at a lower level.[23] For example, the *word* "no-no" may take over the motor impulses toward and against touching the forbidden object, and even the word is later supplanted by more complex thought processes. At every stage of development, the new learning appears within the over-all functional pattern of the organism predominant at any given moment. Learning is *organized* by the prevailing drive systems, which operate according to the "economy" of the personality as a whole.

Like any scientific theory which proposes to analyze fluid part-systems in relation to fluid larger systems—and ultimately to a workable whole—Hartmann's theory requires generalizations. Hartmann writes:

Besides the equilibrium between individual and environment, our knowledge of the psychological apparatus permits us to discern two additional relatively well-defined states of equilibrium. . . . These are the equilibrium between drives (vital equilibrium) and the equilibrium between psychological institutions (structural equilibrium). . . . Actually yet a fourth equilibrium should be added: that between the synthetic function and the rest of the ego, since the ego is not merely a resultant and its synthetic function is, so to speak, a specific organ of equilibrium at the disposal of the person.[24]

In the passage quoted, the word "equilibrium" is used to suggest a play of forces of far more general operation than the "reduction of tension" within a particular system as a biological law. Relations with the environment are given systematic importance in their own right—somewhat beyond the Freudian position, which was always hazy about "reality," although reality was never disregarded and was one of the "three harsh masters" of the ego. Drives may come into conflict with one another. (In a later paper,[25] Hartmann, Kris, and Loewenstein use the model of the excretory apparatus: the child cannot fulfill the desire to expel and to retain at the same time—a drive conflict.) As the ego and superego develop relatively firm organizations of their own, some activities acceptable or even necessary to the ego (as an institution) become unacceptable to the superego. Thus, a new kind of conflict arises on these "institutionalized" or "structural" grounds. This problem is thoroughly familiar to all analysts and follows the outline of our previous discussion of the superego. An activity accepted by the ego may arouse severe tension in the superego, with consequent modification in ego behavior not unlike modifications observable in conflicts with the id.

Hartmann's "fourth equilibrium," the synthetic function of the ego—which is "so to speak, a specific organ at the disposal of the person"—deserves careful consideration. In these long analyses of part-systems as apparatuses and substructures (patterns) of primary and secondary autonomy in varying relations to drives and in complex relation to one another, one tends to lose sight of the person. In one sense, the organism-as-a-whole has been the premise of all the part-functions discussed, in their varying relationships. It is a *person* who wants and fears, who possesses and learns rather special techniques of being human. None of the foregoing pages on ego psychology or the earlier pages on instinct theory would make sense without this premise. It is an essential feature of the dynamic point of view introduced by Freud.

Yet comparatively little is said about the over-all synthesis mediated by the ego. To be blunt, there is very little talk about the "self" as an operating entity in any brand of "Freudian" literature. This statement may sound like a critical comment, but I think it may be considered essentially an item of reporting. Freud and Freudians, especially the ego psychologists, show how the "self" comes about. They deal with it in practice as any good therapist would. But they seem to have been so busy avoiding naive ideas of the "self" in favor of studying the major contours of its development and its major functions that they have neglected the tremendous power of the *synthesis* performed by the ego. We must still look mainly to the non-libido schools, especially to Horney, for careful discussion of the importance of attitudes toward the self.

Among the Freudians, Federn may be mentioned for his emphasis on the dynamic unity of the ego. Following the classical instinct theory in detail, he nevertheless pointed to the ego "as an experience," as one's sensation and knowledge of the lasting or recurrent continuity, in time, space, and causality, of one's bodily and mental life. This experience is thought to rest upon a special cathexis of certain interdependent bodily and mental functions, which are *felt* as familiar and more or less continuing.[26] The energy for this cathexis derives both from the libido and from the death instinct. The boundaries of the ego cathexis shift constantly in a small way and more dramatically if one considers the total life span of the person; yet for the healthy person they have a certain coherence. Under hypnosis it is possible to recover not only memory fragments but a fairly complete "ego state" from early years. For example, subjects who have been "regressed" to their fifth birthday may under hypnosis produce results on the Stanford Binet and the Rorschach tests hardly distinguishable from the performance of a five-year-old child, whereas in the waking state their guess as to what the child might answer is very crude.[27*]

Hartmann's formulation has been presented in some detail here because it offers a careful conceptualization in terms of the libido theory that is useful in integrating a number of widespread and divergent current developments. It is not only the rebels who have seen the need for elaboration in areas of personality function which Freud himself described as neglected. My impression is that an area still neglected is what Federn calls the ego cathexis, or,

* Federn seems to have been more interested in establishing the fact of this ego feeling and its application to the treatment of psychosis (in which the ego feeling is characteristically endamaged—see pp. 288*ff.*) than in studying the effect of specific attitudes toward the self in normal and neurotic people, as Horney has done. Nor has he been interested in the problem of how the sense of self develops during childhood (*cf.* Sullivan) as in any way different from the development of the component instincts in the classical Freudian tradition (to be presented in Chapter 5, on the genetic process). Federn was a close colleague of Freud from 1903. Coming to America in 1938, he exerted his influence more to uphold the classical doctrine than to encourage the further elaboration of his own valuable views on ego psychology.

more broadly, in Hartmann's scheme, the synthetic function of the ego, which must be considered as distinct from the ego as an institution. Hartmann's formulation provides a framework within which the valuable contributions of the rebel schools may be used—without giving up the values of the classical instinct theory. Probably it is only a matter of time until the "self" as a specific organ, so to speak, is given more attention by "Freudians."

Although no one can say with assurance, "This is Freud and Freudianism," there can be little doubt that the developments in ego psychology represent the mainstream of progress in Freudian psychoanalysis. They offer a ready framework for integration of the findings of the non-libido psychoanalytic schools; they supply an approach to those pressing problems which repeatedly led to the radically new theories when Freud seemed to be moving too slowly or to be actively repudiating the problems. Finally, they codify maneuvers every psychoanalyst has been making for years in his "common sense" efforts to understand the patient, to present his interpretations to the patient effectively, and to guide the process of "working through" (see pp. 322ff.).

In a book devoted to theoretical outlines, I cannot go into the details of new empirical studies oriented in the direction we are now discussing. Kardiner and Erikson are outstanding figures whose contribution to investigation of the terms of the milieu will be discussed in the next chapter. Two pieces of work by these authors not discussed later are more directly apposite to consideration of the role of the ego in the psychology of the individual: Kardiner's study of war neurosis and Erikson's treatment of the dream. The study of art by Kris, one of Hartmann's collaborators, is immediately relevant. Rapaport's investigation of the higher thought processes is collated and interpreted in terms of an ego psychology which carries the analysis of these processes far beyond the brief summary of general principles presented in this chapter.[28]*

SUMMARY

In Freud's theory of the terms of the organism, the emphasis is upon instincts (or, better, instinctual drives) which have their *source* in states of excitation within the body. Their *aim* is the reduction of such excitation, an aim which is usually attained through an external *object*. The *object* aspect

---

* This major "book" literature may be supplemented by a sampling of articles which will familiarize the reader with important names in the new area and the topics treated explicitly in their relations to ego psychology.[29]

of the instinct is usually determined by the experience of the individual. Instinctual drives are inborn only in the sense that we all have a common biological heritage. Specific reactions to the outside world are *not* predetermined in the old sense of instincts oriented toward particular external goals, however generalized.

Freud at first suggested two groupings: the sexual instincts and the ego instincts. Later he broadened his concept of the sexual instincts (Eros) to include much that he had originally considered a function of the ego instincts. To this expanded concept he then opposed a death instinct (Thanatos), essentially repetitive and regressive—back to the inanimate state from which life springs. Many Freudians have rejected the death instinct as a metaphysical speculation but accept the concept of an instinct of *aggression* as independent of the sexual drives.

Libido is the term applied to the energies proceeding from the sexual instinctual drives. The somatic source of the instinct of aggression is not clear. The sexual instincts are divided into several *components*: oral, anal, urethral, etc., which normally are finally organized under the primacy of the genital zone. The orifices of the body, equipped with mucous membranes and to a large extent involving the action of unstriped muscles, are called the erogenous zones and seem to supply the major sources of excitation. Reduction of tension (gratification, satisfaction) in these organ systems is experienced as *pleasure*. Until he introduced his concept of the death instinct, or aggression, Freud emphasized the concept of a *pleasure principle* governing the sexual instincts, in contrast to the *reality principle* developed by the ego instincts. The phenomena of masochism and sadism and the repetition compulsion were difficult to explain in terms of the pleasure principle, and Freud revised the concept in *Beyond the Pleasure Principle*. Although it is still considered important, the pleasure principle does not play the simple determining role at first ascribed to it.

Freud's instinct theory is cross-cut by four other *approaches* to the understanding of personality: (1) the *genetic* approach, which considers the actual experience of the child, mainly as regards the fate of the component instincts, aggression, and the development of genitality in his early years (this is discussed in Chap. 5); (2) the *topographical* approach, which considers the role of consciousness, distinguishing between the foreconscious (that which may easily become conscious but is not attended to at the moment) and the unconscious (that which is actively repressed, or instinctual drives which have never become conscious); (3) the *structural* approach, to be summarized below; (4) the *economic* approach, which considers the "quantitative" distribution of energies as tied up in the various suborganizations of the personality, usually in intimate relationship to the demands made by the current situation (this problem is discussed in Chaps. 6 and 7).

THE STRUCTURAL APPROACH

Freud's initial effort was directed toward the clarification of the concept of instinct and toward the delineation of the sexual instinct, which had not previously been observed with anything like the care Freud devoted to its components and their operation. He always stressed "other forces" in the personality that seemed to oppose direct expression of the sexual drives and that often gave rise to pathogenic *conflict*. At first he thought of these opposing forces as themselves mainly instinctual, apparently subserving the need for self-preservation (the ego instincts). But, as he came to observe them more carefully, he took a different tack (mainly in the 1920's). He came to feel that they operate not with the universality of primary instinctual drives but rather as constructs which result from experience. They are, one might say, *necessary* constructs for survival in human society, and hence of quite regular occurrence. Nevertheless, they are later differentiations of instinctual drives, organized with some independence of one another as the child develops, although they always interact.

The undifferentiated state of the neonate may be called ego-id—*i.e.*, it embodies all the reaction possibilities of the organism. Rather rapidly, however, lines of differentiation appear which are oriented toward the outside world and which attain a certain structuralization of their own. This area or sphere of differentiation Freud calls the *ego*. It is known as a province, a structure, an institution of the personality. The point is that although it comes to operate as an independent entity, as it were, it is a precipitate of experience, not a biological given.

After the ego develops as an "institution," the *id* may also be considered as a "separate structure" or "province": the biological substratum which continues essentially unmodified by experience with the outside world. Pressures in specific areas vary with internal changes in the organism (note especially changes at puberty and the climacteric) and with the possibilities for realistic gratification—although the latter is by no means a simple matter of physical discharge. In practice, those impulses are denominated *id* that are *relatively* close to the inherent biological drives, with no great purism as to the slight directedness they attain in early childhood. The Oedipal impulses in themselves, for example, are considered essentially *id*, although their form is always *somewhat* conditioned by experience.

A third "institution," the *superego,* usually becomes crystallized as a fairly distinct structure of the personality around the age of five. Roughly speaking, the superego is the conscience, which Freud considers to be the result of internalization of the child's image of the parents. (How and why this internalization takes place will be discussed in Chap. 5.) Its energies are derived quite directly from the id, although with a type of organization which often severely opposes direct gratification of id impulses, especially those which led to the formation of the Oedipus complex. Although the superego is not inborn—is, indeed, of relatively late development—it tends to function with something of the blind power of the instinctual drives.

Thus, the ego is the flexible structure which mediates among "three harsh masters": external reality, the id, and the superego.

EGO PSYCHOLOGY

Freud himself was profoundly interested in the structure and function of the ego and laid the groundwork for two parallel, interlocking developments which may be grouped under the heading "ego psychology." One of these lines of development concerns elaboration of the concept of the defense mechanisms of the ego. The leader is Anna Freud. The importance of investigating the specific methods adopted by the ego in its task of mediation is hardly a matter of controversy among Freudians. Anna Freud, however, has stressed the fact that much behavior that used to be considered a direct expression of id impulses (with distortion or disguise) must often be seen as determined primarily by a defense maneuver of the ego, and only remotely as an expression of the underlying id impulse. (This problem is discussed in Chaps. 6 and 7.)

The second line of development concerns further investigation of the autonomous, conflict-free functions of the ego, which Freud acknowledged but rather neglected: the sensorimotor apparatus, memory, language, etc. Hartmann has taken the lead along this line with such subtlety that I despair of summarizing his views more compactly than in the nine or ten pages proffered in this chapter. I merely remind the reader that Hartmann and his associates in no slightest sense repudiate either Freud's instinct theory or his elaboration of the defense mechanisms of the ego. Rather, they *add* the concept of the primary autonomy of the ego functions (apparatuses) as operating to organize important aspects of the personality. To some extent, such organization occurs independently of the major instinctual drama, although the subsystems so organized are constantly related to the total life experience of the person.

Furthermore, patterns of behavior developed in the manner mainly emphasized by Freud—that is, out of the conflict among instinctual drives—typically attain a *secondary* autonomy. This secondary autonomy is not freely dissolved with changing circumstances but dictates a measure of persistence of patterns as such. The patterns are then used in various ways as the ego continuously synthesizes its perception of inner and outer demands. The patterns, primary and secondary, may be organized at different levels of function—and here Hartmann *et al.* fall back upon the essential features of Freud's theory as described in the earlier parts of this chapter.

Enough has been said about the over-all synthesizing function of the ego to show that it has a sound *theoretical* place in Freudian theory. Freudians deal with the "self" in practice. In theory, they merely indicate how it is formed and suggest that it has an influence, indeed a profound influence. As an organized pattern, operating as a *pattern* rather than as the quite general "person," the "self" is hardly discussed.

Critical Comment

THE aspect of Freud's theory of instincts that seems to me most significant is its basis in biology. It rejects the whole concept of "instinct" as any kind of psychological adjustment to the external world prefigured in the human mind. This aspect I have presented already, perhaps to the point of undue emphasis.

I would like to postpone detailed discussion of the sexual instincts and the libido theory to later chapters, with only the general remark that Freud's position seems to me a brilliant ordering of observational materials which I feel must essentially be accepted. In fact, my main criticism of the dissident schools presented in Part III of this book is that they dismiss this important ordering of data in far too sweeping a fashion. Freud's position here rests very clearly on somatic sources and is easily verifiable. More-

over, Freud himself in theory extended the concept of libidinal energy to areas of the body other than the erotogenic zones, although he felt that most of our knowledge about the libido stems from study of these zones.[30]

My negative critique of Freudian instinct theory concerns the death instinct and the theory underlying the instinct of aggression. I see no usable bridge between the general fact that a great many vital organizations tend to remain the same or to disintegrate along complex lines determined by their initial structure and the observable tendency of the nursling to bite the breast once teeth have erupted or of the toddler to maltreat his kitten and deliberately spite his elders—or of the child and some neurotics to repeat patterns of behavior in a nonfunctional manner. Freud's general concern with the death of organisms seems to me no more significant (and no less significant) than the concern of many psychologists and philosophers with the *upward* trend of evolution. Of course the living organism dies; under unfavorable conditions it tends to contract, to lose tonus, to maintain itself at lower levels of function down to the point at which only the basic integrative functions built into the human body in the course of evolution remain active as the last manifestation of the organization we call life.

If one fancies the dualistic approach, it is certainly possible to contrast all processes that tend toward creative expansion with all those that tend toward maintenance, retraction, and dissolution, but I do not see that very much is gained unless these two types of process show some sort of special quality peculiar to the dichotomy. If Freud merely wanted to combat the "philosophical" view that life automatically gets better and better, regardless of planned effort, I would heartily agree with him. But instead of remaining at the point of scientific neutrality regarding these processes, he seems in effect to convert a quite obvious quality of any organizational unit (its frangibility as a unit) into a positive drive which actively contributes to the dissolution. He turns it into aggression. I have never really understood how. Freud's elaborate discussion of the death instinct merges into the *clinical observation* of destructive aggression in a manner which I have not clarified in exposition because it is not clear to me. I shall return to this problem later, mainly in the Epilogue. (See pp. 623-636.)

Freud's delineation of the processes involved in the instinct of aggression seems to me unclear and seems often to mix the nature of the instinct with its social effect in a manner quite foreign to the sophistication of his analysis of the sexual instincts. Acts that result in the destruction of property and harm to people or the self are somehow used as proof of the inner need to destroy, a view corrected only in rather special instances— as, for example, the ego mechanism of identification with the aggressor mentioned above. The skeletal musculature is somehow specially involved in turning the destructive instinct outward, and in this manner "aggression" becomes a major *constructive* force when properly fused with Eros. It gets pretty confusing.

The skeletal musculature and the whole complex of bodily stuctures which Hartmann calls the ego apparatuses certainly play a special role in the organization of the personality. But I see no reason to relate the spontaneous maturation of adaptive capacities which are the special evolutionary inheritance of the human species to the inevitable process of "death," or to "aggression" as an active destructive trend. Hartmann's insistence upon the primary autonomy of these apparatuses and their intrinsic possibilities for "pleasure" seems to me thoroughly valid. Furthermore, his view of their instrumental quality in relation to other drives leading to relatively well-defined systems of secondary autonomy and to a complex hierarchical interaction of systems is very close to the psychological framework I shall myself try to develop in successive comments and in the Epilogue. Hartmann and his collaborators dismiss the more philosophical, speculative aspects of the death instinct, but they consider the aggressive instinctual drive as inborn, like the libidinal drives. They have not essentially changed Freud's theory as regards this fundamental dichotomy.

In my own effort at theoretical construction, I would go a step further. It seems to me feasible to contend that any structure which has been built into the human body in the long course of evolution will tend to *act* according to its nature as a system. It is in the highest degree unlikely that the extraordinarily intricate apparatuses of the sense organs and sensorimotor coordination should have come into being as random bits which just happen to hit it off together. The process of natural selection must have been guided by function—not in the crude Lamarckian sense of the inheritance of acquired characteristics, but in the sense that random changes inappropriate to *systematic function* at a viable level could not survive.* The same argument applies to the vegetative systems of the body. Finally, once we take the step of looking at the organism as a viable organization of relatively independent substructures which evolved under the stringent conditions of natural selection, the biologically determined existence of coordinating mechanisms becomes a theoretical necessity.

The organism is pre-adapted at birth, to use Hartmann's phrase, to a level of human survival. I have not continued Hartmann's statement (quoted on p. 96) on this point to "adaptation to average expectation," because for us the average expectation of external circumstances includes social organization and average deference to it. Probably no sort of social adaptation is inherited as such. On this point Hartmann would surely agree. I break his statement in order to sharpen the contrast between the functional patterns established in the human species as a product of animal evolution and the *learned* patterns of its necessarily social existence, which are quite as cogent when we deal with "personality."

In Chapter 1, I presented the idea that science deals with different types of systems. Once established, any system tends to operate according to its own laws. I urge that any system be evaluated carefully as to its intrinsic tightness or looseness and its potential for different types of interaction with other systems.

Here I would like to consider how this "view of systems" relates to Freud's posi-

tion, to the position of the Freudian "ego psychologists," and to the non-libido schools, in so far as my grouping defines them as repudiating the special constellating power of the libido.

In the *view of systems*, any dynamic system will tend to complete itself on its own terms, in relation to simultaneously operating systems. From this point of view, one would *expect* that the "ego apparatuses" would be characterized by cogent systematization of their own and would function autonomously. In precisely the same manner, the vegetative systems tend to function autonomously. It seems to me useful to take as major scientific premise the simple fact that any anatomical structure arising functionally in the course of evolution will tend to behave as a functional unit. It seems to me *theoretically* as proper to describe the movement of the infant's eyes in pursuit of a moving object as a manifestation of a *need* to see as to so describe movements roughly adapted to the satisfaction of hunger or orality. One may call the need a drive to emphasize its active, compelling, quasi-goal-directed character. One may call it pleasure in the broad sense of function-pleasure (*Funktionslust*) suggested by Karl Bühler.[31] I would prefer to leave it at the more neutral level of system dynamics, with the proviso that the familiar instinctual needs and drives are in the last analysis instituted biologically in the same way as the "ego-apparatuses."

This very general analysis is useful only in a negative way in cutting through the artificial mystery which currently surrounds the concepts of instincts, needs, drives, pleasures, etc. If one now examines the various biological substructures whose independent function can be recognized easily, I think one is immediately struck by *difference in the nature of the systems involved.* One may thus understand why the term "instinct" has been applied to some systems and not to others. The visual and auditory apparatuses (systems) and

---

* I refer the reader to George G. Simpson, *The Meaning of Evolution*, Yale University Press, 1949, especially Part II.

many aspects of their intimate connections with the motorium are clearly related functionally to the outside world. That is "why" they developed as systems in the course of evolution. Apparently, the external stimulus is necessary to their functioning as systems. In the absence of such stimulus they simply fail to operate, *without the appearance of inner tension as a consequence of blocking.* (The distress of children born blind or deaf seems definitely to result from their sense of handicap in the world they learn about in other ways and from their lack of freedom to explore, not from tensions inherent in their disability.)

By contrast, the systems absolutely essential to the biological maintenance of the individual and the race would be expected to have a much *tighter* organization, and one much more thoroughly contained within the organism itself. Any aspect of a *tight* organization, correctly identified, offers very high predictability for future events within the system. No systems in the living organism, especially in the human organism, are tight enough to be predictable as the systems of physics are predictable, but the essential maintenance systems are certainly relatively stringent in their demands as systems, and they function mainly within the organism. To put the same idea in more biological-psychological terms, no organismic system is entirely self-contained, but some are more nearly self-contained than others, with relatively rigid or flexible systematic relations to other bodily systems and to the outside world.

From this point of view, one might suggest that the respiratory, cardiac, and digestive systems (and others less generally known) tend to operate with a high degree of autonomy, closely but rather crudely related to the systems oriented toward the outside world and, in more intricate fashion, to one another. The person in a state of terror precipitated by a perceived external danger pants or holds his breath, pales or flushes;

the normal digestive processes are typically suspended. Psychosomatic medicine has amply demonstrated that these systemic consequences may occur and become chronic when the danger is not consciously perceived as external by the adult personality but has become internalized and unconscious. These systems no longer *seem* adaptive because the *systemic* biological reaction is inappropriate. Panting and tachycardia do not help in writing an examination paper, interviewing a potential boss or client, giving a lecture. But if we happen to consider these situations "dangerous," even unconsciously, our basic biological systems react accordingly—to the point of hypertension and ulcers.

No one has considered these very tight, highly automatized systems of bodily function as *drives,* for the obvious reason that they are so internal as to escape any sort of directedness in the external world which is not mediated in a very complicated way. A "drive" is, I suggest, an inner state which the organism is equipped to do something about in a relatively coherent, quasi-goal-directed manner. The inner state of hunger or sexual excitation leads to activities in pursuit of an appropriate object which will reduce the tension. Although the object is not prefigured in the human organism, as it is in many animal species, certain types of activities do seem to be part of its native equipment, and object attachments are quickly formed. Reaction patterns to certain primitive dangers and frustrations also seem to be inborn. They rapidly become more complex and discriminating as the infant matures. (In the Epilogue, I shall relate this observation to the problem of aggression as an instinctual drive.)

Thus, *some* systems of the organism seem to be preadapted to this rather special relationship between the inner state and more or less energetic activity, potentially directed toward the environment. It is convenient to call such systems by a special name—to wit, "drives." They can be called *needs* if one wishes to emphasize the inner state, or one may characterize them by their *goals* if one wishes to emphasize the external complement required for their full operation. I suggest the phrase *drive system* as a useful means of keeping in sharp focus the idea that the drive is essentially one type of system, not a mysterious entity fundamentally different from the other systems of the body.

I suggest the term *interosystem* for those systems (cardiac, respiratory, aspects of the digestive system, etc.) which function essentially within the organism, which are controlled almost entirely by the autonomic nervous system and biochemical patterns, and which are connected with the outside world only in a highly *mediated* manner. The division is not entirely sharp, but it is clear enough to be useful. The need for air is a middling example which may clarify the significant aspects of the distinction. Air is, of course, an external necessity. But it is so plentiful that one can hardly call it a goal. Instinctual activities related to deprivation of air,* when this occurs, seem to be very poorly related to the external problem as such beyond the reflex of deeper breathing. Instead, in many cases, quite massive personality changes may be observed which are not adaptive in the sense that even the most fantastic perversions of the sexual instincts are adaptive. Anoxia, unless it is the result of physical strangulation, is not a problem to which the human organism is at all pre-adapted. It precipitates a very different constellation of psychic events from the patterns resulting from frustration of the drive systems. Mountaineers adapt to a relatively rarefied atmosphere.

* With high-altitude flying presenting an acute practical problem, the reaction of the flyer to conditions of anoxia has been rather carefully studied. See H. Hertzman, J. Orlansky, and C. P. Seitz, "Personality Organization and Anoxia Tolerance," *Psychosomatic Medicine*, 1944, 6:317-331.

It is most unlikely that mountain people show any specific kind of "psychological" drives and goals which may be ascribed to the altitude at which they live. Common features seem much more a consequence of their relative isolation from the complex forms of human society than of a mildly frustrated drive for air.

My argument here is *ad absurdum*. I think it undercuts the idea of biological necessity as a sort of abstract principle underlying "drives." Nothing is more biological than the need for air, but this need is not *systematized* in relation to the environment in such a manner as to become a drive or a goal in the psychological sense. Although breathing requires air, there are no complex air-seeking patterns of behavior. Although the respiratory system is quite easily activated by external stimuli, the activation tends toward a physiological system-wholeness which is often embarrassing and at times seriously pathogenic (for example, the breathlessness or heavy breathing of the emotionally disturbed "normal" person, and psychogenic asthma).

I suggest the term *exterosystems* for the inborn equipment of the body which Freud called the ego functions, Hartmann the ego apparatuses—sensorimotor patterns, phonation (*perhaps* motility, memory, imagination, and the like). The merit of this term is that it brings these functions clearly into the framework of biological systems in the same way as the interosystems and the drive systems. The ego functions differ from the interosystems and drive systems in that they are much more closely related to the external stimulus and much less tightly organized in their operation. They very readily become instrumental for the drive systems—indeed, their evolutionary development must have been functionally related to the major maintenance and reproductive needs of the organism. Nevertheless, they do operate as systems in their own right. Probably the very obviousness of this fact is responsible for its neglect during the period when the importance of "drives" was being recognized.

At the present time, psychological science is in the peculiar position of possessing an enormous amount of information about the exterosystems, collected by "academic psychologists" who had very little conception of the significance of the drive systems, and an enormous amount of information about the drives, collected by psychoanalysts. It is not easy to put these two bodies of information together from the available literature, because an extremely important item is missing from both sets of studies: *how these systems function together in the individual*. It is this functional connection which should, I think, at present constitute the main theoretical focus for both disciplines, although in large-scale research it is usually necessary to isolate one or another system for investigation. The trouble with the great bulk of research in these two areas is that too often no appropriate *setting* for such isolation is reported. In many of the older "academic" studies, the reader is given little or no clue as to the probable *drive* setting; I shall at times point out that even a detailed psychoanalytic study of an individual case typically neglects to report the conditions which are especially relevant to the development of the exterosystems.

I am sorry to introduce new terms into a science already overloaded with terms, and I shall not burden the reader with elaborated refinements of still another systematic theory. In later pages of critical comment I shall sometimes talk of *drive systems* instead of drives, instincts, needs, goals, dynamisms, or whatever. And I shall sometimes use the term *exterosystems* for Freud's ego functions, Hartmann's ego apparatuses, and (after Part III) Sullivan's concept of abilities and capacities. My terms are close enough to ordinary psychological parlance to present no great difficulty as terms. They are, I hope, just odd enough to remind the reader constantly of the *view of systems* which I consider the valuable orienting approach of this book as an attempt at integration. I shall use them only when a reminder seems necessary.

It must be understood that this classification of systems refers not to gross morphological structures, but to *functional systems* which are implemented by neural pathways and by the complex chemistry of the body. The same organ and other mechanisms belong now to one functional system, now to another, depending on the equilibrium of the organism as a whole. Comparatively little is known about the integrative action of the chemical products of the body in their precise relations to the nervous system. It would be foolhardy to attempt refinements of psychological classification on the basis of physiological observations at present, although it seems likely that inborn neurochemical systems play a larger role in the development of specific character trends and disease symptoms than we now recognize. My classification rests upon aim rather than source, to use the Freudian vocabulary, but with the feeling that there is good empirical justification for considering these major differences as in large part source-determined.

As a rule, the exterosystems do not spontaneously build up tensions without external stimulation, whereas the interosystems and the drive systems do. The intero- or maintenance systems are doubtless essentially continuous with the drive systems in that they have internal rhythms, phases of tension and quiescence in their own right. But I think we may profitably differentiate between the kinds of system which function with extreme inner autonomy and the kinds (the "drives") that have rather close connections—neural more than chemical, perhaps—with the exterosystems.

In writing these pages I have avoided using the word *activity,* because I wanted to reserve this term for special consideration. Obviously, neither the extero- nor the drive systems can function without coordinated bodily action. Indeed, the motorium is an intrinsic part of every organismic event. The question of importance here is whether neuromuscular activity is merely an aspect of other systems, the docile instrument through which they operate, or whether it is also (partly) a drive system in its own right.

Observation suggests that the latter alternative is correct. My comments are here derived mainly from Mittelmann.[32] The infant looks and listens, tastes and smells, only in response to external stimuli, but he appears to move spontaneously in response to inner tensions. Moreover, these movements do not seem to be simple discharge phenomena. The baby strives to lift his head, to turn over, to sit, to crawl, to walk, to climb and jump. Although his movements tend to become livelier and more focused when appropriate external or internal stimuli are present, they are very impressive in themselves at all times. The infant struggles to accomplish these new patterns in a manner which at times looks almost painful, cries when he is "helped" inappropriately to achieve what seems to be his aim, or demands help in walking and other activities—and on the whole seems to *enjoy* his "motility" in much the same way that he enjoys oral, anal, and genital pleasures. In order to avoid the complex implications of the Freudian concept of instinctual drives, Mittelmann uses the term "urge" for this inner dynamic quality of the motorium, but he is willing to accept the more neutral term suggested here: the drive system.

Among the drive systems of the organism, motility, hunger, and primitive defense against "danger" (startle reactions, etc.) may be considered as importantly different from the systems Freud has taught us to consider "sexual." The

pleasure aspect of the sexual systems seems to be derived primarily from mucous membranes and perhaps deep diffuse kinesthetic sensation. The *course* of the "sexual instincts" seems to be determined *mainly* by systems of the unstriped musculature and their chemical adjutants. I have suggested that *all* these systems be differentiated from the interosystems of the body on the basis of their relatively direct connections with the outside world. But one may also profitably distinguish between systems focused about hunger, motility patterns, etc. and the "sexual" systems, although they are all drive systems. The former are much more closely related to the outside world than the latter, probably with many built-in connections with the exterosystems—as, for example, the sucking reflex, eye-hand coordination, and the like.

I shall call these systems *nonsexual drive systems,* simply by contrast to the grouping of sexual systems so carefully worked out by Freud. It is impossible to delineate them with comparable clarity at the present time. Probably they do not have the sort of unity Freud ascribes to the sexual libido, although I suspect that there are closer dynamic relations among broad aspects of motility patterns, native sensorimotor patterns, and the like, than is currently recognized. Certainly these systems have a very direct influence on the relationship of the child to his parents and his social world generally. They contribute largely to the development of the sense of self and are related to the problem of aggression.

In my comment on Chapter 5, presenting Freud's view of the genetic process, I shall discuss further the probable significance of some of the nonsexual drive systems in personality formation. I have postponed discussion of *my* view of the problem of aggression to the Epilogue because it represents a rather complex restatement in terms of the view of systems which would take us too far afield right now.

[1] S. Freud, *New Introductory Lectures on Psycho-Analysis*, W. W. Norton & Co., 1933, p. 131.

[2] *Ibid.*, pp. 132f.

[3] S. Freud, *An Outline of Psychoanalysis*, W. W. Norton & Co., 1949, p. 24.

[4] ———, *A General Introduction to Psycho-Analysis*, Liveright Publishing Corp., 1935, p. 306.

[5] ———, *An Outline of Psychoanalysis*, p. 21.

[6] *Ibid.*, p. 22.

[7] *Ibid.*, p. 20.

[8] *Ibid.*, p. 22.

[9] *Ibid.*, p. 23.

[10] S. Freud, "Analysis Terminable and Interminable," *Collected Papers*, London: Hogarth Press, 1950, V, p. 328.

[11] A. Freud, *The Ego and the Mechanisms of Defence*, Hogarth Press, 1937, Chap. 1.

[12] S. Freud, *New Introductory Lectures on Psycho-Analysis*, p. 112.

[13] *Ibid.*, p. 92.

[14] S. Freud, *Collected Papers*, Hogarth Press, 1924, I, pp. 59-75.

[15] ———, *The Problem of Anxiety*, W. W. Norton & Co., 1936, p. 144.

[16] A. Freud, *op. cit.*, Chap. 1.

[17] "Analysis Terminable and Interminable."

[18] A. Freud, *op. cit.*, Chap. 9.

[19] *Ibid.*, p. 124.

[20] K. Horney, *Neurosis and Human Growth*, W. W. Norton & Co., 1950, Chap. 15; *New Ways in Psychoanalysis*, W. W. Norton & Co., 1939, Chap. 2.

[21] S. Freud, *Collected Papers*, Vol. IV.

[22] H. Hartmann, "Ego Psychology and the Problem of Adaptation," in D. Rapaport, *Organization and Pathology of Thought*, Columbia University Press, 1951, p. 383.

[23] *Ibid.*, p. 384.

[24] *Ibid.*, p. 380.

[25] H. Hartmann, E. Kris, and R. Loewenstein, "Comments on the Formation of Psychic Structure," *The Psychoanalytic Study of the Child*, Vol. II, International Universities Press, 1946.

[26] See Edoardo Weiss's introduction to P. Federn, *Ego Psychology and the Psychoses*, Basic Books, 1952, p. 8.

[27] H. Spiegel, J. Shor, and S. Fishman, "An Hypnotic Ablation Technique for the Study of Personality Development," *Psychosomatic Medicine*, 1945, 7:273-278.

[28] A. Kardiner and H. Spiegel, *War Stress and Neurotic Illness*, Paul B. Hoeber, 1947; E. H. Erikson, "The Dream Specimen of Psychoanalysis," *Journal of the American Psychoanalytic Association*, 1954, 2:5-56; E. Kris, *Psychoanalytic Explorations in Art*, International Universities Press, 1951; D. Rapaport, *Organization and Pathology of Thought*, Columbia University Press, 1951.

[29] P. Bergman and S. K. Escalona, "Unusual Sensitivities in Very Young Children," *The Psychoanalytic Study of the Child*, Vols. III/IV, 1949, pp. 333-352; E. Bibring, "On Depression," in P. Greenacre (ed.), *Affective Disorders*, International Universities Press, 1953; M. Brenman, "On Teasing and Being Teased: And the Problem of 'Moral Masochism,'" *The Psychoanalytic Study of the Child*, Vol. VII, 1952, pp. 264-285; M. Brenman and M. M. Gill, *Hypnotherapy*, International Universities Press, 1947 (see especially pp. 107 and 130ff.); G. S. Klein, "Adaptive Properties of Sensory Functioning," *Bulletin of the Menninger Clinic*, 1949, 13: 16-23, and "The Personal World Through Perception," in R. R. Blake and G. V. Ramsey (eds.), *Perception*, Ronald Press, 1951, pp. 328-355; R. P. Knight, "Borderline States," *Bulletin of the Menninger Clinic*, 1953, 17: 1-12, and "Management and Psychotherapy of the Borderline Schizophrenic Patient," *loc. cit.*, pp. 139-150; R. Schafer, "A Study of Thought-Processes in a Word Association Test," *Character and Personality*, 1945, 13: 212-227, and "Content Analysis in the Rorschach Test," *Journal of Projective Techniques*, 1953, 17:335-339; L. Stone, "The Widening Scope of Psychoanalysis," *Journal of the American Psychoanalytic Association*, 1954, 2:567-594.

[30] S. Freud, *An Outline of Psychoanalysis*, p. 24.

[31] *Die geistige Entwicklung des Kindes*, 6 Aufl., Jena, 1930.

[32] B. Mittelmann, "Motility in Infants, Children and Adults: Patterning and Psychodynamics," *The Psychoanalytic Study of the Child*, Vol. IX, 1954.

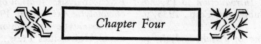

Chapter Four

THE TERMS OF THE
MILIEU

HUMAN BEINGS live in a society. In fact, one of the most distinctive things about us is that we build societies of many kinds and take their dictates with the utmost seriousness. When an adolescent girl says that she would rather die than wear last year's frock to the prom, she is almost literally telling the truth. Certainly her brother in the army submits to fantastic hardships, including killing and being killed, with only minor protest. The triviality and the magnificence of human devotion to *social* goals represent the folly and grandeur of our species.

Two general orientations toward an explanation of this aspect of human life have been offered. One is environmentalist: the structure of society explains how people act. The other is psychological: beneath all social differences, human nature is always the same. As I explained in Chapter 1, I chose the outlandish caption *the terms of the milieu* for a discussion of social phenomena in order to emphasize a third possibility: a relatively unformed organism, the human infant, is born into a complex milieu, his society. What he becomes is an inextricable compound of heredity and environment.

Chapter 3, on the terms of the organism, emphasized the nature of man's biological equipment: his animal needs, his ignorance of how to fulfill them, his capacity to learn, his tendency to develop quite early rather characteristic modes of adaptation which tend to persist as his "personality." But one cannot discuss such topics without constantly dealing with the *environment within which they unfold*. Modes of adaptation are *constructs* which result from the creative adaptation of the organism to the conditions it encounters—for the human infant, mainly social conditions. The present chapter, therefore, discusses the environment, the terms of the milieu.

If one accepts this third possibility (I think that most contemporary scientists do accept it), then certain specific problems may be formulated. In the varieties of external environment, what physiological or psychological needs and impulses are allowed to manifest themselves, are repressed, are evoked, or are further patterned and elaborated? How, and to what extent, do the specific conditions surrounding the infant and young child determine persistent personality trends in the individual, as against the overwhelming directiveness of biological needs? How and to what extent does personality matter at all in the complex economic and political problems of human society?

The persisting problems are not solved, but the questions are posed in such a way that one may work toward useful answers, each discipline contributing toward a common solution.

Freud is generally considered as presenting a radically psychological orientation. It is true that he profoundly distrusted environmentalist theories that attempt to explain "everything" by social and economic causes. He neglected almost entirely in his own writings the possibility of studying systematically the influence of special conditions, historically established, upon the development of personality. His attention was directed, rather, to the origin and operation of deep-lying trends, which he thought of as universal because they are rooted in the biological equipment of mankind. Although their manifestation varies with social conditions, the study of such variation can be considered only as *applied* science. True science, for Freud, involved the investigation of universal principles, and these, he felt, could be found only in the natural sciences and in a biologically oriented psychology.*

My impression is that the majority of Freudians follow Freud's general orientation in this area, the more easily because as doctors treating the individual they are not directly concerned, as a rule, with the broad problems of

---

* "For sociology, which deals with the behaviour of man in society, can be nothing other than applied psychology. Strictly speaking, indeed, there are only two sciences—psychology, pure and applied, and natural science." (S. Freud, *New Introductory Lectures on Psycho-Analysis*, W. W. Norton & Co., 1933, p. 245.)

sociology. As "applied science," or may I say simply as a matter of informed common sense, contemporary Freudians seem to deal imaginatively with cultural factors influencing the behavior of their patients. So did Freud himself. Freud observed that his patients, most of them upper middle class, were subject to pressures which the peasants largely escaped—pressures in the sexual area. The contemporary Freudian analyst, however classical, observes sensitively the great variety of special pressures which affect his patients in a society more complex than that of Freud's Vienna. Variations among analysts in this respect tend to follow variations in their own temperament and experience rather than school affiliation. One need only read a few numbers of the psychoanalytic journals, reporting experience with patients or special groups, to realize that the "Freudian" currently attacked by the "Marxist" is a mythological figure. (So is the "Marxist," in my observation.)

A number of psychoanalysts have carried Freud's *theoretical* concern with social phenomena further, in elaboration or correction of his views. All the analysts discussed in the later sections of this book take issue with Freud on the role of cultural factors in the formation and operation of the personality. Their views will be presented in Parts III and IV. In this chapter I shall discuss the views of Freud himself and of analysts who have written extensively about social theory in what I have here called the "Freudian" vein— that is, with acceptance of the very great significance of infantile sexuality. I have included here a brief mention of cultural anthropologists who have been influenced by psychoanalysis, because the influence seems to derive directly from Freud. Except for Fromm, the analysts who espouse an explicitly "cultural" point of view have not been much interested in specifically social research and have not stimulated such research in other disciplines in as focused a manner as Freud.

In my critical comment I shall take issue with Freud's *restriction* of science to "universals" and suggest some limitations in regard to concepts he considered "universal." Nevertheless, writing this chapter brought me to a greater humility toward Freud's views on group psychology than I began with and than is common for culturally minded psychologists. If I dwell longer than seems quite necessary on such "outmoded" ideas as the hypothesis of the primal horde and the universality of the Oedipus complex, with its implications for superego development, for attitudes toward the leader and one's fellows, my reasons go beyond mere conscientious reporting. I have come to feel that these ideas have about them a flavor of genius which in our time we may criticize but not dismiss.

The outline for this chapter has taken an odd form, stylistically awkward. But it seems to impose itself the more cogently, the more I think about the problem of presenting Freud and Freudians in proper perspective. The difficulty is that Freud has had *two* major impacts on contemporary thinking about the terms of the milieu, leading to developments which tend toward divergence. Both must be reported in their own right before we can attempt any sort of integration.

I shall call one contribution *indirect*. I shall report it first and rather briefly, because, although it stems from psychoanalysis, its techniques and the dynamic systems it uncovers go beyond Freud's own work—at times, indeed, beyond what he would approve, or at least what current Freudian psychoanalytic societies think he would approve. The second contribution I shall call *direct*. Here I shall report first Freud's own position and then the position of Freudians who have tried to elaborate his position within the framework of what I have loosely called the libido theory.

THE INDIRECT CONTRIBUTION

DESPITE HIS OBJECTION to environmental explanations, Freud was, paradoxically, the first major psychologist to give the "culturalists" a valid tool to work with.* We have seen that Freud's instinct theory posits quite vague biologically determined aims *which take their concrete form from the actual experience of the individual*. Next to an absolute *tabula rasa* concept of the human organism, which few observers have found tenable, this formulation *allows* for the widest amount of change in human behavior as a consequence of change in social institutions. It is far more flexible than any list of specific instincts or such broad trends as the hedonistic or utilitarian or "naturalistic" philosophies have posed. In so far as these trends become concrete enough for actual use, they are inevitably both narrow and sophistical in explaining "everything" by the pursuit of pleasure or usefulness, or by the struggle for existence. In practice, they reflect the intuitive psychological insight of the social observer or his prejudices—as when the gross abuses of the Industrial Revolution were justified as the necessary consequence of "natural law."[1]

* Kardiner discusses this point thoughtfully in his introduction to *The Psychological Frontiers of Society*. (A. Kardiner, *The Psychological Frontiers of Society*, Columbia University Press, 1945, pp. xiiiff.)

THE IMPORTANCE OF CHILDHOOD

The vagueness of Freud's basic concept became useful in practice because it led to feasible inquiry into *how* the biological inclinations of the organism are bent into the traits with which the social sciences must ultimately deal: egoism and altruism; self-seeking and gregariousness; competition and co-operation; conscience, morals, ideals; initiative and the need to be commanded; and so on in almost infinite series. The idea that as the twig is bent so the branch inclines is almost as old as human thought, but it played almost no role in the empirical social sciences.

Until the 1920's it would not have occurred to the anthropologist conscientiously recording "a culture" to note down the minutiae of child care up to the puberty rites which obviously inducted the child into his society. The babies and children were dismissed with general comment or colorful anecdote. Indeed, most early observers had the impression that the babies were given *no* training, an impression used sentimentally in praise of the noble savage or interpreted with decorous horror. Careful reporting of the handling of infants and their behavior is now routine; and in some quarters, it is probably over-stressed as the major determinant of social attitudes. We shall discuss the problem in greater detail shortly. The point here is the importance of the *formation* of attitudes in childhood *vs.* the concept of later *imposition* by social forms.

Freud's approach contributed very largely toward this new dimension in social studies. Attitudes are not completely set at birth by our human heritage, or by our race, class, or whatever. Neither are they so malleable in adult life that one may expect to change behavior simply by offering new economic and social conditions abruptly or with a "reasonable" learning period. Peoples as well as individuals adapt and fail to adapt to new conditions in a manner which appears completely whimsical until one begins to understand that the new conditions are *interpreted* in terms of expectations deeply established in the personality. Freud's demonstration of the profound significance of the very early period of life in the development of basic expectations fitted in excellently with the trend toward "functionalism" in the social sciences and with the effort to envisage cultures as innerly coherent, relatively idiosyncratic patterns rather than as stopping points on the highway from savagery to civilization, or as illustrations of the march of economic determinism or race characteristics.

Whether or not Freud's specific views of psychosexual development are adopted, the contemporary ethnologist extends his inquiry to infancy in order to understand more clearly the peculiar tenacity of some attitudes (along with readiness for change) in any cultural group. For example, Benedict points out that the odd mixture of loyalty, honor, face-saving, and downright treachery in the Japanese is not purely a matter of a different set of folkways, still less the superficial consequence of an era of militaristic government. The underlying trends which approximate these traits proceed from the reactions of the infant to the prevalent mode of child care—in conjunction with the deeply characteristic circumstances and value structures of later childhood and adult life.[2]

Although Freud's work on early childhood has been of enormous importance in the development of modern social science, Freud himself contributed very little to this type of social application. On the contrary, he mistrusted it. Many Freudians, notably Roheim,[3] speak out forthrightly against the "culturalist" approach, and more vehemently as Freudian concepts are explicitly borrowed. There is an important reason for this distrust when the "culturalist" assumes that the variations in environmental conditions directly "cause" the variations in later behavior, or in some other way neglects the *course* of instinctual growth which Freud believed fundamental. (The point is discussed further on pp. 138*ff.*) The anthropology of Freud's day did not encourage the kind of integration of external and internal, social and personal factors presented in this chapter, and on this point Freud did not outstrip his times.

In his observation of the universal character of man's inner development, Freud saw no alternative to almost total rejection of theories that pretended to explain behavior by a scientific investigation of the social conditions under which it occurred. The rejective attitude is continued by classical Freudians, even though important modifications have been made in the "cultural" approach, such that Freudian concepts of instinctual development are considered intrinsic to insight into adaptation to culturally determined modes.

THE IMPORTANCE OF THE UNCONSCIOUS

A second fundamental contribution of Freud may be mentioned as having had an influence on the development of the social sciences far beyond his own application of the concept to group psychology: the importance of unconscious, irrational factors in group behavior. In a way, of course, this idea is as old as the observation of society and utterly commonplace. For example, an overworked argument against Prohibition was that if you deny people something, they will want it all the more. Presumably the argument was not naive enough to aver that our sober citizenry consciously decided on unlawful inebriation as the most rational expedient toward repeal of the Volstead Act. Rather, it called upon the familiar generalization that people want what they cannot have, in quite irrational relation to the value of the proscribed object, and very often even without the rationalization that they are defending their personal independence against tyranny.

Freud's work took this kind of casual psychologizing out of the proverb class and put it into the strata of respectable scientific thinking. Whether or not it owns direct allegiance to Freud, almost every publication, radio commentary, or dinner-table discussion in recent years makes extensive use of the irrational unconscious in its diagnosis of social ills. Clearly, Freud cannot be credited or blamed for the vast majority of these statements, except as his ideas brought into focus what had previously been diffuse.

Freud's contribution on this point, too, has been mainly *indirect,* as other thinkers have taken over aspects of his theory or have loosely incorporated ideas about unconscious motivations which have become public domain. Freud is the major, though obviously not the only, source of the widely current inclusion of the irrational *as a factor to be understood* in any social investigation. Again, as in the elaboration of the social consequences of cultural variations in the handling of infants, the modern trend has gone far beyond what Freud suggested or even might approve. His own concept of the role of the unconscious in group behavior was much more precise. He tended to repudiate with vigor, and perhaps with insufficient discrimination, developments that used his basic concepts loosely. Freud's precision in this area has seemed unduly limited, even to Freudians, but it has great merits. The bulk of this chapter will present Freud's own ideas on group psychology—with intercurrent critique and elaboration.

THE PSYCHOSOCIAL APPROACH: KARDINER

Before entering upon the account of Freud's group psychology, however, let us examine in some detail the ideas of Abram Kardiner, who has fully accepted the two aspects of the Freudian contribution here presented as basic —the significance of infantile experience and of the irrational unconscious— but who has *not* followed out the implications of the libido theory as a necessary sequence to be considered as providing the focal aspects of behavior. For him the psychosexual development of the child as described by Freud in "biological" terms is profoundly illuminating—but not determining in the more or less linear causative fashion too often suggested in the strictly Freudian approach or in some of the "culturalist" approaches which borrow from Freud.

Kardiner constantly uses the irrational unconscious (he calls it emotionally polarized thinking) to show how infantile experience is related to the institutions of a given society. He has proposed a methodology which he hopes will serve to integrate social studies with deep-level studies of the individual. Furthermore, he has implemented his approach by a long series of studies of special cultures which, to an increasing degree, he is able to select as especially relevant to particular problems. Kardiner remains an armchair anthropologist, but in firsthand contact with ethnologists and some informants he has developed a direct feeling for cultural differences rare enough among psychoanalysts. Finally, he has attempted to systematize his approach to the social sciences, explicitly using psychoanalysis as one tool among others.

Kardiner points out[4] that social scientists have quite generally recognized that they needed a "psychology" to supplement their interpretations of the consequence of social institutions in human affairs. The scientific psychology of the university and the laboratory—Wundt, behaviorism, Gestalt psychology —is not very old and has not been very helpful. Its methodology has aimed at accuracy but is applicable only to relatively minor aspects of the human psyche (mainly motor reactions and perception). Psychoanalysis, on the other hand, aimed from the outset at the understanding of *action systems,* which were conceived as constellated around emerging goals of profound moment to the person. Psychoanalysis was aware of the multitudinous *substitutive* efforts made by the person to attain his goals, many of which are unconscious. It could, Kardiner believes, be used to trace the fundamental psychological dynamics operating in alien and changing cultures and, hence, could throw more light on our own culture.

Action systems arise in various ways in all cultures. Some, which Kardiner calls the *projective* systems, are derived from the most profound inner experience of the maturing organism, although they become generalized, systematized, and rationalized in the course of life. Projective systems involve the deepest expectations of the individual, his fears and longings, his mode of finding security (unconscious), his conscience and ideals. These systems are learned, in the sense that they result from the actual experience of the person, and they are not to be thought of as special instincts existing in the same quality and degree throughout the world. However, since all men have the same basic problems to solve in establishing the relationship between their biological needs and the requirements of the outside reality of people and things, the solutions adopted can be examined within a rather definite framework of expectation.

The immature nervous system of the infant requires protection against flooding by stimuli which it cannot master and needs gratification of its biologically structured pleasure strivings. When protection and gratification are insufficient, anxiety and substitutive efforts toward gratification *must* result. The notion the child forms of the world at this period and the methods he devises for coping with the world (in relation to himself) tend to persist throughout life, basically influencing his interpretation of later events and to a considerable degree determining his characterological orientation.

This position is supported by all the psychoanalytic schools and is elaborated in many places throughout the present book. (See especially Chap. 5, on the genetic process.) An important feature of Kardiner's early work[5] is his observation that where children are quite regularly cared for in a specified manner by a given culture, all or most of them are likely to develop a similar "basic personality." At the deep level sketchily indicated here, their attitudes toward the world and themselves are similarly constituted and have far-reaching consequences through the projective systems of the society. For example, where the child is regularly asked to renounce its pleasure strivings early in obedience to a higher power (the parent), a sense of sin, with belief in the possibility of atonement and redemption by a savior, is readily understandable. This pattern of child rearing is by no means unique to our society, but it is not universal.

With more permissiveness toward infantile pleasure strivings and a more diffuse method of inducting the child into social restrictions, the ideas of evangelical Christianity become thoroughly incomprehensible to the adult—as many missionaries have discovered. The white man's magic is often adopted on quite other grounds—occasionally closer to what most of us prefer to consider true Christianity—but typically with distortions peculiar to the tribe which is converted or acculturated. Understanding of the "basic personality" of the culture, and of the projective systems rooted in it, may be of profound importance in evaluating the strengths and weaknesses and special directives of the culture as they come into sharp focus in a rapidly changing world society.

Society is, of course, made up of individuals each of whom develops a unique personality structure through his unique experience. By its institutions, however, society provides not only the practical mechanics of living together, but sufficient community of significant emotional experience to ensure that the basic attitudes of the members of a given culture are similar enough for a common psychological orientation. In his first book on this subject, *The Individual and His Society*, Kardiner drew a distinction between primary institutions, organized around the basic needs of man (family organization, in-group formation, basic disciplines, care and training of children, sexual taboos, subsistence techniques, etc.), and secondary institutions, such as taboo systems, religion, rituals, folktales, and techniques of thinking.[6] The secondary institutions Kardiner thought of as derived from the primary and as more subject to change—except for the subsistence techniques, which he recognized as basic but readily influenced by changed external conditions.

In his second book, *The Psychological Frontiers of Society*, Kardiner noted some confusions resulting in practice from this distinction and analyzed the difficulty. The concept of primary institutions had been envisaged more from the point of view of the *culture* than from the point of view of the individual growing within his culture. For psychological purposes, it seemed preferable to substitute the *system* for the institution as an operational concept. The system may operate through different institutions.

Kardiner offers a long but admittedly incomplete list of key *situations* which have been found to influence personality formation profoundly, ranging from aspects of maternal care to differentiation of function in the techniques of production. He then suggests a grouping of systems which cross-cuts institutions and significantly extends the customary psychoanalytic groupings— *i.e.*, it includes aspects of growth beyond those determined by libidinal development. The first category is that of the projective systems described above. The hierarchy continues with *learned* systems taught as such by the culture, taboo systems (which may be taught and persist as "reality" apparently with no precise relationship to basic personality), pure empirical reality systems subject to demonstration, and, finally, value systems and ideologies (which cut across all the previous systems).[7]

These various classifications have been presented too compactly to have much meaning for the reader who encounters Kardiner's thinking here for the first time. They are included to suggest the manner in which he attempts to integrate psychoanalytic insights (mainly the projective systems) with other factors clearly operating psychologically on the individual in any society. Kardiner avoids the error of suggesting that every item of social behavior can be interpreted immediately and sufficiently as a projection of deep unconscious drives, whether these are conceived as universal or as contingent upon the handling of infancy. External influences, such as geographical placement, climate, and available food supply, and historical events undoubtedly play a major role in the development of *institutions*. Once the institution is established, interlocking prescriptions for behavior and attitudes are explicitly taught (learned systems) and are not easily changed. In our culture especially, the rational-empirical system has been so elaborated in the guise of science as to exert a profound influence both indirectly through changes in our way of life and directly on our values and ideologies.

In this hierarchy of action systems and institutions, the projective systems play what Kardiner calls a *polarizing* role rather than a determining one. The same institution is differently interpreted and used by different cultures according to the attributes of the "basic personality." External changes may be skillfully integrated with existing institutions where they are syntonic with the basic personality, may be rejected altogether when they are not, or may prove disastrous. For example, the Comanche in the late seventeenth century adapted themselves with remarkable success to a shift from the Montana plateau to a different mode of life on the plains of Texas. They readily assimilated the horse and the gun, resourcefully exploited all the conflicting groups of whites and Indians around them, and constructed a highly effective though simple culture. Many aspects of the white culture to which they were exposed they ignored. They went to pieces promptly when confined to the reservation—that is, when the enforced way of life no longer provided the special opportunities and curbs suited to their particular culture.[8]

Techniques of child care are, for Kardiner, of very great importance, probably of primary importance, in determining basic personality and the projective systems. *They do not determine the whole life cycle.* The infant in Alor[9] is adequately fed by primitive standards, but the social organization puts the heavy burden of work in the hands of the women and requires that the mother absent herself from the child except for a brief period in the morning and evening. The father takes little responsibility for the child or the home, expending his energies in complex financial transactions which seem a grotesque travesty of the worst aspects of our own "business" pattern—an intricate exchange which benefits no one. Older siblings are responsible for minimal care of the infant and consider their charges a burden, which they typically neglect. In these circumstances, the infant can rarely develop strong attachment to any specific person as an "ideal image" or even learn how to focus its protest effectively. In the crucial period during which the outlines of its view of the world and people are being formed, the child is denied the maternal figure, which in most cultures not only gives food but creates the sense of personal warmth and recourse to a higher being. The aggression of the child, stored up as its legitimate biological needs are consistently frustrated over long periods, readily becomes the pattern of the adult attitude—with the further characteristic that aggression ultimately just has to be "swallowed" (internalized) and cannot be focused in continued activity toward self-help or even *against* the frustrating persons.

Observation (in this case by Du Bois) shows a culture with very little elaboration in technology or the arts—unless a financial system of meaningless intricacy is so considered. There is little political organization or differentiation of status. The people are mostly distrustful, suspicious, procrastinating, lacking in initiative, noncooperative with one another, quick to anger, and amenable to casual reconciliation—in short, about what a psychoanalyst might expect from the quite drastic deficiency in early affectional care of the child.* The culture is an old one, static at a low level of accomplishment and of satisfaction to its members. Despite the instability of marriages and constant minor quarreling, it survives, Kardiner thinks, because subsistence needs are adequately cared for, there have been no external enemies, and the pervasive aggression is too disorganized to do serious damage.

It should not be supposed, Kardiner says, that this society could be promptly ameliorated by the forcible introduction of better child care. To change the pattern of child care would involve reorganization of the entire culture. Redistribution of work load and a total realignment of values and techniques of interpersonal relations, especially the concept of male and female roles, would have to be accomplished at the same time. Mothers brought up themselves like the Alorese girls probably would be for generations incapable of giving their children the desired affectionate understanding, even if they were released by external fiat from their heavy burden of work; the men probably would be puzzled and embittered by the necessary interference with their complex financial operations. Imposition of new values through peripheral institutions such as religion would be hopeless. The personality is built on values with which Christian doctrine is in complete disharmony,[10] as is also the ideal of enterprise embodied in the Western concept of trade. Effective change in any society must take account of the dynamic relationship between personality and institutions.

Kardiner has now published a careful analysis of many cultures and has several more in preparation. His methodology includes an account of the institutions of the culture by an ethnographer, with especial attention to child care and to characteristic attitudes and emotions connected with life activities. Myths, folktales, religious ideas and practices, dreams, any organized ideologies, art forms, and techniques of thinking are considered. Biographies of individuals are collected if possible to provide a clearer picture of the developmental process and attitudes within the individual.

In studying subgroups of our own culture, Kardiner has used the full psychoanalytic technique on a few individuals selected as reasonably representative. Psychological tests, notably the Rorschach, are used when feasible.

* On my own responsibility I cite the studies of "institutional" children in our own culture during a happily brief period when Western ideals appeared to dictate good physical care with widely spaced feedings, early toilet training and diminution of interpersonal contacts. Where this "scientific" regime was carried out with real effectiveness, many children developed a personality not unlike that described for the Alorese. In our culture they often became delinquent and presented an extremely difficult therapeutic problem. (See references on p. 187.)

On the basis of such multidimensional materials, he tries to analyze the major trends and lines of integration within the culture. Thus far, he cautions against predictions concerning unknown aspects of a culture or its possible reaction to change from any limited inquiry into its institutions, not excluding institutions relating to child care. No matter how essential these may be in forming the basic personality of the group, and no matter how strongly "polarizing" the basic personality may be, its significant expression is profoundly and often unexpectedly influenced by other conditions in the way of life adopted by the society or forced upon it. Careful comparative study of fifty cultures might, he suggests, offer some basis for reliable generalization. In the meantime, "the chief merit of [the concept of basic personality] is that it offers us a basis for examining the structuralizations in society and for relating institutions to each other, not directly but through the medium of the individuals who compose it."[11]

The multidimensional approach, polarized around the basic personality, can explain why the Comanche maintained an extraordinary cohesiveness as a cultural group over a period of three hundred years under changing conditions despite a minimum of institutionalized group organization. Aggression and competition were prominent features of the culture—traits in themselves frequently disruptive. From infancy, however, the trend of Comanche culture was toward externalizing their aggression, to the cost of their neighbors. The hunting of buffalo and raiding parties for horses and captives were the main economic resources. Competition was channeled in socially acceptable ways, and its rewards were short-lived. From his early exploits the aging warrior retained no goods and little prestige. There were no vested interests, no durable or inherited status, which would compel the formation of passive attitudes of the weak toward those in power.[12] There were positive institutions fostering friendship among young males and toning down interpersonal rivalries. Individuals who were perhaps constitutionally unable to tolerate the extremely extraverted, warlike pattern of the tribe found a sort of niche in society as "the contrary ones," but they had no special power and accepted the cultural ideal even in their contrariness. Some of the old men engaged in malevolent magic, rather clearly in psychological compensation for their inevitable frustrations, but such magic was not greatly feared—as it is in many cultures. Religion was simple, and magic consisted mainly in the transmission of "power" by supernatural devices.

The structure of the adult culture provided outlet and control for the trends fostered by the basic disciplines of childhood. Maternal care was constructive, consistent, devoid of contradictory elements. "Tensions . . . were not permitted to accumulate to such extent as to cause undue anxiety, hostile attitudes to the parents, and eventual distrust in one's self."[13] The child was not crowded with premature responsibilities in controlling hunger and oral pleasure strivings or in establishing sphincter control. Sexual activity was not restricted. Early childhood training and games were oriented toward the later activities of hunting and war parties, the father serving as model and playmate rather than as disciplinarian. (Women were the chief disciplinarians and remained the chief butt of later unconscious hostilities.)

In such circumstances, a strong and sharply realistic ego is very likely to develop—of course along the lines of reality control fostered by the culture. Kardiner's point is that the child was prepared *emotionally* for the kind of culture within which he lived; the culture could "work" because of this preparation.*

A sharp break anywhere along the line could cause disintegration of the culture. Preservation of the forms of child care could hardly be expected to create effective personalities when the ensuing stages of close relationship between training and future activities and values were radically broken. When Comanche war parties were effectually put down as mere thievery, kidnaping, and murder in American society—and no emotionally congruent reality substitute was offered—the Comanche went to pieces. Admirable by our own ethos in many respects, these people could have little sense of "higher values" in a sedentary culture in which vested interests play a major role. They would not even make good racketeers by capitalist standards, and they were wholly unprepared for the ethical and religious standards we like to consider universal.

Kardiner's interest has become even more definitely focused on investigation of lines of tension and stability within specific social groups or identifiable subgroups—e.g., the American Negro, who is forced into a special group by virtue of his color, although he participates extensively in many aspects of American culture. "Basic personality" continues to be a useful concept, but instead of building up this concept further as a sharply definable psychological system, Kardiner has devoted his attention to its mode of operation under different conditions.

In the framework of this chapter, I may point out two trends in Kardiner's work. The first is toward a rather direct application of the Freudian view of infantile experience as determining basic personality development, and hence the way in which people in a given culture tend to react to the vicissitudes of adult life. This understanding of basic personality applies both to old societies

---

* It should be noted that this point is different from the efforts of a few writers to explain an entire culture by its practices regarding swaddling, weaning, or toilet training. It carries the training process further, in close relationship to modes of adaptation in later years, which are then seen in relationship to one another and to the external demands which the society as a whole has to meet.

in which some sort of viable relationship between basic personality and modes of adult living has long been established and to instances of social change in which a society—i.e., most of the people in it—react in a manner which often seems stupid, aggressive, or even suicidal. Kardiner observed that these oddities of adaptation and maladaptation had strong psychological determinants, traceable to infancy.

Kardiner's second point is that the basic psychological needs of the person may be fulfilled in various ways—or somehow frustrated—not only in infancy but throughout life. *Through its institutions,* a society provides fulfillments and frustrations, continuity with early patterns and discontinuities. The consequence is a kind of adjustment, not necessarily a good one, which varies from one society to the next. The Alorese make out over the centuries at a low level. The Comanche adjusted well (*i.e.,* maintained themselves as a strong society) to change compatible with their brand of continuity but went to pieces when social requirements on the reservation destroyed the basic continuities of Comanche society.

Kardiner's later efforts, I gather, concern the second point more than the first. He is interested in the *dynamics* of the major institutionalized trends in various societies in relation to the basic personality of its members. He has long since corrected any tendency toward reification of a "basic personality" as a sort of entity identifiable for each culture. (Indeed, such reification is more a matter of what people say about Kardiner than what he himself says.) His major concern is with the way in which significant action systems *interact,* whether they are determined primarily by the needs of the individual (inborn or having the cogency of attitudes powerfully established in infancy) or through the various levels of social patterning. Social tension, stability, potentials for change cannot be understood either in terms of the universals of a psychology of individuals or of social institutions. The study of social dynamics requires investigation of the specific *relationships among* the various types of action system operative in any given group.

Although he does not think of society as an organism comparable to a living individual, Kardiner does find the concept of *social homeostasis* a useful one. Operating through the characteristic reaction patterns of its members, socially consolidated trends (institutions) interact with one another in a manner which may foster cooperation and creative expansion or may lead to mutual destruction. No science of institutions can succeed unless it considers the psychological meaning of the institution to the people who make it and how change will affect their deep feelings and habits and other, apparently independent, institutions. No psychological science can be successfully applied to the problems of social living unless the relationship of the individual to the special institutions of his group is carefully examined.

Although Kardiner does not discuss Lewin, the concept of social home-ostasis seems in essence rather similar to the Lewinian concept of group dynamics now being ably developed by many "psychologists." The difference is, of course, that Kardiner has concerned himself only with very large social groups and has emphasized the psychological background of individuals within the group more heavily than Lewin, with more concentration on what we may loosely call "psychoanalytic" interpretations of human motivation. Perhaps the similarity begins and ends with the idea that a group—any group—has a dynamic of its own, which must be studied as such. This is a very important similarity.

Critical Comment

I SHALL NOT attempt to discuss the views of the "culturalists" who have borrowed from Freud in one way or another. The danger of such borrowing is, of course, a one-sidedness and superficiality which may reduce Freud's careful genetic approach to a few stereotypes about suckling and toilet training and his analysis of unconscious factors to a bit of blather about sado-masochistic trends.

It is difficult for me to see anything wrong with Kardiner's theoretical approach to this problem. I am no judge of the specific accuracy of his statements about the cultures he reports. It is quite possible that he has made many rather obvious mistakes, either because his ethnographers gave him incomplete data or because his psychoanalytic interpretation was faulty. Perhaps, as some people say, he is too Freudian. Perhaps he is not Freudian enough. That is said too. Perhaps he doesn't know enough about sociology and economics.

But the effort to discover the *specific operating relationship* between social institutions and psychological trends in each culture is a new venture. The task

is gigantic. It requires at the very least a realignment of principles which sociology and psychology as independent sciences have tended to consider fundamental→universal. It requires a new set of operating generalizations, the *invention* of new ways of systematizing observational data. Benedict, Mead, and Kardiner began with cultures in which the psychological pattern was fairly clear and unified, much as Freud began with the pathological syndrome of hysteria. But they did not thereafter continue to elaborate on theoretical grounds the principles initially formulated. Like Freud, Kardiner expanded his principles to meet the new empirical observations which he constantly invited.

One could hardly expect sociologists or psychoanalysts to be immediately enthusiastic about a point of view that, in a way, undercuts their most cherished scientific principles. Kardiner has been severely criticized by both camps, often with justice. He overgeneralizes at times, and he generalizes prematurely. But what else can he do? A supremely careful methodology in the extremely expensive area of research on societies is beyond the reach of any individual.* Kardiner has from the outset been profoundly interested in the *methodology* of research in this area, but people do not initiate new ideas and enlist support without a very real concern with *results.* The way of scientific progress is the way of demonstration of the value of a new approach, with indications of method. It is the new ideas which give impetus and meaning to the method, with some reciprocity.

In Kardiner one finds a fusion of desired result and method which is highly instructive. Kardiner insists that if one accepts integration as a basic psychosocial concept, one must study *how integration takes place* between the individual and his society. Methodology is here intrinsic to the new aim, carrying it beyond verbal formulation into the concrete study of societies. Kardiner's methodological approach *implements* ideas about society which are quite general, somewhat in the way in which Freud's methodological approach *implemented* deeper study of the individual.

To my mind, Kardiner has seen the essential problem of social research more clearly than any of the other analysts presented in this book, including the *sociologist,* Fromm. Except for Roheim, he is the only analyst reported who radically goes beyond our own culture for understanding of the psychological aspects of social patterns. In my opinion, Fromm presents interesting ideas about the psychological aspects of *European-American* culture, which are useful in educating us to look for particulars of the kind of integration of psychological and social patterns I consider basic. But Fromm's presentation is elaborated in a philosophical direction, via a *dialectic* analysis of the basic needs of man. Although his clinical understanding of in-

dividuals is essentially Freudian, his social generalizations tend to follow his philosophy. He has not even attempted to explain cultures radically different from our own. In later chapters I shall criticize Fromm's position as "reductionist," because it depends too directly on generalizations about human needs, neglecting the difficult step-by-step integration emphasized by Kardiner.

Roheim presents the "psychoanalytic" point of view very ardently—in fact, rather more ardently than many of his own colleagues approve. I shall discuss Roheim's position at some length in this chapter (pp. 137*ff.*), with appreciation of his extension of basic "Freudian" concepts to cultures radically different from ours. In my opinion, Roheim makes the only adaptation possible for a Freudian who considers the Oedipus complex "universal"—that is, he brings into the picture the significance of pregenital factors in the formation of the Oedipus complex. In this manner, Roheim maintains the Freudian thesis of psychological "universals" and the essential unity of mankind.

Kardiner might agree rather thoroughly with Fromm about the essential contours of our own culture, and with Roheim about significant universals derived from the nature of the human infant. Disagreement *at the level of factual observation* is at least subject to reconciliation as more facts accumulate. What is not tolerable to Kardiner in Fromm's position is his tendency to interpret clinical and social phenomena from a dialectic standpoint rather than from direct observation. What Kardiner must object to in Roheim's work is not so much his observation of important trends in the societies he studies as his contention that this is all one ought to study in a society —that these are the true "universals" which Kardiner and the culturalists have missed.

I share Kardiner's impatience with any psychosocial point of view that does

* In point of fact, Kardiner has personally financed many field studies, in whole or in part.

not aim at investigation of the rather specific needs of the human organism, infant and adult, in *reciprocal relationship to codified social patterns*. The concept of action systems, variously developed and variously related to social and individual continuities, allows for a functionalism which does not neglect the importance of institutions—*i.e.,* patterns of personality and society so crystallized through past experience as to function in their own right.

For societies as well as people, systems of secondary autonomy are often very powerful; they often operate beyond their current "usefulness," either to society or to the individual. Some systems are doomed to failure because they are engulfed by wider social trends;

some, because they frustrate the fundamental biological needs of the organism ultimately beyond human tolerance. This fact is well known. What is *not* known is how these systems of secondary autonomy are related to primary social and personal needs in a specific society. The essential problem is handled by rule of thumb. The Marxists recognize variations in the psychological readiness of different peoples for communism. The Freudians recognize that society conditions the way human "universals" are expressed. Kardiner's concept of *action systems* developed in various ways provides a means of organizing basic relationships within the society for further study—for generalization beyond a single society.

THE DIRECT CONTRIBUTION

THEORETICAL POSTULATES:
THE OEDIPUS COMPLEX; PREHISTORY

The emphasis of contemporary cultural anthropology owes much to Freud. Nevertheless, this was not Freud's concept of group psychology. Like LeBon, Trotter, McDougall, and others, Freud observed that men behave differently in groups from the way they do when they are alone. Civilization has a continuity apparently independent of the individual, although it must inevitably express itself *through* the individual. The individual is continuously influenced, *consciously and unconsciously*, by group sanctions as compelling as instincts, although they are not part of his biological equipment. What are groups? How are they formed and changed? What is the source of their power over the individual, sometimes leading him to actions opposed to his own interests? What is the source of those social and moral feelings which continuously modify our animal needs, sometimes to the point of frustration and even death?

In accordance with the scientific temper of his age, Freud sought a universal answer to these questions, one which would be independent of the contingencies of specific groups.* He found it in the relation of the child to the father. I shall preface detailed discussion with a skeleton summary of the childhood events that Freud considered crucial to group psychology. (See Chap. 5 for full treatment of Freud's concept of the genetic process.)

In the transition from the state of primary narcissism characteristic of the newborn to adult mastery of his environment and his instinctual needs, the child almost necessarily acquires special attitudes toward the parent. These are compounded of love and dependence as boundless as the needs of infancy, of rebellion against frustration, and of murderous rivalry coming to a focus during the Oedipal period. The infant (1) transfers his own primitive sense of omnipotence to the parent and (2) *identifies himself with the powerful figure* he has thus created. Especially toward the end of the phallic stage, the child typically solves the problem of his ambivalent reactions to the parent by *introjecting* the parental image, incorporating it as part of his own self in the form of his conscience (superego). The parental precepts now come from within himself. At the same time, he typically takes the parent as model for his own behavior, while retaining a sense of the parental figure's awe-ful power for good and ill.

It appeared to Freud that the emotional relationship to the leader is the quintessence of all group formation and behavior, with the exception of panic, which seemed to reveal the disorganization of a leaderless condition. The need for a leader and the quality of the relationship to the leader are for Freud the consequence of the infantile experience with the parent, which would inevitably mold the child's attitude toward other persons. A group is constituted by its members' adoption of the same object-ideal (leader). The power of the leader is magnified, like the power of the parent, and, above all, the follower identifies with the leader (parental) image. The irrationality and complexity of group behavior can thus be interpreted along the same lines as the attitude toward the parent in individual behavior. Under group conditions, the group

* Having severely criticized such "universalization" in foregoing comment, may I suggest an orientation to Freud's own position. His view of the Oedipus complex as "universal" requires correction in the form he outlined. It derives too much from Judaeo-Christian culture, from Vienna at the turn of the century, from Freud as a person. Correction has been made by many "Freudians" without significant change in Freud's fundamental postulates, retaining his sense of the unity of mankind (cf. the discussion of Roheim, pp. 137-140).

Since we are part of Judaeo-Christian culture, however, Freud's comments have very special value for us. Rejection of undue "universalization" has too frequently led to neglect of extraordinarily sharp insights into our own society. *Our* relationship to the father-leader is, I think, well described by Freud—and for many problems this description is extremely valuable.

Too often Freud's critics ignore a brilliant analysis of group psychology in Europe and America because it does not fully account for group psychology in the Trobriand or Marquesan Islands. I suggest that the reader take Freud's "universalizations" in modern perspective, but that he consider very seriously whatever Freud has to say about our own culture. Corrections and elaborations are still in order, but Freud's own analysis has a kind of penetration often lacking in contemporary psychosocial theories.

ideal or leader may be substituted for the individual superego, thus permitting acts of heroism and cruelty impossible for the individual alone.

The relationship with the parent, however, comprises only part of the early contacts of the infant which mold his basic attitudes toward people. The young child soon finds that his relations with the parent do not take place in a vacuum. There are competitors for parental love—mainly siblings. (Other commitments may take the parent away from the child far more effectively, but the toddler cannot appreciate their significance. He understands vividly how another baby qualifies—sometimes, indeed, seems to destroy—his dream of total love.) Moreover, the rivalry of the siblings *vis-à-vis* the parent and one another is for absolute power—the only kind of power the young child can conceive. Freud's position is that children are born neither sinful nor virtuous but so innocent that they take their emerging awareness of the world as the whole truth. In this world, sibling relations must have a component of murderous rivalry, dictated by relations with the parents long before social competition arises (*cf.* the discussion of Adler, pp. 373-375).

The sibling problem, too, is handled by the process of identification. Instead of killing his brother, the individual cherishes his brother "as himself." The bond among members of a group lies in their common relationship to the leader (father). They are "brothers in Christ," "brothers in arms." So long as love and hate for the leader provide a powerful group focus, the members of the group become *one* quite literally. Freud describes a primary group as "a number of individuals who have substituted one and the same object for their ego-ideal [later called superego] and have consequently identified themselves with one another in their ego."[14] The process of development in sibling relationships is also complicated. We shall see how it gives rise to the virtues of justice and loyalty, as well as to intolerance, conformity, jealousy, and sanctioned hatred.

Thus far, our presentation has been limited to the experience of the child. Most Freudians today find ontogenetic factors—actual relations among siblings in the family—sufficient to account for the phenomena Freud observed. His contribution to group psychology is still widely considered valid and valuable, since it seems to the Freudians to offer a coherent, dynamic explanation of the many contradictory trends so readily seen in group behavior. Freud himself proposed another, supplementary line of origin: phylogenetic memories of human prehistory. Developments in anthropology and in genetics have made this aspect of his theory seem untenable to most scientists, including Freudians. Freud's position is presented here with immediate critique of this aspect of his theory. The reader may wish to follow the advice of a strong adherent of Freud: "Take the primal horde *as a figure of speech!*" Indeed, Freud himself refers to the "scientific myth of the father of the primal horde."[15]

Freud published his view of prehistory[16] in 1912, resting his case mainly upon comments by Darwin and Robertson Smith. He reaffirmed it in *Moses and Monotheism* (1938). According to this view, man originally lived in small hordes dominated by a single male, originally the biological father, although other individuals might enter the group by conquest or by chance. (Formal adoption into a blood clan is common in primitive societies today.) The father possessed all the females and jealously guarded his rights against his own sons. He was deposed only by the son who overcame him in combat and who became "father" in his turn. A similar primitive social structure exists today among some animals, notably the seals, vividly portrayed in Disney's film *Seal Island*. The Greek pantheon before Zeus also offers a familiar parallel.

In human prehistory, the sons eventually banded together, murdered the father, and set up a sort of contract among themselves to prevent recurrence of the old sequence. The father's group of women was made taboo for all of them, wives being sought outside the clan—the beginning of the virtually universal incest taboo and exogamy. A matriarchal form of society followed, very gradually supplanted by the return of the repressed patriarchal. The incest taboo remained, but there were many fathers instead of one. In poetry and in real life, there is a tendency for the hero to reinstate the full magnificence of the primal father—an eventuality longed for and deeply resented by the followers (sons), who eventually combine against him in a renewal of the old father murder.

Freud believes, on the one hand, that the traces of the primal horde surviving in currently observable practices (dictated by the unconscious, of course) are sufficient to warrant a reasonably firm scientific assertion that events in prehistory actually happened approximately as outlined. There is a noteworthy similarity between savage and civilized religious rituals (in fragmentary example, the totem feast and the Eucharist). Further evidence may be found, he feels, in the spontaneous play of children, the productions of the insane, art forms, and dreams. On the other hand, Freud uses the *memory* of these events, the unconscious heritage of the race, to explain the extraordinary power and universality of the Oedipus complex today. For him this is not circular reasoning. This explanation and no other appears to account for *all* the facts from anthropology, sociology, and his own experience of psychology.

CRITIQUE ACCEPTED BY MOST FREUDIANS

Contemporary ethnologists are timid about *any* assertions concerning social organization in this very remote past, because direct evidence is not available. The earliest available evidence suggests a great variety of social forms apparently dependent more upon the physical conditions of maintaining life than upon the relatively malleable sexual instincts. The animal kingdom, too, seems more instructive in the variety of forms of sexual adaptation observable even among mammals, even among anthropoids, than in suggesting any single biological solution. Although Freud's view is not *logically* excluded, its support must come entirely from psychoanalysis in its most subtle aspects—at best, that is, from a method which the ethnologist is not qualified to use. Moreover, the psychoanalyst is severely hampered in applying his usual techniques in markedly alien cultures. At present, only a few very determined Freudians accept the events in the primal horde as a completely tenable literal reconstruction of prehistory. Hypotheses more in line with contemporary observation are usually preferred, in so far as the analyst or ethnologist concerns himself with a question to which no fully satisfactory answer can be given at present.

The second general criticism pertains to Freud's concept of phylogenetic memories—that is, the direct influence of dim recollection of the primal events on the developing attitudes of contemporary man. This concept requires a mechanism for the hereditary transmission of acquired characteristics, no matter how dim the recollection or how long mankind lived under such conditions. With the exception of Lysenko and Soviet scientists, modern geneticists consider such a mechanism definitely excluded by the enormous weight of evidence about the course of evolution and the data from their own science. Almost all Freudians today, in accepting the importance and universality of the developmental processes outlined by Freud, reject his view of phylogenetic memories and indicate that the conflicts noted are created anew in the experience of each child. It seems possible to retain almost the whole of Freud's theory of group psychology by the simple expedient of laying still more stress on the as-it-were necessary fate of biological impulses under conditions which are virtually universal in human experience.

EMPHASIS ON THE OEDIPUS COMPLEX: ROHEIM

Even granting this correction of Freud's views, however, many analysts as well as "outsiders" feel that Freud laid too much stress on the role of the *father*, on the Oedipus complex, in his evaluation of group structure. It has become commonplace to remark that Freud lived in an authoritarian culture in which the father was allotted the socially dominant role; that Freud's own personality was authoritarian. Furthermore, psychoanalysis began with the study of hysteria in which problems of the phallic stage are especially prominent (see Chap. 7).

Psychoanalysis came later to the investigation of pregenital phases and ego mechanisms. It is fair to say that most psychoanalysts nowadays have broadened Freud's formulation to include more of these later contributions to a theory of human development. Some analysts, such as Fromm and Kardiner, specifically reject the Oedipus complex as universal in any meaningful sense. Others, such as Money-Kyrle,[17] stay more securely within the framework of Freud's thinking but point out that the father is always partly father-mother and that attitudes toward the *parent* image are more various and more complex than they appear in Freud's initial observations. Still others, such as Roheim, ardently defend the concept of the universality of the Oedipus complex or, like Bychowski, apply it very directly to the understanding of historical events.[18]

Since Fromm and Kardiner are discussed elsewhere in this book, we may concentrate here on a review of Roheim's position. Although he rejects phylogenetic memories as determinants, Roheim follows Freud in other respects. Despite Roheim's polemic insistence on the Oedipus complex, it seems clear (at least to me) that his work helps to define *in what sense* it is "universal," and to lay a more substantial groundwork in ethnology for the ideas of the middle group of analysts who elaborate Freud's views without explicit repudiation of his somewhat exclusive emphasis on the father-son relationship.

Malinowski was one of the first anthropologists to apply a psychoanalytic orientation to the study of primitive peoples. In 1924 he published "Mutterrechtliche Familie und Oedipus-Komplex" ("Complex and Myth in Mother Right"), an account of a matrilineal society. Among the Trobrianders, the mother's brother holds the authority over the child allocated to the father in our society. Attitudes toward sexual play in childhood are permissive. Under such a social framework, "complexes" in the sexual sphere seemed to be weak and to be focused around the maternal uncle and the sister rather than around the father and mother, as in our society. The obvious conclusion was that *cultural* conditions largely determine the course of sexual and emotional development.

We have already reported the views of Kardiner on this point, carefully developed through cultural studies more sophisticated than Malinowski's pioneer work. Kardiner frequently observes "traces" of an Oedipus complex but does not consider it determining *as such* even for the basic personality in many of the cultures he has studied. Most psychoanalysts were impressed by Malinowski's findings. Fenichel, a staunch Freudian, writes, ". . . it was the family that created the Oedipus complex."[19]

In his opposition to a modified culturalist approach, Roheim has had to battle with his own colleagues as well as with outsiders. *Resting his case on the actual experience of the child,* he points out that by Malinowski's own account the father does play a role in the very early years of Trobriand infancy quite similar to the one he plays in our own society, and that one may see the father figure behind the myths and taboos which apparently concern the uncle exclusively. Roheim believes that the uncle in matrilineal groups he himself has studied carefully can be shown in dreams, myths, and other materials to be a combination of mother and father—a man endowed with a vagina. The social institution arises from and constantly recreates special attitudes toward the parents. Roheim takes pains to indicate how the phallic mother remains dominant in these societies. He points out how she becomes the Witch, who is either symbolically received or rejected in later ceremony, especially bridal rites, and how the primitive infantile evaluation of coitus is repeated in these ceremonies.[20]

In a later paper,[21] Roheim endeavors to show how the Oedipus complex emerges from earlier biologically determined relations between the child and the mother in a manner independent of specific cultural experience—and also independent of phylogenetic memory. The manifest differences in overt cultural attitudes are explained, culture by culture, by the particular conformation of the Oedipus complex resulting from specific pre-Oedipal experiences and the specific manner in which the father enters upon the scene.

In fact, in Roheim's book *Psychoanalysis and Anthropology,* the emphasis is less upon the Oedipus complex as such than upon the helplessness of the human infant, coupled with a relatively precocious libido and rapid development of the brain. It is because the brain continues to develop in the sheltered, libidinal, mother-child situation that man possesses his characteristic powers of symbolization and his capacity for identification with adult figures.[22] The fundamental pattern of his personality is determined in this early situation, along lines which must be the same the world over. Roheim's own interest in *pregenital* experience as significant for the conformation of the Oedipus complex probably made him especially sympathetic to the work of the English school, Melanie Klein and her associates (see pp. 211ff.). In any event he seems to have changed from his original adherence to the Oedipus complex as presented by Freud and to use the formulations of the English school more freely than most American analysts.*

To suggest Roheim's final view of cultural differences as vividly as possible in brief compass, I quote part of his summary of cultures reported in *Psychoanalysis and Anthropology*:

* The shift may be confusing to readers of this book. For example, the term *superego* is used in the paragraphs quoted below in the Kleinian rather than in the classical Freudian sense reported here. Cf. Roheim's statement: "My definition of the word superego is *unconscious aggression inverted against the ego, and the parent regarded as responsible for this aggression.*

"Obviously, this differs from Freud's definition. Freud defines the superego in two sentences: (*a*) You must be like father. (*b*) You are not allowed to do what father does" (*Psychoanalysis and Anthropology,* p. 8).

We then proceed to analyze the cultures of various human groups. In Australia we find an essentially Oedipal culture with projection as the main defense mechanism. In Normanby Island we find people who because of the insecurity experienced in the mother-child situation fail to identify with their fathers and regress to a combination of oral and anal mechanisms. Keeping within or introjection is more important than projection.

But it would be absurd to say that there is nothing oral in Australia or that they do not introject, or vice versa, that the Normanby Islanders have no Oedipus complex or that they do not project. In Alor we again have the "bad mother" as a starting point. Since separation anxiety is so overwhelming, it follows that castration anxiety must also be very strong and the data fully confirm this assumption. Early frustration obviously means a strong Super-Ego; anal magic (wealth), phallic ostentation and aggression are mobilized to ward off "aggression turned inward" (*i.e.*, the Super-Ego). Among the Marquesas Islanders with their peculiar system of polyandry and loveless weaning, we still find the Oedipus complex but the guilt feeling is so powerful that the father makes a symbolic surrender before the battle has started. With the Kaingang we have the very traumatic custom of piercing the lips at the age of two. Here we recognize that not only the events of the childhood situation influence the personality or culture of a group but also history. The traumata of adult age can be resisted on basis of childhood security but a combination of both is likely to be disruptive. The oral trauma plus the loss of their lands has produced a society with nearly open Oedipal hatred and endless aggression. The question can be asked, of course, whether similar factors could not produce quite different results (regression) and we really don't know enough to answer this question. The Yurok are discussed as an extreme case of oral frustration, anal character and Super-Ego pressure. The Navaho serve to show the obvious Oedipus and Super-Ego structure of these people.[23]

Critical Comment

ROHEIM has modified Freud's original position to include variations which Freud himself suggested in regard to the *formation* of the Oedipus complex—variations which every analyst observes in practice and which for the English school have almost superseded the Freudian formulation.

Roheim's differences in basic theory from the "culturalists" he bitterly attacks become increasingly obscure to me, especially his differences from Kardiner, unless he interprets the concept of "basic personality" in far more sweeping terms that Kardiner himself.* He is especially

* Roheim says, "The outlines of what has now become the theory of *basic personality* dawned upon me in the process of fieldwork" ("Introduction: Psychoanalysis and Anthropology," in *Psychoanalysis and the Social Sciences,* I, p. 18), and, "Kardiner has developed what was little more than a hint in my publications into a systematic theory of basic *personality.*

critical of "culturalists" who attempt to explain "culture" in terms of the psychological consequences of special culturally determined modes of handling babies. So is Kardiner; so are most of the culturalists Roheim cites.

Roheim is correct in observing that the human organism is a symbolizing organism and that it tends to *identify* with the ministering adults in a way that we can call projective and introjective. For that very reason, it becomes enormously important to investigate the precise nature of the adult model and the specific satisfactions and frustrations the child encounters. I would add to these topics of investigation, investigation of the manner in which the symbols and roles of his society are taught him in middle childhood (see my final comment, pp. 170*f*.). Certainly, the continuing opportunities and disappointments in adult life offered by his society cannot be a matter of total indifference. Social *forms* tend to persist. They are also subject to gradual modification and to drastic impacts of an external nature which impose more or less abrupt changes, requiring new social forms. Roheim recognizes all these problems, but he is strangely unwilling to consider the idea that they might be investigated systematically and systematically related to universal trends rooted in man's biological equipment. He objects to the mere fact that anthropologists study cultural differences and take them seriously. When Benedict cautions against the use of such words as *conscience* and *responsibility, superego* and *inferiority complex* in connection with Japanese culture because they have profoundly different connotations from those in our culture, Roheim seems to feel that she is throwing overboard all sense of the unity of mankind.

This is not my reading of Benedict's work. On the contrary, she seems to me to stress the *universal* needs of children in quasi-psychoanalytic terms, to try to study how they are influenced by the institutions of society and how, in turn, they influence society. The series of cultural studies which she guided as a project, the Columbia University Research in Contemporary Cultures, arose out of sober recognition of cultural clashes as our top policy-makers and our armed forces found it necessary to deal intimately with alien peoples. Studies of American Indian groups, pioneered by Benedict on a research basis, had already proved useful in the administration of the Bureau of American Ethnology.

Pioneering work, and work done under pressure of immediate need, are likely to fall short of our lofty ideals of scientific method. But Roheim's criticism seems rather petty. As I remarked in the discussion of Kardiner, criticism of conclusions about specific cultures is beyond the province of this book, and beyond my own area of competence. It can hardly be expected that an anthropologist who reads about psychoanalysis would have a full understanding of its deepest implications for the investigation of "universal" unconscious trends. Concrete integration of psychoanalytic and cultural data must require further understanding of *both* aspects. Undoubtedly Benedict's* formulations require correction from both angles.

But one cannot get on with a study of integrative action unless one studies integrative action. Mistakes in integrative formulations about specific cultures are far less damaging, in my opinion, than efforts to universalize one or another aspect of the complex problems of the psychological and social sciences. Benedict

---

. . . Kardiner is prone to make generalized statements based upon an insufficient knowledge of anthropological data" (*ibid.*, pp. 29*f*.).

* Throughout this book I have used Dr. Ruth Benedict as a sort of symbol for cultural anthropology. In part this is a personal tribute to her. She wrote the first book in this area— *Patterns of Culture* (1934). She *taught* Kardiner, Mead, and others in their early approaches to this problem, and I think herself avoided excesses of enthusiasm.

and her fellow anthropologists, Kardiner, and in his way, Erikson (to be discussed) are aiming at an integrative science. Roheim's polemic emphasis on the unity of mankind neglects half the problem and brings false accusation against the *aims* of these "culturalists."

I am indebted to Roheim for a passage he quotes from Murray, which to my mind expresses the problem well in a psychoanalytic vernacular:

> "My guess is that we would have no more than a fraction of the clarifying psychoanalytic concepts we have today if Freud had had a highly developed scientific superego." [Roheim follows up with an interpretation]: What Murray really means is that if Freud had had the kind of scientific scruples that are regarded as necessary in certain circles, then—and the rest follows.
>
> This is one of those cases when a word is twisted and turned till it becomes completely unrecognizable.[24]

My own emphasis would be on the meaning *Murray* attempts to convey— *i.e.,* tolerance for the fact that creative ideas are not developed or "proved" by rigid methodology. To me one of the most impressive testimonials to the essential value of Freud's terminology is that it *can* be used as scientific slang. In my opinion, Benedict and Murray are not "twisting meanings" but are using an argot to suggest thoughtful criticism of an essentially "Freudian" approach to the problem of how the biological equipment of the human infant produces the deep-lying psychological trend of the adult. I repeat that Kardiner, Benedict, Mead, and the "culturalists" are probably wrong on many points. But they are studying a new problem of acknowledged importance: the problem of integration. Surely they may be allowed errors in initial formulation, as Murray suggests for Freud.

In my opinion, Roheim follows Freud's *mistake* in his effort to achieve psychological universalizations in their own right with active repudiation of a study of social patterns *creatively integrated with* biologically focused patterns. Instead of helping to correct the factual shortcomings of these integrative efforts, Roheim takes the negative line of attacking them all and is especially caustic about those that use a "quasi-psychoanalytic" approach.

FREUD'S CONCEPT OF GROUP BEHAVIOR

The Leader

Freud's more specific comments on group behavior are definitely related to the formulation of attitudes toward the father and toward siblings that are *characteristic for our culture*. In all probability they fall short of the universal applicability he envisaged, but, after all, we live in a culture that has this kind of structure. *For us,* therefore, they do have cogency. In *Group Psychology and the Analysis of the Ego* (1921), Freud proposed a group psychology based on relationship to the leader and fellow followers—long before the Duce and the Führer and Stalin made *leader* a term of horror. Freud was almost frighteningly right about group behavior in our culture. We may correct and elaborate his position, as I remarked earlier, but it cannot be dismissed.

The essential feature of Freud's position is the *developmental* nature within the individual of group "instincts," however profound and universally operative they may appear. There are no inborn trends toward gregariousness, leading and following, imitating, or any of the long roster of traits frequently considered native to man as a social animal. Freud's position is that the observable trends grow out of the experience of the helpless infant with specific biological needs as he necessarily encounters the ministrations and frustrations of parents and—a little later, but still prior to a sophisticated appreciation of external reality—the rivalry of siblings. Such experience inevitably leads to many of the traits which social thinkers considered "instinctive" because of their widespread occurrence. The merit of Freud's analysis is that it provides a means of understanding the irrationality of group phenomena more precisely by aligning them with psychological dynamics as established for the individual. Socially oriented feelings are *built* in infancy and necessarily contain the longings, contradictions, and ambivalences of their origin. Freud points out, furthermore, their close relationship to the self, to ideals and conscience.

The individual is thus prepared to expect almost complete support and gratification from the outside power which awakens attitudes toward the father-leader. The pattern of total self-abnegation and blissful repose in the almighty reaches deep into infancy and can fulfill itself toward God or toward any person, idea, or whatever that fits well enough to serve as adequate stimulus. All of us to some extent, some of us to a very great extent, have a nostalgia for this early peace. Expectation always runs along lines of magic rather than of rational evaluation of what the leader might accomplish, least of all rational appreciation of the assets and limitations of a specific leader. The follower tends to build up the power of any leader out of his own psychology. The demagogue typically panders to this deep will-to-believe by demonstrations of power and solidarity at a primitive level. Appeal to reason by outsiders can rarely be effective in such circumstances. Even personal hardships are not critically evaluated in relation to the leader's claims, because he has a right to demand sacrifice, just as the parent had in childhood.

The attitude toward the leader, however, is always ambivalent. Loving magnification of his power is accompanied by fear and hatred, rebellion and rivalry, as with the primal father. Hence the ease with which a group can turn against a leader formerly adored. The fickleness of the mob is the natural consequence of the psychological ingredients of group psychology—is, indeed, predictable in its very fickleness when the psychological roots of group devotion are known. Love of the leader contains, as an integral part of its development, hatred to the point of murder. Murder may always gain the upper hand, as in Freud's concept of prehistory and as may be observed with impressive frequency throughout history. Actual murder and the more pervasive *fantasy* of murder then lead to a *sense of guilt* in the follower, which makes him more than ever compliant.

This statement of the fundamental ambivalence of attitudes toward the leader is still grossly oversimplified. Love and hate are experienced toward the same object, a divided feeling difficult enough to assimilate by itself. But, further, the love and hate are magically overstated in the infantile psyche, projected upon the parental image, *and then introjected as the superego.* The adult does not alternately love and hate the leader as the young child can love and hate. The adult can no longer feel simple remorse for a given act, relieved by simple forgiveness or expiation. The leader's attitudes have been incorporated into his own personality, where they are subject to the revamping of complex individual dynamics. Overt action against the leader lowers the pressure of the instinctual need which prompted it—and by this very fact automatically increases the *relative* strength of other aspects of libidinal ties. Thus, the murder of the father does not bring only a welcome relief from his tyranny. The relief itself allows concomitant feelings of love to gain the ascendancy, along with feelings of severe deprivation of the father's powerful support. Freud here offers an explanation of the often cited phenomenon of deification of the fallen leader by the rebels themselves, the turning of the populace against the leaders who performed the execution in the name of the people, and the unfortunate tendency of revolutions against dictatorship to result in even more severe dictatorial regimes.

To be sure, the overthrow of existing institutions by sudden violence leads to a *factual* dislocation of services normally rendered by the state in a complex society; at such periods, the state is often attacked from the outside. The individual frequently finds himself worse off than before, for reasons which might *rationally* be tolerated as temporary. Yet in fact moderate revolutions are almost always swept aside by the intolerance of the masses, who seem then to show a disconcerting love of the whip which goes far beyond rational necessity. Group mobilization of aggression against the leader is followed almost regularly by group mobilization of love and longing for him—and the guilt-laden belief that whatever unpleasant events still occur are the merited punishment of the all-powerful leader—*i.e.,* father.

Freud discusses this attitude in detail in *Moses and Monotheism.* Moses, he believes, revived for the Jews the repressed image of the primal father and stringently impressed upon them a difficult new ethic (probably derived from Ikhnaton). Eventually Moses was murdered by his followers (Freud cites probable historical evidence), thus renewing the primal guilt. As the chosen people, the children of Israel were told, and believed, that they were especially close to God—that is, to the single, all-powerful father. As external vicissitudes mounted, they never *seriously* reverted to the concept of a tribal god (current at that early period) who could be worshipped, scolded, or abandoned if he failed to measure up to rival gods in fulfilling concrete expectations. The succession of prophets belabored the chosen people for any such backsliding, constantly refreshing their self-confidence and belief in the father.

Instead of leading to repudiation of an ineffective god, the external distress was ascribed to merited punishment from a genuinely all-powerful God. (Later psychoanalytic authors have shown how the peculiar historical role of the Jews played into the religio-socio-psychological problems of other peoples, with reciprocal reinforcement of attitudes within and without Jewry.*)

Leader and Superego

The irrational submission to increasingly tyrannical leaders and the acceptance of hardships even beyond those that originally provoked the revolt have still another dynamic source, according to Freud's view. Frustration of libidinal needs naturally arouses aggression. The aggression cannot be openly expressed against the father. In part it may be displaced to other individuals—often the unlucky innocent bystander, more often a scapegoat unconsciously selected as somehow appropriate. But in large part such aggression is *internalized* as part of the superego. The very young child and the psychopath may be relieved of remorse if their crime goes undetected or is forgiven by the external authority. But the superego is immediately aware of aggressive impulses, whether or not they come to action or even to consciousness. Thus, every undischarged aggression tends to be experienced in the overly conscientious person as guilt, as meriting the just retribution of the all-powerful external authority which has *now become part of the self*. Such retribution is often directed against the self, regardless of immediate external circumstances.

As a problem in individual psychology, the aggressive and self-punitive aspects of the superego are treated elsewhere in this book (Chaps. 3 and 5). Here they are important as a component of the relationship with the leader in group psychology. The group member does not merely childishly love and hate, depend upon and rebel against, the father image, and, after periods of overt rebellion, submit blindly to punishment merited for his misdeeds. The internalized leader, the conscience, builds up aggression in itself. In the name of the gentle Christ, the Christian world has shown plentiful examples both of self-flagellation and massacre of unbelievers. In rejecting the external power of the priests, the Protestant ethic did not reject these excesses. On the con-

---

* *Cf.* the admirable book by R. M. Loewenstein, *Christians and Jews*, International Universities Press, 1951.

trary, the Calvinist conscience became one of the most cruel and intolerant forces the world has known.

How, then, does this complex relationship with the leader function in group psychology? Generally speaking, the leader and the admonitions of the leader are substituted for the ego ideal or superego. The great man—in some circumstances, the abstract idea—takes over the individual conscience. Too often this substitution involves a lowering of the intellectual and moral capacities of the individual. By himself the Nazi guard was often as decent a human being as the rest of us, with as little relish for wholesale murder. He did not execute mass murder solely because he dared not disobey, or even because he rationally believed that Hitler knew what was best for the world. These motives and others played a role, but the main determinant of his actions was merely that the leader became his conscience. Our sturdy New England forebears rarely had qualms about persecuting poor old women as witches or dragging sickly infants to baptism in wintry weather. The Puritan father could grieve over the consequent death of his child and comfort himself with the thought of the salvation of the little soul, but it would not occur to him to feel *guilty* about his action. In fact, guilt was far more likely to attach itself to the hesitation with which he had taken the child to church because of his human fear.

Once the leader or leader-idea is identified with, its dictates become the dictates of conscience. Interestingly enough, people usually do not feel acute remorse for actions committed under conditions of leadership conscience. The Nazi, the participant in a lynching party, may have a morning-after headache as he reviews his actions, perhaps with shame at having allowed himself to be so misled. Yet despite the absence of external coercion in most cases, the individual usually feels—with some psychological justice—that it was not *he* who committed the crimes but Hitler or the mob or even the Puritan ethic. This attitude was reported as characteristic for most Germans at the end of World War II.

Assets of Group Behavior: The Great Man; Peripheral Precepts

Freud brought into scientific discussion the *assets* of such group behavior and closer analysis of its origin and its frequent *value* to the individual and to our ethical ideals. The same identification with the leader permits the soldier to face calmly and bravely dangers which he would find hopelessly terrifying as an individual. Freud points to *panic* as the consequence of a breakdown in the leader relationship. It is well known that troops may go to pieces in the face of quite ordinary danger when the leader somehow fails and that they often surpass themselves in heroism when effective leadership is present.

Under the leadership of Moses and the prophets, the Jewish people reached a moral status impossible to individuals in a rude primitive tribe and of value to the whole world as the new teachings became solidified as a group ethic, constantly renewed in the transmission from father to son. Identification with Christ or with concepts of the state and science has led to group achievements and to much that we consider valuable in civilization. When, as so often, the great man is reviled and killed, his image exerts itself the more strongly as the very personification of conscience. His precepts become the superego of the group and are even more firmly adopted by every member.

Freud further asks, "Who becomes a leader and why?" In *Moses and Monotheism* Freud asks: What is the great man? He points out that the definition can be only partly objective.* To be sure, the great man must have superior capacities, but his greatness resides mainly in the fact that he can formulate with especial clarity and cogency *the trends which are already present in the group.* Christ could not speak in the hearts of the rich or of the organized priesthood. The task of identification with the strange goals set by an itinerant preacher was too severe. At first only the lowly, the downtrodden, and the anxious sinners found the new message close enough to their own (largely unconscious) trends to be accessible to it, to recognize and in some measure participate in the creation of its divinity. As Fromm points out (see pp. 390*f.*), Calvinism could hold no sway over the consciences of men during the Middle Ages because their inner needs had a different structure. Freud differs from Fromm in his analysis of the underlying structure, giving more emphasis to problems revolving around the father, but there would be essential agreement on the *two-way dynamics* of the problem of leadership.[25] *The members of a group determine (largely unconsciously) who can be accepted as leader in the full sense of substitution for the inner ego ideal.*

Having made this full acceptance, however, the members are innerly committed to the *precepts* of the leader-dominated conscience well beyond the specific emotional needs which led to its adoption. Ideals of the leader relatively peripheral to the message of immediate appeal which made him the leader take on the cogency of conscience and are subtly removed from full application of rational criticism. Freud uses the precept "love thy neighbor as thyself"[26] as an example of a group ideal that cannot be defended with any literal rationalism and that combines the best and the worst of sustained group ideals.

To emphasize the limited point of how specific peripheral precepts operate, I return to the example of the Puritan father who takes a frail infant to

* *Cf.* "objective" studies of leadership qualities by "psychologists" indicative of the same point. See T. M. Newcomb, *Social Psychology*, The Dryden Press, 1950, pp. 650*ff.*

church on a winter's day. Most of us know this distressing practice either through textbook accounts or through dramatized versions of those situations in which somebody was in conflict about it. Often we do not realize that the Puritan father generally felt about the problem a kind of conviction we can liken to the modern father's hardness toward his son's visits to the dentist. His conscience demanded adherence to the *precepts* of Puritan theology as unswervingly as the modern conscience adheres to the dictates of modern science. A gentle man may suffer, a cruel man may (unconsciously) exult, through the sufferings of his son. A reasonable man may wonder how far the pains we inflict on children are genuinely "necessary," but he is often helpless. Now, as then, no parent can adequately detach his judgment on such points from the judgment of his time. We can freely criticize and analyze the father of yesteryear. If we want to be "reasonable," we may fairly doubt whether straight teeth have in themselves such impressive survival value over moderately protruding ones as would rationally justify keeping a youngster in painful, disfiguring braces during the years when he is building his social personality. Christening and orthodontia may perhaps seem almost equally absurd to the "reasonable" man. Parents in our society, however, will still strain their budget and their tender emotions to ensure acceptable teeth to their children. *Our* current group ideal demands them.

This example is intended to show how ideas clearly peripheral to basic emotional and rational attitudes develop psychosocial power in their own right. In so far as they are intimately connected with the introjected leader, they are invested with especial authority. They become an integral part of conscience and are followed or rebelled against far beyond rational critique and far beyond the immediate action of the pleasure-pain principle. In this manner the great man (or idea) may lift the individual beyond himself. The same process is responsible for the glories of Judaism and Christianity, and for their failures.

Long before such ideas were commonplace, Freud warned that the Communist approach as he saw it in Russia was doomed to disaster. His complaint was not against the Marxist theory of economics, a point on which he studiously avoided comment of any sort on the plea of insufficient information. He was convinced, however, that the communist *promise* was essentially the same as the religious promise. It seemed to him rooted in the same magical hopes and irrational fears that originated in the childhood relationship with the father. Redistribution of the world's material goods could not *in itself* usher in Utopia.[27]

Freud was aware that man can change his overt behavior overnight with a change of leader as the peripheral precepts of the new leader supersede those of the old leader. The change, however, is not so profound as it appears. Partly it is superficial, almost whimsical, because it depends upon the fundamentally irrational love of the leader, with all its basic ambivalences. The main problem is, however, that in any protracted group situation peripheral precepts too distant from the fundamental psychological needs of the individual either tip the balance sharply against the whole leader identification with kaleidoscopic change or are gradually modified to suit the people, with some retention of the leader's ideas.

The Israelites showed a distressing tendency to worship the Golden Calf and required repeated leadership reminders of the universality of God. The second commandment, *Thou shalt not make any graven image,* is a prime example of the role of peripheral leader precepts. For many centuries this commandment has been an awkward intrusion in Jewish and Christian ethics. It can hardly be taken literally in modern times as a prohibition against art forms and has been gradually rationalized away as a figure of speech. Originally, Moses' precept was a direct attack upon the religious practices of the Jews and the primitive peoples around them. By enforcing this commandment, Moses and the prophets forced the Jews away from the then current concretizations into a more spiritual, abstract concept of the deity.[28] Or, at least, the peripheral precept, accepted because of the deep emotional relationship with the leader, worked *in the direction of* greater spirituality.

One may easily observe how leader precepts are partially converted to popular need. For many Jews, ritual became almost as concrete a representation of God as the graven image. Jesus, like the prophets, vigorously protested against ritual and renewed the exhortation toward spirituality. Yet Christianity, too, became encrusted with ritual, with pomp and ceremony. The babe in the manger is clad in gold; the quiet simplicity of Jesus' last supper with his humble disciples becomes a sacrament which the papacy could use as a kind of sanction against rebellious kings. Relics of the saints are sometimes used in a manner hardly different from that in which the fetish is used. Converted "savages" often merely add saints to their pantheon. In the long run, the leader tends to become identified with such of his precepts as reach the hearts of his followers; the rest are sloughed off or modified.

The two-way dynamics between the great man and the people can thus be applied not only to the immediate relationship between them but also to the body of ideas or code of behavior presented by the great man. Up to a point, the leader may *impose* practices, ideas, convictions that are foreign to the people and even to those emotional needs that made identification with him possible, just as the parent as primary model trained the child to specific behavior quite far removed from infantile biological impulses. The acceptable leader cannot go *too* far afield in his initial doctrine, and, in the course of time, his doctrine is revamped to accord with deeper emotional needs. No view of Judaism, Christianity, or communism can omit Moses, Jesus, or Marx. In fact, Freud shows how the precepts of these men became pre-eminent among their followers *because of* identification with them as father images, with the sophisticated detour through the superego. But it is equally absurd to hold Moses, Jesus, and Marx personally responsible for everything in their derivative isms.

The word *idea* has sometimes been used in company with the word *leader* to indicate that the Freudian position does not necessarily imply a keen sense of the *person* of the leader. Freud discusses types of group structure very sketchily, but from the variety of examples he uses one may safely infer that he considers *any* series of individuals actively sharing a common ego ideal as constituting a group. The group may be quite transitory, as in the case of the crowd or mob. The binding factor may be limited to a very narrow segment of the personality, so that the individuals involved operate as a group only in so far as this aspect of their relational ties comes into play. For example, a college alumnus may be quite frantically identified with his alma mater at football games and reunions but indifferent and resistant to requests that require any real sacrifice of time or money. His college, after all, represents only a small segment of his current group identifications. Freud remarks that we all belong to many groups, mentioning such extremely broad classifications as sex, race, and class as well as the more obvious religious groups, nations, clubs, and other organized units.

IDENTIFICATION AMONG MEMBERS OF THE GROUP

Thus far we have discussed the leader as parent image, partly as an external *force majeure* to be loved, hated, depended upon and rebelled against, and taken as model, partly as an internalized force which through the mechanism of identification and introjection becomes the conscience of the individual. Temporarily or more permanently, for good or ill, the leader or the group ideal may be substituted for the superego of the individual. We have seen that the substitution can occur only when the leader somehow answers to the pre-existing inward pattern of the individual, that peripheral precepts of the leader may be obeyed because of the strong emotional tie, but that they are eventually sloughed off or remodeled in closer correspondence to the enduring psychological trends of the individuals involved. The great bulk of psychoanalytic discussion of sociological and historical phenomena even today is oriented around this continuity between the parent-child and leader-follower relationship.

Freud early pointed out, however, that the process of identification in group psychology takes two directions: one toward the leader, one toward fellow members of the group. He observed that members of the group are neither indifferent to one another nor bound together on purely rational grounds. Freud notes in passing that most human tasks require cooperative effort and considers the idea that working together might constitute the basis of group formation. Yet, in practice, groups formed *merely* on the basis of work tend to dissolve when the task is completed, whereas people who have never seen one another, much less worked together on a job, often have vivid emotional ties. Freud's view of the problem was that the members of a group come together in their common *aim*: having substituted one and the same object for their ego ideal (superego), they consequently identify themselves with one another in their ego. They become brothers in Christ, brothers in arms, or, in Freud's concept of prehistory, simply brothers—*i.e.*, sons of the same father. In a very profound sense—actually a quite literal sense, via the mechanism of identification—all the members of such a group are one. Jesus, the son, said, "Whatsoever ye do unto the least of these my brethren ye do also unto me." The passion of Christ could redeem all who believe in him because he became the son of man, one of us, and could therefore take upon himself the sins of the world and expiate them.

Neither Freud nor Freudians have greatly elaborated Freud's early statements on this point, doubtless because the major dynamic tension was described as the one between father and son, and the "sons" were mainly equated with one another. Freud saw the problem essentially in terms of his concept of prehistory, for which most Freudians now substitute family history. The infant's earliest and strongest ties are with the parents and later substitutes. In attention to the concrete details of the patient's life story, the Freudian analyst frequently makes use of sibling rivalry to explain the dynamics of the individual case—but always in relation to the parent. In Freud's group psychology "the sons" are all banded together against the father and in love for the father. Any differentiation among members of the group in their feeling for one another is ascribed to the role played in the parent-child relationship.*

The community of the sons in relationship to the father suggested to Freud the origin of *justice*. Originally, perhaps, there is only the need to satisfy pleasure strivings and the aggressive instinct, gradually modified in terms of reality and of the powerful dictates of the parent-child relationship. Originally, there is unbounded striving among the sons to supplant the father. The banding together of the sons in prehistory, however, led to curtailment of the potential struggle for absolute power and to the sharing of love.

* This emphasis is in contrast to Adler's emphasis on competition among siblings as a primary factor in personality development. Indeed, for Adler the child-parent relationship is essentially competitive, not the direct love and hate rooted in biological need which Freud suggests.

In the contemporary family group, the little child is typically baffled and resentful at the intrusion of siblings into its early fantasy relations with the parents. Sibling rivalry appears very frequently, despite every effort of the parent not to show partiality, not to neglect the toddler in favor of the new infant. Often, indeed, it is the favored child who is most jealous of any attention whatever paid to the siblings, obviously because his personal expectations are higher. A parent lamented recently that he and his wife had tried to be scrupulously fair to both children in the endless minutiae of childhood fairness —with the unfortunate result that although both children in their late teens seemed to have come through to a warm appreciation of their sound upbringing, they *each* retained grievances about the favoritism shown to the other. The problem goes deeper, according to Freudians, than parental tactlessness and also deeper than the more socially oriented rivalry noted by Adler (see pp. 373*ff*.). It resides in the essential relations of child to parent.

The fundamental jealousy is relieved by the mechanism of identification among the siblings, with strict equality before the parent. God, the Church, the army, the law, loves all its children equally and punishes them equally. In so far as this equality can be maintained, the "children" are relieved of competition with one another and can join together wholeheartedly in a fellowship premised on the community of their attitude toward the leader. Many young officers in the American army found the regulation against dining in public with an enlisted man absurd and uncomfortable. With no army tradition behind them, these young men evaluated the situation on the human terms familiar to civilian life. But the regulation seems psychologically sound from Freud's point of view. The officer is commissioned to represent a leadership which must be powerful enough, in one way or another, to make men work together at tasks ranging from extreme dreariness to extreme danger, which they have not chosen themselves. A leadership so great must, even in its delegated authority, show no partiality toward its "children."

The members of the group, the sons, band together in resentment and guilt as well as in love. Freud sees the model of this relationship in the intolerable despotism of the primal father, culminating in his murder by the sons *jointly,* and in the memory of this event buried in the unconscious of the human race. Any psychoanalyst may retain the idea of a basic resentment against authority as an almost inevitable part of infancy. It is easy enough to see in any group situation how the members solidify their interpersonal relations in common protest. *Up to a point,* the "gripes" of army personnel against regulations are almost as useful in bringing the men together as the positive virtues of the regulations. It is kindergarten wisdom in group leadership to permit criticism, even to let it build up in the group—provided, of course, that it does not reach the point at which the essential ambivalence toward the leader turns into mobilized hostility. In the meantime, it serves the purpose of fostering intragroup identification (plus the more familiar "blowing off steam" mechanism described earlier, in which discharge of aggression actually lowers its action potential relative to the constantly present love aspects of the follower-leader relationship). Confronted by a group partly organized *against* him, the skillful leader, using the basic psychological mechanisms described earlier, can often redirect the organized resentment so as to reinforce his own position in an organized way.

Freud devoted especial attention to the problem of handling *guilt* in the group, because for him the death wish toward the father plays a great part in group psychology. Religious ritual among primitive tribes and even in the Western church seems to concern itself quite specifically with the matter by (1) dispersing the guilt among all individuals so that the crime becomes anonymous and hence easier for each person to bear, and (2) ritualistically dedicating a scapegoat to the purpose. In religion it is easy to see the sacred character of the scapegoat—how it is hallowed before its sacrifice can have meaning. The Christian ritual (and the almost sacred hatred of rather primitive Christian peoples for the Jews, who "killed God") lends itself readily to interpretation along these lines. In fact, Freud remarks that Robertson Smith's interpretation of the Christian communion together with instances of savage ceremonies suggesting oral incorporation of the dead leader contributed largely to his (Freud's) initial formulation of the group problem. Christ, the son, is a striking example of the "divine scapegoat," the redeemer-hero who dies for the tragic guilt of all. Many writers[29] have pointed out that the Jews could not have survived their dispersion and socially anomalous position if the attitude of Christians had not been complementary to their own. The chosen people who produced the God of Christendom could also be elected to allay the common guilt of man in the slaying of the Father. Except under Nazism, which was anti-Christian as well as anti-Semitic, Jewry has been preserved *while it was being persecuted* because of its unique role in the group symbolization of problems inherent in the parent-child relationship, as formulated in Western civilization.

Critical Comment

MY COMMENT on this phase of Freud's thinking falls into two distinct parts. The first concerns the role of the *great man as a psychosocial factor in the development of Western civilization.* The second concerns problems attendant upon membership in conflicting "groups."

The Great Man

I have given Freud's concept of the great man especial emphasis, because it is here that Freud's concentration on the Oedipus complex is most closely related to social change. Freud saw very clearly the *to-and-fro* relationship between leader and followers, an insight which Jung and Rank seem to lack. Very possibly the authors whose integrative psychosocial approach I have generally espoused have also neglected an important point. I refer mainly to Kardiner, Erikson, and, above all, Fromm. In a democratic society, we are so busy criticizing the *bad* aspects of authoritarianism and the narrow application of the Oedipus complex as the determining universal principle that many of us have lost sight of the great man. Very often it is *a* great man who sees beyond the everyday problems of adjustment (social homeostasis) and leads a whole society in a new direction. *Freud's* point is that this change does not happen just because somebody is born who is unusually wise or who in himself achieves wisdom and power. It happens because of a specific relationship between the great man and his society.

Even if we grant that Freud overgeneralized the role of the father, it has occurred to me to wonder whether nonauthoritarian ideals for society really allow for the contribution of genius. Native genius may be expected to occur with some regularity—perhaps once in a million births, perhaps much more often; any figure is a wild guess. But genius *potential* is much more common than we think. The decisive factor is the leader's following—that is, the relationship of the rare but expectable great man to other people in his times. If everybody grew up with trust in himself and his own powers of reason, without capacity for blind devotion to a leader, society would doubtless be spared many bloody mistakes, but it would also lose in the creative expansiveness which is *partly* the consequence of the heroic vision of a few, adopted by the many well beyond their own small powers of reason.

One factor in the enormous, aggressive spread of western culture would seem to be the small, patriarchal family group which encourages a sort of deification of the leader on the model of early attitudes toward the parent, *along with a very considerable training in criticism and personal initiative.* Pop is compared with many other fathers. Emulation in a changing society usually requires resourcefulness along lines quite different from those followed by "the old man." This difference cannot be explained by the Oedipus complex alone. It is the resultant of many trends, mainly social and economic—that is, it is focused around institutions rather than personalities. Yet these extremely important modifications do not change the essential power of the Oedipus complex for *our culture.*

Perhaps I am really "original" in pointing out the probable relationship between *our form* of the Oedipus complex and the *socially* fructifying role of the great man. I have elaborated Freud's sentences and tried to bring them into relationship to a psychosocial view he did not have. People are so much for or against the Oedipus complex, so little used to a psychosocial orientation, that I shall perhaps be accused of misreading Freud as well as his critics. It is my earnest belief, however, that, with the perspective of Roheim and Kardiner for critique of Freud's "universals," the Oedipal relationship of the person to the great man in our culture is not only valid for individuals but has implications for culture itself which even the analysts have mainly overlooked.

"Group" Membership

Neither Freud nor Freudians discuss *systematically* the reasons for feeling oneself vividly a part of one group rather than another, or the consequences of vivid simultaneous membership in groups whose effective precepts may be quite different. For example, a recurrent problem in American politics has been loyalty to the federal government *vs.* local loyalties. Where should the loyalties of a professional woman lie—with her job or her family? Should a worker follow his union, his party, his ethnic group, his religion, his personal loyalties to the boss, etc., etc.? On such matters the Freudians are discreetly mute or state openly that their offerings should be considered a relatively small contribution toward the understanding of events largely determined by other forces.

The truth of the matter seems to be that Freud never appreciated the repercussions of group membership in actual behavior. One may accept his analysis of the basic dynamics of group psychology and still point out that at any given moment acceptance of the group ideal entails rather specific action and concretely formulated codes of values. All too often in our complex culture, the same basic dynamics lead us to such gross inconsistencies of behavior as must offend our sense of rational integrity, and often to a baffled sense of guilt as actions conscientiously performed according to one internalized group ideal are heartily condemned as we shift to another group-psychological context. In Freud's Vienna, it was probably easier to dichotomize instinctual drives and "society" and to neglect the specific demands of society in favor of investigation of individual modes of adaptation to relatively unified external requirements. At present, such neglect clearly omits aspects of intrapsychic dynamics which can be understood *only* in terms of differentiated sociological analysis. The Freudians need not abandon their previous views, but I think they must bring themselves to include more systematically in their theorizings the dynamic importance of group structures and attitudes in a mobile society.

COMPLICATIONS AND ELABORATIONS

THUS FAR I have presented Freud's view of the basic dynamics of group psychology in rather gross terms. I have suggested that one may accept the widespread criticism of a broad cultural bias on Freud's part in considering the Judaeo-Christian form of the Oedipus complex as universal. Yet Freud's idea that the adoption of very deep attitudes toward one's group affiliates depends on the image of interpersonal relations *developed* in childhood rather than inborn as a series of discrete "instincts" or purely contemporary reactions to factual conditions was a brilliant innovation, with profound implications for sociology. In broad outline, Freud's analysis of the relationship to the leader and fellow followers seems so fruitful *for our society* that I have warned against dismissing it because it does not have quite the universal validity Freud supposed. I have tried to show how "peripheral precepts" of the leader (or idea) are accepted beyond the immediate psychological needs of the individual and are changed, abruptly or gradually, as the relationship to the leader changes.* I have suggested that subsidiary comments of Freud on this point indicate the mechanism whereby the more enduring aspects of social change occur—those aspects, that is, which depend on the human factor.

In the following pages I have used an informal grouping of my own to suggest factors of constitutional or broadly social origin which complicate the terms of the milieu for individuals in our culture. Such factors may be studied in their own right—in fact *are* so studied by other disciplines, which often tend toward a reductionism of their own along different lines unless brought into some such creative integration of action systems as Kardiner suggests. In these pages they are merely mentioned as factors that a good clinician takes into account in evaluating patients—or, it may be, students, or people in a housing project, employees—any situation in which the individual or a special sub-group becomes the focus of study with the intent of practical help.

In a book on psychoanalysis, I have taken examples mainly from the "patient" category. It is easy to observe the attention of analysts to complicating factors in the individual case. This has long since become routine. Psycho-analysts still tend toward overgeneralization in group studies, but I think this tendency will correct itself as their experience with group problems widens.†

CONSTITUTIONAL VARIATIONS

Constitutional variations may grossly affect the capacity of the individual to act acceptably in accordance with his natural group affiliations. The rape

* I think that shifts within the group identification with one's fellows *could* be analyzed in the same way. In fact, such analysis is constantly made in practice. I mention a single example: R. S. Eissler, "Riots. Observations in a Home for Delinquent Girls," *The Psychoanalytic Study of the Child*, Vol. III/IV, International Universities Press, 1949. So far as I know, identifica-tion with one's fellows is not much used in *theoretical* discussion of social problems by "Freudians," although it is recognized in practice.

† At this writing, it is my observation that psychoanalysts may do a brilliant job in handling group situations or may fumble rather badly. This aspect of psychoanalysis has not been system-atically developed. The work of Aichhorn, Redl, and others may be mentioned as specifically related to group problems of a practical nature (mainly delinquency), but on the whole psy-choanalysis is a Johnny-come-lately in group problems. My own conviction is that, with more practical experience with group problems, analytic thinking will quickly adapt itself to the study of mediate subsystems operating in groups. Furthermore, although I consider the main subdivisions in this section of continuing importance, the treatment given them here has the imbalance of not-yet-codified materials. The imbalance is exaggerated by the fact that I have merely alluded to the generalizations familiar to most of us and have devoted space to aspects of the problems which are just beginning to gain recognition. It would be impossible to provide a balanced review of the new material now rolling in from all sides. My hope is that some discussion of relatively unfamiliar aspects of the problem will suggest similar sidelines to the reader and ways in which they may be integrated with the major psychoanalytic concepts.

and murder committed by the well-intentioned moron in Steinbeck's touching play, *Of Mice and Men,* illustrate the disastrous consequences which may ensue when the individual simply does not understand the external situation adequately. Intelligent work with the feebleminded assumes group feelings similar in nature to our own but recognizes the necessity for simplified demands from the environment.

Superior endowment is less often recognized as a complicating factor in group psychology, but it is clearly important. We have noted that the great man is definable in practice only as he is related to his group. How many simple monks like Mendel have carried on brilliant experiments in the monastery garden without belated recognition as founders of a new science? Too often genius is wasted because it finds no suitable medium of expression or wholesome encouragement. Too often a superlative mind becomes a positive handicap as the child born with an exotically high I.Q. tries to adjust to an educational and social environment geared to a different order of perceptiveness. Many psychologists have encountered at least one such pathetic specimen.

Smaller deviations in endowment have less dramatic but very far-reaching effects, depending upon the nature of the group situation. Freud constantly speaks of constitutional variations as something important which we know little about. He tends to neglect or flatly discount items which social psychologists can now demonstrate with some confidence. The child with an I.Q. of 100 in a private school geared to a median of 120 may have special difficulties in learning beyond those of children with the same I.Q. attending ordinary public schools—partly because the actual teaching methods in the private school may be unsuitable, but also because he easily develops emotional attitudes toward learning as a function of a *group situation* in which he must usually either work harder than his classmates to maintain the schoolwork ideal, and accept attitudes of passive compliance, or transfer his emerging sense of group relationships to other areas in which he may be more successfully aggressive. His academic problems snowball. It is *factually* much harder to learn second-year French if first-year knowledge is hazy. Even with a genuine change of attitude toward work, or in a more suitable school environment, such a child encounters realistic defeats which the sturdiest character would have difficulty in assimilating.

The problem in these cases is quite different from that presented by very bright children whose school achievement is hampered by emotional blocking of a more specialized nature (see the discussion of Freudian views of inhibition in learning, p. 201). The latter can catch up with their classmates easily enough once the block is removed by therapy or spontaneously with a favorable shift in environment and attitude. Freud was aware of native differences in intelligence to the point of making "good intelligence" a prerequisite for successful analysis. He did not understand how level of intelligence is related to social participation in various social groups and that it *therefore* strongly influences the formation of group attitudes. He tended to generalize from clinical observation of inhibition in learning among bright patients to the learning process as a whole, with serious neglect of factors more commonly encountered in the classroom situation.

Variations in "temperament" of constitutional origin doubtless operate in much the same manner. An active, vigorous, restless child becomes a happy leader when his surroundings value this energy and provide suitable opportunities for wholesome group identifications. In a Hopi pueblo or in the polite atmosphere of many well-regulated families and schools, abundant energy almost automatically makes for trouble. Conversely, Ferdinand, the placid bull, rapidly became a symbol for the constitutional deviant who would rather sit and smell the flowers than participate in the belligerent activity of his culture. Again Freud *justly* observed that many people are hyperactive or unduly passive because of specialized neurotic patterns, and again he overlooked the fact that constitutional predispositions in this direction influence the process of adaptation for many individuals. Measures of these "temperamental" factors are even less accurate at the present time than measures of native intelligence level, so that practical application is especially difficult. Nevertheless, the evidence from observation of individuals over a period of time and from controlled research sufficiently demonstrates the principle.[30] Case reports nowadays frequently state that the patient was an energetic child, a sensitive child, or whatever, quite clearly as an independent factor considered in explaining the course of his development.

INCURSIONS OF DISEASE

The epileptic, the encephalitic, the syphilitic, some psychotics, and other sufferers from known "brain" diseases are obviously affected in their group behavior by the disease process itself on a purely organic level. One might add the problems of "the lame, the halt, and the blind" as a general phrase for any organic defect of social importance, even though it makes no direct attack on the brain.

The recognized "psychosomatic" diseases, such as ulcers, asthma, hypertension, may be included because they have a clear somatic component which in some measure follows its own course regardless of the psyche. Only a few extremists have attempted to deny the factor of organic disease in these conditions. There has been a tendency, however, to neglect the psyche altogether once the organic disease is recognized or, conversely, to ignore the disease once the psychological components are observed.

The problem is highly complex. More than any other "school," the Freudians have investigated two areas: (1) the actual production of organic conditions by continued psychological pressures at the unconscious level, and (2) the incorporation of the organic symptoms into psychic function at the unconscious level. An illustration of popular acceptance in regard to the first area is the emergence of reference to "ulcers" as a stock joke even on many comedy programs. The second is less a matter of common knowledge but is very easy to demonstrate. For example, a college student was extremely self-conscious about his hands, which had been severely burned at the age of five and showed unsightly scars. His general behavior was furtive and guilt-ridden; he refused operations which might have improved the appearance of his hands, habitually did not wear gloves, tended to explain any social rejection on the grounds that the person, often a girl, could not tolerate his disfigurement. Probably the original mishap *was* purely accidental. It occurred, however, at a time when the boy was worried about masturbation, and it was interpreted by him as a merited punishment. At the age of 20, he was not consciously anxious about the practice—indeed, he elaborately justified it as a legitimate recourse for a young man denied normal contacts because of his injury. But it requires no great subtlety to relate the boy's reaction to the accidental burn to his masturbation guilt, or to observe that his odd parading of his injury suggests a continuing conflict of the same nature.

I have chosen the foregoing example because the unconscious psychological mechanism is especially clear, and because the social consequences of scarred hands are obviously less drastic than the boy supposed. The case shows the Freudian contribution at its purest. Probably in any case of incursive trauma or disease a similar interpretation takes place which somehow integrates the new factor with the current psychic economy—at an unconscious level by no means identical with the person's conscious judgment of the event. Further comment should be considered as an *addition* to this important observation, not as a substitution.

The *addition* to the major Freudian contribution suggested here is the factor of how the group reacts to the disability of the individual—a factor which Freudian theory often ignores. Probably girls *did* sometimes shudder a bit when the boy's scarred hands approached them. Because he was neurotically timid to start with, his clumsy adolescent advances almost inevitably met with more-than-average rebuff. If we consider the peculiar psychological constellation of this boy's problems at puberty, it is very easy to see how quite mild socially conditioned reactions from people important to him would *confirm* his neurotic reaction and how, contrariwise, good luck in finding a girl who honestly was not troubled by the appearance of his hands might have led him toward spontaneous improvement.

No Freudian would object to this formulation of social factors in an individual case. On the contrary, most of them report such items in the literature, and a great many Freudians actively try to help the patient with a frank organic problem to handle consequent social problems expediently. I know whereof I speak, because many analysts ask my help for a patient with disease or a defect, either in direct placement in schools in which my word might carry weight or in testing aimed at discovering special aptitudes useful in practical orientation.

Many recent Freudian publications stress social factors in the etiology and course of neurosis in a manner which demonstrates widespread incorporation of a new appreciation of the importance of group values into the traditional theory of the libido. There is still, however, widespread distrust of *systematic* consideration of these matters. A concept such as Adler's notion of organ inferiority (pp. 337*f*.)—essentially social in its formulation—is still vigorously repudiated. The Freudian typically prefers to consider each case in its full particularity.

THE STRUCTURE OF SOCIETY

The problem of social structure can be considered from two points of view. One of these considers the essential structure of the wide social group or subgroup within which the individual functions. In the earlier pages of this chapter, the contribution of Freudians toward the understanding of basic character trends of major social groups was discussed, with emphasis on the mechanism of transmission through significant variations in the handling of infancy—*i.e.*, the period during which basic trends are formed and where the unconscious ideals of the parents are most operative.

Comparatively little was said about the second point of view, which considers the nature of subgroups and their relationship to the wider society within which the person lives. In fact, I mentioned in critical comment (p. 154) that Freudian theory largely omits consideration of problems of intergroup dynamics in a society in which most individuals have strong intragroup relations with a variety of subgroups. The problem of any subgroup in relation to the wider group is important—and has been very frequently discussed.

Not so familiar is the problem of the relative homogeneity or heterogeneity of the total society* and the attitudes of the society toward its deviant members or toward minority groups. Many simple, relatively homogeneous societies tolerate or honor individuals whom we would call feebleminded or psychotic; many either show no discrimination against "our" minority groups or give them a peculiar status which protects while it limits. For example the "nigger" who accepts his place is better treated in many respects in some "backward" Southern communities than the Northern Negro, who has formal equal rights but encounters severe prejudice. Certainly the naive "nigger" usually feels the race problem less acutely.

At the other extreme, an essentially heterogeneous society such as New York's allows for an almost endless number of subgroups of various size and structure, so that most individuals can to some extent find a milieu related to their special needs. The structure of any subgroup in the city may be as tight as that of a small town, but the outcast can with moderate resourcefulness find fellowship to his taste and groups in which his behavior is quite acceptable. Very often, of course, there is a kind of utter loneliness or irresponsibility in the city impossible in a more closely knit social environment. We shall see (Chap. 9, pp. 393f.) what Fromm has to say about the disadvantages of the "market orientation," in which interpersonal ties have become extremely diffuse. Erikson also discusses this problem as a difficulty in finding one's own "identity."[31]

Obviously a great many factors that are not primarily psychological enter into the determination of the structure of society: climate, food supply, material inventions, incursive wars and diseases, and, above all, economic and political trends. The diffuseness of society in New York, for example, is partly a matter of urban as against rural or small-town organization, partly of modern capitalism as against feudal, agrarian, or other types of economy, partly of developments peculiar to an *American* city with a special history and special geographical location. Attitudes toward specific subgroups have their general history and their special modifications in any given locality.

In the case studied by Erikson (about to be described), the social problem was not simply that the child was Jewish. His family had become a minority of one in a new community as a means of "bettering themselves financially"—an honored American venture which in this instance meant encountering the mores of a different town and a different class plus the special filtering of the age-old Jewish problem through the child's own family. Every phrase in this sentence implies long-term social structuring which could be conceived as

---

* Roheim discusses this problem at length, but mainly to refute the idea that one may deduce the pattern of a complex culture from study of modes of infant training. He does not make the points I suggest here.

exerting a "force" of its own—in fact, *is* so conceived in much scientific literature and in fiction down to the popular story of the small boy in a new town, the boy from the other side of the tracks, etc., etc. Both science and the popular story have tended to isolate one or two or three aspects of the child's experience and to neglect the others. I applied the adjective "American" to the business venture. "Jewish" business enterprise is an equally familiar stereotype. I might have used the adjective "capitalistic" out of deference to a broader economic interpretation of the action of this family.

INTEGRATION

The case of little Sam,[32] used by Erikson to introduce his book *Childhood and Society,* is presented here in summary to show how a respected Freudian envisages the interlocking of libidinal development (see Chap. 5) with the special factors mentioned above under the headings of constitutional variations, disease, and social structure. Erikson's special theoretical formulations are summarized in the chapter on the genetic process. It would be too much to say that his *formulations* are generally accepted by Freudians, but his discussion of a case can serve in general example. Among practicing analysts as I know them, there would be variations in *emphasis* on one or another aspect of little Sam's problem. At the level of working with an individual case, however, all the factors stressed by Erikson would be observed and utilized in treatment. *It is at the level of the individual case* that the integrative approach appears in the work of any good analyst. I would not be wide of the mark in stating that most analysts distrust *theoretical* approaches to the problem of psychosocial integration because they are inevitably meager in comparison with the integrative understanding of the patient in its shifting, dynamic complexity. The patient's life must be understood in its rich ramifications if the analyst is to offer fructifying interpretation at the moment meaningful for the patient.

Thus, to summarize the most general current psychoanalytic approach toward the problem of integration, I have chosen a case rather than a theory. To show the difference from Freud's early work as regards the approach to psychosocial factors, a comparable case—little Hans—will be briefly discussed.

Erikson's "Sam" was also about five when he came for treatment. He is described as especially bright and energetic by constitutional endowment. He suffers from spells of "dimming out," the kind one sees in epilepsy of the petit mal type. As we have just noted, his family presents a complex social picture, by no means unusual in America. His close family group has special features, like any family, distinctive but not extreme. Our abbreviated recapitulation cannot do justice to the vividness with which Erikson moves from the presenting problem, epileptic attacks, to consideration of the immediate and remote interlocking factors gradually uncovered in therapeutic investigation.

The first epileptic attack followed the death of the child's grandmother and was rather similar to her symptomatology during a heart attack the boy had witnessed. Subsequent early attacks seemed to be precipitated by incidental encounters with "death" (a crushed butterfly, a dead mole). After the grandmother's death, the child had been told that she had gone to Seattle, her home, and he apparently accepted this version of her departure. The encephalogram was not conclusive, since it was a type characteristic of individuals who do have attacks and of others who do not. Thus, at first blush one might suppose a psychogenic origin based on fear of death, precipitated by the actual death of the grandmother. Indeed, the boy admitted later that he knew she had died, although it seems clear that like most little children he frequently "did not know" when it suited him, without having to construct a deliberate lie.

One may fairly ask why one little boy should be so upset by the death of a grandmother, an event which most children take in their stride. The epileptic attacks began to appear under many conditions when the child felt aggressive. Two years later Erikson precipitated a minor spell during therapy by making the child lose consistently at dominoes. The child hit the therapist in anger, then dimmed out. Coming out of the spell, the child arranged the dominoes in rectangular form like a coffin—a pattern he had used with big boxes in the nursery school. At this point the therapist offered the child the interpretation that he thought he had killed the grandmother and must die himself, an interpretation accepted by the child. (The bit of "play therapy" is mentioned to suggest how the child participates in therapy at this age.) Erikson had learned from the mother that the child had probably misbehaved when left alone with the grandmother, although he had been urgently warned against annoying her—and the grandmother had had the heart attack from which she never recovered. By childhood logic, the boy had killed her; his teasing aggression had killed her.

Many psychological interpretations have stopped here. But, again, other such unfortunate accidents have happened without being taken to heart so vehemently by the child. Erikson tells us, further, that the mother, generally kindly and intelligent, had been under special strain prior to and during the grandmother's visit. While she was intensely busy preparing for the visit, the child threw a doll at her, dislodging one of her teeth. The mother hit him back with far more anger than she knew she possessed. The episode is not presented as in itself traumatic but as an epitome of tensions quite pervasive for the child at that period—tensions which were especially difficult because of the fundamental libidinal relationship with the mother. The child himself was in a phase where the talion (eye-for-an-eye) principle was powerful, so that a dramatic event of this nature would easily be seized upon in symptom formation.

Erikson stresses two factors in the situation that go beyond these common interpretations of little Sam's problem. The first is that the *timing* of the repressive and traumatic events was especially unfortunate in relation to the boy's inner development. They occurred just when he was "naturally" most energetic, outgoing, and healthily aggressive, with a "rapid increase in loco-motor vigor, in mental curiosity and in a sadistic kind of infantile maleness which usually appears at the age of three or four."[33] Earlier or later in the child's maturation the same conditions would probably have been far less devastating.

The second factor is the general social situation, mainly as it affected the parents. It was remarked earlier that the family had recently moved to a gentile neighborhood, opening a small store. The parents anxiously impressed upon the vigorous child the need for propriety—the more anxiously because they deeply feared for their own status as Jews in the new environment. Furthermore, the mother was anxious to prove herself to her mother-in-law as a good wife and mother in the Jewish tradition. Thus, over and above the ancient conflicts of the Jews, as discussed by Loewenstein and others, there were contemporary social tensions in the relationship to the community and the past generation in the family.

After this case summary from Erikson, I return to Freud. Freud often confessed his inability to understand why one person develops a neurosis in a given situation and another does not. In general, no complete answer can be given to this question. One can only find an increasing number of significant determinants. Freud felt that the answer must lie in the "quantitative" distribution of energies of various kinds rather than in a necessary qualitative sequence of cause and effect. This opinion has been justified by later developments. The work of contemporary Freudians seems to show with increasing clarity how such variations in "quantity" occur. Little Sam is very like little Hans (see below) or, indeed, any bright, energetic little boy; his parents are human beings, indeed very likable human beings; the social situation is essentially good. But lines of tension are observable in all of these areas, and they become pathogenic for Sam as pressures from many sources mount in an area where he is himself *at the time* especially vulnerable.

In comparison to Erikson's case, I shall mention briefly the case of little Hans,[34] which Freud himself reported in detail in 1909. He describes the analysis (mediated by the father) of a five-year-old boy, Hans, who developed a phobia of horses so extreme that finally he was unable to leave the house. The case has become a classic for Freudians. I think no one can read it without being impressed by the evidence for the Oedipus complex as Freud described it. Certainly I have no intention of criticizing any of Freud's comments on underlying dynamics in the case of little Hans, or his generalizations about little boys—especially in our culture.

Today one may review the case from the point of view presented in the foregoing pages. Why did *this* intelligent, apparently well-cared-for little boy become neurotic in the course of handling a problem common to all little boys? In a postscript written many years later, Freud states that the boy maintained his cure despite the later divorce of his parents. One may suspect that tension between the parents complicated the early problem beyond the circumstances Freud reports.

I am indebted to a psychoanalyst of mainly classical orientation for a remark in conversation which suggests still another line of speculation. If one follows carefully the description of the child's actual life situation, it appears that little Hans was apparently very seriously deprived of "normal" companionship with other children, except for the peasants on his father's estate during the summer. Even adult companionship seems to have been largely confined to his parents and servants. The most important difference between Freud's and Erikson's case descriptions is that in a very long, minutely detailed report on the child, Freud saw no reason to mention his social situation except as it related to the clarification of particular symptoms. Freud understood very well that a protected child might be especially impressed by "sexual" events on the farm which were not considered "sexual" by other people, including the country children; there were some clearly sexual episodes with country children and servants. Freud contrasted the sexually uninhibited quality of the lower classes with the neurotic inhibitions of "cultured" people —and tended to conclude that neurosis was an almost necessary consequence of civilization.

Freud did not see that the isolation of little Hans in the upper-class nursery would isolate the development of the Oedipus complex with almost experimental precision. The child was left pitifully alone with the problem of integrating his emerging biological impulses with the precepts of his society. He had no opportunity to enlarge the pattern of interpersonal relations through the sharing of activities and interests with other people, to relate his sexual feelings and curiosities with other aspects of life. Indeed, sexuality was very sharply condemned, both directly, by castration threat from the mother when he masturbated, and indirectly, through the snobbish attitude of his parents toward the country people and servants who gave him sexual and other types of stimulation. Under these general life conditions, the development of a classical phobia was a very likely denouement, with concentration on phallic strivings directed toward the parental objects, and with hysterical repression.

Since little Hans's nursery was doubtless fairly typical of upper-class Vienna, it is not surprising that Freud found the development of little Hans common enough to serve as a universal model. The contemporary Freudian would not suggest that Hans's neurosis was *caused by* his loneliness, the castration threats, etc. But he might say that the exaggerated focus on the Oedipal problem in the form of a hysterical repression was fostered by the limitations of the family situation in a special society.

CIVILIZATION AND ITS DISCONTENTS

I conclude this chapter with a brief statement of what I am leaving out of my presentation of Freud's views on society—namely, his summary pronouncements on this topic. Many people think of Freud as saying that civilization is essentially the product of conflict and repression; that the inborn instinct of aggression threatens to get the upper hand and requires constant control. In a very general way, this version of Freud is correct, but it is extremely limited. The frequent corollary that people who have constructive hopes for mankind should avoid the "pessimism" of Freud is quite incorrect. When Freud states that civilization grows out of frustration and conflict, he is no more "pessimistic" than Fromm, who says exactly the same thing as part of a highly affirmative view of the human potential (see Chap. 8). Freud hardly goes beyond ordinary common sense in this dictum. If we are completely satisfied with what we have, why would we try for anything new and better—especially if the trial is costly in terms of immediate comfort, and the reward distant?

Freud's position would be pessimistic if he stated that man's sexual and aggressive instincts inevitably doom him to disaster. Freud's point is, rather, that through understanding his own nature, man can begin to guide his destiny. Like so many others, Freud was deeply alarmed by the destructive power of the weapons man has recently invented. In *Civilization and Its Discontents* he writes:

> The fateful question of the human species seems to me to be whether and to what extent the cultural process developed in it will succeed in mastering the derangements of communal life caused by the human instinct of aggression and self-destruction. In this connection perhaps the phase through which we are passing at this moment deserves special in-

terest. [Freud writes shortly after World War I.] Men have brought their powers of subduing the forces of nature to such a pitch that by using them they could now very easily exterminate one another to the last man. They know this—hence arises a great part of their current unrest, their dejection, their mood of apprehension. And now it may be expected that the other of the two "heavenly forces," eternal Eros, will put forth his strength so as to maintain himself alongside of his equally immortal adversary.[35]

I believe that a valid appreciation of Freud's statements concerning broad social problems must be firmly rooted in an understanding of his psychology of the individual. This psychology is extremely complex. Freud was himself modest in his claims for his analysis of social phenomena. The one generalization I have quoted is presented as a rather colorful summary of an intricate discussion of the operation of instinctual trends *within the individual*. The common practice of tearing such generalizations loose from their moorings in clinically oriented reflections leads to misapprehension. I have expressed the opinion that Freud tends to overgeneralize in this area, with insufficient appreciation of the dynamics of systems constellated around the structure and substructures of organized societies. But Freud's guarded generalizations are paltry in comparison with those attributed to him by both his critics and his fanatical adherents. I have tried to show throughout this chapter that, far from being intrinsically inimical to the contribution of "environmentalist" schools, Freud makes possible the kind of *integration* suggested in the introduction to this chapter as a third possibility in the environmentalist-psychological controversy.

SUMMARY

FREUD'S CONCEPT of personality and social attitudes as constructs resulting from experience gave the "culturalists" a valid tool with which to work. Psychological "universals" proceed from the biological equipment of the species *as it encounters life conditions*. The idea that the experience of the infant and young child is of enormous importance in determining basic trends in the psychology of different social groups has been widely adopted. So also has the idea of "unconscious" trends in a culture. Freud's influence in this direction was called *indirect,* because conclusions are often drawn beyond what Freud himself suggested, often beyond what he might approve.

Kardiner's theoretical position and methodology offer a means of integrating biopsychological trends as seen by psychoanalysis with organized social trends in different societies. Kardiner's concept of action systems offers an adaptational approach to problems of integration.

Freud's view of the primacy of the leader-follower relationship in group psychology was presented at first in its "anthropological" implications, the primal horde, followed by a critique and a discussion of Roheim's elaborations, which preserve Freud's sense of the basic psychological unity of mankind (because of common biologically determined experience) but modify his view of the formation of the Oedipus complex to include cultures that differ radically from our own in pregenital experience and the social role of the father.

Freud's own discussion of the implications of leader-follower dynamics, rooted in the early experience of the child in the family, was presented as valuable, at least in our culture. Emphasis was laid on the adoption and adaptation of the *precepts* of the leader (and the great man) in relation to the biopsychological needs of man.

A discussion of "complications and elaborations" was offered, in which I tried to group factors which Freud and Freudians commonly take into consideration in the individual case but which have not yet been codified as part of Freudian psychoanalytic theory. As summary for this section, I used a case described by Erikson, a "Freudian," in his introduction to a book aimed at showing the intricate relationship between the emerging biological needs of the child, pretty much as Freud saw them, and the special circumstances of his life in a society.

Freud's own generalizations about social problems were mentioned briefly, mainly with critique of those who take them out of context and overgeneralize beyond the guarded generalizations of Freud.

Critical Comment

FREUD'S ANALYSIS of group psychology in terms of leader-follower relationships has the great merit of linking adult attitudes with those which were *developed* in childhood rather than with a series of more or less special social "instincts." Both Kardiner and Roheim have shown that the specific attitudes that Freud describes are more closely related to the specific form of family structure in Judaeo-Christian society than Freud realized. Recognition of this fact does not vitiate the importance of Freud's analysis for most of the group problems we encounter in our own culture. As a generalization, Freud's position requires still further generalization, doubtless with more emphasis on pregenital factors in the formation of the Oedipus complex, as Roheim suggests.

A defect of Freud's and Roheim's position is that too little attention is paid *in a systematic manner* to what I have called "complications and elaborations." Kardiner has tried to make the special institutions of a society an integral part of his study in a manner which seems to me highly suggestive in theory and basic methodology. Kardiner's radically cross-cultural approach, focused on basic problems of *social* organization, is difficult for most of us to understand. When applied to our own culture, it seems oversimplified—in fact, *is* oversimplified, as Kardiner himself emphasizes. New ways of generalization require bold reorganization of current systems of ideas, and one can hardly hope that it will be entirely correct at the first try.

Thus, in discussing group psychology *in our own culture*, I have tried to summarize the kinds of complicating factor Freudian analysts consider in practice. I used a case presented by Erikson to show how interpretation is modified by appreciation of constitutional and environmental factors seen in close interaction with libidinal development. This kind of integration *in the individual case* is perhaps more immediately useful to clinicians than is Kardiner's study of the dynamics of societies, and it arouses less controversy. It seems to me clear that both types of study are needed. It is unclear to me why either should be rejected in principle, although we are entitled to quarrel with specific conclusions and to suggest better methods of investigation.

Erikson goes on to describe eight stages of life, with specific attention to how the individual relates to society in each. After some hesitation, I have reserved report on these stages to Chapter 5, on the genetic process, because Erikson sees them primarily in terms of

needs intrinsic to the individual.* They seem to be an extension of the libido theory and are suggested as probably universal. Although he is much more consciously alert to the importance of social conditions than most Freudians, Erikson does not seem to envisage the terms of the milieu as susceptible to codification in themselves, in relation to personality—*i.e.*, in terms of action systems constellated in various ways, with different types of interaction, as suggested by Kardiner. In *Childhood and Society*, Erikson proposes no methodology for group studies, and he uses alien cultures more to illustrate how adjustment varies with cultural conditions than to suggest that basic personality needs shift with basic differences in the structure of the culture. Thus, to my mind, Erikson's book is extremely valuable for its suggestions about the terms of *our* milieu, but it does not cut so deep into the general problem of the dynamics of societies as the work of Kardiner.

If I may be permitted a personal comment on *areas of inquiry* neglected by all these schools, I return first of all to examination of the development and role of the "nonsexual" systems (*cf.* my comment at the end of Chap. 3). In many cultures babies are swaddled, held on the mother's hip, or in various ways prevented from exercising free motility apart from mother. In our culture, motility is generally rather free (in the crib), with early separation from the mother. In fact, a psychologist, Skinner, devised a "box" in which the infant can be left in comfort without hampering clothing and blankets, although presumably the parents fondle it and play with it as usual. I have no intention of even speculating on what these very impressive cultural differences in early motility ex-

* I came to a contrary decision as regards the placement of Sullivan's outline of stages of development, for the same reason. Sullivan does not present his stages as "needs" but as conditions for aspects of acculturation.

perience mean in terms of later personality development. To describe Russian culture in terms of the effect of *swaddling* infants* is not only one-sided but premature as to the significance of such practices for personality development. More information is needed about the dynamics of individual development in this area before firm conclusions may be drawn concerning the role of variations in motility patterns for varying social constellations. The problem will be discussed further in the next chapter, on the genetic process. But this area of early experience certainly merits further study.

Another area in which systematic cross-cultural investigation seems especially needed is the period of childhood from five or six to puberty, what Freud calls the latency period. Two aspects of this period are of especial interest: the sexual manifestations and the child's relationship to his milieu. According to Freud (see Chap. 5), infantile sexual development, so crucial for the development of character, comes to a temporary resolution at the age of five or six and remains latent until the biological changes of puberty reopen the old problems. Freud suggests that this latency period is biologically determined by a bimodal sexual development in the human species. The sexual aspects will be dealt with in the next chapter. Here the child's relationship to his milieu will be discussed.

It may well be that there is no basic change in the general configuration of the deep personality after the age of six, or at least that the special problems and tensions emphasized by Freud enter a phase of relative stability. But this is precisely the period during which the child seems to be learning about his culture most avidly. Partly his learning is thrust upon him by school and by increased

* I cite the reference to G. Gorer (*The People of Great Russia,* London: Cresset Press, 1949) with some hesitation, because Gorer is himself more cautious in the matter than I imply.

participation in the chores of the household. Partly, however, the little boy explores his world very actively, especially the world he shares with his contemporaries.

The early school age is inarticulate, probably even to itself. Its aims are diffuse and seem to be related more to the culture than to the individual. A little girl, aged eight, wanted to be a maid so that she could make pies—an interesting sidelight on a middle-class urban home, in which the appealing feminine activities were primarily the province of the maid. Little boys often want to be firemen or policemen, garage mechanics, fishermen, flyers—an assertion of masculinity on broad cultural terms. Identification with the father's profession, or rebellion against it, is much more characteristic of the very young child or the adolescent.[36] What teacher says, what the gang says, becomes much more important in middle childhood than what the parents say. Indeed, Mummy is likely to be something of a nuisance much of the time, with her eternal fussing about health and safety and manners. Dad is valuable mainly for direct support and for status in the *boy's* world, although father and son often develop a comradely, man-to-man relationship during these years quite different from the more queasy adulation and rebellion of early childhood and adolescence.

It seems safe to suggest that there is in our culture (and probably in many others) a rather clear-cut period—roughly between the ages of six and twelve—during which the child is extremely responsive to the contours of the world around him and to its *culturally organized* impact of indoctrination. The important factor culturally must be how this period of direct indoctrination is handled. Some cultures—perhaps especially the subculture of psychologically oriented American parents—tend to soften the break as much as possible, both by giving the child more responsibility in earlier years and by babying him along in school. Other cultures simply hurl the youngster into independence, like the English upper classes—or like the Balinese, who give the boy a water buffalo and a knife and expect him to make out pretty much on his own.

There has been very little cross-cultural study of this age period, although any fairly intensive study of a single culture includes some account of the activities of the "juveniles." It would seem to me that classification of the ways in which the child's first eager interest in the world beyond the family is handled by different cultures would add greatly to an understanding of basic social attitudes as well as of important aspects of individual development. Surely some of the puzzling discrepancies between a warm, permissive infancy and an anxious, driving adulthood[37] might be clarified by recognition of a culture pattern which demands too much of the older youngster.

We may *guess* that highly institutionalized practices, however cruel, may be psychologically more tolerable, because the child expects them and suffers with his kind, than unstructured situations in which the child is somehow expected to behave like an adult but is given spotty or erratic training—in which he is given an adult pattern without appropriate bridges between his six-year-old ignorance and the complexities of adult know-how.

Such situations occur all too often in our own culture. The best of schools devoted to specific training cannot supply the over-all comprehension of adult requirements necessary to the child in this phase of his growth, partly because the school is limited in its impact, partly because the inevitable continuities for the emotional life of the child are with the immediate family, which has thus far provided its setting. Thus, *how the family fits into the culture* must be an important aspect of the provision the culture makes for the way in which the youngster relates his early attitudes to the new concerns of the broader, less personalized world he now encounters.

Clearly, my intention is not to recommend a school-age series of cultural conditions as *rival* determinants to the intrafamily conditions emphasized by the Freudians. The latter must have a systematic effect on the developing personality of the order described by the analysts (however faulty their judgments may be in detail concerning a given culture). It must be this already rather developed personality which reacts to the mores and attitudes characteristic for handling the six-to-twelve-year-olds. Furthermore, there is not a clear break at the age of six in any culture. The young child remains partly with his family, is partly delivered over to other institutions, is partly allowed freedom for relatively unstructured exploration. We cannot expect to arrive at a neatly universal explanation of basic personality in relation to culture by adding oversimplified codifications of middle-childhood experience to oversimplified codifications of babyhood. But we might hit the point more exactly in cultures that happen to be well systematized on the matter of training children at this age, and we would be more aware of important trends in cultures that defy easy codification along these lines.

A third area of inquiry is the cultural attitude toward the "self image" of the individual. Since I have not yet adequately explained what I mean by this term (the quotes here refer to my own rather special usage), I can only vaguely indicate the kind of inquiry I have in mind. A recurrent critique throughout this book has to do with the systematization of the self image, which I think is too far neglected in Freudian theory and *overstated* with some naiveté in the nonlibido theories (Part III). Indeed, I shall suggest (see Chap. 8) that these theories might fairly be called, in more positive recognition of their special quality, psychologies of the self. Doubtless everyone has some sense of being an individual— a sense rooted in deeply integrative biological patterns: in the interosystems, with primitive connections to drive systems, to use the vocabulary presented in Chapter 3; in what other people think of us—our "role" behavior. Freud shows how the latter derives from the former, via intrafamily relationships, and surely he is *mostly* right about basic dynamics, despite the plentiful corrections introduced in this chapter. He explains well how some attitudes originate and continue; how they attain the status of an ideal for which the person will fight to the death; how a person kills himself for his "honor."

But Freud does not relate this behavior to the concept of the "self," except as a function of the superego, definitely related to intrafamily experience. I shall try to suggest that the ego ideal (Freud's term, little used after he introduced the term "superego" and closely related to it), Horney's "idealized image of the self," the "self" of Fromm, and, in a different way, the "self" of Jung, the "will" of Rank and even the "self dynamism" of Sullivan—that all these versions of the "self" fail to take into account the role of the individual "self" in a particular culture. I shall suggest (following Fromm, with reservations) that it is *in our culture*—capitalist-democratic, if you like, but recent and still mainly American—that the "self-image" becomes a highly individual construct of enormous psychological importance. In an established democratic society, organized on the principle of geographic and social mobility, the "ego ideal" must be quite distant from the actual precepts of the parents or of limited, well-structured social groups. It must depend increasingly on what "I" am as a single individual. Thus, Horney's "idealized image of the self" be-

comes an important *pathological* clinical entity which cannot be fully explained as a direct derivative of the superego; thus, Fromm's concept of the "marketing orientation" becomes significant—an orientation in which the "I" is continuously modified by what the group demands, without inward stabilization. In later comment on these authors (Part III) I shall take a "cultural" line in critique, addressed to the problem of the role and function of the "self-image" *in our culture.*

Very likely the reader has not been able to follow these comments, which depend upon later exposition. I present them here as advance notice of a position I shall try to make clear: the *idea* of the self (self image) is a construct, not a biological given. Not only its content but also its "tightness" as a dynamic system depends upon the nature of the culture. I shall constantly rely on this position in my efforts toward integration of the various psychoanalytic schools.

Perhaps I can sum up my position in this way: Freud's social theory overgeneralizes the form of the Oedipus complex as it appears in our culture. A parallel comment is that Horney overgeneralizes the form of the "idealized image" as it appears in our culture.

I have suggested three areas in which further inquiry is needed: the role of the "non-sexual" systems in early personality development; opportunities offered to the older child in transition from the predominantly intra-family environment of babyhood to the requirements of adult society; the growth and function of the self image, especially as related to varieties of social structures and substructures.

These points still imply the relatively independent problems of social structures as Kardiner sees them in theory, and as sociologists, economists, and political scientists see them. I think they extend the specific contribution of an approach oriented toward the individual (psychoanalysis) in a manner which may make it more relevant to the work of other disciplines, less biased toward a view of personality determinants which avoids the universality of special instincts but which too often stops at the cradle.

The view of systems requires attention to the wider social systematizations within which the individual develops and functions. The relative modifiability of such systematizations must be seen in relation to their developmental and sustaining role in relation to the systematizations inherent in man's biological equipment. Insight into the reciprocal relations between the individual and his society must derive from greater insight into the emergent adaptive capacities of the human organism in intimate relation to its own past as a creature able to store up and use its experience through "group" symbols, "group" codifications reworked by each person through many generations.

[1] Cf. H. M. Lynd, *England in the Eighteen-Eighties*, Oxford University Press, 1945, pp. 70f.

[2] R. Benedict, *The Chrysanthemum and the Sword*, Houghton Mifflin Co., 1946.

[3] G. Roheim, *Psychoanalysis and Anthropology*, International Universities Press, 1950, Introduction.

[4] A. Kardiner, *The Psychological Frontiers of Society*, Columbia University Press, 1945, p. 1.

[5] ———, *The Individual and His Society*, Columbia University Press, 1939.

[6] *Ibid.*, pp. 471ff.

[7] A. Kardiner, *The Psychological Frontiers of Society*, p. 34.

[8] *Ibid.*, Chaps. 3, 4.

[9] *Ibid.*, Chaps. 5-9.

[10] *Ibid.*, pp. 257f.

[11] *Ibid.*, p. 30.

[12] *Ibid.*, p. 100.

[13] *Ibid.*, p. 85.

[14] S. Freud, *Group Psychology and the Analysis of the Ego*, Boni & Liveright, n.d., p. 80.

[15] *Ibid.*, p. 112.

[16] S. Freud, *Totem and Taboo*, in *The Basic Writings of Sigmund Freud*, Random House, Modern Library, 1938.

[17] R. Money-Kyrle, "Varieties of Group Formation," in G. Roheim (ed.), *Psychoanalysis and the Social Sciences*, Vol. II, International Universities Press, 1950, pp. 313-329.

[18] G. Bychowski, *Dictators and Disciples*, International Universities Press, 1948.

[19] O. Fenichel, *The Psychoanalytic Theory of Neurosis*, W. W. Norton & Co., 1945, p. 97.

[20] G. Roheim, "Introduction: Psychoanalysis and Anthropology," in G. Roheim (ed.), *Psychoanalysis and the Social Sciences*, Vol. I, International Universities Press, 1947, pp. 16ff.

[21] ———, "The Oedipus Complex, Magic and Culture," in G. Roheim (ed.), *Psychoanalysis and the Social Sciences*, II, pp. 173-228.

[22] ———, *Psychoanalysis and Anthropology*, pp. 489ff.

[23] *Ibid.*, pp. 488f.

[24] *Ibid.*, p. 7.

[25] Cf. T. M. Newcomb, *Social Psychology*, The Dryden Press, 1950, pp. 650ff.

[26] S. Freud, *Civilization and Its Discontents*, Hogarth Press, 1930, pp. 81ff.

[27] ———, *New Introductory Lectures on Psycho-Analysis*, W. W. Norton & Co., 1933, pp. 241ff.

[28] ———, *Moses and Monotheism*, Alfred A. Knopf, 1939, pp. 177ff.

[29] Cf. R. M. Loewenstein, *Christians and Jews*, International Universities Press, 1951.

[30] M. Fries, "Research in Problems of Infancy and Childhood" (by Malcove), *The Psychoanalytic Study of the Child*, Vol. I, International Universities Press, 1945, pp. 405-414; R. A. Spitz, "The Importance of the Mother-Child Relationships During the First Year of Life," *Mental Health Today*, 1948, 7:7-13; etc. See Chap. 5.

[31] E. H. Erikson, *Childhood and Society*, W. W. Norton & Co., 1950.

[32] *Ibid.*, pp. 21ff.

[33] *Ibid.*, p. 27.

[34] S. Freud, "Analysis of a Phobia of a Five-year-old Boy," *Collected Papers*, Vol. III, Hogarth Press, 1925, pp. 149-295.

[35] ———, *Civilization and Its Discontents*, pp. 143f.

[36] Cf. E. Ginzberg, S. W. Ginsburg, S. Axalrad, and J. L. Herma, *Occupational Choice*, Columbia University Press, 1951, pp. 60ff.

[37] Cf. C. Kluckhohn, "Some Aspects of Navaho Infancy and Early Childhood," in G. Roheim (ed.), *Psychoanalysis and the Social Sciences*, I, pp. 37-86.

Chapter Five

THE GENETIC PROCESS

THE GENETIC PROCESS is one of the most important aspects of Freudian theory, perhaps *the* most important in differentiating the Freudian from other psychoanalytic schools. With his essentially biological orientation, Freud believed that psychological phenomena should be traced back to their origin in the growth of the organism in its relations with the outside world. Furthermore, his clinical investigation of patients revealed consistently the persistence of infantile material—unconscious, but almost unchanged and very much alive. In fact, their neurotic symptoms appeared to be directly related to such material. Variations in adult behavior became understandable in terms of variations in the type of infantile problem still urgent for the personality, and how it was handled. Even the *mode of handling* such problems adopted by the patient seemed to hark back mainly to techniques developed before the sixth year. The history of the early years, therefore, became the cornerstone of Freudian theory.

Three concepts are basic to the understanding of the genetic process in relation to later dynamics: *stages* of infantile development, *fixation*, and *regression*. By virtue of his biological equipment, the child goes through a fairly regular progression which depends on the coming into prominence of various organ systems. The psychological aspects of the very earliest stages, birth and primary narcissism, are relatively generalized. The mouth, the excretory organs, and the genital organs successively appear to become the *foci* of more specific *distributions of psychic energy*—that is, of the libido. These stages may be roughly assigned to age levels, much as sitting, creeping, and walking may be expected with some regularity at a given age, although, of course, with a considerable range of individual variation as to the exact date. They may be thought of as due in large part to a maturational process.

At each stage, the personality attains a considerable degree of *organization*, so that contributing elements are not freely movable independently. An analogy may be drawn with the patterns of motor development, which have been carefully studied by "psychologists." Creeping involves a highly complex organization of movements which tends to be perfected as such before walking is attempted and which may even interfere temporarily with the development of the new organization. For some time, the toddler is likely to revert to all fours under special stress. Furthermore, as McGraw[1] and others have shown, such patterns have a sort of maturational timing. It is impossible to train a child to walk before he is "ready" for it, but once ready for walking he can be taught skating and other complex related activities very easily—apparently more easily than after the walking pattern is firmly established. The same observation holds for embryological development.[2] Apparently there is a tide in the affairs of babies as well as men, which, taken at the flood, leads on. In the psychic realm as well as the physical (the two are very closely related), Freud points out fairly definite stages of development during which the mental and emotional growth of the child is focused around the emerging sensitivity of the major erogenous zones of the body.

The various stages of development naturally show a great deal of overlapping and interaction with one another. *No phase is ever entirely given up.* Freud uses the simile of an army which, as it advances into new territory, leaves strong garrisons en route serving both to forward supplies and to offer a place of retreat in the event of insuperable difficulties ahead. The tendency of the personality to cling to one stage of development is called *fixation*. The advancing army may come to a halt quite soon, digging itself in solidly, sending forth emissaries in disguise or in pretended friendship. Or the army may hold titular sway over the whole country, fearing to exact real tribute and homage, ready at any moment to retreat to its position of safety.

The process of return under adverse circumstances to the point of fixation is called *regression*. The neurotic does not break along the lines one might expect from the nature of the difficulties of the current adult environment. Rather, the libido retreats, at least in part, to an earlier stage, which then becomes "overinvested with energy" to the point at which the ego can no longer handle it in an integrated, mature fashion. Such regression does not mean that a man of thirty who develops an obsessional neurosis behaves like a child of two. It means that the impulses and fears proper to that period regain such power that the weakened ego cannot cope with them in the customary adult fashion but must resort to special devices—that is, to symptom formation. The kind of symptom that appears reflects (usually as a sort of unconscious compromise) the impulse whose expression is so greatly feared. It is in this manner that Freud finds it possible to explain the bizarre nature of many neurotic symptoms. Through repression, the infantile material remains unassimilated and timelessly vigorous. Through regression it gains such power that the maintenance of repression exacts more and more effort from the developed ego. The effort must be focused with increasing narrowness on control of the earlier points of fixation of the libido.

These schematic sentences have been discussed in Chapter 3 and will receive further explanation and discussion in the later chapters on dynamics and pathology (Chaps. 6 and 7). They are presented here for orientation toward the long chapter on early childhood.

THE TRAUMA OF BIRTH; ANXIETY

WE COME NOW to the actual story of child development. Rank (see Chap. 14) emphasized that the process of birth itself is a very dramatic—indeed, a traumatic—occurrence, fraught with consequences. Freud criticized the details of Rank's theory,[3] pointing out that the infant's perception of his own birth can scarcely be accurate enough to allow recognition of similar occurrences later on in the highly specific manner Rank suggests. Freud further remarked that variations in the difficulty of birth *might* have the implications suggested by Rank—or they might not: an empirical problem which ought to be empirically studied.*

In more general terms, however, Freud considered the birth trauma as the prototype of later anxieties, the first experience of severe threat, which

---

* It is characteristic of Freud that he urged not only empirical study of variations in the human birth process but also comparative studies among mammals and contrasts with nonviviparous birth. His broad biological orientation cannot be too often stressed, especially since it is usually lacking in his followers. Many of Freud's speculative generalizations are based upon the biology of his time and now seem "wrong." They are too easily accepted or rejected in a different frame of reference toward biological science. Collaborative study oriented toward problems currently acute for the biologist and the psychologist is one of the very promising developments of our time.

could provide the pattern for subsequent reactions.* It is characteristic of Freud that he could not accept even anxiety as a simple fact but felt that it must be biologically explicable. Realizing that the infant can have no conceptual appreciation of his passage through the birth canal, Freud pointed to the sudden *flooding* of the immature nervous system with sensory excitation and to the prominence of motor discharge, primarily through the respiratory and cardiac systems, as the foetus begins to breathe independently and to rid itself by increased heart action of the toxic products accumulated in the bloodstream during birth. Later anxiety states typically involve a similar sense of being flooded by stimuli, difficulties in breathing, and rapid heart beat. In short, they seem very much like the neurological state of the newborn child.

The first experience, therefore, may create an enduring pattern of reaction to "danger." The newborn infant can scarcely be afraid of death as such, or of other specific hazards. Any subsequent happening, however, that suggests danger may act as a signal for the reinstatement of this first overwhelming distress. Quite limited problems in later life may thus provoke generalized anxiety by a process which one is tempted to call "conditioning" in the broadest sense of the term.

The birth trauma has not received much attention in recent years. It remains on the books in theoretical disquisition but is otherwise neglected. Probably the reason for neglect is that the concept cannot be used in practical analysis. The patient cannot reconstruct how he felt at birth. The birth trauma as such is untreatable. It joins "constitutional factors" in the limbo of concepts of theoretical importance which cannot be handled in practice and hence tend to be ignored. A useful observation has been made by Greenacre that children born prematurely often show a generalized hypersensitivity to sensory stimulation even after they have caught up to normal development and may in treatment as adults show a large amount of generalized anxiety which escapes analysis along the usual lines. The nervous system of the premature infant, Greenacre points out, is even more subject to "flooding" by stimuli it cannot master than that of the full-term infant.[4] This observation is in line with Freud's idea of birth experience as the prototype of anxiety due to excess stimulation. It offers some support to Rank's idea that the type of birth is important (which Freud considered possible), although Greenacre selected subjects whose early months were hazardous far beyond the ordinary, and she, too, specifically rejects the conceptual elaborations of Rank's theory.

At the present time, therefore, Freud's idea of birth itself as the first "conditioning" experience of anxiety, of catastrophic danger, retains its original speculative value. It has not been empirically confirmed and has been largely ignored in practice.

* The following discussion derives mainly from *The Problem of Anxiety* (1926).

PRIMARY NARCISSISM;
OMNIPOTENCE; MAGICAL
THINKING

THE NEWBORN INFANT is presumably without clear consciousness of the outside world. In the phrase of William James, the baby's world is probably a "booming, buzzing confusion," with sharp foci of awareness developing from acute bodily sensations: hunger, cold, discomfort, and gradually positive longings for the pleasurable sensations, among which oral gratification soon takes a prominent position. At first, the baby distinguishes imperfectly, if at all, between what is himself and what is the outside world. This state Freud calls "primary narcissism." The infant loves himself with supreme egotism—but only because he is largely unaware of any difference between himself and other people or the "things" in his environment. Freud uses the term "objectless" to describe the condition in which no relation to "objects" yet exists. (We shall see that "object" in psychoanalytic parlance almost invariably means a *person* rather than a thing.)

The ministrations of the mother to the baby's general comfort are too complex and varied to be perceived clearly at first. Above all, they do not require the baby's active cooperation. He is uncomfortable, and then he becomes comfortable. He may early make an associative bond between his own crying and this happy change in circumstances. Purposeful crying, however, must at first involve a purely magical interpretation of its effectiveness. The infant can scarcely be expected to grasp the intermediary reality step of setting in motion external forces to operate in his behalf. He does not even know that external forces exist. The first formulation must be simply cry-relief. The cry itself must be conceived as the effective agent, in so far as anything is "conceived" at that stage.

This primitive connection was pointed out by behaviorist psychologists under the label of conditioning. At one time mothers were advised to let their babies cry (if the infants were physically comfortable) in order to prevent the formation of this undesirable stimulus-response bond—until it was observed that repeated experience of helpless frustration was probably itself poor conditioning and that babies need more than physical comfort. The infantile formulation received attention from analysts also and was given a label by Ferenczi: *omnipotence*.

Ferenczi[5] especially stressed the developmental importance of the stage during which, according to the child, events occur because of his cry (later his "hallucinatory" image of the breast, his word, or even his wish) without the mediation of objective activity in a "real" world. Magical thinking, so often observed in the young child and in primitive peoples as well as in the insane—and in much "normal" thinking—thus has its roots in the earliest phases of actual experience. Unaware of the steps intervening "in reality" between his own feelings and actions (the two are merged) and later events, the infant naturally assumes a quasi-causal connection. What he feels and does has unlimited power. Techniques of "real" mastery over objects are very laboriously acquired, both on the level of motor coordination and on the level of intellectual appreciation of the external situation. We shall consider a little later how they are acquired. Just now the point emphasized is the child's primitive "omnipotence," which seems to be really a rather poetic statement of a view of the world the baby could hardly avoid.

These sentences sound adultomorphic and as if we were reading into the child the concerns of a philosopher. Let us remind ourselves once more that the newborn infant simply does not distinguish between himself and "reality." His inner experiences assume a patterning far in advance of his insight into the objective structure of his surroundings. In every specific situation, the *child's* experience is one of an immediate bond between his inner pattern and the external event. One need not posit conscious generalization to arrive at the concept of infantile omnipotence. In so far as a child has expectations, they must be of this order. It is appreciation of reality limitations and expedient use of reality means that requires sophistication.

Critical Comment

FERENCZI'S term *omnipotence* expresses the *generalization* of the infant's expectation. The concept of the conditioning process explains quite neatly how the infant comes to cry "in order to" achieve his ends, but the explanation tends to connote a fragmentary and mechanical event. The value of the concept of omnipotence is that it highlights the continuous action of the child's expectation in relation to everyday circumstances.

We can understand the curious behavior of children far better when we see that *for the infant* what he wants or fears always has immediate consequences, that for him thinking and feeling are largely equated with doing and with outside events. This formulation orders a host of phenomena which otherwise remain discrete.

Ferenczi's term also connotes, for adults, a *gratifying* sense of personal power, and one may wonder whether the infant's emotional state is really correctly described. The *flavor* of the word "omnipotence" is misleading. It is in curious contrast, superficially, with the concept of infantile helplessness so heavily stressed by Adler, Horney, and Freud himself. Also, it accords ill with our earlier discussion of infantile anxiety states and the catastrophic flooding of the immature nervous system by excitation which it cannot master.

An example may clarify the problem. The other day I watched a little boy of about four with his parents at the beach. The father repeatedly whirled the youngster through the air, ignoring the mother's protest. Each time the child seemed abjectly terrified—white and sobbing. The father said, "Oh, he likes it . . . he ought to get tougher." And truly, in a matter of seconds after he was restored to his feet, the child half-laughingly pummeled the father. "I can beat you up," he cried. "I am the biggest man in the world."

It is most unlikely that the boy felt gratifyingly omnipotent while he was being whirled around, or that younger infants feel constructively all-powerful during fits of paroxysmal crying. But they have in a sense a *reserve* of gratifying omnipotence feeling that is denied to the mature adult. The terrified child can solve his terror by beating up his father and becoming the biggest man in the world without reference to the reality item of his miniature stature. His will *is* his deed. Later on, if he has developed normally, he will be forced to consider his actual chances of vanquishing a man five times his size, and he will recognize that they are poor. In this sense, reality is "really" quite a come-down from being the biggest man in the world whenever you so will.

Thus, the child retains the fantasy not so much of a golden age when he always felt powerful as of a period when complete power was at his command. For the young child (and for such childishness as survives in the unconscious of all of us), opposites can stand side by side. Either may usurp the picture completely, like the shift in an ambiguous figure. Both may become simultaneous determinants in the later compromises effected by the ego (reality principle). We saw in Chapter 2 how the same neurotic behavior can unconsciously express two entirely opposite unconscious needs. If mature appreciation of reality helps the little boy in our example to limit his terror (I won't be dropped. A tumble on the sand wouldn't hurt much), it also limits his sense of power (I am not the biggest man in the world. I cannot beat up my father).

PASSIVITY; LOSS OF LOVE

Freud points out that the human infant is born more immature than most mammals* and for some time lives in a state of passive dependence. His state is almost comparable to the kangaroo young in the mother's sac, except that the human mother plays a more active role and the environment is actually constantly changing. The early postnatal period may be seen almost as a continuation of the embryonic stage. The chief need of the neonate is simply

* The importance of this biological fact had been recognized, of course, by many authors prior to Freud. It is stressed by other psychoanalytic schools also. Doubtless the superior adaptability of the human species is directly related to the absence of inborn modes of reaction to complex external circumstances and to the long period of relatively flexible learning.

relief from all stimulation. At first his wish is not so much for gratification as for relaxation of tension, for sleep. Long before he can experience the competitive helplessness stressed by Adler (which requires capacity for comparison in relation to "objects"), the baby "longs for absolute passivity."

Following his general practice of trying to understand later developments as partial reinstatements of earlier conditions, the mystical longing for union with the infinite (or at least something far beyond ourselves) which probably all of us experience at times Freud interprets as derived from the objectless stage of infancy. He uses the term *oceanic* to describe the feelings of the infant at this period and emphasizes the *passivity* of the neonate both as regards giving itself over to quiescence and sleep and as regards the infantile terrors which must be passively endured the moment they overstep the very limited abilities of the immature nervous system to engage in any sort of patterned reaction to noxious stimuli. This early state is recaptured in later life in some states of ecstasy and of panic and is characteristic of many psychotics who have largely regressed to the early narcissistic state. Adults smile as the absolute terror or misery of the baby gives way to gurgling pleasure or sleep in a matter of minutes. His distress seems unimportant. However, repeated experience of absolute terror constitutes evidence to the baby that absolute catastrophe does exist. It is of no importance *to the baby* that his mother lets him cry "for his own good" and that he is not threatened by any "real" danger. The poignancy of later fears often dates back to the objectless fear of infancy.*

The yearning for release from unpleasant stimulation and from desire is, of course, very closely associated with the mother. At first the process takes the form of *primary identification;* that is, the infant does not distinguish clearly between the mother's breast (then the face and gradually the person of the mother) and his own self. Later on, as we shall see, he comes to identify with the mother *secondarily,* as an external object which is nevertheless taken into his inner world. Also, he later develops more or less rational attitudes toward her as a person in her own right. The early relationship remains of

* Combat neurosis, when the danger is real enough, is most likely to break out when the soldier has had to sit and "take it," or when his adult ego is insufficiently involved with his duties. Ground crews, for example, helplessly subjected to bombardment during the menial tasks of caring for the planes were prone to a more regressive type of nervous collapse than pilots engaged in even more dangerous enterprises, partly because the duties required of the latter kept them oriented toward *active mastery* of a limited external reality as against the reinstatement of infantile passivity. Also, the greater romance and prestige of flying and the more intense "object-relations" typically established among the members of the crew on a mission kept the more mature ego development of the fliers at a constant level.[6] Any officer knows the value of keeping his men *busy* under danger, even when the work assigned can be of no real assistance. Glamorizing the Sea Bees and giving them guns for self-defense definitely improved their effectiveness as construction workers. According to Freud, such techniques are effective because they encourage the ego-orientation of later genetic development and prevent reversion to the early objectless state we have described.

profound importance, however, as suggested by the power of the mother symbol in such phrases as Mother Earth and the Mother Country. Every experienced babysitter knows the difficulty of alleviating the distress of the baby *at some stages* when, if he happens to awaken, he wants *mother* and will accept no substitute. Usually this distress appears around the eighth month of life, when the child has learned to recognize the mother as an individual but has not progressed far enough to be able to appreciate the temporary character of her absence and to wait for her return.[7]

The early period of quasi-total dependence on people, especially on the mother, who gradually emerges as the *external* source of relief or gratification, leads to another aspect of infant psychology which tends to persist: fear of *loss of love*. Again, one may mention the process of conditioning. Some activities meet with punishment and are therefore inhibited. The experimental animal can be conditioned *not* to seek food by administration of an electric shock the moment it makes an advance even more easily than it can be conditioned to a buzzer forewarning of gratification. Again, the psychoanalytic contribution is the *generalization* naturally made by the child: any action displeasing to other people may become a signal for withdrawal of "love"—*i.e.*, the relief or gratification now "expected" from people.

Once more, the value of the psychoanalytic formulation lies in its contribution toward ordering a host of phenomena. Very early in life a frown from mother typically exacts a compliance otherwise obtainable only by the most drastic physical punishment on a purely "conditioning" basis. Why? In some few cases the parents have, indeed, administered so much physical pain that compliance is perhaps explicable in terms of direct conditioning to the rod. One occasionally observes an obedient child who ducks involuntarily when the father's arm is raised suddenly, in mute testimony to plentiful cuffing. Typically, however, obedience has a much more subtle derivation. Long before the baby can understand "why," and prior to the more complicated relations with his parents that lead to the formation of the superego, the infant is sensitive to disapproval far beyond fear of direct punishment for any specific act. Without mother's "love," he feels delivered over to overwhelming exposure to stimuli (flooding, anxiety) that his passive techniques cannot hope to master. The later, more specific parental threats, even the fear of castration itself, gain strength from the reactivation of the primitive fear of total catastrophe attendant upon withdrawal of that vague but vivid experience which can for convenience be called "love."

Responding at this age primarily to tactile, kinesthetic, and proprioceptive cues, the infant is extraordinarily acute in discerning the genuine attitudes of the adult (*cf.* Sullivan's concept of *empathy*, p. 359). The nurse who handles the baby correctly but coldly gives him less reassurance than the fond, foolish mother who pours out her adult troubles into the ears of the uncomprehending baby. This example is drawn from Spitz's description of the practice of a number of unmarried mothers in one of the institutional groups he has studied carefully. He observes that many infants thrive as "confidantes" even if stealthily awakened at unholy hours, and others fail to flourish under conditions of pure hygiene. With some wryness about "science," we may say that old-fashioned mother love, no matter how neurotic or simply pathetic, has currently regained the blessing of science.

"Loss of love" is an important Freudian concept and is also very close to the emphasis of the non-libido schools on general warmth and affection as the chief desideratum in training the child for mature adulthood. It is one of those concepts that doubtless are most effective if left somewhat vague pending much more knowledge of infancy than is currently available.

With his usual desire to relate psychological phenomena to strictly biological processes, Freud has emphasized the role of the fact of *separation* from the mother's body at birth and the partial continuity of early infancy with intra-uterine life via the constant care of the mother. "The psychic mother object replaces for the child the biological foetal situation."* Separation from the mother *as object* thus repeats the initial unpleasurable situation of birth and becomes the first "danger signal" for the nascent ego connected with the outside world. "Separation anxiety" is the term used for this experience.

TERMINOLOGY

THE ROLE of the mother in early infancy has been explained in essentially Freudian terms, and the reader should here be forewarned of a vocabulary he will need later on. The dependency and helplessness of the infant, his inability to appreciate with anything like adult perceptiveness the reality factors of the situations he must confront, are key observations of most psychological

* S. Freud, *The Problem of Anxiety*, W. W. Norton & Co., 1936, p. 102. See also Rank's views, Chapter 14.

schools, not to mention of most mothers. Applying the label "primary narcissism" to this condition serves the purpose of easy dynamic summary. The label "object" for the mother, with analysis of how "object cathexis" toward her takes place, sounds wordy beyond necessity at a stage where there is little disagreement as to basic events and their meaning to the neonate. Again, however, the verbal formulation leads toward continuing generalization in the scientific sense of *ordering* observations. Describing the early experience with the mother as first "object" during the stage of "primary narcissism" offers verbal techniques for grasping later happenings developing out of and in relation to this first experience in interpersonal relations.

The structural description of id and ego must also be brought into this more concrete picture of genetic development. The ego develops out of the primal ego-id through contact with reality (mainly people) as the mechanism whereby bodily impulses are *expediently* gratified, regulated, or inhibited. It becomes the mediator between the inner world and the complementary outer world. We may call it, if we like, the *sum* of "conditionings," provided that we focus attention very much on the *dynamics* of the sum. The ego develops its power in large part through the *cathexis* of objects—that is, by allocating to external stimuli the emotional charge originating in purely biological processes. Free psychic energy gradually becomes "bound" as object relations are formed and ego mechanisms are developed. These concepts were discussed in Chapter 3 and will be dealt with in more detail in Chapter 6. They are mentioned here to suggest the usefulness of a vocabulary which at this juncture is likely to seem needlessly obscurantist.

CONTROLLED STUDIES OF
INFANCY AND EARLY
CHILDHOOD

THUS FAR, our discussion of infancy has been based on what Freud and other analysts have *reconstructed* as theoretically probable. Freud and his associates did not exhaustively study infants as such. Freud had six children of his own about the house in various stages of development. He did not examine them systematically, as did some psychologists in efforts at controlled observation, but at least he knew very well what an infant looks like and how it acts. The theoretical infant of Freud is always a substantial human being in its own right, never a logical abstraction.

In recent years, however, psychoanalysts have begun to study infants *as infants*, with the paraphernalia of scientific method. I shall here report only the research of René Spitz as illustrative of the new, direct approach to study of the infant, but Anna Freud, Fries, Ribble, Katherine Wolf (as Spitz's collaborator and in her own right), Escalona, Isaacs, Mittelmann, and others have also carried out noteworthy psychoanalytically oriented studies of infant behavior.* The enormous literature reporting investigations in this area by "psychologists" has been largely overlooked by psychoanalysts, usually because the investigations were too narrowly focused on one or another aspect of "ego" development. The extensive sequential studies of Gesell, Charlotte Bühler, and Piaget command the respect of psychoanalysts and are often used, despite the difference in theoretical orientation.

Spitz followed the development of 34 infants in their own homes, but he has not reported on these observations; he used them, instead, as a control for two contrasting institutional groups, each with a population of 90 to 100 babies.[9] In one institution, called the Nursery, unmarried mothers were encouraged to care for their babies themselves, or with *fairly* adequate substitutes—*i.e.*, other young women in the institution—when the mother had to be away. The over-all ratio of care was about two babies to one "mother." The other institution, called the Foundlinghome, had facilities for physical hygiene and nourishment at least as good as in the "Nursery," in fact, better as regards professional medical standards. Here there was no positive cruelty toward the babies, but the nursing staff was so limited that each nurse cared for about ten babies. The two institutions were selected for study because the groups involved were essentially similar in ethnic and economic background and the infants apparently about equal in endowment at the age of four months. (In the "Foundlinghome" regime, the mothers usually suckled the babies for a few months but then renounced their motherhood completely.)

Considered as a group, the Nursery babies made normal progress as determined by (1) the general impression of activity and emotional responsiveness, (2) maintenance of the developmental quotient (DQ) on regularly administered psychological tests, and (3) physical examination and

* For a sample of the work being done by psychoanalysts and psychoanalytically oriented psychologists see references at the end of this chapter.[8] Other studies may be found in the annual publication *The Psychoanalytic Study of the Child.*

health record.* There were no deaths and no serious epidemics, even though only common-sense precautions were taken against infection.

The fate of the Foundlinghome babies was tragic on all these counts: (a) The general impression was one of apathy and deathly silence. (b) The mean DQ of the group dropped progressively with age to a group mean of 45 (low-grade moron). This statistical finding is made more vivid by the statement that among 21 children aged 2½ to 4½ years (there were 91 in the total group), only five could walk unassisted, eight could not even stand alone, only one had a vocabulary of a dozen words, six could not talk at all, and eleven had only two words. (c) The health record shows that, despite elaborate medical precautions ("No person whose clothes and hands were not sterilized could approach the babies"), 34 of these 91 babies died. All but one of the older group was seriously underweight, despite a carefully supervised and varied diet.

From these contrasting data, Spitz draws the conclusion that "mothering" is essential to the infant far beyond the mere provenance of physical care. He supports his intergroup observations with instances of variation within the Nursery group. When the mother left for a period of several months, the child very often developed a condition which Spitz calls "anaclitic depression," similar in kind to the condition of the babies in the Foundlinghome. The condition was dramatically reversible on the mother's return, although it is not certain how long a delay can be tolerated before the extreme and apparently irreversible condition observed in Foundlinghome infants sets in. (The older children in the Foundlinghome can hardly be called "depressed." They go into a marasmus similar to, though not identical with, catatonia in adult psychosis.)

The anaclitic depression may be forestalled by a fully adequate mother substitute. (In the Nursery, the substitute mother was another inmate, not always as attentive to the extra child as one might wish.) Interestingly enough, the striking depressive reaction occurred less often if the real mother was a "bad" one, so that the substitute could hardly be worse. It was the especially responsive, friendly, alert children of warmly affectionate, devoted mothers who showed the most severe depressions under deprivation and who could hardly be reached by the most determined effort of the well-meaning doctor, although they responded brilliantly to return of the mother or to prolonged "friendly" nursing.

Spitz mentions further complications which would merit special study.

* Spitz also used the motion-picture camera as a recording device. His films, notably the sequence called *Grief* (produced by Dr. René A. Spitz, distributed by The New York University Film Library), are more revealing and convincing than words. The films include simplified statistical tables which support his contention that he has not merely photographed a few isolated instances.

When the mothers were absent, the Nursery babies had to be kept mostly in their cribs, since free play for the very young demands an impossible amount of watchfulness. The babies were given toys and seemed to develop normal agility in their cribs. Nevertheless, it seems likely that subsidiary attachments to people other than the mother, to a variety of "things," to their own motor achievements, might be relatively lacking for this group. By corollary, the role of the mother might loom especially large in the lives of these children, since most of their general activity took place through her, or at least rather specially when she was present.[10]

Spitz points out the importance of *timing* in the discussion of the events of infancy and childhood—a point also emphasized by Freud. It is apparently around the sixth month and after that the child becomes sufficiently aware of the mother as a person and an individual to be *capable* of the kind of reaction Spitz describes. After the second year, the child's ego is sufficiently developed, as a rule, so that abandonment by the mother does not have so *generalized* a catastrophic impact on the child. The consequences tend to be more specific.

The general emphasis of Spitz's study is confirmed by the work of Goldfarb[11] relating the psychological difficulties of older children to their early institutional care. None of the children reported by Goldfarb is as hopelessly retarded as the Foundlinghome infants, perhaps because the nursery was not quite so lacking in human contacts, although it too was conducted with a primary focus on the *physical* welfare of the child. Degree and kind of psychological difficulties were nevertheless found to be dramatically correlated with duration of stay in the institution, age at entrance, amount of parental interest (even though very crudely measured), foster-home placement, etc.

Goldfarb's studies represent an essentially statistical, carefully controlled analysis of older children whose babyhood is known only in the gross manner of social records. Such studies are very satisfying to "psychologists" and social workers who distrust the personal and theoretical bias too often involved in a "clinical" approach to such problems. The reports from the English nurseries* for evacuees, war orphans, and displaced children are also confirmatory. These studies are not so well controlled, because there is little time for paperwork under such drastic "experimental" conditions of child-parent separation, but a few nurseries were set up to allow reasonably good facilities for care of these children, with Anna Freud as consultant. And somehow these nurseries did keep records, almost daily, of the behavior of the children and the small ups and downs of the adults in the institution and outside.

The need for "mothering" appears in these reports, along with a wealth

* The publications of Anna Freud and her associates based on their observations in the nurseries contain a wealth of material.[12]

of information about the effect of *timing* in maternal loss, and how the loss is absorbed in relationships with other people and things—or modes of living. These reports are too complex to summarize here, but I suggest that they be read carefully not only in relation to the studies by Spitz and Goldfarb but for their relevance to the later stages of the genetic process presented in the following pages. Though Anna Freud is a "Freudian," I think she deals with the "Freudian" concept of stages in libidinal development in much the way the very flexible genius of Freud would have dealt with them. There is no reverence for dead rubrics. There is an alive understanding of what the infantile stages *mean to the child* and how they relate to his actual experiences, with creative insight into what happens when he has been drastically torn from the family setting. (These reports express directly in clinical description most of the ideas I shall try to expound in the next chapter, plus most of my critical comment.)

THE ORAL STAGE

THE MOUTH as an erogenous zone is familiar to the most naive observer of babies. Every mother recognizes the stubborn, passionate character of thumbsucking. She is delighted with the bubble-blowing and gurgling oral playfulness of her child and is constantly on guard lest his habit of transferring everything promptly to the mouth should result in the injudicious swallowing of a pin or too large a quota of germs. Indeed, it is surprising that the experts long confined their theorizings to oral activities in relation to *hunger,* so that thumbsucking was considered merely as a bad habit to be corrected because of damage to the teeth, and the mouthing of objects as merely unhygienic. For years, the homely "pacifier" was condemned by science and repudiated by conscientious mothers, who dutifully equipped their babies with aluminum mitts or elbow splints to prevent sucking. Teething rings, carefully sterilized, supplied the supposed functional need for some firm object to facilitate the irruption of teeth through the gum tissue.

With unconscious puritanism, scientists ignored the *pleasure* aspects of oral activities beyond all common sense. The pediatrician in a nursery school in the 1920's, who had psychological leanings, as befitted the doctor in a modern establishment, remarked that all but two or three of the forty youngsters were, to his own observation, at least occasional thumbsuckers. His conclusion was not the obvious one that all children like to suck their thumbs but that the entire group was badly brought up and showed psychological problems! At about that time, David Levy introduced a positive crusade for the old-fashioned pacifier, along with studies indicating that babies and puppies and kittens tend to indulge more in excessive oral activity if they receive nourishment too rapidly—that is, if the desire to suck per se fails to receive adequate gratification along with their hunger.[13]

Kissing is an important adjunct to genital sexuality in adults. Common sexual perversions involve a substitution of gratification through the mouth for genital satisfaction. The very general habits of smoking, chewing, nibbling candy or nuts, and the like testify to the continuation of direct oral pleasure beyond infancy. Billion-dollar industries are built upon it. The emergence of the cigarette as basic currency in the dislocated economy of postwar Europe deserves special consideration. The factor of "orality" indicated by this over-evaluation of an object serving a pure pleasure need of the mouth suggests to the Freudian theorist an emotional constellation (see p. 469) which corresponds uncomfortably well with the allegations of isolationist congressmen concerning the attitude of Europeans—an attitude of passive demand for support without personal initiative.

It was Freud who first pointed out systematically the dual function of the mouth as a utilitarian organ subordinate to the hunger drive and as a pleasure organ coordinate with other zones of libidinal satisfaction. It was Freud who showed how the fate of this pleasure drive is bound up with the development of personality. Hunger is freely acknowledged and in our culture is regularly satisfied for most of us before it can attain the status of a complex psychological drive. It is an intellectual artefact to say that we work to obtain food—most of us, that is, most of the time. In the last analysis, we do, of course, but Mr. Smith goes to the office because everybody works, because he is ambitious, because he is responsible for his family, etc., etc. He brings home the bacon only figuratively. The oral *pleasure* drive is, in our culture, more continuous and more subject to frustration.* Because the infant has to cope with the problem of gaining satisfaction from the start, it becomes one of the major determinants of the habitual patterns of coping that he develops—*i.e.*, of his personality.

Orality must be brought into connection with the problems of perception

* Other cultures supply important comparative data. Among the Arapesh and elsewhere, the infant is nursed whenever it cries. Weaning is a protracted, gentle process. The character of the majority of individuals in these groups seems to be definably different from ours. (M. Mead, *Sex and Temperament in Three Primitive Societies*, Wm. Morrow & Co., 1935.)

In some cultures, *e.g.*, among the Marquesan Islanders studied by Linton, actual deprivation of food may make hunger itself a drive of psychological importance, institutionalized by the culture. (A. Kardiner, *The Individual and His Society*, Columbia University Press, 1939.)

and the developing awareness of the outside world as differentiated from the self. The infant naturally begins to "perceive" at the point of his greatest interest. In his early longing for absence of stimulation, he is most frequently disturbed by pangs of hunger. Leaning on the utilitarian hunger drive, the drive to oral pleasure gains in focus.[14] The neonate's inner distress from hunger is recurrent but intermittent and is followed by the most clear-cut type of relief from external sources. Having his diaper changed, being turned over, being kept warm or cool, and all the special hazards of infancy, such as illnesses or the discomforts attendant upon trips, are for him experiences so variable and complex that they do not lend themselves, as a rule, to stable patterning of inner and outer states in quasi-causal connection. Thus, by experience alone, it would seem to me* that orality is likely to play the major role in the early establishment of the ego—that is, in the shift from the biological unity of experience (primary narcissism) to active interpretation of external events.

Spitz points out that typically the infant gazes fixedly at the mother's face during nursing, a circumstance that further conditions the transition from the purely biological experience of oral gratification to an incipient inter-personal perceptiveness.[15] Freud himself[16] tends to emphasize the instinctual quality of orality and to suggest that bottle-fed babies show the same course of development as breast-fed babies in relation to the mother or mother-surrogate because of a *phylogenetic* factor (*i.e.*, inborn by virtue of the ex-perience of the species).

The nature of this first focused relationship with the outside world has very important implications. As the infant develops, it seems likely, according to the Freudians, that the sequence cry-relief acquires an intermediate step: the *hallucination* of the object that brings relief so recurrently—that is, the breast or bottle, very soon the face, and finally the more or less whole person of the mother. Thus, a sense of "object" is achieved. However, the fate of the object is to be devoured—in fact, destroyed. The satisfied infant actively repu-diates (spits out or avoids) the nipple so heartily welcomed a few minutes earlier. Its object value has vanished in the fulfillment of immediate inner satisfaction.

The tendency of all infants to explore by the mouth and to swallow is the bit of behavior which most requires maternal watchfulness. For the first months, "love" and "destructiveness" via the mouth go hand in hand. The most primitive reaction to perception of the outside world is to incorporate it, to make it part of oneself by swallowing. This is the process of *introjection*. As a mechanism, introjection continues throughout life in much more com-plex form. Its prototype in the experience of the baby is that the "object" can

---

* This particular comment may be original with me, but it seems compatible with the Freudian emphasis on the role of orality in interpersonal development.

easily be absorbed into the "me," at a period where these two concepts are largely merged and the infant is struggling toward their differentiation. For a long time in early childhood, the process of introjection may lead to quite astonishing interpretations of the nature of the objects, mainly people. Child analysis* uncovers *in statu nascendi* the, to us as adults, extraordinary misconceptions of the very young child about his surroundings, mainly his parents, previously inferred from analysis of adults.

Or perhaps it is not really surprising that a baby, who knows the world almost exclusively through his own body, should interpret the world in the only terms he knows. We shall come later to consideration of the processes whereby specific early interpretations are renounced, in consciousness, as dangerous or stupid. And we shall see that there are few bridges between the early infantile concepts and adult concepts in the area of sexuality, and that many of the more formulated infantile concepts are simply cut off from the emerging conscious insight (repressed) with more or less violence by the developing ego and superego, while they continue to function unmodified in the unconscious.

Early orientations so general, so vague, so little subject to consistent correction in the individual instance are very likely to survive. Thus, the notion that the outside world may become "me" (by introjection) and vice versa (by projection, in which "my" feelings are attributed to others) survives as a readily observable unconscious mechanism in the adult. We shall see that the processes of internalization of outside influences so that they are experienced as one's own and of externalization of one's own feelings as if they were outside happenings are emphasized even by psychoanalytic schools which repudiate the libido theory. The Freudian† position relates these processes specifically to the period when the object is literally incorporated and the "object" pleasure of having mother near as *instrument* of pleasure is not clearly distin-

* The following example will serve to illustrate how these ideas are used in practice: A child developed eczema as a 9-month-old infant. When he was two years old, his hands were tied to the sides of his crib, while he was in the hospital, to prevent him from scratching. His mother continued this practice for several months at home. At the age of eight, he still felt indignant over this. In the course of his analysis, he recurrently repeated the fantasy that "the doctors will want to operate on me to cure me of my sores." On being asked why he would be operated on, he would say, "To take out bad things inside." He blamed his mother for "having given him eczema" by giving him chocolate as a "small child." The construction is warranted that the experience of the eczema and the hands' being tied, particularly by the mother, aroused his anger and anxiety. Attributing evil intentions to the bad mother, he assumed that she gave him bad food ("poison"). Along with this, he introjected and incorporated the bad mother. All of these turn into bad things inside. In his perception of the world, his mother and the doctors thus became distorted by two mechanisms. He will be punished (killed) for the bad things inside by being "cut open." Projection is also at work. He had fantasies of killing the doctors, and his fear is that they will do to him what he wants to do to them. (A. H. Maslow and B. Mittelmann, *Principles of Abnormal Psychology, Revised*, Harper & Bros., 1951, p. 277.)
† Melanie Klein has emphasized the importance of this phase of development even more than Freud. (See pp. 211*ff*.)

guished from concomitant inner reactions coming from within the body.

The first relations with the outside world are intrinsically ambivalent. The "loved" object (food) taken in by the mouth is in actual fact destroyed. Freud points out that the infant at this stage is incapable of either love or hate and cannot truly be termed ambivalent. As appreciation of the objective facts develops, however, he is inevitably confronted by the observation that you cannot eat your cake and have it. The old saw is here appropriate in a very literal sense!

LATER ORAL STAGES

THE INFANT'S ATTITUDE in the early oral stage is *passive and receptive*. When the teeth irrupt and the general maturing of the nervous system allows more active mastery of stimulation, he enters upon the *oral-sadistic,* or cannibalistic, phase, in which he bites with all his strength. Fluted edges on the pewter mugs in our house are enduring evidence of the energy with which our babies went about their biting. Bare spots in the hooked rugs, chewed bits in the jigsaw puzzles, tooth marks on the corners of an occasional book incautiously left accessible testify to a similar stage in the puppies and kittens who have lived here too.

The infant still has no clear comprehension of the object as thoroughly distinct from himself. The object is still closely bound up in "meaning" with his own instinctual demands, the mode of response being characteristically one of incorporation. Certainly not all biting at this age has a definitely sadistic coloring, *but it readily becomes fused with truly aggressive impulses.* The baby comes to use his teeth more and more in direct offense or defense or as a punishing response to frustration. By the mechanism of projection, he fears similar aggression in others, mainly in powerful adults. Thus, the primitive experience of devouring can take an aspect of genuine destructiveness. The more the child himself bites in anger, the more he attributes the same impulse to others. Since oral activity is still the main source of pleasure and its object is genuinely loved, the addition of a sadistic component now makes for a real ambivalence, in contradistinction to the quasi-ambivalence of the earlier period.

Evidence for the interpretation of such "meanings" comes from various sources: the fantasy life of little children still close to the infantile formulation but able to express themselves to some extent verbally and in the manipulation of objects (play techniques); the speech and behavior of psychotics who have regressed to the narcissistic stage; the dreams of neurotic and normal adults; enduring myths, turns of phrase, and the like found all over the world in the codification of language. On pages 211ff. we shall see the special use Melanie Klein has made of this formulation. And in Chapter 6, on dynamics, we shall discuss also the character structure of persons who have remained more or less fixated at or who have regressed to the oral stage. Typically, oral habits persist openly along with the sublimations and aim-inhibited expressions developed in the long process of growth toward adulthood.

By virtue of the biological equipment of the species, every child goes through the oral stage. The duration and precise course of this stage, however, depends upon individual constitutional factors and upon the environment.* Of the constitutional factors, little is known. Paradoxically, excessive gratification and excessive frustration of primitive oral needs by the environment both appear to result in a tendency to fixation. The baby who has been too happy at the breast seems unusually loath to give up this source of pleasure, especially when stimulus to advance is lacking or when later stages are somehow made too painful. Libidinal attachments are never given up except for libidinal gain. The mother (or nurse) who herself enjoys suckling the baby more than playing with him, who is so much influenced by his inevitable protest at weaning that she does not gently insist on his renunciation of the breast, may fail to provide the necessary incentive to growth.

Apparently some measure of deprivation, as against passive contentment, is the condition for growth of mature object relations. It is through *delay* in gratification that the child learns to appreciate the difference between his own feelings and the object that brings relief. It is through finding reward to some extent contingent upon his own participation, whether active or in deliberately patient endurance, that the child develops techniques of independent mastery.†

Furthermore, once the infant's natural tendency to go further is stifled, the final weaning is likely to become extremely painful, both to the child and to

* In this discussion I have made free use of ideas emphasized by Abraham and Fenichel, among the older psychoanalysts, and those brought to the fore by the contemporary ego psychologists discussed in Chapter 3. References are given for relatively specific formulations but not for concepts in general use among Freudians.

† Cf. H. Hartmann, E. Kris, and R. Loewenstein, "Comments on the Formation of Psychic Structure," *The Psychoanalytic Study of the Child*, Vol. II, International Universities Press, 1946, pp. 11-38. Rapaport has emphasized the factor of *delay* in careful analysis of psychic mechanisms, even in interpretation of reactions to test materials. (D. Rapaport, *Organization and Pathology of Thought*, Columbia University Press, 1951, pp. 689ff.; *Diagnostic Psychological Testing*, Vol. II, Year Book Publishers, 1946, pp. 189ff., 214ff., 239f.)

the overtender mother. The snowball effect of "spoiling" appears in other activities as well. It becomes continually more "necessary" as the child's protests become louder and his resentment against the withholding of total gratification becomes more violent.

On the other hand, it appears that the infant positively requires a considerable measure of gratification of oral needs and may continue to demand it long past the normal period of renunciation (he may be an "oral character" throughout life) if too severely frustrated in infancy. With undue frustration, the normal early oral dependency is likely to turn either into extreme, effortless pessimism or into a fretful, demanding aggressivity still without constructive effort by the individual himself. It seems probable, nowadays, that the rigid training of the child to regular hours of feeding and early weaning "scientifically" recommended some years ago is psychologically inexpedient. Most normal infants quickly establish a rhythm of their own in feeding which can be judiciously encouraged. Although minor deprivation is positively helpful, it appears that, for the most harmonious development, the balance of experience should be on the side of gratification.

The more focused libidinal desire for oral gratification should, of course, be viewed in relation to the previous discussion of the more general longing for freedom from stimulation and the fear of loss of love. The mother at this stage is primarily the source of oral gratifications, and the emerging object relationship with her is strongly colored by this fact. Her general attitude and presence are crucial not only for the specific oral drive but also for the reasons discussed earlier. The infant can tolerate fairly well the oral frustrations sometimes occasioned by illness or scientific misdirection *provided he has general loving support,* whereas flawless nursing as such may leave him distressed. In most cases, the two aspects of early care go hand in hand. The affectionate, wise mother feeds her child wisely; the overly tense or rejecting mother either spoils or frustrates the baby orally as well as in other aspects of his life.

THE ANAL STAGE

THE PLEASURE ASPECT of activities connected with the anal zone is difficult for the adult to recognize because it undergoes a much more thorough repression in the course of social development than do oral activities. In fact, it is turned mainly to "disgust." The early attitudes survive almost exclusively in jokes and colloquialisms of the more vulgar sort, in dreams, and in some neurotic symptoms. Nevertheless, Freudians consider this phase of infancy especially important in the normal growth of object relations and in the etiology of neurosis.

The neonate voids and defecates passively (reflexly). Probably the sensation of movement in the aperture is itself pleasurable, as is the warmth about his buttocks. It is only as the excreta turn cold that discomfort arises, which at first, like the distress of hunger, is remedied by the mother. Probably some spontaneous pleasure in control of defecation sets in even before training is instituted. At any rate, it seems as though holding in, as well as its opposite, evacuation, is enjoyed for its own sake. Certainly it is in this area that *active mastery of his own impulses* by the child makes its most vivid debut, promptly commingled with external enforcement.

Very young babies typically exhibit a definite, occasionally a marked, coprophilia until discouraged by their nurses. They "love dirt," especially their own dirt. Smearing the crib with the contents of the diaper seems to be naturally an agreeable pastime. Since by the time they are capable of such manipulatory activity, children are very sensitive to "loss of love," the typically strong disapproval of the mother usually suffices for discouragement. In nursery years, such pleasures are thinly disguised in the joy of making mud pies or playing with finger paints and other smeary materials. Often it is the tense, overly neat child who, instead of constructing a design or picture, positively wallows in the finger paints once his inhibitions about using them are removed.*

The preoccupation of many young children (all children to some extent) with anal matters is obvious through play techniques or observation of spontaneous play when external taboos have not been too stringent. My three-year-old son and his progressively reared friends used to tug a heavy bureau from the wall, quite frankly "to play with its buttocks." They *invented* a term of extreme vituperation: "You old b.m.!" (nursery talk for bowel movement), sometimes used jocosely like the adult monosyllabic version. Personal modesty first took the form of covering the buttocks with a towel, leaving the front cheerfully exposed.

In brief, there can be hardly any doubt that anal activity and anal products are of very great emotional import. At the stage at which appreciation of objects is just beginning, this early "object," the first one under the baby's own control, attains enormous significance. Like the object he swallows, it is

---

* This observation is strikingly recorded in the film *Finger Painting*, produced by the Department of Child Study at Vassar College, distributed by the New York University Film Library.

also part of himself. In many primitive societies children are taught to *hide* their feces because an enemy attack upon them would be tantamount to an attack upon the whole person. We have seen that the boundaries between self and not-self, between people and the inanimate, are very fluid at this period. Thus, the infant cannot avoid making all sorts of curious connections between his excreta, himself, and the people and things around him.

The connections may be very strong indeed in consequence of the highly charged atmosphere in which they are formed. But they are made at a time when "the ego is weak," and they are typically not corrected by later learning because they are "repressed." That is to say, the connections are made when verbal and logical tools are rudimentary, offering none of the usual cues for rational memory and correction. The early formulation: "All objects, or certain types of objects, are feces," is incomprehensible even to the toddler, who has in the meantime learned a quite different set of ideas under the tuition of his elders, and whose prideful delight in his product has turned to shame. Again, because the ego is weak in infancy, the child cannot possibly understand that his first formulation was simply too narrow. Instead, he drops it altogether "consciously," especially if it has met with marked disapproval in his developing rational scheme of the world and his own role.

In treatment, the psychoanalyst can often see very plain traces of the anal connections. For example, a patient who could not bring herself to throw away the most worthless trifle invented the scheme of attaching such items loosely to her apron string behind her and going for a walk in order that they might drop off (out) unawares.[17] The patient, of course, not only fails to recognize spontaneously the underlying meaning of the bizarre symptoms but typically repudiates the interpretation offered by the psychoanalyst. We must postpone to the next chapter further discussion of anal components in adult life, here confining ourselves merely to brief mention of the Freudian view of their continued functioning.

Freudians find it useful to draw a sharper distinction between excreta as *object* to the child and the significance he attaches to the *act* of elimination. The way in which this first important impulse toward control and self-determination is handled seems peculiarly fateful for the development of those enduring attitudes toward the self and the world that we call character. Unfortunately, anal pleasures, and infant mastery of the world and himself in terms of this function, *must* be drastically regulated by external demands. Toilet training thus becomes the arena of dramatic conflict among the emerging self-control (ego) of the infant, his instinctual drives, and the requirements of the outside world. The manner in which this first conflict is solved easily sets the pattern for the solution of later conflicts.

Hartmann, Kris, and Loewenstein put the problem succinctly in an article on the formation of psychic structure:[18]

> The situation of the child during the period of toilet training represents in a nutshell the nature of its conflict situation at that age. That conflict situation is threefold: first, there is the conflict between two instinctual tendencies, that of elimination and retention (instinctual conflict); second, there is the conflict between either one of these tendencies and the child's attempts to control them and to time his function: it is a conflict between the id and the ego (structural conflict); and third, there is the conflict with the external world that has made the structural conflict necessary: the mother's request for timing of elimination.

Techniques of toilet training and, above all, the attitude of the mother are, therefore, of great moment in personality development. The child must give up his narcissistic omnipotence. If he can identify happily with the mother and accept her requirements as his own, the emerging pride in his personal mastery of instinctual impulses can be constructively directed toward socially acceptable regulation. His own sense of achievement is enhanced by parental praise. On the other hand, if he is forced to *give up* his self-determination out of fear, whether of direct chastisement or severe loss of love, his inner determination tends to develop *in opposition to the outside world*. The upshot may be anxious effort at compliance, not from a shared interest in regulation but from fear of authority. Or there may be defiance instead. Or, most common of all, a mixture of the two.

In Chapter 6, on dynamics, we shall discuss further the paradox of the adult "anal character," which is typically lacking in self-confidence and at the same time is stubbornly self-righteous and scornful of others; convinced that there is only one way of doing things right, namely, "mine." And since anal activity produces an object—a highly cathected object, as we have seen—the anal character is also likely to have very special attitudes toward *possessions*. Things, and people considered as things, are important not so much for their material or esthetic value as for their symbol value in an eternally re-enacted drama. The ego taking form under these conditions must constantly defend itself against encroachments from the buried id, the reactive fears and hostilities developed during this first essay at independence, and later consolidations in the form of ego-ideal and superego.

Thus far, we have discussed largely only two aspects of the anal phase—its biological determination and the demands of society as mediated by the mother, who already has powers far beyond those of physical punishment. The discussion has not been simple, but it must be still further complicated. The baby does not forget his oral needs for the convenience of the scientist, who would prefer neatly demarcated stages, needs, drives—or any sort of stable rubric. At the time when toilet training is begun, the baby's little psyche is already organized with some firmness at the oral level. Indeed, toilet training very often coincides with weaning, which itself represents a sort of crisis in infantile ego development. No Freudian has attempted to describe the "oral-anal character" as an entity, but comment on the dynamic interplay of the two partial instincts is universal and is supported by a very large amount of published case material, appropriately complex.* If everybody nursed and trained children in the same way, with a few exceptions amenable to special study, such an entity might well appear. In actual fact, of course, there is so much variation in our culture as to the timing of the two events, and as to the course of each drive separately, that one can only hope to trace their interaction in the individual case. It would be interesting to study cultures in which the timing of these two aspects of the child's experience is more definitely prescribed by custom.

Special difficulties in the anal phase may throw the child back to oral satisfactions. Breakdown in training and relapse to babyishness, even with a desire to suck the bottle, are common enough reactions to the birth of a sibling, only partly to be explained as direct imitation of the favored newcomer. They must also be seen as a type of regression under stress. Undue passivity or resentment developed in the oral phase may hamper the child in learning sphincter control. Without physical cause, some babies even seem unwilling to undertake elimination independently. They require enemas—or at least the doting mother thinks they do. Such children may show a peculiarly extreme dependency and lack of initiative throughout life and may be very resistant to treatment.

Psychological connections may also be made by the child between the organ systems themselves. A schizophrenic girl had the habit of covering her mouth with her hand. This, she explained, was because of the smell, which she described as coming from her rectum. Her name, she insisted, was Miss Mud. Her parents were "farts"—a statement intended quite literally and apparently not considered opprobrious.[19] The nonsense of the schizophrenic seems often to be the *sense* of the stages of infancy, in which the objects of the real world are merged with the objects of libidinal importance to the child and with his feelings, wishes, or fears.

* The point is so obvious that there is no literature specifically devoted to it. The great majority of published cases cover it more or less explicitly if the infantile material is presented in detail. The practicing analyst takes such interrelationships "theoretically" as a matter of course and expends his effort on discovering how they have worked out in the life story of his patient. *Cf.* also the discussion of Melanie Klein's position (pp. 211*ff.*) regarding toilet training as a complication in the mounting sadism of the infant, deriving essentially from the oral sphere.

THE PHALLIC STAGE

ABOUT THE FOURTH YEAR, the *focus* of libidinal energy apparently shifts to the genital zone. (This statement does *not* mean that *no* genital activity may be observed earlier.) Undoubtedly the child experiences pleasurable sensations in this area. Erections occur frequently, and masturbation and sex play with other children are virtually universal.

Freud was especially impressed by the *diphasic* nature of genital development in the human species. There is, he thought, a fairly continuous growth of sexuality through the partial instincts (oral, anal) to concentration on the organs of reproduction with some sense of the special love object up to about the sixth year. The sex drive then subsides for a number of years—during the *latency period*—reappearing again at puberty. The early bloom of sexuality, which cannot possibly come to fruition, is called the *phallic* stage to differentiate it from true genitality leading to mature mating and reproduction. At this period, attitudes are formed which are crucial for later heterosexual fulfillment and good relations with people generally. For this reason, it is the stage most fraught with potentialities for neurotic distortion.

The problems and solutions of the phallic stage are not erased by the latency period. When the adolescent enters upon the genital pursuits proper to his age, he is already equipped with attitudes, mostly unconscious, formed before the age of six.

Thus far, it has been possible to speak of the infant regardless of sex. Except for the conventions of language, the pronoun *he* could equally well have been *she*. (Some authors, however, notably Helene Deutsch, note a greater passivity in female infants from the outset.) In the phallic stage, the sexes must be differentiated. From now on, the pronoun *he* refers specifically to the boy; the girl will require separate discussion immediately following.

Crucial to the Freudian interpretation is not only the pleasurable excitement associated with the phallus but the value placed by the child, male or female, on the organ itself. This high valuation of the penis is thought to appear spontaneously in both sexes. We shall soon see that loss of the penis is considered of major dynamic import for the little boy and that the *castration complex* is a potent source of neurotic manifestations in later life.

The little boy's first love object is his mother. At times, Freud speaks as though this object choice were of phylogenetic origin and bound to occur regardless of individual experience. He clearly states, however, that it is not the biological mother as such but the woman who has taken the maternal role toward the child who attaches to herself his nascent genital longings. Her care of his body is a potent influence toward this first "seduction" (the word is Freud's), as must also be the fact that during the oral stage he was identified with her and came to appreciate external objects mainly through her mediation. We cannot repeat too often the lack of sharp differentiation between self and cathected object in these early years (or later on, for that matter, at the unconscious level). Thus, on many counts, it seems altogether natural that the first orientation of the phallic stage should be "incestuous." As in all infantile trends, the initial orientation is extremely potent and is typically handled by repression, among other mechanisms.

Sooner or later, the mother rebuffs behavior in her son that is dimly recognized as "sexual." The social taboo begins operating in a variety of ways. It is especially important that the little boy observes that the father enjoys privileges with the mother from which he is excluded. It may be that the privilege of creeping into mother's bed is revoked when father is home. The child may have witnessed the primal scene (i.e., his parents in intercourse) or have suddenly remembered such scenes witnessed at a time when he was too young to "understand" them even in the confused way typical for infancy. Freud suggests that phylogenetic memories of the primal horde in which father and sons were in open competition for sexual possession of the women (mother and sisters), may also be a factor in the attitude of the little boy toward the father.

In most psychoanalytic writings, especially those of Melanie Klein, it seems as though the little child knows instinctively, though dimly and confusedly, the general nature of intercourse and the process of birth. His first strong intellectual curiosity is directed toward clarification of these matters. Little children are normally, it seems, peeping Toms to some extent, normally voyeurs and exhibitionists. (Indeed, Freud classifies these trends among the component instincts.) They normally undertake exploration in company with other children. Normally, all sorts of misconceptions occur, with substitution of one organ for another, displacement of concern about the genitals to other parts of the body, interpretation of external objects in sexual terms.

Harsh repression of infantile scoptophilia (pleasure in looking) may have serious consequences for the development of intellectual activity generally and may be responsible for later failure in school. This Freudian analysis seems to many very far-fetched, and it is modified by the ego psychologists. It should be remarked, however, that concern with body structure and function *must* be altogether natural at a time when the child knows the world mainly through his own bodily feelings. He is often punished for this interest, rarely effectively helped in learning. Thus, if the attitude of curiosity and inquiry meets with too severe a threat, reinforced from within by the fear of castration, it could change to an attitude of inhibition toward all learning, by the process of generalization from early experience that we have so often encountered.

Or, as we have seen in other situations, the inhibition in learning may apply only to some areas that happen to have strong symbol value. A bright boy had trouble with arithmetic, culminating in total inability to learn fractions, an inability coupled with great anxiety and distress. The therapist, not a Freudian, discovered that for this youngster the numbers represented people—*e.g.*, 8 was a fat woman, 9 a man with a big head, etc. Fractions were so clear a symbol of intercourse, so definitely taboo, that he couldn't even look at them, much less venture to manipulate them himself.

Cases of extreme inhibition of learning on this direct symbolic basis are fortunately rare. It seems likely enough, however, that in a more general way attitudes toward spontaneous inquiry are deeply influenced by the reception of the strong early interest in body function. The naive "psychologically informed" approach of telling the young child all the facts of life does not seem to dispose of the problem. Often the child simply does not understand. Tests following straightforward, clear lectures on sex, even in adolescence, often show the most fantastic mistakes in understanding on the part of intelligent, earnest pupils. The very young child is poorly equipped to grasp verbal concepts, and in our culture his natural experimentation *must* be limited. The restriction applies *in our culture* even to free exploration with other children and is inevitable as regards the parents. In discussing her neurotic boy with the therapist, one poor "modern" mother confessed with tears that she had allowed him to inspect her genitals because he had been so insistently interested. I fear the comment of any psychoanalyst, as well as any layman with common sense, would be that such encouragement of intellectual interest in the boy was itself a demonstration of neuroticism in the mother, which would doubtless operate in other directions as well.

Critical Comment

THUS, in our culture, full gratification of infantile curiosity on points of deep interest to the child is impossible. We have seen earlier that moderate privation is positively helpful in developing active mastery. Primitive cultures, and those groups in our own society in which almost unrestricted observation and experimentation are permitted, have contributed very little to the advancement of knowledge. The true scientist has been described as one who preserves a sense of mystery and who wants to "find out" simply for the joy of finding out. Some psychologists have suggested that curiosity be considered a primary drive.

Hartmann and others point to ego functions of primary autonomy which contribute toward "curiosity." The classical Freudian would consider it a derivative of normal moderate frustration of a deeply rooted drive toward a kind of ego-mastery of important biological impulses. Moderate frustration may well produce an attitude of independent endeavor to discover the truth.

THE OEDIPUS COMPLEX

The infantile formulation in the phallic stage becomes in time one of rivalry with the father for possession of the mother. In the form of demands upon her love and attention *generally,* this tension between father and son is a matter of very common observation. It appeared in literature long before the Freudian era, and no psychoanalytic school would question the frequency of the problem in our culture. The specifically Freudian position is that in the phallic stage possession of the mother has the specific orientation of sexual possession in a quite literal sense—although we should keep in mind that the four-year-old does not grasp the implications of his impulses in anything like adult terms.

The development of object relations connected with the phallus thus inevitably spells the *Oedipus complex,* the term being taken from the Greek tragedy in which Oedipus murders his father and marries his mother. The criticism has been made that in the old story Oedipus is in the grip of fate (his doom was prophesied before his birth) and committed his crimes unwittingly, so that he cannot be held psychologically responsible. For Freud, these frills on the legend only make it a more apt recapitulation of the infantile story. Every boy is fated to kill his father (in fantasy) and to marry his mother, by virtue of the almost inevitable course of libidinal growth in the phallic phase. The incestuous murder is almost always unwitting because it occurs (in fantasy) at an age when the little boy has no reality framework for evaluation of his feelings along adult lines, and he is not given the opportunity for gradual growth in understanding. Instead, the moment he is old enough to perceive external events on any terms but those of direct satisfaction of biological need, he encounters the structure of society at its firmest point, mediated by parental attitudes which, if not inborn, are so deeply rooted in society that one looks in vain for instances of socially sanctioned mother-son incest in the varied roster of social forms reported by modern anthropologists.

Freud remarks that the boy is indeed fated like Oedipus to go through the psychological drama, and that like Oedipus he does not know what he is doing. Amnesia, loss of memory, for these primitive reactions is a *normal* phenomenon. By and large, it is the neurotic and still more the psychotic individual who in one way or another preserves concrete memories of the events occurring in the phallic stage, or, rather, memory fragments easily expanded in this direction. The common complaint of the normal scientist that neither he nor his friends can report anything like an Oedipus complex in their own recollections or in their observations of children is not—for Freud—any disproof of his position. The unanalyzed neurotic manages to function successfully largely by active "successful" repression of his Oedipus complex. The normal person has worked it through adequately, also with amnesia for the early longings and misconceptions. Even children in nursery school have learned to guard against expression of their inner feelings. Moreover, even their fairly open expression is likely to be viewed by the adult observer as highly "symbolic," because it is not subject to the abstract conventions of adult thinking.

Repression of the Oedipus complex is by no means wholly a consequence of the social taboo. Rivalry with the father represents a very severe *inner* threat to the little boy, as Freud makes clear in *The Problem of Anxiety*.[20] We must remember that at this age the child still confuses the wish or the thought with the deed. His perception of reality is so rudimentary that he can plan no very sensible means of handling his dilemma. Typically he entertains —at times—death wishes toward the father* who gets in his way, or he wishes to see the father hurt, diminished, or *away*. However, since he can understand the feelings of others only as a projection of his own feelings, he naturally ascribes to the father similar wishes toward himself; hence he walks in terror of extreme paternal retaliation.

His problem is further complicated by the fact that he also is dependent upon the father's support and authority and has begun to develop genuine love for him. Thus, the death wish arising out of the Oedipus complex comes into conflict with positive attitudes in the child's own psyche, over and above the fear of direct retaliation by the father and the more general fear of loss of love attendant upon all acts or wishes or thoughts which arouse disapproval in the important adults.

* Any annoyance with another person easily leads at this age to a "death wish," which may have important repercussions—for example, the life-long "guilt" of the patient described on pp. 255f. after her sister died of meningitis—because, as the patient then thought, of her death wish during a period of strong sibling rivalry.

The death wish toward the father is more continuing and more powerful, according to Freud, because of its role in the all-important drama of genital development.

One further ingredient must be added to the amalgam typical of the phallic stage. We discussed earlier the baby's sense of omnipotence. The first step beyond the primitive formulation "My cry brings relief" is "My cry brings mother, a little later father, and *they* bring relief." *Normally,* the little child comes to ascribe to his parents the omnipotence he once experienced as his own. *Normally,* the parents are for the young child godlike creatures who give or withhold or punish at their will. The little child has no sense of things happening as impersonal events. His concept of causality necessarily reflects his own experience, in which truly the moment active mastery supplants, here and there, blind passive endurance, the mastery is and must be "personal." In early infancy, "I" did it—that is, the primitive, scarcely differentiated self did it. For a long time (months are as important as years in the whirlwind growth of infancy), "they" did it—that is, the parents as first representatives of the outside world.

Many intelligent modern parents have disliked the uncomfortable omnipotence thrust upon them by their children and have tried to "reason" with them from the start. It is true that parents take a fall as the child corrects his early personalization of causality (animism) and sees his godlike parents in perspective, and it is also true that the higher you rise the farther you fall. In the very early years, however, the parent really has no choice. If he denies his child that pretty bauble the moon, the infant is just as frustrated as if the glittering glasses of papa are removed or as if the rattle is teasingly withdrawn. What counts in these early years is not the reasonableness of the parent trying not to play god but the attitude toward the infant of the god that the infant inevitably creates.

Critical Comment

IN MY salad years as psychologist, I was often appalled by episodes of *teasing* in families observed either in line of professional duty or socially. An extreme example is not a personal observation but a "funny" story. Papa asks son to jump off a high place into his arms and deliberately does not catch him, so that the child falls and is hurt. Papa says: "That'll teach you not to trust anybody but yourself." Doubtless an effective lesson, and doubtless it is my heavy-handed psychologizing which makes me unsusceptible to the humor.

Certainly the baby learns the concrete reality contours of his world by methods far more direct and at the same time more subtle than the verbal preachments of his parents. Like it or not, the parent is a way station between infantile omnipotence and reasonable adaptation to reality, and for a time he must wear the mantle of omnipotence. Although I still cannot stomach even in fun deliberate teaching of mistrust to the extent illustrated in the "funny" story, I have come to see that the small teasings of the affectionate parent are of positive value. In trivial situations—the more valuable because they *are* relatively trivial and do not mobilize overwhelming instinctual drives—the child learns to discount his excessive trust in the parents and his excessive fears of their sublime retribution for his quite natural impulses.

The only danger in normal affectionate teasing and normal fallibility in discipline is a too consistent or too strong impact in areas of deep emotional import *to the child*. Thus Mead and Bateson report that the quite general practice in Bali of handling the infant very affectionately and then deliberately exciting him by pseudo-rejection and petting of other children is reproduced symbolically in typically Balinese myths, traditional dances, etc., and perhaps in the whole Balinese character.[21]

The *normal* jealous demand of the young child for the full attention of his mother makes teasing in this area *potentially* a very severe threat. Momentary teasing when the child feels good, immediately followed by sound reassurance, is probably good training in emotional reconciliation with the facts of divided love. Probably the child can to some extent share the "joking" attitude of the adult and is thus helped to laugh at himself—that is, to gain some objective "distance" from his problem. His feelings are in a way clearly acknowledged and clearly not taken too seriously by the all-powerful adult.

Intense fear followed by intense relief is too difficult for the child to assimilate. Portentously solemn sympathetic adjuration to be nice to little brother, with solemn verbal affirmation of parental love, may also be far less reassuring than brief, essentially benign teasing. The child at this point is "introjecting" parental attitudes, as we shall see. A certain warm light-heartedness toward common infantile reactions is probably a better attitude to "introject" than the most carefully controlled handling of special problems. The child needs *practice* in inhibition, practice even in experiencing disappointment and fear. Parental omnipotence can be used paradoxically to limit its own power by homeopathic doses of disillusionment and abdication.

In the phallic stage, however, the parents are still mainly considered all-powerful, especially in relation to the deeper instinctual attitudes of the child. The most gentle father is easily cast in the role of ruthless avenger because of the boy's own guilt about his sexual wishes and rivalries. In fact, the excessively gentle, permissive father does not supply sufficient *external* force to reassure the child that his own destructive fantasies will not be fulfilled. The full burden of control is left with the child, who then creates an especially tyrannical image of the father (unconsciously) in order to accomplish his task. Students reasoning from the evidence of this image as it appears in projective tests typically deduce that the subject's father was really a brutal person. As teacher I constantly caution them against this conclusion as to the reality background, and, indeed, I have come to feel that unusually pervasive unconscious fear of the father-image in the adult *of good family* (my judgment here does not venture beyond subjects from relatively privileged groups) is more likely to mean a weak or indifferent father than one who actually punished the child severely.

CASTRATION FEAR

The fear attendant upon the Oedipus complex is partly the fear of loss of love so often mentioned before. It also takes a more specific form: *the fear of castration*. Many parents actually threaten cutting off the penis in the effort to stop infantile masturbation. Probably this overt threat is less common now, at least among educated parents, than when Freud began his investigations. It was by no means universal then, so Freud suggests the possibility of phylogenetic memories of the primal horde to account for the quasi-universal fear of castration in little boys as observed by Freudian psychoanalysts. Most contemporary psychoanalysts, even Freudians, feel that the general attitude of parents and society is so hostile toward masturbation and the early Oedipal relationship that the phylogenetic memory is not necessary to account for the fact that verbal threat is not essential. Perhaps the little boy always hears a direct threat somewhere—from servants, from other children. Perhaps it is enough that the penis is enormously important for him, so that any condemnation is creatively turned into total elimination of the organ by the "magic" of the child's own thinking. At any rate, Freud maintains that the early phallic development is brought to a close by the fear of castration, which somehow or other is experienced by every little boy.

The more or less tentative formulation "They could cut off my penis" receives confirmation when the boy sees the female genitalia—or rather when he sees the absence of the penis. The observation of someone without a penis is a sort of demonstration that it *can* be cut off. This early bit of testing of reality thus has the unfortunate consequence of consolidating the castration fear. It does not help much to bring boys up with full knowledge of the anatomical structure of little girls. In homes and nursery schools, baths and toilet facilities very often supply such information from the start, but the child ignores it until he is ready for it. Then he quite suddenly "sees" what has been before his eyes all the time, or he remembers past experience in a new context. According to Freud, castration fear is so deeply embedded in the very nature of the sexual instincts during the phallic stage as to be practically unavoidable. Individual differences are to be found in *quantitative* variations in its intensity, and in the different ways in which it is handled by the growing child.

Obviously, castration fear is very closely bound up with the attitude toward the parents, via the Oedipus complex. We have seen that at this stage the parents are conceived of as omnipotent, and that their actual training procedures are supplemented or even distorted in the child's mind by the fantasy of their reaction to his emerging genital desires. At this point, the mechanisms of identification and introjection, which we have already discussed in tentative operation, come into full action. If the little boy identifies himself with the father, in a rather literal sense unconsciously *becomes* the father, then he can both enjoy the mother and can *himself* inhibit his own dangerous proclivities. This statement is too sensibly purposive in tone, although essentially correct according to Freudian theory.

What happens is again more direct and more subtle. We have seen that the newborn infant has no "self" in the sophisticated psychological sense of the term, and that he has for some time been building up the differentiation between me and not-me in curious ways. We have seen that it is much more difficult to see the breast as not-self than to incorporate it with the inner sequence of bodily events as part of the self in the stage of primary narcissism. For a long time (always, in the unconscious), the boundaries between object and self and between self and object are very fluid. And the determining associative bond is typically the inner biological, libidinal one important to the young creature at that moment.

Thus, the introjection of parental demands (or, better, what the child fantasies the parental demands to be) is by no means a new psychological development. It is part and parcel of the general process of ego development— that is, of the differentiation of self and not-self, of things and other people— in short, of reality. In the phallic stage, however, the child is already a fairly complex little person, with fairly complex, though not very accurate, concepts of the outer world. Thus, if, in his panic about the Oedipal situation and possible castration, he pursues his previous methods of understanding with the familiar fluidity of introjection and projection, what he introjects is a very large gob of "parent." At this stage of development, it is not *fragments* of fact and attitude absorbed through the relationship with the parents that are incorporated with the emerging self. Instead, *a fairly well-organized complex of attitudes* is introjected, typically those *attributed* to the parent by the child during the crisis of the phallic stage.

THE SUPEREGO

We return now to the formation of the *superego*. Partly the boy identifies with the father and so vicariously enjoys the masculine role *vis-à-vis* the mother and socially. He is still partly identified with the mother as of his earlier incipient object relationships. And partly his more sophisticated appreciation of parental views involves identification with their prohibitions as well. Since the child at this stage, according to Freud, is still *mainly* preoccupied with his sexual urges, the focus of the introjected parent image tends to be sexual in the direction just described. When Freud makes the general comment that the superego is the inheritor of the Oedipus complex, he means that the child—denied direct biological fulfillment—typically solves his problem by *incorporating his view of parental attitudes as his own.*

From this point on, musts and must-nots come from within. The child no longer merely obeys outside authority because of the fear of external compulsion, real or fancied. The parent now speaks from within as "conscience." One potent reason why "conscience" can make cowards of us all, and can be severe beyond all good sense, is that "conscience" is formed as a resolution of the Oedipus complex. It is established at a time when the little boy fears extreme retribution for his incipient phallic impulses because at this period "magic" is still for the most part the normal mode of evaluation. At a time when wish is tantamount to deed and infantile omnipotence has been transferred to the parent, this formulation is by no means absurd. On the contrary, it is the most "reasonable" formulation a little child can make. We should keep in mind that the child is handling ideas that are for him quite literally a matter of life or death.

Thus, for Freud, the still, small voice of conscience is established at about this age, via the Oedipus complex. We mentioned this origin in the structural account of the anatomy of the mental personality (pp. 82*ff.*), but we can now understand better both how the superego comes about and why conscience is so "instinctual," often so irrational and punitive. The introjected parent is always to a large extent the fantasy product of the child guilty about his sexual inclinations.

With this background in genetic development, the statement that the superego is a relatively late differentiation of the id becomes intelligible. The irrational demands of conscience, as seen in the pathological condition of melancholia, for example, can now be understood as the introjection of the irrational guilt and fear, sensible enough at the phallic stage of infantile development but inappropriate to adult problems.

No matter what the exact ingredients of the superego or precisely when it develops, it is easy to see that strong self-punitive attitudes of irrational violence are likely to be incorporated into it along with more constructive and socially oriented parental judgments. The early modes of defense against the infantile wishes and hostilities, formulated by the child himself, combine with the admonitions of the adult to form this *internal* control of impulse necessary to adequate social function.

Parental admonition requires some analysis too. It is typically more severe toward the child than toward the adult. The mother who would not dream of eating oatmeal and spinach herself, or of forcing these estimable comestibles upon her husband, dutifully crams them down the throat of her reluctant offspring. She may be even more severe in other areas. She wants to bring him up *right—a fortiori* in regard to training in the fundamental decencies associated with instinctual needs. Most adults have forgotten their own childhood and see their current "liberal" attitude toward infringements of the moral code either as the due prerogative of mature experience or as sins from which the children should be protected. In any event, the parent is typically far more "idealistic" for his child than for himself and his contemporaries.

Again, the rational solution of this problem espoused by some "psychologically informed" parents has not proved expedient. The little child is not a rational being. In his struggle against natural impulses which *must* be controlled, he very much needs the firm assistance of the parental "no" at the level of his own understanding. The "psychologically informed" parent who tries to spare the child the pangs of the Oedipus complex and other infantile hazards too often leaves the child without the necessary guideposts. The child cannot grasp the subtleties of situational values so apparent to the adult. "Reasoning" with him, or accepting his misdoings beyond the point of social acceptance because they are natural to the child, too often fails to give him the framework of potent correction at the level of "emotional" understanding he is equipped to grasp.

An example of this sort of parent-child relationship involves my son's swearing. As psychologically informed parents, we were prepared to "understand" the innocent naughty words of the little boy. We carefully explained to him that certain words are "not used," but without punishment or much parental emotion. However, as his language became settled in a prurient direction, parental admonitions took on increasing forthrightness and forcefulness until disciplinary measures at the age of about eight strongly resembled the direct means ordinarily applied much earlier. We did feel that our parental responsibility demanded censorship prior to expulsion from school and ostracism from any "nice" home.

The child learned the words from other children, mainly country neighbors, whose approval he deeply wanted. These children had been promptly swatted the moment they swore in public, and *their* language was irreproachable in our presence or in school, though definitely not in private. But *they* knew the difference in their bones. Our little boy had to learn the difference as a straight ego problem. Acknowledging the justice of our disapproval, the poor youngster would still let loose an appalling vocabulary the moment he was emotionally aroused—*i.e.*, when his ego control was transiently weakened. Of course he learned, as time went on, not to swear inappropriately, since his ego and superego control is generally sound.

The superego accomplishes basic controls necessary for social adaptation by quite directly taking over parental admonitions which the child endows with emotional power. The parent can escape this condition of socialization no more than the child. He must accept himself in the role of divinity and use his reason in the direction of being as benign and perhaps as *sensible* a deity as possible. It will help him to know that his throne will crumble and mysteriously reassemble from time to time as the child gets on with the business of growing up. It is his job to teach the child the essentials of adulthood in the culture in which they live. Naturally, the Freudian does not consider the actions of the specific parent a matter of indifference. The example about swearing illustrates the point. The Freudian does remark that *over and above* the actual merits and sins of the parent is the emerging personality of the child which has a biological sequence of its own, with demands which must be subjugated or transformed as the price of living in a civilization.

It is, then, impossible to avoid the Oedipus complex, at least in our society. The woes of this period can be minimized and handled constructively in so far as the child is able to identify happily with a gentle but firm parent in harmonious relationship with his culture. To drive home the moral of the example given above, our son could have learned the deep social attitude toward swearing from us directly if we had used the power he ascribed to us normally in early childhood—by virtue of *his* inner feelings—to censure the naughty words. It was the child's different emotional relation to his parents that made the *later* "reasonable" learning actually more difficult.

In the *absence* of adequate parental figures, the superego often fails to develop properly, and object relations tend to remain at the narcissistic level. Here the difficulties of children brought up in institutions may be mentioned again. Too often, the lack of a person to identify with results in a conscience-less individual—in the kind of personality development known as psychopathy. The child, and later the adult, can love only himself.

Unusually harsh or anxious handling by the parent also predisposes the child to later difficulties, especially if the parents are truly loved and respected. The superego makes too stern demands upon the ego for repression of the continuing id impulses. Even when the parents have died, or the child as adult rarely sees them and feels consciously indifferent or hostile, he still acts as if they were at his elbow censoring his every desire. Many a patient who prides himself above all on his rationality suddenly finds himself crying like a baby during the analytic hour over some childish episode. Or it may be that he weeps for the death of a father whose funeral he did not bother to attend some years earlier in his repudiation of "sentimentality" or in conscious hostility to the parent.

THE ENGLISH SCHOOL: KLEIN

This seems to be the best point at which to insert a brief account of the views of Melanie Klein, one of the leaders of psychoanalysis in England. She considers the superego as a much more gradual development than the one here presented as essentially Freudian, and as operating—after a fashion—in early infancy. She takes her departure from the earlier works of Freud and Abraham, with rather more exclusive emphasis upon the earlier (pregenital) modes of infantile sexuality and the death instinct (aggression) than most of the authors discussed, including Freud himself. Basing her theory mainly on observation of children in analysis (she was one of the first to apply the psychoanalytic technique to children and is one of the main originators of the now familiar "play technique" for overcoming difficulties in verbalization for the little patients), she was led further and further back into infancy in her search for the origins of the phenomena she encountered. So far as I know, neither Klein nor her followers have undertaken the kind of direct observation of infants illustrated by the work of Spitz. On the contrary, they would probably criticize such work as too external to the child and would prefer their own method of theoretical extrapolation from the earliest periods of relatively direct expression by the child.

In any event, the major dynamics of ego and superego development are pushed back to much earlier periods—the first year of life. Passive sucking gives way to active biting around the sixth month; that is, the child is able to *do* something about his states of "anxiety" beyond mere endurance. Furthermore, he has developed some sense of "objects" as different from himself, and of himself as "object." His appreciation of "objects" is, however, still rudimentary. It is dominated by the organs and biological processes which his own experience has allowed him to recognize (plus dim phylogenetically determined images, according to Klein, of the penis, the vagina, and the general idea of coitus and childbirth). The breast of the mother, his own feces and urine, the genital organs, the process of incorporation and expulsion, the presence and absence of the mother—these are the essential materials the

infant has available. (Klein does *not* emphasize the development of the musculature, which allows the child to grasp or escape from the object in a more
discriminating manner; and to identify his own body as object.)

Arguing from the major instinctual trends described by Freud and
Abraham, and from her observation of how they operate the moment her
techniques can be used with little children, Klein develops the position that
oral sadism is of crucial importance for personality development. (1) It is a
natural function of the mouth, pleasurable in itself, and it may be intensified
by constitutional variations in the structure of jaws and teeth. (I would add
the general "activeness" of the infant described by Fries.) (2) This rather
incidental sadism of *biting* is intensified and given a definitely hostile direction by the experience of oral frustration in weaning or even in waiting for
food. The longed-for breast thus becomes an object of hostility as well. (3)
The rage derived from frustration "serves to strengthen the sadistic instincts
of the infant."[22] Klein accepts Freud's concept of the death instinct as an
active aggression against the self. (4) The emerging anal sadism of the child
and his observations (or phylogenetically determined fantasies) of coitus are
woven into the prevailing oral-sadistic trend and also serve to heighten his
hostile aggressive impulses. Coitus is fantasied as an act of biting, leading to
oral incorporation of the penis by the mother. The penis and vagina are
conceived of as dangerous weapons—the penis largely equated with the breast,
the vagina with the biting mouth.

At this point, in Klein's theory, the narcissistic (pleasure-seeking) libido
is necessarily at odds with the increasing and increasingly focused sadism of
the child. The infant weaves into this picture its increasing awareness of
external objects on the one hand and of its internal processes on the other.
Therefore it conceives the object as something to be incorporated or ejected,
with the polarity of "good" and "bad" so often cited in analytic schools as
the first possible autonomous "judgment" of the child. For the most part, the
definition comes from within and is determined by the instinctual conflict
itself. Klein writes: "In my judgment, reality and real objects affect [the
child's] anxiety-situations from the very earliest stages of its existence, *in the
sense that it regards them as so many proofs or refutations of its anxiety-
situations* [my italics]."[23] Owing to the interaction of the mechanisms of introjection and projection, which make the object part of the self, as it were,
external factors come to influence the formation of the personality.

These mechanisms are derived from swallowing and spitting out; excret-
ing and retaining the stool—processes which Freud (and Abraham even more
systematically) pointed out as dominating in the experience of the infant.
The mechanism of projection is further aided by the tendency of the organ-

ism to turn the essentially autoaggressive death instinct outward in self-protection. Thus, the infant falls into what Klein calls the *paranoid position* as the first phase of his active relationship to the world, attributing to the parent its own hostilities. She writes:

> The idea of an infant of from six to twelve months trying to destroy its mother by every method at the disposal of its sadistic tendencies— with its teeth, nails and excreta and with the whole of its body, transformed in imagination into all kinds of dangerous weapons—presents a horrifying, not to say an unbelievable, picture to our minds.[24]

Nevertheless, Klein feels compelled to acknowledge the truth of this picture from her studies of three-year-olds in whose lives constitutional factors or actual frustration have built up these normal hostilities to the point of making them unmanageable. These hostilities, projected outward, become the bad mother. The infant expects and fears menace from the outside world as the exact counterpart of its own sadism. It is easily frightened and easily gives vent to rage.

But, of course, there is always the good mother, who facilitates the pleasure seeking of the libido, and there are libidinal urges which find gratification, or at least strive toward gratification. Very early, the infant ego mobilizes one part of the id against another—a division which is the first step toward instinctual inhibitions and the formation of the superego.[25] In this process, the incorporated object (the child's view of the parent) plays an important role at once. Fear of the parent and love of the parent aid the infant in mastering its dangerous hostilities, in alliance with its instinctual erotic strivings.

A little later, the child enters what Melanie Klein calls the *depressive position*. The significant change rests upon the growing recognition that the object (mainly the mother) has an intrinsic wholeness. Mother is perceived as being in herself both bad and good. One cannot attack the bad mother without also destroying the good mother. Following in general Freud's outline of the dynamics of melancholia (see pp. 288ff.), Klein feels that now the "whole object" is introjected, and the hostility projected in the paranoid position is now experienced by the child as again internal and directed against the self. This shift is essentially intrinsic to the psychic development of the child. External factors again operate to reinforce or diminish instinctual drives in a manner which may so change the balance of forces as to produce qualitatively different results. Nevertheless, the main determinant, for Klein, is the child's realization that the object must be preserved, and that the bad mother cannot be separated from the good mother. In the depressive position the child internalizes the conflict.

Klein does not like to assign chronological dates to these "positions," but

I think I am correct in saying that they are now assumed to occur within the first year of life and to set the stage for all future developments, neurotic and normal.

Two points prominent in Klein's thinking have been underemphasized in this schematic report. One is the child's concern with the "insides" of the body, including the genitalia and "children," which it assumes are present inside the mother. Such childhood distortions of anatomy are familiar to every Freudian from the analysis of adults as well as of little children, and they may be considered a quite natural interpretation if one considers the experiential concepts available to the infant. However, many Freudians feel that Klein ascribes greater powers of conceptualization to the infant than is warranted when she attributes such complex fantasies to the first year of life, or even to the second.

The second point is Klein's view of the Oedipus complex and the superego. We have seen that, in Freud's view, these phenomena are of relatively late development (third to fifth year at the earliest), whereas Klein sees traces of genital-organ fantasies from the outset and considers that the superego begins the moment the infant introjects his view of the parental command and uses it in the *economy* of his inner instinctual adjustments. The superego has a gradual development thereafter as the child consolidates his attitudes toward the parents as whole objects—attitudes requisite for the full development of the Freudian superego.

Classical Freudians are willing enough to accept the data Klein adduces as evidence for the fact, observed by other analysts as well, that the Oedipus complex and the subsequent castration fear have *antecedents* in the pregenital period. Many Freudians feel, however, that the main significance of the superego lies in the peculiar organization of id impulses described by Freud, which can be attained only after the child has established a relatively sophisticated relationship to the persons of his parents at a later age. This consolidation of attitudes, the true *conscience*, is neglected by Klein.

A corollary of this Freudian critique* of Klein's position suggests also that she overemphasizes the importance of the oral-sadistic phase in two ways to the neglect of points considered essential to Freud's doctrine. The first point concerns the instinctual life of the child. No Freudian doubts the importance of the oral-sadistic stage or the possibility that it may be decisive for *some* types of pathology and character formation. But it is not necessarily decisive for *all*. The child may negotiate this stage quite well and come to grief because of

---

* Although Klein has a large following in England, her theoretical views are not widely accepted in America. My critical comments here are taken in large part from R. Waelder, "The Problem of the Genesis of Psychical Conflict in Earliest Infancy," *International Journal of Psycho-Analysis*, 1937, 18:406-473.

special difficulties in the anal or phallic phase. Obviously, these difficulties will show certain oral components, since no vital function is abandoned, nor are its special problems ever completely solved. Nevertheless, the focus of disturbance may be constituted so differently as to make Klein's stress on the early oral sadism one-sided to the point of error. (This is the error I have called reductionism.)

A further point of Freudian critique concerns Klein's neglect of the structural aspects of the personality developed by Freud. We have already seen that equating the superego with the scattered instances of instinctual inhibition achieved by introjection of the object does not meet Freud's concept of the *consolidated* power of conscience as organized at a later date under special circumstances. The same difficulty may be extended to the formation of the ego, and it is here that the rift between Anna Freud and Melanie Klein shows itself most clearly. In Chapter 3, Anna Freud's position in the new ego psychology was described as emphasizing the relative autonomy of the systems, big and little, which are erected by the *ego* as defense mechanisms *vis-à-vis* reality and instinctual conflict. Anna Freud believes that these systems must be understood, respected, and helpfully modified by the therapist, especially in the treatment of little children who are still in the process of forming necessary defenses—that is, expedient ways of dealing with the recurrent ups and downs of instinctual drives. Melanie Klein drives straight to the instinctual conflict, with prompt interpretation to the child. One reads almost nothing about the actual life situation of the child in a Klein report. She largely ignores the autonomous institutions of the ego (as suggested in Chap. 3) as well as the institution of the superego.

Many readers must have shared with me a naive repugnance to Klein's description of the monstrous concepts of the very young, and to her application of terms denominating adult psychosis to the normal stages of infancy—*i.e.*, paranoid and depressive. The classical Freudian does not object to the *monstrosities* as such. He encounters them every day in the analysis of the unconscious, and if the reader has not become aware of this fact, it is the fault of my reporting. I have tried to emphasize that these horrid notions are the natural ideation of the infant prior to full experience in the outer world. The *Freudian* critique on this point attacks Klein's view of the age level to which they may be ascribed and her strong emphasis on oral sadism.

Freudian critique of the use of *psychotic labels*, however, is not a matter of disagreeable semantics in equating normal infancy with insanity. The classical Freudian position is that adult psychosis, especially "depression," presupposes conflict among rather well-systematized personality institutions and cannot be considered as in any sense the equivalent of the infantile conflict.

PSYCHOLOGICAL DEVELOPMENT OF THE FEMALE

As we noted earlier, this discussion of the phallic stage and the Oedipus complex leading to the formation of the superego has been oriented specifically toward the male. Freud considered the comparable development of the female child during the same period as very much more complex, although it too is essentially biologically determined and has similar repercussions in later personality development. I shall here report briefly Freud's position as he explained it in Chapter 5 of the *New Introductory Lectures.** With relatively small variations in emphasis on special biological or social factors, Freud's statement is still accepted by most classical Freudians, although it is repudiated by most of the "non-libido" schools. Since I shall not discuss the topic of female psychology in presenting these schools in Part III, I shall take this opportunity of referring the reader to a relatively focused rebuttal of Freud's position, substituting emphasis on special aspects of woman's cultural experience, written by Clara Thompson.[26]

Freud considers the very early psychological development of the two sexes as entirely similar, with the *probable* exception of a greater degree of "activity" in the male on constitutional grounds. (Freud is clear on the meaning of statistically observable differences in this respect, remarking that *some* female infants seem constitutionally more active than the average male.) However this may be, the female infant goes through the same stages as the male, with varying emphasis on active and passive modes; the same organically determined foci in the oral, anal, and genital zones; the same relationship to "objects"—mainly to the mother. In fact, Freud emphasizes the *bisexuality* of the human organism even in its anatomical givens as an important part of his theory.† He rejects the notion of traits *inborn* as masculine or feminine, associated with special organs

At the beginning of the phallic stage, the little girl is still a "little man," finding her new focus of libidinal concern in the clitoris, as the boy finds it in

---

* The reader interested in further developments and ramifications of this point of view will find a comprehensive statement in Helene Deutsch, *Psychology of Women*, Grune & Stratton, Vol. I, 1944; Vol. II, 1945.

† The problem of bisexuality was important to Freud in his early years, partly through the influence of Fliess—the friend whom he placed in a role not unlike that of the analyst in contemporary treatment. *Cf.* E. Jones, *The Life and Work of Sigmund Freud*, Vol. I, Basic Books, 1953, Chap. 13; S. Freud, *The Origins of Psychoanalysis: Letters to Wilhelm Fliess, Drafts and Notes: 1887–1902*, Basic Books, 1954.

Stekel made this concept one of the key points of his theory, deliberately searching out the masculine and feminine aspects of the patient's reactions and the manner of their interaction.

the penis. (Anatomically the clitoris is homologous to the penis. It seems to be sensitive and erectile in a similar way.) She normally begins masturbatory activities like the boy—activities which rarely if ever include the vagina—the passive organ of adult female sexuality. Thus, at the very outset, the problem of her genital development is more complex, since she must make a change in the organ of gratification from the clitoris to the vagina, whereas the boy's penis remains the main organ involved in gratification.

A second complication arises from the fact that the little girl must somehow change the object of her libidinal attachment from the mother (whom she initially loves in the same way the boy does) to the father, whereas the boy merely continues his early tender relationship to the mother under the new circumstances arising in the phallic stage of more focused genital desires for the mother and more focused rivalry with the father. The little girl must come to "hate" her mother and become her rival with respect to the father. (Freud never questions the idea that girls go through an Oedipal phase, sometimes called the Electra complex, from a Greek myth in which the daughter connives at the murder of a faithless mother.)

Hostility toward the mother is latent in children of both sexes because of the role she must play in weaning and toilet training; that is, the necessary disappointments and frustrations of the infant's acculturation prepare a pattern of "hatred" available to the child when the positive aspects of normal developmental ambivalence are overwhelmed. The shift toward hatred of the mother, following upon tender attachment, occurs when the little girl first becomes aware that she lacks a penis. Freud writes:

> She is wounded in her self-love by the unfavourable comparison with the boy who is so much better equipped, and therefore gives up the masturbatory satisfaction which she obtained from her clitoris, repudiates her love towards her mother, and at the same time often represses a good deal of her sexual impulses in general.[27]

At first her lack doubtless appears to her a personal misfortune, but as she learns that all females, including her mother, are afflicted in the same way, she comes to depreciate all women. "The incentives to hostility [toward the mother], which have been so long accumulating, get the upper hand."[28] The little girl obscurely feels that her mother is responsible for this new, special deprivation. Also, the active and passive genital wishes toward the mother that she, like the boy, has entertained must undergo a serious setback.

This unlikely series of events was so neatly illustrated by my small daughter as to reverse my own initial skepticism toward the formulation. She and her brother usually shared the tub in a rather gay nightly bathing ritual. One night, when she was three or four, the little girl suddenly burst into tears. "My weewee's all gone!" Apparently this was the first time she had *noticed* the anatomical difference. Presumably I tried to reassure her with the explanation that little girls have a different kind of weewee. At any rate, for some weeks she objected violently to being called a little girl. This attitude soon faded out, and she became, if anything, overfeminine in her interest in clothes, housekeeping, and the like in later childhood. The small episode was sufficiently convincing to me that the female castration complex exists. Whether it inevitably plays the very important role in the psychology of women ascribed to it by Freud is a different problem, beyond the purview of the present discussion.

Freud goes on to consider what happens in the life of the little girl after the crucial "discovery of her castration" and the development of her *penis envy*. We saw that for the boy the Oedipal phase is a natural elaboration of existing attitudes and is given up because of the threat of castration. The same threat, already fulfilled in the case of the girl, drives her *into* the Oedipal situation. She now wishes to regain a penis via the male (in early childhood, the father) and develops the equation of the penis with a child so frequently observed in psychoanalysis. It is having a child by the father that will, she fancies, restore the lost organ. Having renounced much of the activity involved in clitoric masturbation because of the inadequacy of the organ,* she is now dominated by the passive aims of the vagina in the development of normal femininity.

From this point on, it is not difficult to understand how the girl's Oedipus complex will have much the same contours as the boy's, although the sexes are reversed. She will love the father and hate the mother because the mother is a rival for the father's love, as well as because of earlier resentments. And the girl will tend to *identify with the mother* as a means of handling the problem, just as the boy identifies with the father.

It will be noted, however, that the castration complex has for the girl prepared the way for the Oedipus complex during the period of superego formation, instead of destroying it, as in the case of the boy. Under these circumstances, there is less motive for her to overcome it as sharply as the boy, and according to Freud it tends to remain operative far longer—in fact, indefinitely. Deutsch's second volume, on motherhood, presents the many ways in which the mother's attitude toward her child reflects rather directly the problems and relationships of her own girlhood. The superego of the woman

---

* Deutsch remarks that the inadequacy derives not only from the social comparison with the male organ but from the nature of the clitoris itself as inadequate to full sexual gratification. Thus, the little girl becomes "organless" and must await development in the passive vaginal area, which requires the action of the male. (H. Deutsch, *op. cit.*, I, pp. 228*ff.*)

generally, according to Freud, does not attain the strength and independence of the male superego, a position which seems similar in flavor to the wide-spread idea that her values are more personal and humane, and—for good and ill—less concerned with purely abstract principles.

TERMINATION OF EARLY CHILDHOOD

AS SHE ATTAINS school age, however, the little girl, like the little boy, has reached some sort of integrative handling of the major instinctual urges implicit in the bodily structure of the human race, in more or less effective relationship to the "objects" of the outer world—mainly the figures in the child's own family. In reporting the classical Freudian position, I have confined myself to fairly typical developments in our culture, but the importance of variations in the environmental approach has been discussed often enough to suggest that the Freudian position can readily absorb the variations due to cultural differences mentioned in the preceding chapter. It should not imply a biologically fixed series of psychological events, statable in terms of traits observable at different maturational periods. The problem is rather the successive focus of the libido on various zones, which call forth relatively characteristic modes of reaction. (I am here using terms that Erikson has emphasized.)

The characteristic mode of reaction for the organ zone involved may be passive or active; it may be related essentially to the inner equilibrium of the person or to the object; it may meet with ready welcome or condemnation by the people to whom the child is attached. To these factors must be added the maturation of the basic ego apparatuses: the sense organs, motor coordination, locomotion, speech. All these aspects of the child's experience interact creatively with one another at every stage of development.

By about the age of six, however, Freud believes that the major instinctual problems in their major object relationships have reached a type of organization for each person which remains fundamental throughout life. We may call this fundamental organization his character or personality. Later circumstances allow for expansion, generally or in particular directions. Or later conditions may be especially restrictive; or they may lay such heavy burdens on the personality in one or another area of function that the organizational pattern of the personality established in early childhood becomes more or less permanently distorted. Yet even the distortion is characteristic for the personality, and cannot be explained directly by the pressure of special circumstance.

The family drama and the process of instinctual maturation are in a way complete. The basic personality is equipped, well or badly, for its part in the wider social world.

THE LATENCY PERIOD

WE HAVE SEEN that Freud was deeply convinced of the diphasic quality of human sexual development. The settling of the Oedipus complex, as described earlier, is aided, he thought, by a biological lessening of the sexual urge from about the age of six until puberty, when it again becomes powerful with a recrudescence of earlier problems. Its aims during the latency period have become mainly "desexualized."

A psychological theory so firmly rooted in consideration of the fate of the sexual instincts might be expected to neglect the period when they are in abeyance. This is in fact the case. In a common-sense way, oriented by his special knowledge, every analyst uses the events of the school years for the better understanding of his patient, but there is little systematic, codified scientific treatment of these years to report.

I quote from Erikson, one of the few analysts who has written specifically about this period:

> with the oncoming latency period . . . [the child] now learns to win recognition by producing things. . . . He has experienced a sense of finality regarding the fact that there is no workable future within the womb of his family, and thus becomes ready to apply himself to given skills and tasks, which go far beyond the mere playful expression of his organ modes or the pleasure in the function of his limbs.[29]

If he has been well prepared emotionally for confidence in himself and the world (Erikson prefers the word *trust* as more applicable to the very early infantile state which grows into the more focused connotations of *confidence*), if his native abilities allow the development of skills prized by his culture, if the wider society, mainly the school, offers good ways of "admitting the child to an understanding of meaningful roles in its total economy"[30]—then this period of life has enormous functional importance in preparing the child for his later contribution to society and to his own later family in the area of work.

Conversely, if early family life has not prepared the child for school life, if the school fails to sustain the initiative and confidence of the child, if the child's constitutional endowment makes it impossible for him to keep pace with his fellows in learning tools and skills—then a sense of inadequacy and inferiority is very likely to develop. His capacity to identify with others on the basis of common goals of "industry" (Erikson here uses the term in the general sense) does not develop adequately, and the child is often led back to "the more isolated, less tool-conscious 'anatomical' rivalry of the Oedipal time."[31]

In this manner, and rather sketchily, Erikson outlines the values and dangers of the latency period. We shall see that Sullivan emphasizes competition and cooperation with one's peers as normal developments in what he calls the juvenile period, premised upon the growth in sheer capacity to envisage the other fellow with some objectivity, and to develop the tools of competition and cooperation (see pp.407f.). Both Erikson and Sullivan consider these phenomena as significantly different from the early childhood drama, although their theories of basic development differ as regards the relative importance allotted to the erogenous zones in the constellation of early modes of reaction ("dynamisms," in Sullivan's vocabulary). Both emphasize the need for early preparedness for the typical juvenile experience, the tendency toward regression to earlier patterns if the child's experience proves too harsh at this period, and the danger of a development into the roles provided by his culture that may be too one-sided for mental health.

ADOLESCENCE

ANNA FREUD[32] comments that psychoanalysts have been mainly interested in the *similarities* among the mechanisms of the phallic, pubertal, and climacteric stages, all rooted in the course, denouement, and re-emergence of the Oedipus complex. She points out the importance of observing the *differences* peculiar to these stages, showing in particular that the adolescent disturbance is not merely a temporary exaggeration of mechanisms set for all time in childhood but has a pattern peculiar to itself. The frequent extreme asceticism of the teens, for example, often appears to represent a fear of *all* libidinal impulses, punctuated by an almost orgiastic giving way to them regardless of the taboos peculiar to the individual which will set the pattern of his neurosis in the event that the flare-up of the teens continues. Helene Deutsch, in her extensive writings on female adolescence,[33] suggests that the commonly observed drive toward independence and self-reliance is a primary factor and remarks that many activities which superficially appear to be sexual (even to the psychoanalyst) are actually manifestations of the impulse to growth. The psychoanalytic journals contain many case studies of older children, with relatively brief comment on one aspect or another of analytic theory.

Erikson generalizes beyond the sphere of instinctual development—which he also accepts. He points out that the child, now the young adult, must find an *identity*. This identity is by no means a mere repetition of identification with the father in consequence of a renascent Oedipus complex, or of the rebellion and compromise instituted earlier. It is the accrued experience of his own identity, matched with his perception of his potential meaning for others—"as evidenced in the tangible promise of a 'career.' "[34] The problem of the adolescent is not only the renewed influx of sexual drives based upon bodily structure—what Sullivan calls the "lust dynamism" (see pp. 357f.)—but also establishing his own self (identity) as against the great variety of roles open to him in any flexible society—notably in America. Erikson writes:

> It is primarily the inability to settle on an occupational identity which disturbs young people. To keep themselves together they temporarily overidentify, to the point of apparent complete loss of identity, with the heroes of cliques and crowds. This initiates the stage of "falling in love," which is by no means entirely, or even primarily, a sexual matter —except where the mores demand it. To a considerable extent adolescent love is an attempt to arrive at a definition of one's identity by projecting one's diffused ego images on one another and by seeing them thus reflected and gradually clarified. This is why many a youth would rather converse, and settle matters of mutual identification, than embrace.[35]

In Chapter 4, I used Erikson's presentation of the case of little Sam as a kind of penultimate summary of the *clinical* view of relationships between the terms of the organism and the terms of the milieu, which I felt would be acceptable to most analysts. With more diffidence concerning its general acceptability to analysts, I reproduce here the diagram he offers of what he calls the eight stages of life. It suggests how the stages of libidinal development familiar to classical theory may be related to phases of ego development now being energetically brought into consideration by psychoanalysts.

Erikson is himself tentative about his classification of what he calls "enduring solutions" of the problems posed by the nuclear conflicts of the child,

	1	2	3	4	5	6	7	8
ORAL-SENSORY	TRUST VS. MISTRUST							
MUSCULAR-ANAL		AUTONOMY VS. SHAME, DOUBT						
LOCOMOTOR-GENITAL			INITIATIVE VS. GUILT					
LATENCY				INDUSTRY VS. INFERIORITY				
PUBERTY AND ADOLESCENCE					IDENTITY VS. ROLE DIFFUSION			
YOUNG ADULTHOOD						INTIMACY VS. ISOLATION		
ADULTHOOD							GENERATIVITY VS. STAGNATION	
MATURITY								INTEGRITY VS. DISGUST, DESPAIR

which require progressively new ego strengths for their mastery. Each solution is based upon the earlier ones. Mature integrity depends upon the basic development of trust, autonomy, initiative, etc. in the phases of growth characteristic for the organism. They must be supported by sound cultural institutions—at first mediated primarily by the parents but ultimately extending to all the opportunities and restrictions of society. Erikson presents these "solutions" as a diagonal in order to suggest the need for further elaboration of the precursors and derivatives of an ego development as yet insufficiently studied.

Some analysts may object to the specific formulation Erikson has devised for the relationship among the aspects of the genetic process emphasized by Freud, stages of ego development, relationship to the environment, and changing concepts of the self. Some may feel that the basic libidinal forces are insufficiently emphasized. Others—Kardiner, for example—may feel that the progress of ego development is stated too rigidly—that growth in these complex areas of the personality is fundamentally more variable, more dependent on the specific social constellation within which the child matures. At the very least, however, one may say that Erikson shows how the classical Freudian genetic scheme may be broadened to include muscular and locomotor aspects of growth and may be related to the development of deep personal and social attitudes with some regularity.

Both Erikson and Kardiner, in different ways, provide a bridge between a theory initially too concentrated on infantile sexuality—as Freud himself repeatedly remarked—and the extreme rejection of this aspect of the genetic process characteristic of the non-libido schools. I trust, however, that this chapter as a whole will help to correct the still-prevalent notion that classical Freudian theory is *exclusively* concerned with infantile sexuality, regardless of how the needs of the child are met by his family and his society.

SUMMARY

Early Infancy. The human infant is born without a clear perception of the outer world and of the boundaries of his own self. The main danger he experiences is the flooding of his immature nervous system by stimuli which he cannot master. The birth trauma may be considered as the prototype of later anxiety states which tend toward reinstatement of this early condition. The presence of the mother becomes the infant's main guarantee against such totalistic disaster. Thus, fear of *loss of love* (separation anxiety) plays a cardinal role in infancy and in certain types of severely regressive pathology in later life.

The concepts of omnipotence and magical thinking are necessary consequences of the infant's lack of knowledge about the external world in its own right, or even as different from the internal world. Processes of differentiation and conceptualization available to the infant were emphasized in preparation for understanding of the sexually oriented fantasies attributed by Freudians to the child in later stages of development.

The Oral Stage. Oral pleasure is described as an instinctual (sexual, libidinal) need more significant for personality development than hunger in our culture, although the two are related. Passive suckling, closely connected with the growing perception of the mother as the external source, gives way to active biting. Perception of the object (the mother) appears primarily in connection with the bodily function of swallowing (incorporation and introjection → identification) and spitting out (projection). At a period when the infant does not clearly distinguish between the inner and outer world, between function and object, these trends are necessarily highly generalized. Melanie Klein's position as a theorist is rooted in this phase of the infant's experience with an emphasis most classical Freudians in America consider excessive. All Freudians consider that essential modes of relationship to objects stem from this period, and that the infant's expectations of the outer world are profoundly influenced by this initially oral contact.

The Anal Stage. Reflex evacuation, of course, occurs from birth and is presumably pleasurable to the infant. Probably withholding of the feces also becomes pleasurable spontaneously at a later date; certainly the withholding appears in every culture. The infant appears to value his excreta as "object"; the *activities* of expelling and retaining become his first efforts at direct control of instinctual drives. Furthermore, the mother, already a highly cathected object, demands control on *her* terms. The infant approaches this new focus of instinctual concern with attitudes already partly formulated during the oral stage. Indeed, the two stages overlap; the two foci of concern are only partly independent and necessarily interact with each other. The special feature of the need for autonomous control of a powerful instinctual pattern (itself diphasic as regards expelling and retaining) plus the need for adaptation to the external demands of the mother make the modes of adjustment worked out by the child at this period especially significant for later attitudes toward (1) his own autonomy *vs.* giving in to others and (2) his own possessions (originally his excreta) *vs.* more general valuation of objects.

The Phallic Stage. Here again, the focus is upon an organ that has always been there but has not been of primary importance to the child. At about the fourth year, it tends spontaneously to become predominant. Again, the three-year-old approaches concern with the genitals as a little person whose attitudes have already been rather definitely formed in the course of experience in the oral and anal spheres. These attitudes are never simply renounced. (They may be repressed or, in normal development, partially dissolved in new patterns.) But the three-year-old develops keen desires in the genital area, which he (or she) must somehow try to gratify. Partly the desire is handled by masturbation—a solution seriously condemned by the external objects (parents) whom the child has come to respect, to love, and to fear. Partly the desire demands an external object for its fulfillment, and the child is forced into the *Oedipal* situation. His mother is the object of his genital desires, and his father therefore becomes his rival.

Superego. Prohibition of the natural aim of the libido in the phallic stage leads to formation of the superego. Blocked in direct fulfillment with the mother; conflicted in attitudes toward the father as successful rival (whom one would like to kill and emulate) and as powerful, loved protector (whom one needs and wants); *threatened by castration* if he attempts to compete—the little boy solves his problem by a massive *introjection* of the parental attitude, as he sees it, by *identification* with the parents.

Psychological Development of the Female. In the early years, little girls are very much like little boys. In the phallic stage, they must shift the organ of gratification from the clitoris to the vagina; the object from the mother to the father. Castration is for them the observed fact that determines the formation of the Oedipus complex, and penis envy becomes their dominant motif. The Oedipal situation is not renounced so abruptly as in boys, and the superego of women is not so sharply demarcated and independent as that of men.

Latency Period. After the repression (or resolution) of the Oedipus complex and the development of the superego at about the sixth year, Freud believes that the infantile sexual urge goes into eclipse until the renewed biological forces of puberty again bring it into prominence. Because the years of later childhood do not contribute directly to the course of instinctual development as Freud conceives it, they have been largely neglected by Freudians as an area for systematic investigation, although every analyst uses information about these years in his effort to understand how instinctual trends are operating in the individual case. Erikson points to the importance of finding tools and skills during this period which allow the child to identify with others on a more socialized level than the early organ fantasies.

Adolescence. The classical Freudian position emphasizes the reinstatement during this period of early attitudes and quasi-solutions of the Oedipus complex. Without denying the crucial importance of this position, some authors now point to the *special* structure of libidinal problems characteristic for this age. Erikson emphasizes the need of the adolescent to find his *identity* —that is, a social role which enables him to match his early instinctual relationships within the family with the social roles proffered, more or less expediently, by the society within which he must function.

Critical Comment

THIS CHAPTER has been written as a sympathetic account of *Freud's* views on a topic crucial to Freudian psychoanalysis and, in my opinion, to any valid psychological science. I have occasionally reported controversial views within the Freudian camp and have a few times ventured small elaborations of my own. Possibly I have emphasized the consequences of *how the sexual instincts of the child are handled* beyond what is usual in presentation of Freudian theory but certainly not beyond the writings of Freud and Freudians, even of the vintage of Abraham and Ferenczi. There is less general agreement among "Freudians" as to the consequences of handling than as to the nature of the basic trends. Nevertheless, the concept of variations in the concrete fate of the sexual instincts and of the complex role they play in the unique structure of the individual personality is as fundamental a part of Freud's contribution as the delineation of the component sexual instincts themselves. I think no Freudian would disagree.

I have tried earlier to suggest the enormous importance of an essentially genetic approach to the understanding of personality. In Chapter 10, which is homologous with this one for the non-libido schools, I shall protest strenuously against the general neglect of differentiated study of the developmental aspects

of basic psychological problems, and against the active repudiation of the profound significance of the sexual systems in the formation and continued functioning of the human psyche. Freud's own criticism of psychoanalytic theory— that it was too narrowly oriented around the libidinal drives, pending time and insight for more careful investigation of the aggressive instinct and, above all, of the development and function of the ego—is easier to accept.

If the emphasis of the following pages seems remote from the Freudian discussion of libidinal development reported in this chapter, it is only because I take its values for granted. I have preferred rather to concentrate on *additions* which seem to me worth considering, with some further presentation of the theoretical perspective I see as integrating other important factors with Freud's major contributions. No rejection of the libido theory is intended.

Early Infancy

The concept of *loss of love* has gained in prominence lately among Freudians and seems often to come very close to the emphasis on the general insecurity of the infant and his general need for human warmth and protection expressed by the non-libido schools presented in

Part III. This concept is by no means foreign to Freud, as we have seen. Freud's comments on its relation to the primitive fear of "flooding," to the essentially passive psychological role of the neonate, and to separation anxiety should be kept in mind. That the concept of *loss of love* can be generalized beyond Freud's early practical evaluation seems to me obvious and necessary. That it should be generalized to the point of becoming almost the *sole* genetic principle (as in the schools presented in Part III) is something else again, and in my opinion a genuine mistake.

I would like to make a few personal comments on this phase of infancy. As one cares for a very small baby, its almost constant need for release from stimuli and its helpless passivity are indeed striking. One normally coaxes it to make it drink its fill from breast or bottle —else it takes too little and awakens crying in a very short time. Little babies seem to *want* to go to sleep. Yet they often seem to be unable to do so unless one jounces them gently or talks to them in the peculiar cooing tones appropriate to infancy. Possibly the jouncing of the cradle is reminiscent of the movements of the mother's body before birth. I suspect, however, that there is a sort of *need for stimulation* as inborn as the need for release from stimuli. Although one should not neglect Freud's positive formulation regarding the passivity of the neonate as an observable fact, the concomitant need for gentle stimulation is also observable and might well be considered with the same seriousness.

The infant is passive and helpless and mainly has to endure the assaults of the outside world. Yet if one looks at little babies as it were from *their* point of view, it seems as though they were also trying hard to do the best they could to master their bodies and, fairly soon, their environment. Here I do not mean the unconscious tyranny of the crying infant over doting adults who try to make him stop for their own comfort and their sense of his general welfare. I mean, rather, the strenuous efforts of the infant to lift his head, to roll over, to reach the rattle—to listen, to see, to make noises. These efforts *look* spontaneous and, on the whole, pleasurable. Moreover, they follow quite definite stages, as Gesell and others have fully demonstrated.*

Ives Hendrick writes of an urge to *mastery*, which he considers as instinctual as the pleasure seeking of the erogenous zones.[36] Hartmann and others point to the primary autonomy of ego apparatuses. Mittelmann speaks of a *motility urge*, which develops in its own right, although in constant relationship to the coordinate urges emphasized by Freud (see Chap. 3). All of these recent approaches (I here give merely a sample) are made within the general framework of the libido theory as an *addition* to its resources. Indeed, throughout Freud's own writings, from *Three Contributions to the Theory of Sex* to the *Outline of Psychoanalysis*, one may find instances of the theoretical position that other parts of the body may show the same libidinal quality as the famous zones,† and the clear statement that he was forced to concentrate as he did on the sexual components because so little was known about them. (In practice, of course, Freud's emphasis was almost exclusively on the organ systems described in this chapter.)

The View of Systems

My position, as explained in comment at the end of Chapter 3, is that *any* bodily apparatus tends to function systematically in its own right almost by

---

* A good summary of Gesell's work is contained in A. Gesell and C. S. Amatruda, *Developmental Diagnosis*, 2nd Ed., Paul B. Hoeber, 1947. For similar findings by another author, see C. Bühler, *The First Year of Life*, John Day Co., 1930.

† These statements are quite different from the familiar idea of the erotizing of body parts by displacement from the penis.

definition and thus constitutes a sort of "drive" in its own right. In this sense, it seems unnecessary to posit a series of "drives" or "instincts" different *in kind* from the structures of the body. In Chapter 3 I suggested the term *drive systems* for bodily structures that involve *inner tensions* to a high degree but that are also oriented toward the external world in the sense that they require an object for their fulfillment as systems. I suggested that one would expect systems as fundamental to life as the neuromuscular, auditory, and visual systems and phonation to have a spontaneous "need to function" and to carry a "pleasure" aspect, as well as the organ systems known as the erogenous zones. The "inner tension" aspect is, however, less prominent.

The intensity and continuousness of *drive systems* so defined, and their relationship to the outside world, must vary with the type of system involved. Evidence is accumulating to suggest that their relative strength varies also from person to person, probably on a constitutional basis. Some infants are active, others quiet; some respond vividly to visual stimuli, others are more alert to sounds; and so, one may guess, through the gamut of body systems. (For that matter, some infants seem spontaneously more responsive or more indifferent than others in the oral, anal, and genital zones.)

I remarked upon a general difference between the "sexual" systems and others within the general rubric of "drive systems," which I called "nonsexual." The "sexual" systems involve mainly action through mucous membranes, unstriped muscles, glands of internal secretion— that is to say, action regulated primarily by the autonomic nervous system and its adjuvants. As drive systems they are, by my definition, related to external stimuli much more closely than are the interosystems. Tensions come to awareness more easily, along with some notion (inborn or acquired early) of what to *do* about them. There are large components

of control by the "voluntary" nervous system in two directions: (1) External cues *in variety* come to inhibit or facilitate expression of anal and genital instincts. (2) To some extent, we can *voluntarily* control the expression of excretory and genital urges.

It seems to me clear, however, that these "sexual" drive systems operate in a manner I shall call *global* in contrast to the great flexibility and differentiation of the "nonsexual" drive systems. By global I mean essentially that the sexual systems tend to act as a whole—holistically, on an all-or-none principle. I do not want to use terms which sound so *rigorously* all-or-none, because I am talking about pronounced trends rather than strictly definable entities. The main point is that we do not, with few exceptions *cannot*, perform the major acts of excretion and genital intercourse *partially*.* There are instances in which a *part* of these processes is brought under voluntary control—the deliberate breaking of wind perfected by some classes in our own society, the polite belch required in many Arab tribes, the coitus interruptus institutionalized in some communities. Spitting can become an art. I submit, however, that such instances of direct control over parts require very careful training, and perhaps some inborn talent. The general pattern of these systems is much more unitary than the systems involved in motility and the other nonsexual drive systems.

Furthermore, it seems likely that for the small child the global quality of the experiences associated with the "sexual" systems is even more striking than for the adult. For that reason, external stimuli and fantasies closely woven into these systems are very likely to entail much more extensive reaction patterns, often "unconscious," than the more flexible systems. These patterns are likely to re-

* The oral system is probably equally global (all-or-none) in earliest infancy but becomes more differentiated later and does not undergo the same extensive repression.

tain an infantile quality because of the massive quality of the underlying system. In some such manner it seems possible to explain the observational data Freud and Freudians adduce for the sexual instincts, without recourse to a "mysterious" specifically sexual libido.

Nonsexual Systems

Fully as important as the *biological* differences between these various types of system must be their fate during the early period of growth. This chapter has described the Freudian view of the course of development *in the erogenous zones*, and the more general modes of behavior patterned upon them, *in relationship to the actual handling of the child*. I believe that this view is essentially correct and important—except in its exclusiveness. The neuromuscular and other systems which I have called "nonsexual" seem, in the classical Freudian view, to develop merely as a matter of biological maturation. Implications for character formation are not stressed, except as they relate to personality trends arising from the "sexual" modes. My suggestion is that these ego functions and apparatuses have implications for character formation in their own right; that the ways in which the "nonsexual" systems of the child are handled must be more carefully studied.

From the very beginning, the infant is dandled, talked to, and stimulated visually, usually by the adults who also care for its "sexual" systems. If one watches a good professional baby nurse with her charge, the actual feeding, changing, and other routines seem a rather small part of *her* activity. "You have to *talk* to 'em," one such professional said recently, a little defensively, as she gushed sentimentally to a small red mass of indifference who was being briefly inspected by sophisticated guests of its parents. The marasmus of the institutionalized infant who is rarely

"talked to" may well be explained by the absence of the usual appropriate stimulation to the "nonsexual" systems. The often astonishing alertness of infants with severe handicaps in the erogenous zones may also be explained by this factor.*

Very little babies will stop whimpering with almost any intercurrent stimulation: rocking the cradle, patting, changing their position, "talking to them," or even sounding a buzzer when they start to cry. (Such techniques will not, of course, stop the cry of strong hunger or discomfort.) As they grow older, the human voice and human movements become increasingly necessary, and the impersonal cradle and buzzer lose effectiveness. Increasingly, too, *familiar* humans become essential. In the second half of the first year and for a year or two thereafter, *all* normal babies tend to show some degree of shyness with strangers—sometimes so quickly mastered as to be hardly observable, sometimes painfully marked. The eight-month anxiety that Spitz describes and the depressive phase that Klein points out may be cited as observations by psychoanalysts of this process.

It may be that human infants respond mysteriously to humankind "by nature." I think this unlikely. I think they respond initially to appropriate stimulation of *all* of the major body systems equipped to function. Initially any of these may become preponderant momentarily,† although sleep (fatigue), hunger, and the "sexual" components are

---

* I knew well an infant whose congenital cleft palate made every feeding a nightmare but whose general disposition was remarkably cheerful, alert, responsive. He received rather more than his share of fondling, etc., between feedings.

† Mittelmann includes, in a film recording the sequentially developing motility patterns of a socially responsive infant, one scene in which the infant is so preoccupied with his feet, recently discovered, that he does not respond as usual to the efforts of his mother to provoke a smile reaction.

doubtless preponderant most of the time. For the baby, however, all these stimulations are very closely associated with the ministering human figure. Initially roughly coordinated by the organismic self, they attain an *external* focus in the human figure, eventually in the specific figure of the mother and other familiars. I shall return to this point in the discussion of Sullivan's views of the fundamental nature of *interpersonal relations* in the development of personality, but I should like to point out here that the Freudian emphasis on the development of attitudes toward the "object"—a person—as fundamental to personality configurations is not very different from Sullivan's emphasis. (See Chap. 9 for my effort to clarify the difference.)

The special rhythms of development in the "nonsexual" systems have been studied extensively in the normative fashion of what most babies can do or respond to at a given age (notably by Gesell), but very little has been done to investigate how these patterns relate to affective and interpersonal patterns of growth or to the sexual sequences. Here I should like to make a few suggestions as to *likely* relationships, based on fragmentary, mostly unpublished evidence. These remarks are in the nature of illustrations of tie-ups which might be systematically studied.

A little child is prone to imitate its elders in any activity *with which it can identify*. This is not due to an "instinct of imitation" in the old, outmoded sense. It also is different from the more global mechanism of identification, with emphasis on oral incorporation described by Freud—although this mechanism seems likely enough as a general underlying trend. I have in mind the interplay between adult and child in activities beyond those related to the erogenous zones. Adults playing with babies are prone to imitate the baby! Whatever gurgles, shouts, or other activities the baby produces spontaneously the friendly adult tends to reproduce by way of con-versation with the small person, and the very little baby will often delightedly repeat the performance. At first the process is probably nothing more than doing what he was already doing under heightened general tonus, but quite early, when the baby is in a good mood, the parent can initiate such little games and note a true imitation of the adult behavior. A little later the child will very often do what the adult is doing—not yet in sophisticated play, aping complex adult concerns, but in duplication of the small activity that appeals to the child. Mittelmann shows in motion pictures a typical sequence of a child of two and a half watching him with interest as he shaves, then herself lathering him with the shaving brush, and finally lathering her own face.

Later on, the intermediate stage of self-initiated control of the new technique tends to drop out, and finally the child acts out its idea of the adult concern rather than a mere reproduction of a behavior fragment. This later period, in which the child can conceptualize the role of the adult in games, doubtless corresponds roughly with the period of true object love in libidinal development, and with the formation of the superego through a more complex process of identification—*i.e.*, identification with the image of the parent as constructed out of the sum total of the child's experience.

The nonsexual systems must contribute enormously to the actual contours of the developing psychological self and of the superego and self image. Although the general evolutionary function of these systems is a more differentiated, adaptive response to the milieu, it is also true that *the relationship between child and adult* is more differentiated in these areas, more complex, more intimate, and more open. The little child is constantly helped, taught, and disciplined in a host of small separate activities, carefully limited as to the time and place in which they are appropriate. If he undergoes a frightening experience—a fall, a burn, an attack from an animal—efforts are made to overcome the *generalized* fears which so often develop in consequence, by means of immediate reassurance and immediate re-education in the safe activities temporarily inhibited. (This procedure is quite different from the generalized adult abhorrence of the child's sexual activities, the failure to understand the terrors the child may experience in relation to his sexual desires, the absence of words and concepts and part-activities to facilitate understanding and education.)

The *general* climate of adult help and discipline must be of *general* import for the development of patterns of reaction for the nonsexual systems in their own right as well as for development of attitudes primarily rooted in the systems of the erogenous zones. The child who is generally encouraged in his spontaneous exploratory activities in these areas, who has plentiful activities to imitate from those adults who continue as powerful figures in his life (usually his parents), who is protected from major dangers or taught how to assimilate traumatic experiences—this child will surely build up a more secure and resourceful image of his own role in respect to the outer world (self image) and a more usable image of the adults with whom he identifies during the crucial introjecting period of the Oedipus stage (superego). Since our culture, even more than cultures generally, tends to emphasize relations with the outer world, *this* aspect of the emerging personality is likely to be most closely continuous with later social experience. It will, I think, tend to endure as the relatively *conscious* self image, and it may determine the major continuing defense mechanisms of the ego.

Perhaps in the majority of cases sound "ego" patterns proceeding from favorable development in the nonsexual systems will suffice for the child's lonely handling of crises in the more global

"sexual" systems as they arise in the course of libidinal development. His greater confidence in himself and firmer sense of mastery will allow him greater courage in facing the disappointments and fantasied dangers of the Oedipal phase. The better image of the parents will make their role in the introjected superego both stronger and more benign. In this way the inevitable conflicts of the Oedipal period may be handled with a minimum of distress, and special problems in the sexual spheres may be adequately integrated.

Some parents (and some cultures), however, may be so exacting or reproachful in the sexual spheres that the child is helpless before his inner problems, no matter how well the nonsexual systems have been handled. Or the parent may unduly stimulate the child erotically (often unconsciously), while condemning with horror any "sexual" responsiveness on the part of the child. Or constitutional variations, special experiences outside the family, etc., may increase the intensity and tight *separateness* of the "sexual" systems to such an extent that their course cannot be integrated with the other developing systems of the child's personality—his "ego strength." Neurotic difficulties may then appear regardless of healthy development in other systems *and may become so severe as to polarize the whole of the functioning personality*. The typical *neurotic* conflict in the adult is between a stable ego structure and intensified regressive demands from the sexual systems.*

Serious failure in fostering active, socialized development in the nonsexual systems naturally handicaps the child in

* *Cf.* Anna Freud, "The Mutual Influences in the Development of Ego and Id," *The Psychoanalytic Study of the Child*, Vol. VII, International Universities Press, 1952, pp. 42-50. In Chapter 7 I shall try to explain the difference between *neurotic* and psychotic or psychopathic defenses. The adjective *neurotic* is used there in a special sense, not as applicable to pathology generally.

dealing with the inevitable conflicts associated with his maturing sexual systems. No amount of permissiveness or supportive "understanding" in these areas per se can substitute for the child's own sturdy psychological self in dealing with such conflicts. In fact, parental permissiveness toward the sexual drive systems seems to leave too great a burden of control on the child, so that children reared in this manner tend paradoxically to become compulsive and fearful.[37]

In the vast majority of cases, the attitude of the parents toward the child's behavior is relatively homogeneous, so that a fairly high correlation may be expected among these various systems as regards health or illness simply on the basis of their *coexistence* in the same person and in the same setting. Of course, *some* dynamic relationships must always be established among systems functioning within the single organism, and it is very likely that such relationships typically follow the general principles advanced by the Freudians. But there are probably relatively few cases in which the sexual systems *as such* actually provide the overwhelming focus for the personality as a whole in the manner suggested by the earlier Freudians. In later critique of the non-libido schools (Part III), I shall urge that there are also relatively few cases in which the developmental systems that these schools emphasize so thoroughly determine the personality as to make the course of the sexual systems in themselves a matter of indifference.

It is, I repeat, mistaken to reduce personality dynamics to *any* universal principles, biological or social. The only valid course seems to me careful study of the predominant system-forming aspects of biological equipment in their relation to system-forming aspects of the milieu *in the individual case*. These systems and relationships may often be fruitfully generalized for a given project, but they should not be thought of as theoretical universals applicable to all people in all societies.

Native Endowment

Thus far, I have discussed the probable significance of the nonsexual systems for personality development as they appear in every child. I now suggest briefly the possible effect of individual variations in *native endowment as regards special nonsexual systems*. Let us consider, for example, the experience of the active baby who learns to walk very early. His locomotor development brings him into all sorts of dangers to himself and to the cherished property of his elders at an age at which he cannot be expected to grasp the complexities of caution and discrimination. He has to be watched every instant, with consequent increase in the amount of time and sheer physical energy devoted to his care. His very activity brings him into closer contact with the ministering adults. It is a rare parent who is not proud of his child's achievements—and who does not become exasperated, tired, and irritable under the excessive demands created by the motor precocity. Thus, a constitutional variation which seems *in itself* neutral for psychological development becomes the condition for a genuinely different climate of adult care.

Some babies never become good creepers but try to walk from the start. They may demand a supporting hand for practical purposes, even though their intent seems to involve a rather high measure of personal enterprise. What are the consequences for the development of the psychological self of *this* early relationship to the adult? Surely it may be expected to modify the over-all passivity described by Freudians as proceeding from the early oral stage and the general aggressivity of the later oral stage.

Such typical individual patterns in motor development could, I think, be studied for their implications in general ego growth in much the same way as individual patterns in the sexual systems have been studied. And they should be studied not only in themselves but also (perhaps primarily) in terms of the kind of relationship to the milieu they provoke.*

Some children seem to be born with pronounced gifts or pronounced handicaps in other modalities. Musical prodigies and the tone-deaf are familiar figures. The special environment created by an *outstanding* talent is obvious— and very difficult to handle constructively by the most well-meaning parents and managers. Probably many such talents go unrecognized for want of early fostering. We have as yet no knowledge of how such gifts—or gifts of less startling dimensions—affect the development of the personality apart from their interplay with the larger social patterns of the culture. This would seem to be a significant field of inquiry, albeit very hard to deal with scientifically in the absence of good measures of giftedness short of actual achievement, with its social ramifications.

Much of the foregoing discussion is at least compatible with Hartmann's concept of autonomous ego development and other findings of Freudian ego psychology. I have presented it as my own partly to avoid the possibility of misrepresenting the ego psychologists, whose relations to the classical libido theory are intricate and varied. But mainly I have wanted to present these suggestions about the independent course and interactive dynamics of the nonsexual systems within the framework of my own introductory chapter. To me the analysis

of the dynamics and interactions of different types of system is fundamental. I have tried to suggest that *in fact* the nonsexual systems do tend to coalesce into a personal-social unit by virtue of the fact that they are the major media of interchange with the milieu, especially in a reality-oriented culture such as our own. It is convenient but perhaps somewhat misleading to label this empirical coalescence "ego." The contrast with the id becomes *overly* sharp. Necessary variations in the specific role of the separate nonsexual systems are too often overlooked. There is too much temptation to view the whole process as a unitary "instinct" (*cf.* Hendrick's instinct of mastery, p. 228) coordinate with an equally overunified view of the sexual instincts (Eros).†

In summary, I see little to correct in the classical Freudian view of the genetic process except its *exclusive* emphasis on the course of development in the erogenous zones. Taken by itself, this view seems to me admirably worked out. I have tried to show that both by their biological nature and by their place in society the sexual systems do form a sort of special entity, relatively global in pattern, relatively private and separated from the highly flexible, differentiated socialized patterning of the nonsexual systems of the body. This aspect of human function *requires* the special study accorded it by Freud. It cannot be repudiated or dealt with casually in any basic theory of personality.

I have suggested, however, that the nonsexual systems of the organism (neuromuscular, visual, auditory; phonation, etc.) also carry the independent dynamic value of any bodily apparatus that tends to function in its own right. These

---

* They also *reflect* differences in the milieu. The *typical* locomotive patterns of infancy vary from culture to culture, doubtless in consequence of adult encouragement of some modes at the expense of others. Probably cultural comparisons would be as fruitful in this area as they have been for the sexual systems.

† Freudian nomenclature is given in parentheses because the correspondence with my own position is not exact. The parenthetical phrases suggest probable tie-ups rather than full equivalence.

systems, too, have their natural course (some of them internal rhythms—"drive systems"), and their handling by ministering adults is profoundly significant for the development of enduring personality patterns for the same reasons adduced for the importance of infantile experience in the erogenous zones. From the standpoint of evolution and by virtue of their role in current society, these systems are primarily concerned in relations with the outside world, physical and personal. Their development is fostered by adults in a highly differentiated way. Their functioning is less global, more voluntary and conscious. Identification with external figures (primarily the parents) occurs via these systems as well as by the pattern of oral incorporation. They play a very important role in the development of the conscious and semiconscious psychological self, and of the image the child forms of his parents —thence of his self image, his superego, and general pattern of expectation from other people: his "character."

Since all these systems operate within a single individual, subject to relatively homogeneous handling by the early family environment, it is natural that they should tend to interact very closely and to coalesce into a kind of unity akin to what Freudians call the "ego." This is a different kind of structure from that proceeding primarily from the erogenous zones (id), and the larger systematizations may be expected to operate in dynamic relationship to one another, in much the way that Freud describes.

I suggested that, generally speaking, parents tend to handle the child well (or badly) in the sexual spheres as well as the nonsexual, so that health or pathology in all systems is likely to *coexist*, over and above special dynamics of interaction between the two sets. Broadly speaking, the child whose general development and relationship to his parents in the nonsexual systems is good will be in a favorable position to handle the more private and undifferentiated terrors arising from maturation in the sexual systems; and vice versa. However, one would expect instances in which special problems in the sexual spheres would be so intense as to overflow into the nonsexual systems.

The condition for such overflowing might be variations either in constitution or in aspects of the environment. The consequence would be those cases we all encounter in which even an oversimplified Freudian libido theory is actually proved up to the hilt. Much more commonly, however, the role of conflicts in the sexual systems is heavily complicated, obscured, at times almost eliminated as an active force by the vigorous functioning of the nonsexual systems (ego defenses), which have a relatively independent history of their own sometimes quite different from that of the sexual systems.

My main theoretical comment ends here, because the significant Freudian theory of the genetic process largely stops with the early temporary resolution of the Oedipus complex. I should like to refer the reader to the discussion of the role of the "latency period" in my critical comment on the terms of the milieu (pp. 170f.). This section could be equally well presented here, but it seems rather more relevant to the wider processes of acculturation emphasized in the preceding chapter. I hope that the reader will not feel that the genetic process is confined to babyhood.

I have given scant attention to the very important topic of the development of the child's sense of self. This will be discussed in more detail in my critical comment on Chapter 8 and in the Epilogue. Another omission is the nature and role of aggression, discussion of which even in its genetic aspects is postponed to the Epilogue.

1 M. B. McGraw, *Growth: A Study of Johnny and Jimmy*, Appleton-Century, 1935.

2 *Cf.* especially G. E. Coghill, *Anatomy and the Problem of Behavior*, Cambridge, England: University Press, 1929.

3 S. Freud, *The Problem of Anxiety*, W. W. Norton & Co., 1936, pp. 122*ff.*

4 P. Greenacre, "The Predispostion to Anxiety," *Psychoanalytic Quarterly*, 1941, *10*: 66-94; *Trauma, Growth and Personality*, W. W. Norton & Co., 1952.

5 "Stages in the Development of the Sense of Reality," in S. Ferenczi, *Sex in Psychoanalysis*, Robert Brunner, 1950, pp. 213-239. "The Problem of Acceptance of Unpleasant Ideas—Advances in Knowledge of the Sense of Reality," in S. Ferenczi, *Further Contributions to the Theory and Technique of Psycho-Analysis*, 2nd ed., Hogarth Press, 1950, pp. 366-379.

6 R. R. Grinker and J. P. Spiegel, *Men under Stress*, Blakiston, 1945.

7 R. A. Spitz, "Anaclitic Depression," *The Psychoanalytic Study of the Child*, Vol. II, International Universities Press, 1946, pp. 313-342.

8 P. Bergman and S. K. Escalona, "Unusual Sensitivities in Very Young Children," *The Psychoanalytic Study of the Child*, Vols. III/IV, International Universities Press, 1949, pp. 333-352; S. K. Escalona, "Feeding Disturbances in Very Young Children," *American Journal of Orthopsychiatry*, 1945, *15*:76-80; M. E. Fries, "Psychosomatic Relationships Between Mother and Infant," *Psychosomatic Medicine*, 1944, *6*:159-162, "The Child's Ego Development and the Training of Adults in His Environment," *The Psychoanalytic Study of the Child*, Vol. II, International Universities Press, 1946, pp. 85-112; M. E. Fries and B. Lewi, "Interrelated Factors in Development: A Study of Pregnancy, Labor, Delivery, Lying-in Period and Childhood," *American Journal of Orthopsychiatry*, 1938, 8:726-752; S. Isaacs, *Social Development in Young Children*, George Routledge & Sons, 1946; M. Leitch and S. K. Escalona, "The Reaction of Infants to Stress. A Report on Clinical Findings," *The Psychoanalytic Study of the Child*, Vols. III/IV, International Universities Press, 1949, pp. 121-140; B. Mittelmann, "Motility in Infants, Children and Adults: Patterning and Psychodynamics," *loc. cit.*, Vol. IX, 1954, pp. 142-177; M. Ribble, *The Rights of Infants*, Columbia University Press, 1943.

9 R. A. Spitz, "Hospitalism. An Inquiry into the Genesis of Psychiatric Conditions in Early Childhood," *The Psychoanalytic Study of the Child*, Vol. I, International Universities Press, 1945, pp. 53-74.

10 ———, "Anaclitic Depression." See also R. A. Spitz, "Hospitalism. An Inquiry in the Genesis of Psychiatric Conditions in Early Childhood," and R. A. Spitz and K. M. Wolf, "Autoerotism. Some Empirical Findings and Hypotheses on Three of Its Manifestations in the First Year of Life," *The Psychoanalytic Study of the Child*, Vol. III/IV, International Universities Press, 1949, pp. 85-120.

11 W. Goldfarb, "The Effects of Early Institutional Care on Adolescent Personality," *Journal of Experimental Education*, 1943, *12*: 106-129; "Infant Rearing and Problem Behavior," *American Journal of Orthopsychiatry*, 1943, *13*:249-265; "Infant Rearing as a Factor in Foster Home Replacement," *loc. cit.*, 1944, *14*:162-166; "Effects of Psychological Deprivation in Infancy and Subsequent Stimulation," *American Journal of Psychiatry*, 1945, *102*:18-33; "Psychological Privation in Infancy and Subsequent Adjustment," *American Journal of Orthopsychiatry*, 1945, *15*: 247-255; "Variations in Adolescent Adjustment of Institutionally Reared Children," *loc. cit.*, 1947, *17*:449-457. See also L. Bender and H. Yarnell, "An Observation Nursery," *American Journal of Psychiatry*, 1941, *97*: 1158-1174.

12 A. Freud, "Observations on Child Development," *The Psychoanalytic Study of the Child*, Vol. VI, International Universities Press, 1951, pp. 18-30; A. Freud and D. T. Burlingham, *War and Children*, Medical War Books, 1943, and *Infants Without Families*, International Universities Press, 1944; and A. Freud and S. Dann, "An Experiment in Group Upbringing," *The Psychoanalytic Study of the Child*, VI, pp. 127-168. See also John Bowlby's comprehensive summary of relevant studies: *Maternal Care and Mental Health*, World Health Organization, 1952.

13 D. M. Levy, "Fingersucking and Accessory Movements in Early Infancy: an Etiologic Study," *American Journal of Psychiatry*, 1928, 85:881-918; "Experiments on the Sucking Reflex and Social Behavior of Dogs," *American Journal of Orthopsychiatry*, 1934, 4:203-224; "On Instinct-Satiation: an Experiment on Pecking Behavior of Chickens," *Journal of General Psychology*, 1938, 18:327-348.

14 S. Freud, *An Outline of Psychoanalysis*, W. W. Norton & Co., 1949, p. 28.

15 R. A. Spitz and K. M. Wolf, "The Smiling Response: a Contribution to the Ontogenesis of Social Relations," *Genetic Psychology Monographs*, 1946, 34:57-125.

16 S. Freud, *An Outline of Psychoanalysis*, p. 90.

17 K. Abraham, "Contributions to the Theory of the Anal Character," *Selected Papers of*

Karl Abraham, Hogarth Press, 1927, p. 386.

[18] H. Hartmann, E. Kris, and R. Loewenstein, "Comments on the Formation of Psychic Structure," The Psychoanalytic Study of the Child, II, p. 27.

[19] Personal observation of a case treated by John Rosen.

[20] Pp. 38ff.

[21] G. Bateson and M. Mead, Balinese Character: a Photographic Analysis, New York Academy of Sciences, 1942.

[22] M. Klein, The Psycho-Analysis of Children, 2nd ed., Hogarth Press, 1937, p. 183.

[23] Ibid., p. 302.

[24] Ibid., p. 187.

[25] Ibid., p. 184.

[26] C. Thompson, "Cultural Pressures in the Psychology of Women," in P. Mullahy (ed.), A Study of Interpersonal Relations, Hermitage Press, 1949, pp. 130-146; "The Rôle of Women in This Culture," loc. cit., pp. 147-161.

[27] S. Freud, New Introductory Lectures on Psycho-Analysis, W. W. Norton & Co., 1933, pp. 172f.

[28] Ibid., p. 173.

[29] E. H. Erikson, Childhood and Society, W. W. Norton & Co., 1950, pp. 226f.

[30] Ibid., p. 227.

[31] Ibid.

[32] A. Freud, The Ego and the Mechanisms of Defence, Hogarth Press, 1937, pp. 152ff.

[33] H. Deutsch, Psychology of Women, Vol. I, Grune & Stratton, 1944, Chap. 3.

[34] E. H. Erikson, op. cit., p. 228.

[35] Ibid.

[36] I. Hendrick, "Instinct and the Ego During Infancy," Psychoanalytic Quarterly, 1942, 11: 33-58.

[37] "The Misapplication of Psychoanalytic Concepts in Education," paper by M. O'N. Hawkins, read at the Annual Meeting of the American Psychoanalytic Association, May 1952.

Chapter Six

THE DYNAMICS
OF THE FUNCTIONING
PERSONALITY

THUS FAR, we have considered the ingredients of the personality according to Freud: the nature of "instinct," the contributions of the component instincts as the organ systems of the child gradually mature, the three institutions of the mind (id, ego, superego) which finally emerge as partly independent forces in interaction with one another. We have seen how understanding of the outside world and emotional ties to people develop out of the original "objectless" state of infancy in close relationship to the pattern of bodily growth, especially as the erogenous zones come successively into prominence.

In this chapter we shall examine more carefully how the personality *works,* the dynamics of adult behavior, with only such reference to origins as cannot be avoided in a psychology so deeply rooted in genetics. The adult normally forgets the whole dramatic sequence of sexual development on which we have dwelt so long. He operates as if he were concerned only with the wishes and fears appropriate to a civilized society. How and why does he accomplish this maneuver?

The pages that follow are largely a review of material already discussed, but here they are directly oriented toward the Freudian concept of the libido, leading to understanding of psychodynamics in the functioning person.

The term *libido,* it will be remembered, is applied to the whole available *energy* of Eros—that is, to the motive power springing from states of tension in the body itself. "There can be no question that the libido has somatic sources, that it streams into the ego from various organs and parts of the body."[1] In the very early stage, before id and ego are differentiated, the libido is entirely self-oriented; it is called *narcissistic libido,* and it remains partly so throughout life. We have seen how as objects are presented to the child they become cathected. Narcissistic libido is thus transformed into *object libido.* The energy previously belonging only to the body itself now streams out to people and other objects. (Or we may put it that the external stimulus now has the same power to increase and reduce tension in the organ systems as bodily processes themselves.) The sight of the beloved person is as potent a cause of excitement as the inner rhythms of the sexual urge.*

Freud notes that an important characteristic of the libido is its high degree of mobility. Libidinal cathexes can be sent out to objects like pseudopodia and then be withdrawn back into the self. Serious hurt in experiences with people may cause the person to turn in again upon himself, object libido again becoming narcissistic libido. Conversely, encouragement to warmth and trust, to independent exploration of the outer world, leads to endless building up of object relations so that more and more it is the stimulation of reality that arouses excitement and pleasure instead of the simpler bodily processes. In this manner (partly) the primitive wishes of infancy for direct organ satisfaction become *sublimated* in mature affection, interest in ideas, activities, pleasure in the beautiful. The kind of delight that first began in anal play, for example, now extends beyond the first body product to manipulation of clay, paints, and the like. Curiosity that began with sexual material gradually becomes genuine intellectual curiosity as the libido becomes attached to more and more objects.

It is also apparent that the nature of the object cathected may be expected to change with age and other conditions, depending on the pattern of libido disposition at the moment. There is a constant *substitution* of new objects for old, always calling forth the same charge of psychic (somatic) energy.

Moreover, the components (the partial instincts, see p. 78f.) of the libido exhibit mobility as well. In the preceding chapter we discussed the shift in the focus of concern with organ systems as the child grows older, so that it seems

---

* A reminder is in order that for the Freudian the "object" is almost invariably a person. Inanimate objects, ideas, etc. are generally seen as derivatives or substitutes developed in the course of working out the relationship with the mother as first object, the father in the Oedipal situation, the growing consolidation of ego and superego.

proper to speak of more or less universal phases of libidinal development. Although each stage does indeed have a characteristic *constellation* of associated feelings and activities, we saw that fusions also take place very commonly. The renewal of gonadal activity at puberty often brings with it a recrudescence of the earlier stages as well. In fact, they may monopolize the scene for a time, as if the new genital energy were actually put into the other organ systems. The frequent plumpness of the pubescent girl is probably due in part to the craving for oral satisfaction. She eats too much. The extreme messiness of many youngsters at this age probably harks back to the anal stage in addition to social factors, and the equally extreme neatness and dressing up that so often ensues is not altogether a matter of pleasing the opposite sex. It seems also to involve the unconscious need to subdue anal trends in the interest of emerging genitality.

In some of the sexual perversions, the substitution of one organ system for another is almost complete. Freud was especially puzzled by the inter-relationships of the component instincts which have no clear organ substratum, namely masochism and sadism. We shall discuss them a little later in order not to confuse the over-all picture of the libido now under consideration.

Of course, the libido also becomes *fixated*, as we have seen. One or another stage of development may remain pre-eminent, or by regression regain an earlier pre-eminence. The patterning of the part-instincts always becomes relatively stable, occasionally rigidly fixed. In the character traits of his patients, the analyst can discern the traces of underlying demands for direct organ satisfaction. He can examine the intricate relations of the instinctual components to one another and to the unduly primitive object cathexes. With knowledge of the inner cause of the fixation at an infantile level, he can gradually help the patient release the unhealthy bindings of the libido in favor of free development of mature object relations and satisfying sublimations.

The theory of the libido has, for Freudians, the merit of showing the dynamic unity of the psychic life, its purposive character as related to native biological needs, and—through the concept of fixation—of providing tools for differentiated understanding of the actual complexities of personality. The limitation of the libido theory for most "psychologists" is the implication of a sort of quantum of "psychic energy" available to the organism which may be distributed in various ways like a head of water whose energy potential can be rather exactly measured. Ives Hendrick uses this analogy in his *Facts and Theories in Psychoanalysis.** Freud was himself quite taken with *analogies* from

---

* First published in 1934, Hendrick's explanation of psychoanalysis for the layman must have had a wide influence on related disciplines. (I. Hendrick, *Facts and Theories of Psychoanalysis*, 2nd ed., Alfred A. Knopf, 1939.)

the physics of his time and seems really to have thought of psychological forces in much the same sense. The qualifying "seems" is appropriate, because Freud never went very far out on this limb and so carefully safeguarded himself with generalizations from biology (sometimes *over*generalizations) and with acute clinical observations that one is never quite certain how *literally* he intended the concept of libido as an energy apart from the actual functioning of the organic systems of the body.

In my reading of Freud, I take it as analogy only, rejecting any connotation of a psychic force as such. Surely Freud's careful analysis of the actual process by which objects become cathected and by which the institutions of the mind become differentiated in the course of experience makes such connotation unnecessary in his general theory. The *figure* of a mobile activation of various psychic systems with areas of tight cohesiveness (fixation, binding) is useful in dealing with major patterns of interrelationship—provided one keeps in mind that the streaming back and forth of the libido is figurative only. It expresses well the observable periods of concentration on the more inward systems of the personality *vs.* systems primarily focused around external objects, and the various types of shift in functional emphasis which occur among the prominent psychosomatic systems of the personality. With this interpretation of the libido, it seems to me possible to accept most of what Freud has to say about its behavior.

Let us return to the id, ego, and superego, again emphasizing their original unity. A confusing feature of Freud's writings is that he sometimes appears to use the word *ego* loosely for the whole self—what I have suggested calling the organismic self. Thus, he writes that in the beginning "the ego includes everything, and only later detaches itself from the external world," that "the ego pursues pleasure and seeks to avoid unpleasure."[2] For the most part, however, he uses the word to refer to the more differentiated part of the personality which on contact with the outer world has learned more and more how to function in accordance with the reality principle, and which takes over the increasingly complicated task of personality integration. It is, then, the *id* that remains under the domination of the pleasure principle, striving always for immediate satisfaction of the needs of the organ systems with some separatism.

We cannot know the id directly. Organs have no words with which to express the tensions arising within them. They do not even care how satisfaction is achieved, so long as tension is reduced. "The id knows no precautions to ensure survival and no anxiety; or it would perhaps be more correct to say that, although it can produce the sensory elements of anxiety, it cannot make use of them."[3] That is the business of the ego. Changes in the interior of the id become conscious as *feelings* in the pleasure-unpleasure series and there become materials for the activity of the ego. The analyst deals with *instinct representatives* in the consciousness of the patient, not with the instincts themselves.

The processes of the id are spoken of as the *primary process* (see pp. 47ff.). The id is subject to no laws of logic, no considerations of external reality or expediency. The ego must learn to evaluate the outside situation and postpone satisfaction either out of consideration of safety or to obtain maximal gratification. The *secondary process* is what we ordinarily encounter in thinking and directed activity. It follows more or less strictly the pattern of common sense or mental discipline both as regards methods of thought and as regards the goals and reasons for behavior acceptable in adult society.

The ego, then, acts upon cues received from feelings produced in the id part of the personality and has learned to *modify* the pursuit of pleasure by attention to the reality principle. Also, it can control the id to some extent by presenting it with danger signals and the threat of pain out of its own experience. The infant *ego* recognizes that the absence of the mother or her disapproval is associated with very unpleasant feelings of being flooded with stimulation or being abandoned. This "recognition" acts as a signal, reinstating the old anxiety state. Any pressure of the id toward the motor pathways (remember that these are controlled by the ego) is therefore blocked by "objective anxiety" (an ego function). Anxiety as *purely sensory experience* also belongs to the id. The ego can, as it were, mobilize the power of the id against its own demands, controlling unacceptable erotic and aggressive impulses by setting in motion the opposing reactions of helplessness and fear. Later on, moral anxiety, developed mainly out of the "objective" fear of castration in the course of the Oedipus complex (see pp. 206f.), also is used to inhibit the unacceptable id impulses from reaching expression. Indeed, the superego condemns impulses on its own account, often beyond the objections of the ego, at times even at variance with the more sensible, reality-oriented attitude of the ego.

Thus, the ego has three *sources* of anxiety to cope with. The easiest to perceive are threats from the outside world which are recognizable as a result of experience and which become signals for anxiety even when no longer appropriate. The second source consists of the inner promptings of the id, wanting expression of a kind which the ego has learned, rightly or wrongly, to consider dangerous. The third is the self-condemnation of the superego when the ego allows the id impulses to get out of hand or otherwise infringes upon the requirements of conscience.

We may regard the same situation as three sources of pleasure available to the ego. The external world offers opportunities for enjoyment doubtless the more keen as object relations develop beyond the phase of sheer physical gratification. The primary process is a source of pleasure almost by definition in so far as its strivings can be granted. And everyone knows the delights of a good conscience when man is at peace with himself.

DEFENSE MECHANISMS

HOW DOES THE EGO handle the problem of (1) controlling unacceptable id impulses, (2) avoiding the pain of constant conflict and unremitting effort to subdue them, and (3) achieving the harmonious synthesis which is its most mature goal? Here we confront squarely the task of this chapter: detailed analysis of how the personality *works*.

From the review just presented, it is apparent that this is now essentially a problem of ego psychology—the latest and least definitely formulated aspect of the Freudian scheme. We have seen that from the beginning Freud conceived the dynamics of behavior as some sort of interaction between libidinal and controlling forces—roughly speaking, ego forces. His first effort was almost necessarily toward clarification of the instinctual components and the primary process, about which so very little was known. Gradually, the attention of Freud and Freudian analysts was more and more concentrated on variations in the ways in which different types of patients handled the fundamental instinctual problems common to all of them and apparently inherent in human biological structure. Such attention led to the formulation of the general categories id, ego, superego, and also to a narrower investigation of special types of reaction as the patient was forced to cope with special stress from one or another of these institutions.

In 1894 Freud used the term *defense* to refer to the effort of the person to protect himself against "dangerous" instinctual demands and the conflicts arising in the course of development. Afterwards, he was so impressed by the dynamic power of *repression* (to be discussed in a moment) that for a time it was substituted for the earlier term and became *the* way of interpreting neurotic manifestations. In *The Problem of Anxiety* (1926), he writes,

I now think that it confers a distinct advantage to readopt the old concept of defense if in doing so it is laid down that this shall be the general designation for all the techniques of which the ego makes use in the conflicts which potentially lead to neurosis, while repression is the term reserved for one particular method of defense, one which because of the direction that our investigations took was the first with which we became acquainted.[4]

Freud reached this broader view of the problem from intensive study of pathological conditions other than hysteria, which had formed the basis of his earlier investigations. In these conditions, mechanisms other than repression appeared to be the major protective devices employed by the ego against instinctual demands. Gradually the list of *defense mechanisms* lengthened as one or another was seen to play a major role in the dynamics of various afflictions. In 1936 Anna Freud listed nine of them (in addition to sublimation) as very familiar in the practice and theory of psychoanalysis: regression, repression, reaction-formation, isolation, undoing, projection, introjection, turning against the self, and reversal.[5]

Most of these terms have already been encountered in this book. Others will be explained presently. Their formulation seems to have grown out of the study of pathological cases classified according to psychiatric rubrics, and we shall return to them in Chapter 7, on psychopathology, as they become appropriate in discussing the Freudian view of the dynamics of outspoken disease entities. Freud is very cautious in his consideration of why an individual chooses one mechanism rather than another. Anna Freud, in line with her father's writings, makes some suggestions as to a chronological classification dependent upon the stage of development at which the ego institutes its defenses. Both consider such classification very provisional. Anna Freud remarks that, apart from repression, "we still feel . . . that we are including under a single heading a number of heterogeneous phenomena."[6] Some of the mechanisms—such as turning against the self and reversal—appear to involve the deepest instinctual impulses, yet they are rarely encountered in very early childhood, whereas others which depend upon a sophisticated appreciation of the outside world are among the first neurotic manifestations of childhood. Freud preferred to continue empirical study of the dynamics of defense and the conditions that call forth the defensive reactions rather than to embark upon premature systematization. Probably new insights will be developed as to the origins and interrelations of these mechanisms.

For me the nine mechanisms cited are difficult to understand as an inclusive list—or as properly exclusive. However characteristic for definite psychiatric entities, their relationship to the various defense mechanisms of daily life among relatively normal individuals is far from clear. Why, for example, should a mechanism such as isolation (see p. 254), the everyday counterpart of which would seem to be, roughly, logic-tight compartmentalization, be included when such general mechanisms as displacement and rationalization (see Chap. 2) are not mentioned? Even in the clear-cut pathological conditions, more than one mechanism is typically operative simultaneously. Not infrequently, the major defense of the patient shifts in the course of illness from one mechanism to the other.

The following pages represent my own choice of mechanisms likely to *illustrate* for the reader inexperienced in psychoanalysis Freud's concept of how the person may handle his instinctual problems, of the various ways in which conscious and unconscious factors may be integrated in his symptoms and in his daily living. This choice is not systematic and does not aim at inclusiveness. We shall consider the problem of the relationship between the defense mechanisms and the other aspects of psychodynamics thus far described at a later point in this chapter (pp. 266ff.).

REPRESSION

The word *repression* has already crept into many paragraphs. The concept is used quite generally, with or without specifically Freudian flavor. Repression means, in essence, thorough dismissal from consciousness. It should not be confused with voluntary refusal to act upon impulse, often called suppression. When a person counts ten and refrains from punching somebody in the nose, he is controlling his anger, not repressing it. In repression he does not feel angry at the person at all. A young girl is angry quite legitimately, let us say, because her boy friend forgets to arrive for a date. Yet she is herself convinced that she sympathetically understands his reasons and is not annoyed, thus perhaps preserving her own pride and the positive aspects of the relationship. But she snaps at her brother or anyone handy with a violence out of all proportion to the provocations *they* offer at the moment. If the girl knows privately that she is saving face in defending the action of her friend, this is *not* an example of repression. It is when the suffering family knows her anger—and easily guesses the cause—and the girl herself genuinely believes in her own loving forgiveness toward her boy friend that we can speak of repression.

The same homely example can also illustrate *resistance*, a term that we shall encounter frequently in our discussion of analytic treatment with somewhat more special implications than are suggested here. If brother is so tactless as to comment on why sister is "really" sore, any family knows the ensuing arguments to the contrary, the withdrawal of confidences about later dates, all the little subterfuges of the girl battling for her own belief. If we are dealing with genuine repression, the closer she comes to acknowledgment of her "true" feelings about the date, the more elaborate, strenuous, and often illogical the defensive repudiation. This active but *unconscious* refusal to interpret her reactions correctly is called resistance. The girl who is consciously saving face is much more adept at handling the uncomfortable family teasing, because she has only to think up a plausible story and stick to it rationally, even conceding that she was a bit put out. She may even listen to a spot of brotherly advice, although she often superficially preserves a haughty silence or tells brother to go jump in the lake.

The girl who has genuinely repressed her anger toward the young man is in a worse situation. Her arguments are more absurd because, in the interest of keeping *herself* convinced, she is forced to leave out a good many reality items. Advice cannot be used (unless thoroughly reoriented by rationalization) because acceptance would mean acknowledgment of those facts and feelings she (her ego) is actively excluding from consciousness—*i.e.*, resisting. Moreover, anger toward the family, which at first was merely displaced (see p. 261), is now augmented by focused hostility toward the person who forces an awareness which is genuinely painful. Brother is often in the doghouse for some time. Often he is held responsible for the dissolution of an obviously impossible relationship—if he has so much as failed to be especially cordial when the young man called up, if sister feels she herself was too cool when he called just after a talk with brother. (Mother, father, friend—above all, psychoanalyst— may be substituted for brother.)

As a rule, the repression in such cases is not very deep, and the active resistance to insight relatively slight. Cause and effect are usually so apparent that the tolerant family puts it all down to "adolescence," with little difficulty in following the psychoanalytic interpretation. Sister certainly *acts* as if she really believed the nonsense she talks and did not want to see the facts. She is irritable beyond reason, while the true reasons seem clear enough to the on-looker. As a rule, the girl sees herself, her boy friend, and her family in better perspective a few weeks, months, or years later. The onset and disappearance of her blindness about her own feelings are fairly obvious.

The repressions most emphasized in Freudian theory and practice are deeper and older, dating back to the techniques used by the infant ego for coping with the problems of the very early years. Unable to face the pain of frustration and the fears attendant upon expression of erotic wishes, the small child denies them altogether. The process is expedient at the moment, but the ego thus excludes large areas of the id from itself—and therefore from the possibility of development under the reality principle. The important repressed material is, then, for the Freudian, infantile in a very literal sense. The crude primary process survives unchanged in the unconscious. It remains as freshly urgent as when the child first resorted to this solution of his dilemma, and the repression continues to require constant effort for its maintenance. What changes during the later life span is *mainly* the technique of defense, the ego mechanism.

According to Freud, problems of the unconscious are timeless. The neurotic man of forty is still struggling with the Oedipus complex. This does not mean that the grown man still literally wants to sleep with his mother or seriously fears that someone will cut off his penis. He can discuss these matters rationally enough, usually with ridicule or resentment, occasionally with honest intellectual effort to feel again the early struggle he is told was so crucial. But this effort cannot be successful with his grown-up ego short of the very special psychoanalytic techniques described in Chapter 7, on treatment. The very words he uses as an adult, the image he has formed of his parents and himself over a lifetime, the whole rational context of his thinking prevent any immediate recognition of the old problems. Nor can the adult who is *intellectually* convinced of the validity of the Freudian interpretation of his own case dismiss his infantile terrors by the reasonable conclusion that they are nonsensical. Unfortunately, as we shall see in the next chapter, the process of insight must be one of *emotional* understanding before it becomes effective.

An episode reported by Reik[7] from the analysis of a young medical student will serve as illustration of how the infantile problems are related to adult patterns. A woman visited the patient in his lodgings by invitation, but the young man did nothing to tidy his room. On the contrary, he expressed to the analyst great resentment of the way in which the hospital had been polished up for a visit from the Queen (the scene is Holland), insisting that it was absurd and hypocritical to change one's ways for royalty or any social conventions. On the second visit of the woman, however, he spent considerable time cleaning up, with special attention to the washbowl, even though it was most unlikely that she would ask to use this appurtenance. By this time he was really interested in her, wanted to make a good impression and even to have things as she would like them. The story is *fairly* sensible as it stands. Slicking up for royalty is mildly offensive to many of us; the hospital may well have been somewhat hypocritical or overimpressed by the honor of the visit. Still, taking a strong position of principle on so trivial a matter is in itself somewhat suggestive of a special character trend. Very likely the patient sees many similar items as "a matter of principle." (Reik does not describe him beyond this incident.)

It seems distinctly odd that the matter of cleaning or not cleaning his room should come up in the analytic session at all. Most young men, untidy or orderly, would not find occasion even to mention the state of their housekeeping unless it had actually caused embarrassment. Furthermore, the quick analogy with the visit of the Queen suggests a certain initial overvaluation of the woman visitor, however covert, and failure to conform to minimum hospitality seems a statement of defiance. One might guess at similar attitudes in his relations with women generally, at least with women of emotional importance to him. The careful preparations for the second visit even suggest a kind of capitulation as his affection mounts.

Almost any psychoanalytic school might draw these conclusions (tentatively, as befits such slim evidence) and might further suspect that the pattern of overvaluation and defiance is related to the patient's early attitudes toward his mother. Here, then, is a second level of interpretation, one which may be very useful in tracing and explaining his characteristic reactions to authority, to women, to ideas. Just because the episode is so trivial, its small oddities suggest an unconscious determination which, if confirmed in further observations, may reveal important underlying trends.

The Freudian asks further: why the emphasis on *cleanliness*—above all, why scrub the *washbowl* so carefully? Further analysis reveals difficulties with the mother on the matter of toilet training, especially urination, and the further fact that at one time the patient had used a washbowl frequently as a urinal. Thus it would appear that those aspects of his relationship with his mother that came into prominence at the anal stage are the ones that currently dominate his attitude toward the young lady in whom he is interested. The advent of a woman whom he could love and respect as he did his mother brings out the defiance experienced as a little child and long since repressed. He makes amends in the same vein by cleaning the object that would most have offended his mother, at least in his infantile fancy, even though the action is irrelevant in the current situation. Beneath his ambivalence toward women lies the further implication of the anal problem unconsciously reconstituted directly as well as through its later derivatives. We shall see a little later that the "anal character" is frequently a stickler for principle, etc. The fact that direct connections with cleanliness or excretory functions are so often visible, plus the resemblance of the adult pattern to the infantile situation of guarding the first self-determined instinctual controls (see pp. 264ff.), leads the Freudian to consider the libidinal origin basic to full understanding of the current behavior.

It must be made plain that when a young man of twenty-five "happens" to scrub his washbowl carefully he is not aware of homage to maternal admonition. Nor is the act a habit or a simple memory of preparation for company in his childhood. The washbowl entered the picture at a later date via the inappropriate use to which he had put the fixture. This memory, too, was forgotten at the moment. No one would rationally spend time cleaning an object because he had dirtied a similar one some years previously. Yet the action is definitely meaningful, as we can see from the vantage point of the psychoanalyst's reconstruction.

We can also see that the repressed anal concerns have not been eliminated or altogether dormant, since one element of direct connection has been added—and who knows how the more subtle development of character has been influenced? We can see the repressed material through its influence upon the structure of memory and current behavior, even though the person cannot himself report what by the definition of repression he cannot possibly know. The example further illustrates how the unconscious material continues to influence behavior and becomes more elaborated *in the unconscious* despite its exclusion from the major materials utilized by the ego in its integrative functions.

REPRESSION AND ANXIETY

With this definition and illustration of repression, we can return to its role in the economy of the personality. Repression is accomplished by the ego. Why? The ego is said to function under the reality principle, and surely, one might think, nothing could be more unrealistic than simply to omit from consideration large segments of reality. The answer is clear in Freud's genetic approach. The ego, or, more correctly, the ego-id, is *at first* the total organism, subject primarily to the pleasure-pain principle (and to the death instinct). The ego *learns*, via pleasure and pain, to modify its decisions in terms of external reality, and in time it takes "reality" as a general principle extending beyond any immediate situation. The fundamental consideration of the ego, however, remains the avoidance of pain and the desire for gratification. The stirrings of certain impulses lead to the very painful feeling of anxiety as certain stimuli, whether from the outside world or from within the body, come to serve as danger signals. If these stimuli are not recognized and are not allowed to enter the network of integrated perceptual interpretations in control of voluntary action, two gains are won. First, it is impossible for the dangerous action thus signaled to complete itself in overt behavior, and hence the organism is protected from the threatened disaster. Secondly, the potential painful anxiety is nipped in the bud. Far from having to suffer the dread attendant upon "correct" evaluation of the danger signal, the ego finds a less disquieting interpretation to which it then clings quite desperately. The interpretation (cats, or the subway, or crowds, or whatever, are "dangerous") may lead to marked inconvenience but not to the catastrophe anticipated from "correct" recognition. Any step taken toward further fulfillment of the "dangerous" impulse—including even such innocent steps as partly recognizing the "true" danger or relaxing the elaborate precautions against the substituted danger— automatically arouses anxiety and is therefore immediately repudiated.

Freud noted very early the close relationship between anxiety and the repression of impulses that appeared to be mainly erotic. His first explanation was that repressed sexuality is literally converted into anxiety.* Later (1926) he specifically renounced this explanation in favor of the one just outlined. Repression does not cause anxiety. On the contrary, *it is anxiety that causes repression.* The ego does not allow further development and integration of meanings that carry so painful a load of potential danger. The repressed impulse becomes a symptom, and the ego devotes itself to making the best it can of whatever "instinctual representatives" do break through to consciousness together with the perceptual representatives of the outside world.

Initially, Freud equated the unconscious with those impulses that the censor found unacceptable. He soon observed that this formulation was only a crude approximation of the truth. The roots of the most cogent moral judgments and many of the devices of the ego seemed also to lie in the unconscious. The chief value of consciousness is that it provides greater freedom and skill with which data from the inner and outer world can be compared and integrated. Undoubtedly, elaboration of the primitive processes does take place at the unconscious level (as we saw in the washbowl incident) but only to a limited extent and without full appreciation of reality implications. Integration of the personality as a whole must always include the unconscious formulations and pressures as well as conscious purposes, always in dynamic interrelationship.

Repression is not accomplished without active struggle on the part of the ego. The pressure of the impulse from within, normally recognized as a cue to activity, must be denied; interpretations based on the logic of its normal relations with the outside world must also be denied, as when the adolescent girl fails to see facts obvious to her brother in our earlier example. In saving itself from the immediate danger and pain of recognizing the potential direction of certain impulses, the ego abrogates its rights and duties over large territories. It weakens its position *vis-à-vis* the id and the superego and perhaps, one may say, even that part of itself most definitely oriented toward reality. The

---

* He continued to believe that something of the sort takes place in the "actual neuroses," in which a current sexual excitation is constantly frustrated.

respective areas of repression are—to use Freud's analogy—encapsulated like foreign bodies within the ego.[8] The ego makes an elaborate secondary adaptation to the limitations imposed. It tries to cover over the gaps by rationalization, or even to make positive use of the neurotic symptoms, as in the secondary gain of illness (see p. 261). The analogy might be improved by substituting "tumor" for "foreign bodies," since, like the repressed impulse, the tumor is a product of the body's own economy, although it comes to act independently, and since it often tends to grow by itself locally or to proliferate malignantly through complex systems.

OTHER DEFENSE MECHANISMS

REPRESSION PLAYS SOME PART in all the neurotic mechanisms, and perhaps one may say that the other types of defense come into play either as a means of integrating the instinctual representatives of the repressed impulses with the rest of the personality (as in rationalization or the secondary gain of illness) or when simple repression is ineffective. In the latter event, other mechanisms may serve to buttress the repression directly or to supplement it as independent lines of defense—occasionally to the point of superseding it as the main mechanism. We must keep reverting to the point that in the vast majority of cases several mechanisms operate simultaneously and usually come into clear focus only as one or the other gains the upper hand to a pathological degree. The cases described here are, like Freud's own cases, drawn from pathology, because such cases exhibit the mechanisms more sharply. It should be understood that these mechanisms are also part of the normal personality (see pp. 278ff. for further discussion of this use of pathology).

REACTION FORMATION

One of the most common defenses against the irruption of unacceptable instinctual impulses is *reaction formation*. The power of the repressed impulse is seen in the exaggeration of the opposite tendencies. Excessive trends in one direction—the "virtues to a fault" of common parlance—typically (*i.e.*, not always but very often) represent a buttressing of the repression of unacceptable impulses of contrary nature. It is not enough for the ego to be officially unaware of pleasure in anal activity, let us say, or of hostile feelings toward people. The lack of awareness is guaranteed by positive development in the opposite direction. We noted that often the overly neat child is the one who wallows in mess when allowed free rein with finger paints. The man who would not hurt a fly, who shudders at the sight of blood, may all of a sudden commit a gory crime. The worm turns with especial ferocity when its wormishness has long been a guard against unconscious hostility.

My children, after relatively free expression of infantile anal interests, went through an exasperating phase of overcleanliness. Wanting everything very clean, they were too fastidious to touch dirt themselves. Someone else *had* to take care of the puppy's mistakes. There were serious controversies because dirty dishwater was intolerable and had to be replaced several times during washing up, despite a desperately limited water supply in the country. The reaction of finicking disgust, very genuinely experienced, was clearly related to the positive pleasures recently renounced. Housekeeping became much smoother as reaction formations involving an extreme if somewhat spotty orderliness also gave way to advancing maturity.

Most children show some such reactions at one time or another, often ignored in the general hubbub of growing up. A high degree of freedom in infancy may precipitate an early reaction formation beyond anything imagined by the parent, who naively hoped to avoid common neurotic developments by an understanding tolerance—or the problem may be delayed until adolescence —to mention only two common situations. The manifestations may be fairly direct, as with our children, possibly reflecting the more conscious appreciation of positive pleasure available to the child permitted fairly direct expression in early years. Or the origin of the reaction formation may be concealed beneath very complicated defenses, hardly recognizable at all. The harshness of the child toward the puppy's mistakes looks for a time like an unanswerable argument against early freedoms, but in the long run it seems merely a phase of development. Perhaps it is after all desirable that the ego should cope with the anal problems in this relatively circumscribed and direct manner in later childhood rather than develop repression and reaction formation at the period when these problems are so largely interwoven with the infant's concept of the world and his own autonomy. This type of circumscribed reaction formation is likely to be transitory and limited, in contrast to the permanent and pervasive characterological trends of the same nature which may set in as reaction formations developed during very early severe toilet training.

Very often reaction formation and direct expression of the impulse in limited areas stand side by side in the same personality, both recognizable by their exaggerated and inexpedient quality. Mildred, a college student, was referred for psychotherapy because she was failing in her studies despite fully adequate intelligence. Teacher accounts of her work were surprisingly contradictory. One teacher felt very strongly that the difficulty was merely lack of judgment in distribution of her time, that she was overconscientious and meticulous. He showed, as proof, exquisite notes taken in preparation for a term paper. The notes were too detailed for efficiency—and the paper was never completed. Another teacher maintained that Mildred was inexcusably careless, messy, and uninterested.

Mildred's roommate complained bitterly that she left the bathroom dirty and never picked up her clothes. In interview Mildred described a recent fuss with the maid during a week end at home because the woman seemed unable to remember that the rose hangers belonged in Mildred's closet and the blue hangers in her sister's. Mildred could not bear such untidiness!

Inspection of her notebook confirmed both teachers' reports. It was a mess, interspersed with areas of perfect orderliness. A casual, unheralded visit to her room substantiated both the roommate and Mildred. It presented a colorful mixture of extreme disorder and extreme order. Since her variability on the matter of order had already been discussed, the girl spontaneously opened her bureau drawers in evidence. One was perfection itself. In the others, one could see the plan of careful compartments for everything beneath a rather disgusting welter of clean and half-soiled clothes, plus a few papers and books hastily stuck out of the way in an emergency and never removed.

The one thing Mildred could not achieve in her work, in her housekeeping, or in her relations with people was an ordinary, common-sense balance. She constantly oscillated between a guilty or defiant messiness and an anxious, self-righteous perfectionism. A blue hanger in her rose closet was genuinely upsetting to her. Once she started to copy her scrawled notes, she could not tolerate so much as a typographical error, let alone omit points emphasized in a text which were irrelevant to the topic of her paper. Of course, the girl was profoundly unhappy most of the time, and her associates suffered both from her anxious meticulousness and her exaggerated carelessness.

The inconsistency of Mildred's behavior is not mysterious for the Freudian. Both facets of her personality have the same underlying significance. More careful analysis would probably reveal more of the unconscious reasoning behind her incalculable shifts. In her Rorschach test, for example, it was easy to see how a response emotionally disorganized beyond the ordinary—e.g., "a bloody mess" in Card II—was immediately followed by sharply accurate forms in small details; that is, the release of uncontrolled emotionality appeared actively to precipitate a finicking overcontrol.

The mixture of direct expression and reaction formation is unusually striking in the case of Mildred. A great many people, however, show something of the same pattern. Generally orderly, thrifty, gentle, or whatever to a fault, these people are likely to display sporadic evidences of the opposite characteristics, either in situations so unimportant as to fall outside the area of ego control, or when the ego is caught off guard, or when pressures mount beyond possibility of control. I remember an unusually tender, sensitive man deep in an intellectual discussion when our cat rubbed against his legs in unexpected friendliness. He gave the animal a vicious kick, out of all proportion to the element of surprise and quite different from his usual gentle manner. This man was by no means a hypocrite. It is very possible nonetheless that his general life pattern is in the nature of a reaction formation against strong hostilities and fears which remain strong precisely because they so rarely are permitted to emerge at all and which therefore cannot be integrated with the bulk of his conscious experience.

ISOLATION

Related to this persistence of direct expression along with reaction formation is the mechanism of *isolation,* clearly observable in obsessional or compulsive patients. The impulse, thought, or act is not denied access to consciousness but it is not permitted normal elaboration in associative connections and in affect. The obsessive fantasy of strangling her child may constantly come into a patient's mind quite "coldly," devoid of the angry feelings appropriate to such a thought, naturally painful to an affectionate mother (see Chap. 7).

One might suppose that so open an expression of hostility would be easy to analyze, but such patients typically experience the greatest difficulty in free association. Their thought processes are often very active—in Freud's language, hypercathected and erotized—but somehow carefully avoid any relation to genuine feeling or any ramification into experiences that might explain the obsession. Instead of a thought, a stereotyped action may express the impulse quite directly, though again in so limited a manner that the action becomes a neurotic symptom rather than a crime. A "Jack-the-Ripper" is so extreme an example that he would not be called a compulsion neurotic. His symptom has taken a fortunately unusual malignant form, but it is easy to see from the mechanism of isolation how a murderer may be a genuinely nice fellow most of the time. His whole personality may work on the principle of dissociating certain impulses from the integrative function of the ego. He does not *forget* that he killed a woman, as the hysteric forgets. He may even have to deal secondarily with horror at his act—as if he were judging someone else. But he may genuinely feel no more antagonism or remorse in the usual sense than the spectator at a movie, except as he recognizes himself in the title role.

By its very extremity, this type of isolation is more familiar to us and in a way more understandable than the senseless, logic-tight antipathies of our best friends and admired public figures, who are generally amenable to argument and generally sympathetic to human values. The Galsworthy character who grinds down his workers and competitors six days of the week and espouses the gospel of Christ on Sunday *approaches* the mechanism of isolation, in so far as he is not a conscious hypocrite, but the example is very complex. Business and Christianity also have social sanction in our culture and subserve superficial self-interest. The mechanism may involve social rather than personal-psychological trends toward isolation.

Isolation is a term originally developed by Freud to explain the observable defenses characteristic of compulsion neurotics in treatment. Extension to a movie version of Jack-the-Ripper and Galsworthy fiction is an elaboration of my own, correct enough if we knowingly restrict our judgment to a single dimension of the personality. To override so drastically the dictates of his superego, Jack must have been more than neurotic. And we cannot fairly call neurotic a man who essentially follows the dictates of his times with concern for his own integrity, even if his behavior seems illogical to the disinterested bystander. I think the extension of *isolation* to these extremes of both pathology and normality is consonant with Freud's idea, but let us quote Freud: ". . . He [the patient] does not want the thought of the impression or the action in question to come into associative contact with other thoughts."[9] Freud had in mind mainly the neurotic mechanisms of his patients, in whom the data were clear and analyzable. The further examples offered here are less clear but seem to invoke essentially the same mechanism.

UNDOING

A further mechanism found clearly illustrated in compulsion neurotics is *undoing*. Freud remarks that "it is a kind of negative magic . . . in which the individual's second act abrogates or nullifies the first, in such manner that it is as though neither had taken place, whereas in reality both have done so"[10]—albeit only on an unconscious level, as a rule. A woman felt compelled to pick up every stone she found on the road, lest someone should be injured. A spinster, she sacrificed herself to the care of her aged, irascible mother with uncomplaining sweetness. Analysis of her dreams and free associations readily revealed a powerful death wish toward the mother, complicated by the fact that her sister had died suddenly of meningitis during the early period of acute sibling rivalry—*i.e.*, when the patient had wished her dead. This event had served, with far-reaching consequences, as confirmation of the normal childish belief in the magical power of the wish. She learned consciously, of course, that she was guiltless of her sister's death, and she herself attributed no special significance to the unforgotten days of remorseful terror that had followed the tragedy.

Of course, the sibling rivalry was part of the Oedipal situation and the whole relation of the little girl to her family and herself; hence there are many implications beyond those mentioned here. One of the major trends shown is the lifelong reaction formation against hostility and self-assertion, as indicated by her mousy sweetness of character. However, the extreme demands of her sick mother, plus the growing sense that life was passing her by while she stayed in the sickroom, put too great a strain on this mechanism. There was increasing danger of a genuine focused eruption of hostility toward the mother, related to the repressed infantile problems. Picking up stones can be understood as undoing the hostility implicit in seeing them as potentially dangerous objects in the first place.

Repression is certainly operative in this instance. As an intelligent woman, the patient was quite aware that the chances of someone's coming to grief over a stone in the road are minimal. She was no more careful than anyone else about a host of small daily hazards. But if she therefore deliberately refrained from removing a stone, she was tortured with the idea that a horse might shy, an automobile skid, a person stumble in front of a car on just that stone. She became so painfully anxious that she retraced her steps simply for her own peace of mind, without the slightest recognition that she was thereby protecting her mother, as it were, from an attack of which she did not even remotely think. "Not knowing" is insufficient. The undoing, which also implies a doing, gives the person a magical certainty and further confirms the isolation of impulses that might otherwise spread.

The ambivalent quality of the symptom is often very clear. A patient has a compulsion to turn off gas jets as the undoing of a suicide fantasy, but she turns them on first. A patient prays obsessively for his mother's recovery from an illness but compulsively slaps his mouth immediately after in negation,[11] like a child making a promise with crossed fingers. This mechanism contributes to many cases of "symmetry compulsion"—everything must be the same on the right as on the left, in order to undo symbolically what has been done symbolically.

The same act with merely a shift of attitude may have a reverse meaning.

Fenichel tells the amusing story[12] of a patient with scruples about unnecessary expenditures of money. He bought an extra newspaper—unconsciously symbolizing a visit to a prostitute, according to Fenichel's analysis of underlying dynamics in this case. He decided to return the extra paper but was embarrassed about the attitude of the vendor and so decided instead to buy still another paper to ease his mind. But the stand was closed on his return. The patient then solved his problem by taking a nickel out of his pocket and throwing it away. Again the patient is not aware of the unconscious meaning of this little action. (Let us assume that it has the meaning Fenichel suggests, with the proviso that other "deep" meanings would do for illustrative purposes, even non-libidinal meanings.) Worry over buying a newspaper is itself neurotic enough. The interesting thing here is that the avowed notion of thrift is explicitly flouted by the next step of planning to buy still another paper and finally throwing away the nickel. Returning the paper makes sense once the premise is accepted. Buying two papers is total nonsense as of the idea of thrift, but apparently the patient here shifts to the attitude of the newsboy and is prepared to spend another nickel to relieve himself both of his unconscious self-accusation and the contempt for his parsimony. The primary significance of the first motivation is cogently shown by simply throwing away the nickel in the absence of any social compulsion—indeed, despite any social connotations of money. He has done and undone—at the realistic cost of a dime, plus the fee to his analyst—and has successfully avoided the more important manifestations of his problems.

The actions of undoing tend to be repetitive, perhaps even more than most neurotic symptoms. Repetition always tends to occur when the basic problem remains unsolved. Compulsive rituals of negative magic are especially repetitive because in one way or another they usually include a positive expression of the impulse either in the undoing itself or in the thought or act which precipitates the undoing. Satisfied at the moment, the newspaper patient knows he has spent two nickels. The one meaning (doing) tends to intrude upon the other, and the patient is never sure just how many acts will undo the eternally recurrent positive impulse.

The normal counterpart of undoing is magical expiation, which has been utilized in religion and other disciplines. Many readers know the joke about the young priest who recommends that his penitent commit the sin of adultery once more so that the priest can calculate the penance exactly. The joke is a burlesque of the recourse of expiation known to all of us as both prophylaxis and restitution. The votive candle is often lighted by persons with no real vision of the grace of God. The church demands a contrite heart, but for many people the penances prescribed are the important thing, in no very close relation to the nature of the sin. We readily acknowledge the folly of these actions, yet we all recognize the magical relief that comes from *token* undoing of our misdeeds. The psychological result goes beyond trust in divine forgiveness to the comforting, if irrational, conviction that the event never happened or, in the case of prophylactic rituals, will not happen. Childhood and superstition are full of this mechanism. The dreaded consequence of spilling salt is annulled by throwing a pinch over the left shoulder, much as the patient annulled the act of squandering a nickel, with evil unconscious intent, by the deliberate act of throwing away another nickel.

DENIAL

During the magical years of childhood, *denial* of reality is much easier and may operate as a mechanism in itself. Two small boys fell into acrimonious dispute in my hearing, both feeling genuinely injured. Just as adult intervention seemed inevitable, one of them proposed a solution: "Let's say none of it happened." I forget just how he phrased it, but the idea was clearly to wash out the whole matter and go back to where they had been half an hour earlier. The other boy readily agreed. Struck by the greater expediency of this procedure over any solution I had been able to invent for the circumstances, I merely listened attentively for further repercussions. There were none. Amicable play was re-established quite as if no interruption had occurred.

Denial[13] of reality is not so easy when the problem is less transitory. A quarrel about who had a toy first is in that respect different from the constant observation of the little boy that he is less of a man than his father. Most children "play" at being grown up, apparently with extreme seriousness during the game but laying the game aside when it is finished. Anna Freud describes a child patient who went further.[14] He carried a hat resembling his father's *at all times*, becoming extremely anxious when required to lay it down. (Ultimately he discovered a satisfying compromise—to tuck it into the flap of his breeches, where, according to the analyst, it really belonged, in its symbolic significance as the father's genitals.) In this way the boy extended the dressing-up magical play into a convinced denial of his obvious handicap in rivalry with the father.

The mechanism of denial of reality should not be confused with the repression of inner instinctual trends more commonly found in adult neurosis. In the repression, the conflict is internalized and related to reality through a complex system of cathexes and anticathexes. In true repression and reaction formation, the individual does not allow the instinctual representative of an impulse full access to consciousness and the voluntary motor pathways because of internal opposition, thus *secondarily* limiting the appreciation of reality features of the external situation. In *denial*, the conflict is still simply between impulse and a reality frustration, and reality is the loser.

As the ego matures in its reality function and the inner life takes on more structure, such a solution must be discarded as a *major* defense. Fairly overt denial of facts—above all, connections between facts—may take place incidentally, as we saw in the mechanism of undoing. But only in very grave pathology—e.g., in psychotic delusions—can the *adult* so override the dictates of common sense as to deny directly an important fact. The neurotic mother whose child dies may preserve its doll as a symbol and weave the doll into a complicated system of feeling. But only the psychotic mother can actually replace the child with the doll and react to loss of the doll as to loss of the child or can otherwise maintain that the child never died.

COMPROMISE

For some time, we have been verging on the technique of *compromise*, whereby the unacceptable impulse is allowed a partial, often a disguised, direct expression but no more. Theoretically, compromise is incompatible with the mechanism of repression and reaction formation. A completely repressed impulse requires no effort on the part of the ego beyond keeping it repressed and dealing with the limitations imposed by nonrecognition of important cues. The whole purport of reaction formation is to guarantee against *any* direct expression by reinforcement of the opposite trend. Nevertheless, we have seen that very frequently overdirect expression occurs side-by-side with reaction formation, and that such mechanisms as isolation and undoing allow a partial expression immediately controlled. The emphasis in the following pages is on techniques whereby the direct expression of an impulse is fused with its inhibition from the outset. The borderlines of mechanisms tend to blur for the excellent reason that they are only rough guide lines to highly complex dynamic relationships, and because etiologically different trends of relatively independent structure coexist in the same individual.

Reaction formation involves all-out opposition of one psychic system to another. Repression involves the adaptation of the psyche as a whole toward carefully maintained lacunae in consciousness. By the technique of *compromise,* however, one and the same symptom serves both to express and to inhibit the impulse. We saw something of this in the mechanism of undoing, in which the expiatory phase is premised upon first allowing some positive expression of the unconscious wish. Such compromise differs from the examples to follow only in emphasis, or, better, in the degree of fusion, as a gross emulsion may be contrasted with a mixture in which the ingredient elements no longer separate out clearly.

In illustration of intimate compromise between expression and inhibition, we may consider the facial tic of Miss L., which was the subject of much ribald comment among my schoolmates when I was ten. Every few minutes her left eye contracted in a very provocative wink. She taught eighth grade in our school and happened to live with her father, a retired school principal, at the same small hotel as my family. On the occasion of my quoting one of the boys at home, my parents explained that the wink was a sad affliction, like St. Vitus dance. I was instructed to be very respectful toward a woman who had devoted her life to the care of her remarkable father. Dealing with Miss L.'s father, however, had its drawbacks, which I finally confided to my family. He often requested small errands to his room, where I was greeted with much fatherly kissing and hugging, increasingly unpleasant. My family quietly arranged that I never saw Mr. L. alone, although admonitions toward respectful behavior were not abated.

This fragmentary case of Miss L. is chosen because almost any community affords similar examples of neurotic symptomatology and is partly aware of the sexual implications. Freud would doubtless agree with the hobbledehoys of the eighth grade as to the provocative intent of the wink; at least, similar symptoms have often revealed such intent on careful analysis. From the life-long exclusive devotion to the father, one may guess at an especially strong tie with him. Although his slobbery interest in little girls at the age of seventy-five is by no means conclusive proof of an unhealthy relationship with his daughter, it does suggest some sexual problems, conscious or unconscious, on his part which may well have affected the daughter.

The blameless life of Miss L. is typical for such cases. One may assume that her sexual wish is normally strong but immediately gives rise to severe feelings of guilt, so that any direct expression or recognition of its nature entails painful anxiety. It is therefore repressed, and, as in the cases of reaction formation discussed earlier, she becomes unusually virtuous. The mechanism of her tic, however, is not so much building up a counter-cathexis as allowing limited and disguised expression. The unconscious wish appears in a form interpreted merely as a disfigurement for which Miss L. is in no way responsible. The power of the denied impulse is shown by the compulsive character of the symptom. Naturally, the patient would stop such nonsense if voluntary control were at all possible.

Direct compromise of this nature is usually combined with more subtle gains to the personality as a whole. The ugly tic makes it virtually impossible for Miss L. to attract a suitable man; hence she is protected from sexual temptation in reality by the very symptom that partially expresses her desire. Furthermore, the symptom is highly disagreeable, an obvious handicap in *any* social situation. Her actual suffering serves as a sort of penance exacted by her superego for the measure of release afforded the id. Here, too, there is a kind of compromise. The guilt feelings are assuaged by punishment.

And, finally, there is a *secondary gain* in her relations with people. She cannot be blamed for something that is so obviously not her own fault, and she need not even blame herself for having failed to marry or to establish the kind of social life expected of a young woman. Very possibly, she could also exact an extra measure of care from her father because of her affliction, although the reward of extra attention is not so clear in this case as in those in which the symptom is more seriously hampering in daily affairs.

A rather similar example, with more definite secondary gain, is reported by Reik.[15] A young married woman developed the phobia that she would be seduced if she was left alone with a man, even momentarily. One episode shows the pattern. Her husband leaves her in a taxi while he buys some cigarettes and, on his return, finds her in such a state of panic about the possible advances of the taxi driver during the few moments of his absence that their evening is spoiled. Clearly, this woman's illness keeps her husband at her beck and call more effectively than the domination of a virago, a point which Adler found sufficiently important to explain the neurosis without recourse to other factors. Reik suggests strong penis envy and hostility toward men in the reactions of this woman. Her symptom may be partially explained as the desire to be as promiscuous as a man and to avenge herself for deprivation of the prerogatives of the male, anatomically and in his larger measure of social freedom. Finally, the highly specific fear of seduction is itself a fairly direct acknowledgment of the wish, by no means as obscure as some of the complicated reaction formations discussed earlier. Compare the familiar jokes about the old maid "hoping" to find a man under the bed. The point of the example here is the *compromise* presented by the symptom itself.

DISPLACEMENT

The neurotic compromise need not be so direct as in the examples cited. Concern about the genitals may, for example, be *displaced* to the head, to the feet, to almost any part of the body, or even to the body as a whole. Symptoms may then appear to be quite distant from the impulse pressing toward gratification. An illustration might be the not uncommon hand-washing compulsion. Often the hand is tenderly cared for almost openly as a love object—because it stands for the organ with which it is associated in the act of masturbation. Again, however, guilt is a prominent component of the psychological situation. Therefore, the hand must be cleansed beyond all reason. Or the hand may be immobilized by a hysterical paralysis. Writer's cramp and the manual difficulties of musicians frequently show some such origin—almost always complicated by fears of failure and the secondary gains of self-punishment and self-protection against acknowledgment of fear of failure.

The Freudian does not deny the importance of the socially conditioned elements, but he does not consider them primary. Freud comments that to do so is like maintaining that a war veteran got his leg shot off in order to live on compensation.[16] The veteran not infrequently makes use of his benefits neurotically. He may cling to his illness as a protection against the pain of resuming adult responsibility. Many doctors who consider neurosis quite as "real" a handicap as a missing leg are uncertain of the value of generalized compensation laws, because they play into the needs and fears of the patient at the level of what Freud calls the secondary gain of illness. This gain does not determine the neurosis, as Adler suggested. It has different dynamics. Nevertheless, it may complicate or even thwart cure by the psychoanalytic method that Freud first proposed.

Akin to these phenomena are *displacements* to other people, external objects, institutions, ideas, and activities. Again, forbidden id impulses may be overtly expressed, but again only in partial and disguised form. A common example is taking out one's hostility on an innocent bystander, as in the example of the young girl who snaps at her family when she is disappointed in a date. The case of Sidney offers a more complex illustration. He came for treatment, reluctantly, because he had flunked out of college despite an I.Q. of 150 and a brilliant academic record in high school. The parents were genuinely bewildered. When he lived at home, Sidney had been a model child in the best sense of the word: responsible, industrious, agreeable, reasonably social, always affectionately respectful toward his parents. At home he was still respectful, penitent, full of promises for reform, touchingly grateful for the understanding patience of his family in the face of the disastrous year away at college. The dean told a very different story. The boy had not done his assignments, had finally cut classes at his whim, was generally impudent, adopting a devil-may-care, rebellious attitude *toward all the college authorities*.

Sidney's father had attended the college before him. Gradually, in the course of treatment, an underlying, repressed resentment toward the parents, especially hostility toward the father dating back to the phallic stage, became manifest. Under the stress of the new environment, plus a belated adolescent concern with sex, the boy's previous pattern of repression and reaction formation had become inadequate. It was still impossible for him to acknowledge his hostilities directly. The dean of his father's college took the brunt of resentments whose real significance was intolerable. Here displacement operated as a defense mechanism of impressive special organization.

RATIONALIZATION AND CAMOUFLAGE

Two more mechanisms may be mentioned briefly: *rationalization* and *camouflage.* These mechanisms are so general and so generally recognized that they hardly belong in a section devoted to specifically Freudian concepts of dynamics, but our outline is not puristic. *Rationalization,* of course, is the tendency of most of us, most of the time, to reinterpret our behavior so that it seems reasonable, or at least fits some sort of rational framework. By preference, the reinterpretation shows us in a favorable light, but we can settle for the excuse "I wasn't myself" when our behavior has been all too clearly reprehensible or foolish.

Camouflage (the word is taken from Reik) is a more conscious application of the same technique, mainly for the benefit of others. Reik presents the pathologically extreme example of a compulsion neurotic, plagued with the necessity to perform small rituals on many simple occasions, who actually went over the route he planned to take on an outing with a young lady in order to work out in advance highly ingenious ways of making his absurd compulsions appear like spontaneous and natural actions.[17] At the extreme of normality is the cough or the dropping of a book or whatever by the inadvertent eavesdropper who wishes to announce his presence without suggesting that he has overheard.

The deeper dynamics behind the mechanisms described in the last few pages (displacement, compromise, rationalization, camouflage) are extremely variable, so that it is rarely possible to use them as such in fruitful understanding of the patient as a person, although the interpretation of specific acts requires awareness of them. However, analysts have come to recognize *some* individuals as prime rationalizers or prime camouflagers, and to deal with them in treatment accordingly. Perhaps just because these mechanisms are so close to human nature *generally* in our highly "rational" culture, they escaped official listing among the Freudian defense mechanisms. Perhaps as analysts work more with character neuroses instead of symptoms (see Chap. 7), such items may enter the listing. Under the heading *overintellectualization,* many of these exaggerations of normal trends in our culture are taking shape as a newly recognized defense mechanism. On the other hand, the normal manifestations of the old defense mechanisms receive emphasis with increasing clarity as "Freudian" thinking penetrates other disciplines and the whole of contemporary thought.

CHARACTER

A special kind of defense mechanism, very pervasive in its influence and lying at the core of the personality, may be called "character." Concern with this problem begins with Freud, but it has been developed further by other analysts—notably by those whom we shall present in Part III. In the opinion of most Freudians, these analysts have carried the concept rather too far, to the point of making it the cornerstone of their theory and practice, sometimes repudiating altogether Freud's concept of the libido, his structural approach, and most of the more restricted mechanisms of defense. This statement applies especially to Adler and Horney.

Among the analysts whom I have classified as Freudian, Karl Abraham[18] is outstanding in this connection. Abraham felt that when the personality became fixated primarily at one or another stage of libidinal development, the adult personality could be fruitfully described in terms of the strivings and attitudes characteristic for this stage. He distinguished an oral passive and an oral aggressive character and an anal character. The genital character is that of the fully mature person. Fromm borrows a great deal from Abraham's elaborations (the original idea was Freud's), although he lays much more stress on the general social constellation within which the child is reared. Fromm's account of these characters is so good that I refer the reader to pages 267ff. instead of repeating the description here.

Another author of especial importance in this area is Wilhelm Reich.[19] Whereas Abraham appears to see character mainly as a kind of continuation of trends established in the developmental stages of childhood, as habitual ways of reacting rooted in the relative fixation of the personality at one or another phase of libidinal growth, Reich's emphasis is on the concept of defense. Character, according to Reich, involves a profound and chronic alteration in the ego which serves the person as a sort of *armor* against those stimuli, external or internal, that he has come to consider dangerous. Far from directly reflecting his libidinal structure, it typically represents a reaction *against* powerful libidinal trends. In the analytic hour, it functions mainly as resistance to

effective emotionally valid insight into the materials elicited by free association and other analytic techniques.

Traits develop in deep relationship to the level of libidinal development
at which defensive maneuvers became especially necessary to the child, and in
relationship to the persons he was mainly identified with at the crucial points
of growth. Reich essentially accepts the libido theory, although he has increasingly stressed what he calls orgone energy.*

The significant aspect of Reich's work for psychoanalysis is his emphasis
on character per se, and on the necessity for handling these organized resistances actively in the psychoanalytic hour. Of especial interest to me is Reich's
observation of typical psychological defenses in postural and other physiological
constellations. This is an area of inquiry that should be developed further.
Related to this observation is his analysis of coherent patterns of reaction
beyond what the patient verbalizes about his problems or his significant productions in free association deriving from the id. Earlier than most analysts,
Reich came to realize how characteristic modes of reaction—self-dramatizing,
cynical detachment, etc.—influence the course of the analysis. He showed
vividly how the ego can muster one aspect of the id impulses against another,
so that the defensive armor becomes as strong *instinctually* as the impulse that
is being repressed and is equally irrational and resistant to change.

I think I am correct in stating that most Freudians nowadays find attention to character (habitual ways of reacting) useful in understanding their
patients. It is often helpful, indeed indispensable, to realize that patient X is
the kind to lie back and let George do it, placidly accepting any interpretation
so long as the great doctor appears to be taking care of him; whereas patient Y
may be terribly hurt by the slightest implication that the doctor may have an
idea beyond what the patient can himself understand about his condition.

This clinical usage of insight into broad character trends is discussed more
thoroughly in Chapter 12, where treatment procedures are presented in some
detail. In theory, Freudians tend to view efforts at "typing" character with
not a little suspicion. They have been more concerned with fundamental
theory and with a careful examination of relatively narrow "mechanisms"
than with broad classification of organized ego devices. They fear lest the
unique constellation of problems presented by each individual will be lost in
such characterological generalization.

At one point in the writing of this book, I had the notion of discussing
rather thoroughly how the key concepts of each school could be translated into

---

* Almost no analysts have accepted his later theoretical developments toward a "biophysical"
statement of psychological problems on the basis of this "universal primordial energy." Since
Reich himself prefers to dissociate himself from psychoanalysis, we need not attempt here to
present his current views. They seem to me quite fantastically wrong.

the vocabulary of the others. In my innocence, I even thought that this might be an easy job. I had in mind especially such concepts as self-esteem, self-assertion, the will to power, insecurity, dependency—that sort of thing. Everybody knows they are important.

I did not find such translation feasible. The Freudians consider such concepts as highly complex resultants, the dynamics of which vary from one person to another. Dependency as a major trend *usually* suggests orality. Self-assertion and the will to power may be rooted in oral sadism, or they may be derived primarily from the problems of the anal period. Fear of loss of love, primary aggression, narcissistic libido—these factors also must be considered, not to mention the whole array of the defense mechanisms of the ego. Insecurity—is it anything more than anxiety? Thus, it would be going against the basic concepts of Freudian theory to attempt any generalized redefinition of these terms for easy comparison with later chapters.

I have tried to understand why concepts basic to some schools of psychoanalysis really have no place as dynamic systems in Freudian theory. I think the reason is that Freud really never considered the "self" as an important dynamic system, whereas the other analysts make it fundamental. Since I discuss this difference at length elsewhere, I here merely alert the reader to the problem. Insecurity is different from anxiety because it involves a sense of the self as something of a unit. Self-esteem, self-assertion, and the other concepts also rest upon this premise. Freud's omission of these concepts is only one aspect of his different attitude toward the "self." Freudians are right in feeling that they cannot be simply added to Freudian theory or easily translated into their terminology.

MECHANISMS AND DYNAMICS

IN OUTLINING THIS CHAPTER on "dynamics," I was startled to find that I seemed to be talking mostly about "mechanisms." Of course, I had defined "dynamics" with special limitation as *how the adult personality functions.* At first, I thought this was merely a semantic problem—that the Freudians said *mechanism* when they really meant *dynamism*—or that my definition was too idiosyncratic to justify use of *dynamics* as a chapter heading.

On reflection, the problem goes deeper. The Freudian concept of dynamics is actually highly differentiated and multidimensional and must be presented in a complex manner. A great deal of attention is paid to mechanisms (*subsystems,* in the vocabulary I have suggested) which are highly dynamic in their implications for the understanding of human behavior but which stand in variable relationship to other systems of psychic events (drives, conflicts, psychic institutions, etc.). The little boy who insists upon carrying a hat (Anna Freud) and the man who throws a nickel into the gutter (Fenichel) both have problems in the genital area probably equally reducible, in deep analysis, to fear of castration, according to Freudian theory. Yet these odd bits of behavior are incomprehensible unless they are seen within the mechanisms of denial and undoing respectively. The term *mechanism* is appropriate because almost any basic impulse may be denied or undone. The term *dynamism* might be appropriate (it is never so used in practice by Freudians*) to indicate that a whole series of events are seen in quasi-necessary relationship to one another.

Let us carry the example a bit further. "Throwing something away" so elaborately in the constellation of thriftiness sounds very much like the generalized syndrome of the anal character, with retention and willful expulsion. This kind of interpretation is by no means foreign to Fenichel's thinking, and very probably he would not object to its being applied to the patient described. His complaint might be that it does not fully explain the particular incident, which appeared to represent *mainly* the magical undoing of the wish to visit a prostitute. By the principle of overdetermination, the action of the patient is almost certain to have roots in several organ systems, often operating through more than one mechanism. Furthermore, the action typically involves tension among the three institutions of the mind—id, ego, and superego. Thus, the token visit to the prostitute probably may be said to represent an id impulse which promptly comes into conflict with the superego.

Freudian dynamics regularly takes account of three systems, which function simultaneously: (1) the genetic system, constellated around the pleasure strivings of the erogenous zones. Experiences of gratification and frustration or punishment in childhood typically determine an emphasis on one zone rather than another, and the zone so selected then exerts a *polarizing* influence on subsequent developments but clearly cannot be considered as fully directive for all future behavior; (2) the structural system (id, ego, superego), representing the general organization of the personality as regards its relationship to instinct (bodily pleasure striving and aggression), to external reality, and to conscience and ideals (the emerging social structure of the personality);

* Sullivan's usage (see pp. 357*f.*) is close to the one I have suggested.

and (3) the defense mechanisms of the ego, which interpret the significance of specific behavior patterns.

To a marked degree, the defense mechanisms seem to cross-cut the first two dynamic approaches. Their etiology is obscure (*cf.* p. 244). In the next chapter we shall discuss a rough relationship between the mechanism of repression and the hysterical syndromes, which are thought to proceed *mainly* from disturbances at the phallic stage of development. The mechanisms of isolation and undoing appear to be especially characteristic for obsessive-compulsive syndromes, which seem to involve *mainly* anal components.

Even these relatively sharply differentiated pathological syndromes typically present a *mixture* of mechanisms and trends genetically and structurally oriented. The specific diagnosis merely suggests a predominant pattern, which to some extent polarizes the whole gamut of personality reactions but which never completely explains the person. In practice, the analyst must always work to and fro among these various system dynamics, choosing whichever is most significant for his purpose at the time. He must always keep in mind that a harsh superego functions differently in a personality primarily constellated around anal trends than in one constellated around oral trends; that any given act must be interpreted in terms of its immediate significance— usually its place in a defense mechanism—and the reality situation of the patient. The distinction between defense mechanisms of the ego and genuine id impulses is not always easy to establish. Anna Freud reports the case of a shy little boy who suddenly began laying about him with a rod and knives at one phase of treatment. This behavior did not yet signify a release of previously inhibited aggression but identification with an external aggressor punishing him for masturbation.[20] By the mechanisms of identification, introjection, and projection, the ego may closely simulate the more internalized commands of the superego. Indeed, some authors (Klein, for example) prefer to consider these reactions as manifestations of a primitive superego, whereas others (A. Freud, for example) feel that primarily ego-determined defenses should be distinguished from the superego.

If the reader finds this account confusing, he has the full sympathy of the author, but I think he will have to struggle through it. Freudian dynamics is a *view of systems* relatively loosely woven together, not a single holistic system by which everything can be explained once the key to the over-all pattern has been found. The theoretical groundwork for a view of systems was suggested in Chapter 1 and can be used in support of this "confusion." In critical comment I have already suggested that Eros and Thanatos represent

Freud's effort to discover ultimate, universal principles and that they tend to be misleading when applied as instincts in the concrete instance.

It must not be forgotten, however, that all these systems appear within a single individual, who must also be considered as a functioning totality. The task of the skilled psychoanalyst must be to understand in so far as possible the currents and cross-currents of the personality in their relationship to one another. Often the bond is highly dynamic, as when a threat of direct break-through of libidinal material is met by a strengthening of the countercathexis or the development of still more elaborate compromise symptomatology. However, different trends may stand side by side in the personality, and the relationship among them may be mainly *quantitative*. Freudians call these *quantitatively* determined relationships the *economic* aspect of personality dynamics (see pp. 85ff.), and they increasingly stress the effect of the preponderance of one system over another at different periods of life—or, indeed, from moment to moment—as internal and external stimuli make varying demands upon the individual. The trend *that is stronger at any given period* mainly determines the behavior of the person, while the weaker trend finds expression as best it can.

Freud uses the example of hallucinatory confusional states in which the patients may report after recovery that "at the time in some corner of their minds . . . there was a normal person hidden, who watched the hubbub of the illness go past, like a disinterested spectator."[21] The example points to a *split in the ego,* which Freud further illustrates from neuroses in which acceptance of reality factors exists along with their repression. The neurotic instance Freud presents in this connection is fetishism, which he analyzes as denial of the observational fact that women have no penis because of the threat of castration implied in this circumstance.* Yet fetishists often exhibit direct castration fear at the same time, demonstrating acceptance of the biological facts. Furthermore, they may also show normal sexual potency on occasion—or, indeed, predominantly. The sexual exaggerations of the neurotic Don Juan are typically in direct relation to unconscious sexual fears. By contrast, the normal sexuality of the fetishist, or concomitant neurotic reactions of different unconscious origin, exist side by side with the denial mechanism and independently of it.

* It would take us too far afield in this book to present Freud's evidence for such a statement. Freud's paper on "Fetishism" (*Collected Papers,* Vol. V, Hogarth Press, 1950, pp. 198-204) may be cited not only for its immediate relevance but as an example of more detailed working out of the libido theory than has been presented in this book. Further examples may be found in almost any issue of the psychoanalytic journals (*Journal of the American Psychoanalytic Association, Psychoanalytic Quarterly, Psychoanalytic Review*).

Fairly often, then, the id impulses are *not* direct contributors toward the reaction pattern exhibited by the person from moment to moment but maintain a separate subterranean existence expressed in fragmentary fashion if at all. They are not inactive meanwhile but may come to the surface only when the *quantitative* relationships of the various trends within the personality are shifted. A delusional system in a psychotic paranoid outbreak, for example, often leaps into prominence full-blown and is *not* prepared step by step as the ego makes successive compromises with various aspects of libidinal demands. According to Freud, whole sectors of behavior may be elaborated in the unconscious *without reference to the prevailing personality trends.* They are sometimes manifested in dreams or in small errors of everyday life, like any other unconscious material, but they come into effective action *only as the balance with other trends is changed.* Usually, the shift is toward pathological reactions as pressure from increased libidinal forces (as in puberty or the climacteric) or from outside circumstances reinforces the power of the normally submerged trend. Freud remarks, however, that the dreams of a paranoid patient often show a correction of a delusional system that is unshakable in his waking life.[22]

This aspect of Freudian doctrine has been stressed somewhat beyond its customary place in Freudian thinking* because of its theoretical contrast with the position of Adler and the analysts discussed in Part III, who strongly emphasize the constant adjustment of the total personality to the life situation at any given moment. Indeed, it is in some contrast to the current very general trend toward a holistic view of the dynamics of the individual organism, a view that owes much to Freud. The problem will be discussed further in Chapter 7, on treatment, and in critical comment, but it may be remarked here that the *split in the ego* just described is to be seen as a complication of Freud's position, not as a denial of the holistic approach. The development of trends side by side still rests upon their meaningfulness to the person and is never thought of as a mechanical linkage of psychological events. The emergence or repression of such independent sectors depends upon the *economy* of the total personality at any given moment quite as much as instances of dynamic relationship seen in reaction formation and compromise in which behavior is interpreted as exaggerated repression or disguised expression of unacceptable impulses. It goes beyond the problem of "character."

The major underlying dynamics of the Freudian scheme seem fairly constant: fear of castration or loss of love. Because of the complex development of the genital function through various stages of growth of the libido and object

---

* Freud himself in a late paper remarks that it has been unduly neglected. ("Analysis Terminable and Interminable," *Collected Papers*, Vol. V, p. 328.)

relations, the final problem always includes the component instincts and the crystallization of the psychic institutions. Thus, although the nuclear conflict is almost regularly considered by Freudians to lie in the Oedipal situation, its actual working out in the individual instance becomes infinitely varied as different points of fixation or regression, of instinct fusion and defusion, of tension among different structural divisions, come into predominant action. In the foregoing pages, the emphasis has been on the *how* of such action. This is primarily a problem in ego psychology. We have discussed typical ways by which the ego performs the task of synthesizing the various demands made upon it by systems developed as such in some independence of one another.

SUMMARY

THIS HAS BEEN so much a chapter of review and integration that a detailed summary seems useless if not misleading. The long discussion of the genetic process was reviewed in the terms of the concept of the libido as a kind of "energy" deriving from the sexual instincts, mobile at the beginning but becoming fixated or bound in the course of development. I suggested that this "psychic energy" can be interpreted, probably with Freud's full agreement, as tension within the sexual drive systems. Its mobility and other courses, fixated and bound, then become useful generalizations of psychic events which require further understanding in terms of more restricted concepts.

Freud cut into this "energic" concept of the sexual instincts in several ways:

(1) The structural approach (id, ego, superego) was briefly reviewed.

(2) Defense mechanisms of the ego were described, although it was explained that the listing of such mechanisms was neither complete nor systematic, and was merged with concepts that are not usually classified as defense mechanisms—rationalization, camouflage, and overintellectualization.

(3) The problem of character types was briefly discussed.

(4) Finally, an effort was made to suggest how all these different ways of approaching insight into human behavior are used *together* in the Freudian concept of psychodynamics, again referring to the economic approach rather sketchily described in Chapter 3. I suggest that the last few pages of text be

considered as a sort of dynamic summary and integration of the disparate materials presented earlier.

The key to fruitful understanding of the Freudian concept of dynamics is emphasis on its *multidimensionality*. Freud does not extrapolate human behavior from a few general principles, handling complications by purely logical deduction roughly checked against experience. On the contrary, he has introduced a whole series of concepts which order observations at different levels, from different angles. This *multidimensionality* is somewhat confusing, and I think the Freudians themselves often get tangled up in it. Nevertheless, I feel so very strongly about its positive value for psychological science that I should like to state here—in exposition—that it is the main strength of the Freudian position. It is, as I suggested in Chapter 1, a necessary concept for any mature science.

Critical Comment

IN REVIEWING this chapter, I find that I have already twice intruded upon exposition with what is actually critical comment. The first intrusion is the discussion (on p. 254) of Anna Freud's listing of the defense mechanisms, with the decision that I would follow my own listing in the absence of any very coherent background for choice in Freudian literature. The second appears in the last few pages, where I have tried to suggest the relationship of these mechanisms to the underlying dynamics of the libido theory and the genetic process.

Yet both these intrusions are so closely related to the writings of contemporary Freudians and to aspects of Freud's own writings that it seems mistaken to claim personal responsibility for them. This is an area in which Freudian thinking is itself in a state of flux and active development, in which it is not possible to rely upon clear-cut "schools" to carry the brunt of differing opinions, in which individual authors stand in varying relationships to the many cross-systems of the Freudian view of functioning dynamics. I believe that my intrusions so far represent "Freudian" thinking that they should remain in the expository section, even though they are not strictly classical and partly represent my own attempt to organize understandably for the reader and myself the new considerations now being voiced on every side. In these last pages, I have already tried, in occasional parentheses, to indicate how the complexities of Freudian dynamics relate to the "view of systems" which I suggest throughout my personal comments. It must be plain that I find the multidimensional approach of Freud in general highly congenial.

In line with the critique offered after earlier chapters, it seems to me that the underlying systems should be *extended* beyond the erogenous zones and the instinct of aggression to include the "nonsexual systems" prominent in the biological equipment of mankind. In discussion of the genetic process (Chap. 5), I suggested that these systems are by their very nature more oriented toward the outer world and that they tend to coalesce as primary ingredients of the "ego"—what I have called the psychological self.* It seems to me possible, even probable, that the fate of the non-sexual systems as the child encounters the controls of his physical and social environment contributes very largely toward his choice of preponderant ego defense mechanisms. Freud and Anna Freud were quoted to the effect that such choice for a given individual remains a mystery, and the problem is too complex and too new to warrant even a speculative blueprint on my part, but I suggest that examination of parent-child relationships in the nonsexual spheres may offer a clue to these choices.

Let us suppose, for example, that the father of the little boy who insisted compulsively on wearing a hat was the kind of person who would make an especially cogent Oedipal figure—and who did not participate in the child's play or otherwise offer *possibilities of identification in the motor sphere or other emergent activity systems*. Let us suppose that there were no adequate father representatives available for these systems. In such circumstances, the *sexual* image of the father would be almost the only one through which the normal identification process could function, and it would not be functionally integrated with appreciation of the father (the male image) in areas closer to reality. "Being a man" would thus be excessively concentrated on the aspect of having a big penis. In the magical years of childhood, this requirement could be fulfilled readily enough by the hat.

Obviously I hold no serious brief for this interpretation in the absence of any information whatsoever about the experience of this child in the nonsexual areas of his life. I suggest it only as a *plausible* explanation, in order to illustrate my concept of the importance of the actual handling of the nonsexual systems. The illustration is further useful in pointing up the fact that Anna Freud, who has made the most outstanding contribution to ego psychology, does not consider such background material relevant enough to report.

Certainly case reports concerned exclusively with matters of habit training, discipline, opportunities for learning, and the like are quite insufficient. I am not advocating a reversion to the pre-psychoanalytic efforts of many child psychologists. I am urging, however, that such materials be reported *by analysts;* that they be analyzed for their systematic implications as regards development of the nonsexual systems—in constant relationship to development in the erogenous zones. In practice, Freudians do pay attention to such matters. The report of the actual development of refugee children in a small school supervised by Anna Freud herself[23] offers abundant testimony to such attention. Her recent papers and lectures do seem to lay more stress on activity, the nature of the "models" offered the child, etc. But there is still little systematic attempt at *codification* of development in the nonsexual spheres in its relation to libidinal growth and to general patterns of parental or cultural handling. Here is a field wide open for investigation.

The Self Image

To my mind, there is a major omission from Freud's statement of the important dynamic groupings of systems (structures, institutions) that come to function more or less independently in the mature personality. That is the self-image. Freud himself used the term *ego-ideal* for some time, but as he came to envisage its major dynamics in terms of the introjective identification with the parents at the end of the Oedipal phase, he emphasized the term *superego* instead.

* The terms are almost equivalent as regards *Freud's* "ego" but not quite. My "psychological self" implies a vague sort of integrative process which includes conscious, preconscious, and unconscious processes, whereas the Freudian "ego" is a still broader concept applied to part functions as freely as to this integrative function.

The ego-ideal is now considered a subsidiary aspect of the superego, or a derivative of early narcissism, and in my opinion has not been sufficiently investigated.

It seems to me that people build up a rather clear-cut picture of themselves which goes beyond "conscience" and which has more definite and more *socialized* contours than narcissistic libido. This image is surely strongly influenced by the superego, but it is also a reflection of what other people think of us—as interpreted by ourselves; of what we consider our assets and limitations according to the social values we accept; of the role we think we play in our own world. Attitudes developed in interplay with our material and cultural surroundings tend to coalesce around the focus of our concept of our "self," which, after all, plays a constant role in our everyday activities and in important life decisions.

I offer as example a significant psychotherapeutic result in one interview from my own experience. I had administered the group Rorschach to a college class simply to demonstrate the technique, but one student asked whether I would not go over the results with him privately, because he felt so desperate and miserable. His Rorschach looked to me essentially sound, but with striking indices of an almost panicky sense of inferiority cropping up repeatedly as a kind of *extra frill* on his responses. I suspected some sort of traumatic experience. On being questioned about this possibility, the young man (aged 20) described a protracted illness in late childhood which had made it impossible for him to participate in games. He was taunted by his fellows as a "fat slob"; he was "yellow"; girls snickered at him. He had obviously preserved this image of himself in his own mind, although it had happily become illusory.

With the Rorschach as backing, I explained the mechanism to him, energetically suggested that he look carefully in the mirror (he had become handsome), and reviewed with him his actual achievements, which were quite impressive. We analyzed together a little how girls and employers *really* acted toward him, and how his timid behavior tended to chill their early advances.

Follow-up in this case consisted in occasional brief after-class reports of a successful job interview and the appreciative comments of his new boss, of successful dating, and, finally, of sustained interest in a particular girl. When I met him by chance a few years later, he smilingly told of his marriage, his successful army experience, and his good professional prospects.

Unfortunately, this case is by no means typical of the results I expect from one interview with a disturbed college student. The technique employed worked so well because all that ailed *this* boy, I think, was a poor self image of late and relatively circumscribed development. Symptomatically, it was affecting every aspect of his life because he carried it into all his interpersonal relationships. Eventually, it might have *become* much more thoroughly integrated with his entire personality, and hence much more resistant to treatment. Dynamically, it was still something of an excrescence, whose independent identity was clearly observable and easily handled by the boy himself, once the respected professor, fortified with the objective test findings, gave him a new orientation.

In its slight but clear-cut pathology, this case illustrates well the independent structure and power of the self image I am suggesting as an addition to Freud's structural approach. In the vast majority of cases, the self-image is much more closely related to the superego, because as a rule it is the parents who induct the child into society, and there is no such sharp introduction of social attitudes constellated around a special, relatively transitory phase of development (the illness in late childhood). Self image and superego, then, have such close dynamic relationships that it may well seem appropriate to subsume the ego-ideal under the rubric *superego*.

Probably this fusion was especially cogent in the Vienna Freud knew, which was still relatively stable as regards social mobility. In America, the adaptation of the second-generation immigrant to his social environment as well as to the Old World ways of his parents has long presented a dislocation in the process of growing up. Even the American of native stock has almost typically lived a life as an adult very strikingly different from the pattern set by his parents. Margaret Mead points to the peculiarly American ideal of having things so much better for our children that outstripping their parents becomes almost the normal expectation.[24] Under these conditions, it seems likely that the self image would attain a firm structure of its own, very heavily influenced by social values quite often at variance with those of the parents.

From the point of view of Freudian dynamics, I would classify this self image as a substructure primarily of the ego rather than of the superego. Like all ego structures, it must "borrow" much of its power, and very probably it borrows mostly from the superego. If Freudians prefer to call it mainly superego, highlighting the special role of the parents via the Oedipus complex, I see no reason to quarrel about verbal classifications. One might call the maintenance of the self image a defense mechanism! But it is one of such extensive proportions that the term becomes rather silly.

I have tried to make very clear that I think of the self image as a developmental construct, in no sense an "instinct." I do not like the idea of considering self-esteem, self-assertion, etc. as primary phenomena, or considering the "self" as the irreducible unit of a theoretical system of psychology. This argument will be continued in comment on the authors presented in Part III who take some such position. Nevertheless, it seems to me that Freudian dynamics neglects or misinterprets a psychic structure which, at least in our culture, has enormous power as a fairly integrated system.

Freud's very broad definition of the ego seems to me extremely useful, as I have said repeatedly. It allows for multidimensional study of learned subsystems in intimate relation to inborn drive systems. But its *integrative* function, always mentioned, has not been adequately studied. It remains a source of confusion to the Freudians themselves. Some of the best of them fall into the error of mistaking this integrative function for the "ego." (This is the criticism leveled against Federn's original contributions, reported briefly on p. 103.) Too many analysts fall into the opposite error of failing to recognize the organizing power of this ego function in its specificity. They may then misinterpret special aspects of behavior as belonging either to libidinal constellations or to quite limited ego defense mechanisms, whereas actually they belong to the integrative efforts of the ego. In practice, the emphasis on "character trends" prevents serious error. To my mind, however, "character trends," themselves poorly studied, do not sufficiently deal with the observable facts concerning the power of the self image.

The self image, I suggest, is a substructure powerful enough to demand attention in its own right; it is *not* the equivalent of the integrative action of the ego as Freud and Hartmann understand it. Such integration is much closer to what I have called the "psychological self," what Sullivan calls the self dynamism. If I may anticipate later chapters, "my" self image is fairly close to Horney's idealized image of the self and to Jung's persona. In critical comment after these chapters I shall discuss the values and demerits of these other concepts, trying to disentangle them from their theoretical matrix and to suggest how they can be used in a "view of systems."

The integrative function of the ego in the Freudian sense is a much broader concept than the self image, much more "unconscious," much more deeply related to drive systems and even to interosystems. Far from criticizing this concept, I think it should be retained as a protec- tion against the reductionism of the self psychologies. But in its more generalized, biologically determined efforts at integration, the ego does, I think, quite regularly develop a sense of "I" which operates much more systematically (and hence more dynamically) than Freud and the Freudians have envisaged in their theories.

[1] S. Freud, *An Outline of Psychoanalysis,* W. W. Norton & Co., 1949, p. 24.
[2] *Ibid.,* p. 16.
[3] *Ibid.,* p. 108.
[4] S. Freud, *The Problem of Anxiety,* W. W. Norton & Co., 1936, p. 144.
[5] A. Freud, *The Ego and the Mechanisms of Defence,* Hogarth Press, 1937, pp. 46f.
[6] *Ibid.,* p. 54.
[7] T. Reik, *Listening with the Third Ear,* Farrar, Straus & Co., 1948.
[8] S. Freud, *The Problem of Anxiety,* p. 33.
[9] *Ibid.,* p. 74.
[10] *Ibid.,* p. 69.
[11] O. Fenichel, *The Psychoanalytic Theory of of Neurosis,* W. W. Norton & Co., 1945, p. 154.
[12] *Ibid.*
[13] A. Freud, *op. cit.,* Chaps. 6, 7.
[14] *Ibid.,* p. 95.
[15] T. Reik, *op. cit.*
[16] S. Freud, *The Problem of Anxiety,* p. 33.

[17] T. Reik, *op. cit.,* pp. 288ff.
[18] K. Abraham, "Contributions to the Theory of the Anal Character," *Selected Papers of Karl Abraham,* Hogarth Press, 1927, pp. 370-392; "The Influence of Oral Eroticism on Character-Formation," *loc. cit.,* pp. 393-406; "Character-Formation on the Genital Level of the Libido," *loc. cit.,* pp. 407-417.
[19] W. Reich, *Character-Analysis,* 2nd ed., Orgone Institute Press, 1945 (first German edition 1933).
[20] A. Freud, *op. cit.,* pp. 123f.
[21] S. Freud, *An Outline of Psychoanalysis,* p. 115.
[22] *Ibid.,* p. 115.
[23] A. Freud and S. Dann, "An Experiment in Group Upbringing," *The Psychoanalytic Study of the Child,* Vol. VI, International Universities Press, 1951, pp. 127-168.
[24] M. Mead, *And Keep Your Powder Dry,* Wm. Morrow & Co., 1943, pp. 74ff.

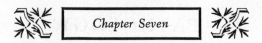

Chapter Seven

PATHOLOGY AND TREATMENT

THIS CHAPTER IS DIVIDED into two parts, which are independent of each other. The first deals with Freud's view of the origin and dynamics of the major entities of mental disease, as classified by psychiatrists. It presupposes some knowledge of abnormal psychology and will be of interest mainly to readers whose professional concerns bring them into contact with the mentally ill. The second part attempts to explain the rudiments of psychoanalysis as a highly specialized method of treatment. The explanation is essentially *continued* in the homologous chapter on treatment for the non-libido schools (Chap. 12), with a different emphasis but a great deal of overlap. In their treatment procedures, the schools have more in common than is generally recognized.

Pathology and treatment are the medical side of psychoanalysis. A book written by a layman for fellow laymen should attempt to provide no more than a general orientation toward the complex problems which are the special province of carefully trained doctors. Too often we tend to judge methods of handling the severely ill in the common-sense manner appropriate to the minor difficulties of our healthy acquaintances and to evaluate talk on the analytic couch as if it were a social conversation.

PATHOLOGY

IT WAS ESPECIALLY the study of hysteria that gave Freud the first clue to the role of the unconscious in psychic life and suggested the basic nature of sexuality in human development. It was especially the study of obsessive-compulsive states that led to a broadening of his concept of psychodynamics beyond the oversimplified idea of repression and transformation of sexual libido into anxiety. The traumatic neuroses brought into unhappy prominence during World War I focused attention on non-libidinal factors in personality organization: on repetitiveness and aggression. Probably one may say that the extension of psychoanalysis *as a therapy* into the area of character disorders has contributed very largely to the recent emphasis on ego psychology in psychoanalytic theory. The patients baring their souls on the analytic couch nowadays frequently have no "queer" symptoms like those that initially challenged Freud for a reasonable explanation. As late as the 1920's, patients with a character neurosis only were considered unsuitable subjects for analysis, even in the rare instances when they applied for treatment. Once they were accepted, however, their treatment was especially instructive as regards the functioning of the widespread *systems* of the personality which operate to control biological demands—that is, as regards the development of ego-psychology.

The oversimplification of Freudian theory in its stages of growth since *Studies in Hysteria* (1895)[1] has been repeatedly corrected by patients who expressed orientations different from those outlined at any given period of theoretical consolidation, with such clarity that the honest scientist was compelled to consider them thoroughly. Such clarity is part and parcel of the pathology, in that pathology isolates functional trends for special study because of their exaggeration, just as the normal role of the thyroid in the general body economy is revealed when it becomes defective or hyperactive. The normal individual can rarely be studied by the exhaustive and exhausting method of psychoanalysis because he has neither the time nor the patience to spend an hour a day for months and years in minute self-examination.* Over and above this practical obstacle, however, is the fact that the normal close

* "Normals" are not entirely unrepresented in analytic experience. The requirement of personal analysis for every doctor intending to practice the profession himself and the increasingly widespread custom for psychologists and social workers to supplement their training in this manner provide many hundreds, even thousands of instances.

integration and full creative interaction of systems make it extremely difficult to tease out essential structuring trends.

Psychoanalysis—and through it psychological science generally—owes much to the quasi-experimental singling out, by various pathological conditions, of special aspects of the personality for scientific investigation.[2] In the sections of this book devoted to "normal" dynamics, I have repeatedly drawn examples from neurosis to illustrate principles that would hardly be clearly perceptible in normal life. For example, the childhood rhyme "Step on a crack and break your mother's back," with the consequent care in measuring one's steps to avoid the regular divisions of concrete blocks in the sidewalk, is a fine illustration of compulsive behavior rooted in magical thinking. Occasionally a normal child will step on a crack in deliberate retaliation for some punishment, and may feel guilty for a while if his mother happens to fall ill shortly thereafter. The perdurance of such "nonsense" through many generations and its wide diffusion in one form or another through child cultures very strongly suggest that the hostile thought and its magical undoing are quite typical of childhood. Nevertheless, for most of us, such bits are so much part of the general process of growing up that even in retrospect they do not seem convincing evidence about our deeper motivations.

I personally joined with my schoolmates in avoiding cracks quite consciously as a *social* gesture, in view of the fact that my mother was already dead. I was rational enough to see the irrationality of the ritual. Fortunately, I was neither rational nor neurotic enough to reflect that my mother might have died because I had stepped on cracks in the past, but I remember feeling slightly dishonest in sharing the game. The main thing was the fun of spacing our steps in unison or competition, and perhaps just of having a ritual. Because of my recent loss, I was probably the only child who consciously thought about her mother at all in connection with the jingle.*

* At this point in my writing, it occurred to me that I did not clearly recall having heard this jingle since my own childhood, and thought that perhaps it had been a local phenomenon, remembered for purely personal reasons. Since my son happened to be entertaining two young intimates, the three just under twenty, I barged in with the odd question "Did you ever worry about stepping on a crack in the sidewalk?" Chorus: "Break your mother's back." Boy 1: "It was just a game." Boy 2 (from a Southern background): "I didn't think about my mother—we thought we might turn into a toad or something." Boy 3: "Nothing to do with my mother, of course. It's just bad luck. I still skip cracks sometimes when I'm in the mood, and sometimes I jump so as to step on all of them. That's not neurotic, is it?" Chorus: "Yeah, sometimes we did that, just to show."

This small inquiry was loaded by the fact that the questioner was a mother figure. Hence, some of the overprompt disclaimer of any reference to mother in the game doubtless can be laid to conscious chivalry. It seemed fairly clear, however, that the ritual had genuine psychological meaning for all of them and that it was thoroughly interwoven with their *social* memories. When I drew a comparison with an example of rather similar ritual in compulsion neurosis, the boys cheerfully accepted a psychological interpretation of unconscious meaning in the neurotic symptom but resolutely denied any real similarity with their own game on the

For most normal children, magical thinking and acts are so closely inter-woven with emerging cognizance of the world of physical and social "reality" that it is incorrect as well as unconvincing to interpret these current ritual games exclusively or even primarily in terms of their specific origin in con-demned infantile "sexual" attitudes and their underlying appeal. Normally, the creative integration of subsystems progresses so rapidly and so thoroughly that it becomes extremely difficult to discern the dynamic components opera-tive at any given moment. Yet it is as absurd to deny their importance as to maintain that the thyroid gland is unimportant because normally it functions in very close relationship with other body systems.

THE FREUDIAN VIEW OF PATHOLOGY

In a book oriented toward the contributions of psychoanalytic theory to general psychological understanding, we shall review very sketchily its con-tribution to strictly medical psychology—that is, to the diagnosis and treatment of the mentally sick. A number of excellent books are already available both for the layman contemplating analysis therapeutically and for the serious student. For the latter, Fenichel's *The Psychoanalytic Theory of Neurosis** offers a compendium of information respected by his professional colleagues and extremely useful to the rest of us for its wealth of documentation, clarity, and absence of bias.

Of major importance to every branch of psychopathology was Freud's effort to discover a dynamic explanation for illness in contrast to the more static description of symptoms that was characteristic of earlier psychiatrists, even such brilliant men as Kraepelin and Charcot. Freud's effort was wel-comed by a few contemporary giants such as Bleuler and paralleled by the work of such men as Adolf Meyer in psychobiology. It had, of course, its harbingers, too. It is largely through the influence of Freud's ideas, however, that the idea of *the symptom as an adaptive mechanism* has become a com-monplace and that its cure is always envisaged as handling of the underlying (typically unconscious) dynamics rather than the symptom itself. This formu-lation applies to all the schools of psychoanalysis and to most contemporary therapies of whatever label.

---

quite sensible grounds that they played it mainly because everyone else did, and just for fun.
    I submit this reaction as typical for older heads as well. "Normal" behavior is too complex in its determinants to offer a convincing example, although the basic trends are quite similar to those neatly isolated in pathology.
* O. Fenichel, *The Psychoanalytic Theory of Neurosis*, W. W. Norton & Co., 1945. The reader may find Fenichel's earlier book, *Outline of Clinical Psychoanalysis* (W. W. Norton & Co., 1934), more comprehensible.

All the "mechanisms" described in the preceding chapter are, of course, used in the understanding of psychopathology. Typically, the same patient, whatever the over-all diagnosis, exhibits several mechanisms in exaggeration, just as disturbances of the endocrine system usually involve marked polyglandular symptoms identifiable separately, even though the major pathology may be clearly ascribable to a single gland. Such mixtures are inevitable in any organismic system in which one organismic event necessarily influences another and in which all subsystems participate in the same process of over-all adaptation to external events. Nevertheless, many patients can be usefully classified according to their *major* symptomatology, now seen as in direct relationship to the "cause" of their illness. (The quotation marks around "cause" are intended as a reminder of the complexity of causal relationships among creatively interacting systems and as a precaution against any linear, one-to-one formulation of etiological factors in the development of fairly specific pathology.)

Freud repeatedly emphasized the idea that the trends and conflicts he discovered were not the specific "cause" of neurosis. Neurosis results from the *quantitative distribution of energies,* not from the mere existence of a conflict. Even the nuclear problem of the Oedipus complex is not peculiar to neurosis. Pathology develops as one or another aspect of the problem becomes quantitatively unmanageable by the techniques that the personality has established.

THE MAJOR NEUROSES

Hysteria. Freud's own starting point was *hysteria,* partly for the historical reason that Charcot's work on this condition was already important enough to draw Freud to Paris for special training in the treatment of mental disease, and doubtless partly for the deeper reason that hysterics typically exhibit with especial clarity the continuing power of repressed material. The symptoms are often dramatic. The patient cannot lift an arm. No medical measures avail, nor can the doctor account for the paralysis on anatomical grounds. Or the patient has clearly irrational fears. He cannot cross a street alone, perhaps not even go out of the house; or he cannot ride in subways; he becomes dizzy on high places; he is terrified at the sight of a cat; he is afraid to go to sleep. Almost any part of the body may become afflicted, almost any bodily function, almost any relationship with external events. Such afflictions of the body are usually called *conversions;* the patently irrational fears are called *phobias.*

Clear-cut instances of hysteria have become relatively rare. Hysterical *spells* with a definite sequence of events as described by Charcot are almost never encountered in clinical practice today. "Monosymptomatic" disturbances involving a single paralysis or a single phobia are uncommon, apparently less common than they used to be. The typical hysterical picture observed nowadays shows a variety of minor phobias and conversion phenomena, often with attacks of frank anxiety more or less temporary, usually in reaction to an external situation whose unconscious meaning to the patient is fairly obvious to the psychoanalyst although by no means clear to the eye of common sense or to the patient himself. These patients are usually outgoing in their general approach to life, capable of warm response to other people, including the therapist, and emotionally labile—that is, their feelings shift readily in response to changes in their life situation and to the changes introduced by the therapist. Indeed, the problem may be that they change *too* quickly, sometimes that there is *too* rapid and dramatic a "cure," in contrast to the obsessive-compulsive individual, whose characteristic emotional reactions tend to remain stubbornly the same.

By the same token, these patients are suggestible—hence in large part the ease with which Charcot was able to confirm his observation of a definite sequence of events in the hysterical spell. Other doctors, not excluding Freud, have at times been misled. The popular use of the term *hysteria* (hysterics, hysterical) expresses common observation of the last two points: an excessive emotionality and a tendency to make false interpretations without conscious prevarication. Worthy citizens are occasionally quite unjustly accused by such "hysterical" people of attempted rape and other offenses in variety following quite ordinary friendly gestures or rebuffs. Most laymen have some acquaintance with this phenomenon. Of course, popular usage often extends the psychiatric concept to persons who are not hysterical in the psychiatric sense at all and fails to include persons who show the fundamental qualities of this syndrome in less dramatic form.

The classification of "hysteria" as a disease entity stems from psychiatry, not from psychoanalysis. Freud began his investigations upon a recognized ailment, still recognized by psychiatrists despite corrections and frequent emphasis on a type of dynamic that shades into the "normal."

Freud *explained* the ailment, using it at first as the paradigm for all mental illness—indeed, for all psychology. He noted very early that hysteria is a special instance of a theory of psychodynamics much more complex. In the case of Anna O., Breuer and Freud discussed the observation that her symptom of paralysis of the arm disappeared when she remembered that it first occurred when she was watching at her father's deathbed and dozed off with her arm in an uncomfortable position. For Breuer, the choice of symptom was accidental, or, rather, was determined by whatever had happened to be important to the patient in a semiconscious state. He anticipated Freud in the important *discovery* that the hysterical symptom is directly related to a memory that has become unconscious. Today we may say that the mechanism of "hysteria" is essentially this, and its familiar name has become *repression*. When Anna O. remembered the episode at her father's bedside, her paralysis was cured. The episode, with insight and cure, seemed to suggest that hysterical illness (then generalized beyond present limits) was due to repressed memories, completely unknown to the patient, which continued to exert an influence—somehow.

Freud went beyond Breuer in the effort to explain *why* a specific memory was repressed, *why* a specific forgetting should have pathogenic consequences. He observed that the forgotten event was always associated with an event painful to the patient, giving rise to severe anxiety and conflict. This event seemed to him at first quite regularly a realistic sexual attack in childhood. Freud's patients described such misfortunes to Freud in the early years as faithfully as Charcot's patients obliged with the sequential pattern of the hysterical crisis Charcot believed fundamental to the disease. Fairly soon, however, Freud came to realize that very often the event had not *really* occurred. Rather, it was a childhood fantasy of something deeply wished and deeply feared—the Oedipal wish in conflict with the fear of castration and loss of love. The Oedipus complex became for Freud the nuclear complex in neurosis; the underlying fear became always the fear of castration. The weak ego of the child was unable to master this conflict directly and therefore resorted to the stratagem of repression.

At times the repression of the unacceptable wish is complete, and one can see it only in the gap left in the personality, in certain absolute prohibitions (hysterical blindness is a striking example), or in the total failure to experience love, rage, etc., in circumstances in which they might be expected. Often the wish is so close to the surface that any "tempting" situation causes an exacerbation of the symptoms that serve the purpose of preventing its eruption into consciousness. Often the symptom allows a very partial expression which punishes and inhibits while it gratifies. Any disturbance in the equilibrium between the impelling and repressing forces (*systems*, in our vocabulary) whether due to increase in libido from within (as during adolescence or the climacteric), to change in circumstances, or even to therapeutic interpretation, if insufficiently assimilated by the mature ego, may bring about an intensification or spread of the neurosis. New material may constantly be included as it becomes associated with the repressed conflict—derivative repressions. Temptations and partial expression constantly renew the anxiety that caused the exclusion of the childhood wish in the first place. Hence, a definitely established neurosis rarely cures itself spontaneously, although under favorable circumstances it may appear quiescent. The repressive defense may have become a character mechanism, used in areas unrelated to the wish initially repressed. Some people resort to this defense so extensively that its use becomes in itself an interference with adequate adaptation.

According to Freudians, hysteria dates from the *phallic* stage of childhood, with relatively slight complication from earlier stages of development. (All neuroses are somewhat mixed.) The reason is clear in its major mechanism—repression—as well as in the unconscious material elicited during psychoanalysis. The very young child (pre-Oedipal—oral and anal stages) experiences the circumstances of its own life deeply, but it has not yet perceived distinctions in its environment and in its own impulses sharply enough to be able to formulate or repress highly specific reaction potentials. *Object* relations have not yet become clearly developed. The pre-Oedipal mother tends to mean the whole world. The phallic mother (*i.e.*, the mother as perceived during the phallic stage, fantasied as possessing a penis) is already something of an individual—still not the actual person the adult sees but marked for the child by such characteristics as are important in this period of its own life. Emergent genital concern is related to a more differentiated view of the world, still very limited and inevitably colored by the family constellation, which still represents the child's main experience. Inevitably, then, the differentiated type of repression characteristic of hysteria *cannot* occur prior to differentiated perception and object relations. Almost inevitably, the repression reflects the preponderant concerns of the stage at which it first becomes possible. Earlier the child cannot formulate his genital wishes and fears sharply enough, or they do not yet exist. Later his ego is strong enough to cope with problems by more realistic techniques. Thus, the etiology both of hysteria as a separate entity and of hysterical components in other conditions can be seen as essentially the repressive technique natural to the phallic stage, however elaborately interwoven with other trends in the personality as a whole.

The other aspects of the hysterical syndrome (emotional lability, outgoingness, ease of transference, suggestibility) also seem related to the stage at which the dynamic of the neurosis is determined. The child has already progressed a long way toward relating himself to the outer world, especially to people. That the gain in general personality development is not lost through the later illness is shown in these subsidiary characteristics, and in the generally favorable prognosis for treatment. The relatively mature development of the capacity for object love facilitates transference (see pp. 305ff.). Patients exhibiting these characteristics can often be temporarily cured of a major symptom by almost anything—a pilgrimage to a religious shrine; Christian Science; suggestive therapy, especially when combined with hypnosis; a change in life circumstances luckily related to the major conflict. Too often, by these methods the patients merely substitute one symptom for another—a situation therapeutically successful only if the new symptom happens to be more socially acceptable than the old one. In general, the patients seem to respond well to psychoanalytic treatment, with more thorough and permanent results as the underlying conflict is really resolved through recognition of its infantile source.

Compulsions and Obsessions. *Compulsion neurosis, obsessions, and obsessive-compulsive states* proved less easy to handle than the cases of hysteria treated early by Freud, and they required an extension of his theory. Again, the classification comes mainly from psychiatry. The patients are literally compelled to go through complicated rituals, on penalty of extreme anxiety. Or intolerable or foolish thoughts run through their minds over and over—*e.g.,* a devoted mother thinks of slashing her child's throat every time she sees a sharp kitchen knife. Such thoughts do not lead to action except in rare, complicated cases and are usually experienced "coldly," without the hot emotion (*e.g.,* intense hostility consciously felt toward the child) that would normally accompany an idea of this character.

Coldness is here a relative matter. Such thoughts are intolerable even to the obsessive patient, and only a schizophrenic can recount them blandly. The obsessive tries to conceal them and often worries over them to the point of contemplating suicide. The hysteric, however, would typically handle such a thought by amnesia, perhaps with a paralysis of the arm or a knife phobia if the thought had sufficient dynamic power. Normals brought up in our culture are unlikely to have such thoughts at all, not because they lack occasional "murderous" impulses toward their offspring but because, in the normal world of symbols, knives belong quite thoroughly in the kitchen. "I'll whale the life out of you" or "I'd like to throttle you" are equally effective lethal sentences, and very common. In any cultural group or subgroup in which knifing is common, the content of the patient's thought would be quite normal in the same manner as our expletives. The normal parent has such ideas in moments of exasperation, but they are consciously experienced, not recurrently, not without the hotness of immediate anger. Despite the repetitiveness of the thought, the threatened child is usually physically safer with the obsessive parent than with an impulsive "normal," whose rage may accidentally go beyond bounds.

Freud's puzzlement arose from the *admission to consciousness* of ideas directly abhorrent or representing the condemned wish in thin disguise with great elaboration. As so often happened in his work, the fairly direct expression of a mechanism gave him the lead for understanding more obscure cases. He felt that in these instances the unacceptable idea and its derivatives were not so much excised, as in repression, as *quarantined*—that is, denied their normal associations and ramifications.

Typically, the same patient shows both compulsive and obsessive symptoms in variable relation to each other and with varying degrees of systematic elaboration. Freud suggested the term *isolation* (p. 254) for the thoughts kept from normal elaboration into the affective, motoric, and intellective fullness of the personality and the term *undoing* (p. 255) for the actions or thoughts that are literally opposed to a prior unacceptable idea. The compulsions of conscience (superego), with feelings of guilt, etc., operate as strongly in these patients as primitive impulses from the id, typically with ready shifts from one to the other. Or the same symptom may serve both institutions. Ambivalence is marked.

In character, these patients usually show trends similar to those described for the anal character on pages 470*ff*. They tend to be reserved, guarded, self-opinionated, stubborn, rigid, addicted to rules of conduct and programmatic modes of thought, often overidealistic. They cherish possessions and people as possessions. Warm, outgoing contacts with people are difficult for them. They are often suspicious or stand upon their rights against the world. They are usually orderly, punctual, fastidious—with areas or periods of carelessness and "messiness."

An important reason for difficulty in psychoanalytic treatment is their repugnance to free association. It is almost impossible for them to relax their self-control sufficiently to let their minds wander freely even when they wish very strongly to comply with the conditions of treatment. Their minutious account of what goes through their minds is unfortunately too often genuinely trivial because unconsciously guided into safe channels, and their report of damaging truths about themselves so "isolated" from the appropriate affect as to be useless therapeutically (see p. 316). The analytic material clearly shows strong anal components in thin disguise, not infrequently quite openly. Often the patient readily sees these components but cannot see that they matter very much.

Freud saw the dynamics of this syndrome as harking back to the sadistic anal stage of genetic development. He did not renounce thereby the concept of the Oedipus complex as a nuclear conflict. He felt that even in these cases castration fear was originally dominant, and that to ward off its threat the patient regressed to the earlier stage. Hence the concept of regression as an active defense mechanism. Sexual function may be adequately preserved by a process of isolating it from its psychological meaning. These patients are often potent in the physiological sense, although they "possess" their partner much as they possess objects in the ordinary sense of the word. By retreating to the personality installations of the anal period, the patient avoids the threat of his impulses toward the mother as object developed during the phallic stage. But since these impulses are the main avenue toward the development of mature object relations, he is very seriously hampered in this entire area—as shown in the typical character syndrome described above. Any genuine attachment to a person carries the danger of castration. The person feels safe only as he stays within the confines of the earlier stage. (The reader is reminded that Freud's ideas are being reported throughout this section. The present author will offer some re-evaluation in critical comment later.)

Of course, the anal stage is not without its own very serious anxieties, described on pages 194ff. Compulsion neurosis often presents a combination of autonomous pregenital fears proper to this stage and pregenital fears that are direct substitutes for or distortions of castration anxiety. A patient had the obsessive fear that a snake might crawl out of the toilet into her anus. Previously she feared that a snake might be in her bed.[3] The sequence suggests the regression from the phallic to the anal orientation, clearly with some retention of the phallic concern. On the whole, however, the symptomatology seems characteristically related to the problems of the anal-sadistic stage. In Freudian libidinal terms, the characteristic ambivalence reflects the dual function of the anus as an actively expelling organ and as a hollow organ pleasurably stimulated by the entrance of feces from above; the dual aspect of feces as a foreign body to be expelled and as a cherished part of one's body.

In terms of social development, the anal stage is the period during which the first self-regulation of a powerful instinctual drive is instituted, at a time when the social "self" is still differentiated vaguely, as vaguely as are the specific aspects of the environment (mainly persons) which inevitably impose regulation according to external requirements. The general developmental picture has already been discussed at length (Chap. 5). Neurosis arises when the *quantitative* distribution of energies is seriously affected, probably partly on unknown constitutional grounds, mainly because of the special pressures of the developmental period.

No child solves the very real problems of the anal period "perfectly." The most normal character shows rather pronounced trends traceable, in part, to the bent given the emergent psychological self at this time. The pressures that produce neurosis are rarely confined to a single area such as toilet training. Even when a healthy, loving mother was exhorted by scientific authorities to train her child at a much earlier age than is now advised by such authorities, she did so lovingly, was warmly forgiving, and was frequently a bit sneaky about "the rules" if not consciously rebellious. The neurotic, rejecting mother can frighten her child about his anal interests even when she refrains from introducing official "toilet training" until the age of two.

The *context* of the training procedures largely outweighs their specific impact and may largely absorb it. The neurotic mother is likely to be tense throughout her motherhood, whether her own anxieties center in the anal sphere or elsewhere. For one reason or another, pressures on the child are likely to be especially intense at a specific stage, with consequences either for his "bent" as a normal person or for the major structure of his neurosis. However, every person and every neurosis show traces of other stages in complex relationship to the main trends, because development never takes place all of a piece and because the unconscious easily tolerates internal inconsistencies or frank contradictions.

THE FUNCTIONAL PSYCHOSES

The essential feature of Freud's explanation of *psychotic* conditions may be stated as the greater depth of the regression. The adult never lapses back to infancy all of a piece, of course. Part of his acquisitions are retained and, indeed, struggle actively against the regressive trend. Freud felt, however, that the truly psychotic manifestations belong to the pre-Oedipal period—indeed, to the stage of narcissism before the ego has properly developed. The mechanisms of psychosis (apart from the dynamically separable attempts of the ego to regain mastery) are the archaic mechanisms of the infant before secure object relations have been established. Freud does not deny the probability of constitutional factors in many cases which somehow predispose the individual toward unduly strong fixations at the early stage or which undermine the structure of the ego later on. Careful studies of heredity[4] and the fulminating character of the disease in some individuals speak for organic components, as yet unknown. In many cases, psychological factors seem sufficient to account for the manifestations, and in all cases the manifestations seem to follow the dynamics of regression to primary narcissism.

Depressive States. Depressive states (including involutional melancholia and manic-depressive psychosis) are thought of by the Freudians as representing a fixation at the oral-sadistic level. The patient's basic relationship with the world is that of a hungry infant dependent upon the outside for its vital supplies. The self-esteem structure at this period rests mainly on the extent to which infantile longings are gratified from without, with fears of annihilation when gratification is withheld. The self is poorly differentiated; object relations follow the principle of oral incorporation, becoming quite literally part of the self. The person identifies with the object, which is then introjected, and functions thereafter as if it were an indigenous part of the personality. In these psychoses the drama is internalized, the contours of the object being largely lost in the introjected equivalent. The patient withdraws from reality contacts, regressing to the narcissistic condition of early infancy.

Noteworthy in depression is the hostility of the patient, directed almost entirely against himself. The self-accusatory trend seems to be mainly the consequence of his orality—that is, of the tendency to identify with and incorporate the object. It is often possible to trace clearly an earlier ambivalence to the external object whose defection so commonly precipitates the depression. Neurotic depression has a similar underlying dynamic, but the ego remains intact and adequate contact with reality is preserved. Normal mourning regularly includes attitudes of hostility and remorse (guilt) toward the deceased—along with the painful feeling of emotional impoverishment and emptiness described above. The more the individual depended on the loved one for narcissistic gratification, or the stronger the ambivalence and undercover hostility in the original relationship, the more likely it becomes for normal mourning to change into melancholia under the impact of bereavement. (Loss of job, money, or whatever may have the same effect. The systematic breaking of object relations in concentration camps, D.P. camps, and even rehabilitation placements has unhappily demonstrated the capacity of presumably "normal" people to develop a depressive syndrome when external emotional supplies are very seriously withheld over long periods.)

Hostility toward the (introjected) object is strongly reinforced by the severe superego of the depressed patient. So striking is the force of the superego in depression that melancholia was the condition that first led Freud to the formulation of this aspect of personality development as a quasi-independent entity. It seems that the patient who becomes psychotically depressed has introjected mainly the harshly punitive features of the parental image, not the protective and permissive features of the actual parents. This is probably in large part because the powerful fixation at the oral-sadistic level had its effect on the formation of the superego during the Oedipal period, interfering with the development of genuine object love for the parents. Harsh control by the introjected parent was necessary to match the harshness of the child's instinctual wishes (see pp. 207ff.). Increase in the force of the id impulses during the climacteric makes involutional melancholia a likely special form of the depressive pattern. However, the deprivation or narcissistic wounds which so often precipitate the other forms of the illness also tend to increase the infantile oral-sadistic demands; hence the counterattack of the superego.

The ego as usual attempts to placate all parties and may suffer the fate of all would-be peacemakers. To be sure, the introjection of the object protects the person against outwardly directed efforts at retaliation or satisfaction which would entail serious complications with reality. By the same token, the mechanism prevents constructive resolution through new object attachments and the establishment of improved relations with the outside world. The ego denudes itself of its major function, reality testing, and in the internalized struggle yields too readily either to suicide or to *mania*—that is, to a violent reinstatement of the infantile omnipotence in which everything is received, every wish granted, with temporary freedom from guilt. The periodicity of the manic-depressive syndrome corresponds, according to many Freudians, to the cycle of hunger and satiety of the infant. The superego (introjected parent) grants supplies after the period of deprivation—but also the period of satisfaction must be followed by distress. In so far as the ego renounces its reality-testing function in psychosis, it falls prey to these archaic formulations.

Schizophrenia. Schizophrenia, the other major functional psychosis, has many points in common with psychotic depression. Again, there is the unsolved problem of a predisposing organic condition, the same deep regression to primary narcissistic states, the same loss in the reality-testing function of the ego. Schizophrenia, however, is a much more variable disease. Perhaps because the ultimate regression is even deeper than in depressive states, its pattern is less clearly attributable to the problems and mechanisms of a specific developmental stage.

Some psychiatrists consider manic-depressive psychosis as a special form of schizophrenia, characterized by the nature of the early fixation. Many psychotic conditions show features of both ailments. Mixtures of psychotic and neurotic syndromes are still more common—in fact, virtually universal.

Freudians differentiate generally between the primary regressive symptomatology of schizophrenia and its restitutive mechanisms. Partly these latter take the form of neuroticlike mechanisms. The very regressed schizophrenic, however, also attempts restitution. World-destruction fantasies become the dream of a mission to save the world. The lost objects of the outside world are reintroduced as hallucinations and reworked as more or less systematized delusions. These truly psychotic restitutive efforts are, of course, unchecked by the mature reality judgments of the ego and employ the shadow rather than the substance of past life experience. The essential feature is still the break with reality.

Freud especially noted among schizophrenics the prevalence of conflicts about homosexual trends. It would be incorrect to say that such trends "cause" schizophrenia, even in the sense that fixation at the oral-sadistic level appears to be significant in structuring depression. The high incidence seems to be due rather to the fact that the parent of the same sex is normally introjected at an early age, normally desexualized in the course of development. The resexualization of the superego and social ego may catch at this midway point between heterosexuality and narcissism, whether in the regressive or restitutive processes of the psychosis. The problem in many cases is not only, probably not even essentially, the homosexual trend as such, but the role of this early formulation of object and superego relationships in the effort of the patient to maintain his grasp on reality.

Critical Comment

SINCE no detailed critique of Freudian psychopathology will be offered later, I offer here my own comments, based on observation of several hundred schizophrenics—mostly borderline cases—tested by a variety of projective techniques. Striking evidence of homosexual trends is rarely absent. However, the evidence is almost equally striking for virtually all the infantile material cited by Freud, or even by the non-libido schools. In some cases, the homosexual conflict seems to supply the main focus of the disturbance or to have served as precipitating cause. Much more commonly it seems incidental to the *general* re-emergence of unconscious material in too naked symbolism, with too little focused repression and critical censorship. These patients demonstrate with startling clarity every dynamism in the books. The *emphasis* on one problem or another tends to shift with the nature of the test, the mood of the patient (sometimes within a single testing session), and surely with the bias of the interpreting psychologist or psychiatrist.

Regressive features are observable in all schizophrenias and obviously gain the upper hand as the disease progresses. In the stabilized borderline cases they appear in curiously isolated form. A generally careful, moral, gentle patient blandly gives occasional extremely "raw" responses—responses such as would seriously embarrass a neurotic patient and which are not socially codified even in the mores of the waterfront or in accepted swear words—with no more than the polite initial query: "Do you want me to tell you everything?" The bland emergence of these fragments seems to be due more to the *disintegration* of ego structure, which allows disconnected infantile repressed material access to consciousness, than to the dynamic force of impulses which finally break through repression despite the focused control of the defense mechanisms. (See also Chap. 12 for Sullivan's views on schizophrenia.)

PSYCHOPATHIC PERSONALITY

There are individuals whose behavior seems primarily characterized by a complete absence of moral scruple. Often winsome and charming when it suits their purpose, or perhaps most of the time, they have no hesitation in selling out their best friends for the sake of personal advantage, and they may not even balk at murder if seriously frustrated. Their only rule of conduct seems to be one of expediency. Moreover, although they may be intelligent (there is no correlation between this condition and intelligence), their judgment of expediency is often poor, apparently because it tends to be limited to immediate advantages. Often very clever about getting what they want at any given moment, they seem incapable of postponement and long-range planning. Their least whim demands prompt gratification. Thus, in a manner which looks positively silly, they frequently sacrifice a greater good just around the corner for a pleasure that is purely temporary but immediate. They may become fiercely angry when opposed but recover their equanimity at once if their end is gained or if something happens to change the direction of their desires.

A psychopath may commit a "crime of passion" on the spur of the moment and begin cold-bloodedly to cover his tracks a moment later. The cheerful indifference or "appropriate" grief he may show five minutes later is not superbly skillful acting. He actually feels calm and may even feel genuinely sorry for his victim, although deep, personal remorse is foreign to him. He may steal impulsively and be caught through carelessness—not because he unconsciously craves punishment, as do some neurotics, but because he quite genuinely forgets about the possible consequences when his mood shifts.

In favorable external circumstances, psychopathic personalities may appear merely irresponsible and childish. They may have no driving ambitions beyond what they can attain by cajoling their associates. They readily confess their shortcomings and, as genuinely as they can make any resolve, they promise to reform, only to relapse into the old ways at the slightest provocation. In unfavorable circumstances, either of poverty or emotional frustration, they easily become criminals—both petty recidivists and major misdoers. They cannot be classified as insane by law, because they are perfectly well aware of the nature and meaning of their acts. Their basic sense of reality is not disturbed (unless the psychopathy is complicated by psychosis). Whatever foolishness they show is due to *lack of stability and capacity for delay*, not to failure in appreciation of the realities of the situation.

The major Freudian explanation for this condition is that there has been a serious failure in superego development. The parental image has not been adequately internalized in the form of conscience but remains the policeman at the corner—an external force. Truly, the behavior of the psychopath is childish, without the limited experience of the child. When the resources of adulthood are used without the inner controls of adulthood, the resultant behavior is very likely to be deplorable. Object relations generally are poor of necessity—since good early object relations would have led to more adequate superego development. By the same token, infantile instinctual drives are prominent. Psychopathy may develop if the process of early identification is interfered with—that is, if there is no stable parental figure—if early experience is extremely inconsistent, or if the adults are somehow too remote to provide a suitable model for the child to identify with.

Bender's attention was drawn to the problem when many children with this condition appeared in her ward at Bellevue,[5] the great city hospital of New York, after infancy in an institution that offered good physical care but little opportunity for affectional ties with adults—or even with other children. Some primitive peoples—for example, the people of Alor—show a somewhat similar underlying character when the cultural tradition of child-rearing works against sustained care and reasonably affectionate attention by continuing ministrants (see pp. 126f.).

Such cases present a difficult therapeutic problem in psychoanalysis because they cannot easily establish a solid transference to the therapist (see pp. 305ff.). Relatively mild symptoms remain stubbornly persistent, although on the surface they appear easier to handle than a severe neurosis. Experiments in treatment are being made, some of which try to capitalize on the fact that the superego is never so *totally* absent as I have perhaps implied but is immature and conflicted. I have been told of one technique in which the psychopathic delinquent is brought before an awesome *panel* of doctors who literally *say nothing* beyond an initial expression of their desire to help the culprit once he is honestly interested in helping himself. This technique is intended to mobilize the socially oriented anxiety of the psychopath in such a manner as to focus his attention on himself, on the feeling that he is running away from himself instead of bamboozling others—to *mobilize* anxiety about the self → superego. Useful in some instances, this technique is extremely costly in doctor time—and if he is at all forewarned the psychopath can sit out the doctors easily enough. I mention it here only to emphasize the dynamics of psychopathy—the peculiar difficulty in relating *personal* demands to that internalized sense of the rights of others and one's own *continuing* self, which is the essence of the superego.

Other therapeutic ventures—of much greater repute in psychoanalytic circles—are based on efforts to understand and to handle the pregenital problems which made normal superego development impossible in the patient's early childhood. The problem of the psychopath is not really lack of anxiety but rather very intense anxiety about infantile fears that are usually transmuted if not resolved in the Oedipal phase, plus a defect in ego formation. Therapy is therefore addressed to the intense anxiety of the pre-Oedipal situation (usually "oral" in its major outlines) which prevented adequate development of the superego. Thus, with the same general theoretical purpose as the one behind the panel of silent doctors, the analyst may deliberately make himself an intensely personal figure to the patient, as all-permissive as possible, belatedly giving the patient the kind of support and trust he missed in his formative years. Therapy should not stop at this point—on the contrary, it *must* be continued beyond this stage, and perhaps better by some other person or institution as the "new" individual goes beyond his initial therapeutic experience. Like the maturing child, he may need the figure of the first therapist in the background as "parent"—loved and hated, but a stabilizing force, like the normal superego.

Short of *active* planned psychotherapeutic intervention (and concurrent with it), treatment of the psychopath is mainly "environmental." Recognizing the psychopath's basic problems, the doctor tries to get him into an *environment* in which the demands made upon him are essentially stable and firm—even beyond the usual firmness of environmental demands. This "environmental" stability may often serve to keep the behavior of the psychopath in line with social demands—the more easily because it is the *social* rather than the deeply personal (superego) values to which he responds.

It sounds paradoxical to add that the environment should also be flexible and tolerant of inevitable backslidings in the constantly renewed resolves of the psychopath to do better. Rewards should be kept related to rather immediate goals; punishments should be direct and short-lived. These people *cannot* keep long-term promises without many vivid short-term reminders. A merited punishment, knowingly incurred, is actually experienced as mere persecution once the initial sense of guilt has worn off. Stability in the sense of an endlessly recurrent routine is anathema to them. In a way, they actually *need* constant change, because they have no means of absorbing ups and downs of feeling through the *inner* stabilization of the superego. What counts is the stability of the basic social judgments of the people they encounter—the secure, inescapable feelings that some things are acceptable and some definitely are not.

I have somewhat elaborated on treatment procedures here because I shall not return to them in the presentation of psychoanalysis as a method of treatment. Such procedures are not "psychoanalysis," but they may be conducted or supervised by psychoanalysts who plan their therapeutic approach in terms of psychoanalytic understanding of the patient's problems. Most of the "Freudians" are insistent upon a clear definition of psychoanalysis *as a specialized therapeutic method* with profoundly important goals and with techniques very closely related to its goals. This definition is in some contrast to the current loosening of the definition of *psychoanalysis as a method* characteristic for the authors discussed in Chapter 12. "Freudians" call the very active or environ-mental kind of treatment procedure "psychoanalytically oriented psychother-apy." It is not, of course, confined to delinquency but can apply to any kind of disorder or environmental condition. It enables the use of psychoanalytic insights in the treatment of patients who—because of the nature of their emo-tional problems, financial limitations, special life circumstances, etc.—cannot be treated by the psychoanalytic method.*

CHARACTER DISORDERS

Psychoanalysts are treating in increasing numbers patients who are free from gross symptomatology but whose general conduct is nevertheless mark-edly *difficult* for themselves or their associates. These people have already been described as "types" with some exaggeration of the normal bent (see pp. 264ff.). The earlier description will serve here, with further elaboration. We have already discussed how character trends within the normal range are related to the developmental process. Normally, the early experiences influence the developing ego, because the ego is always the creative product of life ex-perience. Unduly severe experiences may *bend* the general ego development in one direction or another at almost any stage short of a distinct pathological break.

Initially Freud expressed skepticism as to the value of psychoanalytic therapy for *character disorders* because in these instances the ego is typically involved in the "disorder," whereas in the symptom neurosis the ego seemed a relatively independent agent struggling against the tyrannical demands of the id and superego. Therapy (to be discussed in detail shortly) could there-fore hope to succeed by releasing the ego from its bondage—that is, by giving the mature personality courage to examine the intrusions from the infantile unconscious and to handle them on adult terms. The *symptom* is directly ex-perienced by the patient as ego-alien. *He* cannot raise his arm, although *he* wants to. *He* knows it is silly to be afraid of cats, subways, and the like, or to engage in the absurdities of compulsive ritual. The overdependent or over-

---

* For an example of the application of psychoanalytically oriented psychotherapy to the treat-ment of psychopathy (delinquency), I refer the reader to K. R. Eissler, "Ego-Psychological Implications of the Psychoanalytic Treatment of Delinquents," *The Psychoanalytic Study of the Child*, Vol. V, International Universities Press, 1950, pp. 97-121. Eissler gives the psycho-analytic background and relevance to psychoanalytic theory of his therapeutic procedures with a subtlety I cannot hope to report here and refers the reader to the important work of Aichhorn in formulating and handling the problems of delinquency. See also D. Beres, "Clinical Notes on Aggression in Children," *loc. cit.*, Vol. VII, 1952, pp. 241-263.

aggressive or overfastidious person without symptoms, on the other hand, almost always justifies his behavior to himself on grounds of idealism, morality, or rational necessity. Analytic interpretation encounters resistance from his mature ego as well as from the infantile unconscious. The patient is likely to feel that all he is and wants to be is threatened by the analysis; indeed, it is not always easy for the analyst himself to distinguish between healthy—or at least necessary—reactions to real pressures and those reactions that are irrationally compelled by the underlying infantile bias, because the two are typically so thoroughly intertwined. An irascible boss is a problem for anyone who cannot afford to lose his job. The problems of the patient suffering from character neurosis are always in considerable part realistic and contemporary, his reactions in considerable part justified, *as well as* neurotically determined and neurotically defended.

It was recognized increasingly (especially in the 1920's) that *every* patient presents in some degree a character neurosis over and above his obvious symptomatology, and that every analysis must handle the consequent resistances before constructive work on the specific libidinal problems can be undertaken.[6] The patient must be shown convincingly and repeatedly how his judgments in everyday life and in the analytic hour are conditioned by the *ego* defense mechanisms established over his whole life span. Only then is his ego free enough so that he can avail himself of the new insights obtained by the psychoanalytic method for the handling of the neurotic symptoms. (See the discussion of ego psychology, pp. 89*ff.*).

Many Freudians consider that it is necessary in treating character disorders to *create* symptoms, as it were[7]—that is, eventually to focus the anxieties on the historical infantile conflict, where they belong, to reactivate the old problems by systematically removing the displacements and ingrained, rigid defenses of the ego until finally the reasonable ego can confront the early terrors as alien to itself with the therapeutic aids proper to all psychoanalysis. Until this final step is accomplished, therapy must be considered superficial even if effective. The ego may learn more expedient techniques during superficial therapy, but the pathogenic core remains untouched (*cf.* the discussion of treatment).

At the present time, there is enormous variability even within the Freudian camp as to the relation of character to the underlying libidinal problems, and in Part III we shall discuss those psychoanalytic schools that consider that character is all that matters, dismissing the libidinal entanglements as incidental instead of determining. Generally speaking, the most orthodox Freudian nowadays spends a great deal of time on the analysis of character resistances—ego defenses.

Critical Comment

THIS account of the Freudian view of mental diseases has been of necessity superficial and incomplete. It should, indeed, be remarked at once that my presentation has emphasized the distinctively Freudian (libidinal) aspects of the etiology of pathology rather too heavily to reflect accurately the current views of most psychoanalysts. There is always more vivid consideration of ego and superego aspects of the personality than I have implied. I shall return to this point a little later. There has been no mention of the actual neuroses, of traumatic neuroses, of perversions, addictions, stuttering, tics, epilepsy, and the complex psychological accompaniments of organic lesions of the brain. Elaboration of medical entities seems inappropriate for this book. The general statement may be made that the Freudian explanations of these other disorders tend to rest upon the stages of libidinal development *in complex relationship to variations in the development of the ego and superego* in a manner analogous to those offered for the major neuroses and the functional psychoses.

The merit of the Freudian approach, to my mind, lies in the effort to understand these functional diseases in terms of the functioning of the organism rather than merely to classify them by their prominent symptomatology. It is well known that the "symptomatology" of mental disease is highly variable and offers an insecure guide to diagnosis and appropriate therapy. Etiology is almost completely obscure. The other psychoanalytic schools (except that of Sullivan) have scarcely tried to work out a specific dynamic explanation for specific diagnostic entities (see Chap. 12). They tend to ignore the specificity of the disease in favor of trying to understand the dynamics operating in each patient as a separate individual in the terms that each author considers "universal." Psychiatrists in the Kraepelinian* tradition tend to concentrate on establishing more secure clusters of *symptoms* for purposes of diagnosis and prognosis. They function mostly in the overpopulated institutions for mental cases, where time-consuming psychotherapeutic approaches to the individual are almost impossible and gross therapeutic techniques applicable to major diagnostic categories must be relied on. (See pp. 496ff. for further discussion of the positive values for psychological theory of the kind of observation enforced by sheer numbers in large hospitals.)

The achievements of Kraepelin and those psychiatrists whose concern is mainly with diagnostic classification should not be minimized. However faulty, the current psychiatric classifications do offer a sense of *pattern* in the confused welter of mental disease which contributes importantly to the understanding of the individual case. A good diagnostic label, properly applied, is an aid to the therapist in anticipating many of the reaction patterns of the patient, present and future, beyond the limited sample of patients he has himself encountered in the therapeutic session of a full psychoanalysis. It is recognized that observation of recurrent systems of events may be very useful in practice even when their intrinsic dynamics are not understood—even when the clustering is not truly dynamic at all but due to common underlying "causes." Any tendency to rest content with such systems and to apply them indiscriminately is deplorable—but it is equally mistaken to ignore the assistance they can offer.

* Kraepelin was to psychiatry what Linnaeus was to botany. He developed a workable classification of mental disorders.

Many psychologists and psychoanalysts who pride themselves on their dynamic approach make the error of scorning the substantial empirical systems developed by old-style psychiatry. This point is discussed further in Chapter 12.

After pointing out the general value of an approach that undertakes a specific dynamic interpretation of the specific entities descriptively outlined by psychiatry, we may consider whether the dynamic interpretations seem good and sufficient. I offer my impression that the classical Freudian interpretations are good but not sufficient. In my own work of trying to reach a useful diagnosis of the individual from his performance on a battery of subtle psychological tests, I have encountered the problem at first hand in hundreds of cases—thousands, if one may include large groups of so-called "normals," any one of whom *may* exhibit in the tests a potential pathology, in fact may *be* a "patient" studying or working during therapy. Thus, I am not talking entirely as an outsider but as a participant who has seen a great many people, via test performance, with the explicit purpose of trying to understand the nature of the pathology when the patient is referred by a psychiatrist and (a realistically much harder task) of trying to prognosticate the pathology in groups presented as normal.

From this (testing) angle of vision, one encounters a large number of cases that follow with textbook fidelity even the superficial description of Freudian dynamics given above. The tester must be blind, deaf, and dumb not to recognize the syndromes as Freud described them, not to find independent corroborative evidence in the tests.

But however frequent, and however impressive when they occur, these cases are in the minority. Any simple extrapolation from the libido theory to the majority of cases encountered in unselected practice comes to grief very quickly. The problem of function in pathology is much more complex. Despite the fact that my description of Freudian dynamics underlying the major neuroses and psychoses is taken directly from highly respected Freudian sources, any Freudian analyst would squirm a little at an account so concentrated on stages of libido development. Freudians who emphasize ego psychology in their theoretical framework would protest vigorously against such oversimplification. And in my own work as tester, I would guess roughly that for every case that neatly fits the simple Freudian dynamics here outlined there are ten for which the interpretation requires drastic modification, sometimes to the point at which the major pathological trends seem entirely extraneous to the stages in the genetic process. This is especially true in psychosis as it is understood today, in which the infantile material posited by Freud does indeed appear but in such bewildering variety that the main problem seems to be the over-all ego strength of the patient, and regression to specific stages of development seems of rather peripheral importance.

A major—perhaps one may say *the* major—problem in pathology has in late years become the problem of the ego. How strong is it? What is the nature of its defenses? At a deep level, there must be a high correlation between the nature of the ego's defenses and the type of libidinal problem encountered during the period when the ego was in process of formation. If we assume that the deepest troubles will lie in the areas of frustration of the powerful "sexual" systems, so important for the infant (a fair assumption in a reasonably stable society, able to satisfy the physical needs of the majority of its members reasonably well), then deep pathology is very likely to follow the patterns derived from the libido theory. Such patterns will never be without great import. But if we take seriously the extension of the genetic process into the nonsexual systems, as I suggested in my comment on Chapter 5, the problem of the etiology of pathology also becomes more complex. The fate of the emerging nonsexual systems—their coalescence among themselves; their relation to the self image, the parent image, and specific social demands—must play a major dynamic role in personality formation.

It was suggested earlier that generally speaking "good" parents are "good" all along the line, including handling of the child's sexual systems, and that "bad" ones are consistently "bad," so that by and large concentration on either the sexual or the nonsexual area is likely to show good empirical results in therapy and in the philosophy underlying therapy. But this correlation rests upon a highly complex underlying correlation of adult attitudes, not upon dynamics intrinsic to the growing child. It is all too possible to thwart the child in some ways while encouraging him in others. The specific effects of thwarting and encouragement in the nonsexual systems have not yet been codified satisfactorily, in their own right or in relation to the simultaneously emerging sexual systems.

It is very easy to say that the trouble with the Freudian view of the dynamics of the major psychiatric disease entities as described above is an overemphasis on libidinal development. No one would disagree, not even the classical Freudians. I have tried to say that some individuals do in fact present a very neat confirmation of this oversimplified Freudian view—probably because for one reason or another their libidinal problems dictated the major orientation of the personality. It is by no means heterodox to suggest that *all* cases present complicating factors in the nature of their ego defenses, or even that in some cases the nature of the defense may determine the form of the disease.

One may confidently expect that as knowledge of ego mechanisms increases, the Freudians themselves will extend their views of the dynamics of psychopathology to systematic evaluation of different types of ego development. In my vocabulary, the partially independent pathology of the nonsexual systems will probably be used in its own right as well as in relation to aspects of the personality already emphasized in Freudian doctrine. The often rather forced effort to find a unifying dynamic strictly in terms of the libido theory may be relieved by a more informed and fruitfully codified appreciation of the role of other aspects of mental function.

PSYCHOANALYSIS AS A METHOD

OF TREATMENT

THIS PART OF THE CHAPTER, like the chapter as a whole, has two major subdivisions, but these are not at all independent of each other. The first part—*techniques*—cannot possibly be separated in the actual therapeutic process from an understanding of what helps the patient get well. The second part, entitled the *dynamics of psychoanalytic therapy,* is concentrated on such understanding.

Analysts themselves write a great deal about "techniques" and often attack one another on points that may seem to the outsider rather trivially technical. Should the patient be allowed to sit up instead of lying on the traditional couch? How many days a week must he come if his treatment is to be called psychoanalysis rather than psychoanalytically oriented therapy? Should a warmly sympathetic attitude toward the patient on the part of the analyst be encouraged, or even allowed?

The answers to these questions always depend primarily on the therapist's concept of the dynamics of his therapy. His technique is *his* business, in a way, as much as the technique of the surgeon. No two "psychoanalyses" are the same, because every analyst adapts himself to the needs of the particular patient. No two analysts are quite the same, regardless of school affiliation. Certain generalizations may be made, however, which seem characteristic for the school.

TECHNIQUES

Psychoanalysis began as a *special method of treatment,* not as a psychological theory of general import. On many occasions, the word is still used in this narrow sense. For example, when a Freudian recommends against "psychoanalysis" for certain pathological conditions, he does not mean that they are not comprehended by psychoanalytic doctrine but that a *specific standard therapeutic technique* is inexpedient. A classical Freudian may himself engage in various types of therapeutic endeavor with enthusiastic interest and marked success, but he is careful to label them as "psychoanalytically oriented psychotherapy."

Of considerable historical interest is the period during which psychoanalysis doubted its therapeutic value beyond quite special cases, restricting its value otherwise to a new psychological understanding.[8] This was the period around the 1920's, when confidence gained from early therapeutic successes was damaged by initially unsuccessful efforts to extend the application of the psychoanalytic method to a wider variety of cases, and perhaps by relapses among "cured" patients. Moreover, Freud never believed that he held an easy panacea for all human ills in his hand. Neither Freud nor the Freudians (apart from the lunatic fringe inseparable from any important movement) have ever envisaged psychoanalysis as a therapeutic method in such global terms.

The very first cases treated were hysterics; the method was hypnosis; the rationale was the recovery of memories that had been repressed. The limitation of this method was that many patients were not hypnotizable. Furthermore, the cure proved neither certain nor stable. Some patients did not immediately renounce their symptoms, or got them back fairly soon, or disconcertingly substituted a different symptom hardly more desirable than the first.

We have seen how this state of affairs led to the revision and deepening of the theoretical considerations underlying the treatment—*i.e.*, to the whole complex development of psychoanalysis as a psychological doctrine. Our concern now is with modifications in *therapeutic technique* and (a little later) the rationale of cure.

Free Association. Freud observed that if the patient lay in a relaxed position and was encouraged to speak out whatever thoughts came into his mind, no matter how trivial or shocking, the repressed memories tended to come back of themselves, along with all sorts of material ordinarily excluded by the orderly processes of consciously controlled thought. Moreover, the patient remembered his own productions—as he did not under hypnosis—and was able to use them constructively, with the aid of the analyst, in a conscious reintegration of his psychic life to an extent impossible in the older, "suggestive" approach.

Freud called the technique *free association*. The admonition to report completely the undirected meanderings of the mind became the "basic rule" of psychoanalysis, and it is still fundamental for most Freudians. The only standard equipment of the analyst's office is the couch, with a chair for the therapist behind the patient. The purpose of the arrangement is, of course, maximal relaxation for the patient physically and "socially." Sitting *vis-à-vis* another person tends to evoke our usual interpersonal *directedness* of thought and feeling. Even when trustful relations with the doctor are well established and the patient wishes to confide freely, it is difficult for him to renounce the ordinary forms of social responsiveness. Hence the value of an artificial situation which leaves the patient, relatively speaking, alone with his thoughts and which structures the analyst as an outside interpreter instead of a participant in the realistic, ego-oriented reaction patterns of the patient. The aim of the free-association technique is to get at the unconscious material with as little interference from controlling and defensive forces as possible.

In recent years, many analysts have noted that the recumbent position has implications for some patients far beyond the intended relaxation and impersonality. The patient may feel abandoned and alone when he cannot see the doctor. Or he may feel humiliated by what he considers a kind of inferior status. Patients with paranoid trends are sometimes disturbed by the constant thought that the analyst may be doing something against them behind their back. Often this feeling is rationalized as the idea that he is dozing, or perhaps that he is taking verbatim notes for publication of a case history. One young woman patient had suffered capricious physical chastisement from her father as late as adolescence. Despite an unusually great conscious trust in the analyst, reinforced by his especially active sympathy and practical help in her profession, she could not get over a fear that as she was lying on the couch, he was getting ready to strike her. Even after her vague fear of having someone behind her was understood, the residual unconscious threat was so great that she could not associate freely lying down.

It seems safe to say that every analyst nowadays abrogates the rule of the couch occasionally. Sometimes the "sitting up" allows the patient to associate more freely. Furthermore, the technique of free association itself is used with discretion rather than as a routine "must." Some patients (*e.g.*, compulsives and obsessives and perhaps overintellectualizers generally) either block very badly or fill the hour with trivia so directed as to be really trivial. Some patients (*e.g.*, borderline psychotics) may uncover valid unconscious material so rapidly as to threaten their entire ego-defense system and may require braking from the analyst with deliberate reinforcing of protective devices.

Some analysts feel that any deviation from the technique of free association on the couch is to be considered as a temporary handling of resistances, and that any treatment carried out "sitting up" must be considered as psychotherapy rather than psychoanalysis. Other analysts feel that the proper criterion is the reaction of the patient. Some individuals "sitting up" do appear to uncover genuinely deep materials and to revise their way of living on the basis of a genuine resolution of the buried infantile conflicts. Others on the couch five days a week never get beyond the level of conscious discussion employed in psychotherapy.*

Interpretation of Dreams. A second technique for getting at unconscious materials short of hypnosis that Freud discovered early was the *interpretation of dreams*. The rationale of dream interpretation has already been discussed (Chap. 2), and we have seen that every psychoanalytic school retains this avenue of information about the unconscious, no matter what interpretative rubrics are applied. We have seen, too, that every school interprets *partly*

---

* The verbal quibble about what constitutes a psychoanalysis has acquired practical importance as "being analyzed" becomes a formal prerequisite for social work and clinical psychology. At present, the candidate may do well to avoid the purists who demand the long concentrated period on the couch as intrinsic to "psychoanalysis." The current state of affairs is too confused to endure, but it would be presumptuous to prophesy the exact technical definition of "a psychoanalysis" ten years hence.

according to quasi-universal symbolisms appropriate to the major emphases of the school, and that every school requires further information from the patient to clarify the meaning of idiosyncratic symbols or to confirm the generalized meaning. No psychoanalyst would publish a "dream book" to explain dreams, because the dream is always the product of highly idiosyncratic unconscious systems.

Recounting of the dream in the analytic hour is followed by free association to the dream as a whole or to such parts as strike the patient or analyst as especially significant. It is often accompanied by an account of the happenings of the preceding day, which are very often reworked in the dream. The reader is here reminded of the distinction between the manifest and the latent content of the dream, the former being its actual story and the latter its deeper unconscious structure. Initially, Freud held the opinion that the dream always expressed a *wish*—often, of course, the exact opposite of the aims of the conscious personality. For example, a relatively superficial reaction formation, common in everyday living, is very likely to show the direct impulse under thin disguise in dreams. Study of dreams in traumatic neurosis suggested that the dream might be merely repetitive. Nowadays, if we judge by published cases and by conversation, even the "Freudians" do not limit dream interpretation to wish or repetition or to expressions of anxiety and guilt. General and personal symbolisms, the residue of the day or the life span, almost anything that gives meaning to the dream becomes part of analytic therapy.

The dream always has a multiple determination and can be interpreted on many levels. Some of Freud's reports illustrate the wealth of information to be obtained from a single dream. Dream interpretation is, however, very time-consuming and may be used by some patients actually to avoid coming to grips with important problems. It is not necessary to analyze every dream completely. The significant materials will reappear in other dreams until they are successfully assimilated. Very often the analyst understands more from the dream than he discloses to the patient at any given time. Interpretation is not intended as an intellectual exercise for the patient but as a process of full recognition and assimilation of trends hitherto excluded from consciousness. Insights proposed by the analyst that the patient is not prepared to handle are shrugged off or met with active resistance. As a rule, interpretative comment is based not only on a specific dream but on a long sequence of dreams and other behavior revealing of the patient's state of mind (largely unconscious). Thus, the dream interpretation by the analyst in course of treatment is far less chancy and idiosyncratic than it appears to the layman observing the variability among doctors in their interpretation of dreams presented in isolation.

Occasional faulty or ill-timed comments are inevitable. The skilled analyst quickly recognizes his error, not so much from the active protests of the patient, which may indicate merely his resistance to necessary insights, as from further unconscious productions.

"The Psychopathology of Everyday Life." A third avenue of information about the unconscious that Freud discovered early he called *"the psychopathology of everyday life."* His book by this title is mainly concerned with the small lapses in normal speech and behavior and has already been discussed (Chap. 2). The analyst constantly observes the minutiae of the patient's actions during treatment for their unconscious significance. Coming late or early, fussing about bills or giving presents, forgetting possessions or carrying off items from the office, admiring or criticizing appurtenances or characteristics of the doctor, and the whole host of small variations in behavior supplement free associations and dreams in offering cues to unconscious reactions.

Emotional Concomitants. More recently many analysts have become sensitive to such physiological cues as flushing and pallor, rigidity or relaxation of posture, changes in timbre of voice. A relatively new type of question during the hour is not "What are you thinking?" but "What are you feeling?" with analysis of the transitory states of depression, anger, exhilaration experienced by the patient and previously disregarded because too vague and irrelevant for routine report under the old instructions about the basic rule. For research purposes, mechanical devices have been used with patients to register emotional change.[9] Thus far such devices are too cumbersome for regular, practical use. The correlation between the topic under "analytic" discussion and the bodily reaction has been amply demonstrated, however, and it may be that *eventually* some mechanical device will supplement the analyst's observations.

Whether or not machines are used, it is fair to say that the unconscious emotional concomitants of the "ideas" emerging in the analytic session represent a post-Freudian emphasis entirely consonant with his basic theories but relatively neglected in his initial intellectualized approach. A few dissident analysts, notably Reich and his followers, actively provoke vivid emotional response during the treatment session, either by manipulating muscles or by allowing direct sexual pleasure. Such procedures are anathema to the orthodox Freudian, as we shall understand further in the discussion of doctor-patient relations (pp. 316ff.). They are mentioned here as the extreme of the valid effort to get at and handle genuine feeling in the analytic session in conjunction with the patient's ideas. Freud's own investigations showed how ideas and feelings can become separated in pathology, with the consequent therapeutic problem of reintegration. In a more general sense, the affective participation of the patient has always been considered a necessary part of the cure, as will be seen in our discussion of the dynamics of therapy.

Patterns of Reaction. The happenings of the previous day are usually reported more or less routinely during the analytic hour, not only as an aid to understanding the dream but for the information they yield about the patient's *patterns of reaction.* Very often the events of the day lead back to memories of somewhat similar events in childhood—similar in unconscious dynamics in a manner often quite unexpected to the patient and often difficult for him to recognize at once. The patterns to be observed are partly revealing of id materials and are of especial value in clarifying the defense mechanisms established by the ego. Analysts vary in the amount of time devoted to examination of current behavior, but apparently the trend is generally toward greater emphasis in this direction as against the early efforts to release childhood repression by recapturing "forgotten" episodes.

Every analyst realizes nowadays both that the patient needs to start where he is in order to reach the infantile material with fruitful insight and that he needs constant help in understanding concretely how his present problems are related to the distortions instituted in childhood. Listening to debates among analysts in professional meetings of their own, I have been impressed to note that "revolutionary" advocacy of increased attention to the current life patterns of the patient is met with the comment from the Freudian "die-hards": "We've been doing that for twenty-five years."

There can be no doubt about the influence of new information on the role of social factors in personality function. The study of ego mechanisms demands attention to the life pattern. Psychoanalytic practice has become so flexible that adherence to a theoretical school is no guarantee of rigorously standard techniques, and its theory allows for honest variation. Just now, variations center largely about the *role* of the nonsexual components of the problem presented by the patient, I think, with generally increased attention to their specific dynamic pattern.

Transference. Probably the most important therapeutic device is the emotional relationship between doctor and patient—a device which can be called roughly the *transference.* Freud observed that his patients tended to ascribe to him the attributes of God Almighty—a phenomenon initially acceptable enough to his own ego. The patients also showed a tendency, however, to react to him as though he were the devil incarnate—to a point at which he was glad to conclude that he could not possibly be as bad as their accusations implied. He wryly remarked that he soon found it necessary to discount the flattery as well, recognizing that the patient was not expressing an objective judgment in either direction. On the contrary, the analyst seemed to be merely a stick figure drawn by the patient in whatever role his unconscious prescribed. The analyst *became* pro tem the all-powerful parent, beneficent or malignant as the patient re-enacted one or another aspect of his early experience. We shall consider in a moment the profound importance of this transference phenomenon in the dynamics of therapy. Our present concern is its implication for technique.

Freud felt that because the patient uses the analyst so directly in this unconscious reliving of the past, currently realistic reactions to the actual person of the doctor should be kept to a minimum. There should be no relations of any sort outside the office; preferably the analyst should not have been a friend of the patient and should not be in any way involved with his present practical activities. The analyst's attitude should be one of benign, authoritative objectivity. He should not participate in the patient's current problems by way of concrete advice or even by way of ordinary human sympathy. Detachment was considered essential to analysis of the patient's infantile attitudes as repeated in the treatment session.

The impersonal attitude of the analyst also offered a secure method of handling the phenomenon of *countertransference*—that is, the emotional involvements proceeding from the unconscious of the doctor. The training analysis* was supposed to free the doctor from the irrational bias inherent in his own psyche, or at least give him such insight into his personal trends as would make them innocuous during the process of interpretation to the patient. Obviously, it is not easy to preserve one's objectivity in the face of the egregiously antagonistic or seductive behavior of many patients at one stage or another of their treatment. The temptation is very great to react "humanly," or with one's own vanities and prejudices, to the vivid transference behavior of the patient. The prescribed detachment and Olympian calm offered further protection for the objective course of the treatment, this time against the reality involvement of the doctor.

Moreover, his Olympian calm enhanced the *authority* of the doctor, which Freud felt must be part of the therapeutic process. Often the patient neurotically demands magic help for his problems, so that the analyst is typically forced into uncomfortable omnipotence. He can avoid it no more than parents can. Often, however, the timid efforts of the ego to regain mastery need

---

* Freud went so far as to recommend reanalysis every five years *for the analyst* as desirable routine procedure (S. Freud, "Analysis Terminable and Interminable," *Collected Papers*, Vol. V, Hogarth Press, 1950, pp. 316-357).

the reinforcement of the doctor's authority. New insights tend to arouse anxiety and hence resistance. Cogent interpretation automatically reinstates the old defenses. To break into this vicious circle effectively, the analyst must somehow be a power on the side of the angels. The structuring of his role as a trusted, impersonal doctor who can offer substantial help by virtue of his professional knowledge should antedate the fireworks of positive and negative transference and should be maintained throughout the treatment—with a final period of resolution of transference and reinstatement of normal reality relations.

These paragraphs have been limited to *Freud's* recommendations as to the behavior of the analyst in the psychoanalytic session. Since Freud's technical recommendations proceed from his evaluation of the dynamics of therapy, our discussion has necessarily encroached upon the later section on the dynamics of therapy. Not even Freudians are so rigid in practice nowadays, and the nature of the transference phenomenon will require long consideration (see also Chap. 12).

The Interpretative Comment. The *interpretative comment* of the analyst provides the major integration of the therapeutic procedure. In the long illustrative passages on free association and dreams (pp. 38*ff*. and 57*f*.), it was pointed out that many themes are presented. The account of life situations presents many facets; the patient reacts to the analyst on many levels. In therapy the analyst obviously does not offer the patient a balanced, inclusive review of the complexities of his mental state. His task is to evaluate which of the problems are "hot" at the moment so that the patient can assimilate a new insight and use it for fruitful change. His task is to so time and so phrase his comment that the *patient* will see its implications. Intellectual understanding by the patient is often of secondary importance. Indeed, a pitfall of therapeutic analysis may be the joint pursuit of refined shades of unconscious meaning by two subtle minds during which the patient is as "objectively" interested as the analyst. Interesting conversation, but no therapy.

The valid therapeutic comment grasps the fundamental "emotional" import of the material for the patient at any given moment and arouses an "emotional" response. (The quotation marks are intended to enlarge the meaning from overt laughter and tears to anything deeply *felt* in contrast to the intellectual game of identifying mechanisms.) The therapeutic comment stirs up the patient, in one way or another. It brings his whole personality into the office of the analyst and provides a kind of emotional re-education on the spot. Ferenczi laid especial stress on this active experience *with the analyst,* recom-

mending a realistic permissiveness that Freud could not approve. In our discussion of dynamics, we shall consider several varying points of view on this
point—which merges with the doctor-patient relationship.

What underlying trends the analyst selects for interpretation at any given
point will depend to a large extent on his appreciation of the complex over-all
dynamics of the case, an appreciation closely related to his theoretical approach.
Freudians separate ego defenses and id strivings more definitely than do the
non-libido schools. They may often interpret "defenses" without the slightest
mention to the patient of "id" materials quite obvious to them, and they may
consider proper integration of the two lines of interpretation a late but necessary phase of the analysis. In practice, these phases of interpretation overlap
constantly; but the Freudian analyst prefers to keep them theoretically distinct
(whereas the non-libido schools prefer a merger even in theory).

The outsider or patient frequently does not understand that the interpretative comment is used by the analyst as an instrument almost as highly specific
as the instruments of surgery. Theoretically correct insight on the part of the
analyst obtained by the various techniques outlined thus far is only the background of therapy. Doubtless the patient gains something merely by reviewing
his thoughts and feelings in the analytic situation as such, but this gain is
chancy—occasionally dangerous. (Techniques of self-analysis and such ventures as Buchmanism and dianetics rely primarily on such *unguided* emergence
of personal and interpersonal materials, in which the usual rational controls
are temporarily abrogated.) Psychoanalytic treatment consists in the intervention of the doctor *at the level of understanding the patient can truly assimilate,*
finally taking the patient back to the deepest strata of his personality. The
interpretative comment is the major device employed by the psychoanalyst.

NEWER DEVELOPMENTS IN
PSYCHOANALYTIC TECHNIQUES

Most analysts are less rigidly impersonal and authoritative nowadays than
Freud recommended. A measure of sympathy, appreciation, and encouragement appears to give the ego more support in its struggles than an objectivity
which the patient very often interprets as coldness, disapproval, or rejection.
Some analysts—notably Reich, Rank, Ferenczi, and most of the non-libido
groups—make active use of *any* vivid relations with the doctor, *extending the
meaning of the concept of transference to any attitude of the patient rooted in
his unconscious patterns.* The dynamics of this newer view of the transference

relationship will be discussed in the homologous chapter on therapy for the non-libido schools. It will be dropped here with the comment that most contemporary Freudians do *in practice* handle the therapeutic relationship more flexibly, although *in theory* departure from objectivity is usually conceived as an adjunct to the handling of the important ego defenses rather than as curative in itself at a deeper level.

Newer extensions of psychoanalysis to the treatment of children and adolescents, psychotics, addicts, and other "irresponsibles" have led to a newly concrete concern with the current environment of the patient. Parents and teachers must cooperate in giving information about the young child and even in his treatment during the period when the superego is not yet fully formed. The adolescent is too often yanked out of treatment at the whim of his parents or subjected to reality pressures so great that analysis of underlying patterns is swamped in the need to meet actual demands. Uncontrolled use of drugs or alcohol puts the patient beyond reach of the doctor. Furthermore, analysis may come to a standstill when any close reality relationship is stubbornly, realistically "impossible," as when the neurotic wife must cope with a neurotic husband. As a rule, the husband is sent to a different analyst for elaborately independent treatment. A few analysts, notably Mittelmann, have urged the value in some situations of having the same doctor treat both partners simultaneously.[10] Naturally, the analyst must be especially careful to avoid taking sides, but the two-way account of a controversy, analytically understood with both partners, frequently helps to sharpen insight and to guide the timing of interpretations to both patients.

Some analysts now take a hand in actively encouraging professional or artistic activities about which the patient has been blocked, sometimes for many years. The signed works of many professional artists hang on our walls at home, but guests typically pause before a portrait done by a patient, aged thirty-five, who had given up a deep interest in painting at the time of her marriage fifteen years earlier, with a nagging sense of frustration and failure. After protracted analysis, the analyst's forthright insistence on renewal of her efforts to paint not only provided this woman with an importantly productive interest but seemed to expedite the analytic process itself.

Even persons without native talent are sometimes urged to take up creative pursuits, both for their interpretative value during treatment and for their common-sense value as enjoyable hobbies. Occupational therapy has long been a recognized part of the institutional treatment of mental conditions. In recent years, such activities and products have been brought into much closer relationship to the dynamics of the psychoanalytic technique. A recourse of necessity in the handling of patients who cannot verbalize adequately—children and many psychotics—"artistic" expression is proving to be a useful adjunct to treatment generally.

The narrow definition of psychoanalysis as the verbal productions of the patient on the couch insulated from his contemporary world in so far as possible is thus being extended in two directions: (1) more conscious use of his real-life situation, (2) use of nonverbal techniques. It seems likely that such infringements of the classical procedure will increase in more intimate connection with the kind of insight previously considered specific to the psychoanalytic technique. On the whole, such variations are welcomed by all schools, though the purist prefers to call them psychoanalytically oriented therapies rather than psychoanalysis.

A further adjunct to therapy may be mentioned which has received attention since the war: the use of drugs (sodium amytal, pentothal) and hypnosis, which enable the patient to remember important materials inaccessible to his conscious mind and to express emotions ordinarily withheld. Pentothal is not a "truth drug," but it does relax the ordinary ego controls so that memories and affects intolerable to the ego emerge relatively freely. These techniques came into prominence under the emergency conditions of the war, when the number and urgency of the cases precluded psychoanalysis as a formal therapeutic method. They deserve a place in this chapter only in that they have been used as *part* of a more or less clearly defined psychoanalytic approach.* They were, of course, most successful when used with an essentially normal person who had cracked under extreme stress. They did not prove a cure-all and have become less popular, even as an adjunct to psychoanalysis, as the patient load of the analyst has reverted to the more chronic types produced by the ordinary stresses of civilian life. The relatively direct access to the repressed materials is of some value to the analyst in formulating *his* understanding of the patient and may be of some value to the patient as he is cogently reminded of significant past events. The technique is positively dangerous for some borderline psychotics whose weakened ego cannot tolerate this artificially induced irruption of thinly repressed material. It is positively helpful for some patients, mainly essentially normal people reacting to severe trauma. For the majority it seems distressingly *indifferent*.

The production of repressed memories and affects without the conscious participation of the ego rarely has much therapeutic effect. The recovered

* The various forms of shock therapy and brain surgery are omitted here because they have not been reported to any considerable extent in close conjunction with psychoanalytic techniques. Probably their main value *for the analyst* is in improving the accessibility of the patient to psychotherapy.

materials do not become part of analytic therapy until they are reviewed in a waking state, when they function very much like any other material brought to consciousness in therapy. The process of insight and assimilation must follow the usual pattern. The patient who has never been able to tolerate guilt will not benefit much from recognition that he felt guilty during a particularly difficult situation which he had "forgotten." Actually the time consumed in narcotizing or hypnotizing the patient is very often as great as that consumed in reaching similar material by ordinary methods—and the patient is less helpfully participant in the process.

Thus, a promising short-cut proved as usual to have limited usefulness, notwithstanding occasional spectacular success.[11] The fruitful suggestion has been made that a few "drug" sessions be used when a long analysis has gone stale—that is, when the patient confronted with some deep problem still unresolved tediously produces the same type of material over a long period and has become, as it were, immune to interpretation. The classical psychoanalytic passivity, so valuable in allowing the patient to structure his own cure according to his own needs, may here lead to protraction of analysis and sometimes to its failure when the patient becomes too bored or can no longer afford such expensive tedium. In such situations, pentothal is unlikely to uncover dramatically new data, but it may give patient and doctor a new lead of immediate value. Probably the sheer novelty of the procedure serves to break up an undesirably crystallized relationship to the analysis.*

Pentothal may, under controlled conditions, do a job often accomplished by real situations beyond the analyst's control. It has become a commonplace that shocking reality problems which one might suppose would wreck an unstable nervous system not infrequently pull it together, at least temporarily—e.g., the frequent improvement of neurotics during periods of bombing. Very often the turn of events in the patient's life, even when thoroughly deplorable otherwise, turns the *analysis* in a good direction, as awareness of vivid feeling and its setting is forced upon the patient. Unfortunately, accidental traumatic events too often make the patient worse—hence the value of a controlled dose of trauma. In informal conversation, I have heard many quite orthodox analysts admit the therapeutic value of having lost their temper with a patient—very occasionally and by no means as a technique to be advised. The patient may suddenly improve, not in the popular sense of being overawed by authority

* A few striking efforts to use these adjuncts to psychoanalysis are described in R. R. Grinker, "The Use of Narcosynthesis in War Neurosis," in F. Alexander and T. M. French (eds.), *Psychoanalytic Therapy*, Ronald Press, 1946, pp. 325-337; L. S. Kubie and S. Margolin, "The Therapeutic Role of Drugs in the Process of Repression, Dissociation and Synthesis," *Psychosomatic Medicine*, 1945, 3:147-151. See also B. Mittelmann, "Psychoanalytic Observations on Dreams and Psychosomatic Reactions to Hypnotics and Anaesthetics," *Psychoanalytic Quarterly*, 1945, 14:498-510.

but in the genuine analytic sense of relaxing resistances. A sudden illness of the analyst or a holiday period *may* have a similar good result.

Unfortunately, the occasions when such departures from objectivity have borne fruitful results can be matched by occasions when a personally determined burst of temper from the analyst has been as seriously deleterious as a slip of the surgeon's knife. Most classical analysts therefore tend to repudiate any relaxation of objectivity as a dangerous or at best uncontrollable technique. (It should be remembered that the patient is transferring his major emotional attitudes to the analytic situation, so that what the analyst does *realistically* has an emotional import far beyond the same actions by any other person. He is God Almighty not by his own wish but in surrogate capacity.)

Profiting by observation of these accidental infractions of standard psychoanalysis, some analysts in publication and many more in personal practice have come to feel the desirability of a *flexible* approach to therapy, both as regards the attitude openly expressed toward the patient and as regards the conscious utilization of changes in his life situation. Personal warmth, encouragement and sympathy, tough criticism, direct command may be consciously administered "as needed." For example, after protracted but fruitless analysis of his dilatory behavior, an analyst dismissed a patient (a college student) temporarily, saying that he must finish three overdue term papers before treatment could be resumed. The patient's objective anxiety about his mounting "incompletes" had come to swamp the analytic hour with fruitless self-recrimination. The doctor judged, correctly, that the boy *could* write the papers under this powerful command, and that the experience would be analytically useful, both in relieving the immediate anxiety and *in supplying the material for vivid interpretation of deeper problems.* The fact that finishing the papers also saved the boy from a realistic setback in his budding career is properly a secondary consideration for the psychoanalytic process, no matter how appealing to the analyst as a person.

It is easy to get many types of patient to perform well under the analyst's control. In a few cases (borderline psychotics, deep neurotics), the doctor may feel that he should limit his efforts to this modest aim, putting up with life-long calls on his attention or getting the patient into a protected situation. The aspiration in the present example was higher: to make a brilliant boy truly independent. The direct command was used (1) to relieve the immediate symptom, (2) to show the patient dramatically that he *could* write papers, and (3) to *show* him his neurotic need for authority. After this episode, the analysis resumed its course. The reader should be fully alerted to the difference between use of such a technique as a controlled *episode* in the reality world of the patient, prepared and exploited in relation to the continuity of his deeper productions, and similar techniques used as therapeutic devices in themselves. In so far as treatment is *confined* to this level, it is not "psychoanalysis" for the Freudian, no matter how successful, and no matter what borrowings from Freudian doctrine are considered justification by the therapist for calling his procedures psychoanalytic.

The Chicago group, under the leadership of Alexander and French,[12] has especially emphasized the curative process that goes on *outside the doctor's office* during a psychoanalysis. In part the patient consciously continues a kind of self-analysis between sessions which is almost always helpful when constantly checked by the analyst. Even more important are the unconscious or semiconscious consolidations of insights through actual living or the flashes of deep understanding that appear as the patient suddenly realizes the full import of an interpretation previously accepted on too intellectual a level, or perhaps even rejected. So efficacious is this extracurricular learning that these analysts recommend a large measure of flexibility in the number and timing of the formal analytic sessions. *Some* patients, they point out, do as well in a genuinely psychoanalytic sense with two or three sessions per week—occasionally even one—as with the conventional five.

It may be advisable to interrupt the analysis altogether for a time, well short of completion. This expedient has not only the practical value of reducing the total time and expense of the treatment, they think, but may be a positive aid to therapy. The patient returns to treatment with new insight and new zest; the analysis is kept in closer relationship to his actual adjustments—amelioration of which is, after all, its therapeutic aim. The skill and experience of the analyst should, according to Alexander and his colleagues, be directed in part toward timing of the sessions as well as toward timing of interpretations in a rigidly structured treatment technique. (Most classical analysts feel that this is no longer "psychoanalysis," however successful therapeutically.)

In partial summary of the *techniques* of psychoanalysis as a method of treatment, we may list the following: free association (on the couch, in recent years "sitting up" for some patients); dreams; review of the current and past life situation (1) to facilitate understanding of the infantile repressed materials and (2) for understanding of neurotically determined patterns of reaction; the analyst-patient relationship (transference); interpretative comment.

With some unavoidable admixture of *dynamic* considerations, modifications and innovations were mentioned. The most controversial change concerns the nature of the transference phenomenon and the type of material selected for interpretative comment. Full discussion is postponed to the homologous chapter on the non-libido schools. At the present time, variations in technique are appearing in all analytic schools, with relatively little relationship to basic theory. Most Freudians prefer to use the label "psychoanalytically oriented psychotherapy" when treatment procedures depart markedly from the traditional psychoanalytic session. Variations in fairly common use now are:

(1) Flexibility in the number of sessions per week, occasionally with the introduction of planned interruptions of treatment.

(2) More active manipulation of the environment, especially for children, adolescents, and psychotics. Consultation with associates of the patient, simultaneous treatment of members of the family, direct encouragement of special activities (especially art or hobby interests), occasional direct aid in planning and the like are no longer so strictly taboo as in earlier years. However, in so far as these techniques are considered part of a *psychoanalysis* at all, the intent is to facilitate understanding at a deep level. Their aim is to remove tedious blocking, to reveal underlying problems more sharply, to help the patient integrate new insights with his current life adjustment. "Cure" by such methods is not considered a "psychoanalytic" cure and may even at times endanger the progress toward more fundamental solution of difficulties. Hence alarm in many quarters lest the superficial successes achieved with relative ease in many cases by these techniques jeopardize the essential meaning of psychoanalysis as a distinct therapeutic method.

(3) More systematic observation of the reactions of the patient at the nonverbal level; to a lesser degree, the introduction of techniques designed as aids to such observation or which actually encourage nonverbal expression. Methods and types of observation forced upon the analyst in dealing with patients of very limited verbal capacity (*e.g.*, children and psychotics) are beginning to penetrate the treatment of the ordinary adult patient. Vasomotor reactions, facial expression, voice, body motility offer promising leads. The subjective report of the patient on what he is feeling as well as what he is thinking is useful. It is too early to predict how valuable an adjunct to treatment these techniques may become.

(4) The use of drugs and hypnosis—and, to a much lesser degree, shock—has gained notice as an adjunct to specifically psychoanalytic therapy. This statement does not evaluate these techniques as helpful in therapy generally. They are valuable to *psychoanalysis* in the same way as manipulation of the environment is valuable—that is, in removing stubborn blocks or providing experiences of vivid revelation (*possibly* encouraging also a kind of living through, although this aspect of the therapy is highly limited where by definition the power of the ego is reduced). Most psychoanalysts have come to feel that these techniques are of quite limited value *for psychoanalysis*, however useful they may be in cases unsuitable for full psychoanalytic treatment.

THE DYNAMICS OF PSYCHOANALYTIC THERAPY

Our discussion of the etiology of pathological states and of the techniques of psychoanalysis has constantly skirted the problem of the dynamics of cure: *why*, according to the Freudians, does the patient recover? The following pages, necessarily in large part review, are oriented toward this special problem.

Freud's initial position stressed two points, both of which remain deeply significant despite major shifts in their theoretical setting and elaboration in technique: (1) the recovery of repressed "memories," and (2) the handling of repressed "affects." (The quotation marks are used to emphasize the limitations of Freud's initial formulation.) We have noted Freud's early recognition of the fact that the traumatic "memories" were often fantasies constructed by the child out of his own wishes and fears rather than actual events; hence the development of the libido theory to account for the curious reconstruction of the same type of fantasy in so many patients. The Breuer-Freud formulation of cure resulting from recovery of memory for the traumatic event thus gave way promptly to the more general formulation of recovery from the infantile amnesia resulting from repression of the infantile wishes and fears.

Repression established in early childhood remained the effective cause of neurosis; *release from such repression* was essential to its cure. Remembrance of things past was thus an essential part of psychoanalysis, although the reinstatement of childhood memories was never considered the whole story and now plays a secondary role for many analysts even in the Freudian camp. Alexander quotes an incidental passage from Freud suggesting that it is the result rather than the cause of successful therapy.[13] In so far as the pathological symptoms are conceived as the direct consequence of the exclusion from consciousness of infantile wishes and fears *which remain active as such,* their emergence during the analysis becomes the *sine qua non* of deep analytic therapy.

We shall see in a moment that this emergence takes place mainly via the transference of the original conflict situation to the relationship with the analyst, so that literal remembering of the actual infantile events need not be complete even in classical Freudian theory. Present-day Freudians seem to range all the way from those who merely tolerate the necessity for handling the secondary, defensive elaborations of the patient before coming to grips directly with the significant childhood data to those who are hardly distinguishable from the non-libido analysts in a theoretical and technical emphasis on what the patient has made of the early conflicts. The theoretical dichotomy between the continued, timeless, unchanged infantile unconscious and the patterning in infancy of types of solution for general life problems (the non-libido schools) becomes battered in the actual process of treating patients, once their adult resistances and defenses are recognized. In a theoretically oriented book, however, the different dynamic and hence therapeutic significance of the infantile material should be stated.

Freud's second point concerned *affect*. He observed at once that the repressed memory almost never came to consciousness "cold" and that if it did, no therapeutic result occurred. One could not merely *tell* the patient convincingly about his repressed memories and expect a cure. The process of cure was obviously somehow much more emotionalized. Freud's first idea was that a certain quantum of emotional energy had originally been bound to the repressed situation and remained operative as the motive force behind the repression, constantly seeking expression, until it could finally be worked off. Thus, it was expected that the patient would emote—in more technical language, *abreact*. Psychoanalytic cure was thought to be a sort of *catharsis*.

We have already seen that Freud renounced the idea that libidinal energy was directly convertible into anxiety or that it was so statically bound that it could be handled by an appropriate catharsis. The two cardinal principles of somewhat mechanical recovery of infantile memories and somewhat mechanical abreaction of the emotions attached thereto survive only as the general principles of insight and feeling even among the most classical Freudians. Recognition of the importance of the patient's *feelings* during the analytic hour cannot be overestimated in the dynamics of any school. Freud's own recognition of the problem requires further description of his concept of the dynamics of therapy.

Transference. We have already defined the concept of transference and indicated something of how it is used. As the patient *repeats* in his relations with the analyst the infantile relations with his parents, the buried feelings again find expression and become available for therapeutic manipulation. (This is the classical Freudian position; transference is understood more broadly by some schools.) Freud himself saw the curative aspects of this controlled repetition of the infantile conflict situation as mainly the re-evaluation of the problems by the patient's mature ego, now able—with the benign authority of the doctor as support—to handle consciously the terrors that once motivated the disastrous repression.

Some analysts, notably Ferenczi, felt that this interpretation and its accompanying technique was too intellectualistic. Accepting the basic idea of the transference as a reliving of the infantile situation, Ferenczi came to believe that it should be relived *with a difference directly experienced by the patient*—namely, that as parent-substitute the analyst should supply positive warmth and acceptance. Most patients, according to Ferenczi, fell ill because the real parents were too harsh, or at least the child erected too harsh an image of them. Therefore, the re-experience in analysis should provide a genuine antidote in a new learning situation, as it were, in which the "parent" was actually vividly tender.[14] This formulation seemed to Freud unduly narrow and the ensuing techniques unduly dangerous. Ferenczi's approach is nowhere followed exactly today, but many analysts have taken over the idea of the analysis as essentially a process of living through concrete emotional experiences during treatment, as against the classical Freudian *stress* on conscious insight, which becomes effective through the transference as the patient deals with real feelings rather than intellectual artifacts. Alexander especially emphasizes the importance of corrective emotional experience that occurs when the analyst assumes an objective, understanding attitude "opposite to that of the parents, which caused the neurotic development."[15]

Alexander and his colleagues, like the analysts presented in Part III and many others, tend to see important variations in technique as involving a change in underlying theory. Often they seem to have changed the theory to suit a technique that appears to work well in many instances. Hence, perhaps, the feeling among many of his colleagues is that Alexander is no more "Freudian" than analysts who have formally seceded from the Freudian camp.*

An approach that preserves the essence of Freud's theory and technique while allowing wide variation in practice is that formulated by Eissler.[16] He proposes the term "parameter" for techniques that deviate from Freud's model but that aim at the same goal—namely, a profound structural change in the personality. He tries to use developments in ego psychology to explain the need for variation in the special instance and also the need to return to the basic model as soon as possible.

Freud himself remarked on the need for variation in some instances, notably in the treatment of phobias. Sooner or later, the doctor must *actively*

---

* Alexander is a member of the American Psychoanalytic Association (Freudian), whereas the authors discussed in Parts III and IV are not—except for Sullivan. More important for this book in classifying him among the "libido" analysts is the fact that he has used "libido" terms as major rubrics for research into the dynamics of psychosomatic constellations (incorporation, retention, expulsion, etc.) and has stressed their importance in treatment and in diagnostic evaluation.

require that the phobic patient do what he is afraid to do. The agoraphobic, for example, must come to the office alone. Stekel was so impressed by the success of this *démarche* as to insist that *every* patient come alone from the start, that he be induced to attempt control of his symptoms, whatever their nature. The variation in technique recommended by Freud for phobics at one stage of treatment became for Stekel the basis of a generalized difference in therapeutic approach.

Eissler's concept of the "parameter" allows for variation in technique as radical as any reputable analyst has proposed but he stresses one condition: that the therapist constantly consider how his relationship with the patient, the nature of the transference, is modified by the special technique required for special disorders (not only phobias, but syndromes of delinquency, psychosis, etc.).

It is always difficult, and it may become impossible, for the therapist to reinstate himself in the patient's mind as the neutral, benignly authoritative doctor Freud envisaged as the solid therapeutic force behind the patient's effort to cure himself. At times, it may even be necessary to transfer the patient to another analyst—not because the second analyst has a fundamentally different approach but because the first analyst has become so special a figure in the patient's life that therapeutic detachment is no longer possible. The analyst treating a delinquent or a psychotic, for example, may break all rules of classical analytic treatment in order to meet the problems of such profoundly disturbed patients and bring them to the point of readiness for analytic treatment. It may even be desirable for him to remain in the background as a reassuring or authoritative figure, seeing the patient occasionally if necessary, playing the role of the benignly powerful parent which was somehow missing in the patient's early emotional experience, while the second analyst carries on the task of analysis at a more mature level. In less severe cases, the analyst may merely be alert to the balance between the positive need of the patient for active response from the analyst at some points of the analysis and the general therapeutic need for the encouraging detachment of the doctor which Freud saw as the means of helping the patient toward effective release of unconscious blocks and an independent restructuring of his personality.

Acting Out. The same difference in evaluation of the curative process appears in relation to the problem of *acting out* in the analysis—that is, carrying into action impulses stirred up in the course of treatment. The classical Freudian position argues that so long as the patient *expresses* his impulses, in however disguised a manner, he feels no need to understand them. A tender impulse toward the analyst expressed and accepted on a realistic level dies "analytically" with its gratification, with no furtherance of conscious insight. So also aggression.

A friend of mine described rather resentfully a small episode early in her analysis. She came to the office in a happy mood on a lovely spring day and duly reported a fleeting impulse to buy the doctor a flower from a street vendor she had passed. Her failure to buy the flower became the topic of a long discussion. She maintained that she had properly inhibited the impulse as silly and inappropriate, that the purchase of a flower would have been accepted with an impersonal bow, chilling to the thought of a small shared pleasure. Her analyst used the episode to show her anticipation of his rejection as a concrete demonstration of a much more general anticipation. Very probably he would have reacted to an actual purchase as impersonally as she predicted, but with a different kind of interpretation. Indeed, she would have been a different kind of patient if she were the sort to indulge freely in such friendly whims. Precisely by preventing the realistic consummation of the patient's expectation, the analyst makes the impulse analyzable.

Many analysts nowadays have come to feel that "acting out" is in some measure unavoidable, whether in real life or in the office, and that it should be analyzed rather than prohibited. The pattern of impulse can perhaps be better revealed in its functional complexity than in artificial isolation; the patient learns gradually a better integration of his new insights into his unconscious motivations with his customary modes of reaction. Many analysts would accept the gift of a flower with ordinary appreciation, pleased at the direct demonstration of a freer human relationship, even though it might be necessary to point out further implications in the small gesture. Everyone agrees that the patient must be protected against socially unacceptable license caused by a temporary relaxation of strict ego or superego control, both for the sake of his reality commitments and because the patient may frighten himself back into his old defenses if partial release is achieved earlier than adequate assimilation of improved methods of control.

Above all, the patient must not be allowed to interpret bits of "acting out" as a true resolution of his problems, even when his behavior is positively good. For example, the patient might be so heartened by the analyst's approval of her buying a flower and similar gestures successfully carried out in real life as to believe prematurely that her fear of rejection had been cured.

As usual, it is impossible to know exactly what goes on in the privacy of the office, but probably the majority of analysts now accept *some* "acting out" as useful material, provided only that it is adequately interpreted. The patient as a whole is handled *in statu vivendi* and is not considered as a set of infantile repressions in need of cautious release.

Resistance. The problem of *resistance* was disregarded in our discussion of techniques because it is too complex for treatment at a superficial level. It will be remembered that Freud observed almost at once that *something* kept the patient from effectively grasping the truths about himself which had become apparent to the analyst. Examples have already been given of the cruder forms of resistance in the analytic hour: coming late, forgetting appointments, short or long periods of blocking in free association, abrupt failure to dream or to remember dreams, argumentativeness, etc., etc. The point may be carried further here. Freud came to realize that almost any phase of the analytic process, even dreaming, *may* be used by the patient as active resistance. I remember my gratified interest when my dreams suddenly became so "Freudian" that their symbolism was to me a convincingly patent demonstration of my infantile libido concerns—and how dashed I was when my Freudian analyst as suddenly brushed them aside as not worth analyzing. Instead he suggested that my unconscious was merely having a bit of fun at his expense in a mocking dream-conformance to his presumed expectations. The same phenomenon in another patient, or in myself at a different phase, might be interpreted as a desire to please the analyst, or perhaps merely to escape true interpretation by using the analytic concepts and familiar symbols themselves in an intellectualized manner, short-circuiting, as it were, their proper psychological value.

Childhood memories may be used in the same way to *avoid* recognition of unconscious forces. Weeping over a doll broken at the age of five *may* be nothing but pure sentimentality, or a kind of fruitless acting out, or a means of dodging consideration of problems that were coming uncomfortably close to consciousness. I remember sometimes going to the analytic hour with my mind a complete blank, no dream to report, no significant event of the day before, and semideliberately returning to an intriguing childhood episode left incomplete some time back. Occasionally I got away with it—presumably because the episode was "really" important and "really" there was nothing more immediate on the agenda. More often, the Freudian analyst did not accept this *démarche.* "What were we talking about yesterday?" he might ask, and I would find I had honestly forgotten a very important topic. The most impressive part of such a tale is that a patient intellectually sophisticated about the mechanism of resistance, paying more than she can afford per hour, nevertheless semiconsciously casts about for another red herring. I was by no means unique; many patients act in this way. Since the non-Freudian analysts often write as though they had discovered the use of dreams and childhood material as resistance, this personal testimony of failure to gull a classical Freudian with dreams and memories may be of especial interest. Anything *can* be resistance, and *any* skilled analyst knows it.

Resistance, then, is an *active force* in any type of analysis. What are its dynamics and the principles of handling it? Here there is more divergence among analytic schools, and we are again confronted with the observation that the practice of any analyst cannot be predicted with assurance from his theoretical allegiances. "Secondary" resistances may dictate the line of therapy quite as effectively and in much the same terms as when the same phenomena are labeled "primary" in the theoretical scheme.

As usual, Freud's position is the most complex. He tried—eventually—to differentiate among the various sources of resistance according to his structural approach. Id and superego are behind many resistance phenomena on two counts: (1) The analytic process may threaten a source of disguised gratification. The id impulse itself then presses the more urgently for gratification elsewhere or works against destruction of the disguise. Obviously, this resistance is in no way conscious and can be seen only through its pressure on the ego, which then may become especially fanciful in its protests against the analyst, *e.g.*, through crude rationalizations or the other resistance phenomena suggested. (2) The superego controls (conscience) may be undermined to the point at which they must again be buttressed by the primitive anxieties that brought them into existence, or the relaxation of ego controls over id impulses may indirectly increase the alertness of the superego by reawakening the basic castration anxiety—or whatever. At first Freud was concerned mainly with the drama among the id impulses and their very close derivatives as the main source of resistance, whereas the ego was conceived of as a fairly ineffectual mediator. Later the superego and more recently the ego itself have been seen as major dynamic factors in resistance.

In a strict sense, all resistance is ego resistance, since intellection and the motorium are exclusively under ego control. In a practical sense, id and superego resistance refer to the major dynamics behind the performance of the ego. *Ego* resistance *as such,* is considered as referring to the whole complex of defense mechanisms erected by the ego during the life of the patient. Freud himself paved the way toward recognition of this type of organized resistance, but his followers, notably his daughter Anna, have carried insight into its nature much further. Anna Freud remarks upon the initial concentration of psychoanalysis on uncovering id materials in contrast to later concern with how they function *in relation to the ego,* which alone allows access to them and which requires study in its own right.*

A line of defense, once it is adopted by the ego, becomes a more or less coherent system in itself. If the little boy handles his castration fear by being

* So does Freud himself, but Anna Freud elaborated upon Freud's idea. (A. Freud, *The Ego and the Mechanisms of Defence,* Hogarth Press, 1937, pp. 3*f.*).

a big strong man himself, then anything that interferes with his self-esteem system becomes a serious threat. The fantasy of football hero may change to a fantasy of a great author[17] and may in adulthood present an almost infrangible front of power-striving—rooted in rivalry and fear of failure. Any psychoanalytic interpretation that in his eyes lowers his sense of power is then automatically rejected as positively disastrous. This may mean *any interpretation whatsoever,* if the analyst-patient relationship is construed by the patient as an example of power relationships. The analyst may be correct in interpreting the patient's objection to lying on the couch as fear of his passive homosexual wishes—correct at some deep level of the id. But the patient does not usually resist such an interpretation initially because his *id and superego* are aroused— not unless the patient is psychotic or a borderline homosexual. The interpretation would not *initially* reach the id or superego at all, and if the analyst were so foolish as to proffer it, he is entitled to the punch in the jaw he might well receive *from the patient's ego.* Ultimate correctness in terms of origin and continuing force at a deep level does not fully guarantee the correctness of an interpretation of the main determinants of current behavior. The constellative power of the ego gives established defense mechanisms value in their own right. Interpretations that threaten a firmly elaborated defense system are resisted as such, not because the id impulse which originally conditioned the development of the system is anywhere near irruption into consciousness. The patient is not, *at this point of the analysis,* protecting himself against recognition of his latent homosexuality. He is resisting the idea that he is not a big strong man, the false premise on which he has built his life adjustment.

As Freudians came to recognize the independent power of these false premises—the ego resistances, character problems—their first inclination was to devote a period early in the treatment to disposal of this excess baggage as a preliminary to genuine psychoanalysis. It became apparent somewhat later, however, that ego resistances were not easily handled, even when recognized by doctor and patient. A new step in analysis of the infantile libido naturally resisted by the patient tended to provoke a resurgence of the entire system of ego resistance so carefully disposed of in preliminary treatment. Or a new kind of ego system developed which was still patently defensive. At no point did the patient's ego become a stable, mature, socialized, reality-oriented entity, hampered here and there by incursions from the repressed infantile unconscious. Character analysis became a *continuing* part of every analysis, no matter how prominent the neurotic symptoms.

Working Through. An important phase of the therapeutic procedure is called *working through.* It was early recognized that the flash of insight, even when accompanied by the appropriate emotional reactions, did not establish the cure. Full cure demanded a thorough, detailed and *repetitive* working through of all aspects of the neurosis in the analytic sessions. Originally the concept applied mainly to tracing the ramifications of the infantile conflicts through their essential derivatives at the unconscious level—not once and partially in a sudden episode of abreaction but over and over from many angles and in full complexity the neurotic defenses must be undone. "The ego [must be educated] to tolerate less and less distorted derivatives."[18]

The concept of *working through* the same problems from many directions with fullness of insight and feeling is in a way the quintessence of psychoanalytic cure. Almost any method can achieve a "cure" when the therapeutic device happens to release a specific block, or when a defense mechanism is turned to more fruitful channels. The aim of psychoanalysis is fundamental change in the personality, such that the patient is released from neurotic hangovers (pathogenic defenses) and can confront the realistic problems of his life as a mature human being. This aim is admittedly grandiose to an impossible degree, but its approximation is the goal of a full analysis. To establish firmly a basic change in the personality, the analyst feels that all the important ramifications and derivatives of the neurotic problem must be worked through, and worked through by the tedious route of full insight and feeling on the part of the patient.

Freudians often feel that partial failure or relapse in an essentially successful analysis is due to the fact that some areas of infantile conflict have not been sufficiently worked through. It was observed, for example, that the passive homosexual phase in the development of a boy had not been emphasized enough in theory and was often neglected in practice when it presented no special problems at the time of the analysis. Some analysts (Bergler with especial fervor)[19] point to a universal masochistic trend which ought to be unmasked in *every* analysis.

It is a difficult practical—and even ethical—problem for the analyst to decide whether he should actually *provoke* a sense of problem on the part of the patient in areas that are causing no trouble at the moment and that may be expected to remain quiescent. A young man with the psychosomatic symptom of "gasping," severe work inhibitions, and fear of women was brought to the point of establishing a happy marriage and vocational success. His "gasping" had ceased. He naturally wished to terminate an expensive treatment in order to devote himself more to his new career. The analyst felt that powerful longings for dependency and total care had not been adequately worked through. In this case, the analyst felt in particular that the patient might not be able to tolerate the joys of fatherhood. In fact, there had been some hint of lively difficulties when his wife became pregnant, but since a miscarriage occurred almost immediately, with consequent shift in the patient's emotional constellation, little opportunity had been offered to work through the basic attitudes involved. Moreover, it looked as though the wife would be unable to have a child, as though the current life situation would protect the patient against having to handle this area of difficulty—indeed, it seemed that his job and marriage were as stable as anything one may expect in a troubled world. The patient was therefore dismissed, with a warning that further treatment might become necessary. Eventually the wife did carry through a successful pregnancy. The patient gave her devoted care, with minor exacerbation of his own troubles, up to the appearance of his baby-rival. At this point his symptoms returned with such effulgence that further analytic treatment was unavoidable.[20]

FREUD'S SUMMARY

"Analysis Terminable and Interminable." In a brilliant paper written late in his career, Freud remarks that it is scarcely feasible for the analyst to institute *on his own initiative* the degree of emotional participation necessary for genuine therapy on points that are not otherwise vivid for the patient.[21] The analyst is required to cover the major active derivatives of the neurosis. Should he hunt out *potential* trouble spots? Should the analyst in our example have somehow forced recognition of neurotic needs which the patient did not see and which actually were not significantly determining in a life situation apparently substantial enough as life situations go? It should be remembered that giving the patient intellectual sophistication on such points does not achieve a therapeutic result. The dormant neurotic conflict must be deliberately activated, at considerable expense of time, effort, and suffering. In practice, it has usually seemed preferable to accept the imperfections of the analysis, releasing the patient when the major difficulties have been resolved and accepting the fact that further treatment may become necessary if the life situation so changes as to arouse the hitherto dormant conflicts.

Freud points to the importance of *quantitative* relations in the psychic economy. In our example, the birth of a child introduced a relatively novel set of emotional problems for the patient which he was not prepared to handle. Difficulties may also arise when the ego has to cope with a very severe threat along lines already treated. The increase in the force of id impulses during puberty or at the climacteric, for example, may render inadequate ego controls established during the analysis which were quite sufficient in ordinary circumstances. Freud describes the case of a woman who had been successfully cured of an incapacitating pain of hysterical origin and who had remained "cured" for years under very adverse circumstances. Her family lost their money, and the ex-patient valiantly supported her relatives, withstanding her own disappointment in the shattered hopes of marriage and personal happiness she might reasonably have expected. Some twelve years after her analysis, she had to undergo a hysterectomy, an event very likely to reawaken the conflicts behind the original neurosis, at a time when her defenses must have been weakened by the factual frustrations of her life situation. At this time she had a breakdown, from which she never recovered. Freud is "inclined to think that, but for the fresh trauma, there would have been no second outbreak of neurosis."[22] It is important to note that the second illness followed not upon stress *as such* but upon a piling up of stresses in the area which the patient was least able to handle, far beyond ordinary expectation of misfortune.

In this paper, Freud gently protests the optimism of analysts who feel that a "completed" analysis immunizes the patient against any further emotional difficulties. The working through, he points out, is never complete. Handling of the problems active during treatment and their major ramifications can scarcely hope to be exhaustive. It is difficult and probably unwise to stir up a pathogenic conflict of which there is no present indication.[23] "For the most part our theoretical concepts have failed to give the same importance to the economic as to the dynamic and topographical aspects of the case. So my excuse [for a lengthy discussion] must be that I am drawing attention to this omission."[24] In this compact sentence, Freud reviews scattered comments throughout his work on the significance of the quantitative interrelationships among the psychological trends whose dynamics he did so much to clarify. He abates none of the force of the dynamic concepts discussed throughout the chapters of this book. More clearly than many of his followers, he came to realize the profound importance of the *weight* of impact at any given moment of the various separate components of the dynamic constellation.

Freud writes: "We know that the essence of the analytic situation is that the analyst enters into an alliance with the ego of the patient to subdue certain uncontrolled parts of the id, *i.e.* to include them in the synthesis of the ego."[25] In this chapter we have talked about insight and feeling (abreaction) and transference and resistance and working through as the ingredients of psychoanalysis. They come together in the *synthesis by the ego of the patient,* supported by the analyst. We have seen that insight at the purely intellectual level of ego function does not cure by itself and may even be used as resistance against cure. We have seen that abreaction of a specific repressed emotion gives at best local relief and may be dangerous. The amnesia of an essentially normal adult under severe, clear-cut stress with consequent bizarre symptoms may be cleared up quite easily by a great variety of techniques ranging from common sense through the whole galaxy of isms. The "fundamental change in personality" envisaged by the psychoanalysts turns out to be a change in the whole *stance of the ego* toward the demands of the id and superego and intercurrent reality pressures.

Freud came to realize the importance of variations in the ego itself, constitutional or acquired, which profoundly influence the reaction of the patient to analysis. In 1937 he spoke of an "imaginary" normal ego[26]—in definite modification of the period during which he naively assumed that the ego was somehow a fairly stable entity on which the analyst could rely unless it was very seriously impaired by constitutional intellectual defect, psychosis, or character disorder. Freud accepts analysis of ego defenses as half the task of psychoanalysis, the other half being analysis of the hidden materials of the id. "Our therapeutic work swings to and fro during the treatment like a pendulum, analysing now a fragment of the id and now a fragment of the ego. In the one case our aim is to bring a part of the id into consciousness and in the other to correct something in the ego."[27] The ego itself resists cure, at an unconscious level, and the analyst may become simply "an alien personality" making disagreeable demands. It is essential that the analyst understand and interpret the ego defense mechanisms at their own level of integration—and that he preserve so far as possible the "positive transference" (attitude of affectionate trust in the doctor) which is the strongest support to the patient and his "strongest motive for co-operating in the work of the analysis."[28]

Critical Comment

IT WOULD be presumptuous indeed for a layman to attempt detailed criticism of procedures in a highly skilled medical specialty.* From the outside, we can observe that there are striking failures— by all the varieties in technical approach outlined in this chapter and by the non-libido schools to be discussed in Part III. In a general way, of course, the criterion

of a good therapy must be in its record of cures. Molière's satire on doctors who prefer that the patient die according to the rules of the profession rather than get well in an unorthodox manner is still cogent.

Yet the problem of validation by therapeutic success is complex. One aspect of the problem is the nature of the illness treated. It is no more correct to lump mental disorders together for overall validation of therapy than to subject the treatment of all physical diseases to a single criterion. Some disorders which may look quite dreadful to the outsider

* For an excellent and relatively nontechnical discussion of these problems by an important psychoanalyst, I refer the reader to R. P. Knight, "An Evaluation of Psychotherapeutic Techniques," *Bulletin of the Menninger Clinic*, 1952, 16:113-124.

are very easy to handle by almost any method—on the analogy of measles, simple fractures, some pneumonias. Others are intrinsically more resistant to treatment, or at least are not well understood by anyone at present. The cancer specialist has a higher rate of mortality among his patients than the pediatrician, but one does not therefore consider him a less skillful doctor.

Another aspect of the problem is the question of what one considers a "cure." If a musician recovers from a hysterical paralysis of his arm, the result appears very convincing. But he may have developed blinding headaches, or he may be thoroughly exasperating to his manager and his family. A compulsive patient may give up his flagrant rituals but become so difficult to live with as to place an intolerable burden on his wife, often demanding constant small concessions which *appear* reasonable or trivial but which effectively enslave his intimate associates. Are these really cures?

Or let us consider the not infrequent instance of the patient who keeps running back to the analyst whenever difficulties arise or who repeatedly seeks out new therapists. These cases seem to support the idea that the analyst has not liberated the patient from the dependency which is an almost inevitable phase of treatment. Sometimes the blame does, indeed, rest with the analyst. Very often, however, the explanation lies in the nature of the illness. Some personalities are no more able to become thoroughly independent than some heart conditions can do without drugs administered under supervision of the doctor. If such a patient is enabled to live a fairly normal life most of the time, with the analyst as a continuing bulwark against overwhelming anxiety, then the role of the analyst seems positively constructive. The alternative may be a mental hospital, social failure, or other forms of destructive invalidism.

Furthermore, the external situation of the patient plays an important role in the success or failure of treatment, often in ways that cannot be anticipated. Two examples were quoted earlier—Freud's "cured" hysteric who broke after a hysterectomy following upon a lifetime of serious frustration, and the man whose symptoms recurred after the (unexpected) birth of a son. Conversely, an unusually favorable external situation may mask the continuance of underlying neurotic problems. And, to mention still another complication, the superficial cure of a severely handicapping symptom may in some instances so improve the external situation of the patient as to relieve him from many of the secondary environmental pressures which had strained his "defenses" to the breaking point. Thus, the symptomatic cure may itself create the favorable situation which allows deeper problems to remain inoperative. Not infrequently, indeed, such an effect may so shift the orientation of the personality that the very partial "cure" established at the end of treatment becomes consolidated and extended in a genuinely profound sense.

One may summarize these difficulties in evaluating a therapeutic approach on the basis of its "success" by stressing the very imperfect correlation between the way in which the patient behaves in life situations and the dynamics underlying his behavior. To some extent, the same problem is encountered in physical ailments. The period in my own life when I looked and even felt most superbly healthy (plump, rosy, with a fund of unused energy) was the time when I was confined to bedrest by heartless doctors for minimal tuberculosis—indicated by nothing more than small shadows observable in x-rays and slight noises audible through the stethoscope. Much more is known about specific physical diseases, however, than about mental disorders. And there is much greater trust in the special knowledge of the doctor. Few laymen would rely on their impression of the physical health of the patient against the careful examination of a physician or would see anything surprising in protection for a case of tuberculosis despite the fact that the patient looks and feels perfectly well.

Let us not forget that *any* sort of specialized care for the mentally ill is scarcely more than a century old and that a fruitfully dynamic approach is scarcely more than 50 years old, even if one dates it from its limited and highly controversial beginnings. Let us not forget that we are now calling "mental illness" not only the extreme disorders of frank madness but those smaller distortions previously known as eccentricity or plain wickedness. And, finally, let us not forget that mental illness involves the most flexible aspects of the organism, in which substitutions of one overt pattern of behavior for another can be made with the greatest facility and without change in underlying dynamics. In view of these factors, any *simple* validation by therapeutic success seems childish, whether judgment rests upon what happened to a couple of our friends in analysis or upon elaborate statistical data. One must always ask the further questions: What kind of case was treated? How did the patient make out in later years, in what kind of situation?

This discussion undermines at once the scientific standing of all schools that claim success for all types of patient indiscriminately by the same therapeutic method. We have seen, for example, that it is not *safe* to encourage all comers to release repressions which form a major part of their ego defenses without the very careful guidance of a skilled therapist. Although many patients are unable to achieve such release under the conditions of dianetic therapy (and so remain unharmed if unbenefited), some borderline psychotics are especially susceptible to conditions leading to the emergence of primitive unconscious materials. Such emergence may easily swamp their relatively fragile defense systems, thus precipitating a psychotic breakdown.

Psychoanalysis itself suffered from such incautious generalizations in its earlier years and is not entirely free of them at present. Freud himself learned a differentiated approach only through experience with patients for whom his early formulations were either futile or positively harmful. One of the most remarkable things about this genius is that he *did* learn throughout a very long career, and he guided most of his followers toward a highly complex view of human functioning. He underrated the effect of environmental *systems* on dynamic processes typical for cultural groups, and he himself never fully surmounted a concentration on libidinal forces which he acknowledged to be excessive, but he made a firm place in theory for the elaboration of a more satisfactory ego psychology such as is now taking place within the Freudian group. There are still "classical" Freudians who seem fixated at stages of the libido theory more rigidly than Freud himself. There are purists who defend the letter rather than the spirit of Freud's recommendations for therapeutic technique, who therefore oppose indiscriminately all new adjuncts and modifications in treatment. Yet, under the guise of analysis of defenses and psychoanalytically oriented psychotherapy, even the conservative die-hards very often *use* the new modifications quite as freely as the rebels and contribute toward their development.

One may also suggest that the large conservative element in the American Psychoanalytic Association prevents the rebels from throwing out the baby with the bath and tends to preserve the essential values of the libido theory and of Freud's view of psychoanalysis as a method. Controversy within the Association is disquieting to the onlooker, and it sometimes seems as though the established Freudians took an unduly long time to recognize the value of corrections and elaborations loudly proclaimed by outsiders in variety. Nevertheless, the net result seems to be a complex theoretical approach fundamentally unified in its diversity and capable of assimilating new ideas of great magnitude.

The libido theory narrowly construed as the distribution of energies proceeding from the erogenous zones has long become outmoded. I have urged the point that "energies" of similar nature (*i.e.*, in my vocabulary, the tendency of a functioning system to function systematically) are derived from other bodily apparatuses and undergo processes of consolidation in their own right as well as in relation to the sexual libido and to systematic pressures from the milieu. The theoretical summary of this supplement to the libido theory is my own, but it summarizes points heavily stressed by Freudians in variety under the general label of ego psychology.

I have myself tried to preserve the libido theory, narrowly defined, as an essential *part* of an effective "view of systems." This *part* of the many systematizations of the human psyche was worked out in detail by Freud and the Freudians. I think it cannot be discarded. Freud himself very clearly pointed the way toward investigation of other *parts* of the psyche as they become consolidated in the course of experience. His formulation of the "economic" aspect of personality integration, whereby operative dynamics might shift dramatically with varying *quantitative* pressures from within or without allows for attention to all sorts of system dynamics at any given moment—or over protracted periods in different cultures.

I urge a substitute criterion for validation of a therapeutic approach by its therapeutic success. That approach is most valid scientifically—and ultimately in practice—which can best *explain* its successes and its failures; which can most adequately use its failures to introduce corrections and elaborations honestly integrated with its basic theories.

There is no necessary correlation between the correctness of a theory and its success in producing "cures."

In concluding the Part on the schools which essentially accept the libido theory, it is perhaps well to answer a question often asked of me: "Are you a Freudian?" People seem to want to have the author somehow *placed* as to general school orientation, if only to evaluate her bias in reporting.

My answer is "Yes, I am a Freudian in general orientation." Partly this statement is merely an acknowledgment of Freud's profoundly important contribution to all psychoanalytic and psychological thought, an acknowledgment made even by the rebel schools. My answer goes further, to include Freud's specific ideas and their later developments within the framework of the American and the International Psychoanalytic Associations.

Emphasis on the libido theory is more a matter of the historical development of psychoanalytic schools than a problem intrinsic to psychoanalysis. It takes its place along with Freud's genetic, topographical, structural, and economic approaches, with the theory of aggression, with insight into defense mechanisms, and, finally, with a maturing ego psychology. I hold no brief for a libido theory which reduces psychological science to the push of the sexual instincts and the aggressive instinct. Neither did Freud. His approach is essentially multidimensional. It is not *tied to* simple "universals" but operates through a series of *quasi*-universals whose intrinsic dynamics and major relationships it attempts to understand with increasing perspicacity as new data come to hand. It is multidimensional without losing sight of dynamics. It can correct over- and under-emphases without loss of its general integrity.

[1] J. Breuer and S. Freud, *Studies in Hysteria,* Nervous and Mental Disease Publishing Co., 1936.
[2] *Cf.* J. Dollard *et al.,* Frustration and Aggression, Yale University Press, 1939.
[3] O. Fenichel, *The Psychoanalytic Theory of Neurosis,* W. W. Norton & Co., 1945, p. 275.
[4] See especially F. J. Kallman, "The Genetic

Theory of Schizophrenia," *American Journal of Psychiatry*, 1946, *103*:309-322.

[5] L. Bender and H. Yarnell, "An Observation Nursery," *American Journal of Psychiatry*, 1941, *97*:1158-1174.

[6] S. Ferenczi, "The Further Development of an Active Therapy in Psycho-Analysis," in S. Ferenczi, *Further Contributions to the Theory and Technique of Psycho-Analysis*, 2nd ed., Hogarth Press, 1950, pp. 214f. W. Reich, *Character-Analysis*, 2nd ed., Orgone Institute Press, 1945.

[7] O. Fenichel, *op. cit.*, p. 538.

[8] *Cf.* C. Thompson, *Psychoanalysis: Evolution and Development*, Hermitage House, 1950.

[9] *Cf.* B. Mittelmann and H. G. Wolff, "Emotions and Gastroduodenal Function," *Psychosomatic Medicine*, 1942, *4*:5-61.

[10] B. Mittelmann, "The Concurrent Analysis of Married Couples," *Psychoanalytic Quarterly*, 1948, *17*:182-197.

[11] R. R. Grinker, "The Use of Narcosynthesis in War Neurosis," in F. Alexander and T. M. French (eds.), *Psychoanalytic Therapy*, Ronald Press Co., 1946, pp. 325-337.

[12] F. Alexander and T. M. French (eds.), *op. cit.*, pp. 38ff.

[13] F. Alexander, "The Development of Psychoanalytic Therapy," in F. Alexander and T. M. French (eds.), *loc. cit.*, p. 21.

[14] S. Ferenczi, "The Principle of Relaxation and Neocatharsis," *International Journal of Psycho-Analysis*, 1930, *11*:428-443.

[15] F. Alexander, *Fundamentals of Psychoanalysis*, W. W. Norton & Co., 1948, p. 299.

[16] K. R. Eissler, "The Effect of the Structure of the Ego on Psychoanalytic Technique," *Journal of the American Psychoanalytic Association*, 1953, *1*:104-143.

[17] A. Freud, *The Ego and the Mechanisms of Defence*, Hogarth Press, 1937, pp. 106f.

[18] O. Fenichel, *op. cit.*, p. 572.

[19] E. Bergler, *The Basic Neurosis*, Grune & Stratton, 1949.

[20] Personal communication.

[21] S. Freud, "Analysis Terminable and Interminable," *Collected Papers*, Vol. V, Hogarth Press, 1950, pp. 332ff.

[22] *Ibid.*, p. 324.

[23] *Ibid.*, pp. 332ff.

[24] *Ibid.*, p. 328.

[25] *Ibid.*, p. 337.

[26] *Ibid.*, p. 342.

[27] *Ibid.*, p. 341.

[28] *Ibid.*, p. 335.

Part Three

ADLER, HORNEY, FROMM, AND SULLIVAN

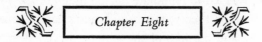
THE TERMS OF THE
ORGANISM

THE FOLLOWING FIVE CHAPTERS present, in a manner homologous with the five chapters preceding, a different view of psychoanalytic theory. Chapter 1 explained the broad distinction made in this book between analytic schools that essentially accept the libido theory and those that essentially reject it. For the purpose of this somewhat arbitrary dichotomy, the libido theory is *very* loosely defined as an emphasis on infantile sexuality—or, indeed, any native biological drives—in the formulation of basic psychological theory—in contrast to an emphasis on the human self and its interpersonal experience. The dichotomy is surely artificial, but it has a historical cogency which cannot be ignored at the present time and which is likely to persist for many years.

One of the most promising in the knot of young doctors who gathered weekly in Freud's home in the early 1900's to discuss the exciting new discoveries of psychoanalysis was Alfred Adler. He was the first to break from the master and to found a school of his own, which he called Individual Psychology.

There can be little doubt that personal factors contributed to the breach. Freud ascribes it to the rivalry of the father-son relationship. Adler, following his own theory of the family drama, comments that Freud was a typical eldest son, whereas he himself was a second son. The breach was unfortunate for both men. It seems clear that in his zeal to emphasize the uniqueness of his new school, Adler was led to repudiate far too much of the Freudian doctrine, notably the entire libido theory, much of Freud's careful investigation of unconscious processes, and portions of the genetic process deemed significant by Freud in accordance with the libido theory. Perhaps Freud, for his part, became more narrowly insistent on these aspects of his approach. One may suspect that ego psychology developed relatively late in the Freudian school not only because Freud was too busy laying the groundwork of the libido theory but also because he actively resisted the "superficial" ideas and practices of his erstwhile pupil. For I take the major contributions of Adler to be an emphasis on social and interpersonal factors in personality function, and the initiation of a psychoanalytic approach to the study of "character."

We have seen that for Freud psychological data found their anchor in biology. Parents, the family, society are necessary to the Freudian scheme, but the influence of special types of experience is not elaborated so much for its effects on the self or ego development as it is for the vicissitudes of sexuality in the broad sense. To the strict Freudian, these conditions of human function seem to be the stuff of common sense for the therapist, at most fairly well-codified derivative phenomena or defense mechanisms which the therapist is trained to take into consideration.

But these "derivative" phenomena are the mainspring of Adlerian dynamics. Drawing attention to the experiences of the young child in mastering his environment as the prototype of his later behavior, Adler built a coherent theory of personality development and function primarily out of attitudes toward the self and toward other persons, toward society.

Two contemporary schools of psychoanalysis, the Association for the Advancement of Psychoanalysis (Horney) and the William Alanson White Foundation (Sullivan), take a position similar to Adler's in that the *primary* dynamic principles are seen in interpersonal relations and efforts at *self-*maintenance, and the primacy of the more specific biological demands so heavily stressed by Freud is repudiated. Fromm is a member of the faculty at the latter institute, but his *special* influence derives mainly from independent books, lectures, and teaching. These schools owe no direct allegiance to Adler. Historically, they represent new revolts from Freud on a more sophisticated level and the independent influence of Adolf Meyer, rather than an expansion of the Adlerian position. Nevertheless, for the purposes of this book, the theoretical additions seem to belong here rather than in the Freudian section.*

* After long hesitation I have decided not to report the views of another rebel, Sandor Rado,

Individual Psychology (Adler's school) had an immediate influence on people outside the analytic profession: on teachers, doctors, criminologists, and the man in the street. This was partly because Adler himself devoted much time to writing and lecturing for the general public and encouraged his followers to direct practical application of his ideas in schools, juvenile courts, and guidance clinics for children and adults. Partly, however, his theories are closer to common sense and common observation, and hence easier to assimilate. People accustomed to remark that "Johnny's nose is out of joint" after the birth of his new brother, could readily grasp the importance of "sibling rivalry." The "inferiority complex" was a gratifying phrase for the uneasiness most of us feel in an individualistic and highly competitive society. Adler's therapeutic approach was sympathetic and direct, consciously using a large measure of open encouragement. People found it, therefore, more immediately appealing than the shocking "pan-sexualism" and "pessimism" of Freud. And it *seemed* much quicker.

It is probably not accidental that the two contemporary schools included in this section also have a large "lay" following. Their theories, too, are *relatively* easy to understand and to incorporate with ideas derived from other sources about the nature of man, for much the same reasons.

Almost all of Adler's specific formulations have become part of the common stock of ideas—one might even say, the stock of clichés. His fate is like that of Heine, whose little masterpiece *The Lorelei* attained such prompt popularity that when he himself asked a group of people singing it for the name of the author, he was told, "Why nobody wrote it—it's a folk song." Societies for Individual Psychology and a professional journal still exist, but with comparatively little scientific status or extensive popular following. *As a system,* the Adlerian theory is no longer vivid.*

Yet I think the reader will find it useful to set the current Adlerian clichés back into the context of his system. The fragmentation of his ideas either in popular adoption or in scientific criticism by his peers was a source of great personal irritation to Adler, and he was justified. He had a vision of how the personality functions as a whole in a social milieu, and this vision has been recaptured by the other psychoanalysts now under discussion. Inevitably,

in this book. The decision requires defense, because Rado was for many years educational director of the New York Psychoanalytic Institute, and later at Columbia University. He has had extensive influence on psychoanalytic thought in our decades.

Rado's approach has been called *adaptational psychodynamics.* I like the name and much of what Rado says, but he has not yet published an over-all view of his position. He changes his terminology rather frequently, and I do not feel that a few technical articles in the field of psychiatry can justify the kind of reporting accorded to the other analysts in Part III.

* I am told that a sort of renascence is now beginning. Certainly other psychoanalytic schools speak more appreciatively of Adler now than they did a few years ago.

Adler made mistakes. So, undoubtedly, have the others. Since they are still in active controversy with one another and exhibit an entirely admirable tendency to change their own minds, it seems helpful to use Adler's *system* as the point of departure. His very shortcomings are valuable in pointing up the crucial problems that have been handled by contemporaries in a more satisfactory manner, but perhaps not with complete success.

It has seemed to me desirable to treat as something of a unit the authors who essentially share Adler's emphasis on the self and interpersonal relations and repudiate the constellating power of the sexual instincts as biologically determined. I believe that one may thus see in sharper perspective the values and limitations of this whole orientation, as contrasted with the theories I have called "Freudian" because they retain this fundamental aspect of Freud's position. The "Freudian" usually characterizes the psychologies presented in Part III as *ego* psychologies. These are concerned with developments and conflicts within a single system—namely, the ego as defined by Freud*—and neglect conflicts with other systems—the id and superego. Appreciation of the *values* of careful investigation and astute handling of ego conflicts is growing rapidly in the Freudian camp, as we have seen. For the "Freudian," the common *limitation* of all the authors discussed in Part III is their failure to give due weight to the psychological importance of trends rooted in the biological functions of the organism—that is, to the libido and the instinct of aggression.

In fairness to these schools, it seems desirable to state that I share the "Freudian" view on this point. Out of deference to current interest and my own feeling for the *usability* of the "ego psychologies" in the social sciences, I have described them in far greater detail than the contemporary "Freudian" variants of the libido theory. I believe, however, that the reader will gain a clearer perspective toward psychoanalysis as a whole if he considers these schools as variations upon the theme of the "self" in its personal and interpersonal aspects rather than as a series of quite separate theoretical systems to be adopted or rejected as a whole.

The material is so arranged and labeled that the reader can, if he prefers, read everything about each author sequentially instead of following my chapter organization. Since these authors have largely neglected to make an elaborately differentiated approach to the terms of the organism, I have used this

---

* The reader is reminded that "ego" is a very slippery word. I use it *here* in the Freudian sense of an institution developed by the personality. (See Chap. 3, especially pp. 86*f*.) I shall often use it loosely to mean simply the person-as-a-whole (a loose usage all too well justified by the authors I quote), and in some chapters—the one on Jung, for example—I shall have to ask the reader to learn a new, quite special definition.

I shall try to keep the contextual meanings of the word clear, but the reader's understanding of its current "polyguities" must be my main safeguard. The neologism is intended to suggest that the word has several quite clear meanings, in addition to loose usage.

first chapter as a sort of advance summary of their main theoretical position, somewhat beyond a strict biological definition of its subject matter. Because their approach to *the genetic process* is undifferentiated, this chapter groups all the authors together for a brief and rather critical discussion. They are grouped together again in the chapter on treatment, since I found it quite impossible to present a fair picture of treatment procedures for any one school, based primarily on its theoretical divergencies from the others. In fact, it seemed necessary to bring "Freudian" approaches back into the discussion very prominently. For the layman learning about psychoanalysis, the similarities are here much more important than the differences. I have tried to make clear the variations in *emphasis* from school to school, while explaining further what they *all* essentially mean by psychoanalysis as a therapeutic method.

ADLER

LIKE ALL PSYCHOANALYSTS, Adler makes a bow to constitutional and hereditary factors, but his bow is perfunctory. His real efforts were devoted to showing how traits commonly considered inborn are usually determined in the life history of the person. In practice, Adler's approach was radically oriented toward the terms of the milieu—that is, toward the environmental situation encountered by the child.

Adler's earliest personal contribution was a study of the effects of "organ inferiority," often a congenital bodily defect, on personality formation. Later on, other aspects of the developmental situation—such as pressures due to the attitudes of parents and siblings—came to outweigh in importance the specifically organic anomalies; but he never renounced his earlier observations. At first glance, the stress on physical defects appears to pertain to the terms of the organism rather than the terms of the milieu. Yet Adler derived his psychology not from biological constitution itself but rather from *the attitude the person adopted toward his defects.* Favorite examples are Demosthenes, who became a great orator in compensation for an early defect in speech; Annette Kellerman, who became a champion swimmer not so much despite as because of bodily weakness; the limping Nurmi, who became a famous runner. Stutterers other than Demosthenes have sometimes used their defect as a devious means of preserving in fantasy their inflated longings for prestige against wounding encounters with reality. What might they have become, if they had not stuttered!

Thus, where the Freudian sees the physical problem of stuttering as the malfunction of an organ because of psychological patterns developed primarily around biological impulses toward oral gratification, for Adler such a physical problem is important only as it becomes a focus for striving or self-protection, the roots of which are otherwise determined. The focus is not always so "conscious" as in the case of Demosthenes. The child who is unconsciously afraid to go to school may vomit every morning because his stomach happens to be his weakest organ. Where the Freudian very often sees in this symptom a specific kind of defense reaction, the Adlerian usually sees merely the organic disability which most quickly reflects a general state of tension.

Adler speaks of "the language of the organs," by which he means that vomiting often tells of a fear which the child does not admit, of which he is often not aware. The child may or may not adopt stomach trouble permanently as a symptom, depending on his general attitude toward life. In any event, the organic root of symptom choice is an accidental consequence of the physical structure of the individual child rather than the consequence of a disturbance in the biological development of an organ system common to all children. The important psychological element is not the physical fact but the attitude adopted toward it.*

Adler's view of the basic biological framework for the conditioning of psychological attitudes is very simple: the infant is a helpless little creature surrounded by powerful adults. Mankind is puny in comparison with natural forces or even some of the beasts of the field. Thus, the basic feeling of any individual must be one of inferiority. By the very nature of his status in infancy and *vis-à-vis* the universe, he starts out with a *normal* sense of helplessness, and his strivings may be seen as compensatory striving for power and for superiority over the people and forces which originally had mastery over him—striving for "perfection."

We have seen what Freud (and, more particularly, Ferenczi) made of the initial helplessness of the human infant. With Adler it becomes the paramount determinant of all later behavior. It is the biological core for his emphasis on the feeling of inferiority and the consequent drive to superiority, power, prestige, or perfection which plays so great a role in his psychological system.

* Freud also acknowledges the likelihood of a genuine organic condition as *one* of the factors determining choice of symptom. See his account of the case of Dora ("Fragment of an Analysis of a Case of Hysteria," *Collected Papers*, Vol. III, Hogarth Press, 1925, pp. 13-146).

In practice, Adler places almost equal emphasis on what he calls *social feeling* or *social interest*. We shall encounter again in the other analysts of this group dynamic trends of very great systematic importance that seem to have no *biological* underpinning in theory. In Adler's writings, social feeling or interest appears as a very important aspect of the child's development, apparently taught by society, especially by the mother. A lack of social feeling in the patient is commonly part of Adlerian diagnosis, and the therapist usually takes steps to remedy this lack.

It remains obscure whether Adler conceives of this truly important aspect of human function as in any sense biological or as the product of training to be normally expected in our society. In later pages we shall describe in more detail the use he makes of the concept. Here this obscurity may be contrasted with the elaborate efforts of the Freudians to explain how the human animal develops social traits.

Adler uses two further concepts in his analysis of the functioning personality almost as frequently as the concept of social feeling, and in much the same manner. These concepts are *courage* and *common sense*. The wholesome, normal (or positively good) person approaches the problems of existence confidently and realistically. He is not so afraid of failure as to retreat from the truth about himself and the situation he confronts. Therefore, both his own helplessness and external difficulties lead to *constructive* striving, whereas precisely the same conditions in the sick personality lead to a turning away from appropriate effort into mistaken or ineffective fantasies and to a constantly growing gap between the real world and the world in which the patient reigns uneasily supreme in his own mind—so as to avoid recognition of his actual difficulties. Adlerian therapy makes large use of *encouragement*, but the purpose of the encouragement is to help the patient close this gap *himself*. It is the patient who must ultimately regain the courageous attitude toward life which will foster a more realistic approach to his problems and enable him to handle them in terms of common sense and social feeling instead of grandiose fantasy. (Clearly, *common sense* does not have here the derogatory flavor of superficiality often implied by the phrase. It is Adler's term for what Freud calls "reality.")

Like social feeling, courage and common sense appear to be, for Adler, the natural attributes of man as he develops unhampered in a good human environment. They seem to be Adler's terms for the valuable human potential so heavily stressed by the other authors discussed in this group. Adler even attempts to show the "striving for perfection" as a demonstrable evolutionary fact. From his later writings, one gets the impression that he himself came to see the drive to superiority as a sort of distortion of man's native propensities under the unfortunate conditions of his actual experience. Normally—that is, by the terms of the human organism—the initial sense of helplessness would be handled with social feeling, courage, and common sense as the infant matures in affectionate, sensibly educative contact with his fellow humans.

Adler is known for the observation of the importance of the drive to power, for stress on the unity of the personality and the importance of fictive goals, for his approach to characterology. The whole "positive" aspect of Adler's later position relative to social feeling, courage, and common sense is often overlooked.* He was a worthy precursor of Horney and Fromm in the quite energetic statement that social feeling, courage, and common sense are the native potential of man—which develop spontaneously unless positively thwarted, and which require no special explanation.

Adler made a further observation of profound importance concerning the human organism: its essential *unity of function*. This principle has frequently been cited as one of the cardinal points of any modern psychology, and it is not peculiar to Adler. In assigning historical credit, however, one must note that Adler was among the very first to grasp the psychological significance of this principle. Every individual, he believed, develops in infancy a *style of life* peculiar to himself which is determining for his later behavior. The theoretical statement that "the organism functions as a unit" was for Adler the starting point for his practical interpretation of personality. Under the term *characterological trends,* this type of interpretation has become important for "Freudians" too, although the Freudians do not go so far as Adler in exclusive emphasis on this point.

We have seen that for Adler inferiority feeling is universal, and that specific defects, often inborn, play a role *in determining the nature of compensatory strivings.* With some unfairness to Adler, discussion of the role of specific environmental influences in such determination is postponed to the next chapter. What we must understand at once is that, however determined (mostly in very early years), the life style of the individual is considered the key to his behavior. His major goal is always superiority, or at least compensation for the basic feeling of inferiority, but he may achieve this goal in a great

* Perhaps the main reason for this widespread failure to appreciate Adler's maturing psychological theory is the nature of his writings. The later ones are extremely difficult to read. They seem turgid, bombastic, repetitious, disturbingly hostile to all sorts of ideas which were doubtless worthy of enmity in the crude form in which Adler encountered them but which have long since been winnowed and developed to a scientific status. No reputable geneticist today, for example, believes that a tendency to thievery is inherited—and he may well resent having his entire science castigated because of misapprehensions prevalent a generation ago. Unfortunately, I cannot recommend that the reader turn to the original sources unless he is prepared to expend a good deal of patient effort in disentangling what Adler meant and to discount the phillipics which are no longer appropriate. Adler's interpreters are much easier to read.

variety of ways. The specific *mode* of achievement, conditioned* by early experience, becomes the life style. The vagaries of behavior in the individual may therefore be understood if one understands his goal and the relation of his behavior to the goal. The phrase used for all sorts of misbehavior—from criminality to neurosis and psychosis—is "erroneous" solution of life problems, a wrong life style.

The indisputable merit of the concept of the life style is that it emphasizes the functional meaning and goal-directed character of behavior. This merit is shared with all schools of psychoanalysis and was discussed in Chapter 2. But Adler goes a step further in stating that each person has a specific goal which is deeply his own, and that he adopts early in life a specific technique for attaining it. The child may come in his first years to feel that he is entirely helpless and that he can maintain himself only by gaining the support of others. Throughout life he will be unable to assert himself constructively, to take direct initiative for his own destiny, and instead he develops obvious handicaps which demand the care of others. The handicaps, which often look very real indeed, also protect him from having to acknowledge his failure as a person. He can nourish his self-respect on the idea that, except for his weak stomach or his speech defect or insomnia or whatever, he could have accomplished great things.

Another child may feel, unconsciously, that the world is hostile and grudging, allowing him his place in the sun only through his own strenuous efforts. He is constantly mistrustful of kindness, uneasily competitive, resentful of the success of others, insistent upon taking what he considers his due regardless of the expense to his fellow men or even to himself in the long run.

To a considerable extent, one may identify the life style with the underlying *character* of the person. Adler was one of the first to see the dynamics of *character trends* as within the province of psychoanalysis, in contrast to Freud's *early* emphasis on the neurotic symptom. Further, Adler's emphasis on the goal underlying the life style led him to envisage the possibility of a radical and almost automatic change in character and behavior once a shift in goal could be achieved. The life style, he felt, would quite naturally adapt itself to the new goal with just as much inner coherence as the former style.

The classical example of such a shift in life style with a shift in values is the redemption of Jean Valjean in *Les Misérables* through the unexpected kindness of the priest. The Individual Psychologist attempts consciously to identify the goal of the patient from study of his life style, and to clarify this goal for the patient. By means of his own encouraging attitude, along with

* Another term commonly used beyond its original meaning. Adler objected to the scientific concept of conditioning current in his time.

manipulation of the environment designed to help the patient in his first steps, the therapist endeavors to educate him toward a new goal.

We shall discuss therapeutic procedures in greater detail later. They are mentioned here for theoretical reasons: to show how deeply Adler believed in the flexibility of human nature, in the freedom with which overt behavior could respond to the major intent of the person. This belief is in some contrast to the *relative* fixity and the autonomy of behavior constellated about the various organ systems and personality structures emphasized in Freudian doctrine. Of course Freud constantly stresses the interaction of these systems and points out how one type of satisfaction may substitute for another. He shows the "secondary gain" to the ego of neurotic symptoms, and he never loses sight of the unity of the organism. Nevertheless, there is a very important difference in principle between the idea of interrelated systems, more or less definitely structured in themselves, and a freely moving psychological field.

SUMMARY

Adler was not much concerned with the terms of the organism as such. He drew special attention to the significance of organic defects, but only as they conditioned or revealed psychological attitudes. The person who happens to have an *organic inferiority* may work especially hard to overcome it, or he may use it as an excuse to avoid realistic effort. If a child happens to have a weak stomach, anxieties which he does not admit even to himself may reveal themselves in vomiting. The nature of the defect or the physical symptom was for Adler an accident of bodily structure of no psychological interest except for the attitude adopted toward it by the person.

For Adler, the only biological fact of importance in itself is the helplessness of the human infant. This is the root of *universal feelings of inferiority,* which supply the motive power for compensatory striving toward superiority. In the last analysis, all impulses, even the most normal, may be explained in terms of such striving. In the healthy personality, such strivings are accompanied by *social feeling, courage, and common sense*—attributes considered natural to man in a human environment that encourages free development and offers sympathetic training. Explanation is required not for their appearance but for their failure to appear. If early experience places too great a burden on the child, he develops unrealistic expectations and does not prepare sound methods of coping with life situations; the striving for superiority becomes distorted. The child makes an "erroneous" solution of life's problems— erroneous because it operates against interest in others and a spirit of cooperation; because it strives for a fantastic superiority without the appreciation of reality offered by a properly maturing common sense.

Thus, very early experience determines the specific kind of superiority the person will strive for and the pattern of his striving. This specific goal and the mode of its achievement Adler calls the *life style* of the individual. The concrete details of his behavior, his fantasies, dreams, attitudes, and feelings have an inner consistency which becomes intelligible once one is able to grasp the life style. They can be modified automatically all along the line once the individual changes his goal.

Despite the fact that the nature of the life style is determined by the milieu, this concept properly belongs to the section on the terms of the organism because the concept implies great freedom of movement among personality elements. It involves a radical holism whereby every element is immediately influenced by the aim of the organism as a whole, in some contrast to Freud's concern with part-instincts, with consideration of the semi-independent aims of organ systems and personality structures which interact with one another.

HORNEY

IT IS DIFFICULT to describe in detail Karen Horney's views about the terms of the organism, because they are stated for the most part only by implication. Like Adler, Horney takes up the cudgels against the Freudian description of the dynamic role of specific biological (sexual) needs and places her entire emphasis on the process of adaptation to life situations (mainly interpersonal). Her attitude toward hereditary and constitutional individual differences is less crusading than Adler's, perhaps because the narrow views of inheritance that Adler tried to combat are no longer prevalent. Horney's discussion of cases takes individual differences in native endowment for granted. The problem is not raised explicitly.

Like Adler, too, Horney feels that her approach is less "pessimistic" than Freud's. She proclaims her belief "that man has the capacity as well as the desire to develop his potentialities and become a decent human being . . . that man can change and go on changing as long as he lives."[1] Especially in her spoken lectures, man's natural wish to enjoy and expand comes to the fore, in deliberate contrast to the exclusive wish to avoid suffering.

> . . . We believe that inherent in man are evolutionary constructive forces, which urge him to realize his given potentialities. This belief does not mean that man is essentially good—which would presuppose a given knowledge of what is good or bad. It means that man, by his very nature and of his own accord, strives toward self-realization, and that his set of values evolves from such striving.[2]

Yet, as we noted in commenting on Adler's concept of courage and social feeling, the biological roots of this "optimistic" belief in human potentiality are left obscure. And Horney does not elaborate a careful philosophical formulation, as do Fromm and, in his own way, Freud.

The qualities of the decent human being, the normal person, *the real self*, this "man" in whom one may have faith, are indicated in many pages as the obverse of the "neurotic" trends that Horney analyzes very carefully. The "neurotic" person is generally more rigidly, more compulsively, set in his modes of reaction and is less able to perceive the "real" demands of the situation. It is decent and normal to stand up for one's own rights. The "neurotic" may fight for his rights when they are in no way threatened, or may tolerate submissively an undue amount of injustice, or may veer back and forth between too great and too little self-assertion. His reactions are determined by his own "neurotic" needs, mostly unconscious, and are therefore often inappropriate to the external situation. Horney writes, in 1945, "Neurosis, it must be said, is always a matter of degree—and when I speak of 'a neurotic' I invariably mean 'a person to the extent that he is neurotic.' "[3]

From this point on, I shall dispense with the quotation marks around "neurosis." It should be understood, however, that Horney uses the word for any deviation from this deeply intuitive concept of basic human potentiality. In reading Horney's books, one is likely to feel that oneself and one's friends are being described very vividly (she was an expert clinician), almost always under the label "neurotic." This label does not mean that we must all worry about our personal mental health as such. Rather, it means that the conditions of human life are such that we quite typically fail to realize our human capacities fully, and that our interpretations of external realities are often distorted by our efforts to maintain the personal stance we have adopted.

The mainspring of neurotic manifestations is seen by Horney as a *basic anxiety*. By this term she means "the feeling a child has of being isolated and helpless in a potentially hostile world."[4] The neurotic patterns are seen primarily as means of handling this anxiety, which is "the most painful experience man can experience." In contrast to realistic *fears,* which are limited by the actual threat of the external situation, anxiety tends to be all-pervasive. It is "hidden and subjective." It covertly determines the behavior of the person, regardless of the real dangers, and is therefore often highly injurious. Dangers may be fancied when they do not exist, inappropriately handled when they do. In his efforts to avoid this *inner* anxiety, the person distorts his view of reality and typically limits his own activities to areas he considers safe—although his "safety" is defined in a highly subjective manner and may on occasion look like precisely the opposite. For example, some individuals may court external danger to avoid inner anxiety.

Horney's emphasis on the helplessness of the infant as determining for the basic pattern of later behavior is reminiscent of Adler's, but her position differs from his in two ways essential to the present discussion: (1) Adler feels that because of his initial helplessness *every* infant feels inferior. In consequence, striving to overcome this normal (universal) feeling becomes the guiding principle of all human activity. Horney's position is broader and more cautious. The infant does not *necessarily* feel helpless in a hostile world. On the contrary, he has multiform capacities for enjoyment and achievement which are operative and valuable in themselves. His helplessness should be seen rather as the primary *condition for* neurotic development when actual difficulties in his surroundings make the outside world seem frustrating and hostile at a time when the new organism is largely at the mercy of its environment.

(2) The second difference lies in the consequences. For Horney, the infant's helplessness leads not so much to a focused sense of inferiority, with compensating drive to become superior, as to an exacerbated *need for security.* This is the need which becomes paramount in all neurosis, even in the neurotically determined quirks of the normal person. The expedients by which the neurotic attempts to cope with a world he deeply experiences as hostile Horney calls *safety devices.* Thus, Adler's neurotic drive to power, clearly demonstrable in some individuals, is interpreted by Horney as the need to pile up personal insurance against the danger of being overwhelmed. Mankind is and should be self-assertive. Assertion beyond the normal range is a means of coping with insecurity. The longing for love (love in excess—it is normal to want love) can usually be seen as the longing for unlimited support—that is, as another means of coping with very deep feelings of insecurity. Submissiveness and altruism (again in excess) frequently suggest either a direct bid for protection or, in many cases, a way of avoiding retaliation for hostile self-assertion which the person fears—usually at the unconscious level—

would break forth furiously in himself and meet with retaliation in kind. (In Chap. 11, on personality dynamics, we shall see the especial vividness of the psychology of opposites in Horney's scheme, the so-called vicious circle.)

Hostility plays a basic role in Horney's thinking different from that in both Freud's and Adler's. She repudiates any notion of an independent instinct toward death or destruction, or even a native "aggression" beyond what she would call normal self-assertion and enterprise. None of the Freudian positions on this matter would satisfy her. But although hostility is not an "instinct," the infant may experience his world as *hostile* in a rather general sense and may develop hostile feelings in response. Again, I have the impression that Horney simply cuts the Gordian knot as regards the terms of the organism. In her working theory, however, hostility as such looms large. The realistic frustration of normal desires directly awakens feelings of hostility. More important for her view of general psychodynamics is that neurotic frustrations *self-imposed* in the interests of security also awaken feelings of hostility. In both instances, the hostile feelings themselves arouse anxiety—harking back to the helplessness of the infant whose hostilities can have no realistic success.

Self-esteem is another concept that bulks large in Horney's operative dynamics. For her, it does not have the intrinsically competitive flavor that Adler derives from the need to compensate for inferiority. Rather, the need to value oneself and to be valued seems to Horney one of the obvious "givens" of human nature. Overvaluation—or undervaluation—of the self is the consequence of special threat in this area, always to be analyzed in terms of basic anxiety and the need for security. But even hostility is thought of as dangerous in most instances, not so much because the person fears annihilation even at the primitive, unconscious level as because recognition of hostility is a threat to his self-esteem. Normally, self-esteem includes the wish to be valued by one's fellows, but only in neurosis does it become merely a sort of reflection of what other people think we should be. Normally, the person has an ideal for himself which serves as an integrating and guiding force in his behavior. Only in neurosis does an *idealized image of the self* (see pp. 454ff.) become so limited and at the same time so fantastically demanding as actually to hamper free enjoyment and productivity. In *Neurosis and Human Growth* (1950), the tension between this idealized image (constructed as an effort toward integration in the face of neurotic conflicts) and both the actual and what Horney calls the real self is given still more emphasis. Self-idealization versus self-realization is presented in this book as the central inner conflict.

Conflict is another concept basic to Horney's system. Much of her work centers about the extrinsic and intrinsic factors in man's experience which foster the development of conflict for all of us—conflicts that readily take on neurotic proportions. (These factors will be discussed in Chaps. 9 and 11.) The question is why conflict should be so painful to the human organism. Horney remarks that conflict is functionally inexpedient to the point of paralysis. If a man wants to go in two diametrically opposed directions at once, he finds it difficult to move at all. Whatever choice he makes goes counter to other impulses, and these—because they are thwarted—tend to become even more insistent and to arouse unacceptable feelings of hostility. A sense of unity in the self is also a deep human necessity. Our self-esteem and our role in society demand personal integrity. It is difficult enough for the ideally normal person to find his way among the complexities and frustrations of an imperfect society. The neurotic must do so with the added burden of his basic anxieties, which typically lead him to see threats even where none actually exists and to interpret them in his own narrow fashion. For him, the problem of choice is at once more urgent (because the real situation arouses his deep anxieties) and more difficult (because his inner dynamics tends to so limit and exaggerate the issues on both sides as to make them quite irreconcilable).

Driven by his need for integration, the neurotic is prone to solve the dilemma of conflict by *repressing* one side of it. Repression does not eliminate. On this point Horney agrees with Freud. On the contrary, aspects of the personality rendered *unconscious* are very likely to function all the more vigorously with narrow, blind insistence because they are cut off from modification by constant reconsideration in close connection with reality factors. This neurotic solution is, therefore, no solution at all and in the long run makes the original conflicting trends still more irreconcilable.

The preceding two paragraphs have gone somewhat beyond the topic of this chapter: the terms of the organism. Concepts have been used schematically that will be explained more thoroughly in later chapters. Yet the crux of the difference between Horney's position as to the intrinsic nature of the human being and that of Adler and the Freudians emerges clearly only as one examines the major operative dynamic concepts in the perspective of fundamental tenets regarding the terms of the organism itself. A summary of Horney's position will perhaps be sharpened for the readers of this book if it is presented in terms of forthright comparison with the authors previously discussed.

SUMMARY AND COMPARISON

Like Adler, Horney is primarily concerned with the movements of the personality as a whole and tends to resist compartmentalization into instincts present at birth or institutions "necessarily" developed later. Thus, she rejects the Freudian instinct theory, and also the Freudian structural approach (id, ego, superego).

Like Adler, she considers her approach essentially optimistic, with faith in the natural creative potentiality of man at birth and at any stage of his life cycle. This position both Horney and Adler see as different from Freud's formulation of man as essentially subject to the instincts of sexuality and aggression (death). Horney does not attempt a general scientific or philosophical justification of her position (as Fromm does for his, and as Freud did). Furthermore, her concept of the normal—actually the ideal—personality is not explicitly and systematically stated but appears as the rich, multiform obverse of the neurotic trends which she describes acutely.

Like Adler, she tends to emphasize one principle as basically determining for human behavior, but for her this principle is the need for security. The need for security does not operate universally, as does Adler's will to superiority, but only when the person is threatened. When the threat reaches unmanageable proportions in infancy, the person readily develops an all-pervasive sense of the world as hostile and dangerous. This feeling Horney calls *basic anxiety*. The individual defends himself against it by *safety devices,* which must be considered neurotic because they protect against this deep *inner* fear and are not expediently related to the realistic dangers he encounters.

Horney works extensively with the concepts of *self-esteem, hostility,* and *conflict.* (Description of how she uses them is postponed to later chapters.) Her position is here *un*like Adler's in his insistence on a unitary theme. My impression is that Horney's main support for these concepts is clinical observation and an appeal to our *deep* "common sense," although I have tried to suggest how they relate to her feeling for the person-as-a-whole (the real self), which is perhaps her most crucial difference from Freud—or at least from the Freudian formulations she attacks.

The emphasis on conflict as intrinsically pathogenic, on repression, on the continuing operation of unconscious trends as such—these emphases bring her closer to Freud than to Adler, who considered any such enduring splits in personality organization as running counter to the free movement of the personality striving constantly toward its goal. But we must also note clearly the difference from Freud. For Horney, the conflict is not only a present rather than a past conflict (a position with which most Freudians would agree, with reservations), but it is a conflict freely restructured from moment to moment, maintaining only the basic attitudes established in infancy. Horney does not tolerate the idea of specific impulses, repressed because of intolerable conflict, remaining encysted timelessly in the unconscious. (The point is elaborated in

Chap. 11.) On this point she goes beyond criticism of a mere overemphasis on sexuality in Freudian doctrine. Her concept of conflict, repression, and the unconscious is fundamentally different from Freud's. It is much more immediately related to her concept of the person-as-a-whole, taking his stance toward a world which he neurotically conceives as essentially hostile and dangerous.

FROMM

ERICH FROMM will be discussed briefly here because, as becomes a psychoanalyst whose major background is sociology rather than medicine, his most original contribution has been toward the psychoanalytic approach to social problems.* His social orientation is deeply related to his concept of the individual, however, and this concept contains at least new emphases.

Fromm seems less antagonistic to the Freudian libido theory than do Adler and Horney, but he does not propose to let it get in his way. Bodily (sexual) needs are frankly acknowledged as universal; individual differences in native endowment and temperament are given explicit importance. "Specifically human" problems, he says, begin where these matters leave off, however, and are to be seen mainly in terms of man's relationship to his human environment.

Fromm's imagination is caught by the panorama of biological evolution. The point he stresses is the growing *individuation* of the organism, reaching its culmination in man. Beyond all other creatures, man has freed himself from the matrix of nature, is least bound either by outside events or by his own constitutionally prefigured reaction patterns (instincts). He *can* follow and to a large extent create his own destiny. But he also belongs to his evolutionary

* Throughout this book, discussion of Fromm's theoretical approach is based primarily on *Escape from Freedom* (Farrar & Rinehart, 1941) and *Man for Himself* (Rinehart & Co., 1947). These books were preceded by a long monograph on the authoritarian society and other articles in German which have not been translated. I cannot here report the background of Fromm's thinking beyond the major reference: his monograph in M. Horkheimer (ed.), *Studien über Autorität und Familie* (Félix Alcan, 1936). His later works seem to be related on the one hand to further development of psychoanalytic theory and on the other hand to religion and ethics. The specifically sociological orientation, considered so important in this book, apparently has not been continued.

past, to his historical past as a social being, and to his childhood, when his individual reactions were very largely conditioned by biological and social forms.

Individuation is not an easy process. On the contrary, it leaves man feeling alone and insignificant, often uncertain and conflicted about what course he should take. The title of Fromm's first book, *Escape from Freedom,* presents his position vividly. Over and above (but also including) the kind of conflict stressed by the Freudians, Fromm sees a general dichotomy between the biologically conditioned trend of the organism toward the matrix of instinct and authoritarian commands (which provides a very deep "security") and a need for freedom—that is, for rational, individual choice—posited by the inborn resources of the human organism as specifically human. These resources constantly pose new problems in adaptation, constantly undermine the old adaptations. In *Man for Himself,* Fromm emphasizes the human potential in a manner which seems at first glance much like Horney's emphasis on the "real self." But he also emphasizes the intrinsic conflict of man's existence in a way which he himself calls philosophical and dialectic. Man, as man, must strive for new, creative solutions of his problems if he is to survive.

There is, according to Fromm, no "drive for perfection" in man and no innate social feeling. The very conflict in man's existence is the basis for a dynamism which drives him to new solutions, because every solution contains contradictions that are solved at new levels. (*Cf.* Rank, Chap. 14.) To put it differently, instead of Freud's evolutionary scheme of libido, there is a dialectic scheme based on the idea of basic contradictions and the unending necessity of ever new solutions. Once man emerged from the animal kingdom, so to speak, his conflicts forced him to seek new solutions, and he has only the alternatives of going ahead or of dying out as a species.

Fromm repudiates any version of "original sin" in man—whether Eros and Thanatos, self-interest, self-preservation in the traditional sense of the survival of the fittest—or any theory suggesting innate undesirable traits. Native to man is the flexibility of his nervous system, which allows creative adaptation to his world, and a tendency to expand and to exercise his powers. Since man's world is primarily social, his powers and natural satisfactions are bound to be socially oriented. *In so far as man is able to accept individuation,* and the potential of his nervous system permitting reasoned coping with his surroundings, he can be happy in the true sense of self-fulfillment through productive work and genuinely loving relationships.

Self-interest in the true sense involves the satisfaction of *all* the powers of the individual, which automatically include love and consideration for his fellows. There is no intrinsic contradiction between self-love and altruism.

On the contrary, only the person who has accepted individuation, who loves himself, his true self, is capable of appreciating the selfhood of others. Only such a person can love others generously for what they are to themselves as distinct from what they mean to him. He may sacrifice himself to a person or a cause if extreme circumstances so demand, but he does so *knowingly* and as a matter of necessity. Self-sacrifice as such is not a virtue—indeed, too often it is a mask for the fear of being alone, sometimes for the underlying hatred of the self and others. The dynamics of this transformation will be discussed later (pp. 466f.).

Whereas Horney believes that man is "normally" secure unless the conditions of his life have fostered "neurotic" trends, Fromm's analysis of the basic problem and opportunity of mankind—man's new individuation—suggests that a measure of uneasiness is universal and that "normally" the person is likely to attempt some means of escape from his freedom. Neurosis then becomes a matter of the degree to which the individual is unable to tolerate his status as a separate self and has developed in consequence seriously "nonproductive" mechanisms of escape.

The instinctual equipment of animals tells them "what to do" without the need for deciding rationally on the most expedient course of action. Laboratory work with animals shows that they, like people, can be thrown into a neurotic-like state when the experimenter places them in a situation in which two or more ingrained patterns of reaction of similar valence are simultaneously stimulated, or in which every attempt at solution of the problem is systematically blocked. We are all familiar with the frequent highly unsuccessful adaptation of animals to new crisis situations—for example, the stubborn insistence of the panicky horse on staying in the refuge of his stall when the barn is on fire. On the whole, however, there is psychological security in knowing what to do by instinct. Man has forefeited this type of security by his very nature. One aspect of his endeavor to escape from his new freedom is his attempt to recapture the comfort of established rules of behavior, which relieve him of the torture of personal decision and doubt. Thus everyone, but more especially the person who is especially frightened by freedom, is prone to seek rules, principles, the fiat of superior authority, regardless of self-interest.

Earlier forms of society and religious beliefs served to alleviate the pain of personal responsibility by a plenitude of codification. The "noble savage," the natural man of early-nineteenth-century romanticism, is a myth. Not always, of course (one of the major contributions of modern anthropology is appreciation of variation among "savage" groups), but typically, the individual in primitive societies is even more hedged in—and more protected—than ourselves by socially prescribed regulations of behavior. Areas of sexual and other types of freedom occur which seem to us free to the point of absolute license, but more careful study of such "free" cultures typically reveals restrictions which seem to us fantastic—for example, the quite common item that one must not address one's cross-cousin by name, and a host of minor and major taboos which vary from culture to culture. Objective study of these natural experiments in widely different types of social organization does not support the romantic idea of individual freedom as a natural outcome of the elimination of the particular social abuses or Grundyisms present in our own society.

Fromm points out the emotional value to newly individuated mankind of social systems, which, like the instinct patterns of animals, tell the person what to do and which, further, supply a sense of *belongingness* to the individual nakedly exposed to the problems of coping independently with the problems of existence. Many social orders, many powerful ideologies, supply the individual with needed protection against recognition of his aloneness and insignificance *vis-à-vis* a world which grows constantly larger (psychologically) with the achievements of the intelligence released by man's individuation. Thus, a primary problem of mankind, a "normal" condition of distress, is the feeling of aloneness and insignificance. The more the instinctual certainties and their surrogates in organized societies and ideologies must be renounced in the progress of biological and social evolution, the more man is forced to cope as an individual with his nostalgic and in part quite realistic yearnings for the power and security of incorporation with a larger entity.

In fact, once man fully appreciates his position in the universe, he is face to face with ineluctable conditions of existence of no mean importance. He is often helpless in his relation to natural forces, to the social conditions he has inadvertently created in the course of his human development, and with some finality he is subject to death.

> Into this universe and why not knowing,
> Nor whence like water willynilly flowing:
> And out of it, like wind along waste,
> I know not whither, willynilly blowing.

> What, without asking, hither hurried whence,
> And, without asking, whither hurried hence!
> Another and another cup to drown
> The memory of this impertinence!

These are the *existential* problems of the human situation. Fromm does not blink them, though he does not recommend as a solution the cup offered by Omar Khayyam. "Uncertainty," says Fromm, "is the very condition to impel man to unfold his powers. If he faces the truth without panic he will recognize that *there is no meaning to life except the meaning man gives his life by the unfolding of his powers.*"[5] "Psychology," he continues, "must be based on an anthropologico-philosophical concept of human existence."

Many of the problems of human existence, however, are *historical.* "The poor always ye have with you" has been taken out of context as Biblical sanction for the necessity of poverty—or poverty has been explained as an inevitable consequence of natural law. War is another constantly recurring phenomenon quite commonly considered as economically and psychologically necessary. These and many other human problems are *not,* for Fromm, implicit either in society or in human nature. They are not existential problems. They can be handled with increased understanding and success.

Fromm fully accepts the contributions of areas of inquiry outside psychology for the general understanding necessary to human welfare. He would like to see the data of psychology used in conjunction with materials from the natural and social sciences. Above all, he would like to see man take his own self more seriously as the true aim of life. Only humanistic ethics, rooted in the powers of man and the potential of his understanding, can suffice to create a good society—that is, a productive society satisfying to its members. The decision rests with man. "It rests upon his courage to be himself and to be for himself."[6]

Subsequent sections on Fromm will deal more concretely with his contribution as psychoanalyst to the understanding of social situations and with his concept of the dynamics of individual behavior.

SUMMARY AND COMPARISON

As I read Fromm, he has no serious quarrel with other analysts except on grounds of omission or overemphasis. He uses joyfully and thoughtfully the concepts of many schools, including the Freudian. Like Adler and Horney, he tends to think mainly in terms of the problems of dependency, powerlessness, hostility, and their counterparts, with greater stress on the development of the self and on the conflict between the need to feel part of a larger unit and the need to be oneself. Like religious and philosophical thinkers, he considers as primary man's need to find meaning in life.

But, for Fromm, the essence of the human conflict is the necessity forced upon man by the very individuation of his biological structure to seek new, independent, and reasoned solutions to the problems of his existence. Man's potential freedom as an individual tends to make him feel alone and insignificant. Fromm therefore sees the basic psychological problem not so much as a need for security, as does Horney, as an escape from freedom and individuation. His major original contribution to psychoanalysis is, to my mind, his effort to relate the psychological forces operating in man to the society within which he lives. This point will be discussed in the next chapter.

SULLIVAN

IT IS POSSIBLE to give the reader one identifying phrase that will serve him in any superficial discussion of Sullivan: *interpersonal relations*. All the schools presented have very strongly emphasized our dealings with one another as crucial both for the development of our personality and for its significant operation. Sullivan presents them as, in a way, the whole story of human psychology. It sounds simple.

Actually, Sullivan's way is extremely complex. Understanding of his views is not made easier by the fact that he introduces a new set of words for almost every psychological concept. The new terms guard the reader against misunderstandings based on preconceptions carried over from different usage in other schools of thought, but such a plethora of idiosyncratic terms makes it difficult for the reader to call upon his past psychological knowledge in a positive understanding of the new position. I am not alone in feeling—when reading Sullivan—as if I were floundering not in a morass but on the precarious summit of a brilliant display of fireworks.

A further reason for this terminology is that Sullivan received his training under William Alanson White and Adolf Meyer rather than Freud. He has greatly enlarged the concepts of psychobiology (Meyer's term for the dynamic theory of psychiatry which he developed parallel to psychoanalysis) in a direction now considered by most people "psychoanalytic." Unlike all the other analysts presented in this book, he was not brought up in the Freudian terminology, so to speak. His position is not so much a rebellion as a qualified *rapprochement*.

Furthermore, Sullivan wrote comparatively little, and that little was usually written for a specific occasion upon which the topic and the audience to a large extent dictated the orientation of his paper.* Although one has the feeling that everything that Sullivan said was for him part of a highly systematized approach which he constantly elaborated, even to the point of

---

* Sullivan was a talker rather than a writer. Since tape recordings of his lectures exist, a number of volumes of his works are scheduled for publication as rapidly as they can be edited by his colleagues.

changing his views on specific questions of great importance, he never wrote a thoroughly systematic book.

Sullivan was the acknowledged theoretical leader of a school in the literal as well as the ideological sense—the William Alanson White Psychiatric Foundation. This school sponsors an excellent journal, *Psychiatry*, and several of its leading spirits have published eminently readable books which emphasize the important clinical aspects of Sullivan's point of view.* The clinically oriented publications of the William Alanson White Psychiatric Foundation seem to me to have fastened upon certain aspects of Sullivan's theory and developed them further. These aspects I shall try to report in Chapter 12, on pathology and treatment.

It seems to me that Sullivan is, *in theory*, the least "reductionist" of any of the authors discussed thus far. He is hardly willing to allow *any* psychological generalization to stand as valid apart from his view of an acting organism whose most important property is that, by its very nature, from birth and even earlier, it interacts with its surroundings. *Modes of interaction* thus become the real focus of psychological inquiry, and for human beings these modes of interaction primarily involve *people*. To speak of impulses, strivings, goals, etc. as if they belonged to the individual is a formulation imposed upon us by the structure of our language and the habits of common speech.[7] All we can ever observe as scientists is how the individual reacts to other people in a given situation. (Sullivan defines all situations as interpersonal, since even our most solitary efforts are related to "fantastic personifications" developed in the course of our experience with people.)

Furthermore, we are ourselves participants in the *situation* we are examining. As such, we directly influence its course in any face-to-face encounter (notably in psychological interview and therapy), no matter how "objective" our approach, and our *participation* influences our evaluation of events not subject to immediate influence. Sullivan is eloquent about the private life of his dog, which is as unknowable to him in its idiosyncratic fullness as the full individuality of any human being.

* Especially in discussing problems of treatment (Chap. 12), I shall refer frequently to Clara Thompson's *Psychoanalysis: Evolution and Development* and Frieda Fromm-Reichmann's *Principles of Intensive Psychotherapy*. A volume of short papers entitled *A Study of Interpersonal Relations* not only presents interesting materials but will serve the reader as a means of becoming acquainted with a large number of authors who essentially share Sullivan's point of view. Patrick Mullahy, who worked very closely with Sullivan over many years, published, with his approval, a brief systematic account of Sullivan's position during his lifetime (he died in 1949). This account appears at the end of a series of lectures by Sullivan published under the title *Conceptions of Modern Psychiatry*, the book I used most extensively in preparing my exposition. A more detailed digest of Sullivan's position may be found in Mullahy's *Oedipus—Myth and Complex*, which also reviews many of the other authors presented here. (See also H. S. Sullivan, *The Interpersonal Theory of Psychiatry*, W. W. Norton & Co., 1953.)

This analysis means more to Sullivan than an exercise in semantics and epistemology. He feels that psychiatry should renounce the futile attempt to define the isolated individual in favor of defining the situation, or, rather, the significant interpersonal aspects of the situation. It will become clear that Sullivan is not an "environmentalist" in the ordinary meaning of the term and that he does in fact concern himself very largely with what most of us call "the individual." His main theoretical concern seems to be with the complete *integration of organism and milieu,* which operates continuously. "An organism," he writes,[8] "is a self-perpetuating organization of the physico-chemical world which manifests life by functional activity in the complex."

Sullivan goes on to point out that maintenance of life *requires* interchange with the environment, that the human infant is relatively poorly equipped for such interchange at birth, although well equipped for ultimate highly adaptive interchange. From birth, however, the organismic functional process is elaborated by support from without, which the organism necessarily integrates with its own growth. "As growth and maturation proceed acculturation is inevitable."[9] There is no human "self" whose nature or whose potentialities could be described *a priori,* which is fostered or hampered by its environment. Nor is the human organism a *tabula rasa* on which the environment may write any characters it pleases. The point Sullivan stresses again and again is the functional unity of the self *developing in its interpersonal context.* Perhaps I overestimate the importance of this point to Sullivan because it is a point I have myself tried to put forward as fundamental for psychological science—with less exclusive emphasis on interpersonal features (see pp. 22f.). Nevertheless, it seems to me that Sullivan's idiosyncratic language proceeds not so much from any superficial emphasis on the importance of *people* as such in our lives as from his deep insistence on the contextual development of all that we call the psychology of the individual.

Obviously, we do not *in fact* deal with other people, physical events, or ourselves in any given situation as if that situation were unique. Like Adler, Horney, and many others, Sullivan points to the fact that very often the contours of the *situation* as viewed from outside seeem to have very little to do with the psychological reaction of the person. Some people surmount easily situations that seem to us crushing, or they may collapse at what seems to us a quite trivial rebuff. This judgment is true even when our evaluation of the situation is not very personally our own but has what Sullivan calls *consensual validation*—that is, when the evaluation is what most of us would agree upon as pretty sound.* Always something of a mystery, and always

---

* In my glossary of Sullivanese, consensual validation seems to be "common sense" of a high order—the things people agree upon because their common sensual apparatus and deeply common interpersonal experiences make them seem objectively so. It is a critical and cautious term for the "reality" so often used by other psychological schools.

rather fluid in their dynamic patterns, the specific interpersonal situations we observe become analyzable as we learn to observe the major *dynamisms* operating more or less continuously in the individual we are scrutinizing—and in ourselves—or the significant aspects of the situation studied.

To make clear Sullivan's view of the coherence of the *individual* in the multifariousness of his reactions to different situations, one should perhaps go on at once to his concept of the self dynamism, the self system, the "self" as Sullivan understands it. This concept—to which he gives great weight—brings his discussion much closer to the orientation of the other authors discussed in this section and corrects the impression of an almost mystical situationalism which may have been suggested thus far. But I interpose here Sullivan's concept of *dynamism,* which seems to me fundamental to his whole position.*

Sullivan defines dynamism as "a relatively enduring configuration of energy which manifests itself in characterizable processes in interpersonal relations." These dynamisms manifest themselves in numerous ways in human situations and are considered only *relatively enduring—i.e.,* they are not "some fanciful substantial engines, regional organizations or peculiar more or less physiological apparatus about which our present knowledge is nil."[10] In basic theory, the "dynamisms" arise out of the interaction between the organism and the interpersonal situations. They do not properly belong to the organism itself in any ultimate fashion, contrary to the theoretical implications of all schools that point to "instincts," no matter how "basic," or to an inborn "self," no matter how "potential." (Neither Freud nor the authors reported here as emphasizing the movement of the total personality really satisfy Sullivan.)

Sullivan's position on this point becomes more clear if we observe how he actually uses the term *dynamism*. He applies it mainly to the emergent "self," which takes on enduring contours in infancy and early childhood—as enduring as those we have encountered in other schools. But he also applies it to part-systems *within* the developing *self dynamism*. Thus, instead of presenting "orality" as a psychological need, stage, or whatever, he speaks of an "oral dynamism," compounded of hunger and oral pleasure, which is very likely to function as a relatively enduring configuration; indeed, it becomes linked with language and organizes very substantial sub-aspects of the self dynamism. Genital impulses become a "lust dynamism," always of importance, occasionally of such importance for some individuals as to overwhelm the self dynamism.

Sullivan uses the term *dynamism* very frequently for such relatively en-

* My emphasis in reporting is here obviously related to my own concern with the structuring power of partially independent systems and subsystems in varying types of interrelationship.

during subconfigurations and would probably use it quite generally if it did not interfere with the stylistic requirements of writing. The semantic frill becomes really necessary for purposes of communication only at those points at which he needs to distinguish sharply between his concept of the relatively enduring configuration and the concept of permanent, inborn drives, impulses, apparatus, or whatever familiar to other schools.

The *self dynamism,* which comes to play a crucial role in the organization of behavior, is a construct built out of the child's experience. "The self may be said to be made up of reflected appraisals."[11] It "comes into being as a dynamism to preserve the feeling of security. . . . It is built largely of personal symbolic elements learned in contact with other significant people. . . ."[12] Detailed discussion of how the self system *develops* is postponed to the next chapter, and we shall note here only that the development occurs in close relation to the attitude of the parents or other significant adults toward the child, and that for Sullivan as for the other psychoanalysts its contours tend to be set rather firmly in infancy and early childhood. Discussion of how it *operates* will appear in Chapter 11, on personality dynamics. Here the important point is that its operation is crucial to Sullivan's version of the unconscious and preconscious—which he calls, in rough parallel to the Freudian terms, *dissociation* and *selective inattention.*

For the present chapter, the phrase in the sentences quoted above that requires immediate elucidation is "the feeling of security," so reminiscent of Horney and so suggestive of a basic need which, after all, transcends experience. Sullivan's theory, like all the others, regards the biology of the organism as the root of its psychology—even though Sullivan lays especial stress on the fact that we never encounter this "root" except as it has developed within its environment. The body demands certain *satisfactions* related to its native organization, primarily the organization of organs and unstriped musculature. "Throughout life the pursuit of satisfactions is physiologically provoked by increased tone in some unstriped muscles; and the securing of the satisfactions is a relaxation of this tone, with a tendency toward the diminution of attention, alertness, and vigilance, and an approach to sleep."[13] Under the heading of *satisfactions,* Sullivan includes all the usual bodily needs, including the satisfaction of "lust."* The bodily organism strives for a state of *euphoria,* of tensionless bliss, an end state best approximated in deep, dreamless sleep. In the very early months of life, the striped, skeletal musculature is apparently

---

* Incidentally, Sullivan feels that "lust" attains significant proportions only with puberty, apparently disregarding the Freudian linkage of the oral- and anal-zone developments with the genital in the concept of "infantile sexuality" and Freud's idea of the diphasic character of human genital development.

considered merely as instrumental to bodily satisfactions, the goal of which is reduction of all tension.*

The pursuit of *security* seems to arise a little later, after the infant has become at least dimly aware of the tension-producing attitudes of the ministering adults around him. It is essentially oriented toward interpersonal relations and requires the feeling of approval and prestige as a protection against *anxiety*. Here the concept of *empathy* must be introduced briefly as the logical bridge between the primitive pursuit of satisfactions (lowering of tensions) and the slightly later development of the pursuit of security. Sullivan believes that the infant responds very directly, intuitively, almost without analyzable sensory awareness, to the *mood* of the significant adult. If this mood is hostile or disapproving, the infant experiences the mood in himself directly as uncomfortable tension. Between the sixth and the twenty-sixth month, he begins to perceive the adult as a separate entity and "catches on" to the fact that his own behavior has a good deal to do with these empathized moods in the adult. He begins to attempt to structure his behavior accordingly. Adult approval brings direct "satisfaction"; disapproval brings heightened tension.

This sequence will be discussed more thoroughly in the next chapter. A word about it is essential here to show how Sullivan proceeds from the purely psychobiological view of satisfaction as release from any sort of tension to the psychological-interpersonal view of security as a positive need for approval and prestige—without considering any psychological needs "inborn."

In later life, the pursuit of satisfaction (essentially bodily) and the pursuit of security (essentially interpersonal) may be roughly distinguished. One can easily understand, however, why Sullivan stresses the uncertain nature of the distinction. Always the two pursuits interact to the point of being dynamically merged. Only in some instances may one type of pursuit so predominate over the other as to be considered fully determining in its own right. Two examples will serve to illustrate this: the lust dynamism, a bodily satisfaction, may become so strong as to overwhelm the self dynamism, which has been constructed primarily out of the reflected appraisals of others. The person may commit suicide in pursuit of the security of his self dynamism.

Mullahy (as well as I) has some difficulty in fitting Sullivan's concept of the *power motive* into his general scheme. Sullivan speaks of states "characterized by the feeling of ability or power" and remarks that "we seem to be born . . . with something of this power motive in us."[14] The infant reaches for the moon in the naive fullness of his effort to handle the world about him and discovers that the moon is unattainable, is in no sense manageable. His

---

* P. Mullahy, *Oedipus—Myth and Complex*, Hermitage Press, 1948, p. 283. Even Mullahy considers this point unclear, and I shall discuss it further in critical comment.

frustration in this matter (of course, only illustrative) results in the discovery of his powerlessness and in the beginnings of "thoughts, foresights, and so on, which are calculated to protect one from a feeling of insecurity and helplessness in the situation which confronts one."[15] In the context of Sullivan's discussion, the reach for the moon merges into analysis of the infant's cry as a tool—the beginning of language and the use of language behavior as one of the "most powerful *tools* which man uses in the development of his security with his fellow man." We shall return later to Sullivan's emphasis on the importance of language.

Sullivan does have the idea, however, that the infant *naturally* tends to use his neuromuscular equipment, his "abilities," in his pursuit of satisfactions and security, and that frustration in this area, no matter how realistic (*e.g.*, the unmanageability of the moon), contributes toward his sense of helplessness and insecurity—and toward the fostering of positive development in the area of competent handling of his social and physical environment. In a favorable environment, the power motive is part and parcel of the child's positive attitude toward himself and others, his normal growth pattern. Only when the self dynamism has developed in a hostile and insecure manner may the power motive become a power *drive*, tending toward fulfillment at the expense of others.*

Sullivan's concept of *loneliness* must also be mentioned here. Sullivan believes that we have an inborn desire to touch one another and to be physically close—beyond the closeness of the sexual embrace per se. Thus, the avoidance of loneliness falls under the heading of the pursuit of satisfactions, although it is so early and so deeply influenced by our cultural experience as to be considered only "a middling example."[16]

The concepts of the inborn *power motive* and of *loneliness* suggest some acknowledgment of terms of the organism beyond the pursuit of satisfaction as instrumented through the organization of vital organs and the unstriped musculature. My impression is that Sullivan means to include them under the heading of the quite obvious "givens" of the biological organism.

SUMMARY AND COMPARISON

Sullivan emphasizes the pervasive interaction between the organism and its environment, mainly the personal environment. This interaction is so per-

* I quote a comment of Clara Thompson: "In my opinion Sullivan uses power impulse where I would use the impulse to growth. That is, he thinks of the child as having a definite drive to develop and express his energies and abilities—*i.e.*, to learn and master his world. I think his use of the word *power* is unfortunate in that the word is generally associated with neurotic power drives."

vasive that Sullivan objects in principle to the concept of *any* organized psychological impulses, drives, goals, etc. that can be distinguished as proper to the organism itself in contrast to the organism-in-the-interpersonal-situation. He uses the term *dynamism* for those relatively enduring configurations that emerge as the organism experiences its living and that come to offer workable constructs for understanding the significant aspects of interpersonal behavior.

Initially, the organism *pursues satisfactions* implicit in its bodily structure. Such pursuit means relief from tensions arising mainly through chemical disequilibrium and action of the unstriped muscles. The skeletal musculature is at first merely instrumental to this end. The end state desired is called *euphoria,* a condition of tensionless bliss most nearly approximated in deep sleep. The pursuit of satisfactions continues, of course, throughout life, but the purely bodily dynamisms become difficult to distinguish sharply from those arising primarily from other sources.

The latter type of dynamisms are grouped together as the *pursuit of security*. This pursuit is culturally determined and comes to involve the need for approval and prestige. Initially, the infant directly experiences tension (discomfort) through a process of *empathy* when the adults around him are disturbed and hostile. He soon grasps the fact that his own behavior has something to do with the uncomfortable attitudes of the adults, whom he begins to perceive as entities different from the physical world and from himself; he then begins to control his behavior in a manner calculated to reduce these tensions. *Anxiety* (to be discussed in Chap. 11, on dynamics) develops in this interpersonal context. We shall see that avoidance of anxiety rapidly becomes the motive behind the formation of new dynamisms related to the pursuit of security.

Although Sullivan repudiates the concept of an inborn self whose actual or potential capacities may be considered generally human, he lays enormous stress on the *self dynamism*. This enduring configuration develops out of the reflected appraisals of the significant adults around the infant and becomes a factor of prime dynamic importance for all human behavior. Discussion of its operation is postponed, but we may remark here that for Sullivan, as for the other psychoanalysts, the major contours of the self are established rather enduringly in the very early years of childhood and provide the main orientation of the personality toward later experience. Sullivan's emphasis on the situational, interpersonal aspects of psychological events should not be construed as supporting any crude environmentalism.

Loneliness is the obverse of a bodily need for contact with others (a satisfaction), however complicated later by the emergent need for security. The *power motive* is probably an "impulse toward growth," an inborn tendency to express one's abilities, probably especially those inherent in the skeletal musculature and the sense organs. Frustration in these areas leads to feelings of discomfort and helplessness—which are immediately incorporated into the trends described above.

Critical Comment

THE point I shall highlight in comment about all the authors grouped in this Part is the emphasis on the self, the person-as-a-whole. The idea is not new, of course. Many philosophers and psychologists have espoused what Woodworth calls a psychology of the self,[17] in some contrast to psychological theories that emphasize laws, drives, instincts, reflexology, even in the modern sense of dynamic patterns. Classical Freudians are offended by any implication that *they* do not deal with the self, with the person-as-a-whole. They do, of course— both in their actual handling of patients and in *ultimate* theory. But they disapprove of taking the self as a primary psychological unit.

I think it is fair to say that the philosophers and academic psychologists who emphasize the self have not contributed very concretely toward the problem of actually handling people as individuals. Only a system oriented toward therapy can do this. In Freudian *theory* the self is a highly complex construct, the special dynamics of which have not been fully studied. (*Cf.* the discussion of Hartmann, Federn, *et al.*, pp. 95ff.) One may confidently hope that the Freudians are on the way toward such study. The "synthetic function of the ego" is a well-recognized concept. So is the superego, which includes the "ego ideal." The operating power of the self is not, in my opinion, adequately formulated by an "ego function" stated too generally and a "superego function" stated too specifically.

In the conceptual framework offered in Chapter 1, the self is essentially a historical system. Until recently, Freudians have been so interested in the factors (loose dynamic systems) that affect the growth of the individual that they have rather neglected the dynamic significance of the complex person he has become. One might think in terms of an analogy: it is as if they had investigated factors such as the nature of the terrain, character of rainfall, etc., that are significant for the formation of rivers but had paid only casual attention to the way rivers act as dynamic units. It is as if they said, "What is the point of focusing investigation on anything so variable as the river itself when we still do not understand how rivers are formed? Let us concentrate on the general genetic principles, and we can apply them as needed in the individual case."

The point of view of the self theories is that the focus of study ought to be the river itself, how it acts as a unit. It is, to be sure, important to learn how it is formed, but the main thing is how it behaves. A few quite general formative principles will suffice for the understanding of how a specific river comes into being, of the major sources of its flow, and its vulnerable aspects. The important problem is the river. Furthermore, if we deal with human beings instead of a river, we may count upon a *creative* modification of the past from the person himself, so that we need not rely wholly on dams and drainage for effective change. Such creative modification does not mean abrogation of the past in some mystical fashion but rather the fact that the human being as "river" can himself start changing his mode of approach, and that this inner change will modify the whole course of his reactions. (This appreciation of the "creative" capacity of the human being belongs also in the Freudian approach, although it is not there discussed in such rhapsodic terms.)

Once we grant this general focus on the self, the four authors reported in this chapter show very interesting differences. Adler presents the focus most clearly and simply. His entire emphasis is on the individual as a goal-directed action system. In my opinion, this *over*emphasis was valuable, especially at a period when psychological and psychiatric science was mainly concentrated on universals that cross-cut the "individual." This period is not yet altogether past. Adler's insistence on consideration of the goal and life style of the individual still carries an important message, even after we correct for his excessive insistence on a *single* goal.

I am less favorably impressed by his description of how the life style comes about. He posits "universals"—*i.e.*, the helplessness of the infant, his inevitable sense of inferiority, and his consequent will to power. This position is a little like saying that the goal of every river is to reach the sea and interpreting all its behavior in terms of its adaptation to the obstacles it encounters. If one interprets the will to power broadly enough (as Adler does), and if one pays assiduous attention to the manner of adaptation to characteristic obstacles, then one arrives at a fairly workable picture of the human being in our culture. It was important to emphasize the goal of the person-as-a-whole and the *current* adaptive quality of every act. The very grave error in Adler's formulation is what I have called reductionism. An important aspect of human experience, the helplessness of the infant, is used as an abstract principle which is then applied generally in all situations. Adler's view of psychological motivation is never entirely wrong and is quite often overwhelmingly convincing. But it is, to my mind, always limited—like interpreting every aspect of the river by a single important determinant.

I took pains to point out that Adler actually includes much more than inferiority→will-to-superiority in his view of the self. Social feeling, courage, and common sense are functioning parts of the human heritage if they have not been distorted during early training. If I understand him correctly, Adler does not believe that these qualities are inborn as such, but neither are their opposites inborn. On the contrary, man's nature is such as to adapt flexibly and energetically to the world around him. Since this world is largely a world of people—indeed, *must* be peopled if the helpless infant is to survive—his adaptation must be primarily social. Thus, it is not necessary to posit any special social instincts, or even love and aggression, to account for social behavior. It will inevitably develop in consequence of experience, and its nature will depend very largely upon the nature of the child's first experiences.

Horney, Fromm, and Sullivan all emphasize this point, each in his own way. It seems to me essentially true and important. The limitation of Adler's formulation is that he construes the experience of the child too narrowly and even, in a way, incorrectly. The infant must feel painfully "helpless" long before he is intellectually able to conceptualize his problem in the realistic, comparative terms required by Adler's basic theory. In fact, this comparative, *competitive* view of his problem is likely to be of relatively late development (at least well on in the second year, sometimes delayed as late as school age). Probably, indeed, Adler's view has cogency mainly within our own competitive, striving culture which subtly influences the child, via the adults around him, from a very early age. No psychoanalyst denies that some (even many) individuals are guided by power strivings just as Adler describes, but most analysts, and I, feel that the *will to power* involves the development of a special psychic constellation. It is not a universal principle.

Horney, too, accepts the helplessness of the infant as a crucial fact in human psychological development, but she does not leap to the concept of compensation for it as *the* guiding principle. If the infant is well handled, he learns that people are generally helpful and warmly satisfying, that they are not always at his beck and call, and that hence he must learn to do without at times and discover ways of handling difficulties by himself. Enterprise is applauded and guided, but within the framework of what other people need. These are, in a way, easy lessons, because the human *potential* readily includes them. Unfortunately, if it is badly handled, the helplessness of the infant easily leads to a *basic anxiety*, a generalized insecurity underlying all his later reactions. Adler's striving for power is only one, fairly common, means of trying to establish security.

In my opinion, Horney's theoretical position is in essence almost as "reductive" as Adler's, since *the need for security* becomes a kind of universal which supplies the dynamic theme upon which the variations in personality development are constructed. But Horney codifies in a much more sophisticated manner the processes behind the development and maintenance of specific modes of gaining security. She shows how the exaggerated formation of one mode almost inevitably creates an *inner conflict* leading to covert exaggeration in the opposite direction, which can no longer be understood merely as an effort to gain security. Rather, it becomes itself a new threat to security, especially difficult to handle because it is unconscious. She shows more clearly how the unconscious processes grow, and how they lead the person further away from sound appreciation of reality (Adler's common sense)

and true satisfaction. (We shall return to these problems in Chap. 11, on dynamics.)

Finally, Horney shows in a more differentiated manner how an *image* of the self develops, which becomes powerful in its own right. She herself comments that this new development in her theory (it becomes of dominant importance only in *Neurosis and Human Growth*) brings her closer to Adler's position, and she speaks with new appreciation of Adler's insight into the efforts of the patient to maintain and fantastically magnify his view of himself. Even in this last formulation, however, Horney considers "the pride system" as essentially a product of the need for security rather than a reflex of an inevitable sense of inferiority, *à la* Adler.

Furthermore, Horney emphasizes a specific tension between the idealized image of the self and a "real self," of which the patient is somehow dimly aware. Especially in discussing therapy, Horney writes as if this "real self" were a kind of developed entity which exists all the time and which can be counted upon to take over once it is given the opportunity. In theoretical passages she is more cautious: the real self is a *potential*, apparently much in the manner described a few pages back.

Horney's view of the idealized *image* of the self as a psychological syndrome of enormous importance as such seems to me valuable. It is an advance upon Adler's idea that all human behavior can be interpreted directly as a matter of building up the "self," because Adler does not really analyze the concept of the "self" at all. He takes it for granted. Horney here approaches a problem that Freudian theory thus far has tended to neglect—namely, our organized picture of ourselves in its full detail. The tension between this picture of ourselves and what we actually are or vaguely feel ourselves to be is undoubtedly very great, and it is not *fully* handled, to my mind, by the Freudian concept of super-ego-ego tension and the ego ideal. Jung handles *part* of this problem adroitly with his concept of the persona (see pp. 558*ff.*), the mask, the social front, which stands in varying relations to ego consciousness and to the total personality. My objection to Horney's position does not apply primarily to the concept of the idealized image as a relatively coherent construct, *a substructure of the ego,* which normally develops in our culture (often to a pathological degree) and which then operates as a dynamic system in its own right. I have called this substructure *the self image* and shall refer to it frequently in later chapters.

My complaint against Horney's latest theory mainly concerns the implication of a "real self" which can be released all of a piece, as it were, if the idealized image is disposed of. This view presupposes a kind of maturing of the human potential under cover, so that the sickest patient, whose attitudes have been distorted since infancy, in some sense "really" is capable of a sophisticated, genuinely mature judgment in complex adult situations—if only his "real self" can be allowed to speak. This view is contrary to all we know of how such judgments are developed. Adler and Jung do not go so far, even though they set out with a somewhat similar concept of the neurotically inflated image of the self and of the importance of this image. The new, more vital relationships of the person to his environment must be courageously sought for and *developed.* They are not merely "discovered."

Fromm's position on this point is more deeply philosophical (he himself calls it dialectic) than those of the other analysts. The sense of self is the product of the evolutionary trend toward individuation and carries within itself the longing for the older status of nondifferentiation, "belongingness" (*cf.* Angyal's emphasis on autonomous and homonomous trends).[18] I reserve full discussion of Fromm's position for the next chapter, but I must here remark on the essential difference between Fromm's view of the self and the clinically derived emphasis of Horney. Fromm insists upon the *potential* of the human being but considers his problems as an essential part of his destiny. In his clinical evaluation of specific difficulties, Fromm is often closer to Freud than to Horney. The real self is not merely "discoverable"; it is considered the *achievement* of the species and of every individual.

Sullivan's position on the self seems to me the most valuable. Mullahy criticizes him as too far neglecting the "individual" in his theory.[19] With some timorousness, because the man who worked closely with Sullivan for years ought to know, I remark that this is not my impression. The *self dynamism* seems to play the preponderant role in Sullivan's actual thinking about people, as we shall see in later chapters. What Sullivan emphasizes is that this self dynamism is a *construct,* not a biological given which can be defined in its important particulars as *the* individual, species *homo sapiens.* Nevertheless, it operates as a unifying system from the very outset. Although it is not coextensive with the total personality and is in all its details a product of the interaction between organism and milieu, it provides the major organizing function of the personality. *As it develops,* it determines which aspects of experience may be freely integrated with one another in full awareness (consciousness) and which are to be neglected or actually dissociated as subdynamisms (subsystems, in my vocabulary) very imperfectly related to the self dynamism. These *sub*dynamisms may take their dynamic focus either from the bodily needs of the organism or from the milieu. (The lust dynamism, for example, demands satisfaction as a bodily urge and becomes constellative in its own right. But the social construct of acceptable attitudes and behavior regarding lust *also* provides a quite dynamic system which tends to be accepted as such in the emergent self dynamism, so that infringements of a *social* pattern may have profound repercussions at the psychological level.)

Sullivan's view of the growth and functioning of the self dynamism will be discussed in later chapters. The theoretical conception of the self as a dynamic construct creatively related to (and relating) subsystems which have varying degrees of tightness of structure (autonomy) seems to me to offer a very useful formulation. It is not unlike the Freudian concept of the ego, as elaborated by Hartmann, Rapaport, and others (see pp. 95*ff.*). In some ways, it cuts more sharply to the heart of this special problem, because Sullivan does not have to deal with Freud's instinct theory and Freud's established structural approach. Thus, he can observe more flexibly the synthesizing power of the self dynamism in its important relations to bodily needs and social patterns, without having to redefine the remnants of instinct universals still covertly present in much Freudian thinking.

By the same token, however, Sullivan *loses* a great deal. Like all the analysts treated here, he underplays the role of the biological demands of the organism. He also seems to underplay important *organized aspects* of the self dynamism itself, so that it often appears to operate too much as a unit. He writes of the development of an "internal critic" of some importance, but this critic seems a very pallid homologue of Freud's *superego*, not well studied in origin or function. (Sullivan frequently borrows Freudian formulations on this point, without making clear what distinctions he would draw, if any.) Neither Sullivan nor Freudians make much use *in theory* of Horney's concept of the idealized image of the self or of Jung's concept of the persona.

All three concepts—superego, idealized image, persona—represent systematizations within the self dynamism which their proponents consider as *developing* in the course of living in human society; as variable both in content and in tight-

ness of structure from one individual to the next, and doubtless from one society to the next. (On the latter point, see Chaps. 4 and 9.) Nevertheless, such systematizations are almost inevitable in human society and may become very cogent indeed as fairly autonomous units, tension-producing in some circumstances.

It would seem quite feasible to incorporate this type of subdynamism into Sullivan's general formulation more "systematically" than seems common for Sullivan and his followers. Once the sting of a philosophical universalization is taken out of these concepts, it seems clear that they are true and important. Every analyst knows that the parents play an enormous unconscious systematizing part in the development of "conscience," and that this "conscience" (*superego*) may attain tragic proportions. Consciousness of role, not altogether conscious, has been stressed by social psychologists[20] rather beyond Jung's concept of the *persona*, and rather beyond what most *psychoanalysts* have considered significant. But one can hardly doubt either the systematic quality of this role consciousness or its importance.

Horney's *idealized image* seems to be a fusion of role consciousness (persona) with the deep compulsiveness of the superego. My guess is that this *fusion* actually occurs so often that protagonists of the superego can solidly maintain their position with secondary attention to social roles, whereas social psychologists can make out an excellent case for the relationship to the parents as merely one aspect of the role-forming process, admittedly the most important.

For the kind of patient most often encountered in a New York City practice, the fusion that Horney calls the idealized image must be clinically recurrent and powerful in much the way she describes. I shall suggest in later chapters that Horney's excellent clinical observations are related to the problems of what Fromm has called the "marketing orientation," that Horney in formulating her basic theory was as much influenced by her times as Freud was by his. I suspect that it is in a culture in which the child *cannot*, for reasons of social mobility, take over any direct, may I say *literal*, role-consciousness from his parents that the self image becomes differentiated far beyond the superego as Freud conceived it and beyond Jung's concept of the persona. Very possibly it is only in certain societies that the idealized image becomes so strongly integrated and plays the preponderant intrapsychic role ascribed to it by Horney. In other cultures, there may more typically be several images of the self, relatively loosely related to one another and much more closely related to specific biologico-social patterns.

Thus, although it seems to me that the Freudians have too far neglected the dynamic importance of the self system, the self theories have left the concept too far undifferentiated, with the result that it becomes a philosophical universal instead of a developmental construct. Sullivan's concept of the self dynamism readily *allows for* further study of significant subdynamisms, although Sullivan did not undertake such study in a systematic way. On the contrary, his clinical approach seems often to reject subdynamisms of all sorts in favor of a "pursuit of security" almost as infinitely flexible as Adler's. Or perhaps I should say rather that he does not stay with any formulation of important subdynamisms long enough to make it very useful—apparently out of fear lest it have a stultifying effect on clinical understanding of the living patient.

My own suggestion is that the formation and functional dynamics of the *self image* or images be investigated in their own right as an addition to the usual psychoanalytic investigations. This suggestion seems entirely feasible in systems in which the self is made the primary psychological unit.

A further point that requires discussion in this chapter is the neglect or active repudiation of Freud's views concerning the constellating power of the biologically determined sexual and aggressive drives. In so far as Freud conceives these drives as instinctual forces operating in a vacuum, I agree with the repudiation. But this is not very far. Freud did have ideas about universal principles—so did everybody else in the scientific philosophy of his time—and his generalizations led to Eros and Thanatos (see pp. 108ff. for my critique). His clinical practice in Vienna probably led to an overemphasis on the Oedipus complex as the nuclear problem in neurosis in much the same way that Horney's practice in New York led to an overemphasis on the role of the idealized image of the self. Shall we therefore say that infantile sexuality plays no significant role in personality development, that the Oedipus complex was a local phenomenon, and that the idealized image of the self was a pitiable mistake?

This is not my conclusion, and again I should like to align myself with Sullivan's *theory*. He writes of oral, anal, and "lust" dynamisms, specifically giving them place in his theory as important constellative systems. But instead of carrying through in Freudian terms, he subordinates these dynamisms to the child's need to feel comfort with the ministering adult, and his position becomes generally hostile to the Freudian emphasis on infantile sexuality.

Let us accept Sullivan's position to the hilt—but then consider what is likely to be comforting and important to an infant and what the infant is likely to do about it. As I read Sullivan's account of infancy—how the baby "catches on" to this and that—I was impressed by an analysis of *intellectual* development beyond anything I had read before in psychoanalytic literature. But Sullivan's infant seemed to be "catching on" to its environment, whereas Freud's infant seemed to be *creating* its environment, as it were—or at least to be posing the major terms on which it would (could) interpret and react to its environment. Freud's infant seemed to me more like the babies I have known and the infant I would hypothesize as an evolutionary product.

Much of my critical comment in the Freudian section of this book has been devoted to the nonsexual systems observable in infancy, because I think they have been neglected by Freudians. Yet I cannot state too emphatically my judgment that the infant *is* overwhelmingly concerned with its profound biological functions (oral, anal, and genital); that its early interpretation of the world *must* be primarily constellated around these functions; that to neglect the constelling power of these functions per se in early personality development is to falsify what I have presented as Sullivan's own approach—an empirical view of emergent dynamisms.

In my opinion, the neglect→repudiation of the sexual systems in Sullivan's writings and among the "Sullivanians" is more an accident of his times, a reaction against a narrow Freudianism, than intrinsic to his theoretical approach. In later chapters, I shall try to point out more specifically where *I think* Sullivan was wrong on this point and others. My "think" is justified at this moment of writing, but I am not at all sure that it will remain justified. Among the schools discussed in this chapter, *I think* it is "Sullivan's" that will survive and that will correct its own errors.

[1] K. Horney, *Our Inner Conflicts,* W. W. Norton & Co., 1945, p. 19.
[2] ———, *Neurosis and Human Growth,* W. W. Norton & Co., 1950, p. 15.
[3] ———, *Our Inner Conflicts,* p. 27.
[4] *Ibid.,* p. 41.
[5] E. Fromm, *Man for Himself,* Rinehart & Co., 1947, p. 45.
[6] *Ibid.,* p. 250.
[7] H. S. Sullivan, *Conceptions of Modern Psychiatry,* William Alanson White Foundation, 1947, p. 24.
[8] *Ibid.,* p. 15.
[9] *Ibid.*
[10] H. S. Sullivan, "Introduction to the Study of Interpersonal Relations," *Psychiatry,* 1938, 1:123n.
[11] ———, *Conceptions of Modern Psychiatry,* p. 10.
[12] *Ibid.,* p. 21.
[13] *Ibid.,* p. 43.
[14] *Ibid.,* p. 6.
[15] *Ibid.,* pp. 6f.
[16] *Ibid.,* p. 6.
[17] R. S. Woodworth, *Contemporary Schools of Psychology,* rev. ed., Ronald Press Co., 1948, pp. 241ff.
[18] A. Angyal, *Foundations for a Science of Personality,* The Commonwealth Fund, 1941, Chaps. 2, 6.
[19] P. Mullahy, *Oedipus—Myth and Complex,* Hermitage Press, 1948, pp. 333f.
[20] See T. M. Newcomb, *Social Psychology,* Dryden Press, 1950.

Chapter Nine

THE TERMS OF THE

MILIEU

ALL THE SCHOOLS discussed in Part III make a very special point of the *adaptive* nature of the human organism. It is, of course, an organism with quite obvious biological requirements, among which oral, anal, and genital needs may be listed. But although the analysts I have grouped as "Freudian" tend to consider such needs as primary determinants of personality development, the analysts in this group consider them as incidental to problems of adaptation to a social (interpersonal) milieu. Toilet training, for example, is considered important not because the *child* is especially interested in the process of evacuation and its products but because *parents* and *societies* impose restrictions in this area. The significant point is not the anality of the young child (or its oral and genital urges) but rather the social (interpersonal) situation it encounters.

The terms of the milieu are, therefore, crucial for the understanding of personality dynamics in these schools. Whereas I found it feasible to comment upon the four authors together as regards the terms of the organism and the genetic process (Chap. 8 and 10) as generally different from Freud and the analysts who essentially accept the libido theory, no such lumping of schools is possible on the topics on which they differ profoundly among themselves.

369

The reader is reminded that he may, if he chooses, read the *expository* material on a single author successively in Chapters 8, 9, and 11 without much loss through omitting the concomitant account of the other three in the same chapters. The double-column material, however is designed to be cumulative. Thus much of the criticism, both positive and negative, presented after the discussion of Adler applies equally well to the other three authors and is not repeated in detail. Instead, comment is focused in a comparative manner on distinctive points of difference among the authors.

ADLER

ADLER'S ANALYSIS of environmental influences was largely concerned with the family group. He agreed with Freud on the crucial nature of the very early years (up to five) in determining personality trends and also on the crucial nature of intrafamily relationships. But where Freud emphasized the fate of the biological impulses of the infant as they meet reality in the home, and the longing of the child for the mother as a love object in the growth of his genitality, Adler based his psychology on the general attitude of the parents, especially the mother, as expressed in training all along the line and on the interrelationships of the siblings.

PARENT-CHILD RELATIONSHIPS

Adler's major rubrics for parent-child relations are the *spoiled* and the *hated* child. For the sibling relationships, he discusses especially the *only* child and the *first, second,* and *youngest* child.

The *spoiled* child, pampered in every wish, develops difficulties for two reasons. First, he forms the expectation early in life that he will always be taken care of and that his whim is law. Adler notes that many criminals were spoiled children. They quite honestly feel that society owes them a living without contribution from themselves, and hence that there is really nothing wrong in taking their due when people seem reluctant to offer it in later life.

Their view of themselves is often grandiose, in consonance with the view taught by their adoring parents. Essentially dependent, they command like princes royal.

Criminality is only one, relatively rare, consequence. "Lovable Lorenzo Jones," whose adventures have entertained afternoon radio listeners for many years,* is an excellent example of the spoiled child. His inflated dreams repeatedly fail to pan out. He plays the role of genius to himself and is not above occasional good-natured dishonesty in his endless expectation of fame and fortune. His wife, Belle, has to remind him of moral precepts, and she wages a losing battle against his failure to appreciate the realities of the household budget as well as his dickers with wider enterprise. Mr. Micawber ("Something will turn up") and the Paycock in *Juno and the Paycock* offer literary examples. In a different key, with more modulation, real families have the same problem with a "spoiled child" personality. The type is very familiar.

Secondly, the spoiled child does not learn techniques of adjustment to real social situations because he is protected from the need for personal effort. Even a first-class intelligence may be used in whimsical fashion rather than in sequential learning. Mr. X was brought up as the only son of a rich man with the idea that he would merely administer the estate and exploit the subtle intelligence his parents admired. Unfortunately, his father developed a mild psychosis in later life, and somehow so compromised a capital of nearly a million dollars that all the son inherited at his death was a few mortgages. This young man faced up to the fact of actual poverty fairly soon, but his efforts to deal with it were extremely trying to his relatives and friends. Ultimately, his own widow and children fell upon public relief.

Mr. X had had training in the law, but he had never passed his bar exams because neither he nor his parents saw any reason for subjecting him to distasteful drudgery. He knew a lot about books, but the public library could not use such scattered, esoteric information. The private bookshop he set up with his tiny remaining capital failed—despite loans from relatives. Relatives who contributed from their hard-won savings were not pleased to learn that Mr. X had spent a third of the money lent him on a lovely but unsaleable first edition, another third on back wages for a maid. Mr. X felt that he could

---

* Incidentally, soap-opera characters offer a curiously cogent example of the life style (not to mention the repetition compulsion). Amos and Andy and the Kingfish *et al.* have been getting into the same kind of scrapes for twenty years. If any one of these people acted out of character for a moment, a million voices would be lifted in protest. The popular short story or novel ends on a note of resolution after a dramatic event. The continued radio story and even the gag shows succeed because of the *characterization*. Schnozzle Durante, Eddie Cantor, Charlie McCarthy, and Mortimer Snerd get belly laughs from jokes that on the "Can you top this?" program would scarcely raise the laugh-meter an inch. The laugh is supplied by audience appreciation of the *person*. So, too, with the comic strip *vs.* the cartoon.

not ask his wife to cook and launder. It was enough economy that he himself lunched at a drugstore counter. A third of the family loan did go to creditors, to postpone bankruptcy by a few months.

Mr. X honestly did not know how to cope with the problems of making a living or getting along with his fellows. His ineptness in handling money and customers was due neither to stupidity nor to ill will. The life style established by early "pampering" was such that he had never learned the techniques of initiative, realistic planning, and interpersonal give-and-take.

According to Adler, these desirable traits develop through the actual experience of the infant and young child in mastering his environment and adapting to other individuals. The overprotectiveness of the parents deprives the child of the opportunity to learn how to master and to adapt, and inculcates attitudes of expectation of total support and unquestionable superiority.

The *hated* child also receives erroneous training. Because the world around him is essentially hostile, he early develops the attitude that people are against him and that he must fight for his rights. This he may do with energy and resourcefulness.* He is typically very difficult to live with or work with and may defeat his own ends by his uncooperative or actively hostile behavior. An example is Miss Y. Her mother died when she was very young; her father, irresponsible and bibulous, found her a nuisance. Relatives brought her up grudgingly, sending her to work in a factory at the earliest possible age. This girl put herself through the commercial course in high school, earned money as stenographer, and finally entered college at the age of 22. Her work was so good that the college authorities offered her a scholarship to spare her the fatigue of self-help and summer work. This assistance she refused. "I can pay my way. I will not be owing anybody." She made few friends among the students.

I knew her rather well when we were both in college, better after graduation, when she was employed by an older friend of mine. She was his confidential secretary and very much appreciated. "She has a head like a man's," he commented in glowing praise. Ultimately, in great embarrassment, he asked if I could help in a situation that had become intolerable. In the small emergencies of office routine, she refused to take dictation beyond her stated job requirements. Because she objected to being summoned by a buzzer, her employer personally invited her to his office each time he needed her. Finally,

---

* One should mention here the deeply rejected children ("institutional" children and the migratory orphans of Europe, who have never known a close relationship with people). These children may become so profoundly discouraged, to use Adler's term, as to go into a state of lethargy (marasmus) or become antisocial out of a fundamental inability to internalize moral considerations (psychopathy). The differentiation of this group has come from later study, although it is consonant with Adler's thinking.

she threatened to resign because he asked her to deliver an urgent parcel, wrapped in brown paper, on her way home. Her employer told me that he had asked in advance how she got home and that he knew that the errand would take only a few extra minutes of her time. "I *told* her she could leave early." The dénouement was that the boss delivered the parcel himself at the expense of an hour of his time, but he was annoyed and perplexed. "Do I really let the best secretary I have ever had go because of a parcel? This is the last straw," he said. "She's a wonderful girl, she does her job beautifully, but everybody complains about her. What can I do?"

The girl, when I asked her about her resignation, was very peevish. "Deliver a parcel? Wrapped in brown paper? I wouldn't be seen on the street with a bundle. Would you?" I remarked that I walked home almost every day with groceries in large brown bags, that her *boss* had not minded carrying the parcel—only it took him an hour to do what she could have done in a few minutes.

Actually it was the brown paper and the "errand running" that had upset this girl to the point of giving up a job she really liked. She had worked so hard against the enmity of her family to achieve "status" that she would tolerate nothing that seemed beneath her dignity. She could not trust the motives of the college authorities and her boss. She violently rejected "charity" and any sort of "imposition." Her life style was premised on being hated, on struggling for her rights in a hostile world.

Ideally, the parent gives loving support to the young child, with encouragement to initiative and self-confidence. The child is helped neither too much nor too little. Discipline and training have a positive character, never "breaking the child's will." His own bent is understood and gently corrected or fostered, as the case may be. In such a home, the child develops courage and social feeling. His normal feeling of inferiority leads to constructive striving rather than a demanding helplessness or hostile guardedness and attack.

SIBLING RELATIONSHIPS

The home environment usually includes siblings as well as parents. The *only* child is typically spoiled, occasionally hated. For him there is no corrective influence for good or ill provided by competition with his siblings. The oldest child, the second child, and the youngest child are subjected, typically, to special environmental pressures and opportunities.

The *oldest* child is the dethroned king. After a year or more of so commanding his surroundings as to expect the exclusive attention and help of adults, he is suddenly confronted with a young usurper. In any family, the new baby takes up much of the attention previously accorded to our hero, the first-born. The adults give the newcomer more attention partly because he is new and appealingly helpless or cute, partly because very young babies necessarily require more care than toddlers, at more regular intervals and in more emergencies. The first-born is likely, therefore, to fight in a variety of ways to regain his lost empire, and to be nostalgically oriented toward the past. The first-born is also likely to be the leader among his younger siblings, especially during the very early years of life. He is also more subject to parental authority and is held responsible for himself and others more insistently than the littler ones. These infantile patterns tend to become his life style: the leader in fear of authority and also of encroachments from below.

The *second* child, if fairly close in years to the first-born, is in the position of having a pacemaker always before him. Furthermore, his status may be encroached upon by still younger children. Very commonly, the earnest zeal of young parents to bring up their offspring "right" has somewhat abated by the time of the second child's arrival, and hence the atmosphere surrounding early training is more relaxed. Thus, the second child tends to be less concerned with authority, responsibility, and absolute power, but he tends to be more directly competitive with his peers. He is likely to carry through life the deep conviction that he is not so able as others, even though, by the time he reaches the second grade, he may have succeeded in outstripping his older brother. This attitude may either discourage him or make him rebelliously striving beyond the ordinary.

The *youngest* child is never displaced in infancy by a new baby who monopolizes the mother's attention. He is often petted by the whole family, although occasionally a late arrival is experienced as a nuisance in lives already oriented in other directions. Thus, he is in many respects like the only child. But he must deal practically as a little child with several competitors, all of whom are stronger than he, thus keeping his strivings in closer touch with real people. His spoiling commonly leads to a somewhat inflated self-esteem, which is also uneasily conscious of actual weakness. It is not surprising, therefore, to find in legends and folk tales the recurrent theme of the youngest son who accomplishes by guile or wisdom tasks in which the brute strength of the older brothers failed. An excellent prototype for the cockiness and realistic striving of the youngest is the biblical Joseph.*

Adler focused his whole emphasis on the kind of experience the child had

---

* The *fact* that Joseph was succeeded by Benjamin serves only to illustrate the importance of the *psychological* situation as against any magical or quasi-biological rule about order of birth. Benjamin, as the child of Jacob's old age, who cost the life of his beloved mother, occupied a position almost outside the family hierarchy. He was always the cherished little one, *hors de concours.*

in infancy. His generalizations about the terms of the milieu followed his observations of what *usually* happens in the early years of children's lives. He himself constantly pointed out the special impact of such general social factors as laws of primogeniture on the experience of the siblings, and also of the special factors within a given family that would modify the problem presented to a specific child. His point was not that order of birth is in itself important but that the place of the child in the family introduces fairly definable problems which—granted the general need to attain superiority—tend to call forth certain characteristic kinds of solution. The essence of Adler's creed is *not* to define the child in any fixed manner but to define, so far as may be done, the problem the child has tried to solve.

The attitude of the parents, especially of the mother, is of major importance in determining how the problem of sibling rivalry is structured for the individual child. (Or, I think with Adler's consent, one could state the principle the other way around: sibling rivalry becomes important to the child in very early years because it so strongly affects the parent-child relationship.) The rubrics *spoiled* and *hated* are quite as important in Adler's later writings as *organ inferiority* and *order of birth*. The good Individual Psychologist sees them in intimate relationship to each other—in a context in which the person is trying courageously or unrealistically, with social feeling or limited self-interest, to overcome his inevitable feelings of inferiority. To state this more positively, the individual is constantly striving toward his own goal, which in the last analysis is always some kind of superiority. The specific kind of superiority he fancies and the methods he adopts toward its achievement derive from the very particular circumstances of his own life. Among these circumstances, Adler has tried to codify some which exert an especially potent influence, so potent that the psychologist should always inform himself about them and try to understand what the child has done about them.

CULTURAL INFLUENCES

Adler's official rubrics are focused on the first five years of life within the family. An aspect of his approach very difficult to report is his attention to *broader cultural influences*. Even more than Freud's, his discussion of individual cases and his incidental comments throughout his work reflect an appreciation of the important role of influences that come to bear later, notably the school. The limitation of these comments of his is that they remain on the level of common sense as regards delineation of specific social impacts. Adler's concern with the individual is portrayed in the very label he applied to his school: Individual Psychology. He was, in part justifiably, very touchy when accused of being too individualistic. He pointed quite correctly to the important place given in his basic theory to social participation, and also to his constant reference to social factors in discussing the individual or even special aspects of theory. Yet, in practice, his contribution along this line was more to destroy bad generalizations then current than to substitute new generalizations.

In theory, Adler was prone to discount altogether the psychological importance of broad environmental factors, such as poverty. He remarked eloquently on the high achievement of many underprivileged boys: Lincoln, Carnegie, Jesus. He observed that in the same poor family one child may become delinquent, another a law-abiding citizen. Therefore, he argued, neither heredity nor environment can be the determining factor. For Adler, the determining factor is the child's *attitude* toward the handicap of poverty—his life style—just as an organ inferiority is not determining in itself but only in relation to what the person feels and does about it.

The only rubrics—or, shall we say, points of orientation for scientific ordering of the data—that Adler offered are the ones we have described. *But,* if a specific child was doing badly in school Adler often commented that the economic and cultural level of his home was so poor that he could not be expected to learn as well as his more privileged fellows—that he did not have enough tools. Or the scolding of a teacher may so discourage a child to whom grades are especially important in his goal strivings that he stops working altogether. In practice, the institutions and attitudes of the wider society bulk large in Adler's interpretations of the individual case, in his therapy, and in his suggestions for the practical application of Individual Psychology. In fact, he makes much of the *three problems of life*: social adjustment, work adjustment, and adjustment to love and marriage. All these problems are essentially problems of adaptation to the milieu conceived in rather broad social terms.

Apparently, however, Adler made no effort to classify social and cultural impacts as he did the early family influences. He was content mainly to point out the effect of the life style on behavior in relation to the three problems of life, and to suggest how understanding of the individual bent could be used in education, in the law, in medicine, in vocational guidance. His general social program, in so far as he formulated one, called for encouraging a more favorable atmosphere; for establishing genuine cooperation rather than competition; for understanding rather than discipline; above all, for trusting in the capacity of each person to arrange or rearrange his life style in a happy and productive manner.

The only exception to the statement concerning the absence of broader social rubrics is Adler's concept of *masculine protest*. Adler denied the existence of any native psychological differences between men and women. Our society, however, like most patriarchal societies, Adler points out, places a premium on masculinity. The little girl is *made to feel* inferior in countless small ways simply by the traditions of a man's world. It is only recently that her rights have been equal before the law. Occasionally, her parents openly regret not having had a boy. Her brothers are very likely to be teasing, excluding, or at best condescending toward "girls" in childhood, however worshipful they may become during adolescence. Thus, every woman has an additional burden of inferiority feelings to carry. Like all the special hazards previously discussed, this one may be successfully handled. With an extra-heavy dose of experience in derogation of her sex—perhaps especially if the mother, because of her own suffering, is unable to help her—the female child may try to reject her sex and compensate in the direction of becoming as masculine as possible. This becomes her path toward superiority.

As usual, the situation presents wheels within wheels. The girl with a strong unconscious masculine protest may exaggerate her femininity—sometimes because she is afraid to be "different," sometimes as a weapon against men, whom she considers as so many scalps to be hung as trophies. Moreover, many men whose life style is fundamentally tender, timid, sensitive, artistic—*i.e.*, "feminine," in our culture—becomes so ashamed of their failure to live up to the cultural masculine ideal that they too develop a masculine protest. A woman may relish having been a tomboy in her childhood, but even a mature man cannot smile genuinely when an acquaintance reminiscing about the old days exclaims, "What a sissy you were, pal! Remember in eighth grade . . .?" The young sissy is very likely to become the aggressive he-man in compensation. In discouragement, or in rebellious flaunting of his own "feminine" tastes, he may become a homosexual.

The masculine protest, like organ inferiorities and aspects of the family constellation, must be seen in relation to other factors in the upbringing of the child. It has been described at some length because it is a label for a specific set of *social* influences beyond the person and his family, which makes for a heightened sense of inferiority. It is the one social influence that has acquired the dignity of a special Adlerian term; it is the one *codification* of the implications of a social attitude for personality structure.

SUMMARY

Adler, like Freud, believed that the first five years of life are crucial for personality structure. It is then that the life style is set up, largely under the influence of the family. Psychologically, all children, except those who have a gross brain defect, are born equal, and all of them normally feel inferior. The point at which they feel most inferior—and hence the direction assumed by the compensatory striving for superiority—is determined partly by specific organ inferiorities, partly by the interpersonal situation in which they first learn to adjust themselves to life. The general style of coping with events and people throughout life is developed through the actual experience of coping with their parents and siblings.

Adler distinguished several types of family situation which set a special kind of problem for the infant and therefore tend to call forth a characteristic kind of solution. The child who has been *spoiled* or *hated* tends to expect pampering or to anticipate hostility all his life. Order of birth also modifies the influences of the milieu for the little child. The only child, the first-born, the second-born, and the youngest child are likely to show a life style typical for the kind of rivalry, pampering, and rejection they had to meet.

Despite the preponderant influence of the first training, Adler was very much concerned with later social impacts, especially the school, where the child may learn better techniques of cooperation and more self-confidence and enterprise, or where he may become seriously discouraged. He stressed the importance of understanding the goal and life style of each child, and the value of encouragement as against harsh discipline.

In his discussion of cases and his comments on the application of Individual Psychology to groups, Adler constantly related the personality of the individual to the broader social influences he encountered. He emphasized three life problems everyone must somehow solve: social adjustment, work adjustment, and adjustment to love and marriage. He made much of the need for proper training along these lines and often spoke of the limitations imposed by poverty, harsh authority, bad companions, unsuitable work, and the like.

At only one point, however, did he generalize with anything like the clarity accorded to intrafamily relations the problems set by wider social influences. Social attitudes toward sex differences in our culture are, he felt, so strong as themselves to have a constellating effect on personality development, especially in cases in which the social impact has been especially strong. "Feminine" qualities (what are called feminine—he denies any real psychological difference between the sexes) are held in such low esteem that women carry an extra measure of inferiority feeling and may compensate by what Adler called the "masculine protest." The exaggerated he-man also is usually compensating for an inferiority complex centered about fears of so-called feminine traits in himself.

Critical Comment

IN CRITIQUE, I stress again Adler's formulation of the role of the environment in psychological development. He stated the issue very early in a manner which deserves especial applause: No environmental factor "causes" a psychological result. What the environment does is set a relatively special kind of problem which the human organism attempts to solve in its own way. Since human resources, especially the resources of the infant, are not unlimited, babies confronted with much the same problem are likely to solve it in much the same manner. The type of solution hit upon during the extremely malleable years of early childhood tends to orient the person's whole approach to life (his life style). Only in this roundabout way can environmental factors be seen as "causative."

Adler attempted to codify the situational differences in the life of the young child that are recurrent enough and important enough to represent types of solution characteristic for adults: the general attitude of the parents, and relationship with siblings. No one nowadays doubts the importance of these matters. But almost everyone doubts that their orienting role is as *preponderant* as Adler suggested. He himself observed that special factors within a particular family may so drastically influence the situation encountered by the child that the usual cultural inferences would not operate in his case. So far as I know, he never discussed the problem in terms of gross cultural variations, such as those presented by societies (*e.g., Samoa*) in which the family unit is so large that no child *experiences* being the eldest or youngest in anything like the way Adler describes. I cannot imagine that Adler would attempt to force his views of the psychology peculiar to order of birth on peoples of such radically different background. He came, indeed, to lay more stress on the attitude of the parent. In this area, his early formulation comes very close to the emphasis in all current psychoanalytic schools on the need for general warmth and realistic encouragement from the ministering adults.

In a general way, Adler emphasized the importance of later experience more than was fashionable for the psychoanalyst of his day, and in a general way he was right. His insistence on social and vocational adjustment as well as love and marriage represented a valuable extension of psychoanalytic thought beyond the office, beyond the alleviation of neurotic symptoms thought to be mainly sexual in origin and implication. But again he was right only in a general way. He was so active in repudiating the *bad* social generalizations of his time that he tended to take up arms against *any* generalizations. It is ridiculous to deny the general situational influence of poverty because a few individuals have surmounted it—just as it would be ridiculous to deny the importance of order of birth because some individuals are preponderantly influenced by other aspects of their early family experience. Surely the way of science is to follow Adler's own admonition as stated earlier in this critique: *What special problems do typical situations of broader social structure set for the individual, and how is he likely to find a solution psychologically?* The answer is more difficult when one considers the problems of the older child and the adult, because their resources are more varied than those of the baby. The nature of the scientific question is the same, although Adler did not fully recognize this problem.

I suggested that Adler did make a

social generalization on one point: the masculine protest. Again, he was right in a general way in stressing the importance of cultural attitudes toward women and "feminine" traits in men. But our society, and subgroups within our society, are much more variable on this point than Adler recognized, and their attitudes are much too complexly wrought of idealization and devaluation to be subsumable under the single rubric of female inferiority. Furthermore, no analysis of the influence of social attitudes, however correct, precludes the idea that psychological differences directly related to physiologically determined sex differences are *also* operative. It was useful historically for Adler to speak out firmly against the idea of the biological inferiority of women, current at the turn of the century, and in a way fostered by the Freudian view of sexual differences. But today the concept of the masculine protest seems too limited to be considered valuable.

The major criticism of Adler's position about the terms of the milieu is that it is based upon an oversimplified view of the dynamics of the individual. I have already suggested that the life style is not so simple a continuum as Adler implies and that it is not built entirely out of the need to feel superior. Adler construed the problem of the infant and the young child too narrowly, and he was insufficiently aware of the complexity of adult dynamics. His reductionism in the area of the psychology of the individual actually prevented fruitful elaboration of his admirable initial approach to inquiry into social factors. The very great merit of the latter has had to be rediscovered by other analytic schools and by "environmentalists," who often did not see the basic problem so clearly as Adler did.

HORNEY

LIKE ALL PSYCHOANALYSTS, Horney grants the profound effects of early experience in the family upon personality development, although she seems somewhat less insistent on the point than Adler and Freud and more ready to envisage the dynamic significance of later impacts. The infantile pattern receives *heavy* stress only in cases of deep neurosis, in which, she points out, the basic anxiety of the patient always derives from the child's feeling of being helpless in a hostile world. She distinguishes this condition from the "situational neurosis," in which the person whose early growth was essentially normal breaks under intolerable strain from present circumstances.

Probably it is fair to say that for Horney childhood experience, although always important, is determining as such only in serious pathology. A reasonably satisfactory childhood leaves the person free to respond fairly directly to the opportunities and pressures of later life. For the general run of people, close examination of their preschool life is less rewarding than study of their subsequent career: what conditions they had to meet, what they did about them. Any six-year-old is entitled to a bit of fearfulness in the new environment of school and must react to this impact with the techniques he has thus far acquired. If his techniques are reasonably flexible, if his real self has not already been stifled, the way in which he responds will depend largely on the offering of the school. Harsh, inhibitory treatment may turn the scales one way; tender, encouraging treatment the other—with modifications by the special bent of the child and the climate of his home. Only the deeply neurotic child will turn the school experience into a reflection of his own needs almost regardless of the real situation.

With this general orientation, Horney is more sketchy than Adler about the specific intrafamily situations which determine character development. In individual cases she may often find the Adlerian rubrics helpful. She would feel no need to make a bow to Adler in pointing out the role of parents or siblings, but she would certainly inquire into them, occasionally giving them great weight. In her writings, Horney is not much interested in *generalizations* about early conditions of specific import for specific personality development. She is more concerned with what the person is doing with his attitudes here and now.

Thus, Horney's account of the early family drama is less elaborated than Adler's or (on a different basis) Freud's. She states that *"the basic evil is invariably a lack of genuine warmth and affection [from the parents]"* (my italics).[1] The reason for this lack she traces back to the neurotic personality of the parents themselves, plus their own entanglements with social patterns. The parent who is himself neurotically compliant, aggressive, or detached in his social relations is likely to foster similar attitudes (or their dynamic opposites) in the child. Lacking the early warmth, love, appreciation, and security which allow the real self to develop soundly with flexible, realistic responsiveness to later social events, the child of the neurotic home is oversensitive both to the neurotic social values of its parents and to the later impacts of social groups. "Normal" self-esteem and feeling for others and for the realistic contours of life situations are hampered.

An example is Shirley, who came to my attention when she was a college student. Her work as a freshman was poor almost to the point of failure. She seemed irresponsible, only moderately intelligent, superficial, and bigoted. Her parents were annoyed by reports of inadequate achievement, due primarily, according to her teachers, to lack of effort. Late in the freshman year, Shirley began to improve scholastically. In her second year her teachers gave her better grades and expressed appreciation of her growing earnestness and concern with intellectual and social issues. In February of her second year, the girl brought me a letter from her mother accusing her of frivolity. An unattractive girl, the mother wrote, should make the most of the opportunities for which her parents were sacrificing so much.

Shirley's "frivolity" seemed to consist in occasionally staying at the college over the week end to study and in going out with groups of young intellectuals of "dubious character." The "dubious characters" included the very upright son of a poor clergyman—in fact, anyone who would not be a first-class catch as a husband. The parental "sacrifice" seemed to involve mainly the second housemaid, who might have to be dismissed to balance the budget. Hostility to her daughter spoke from every line of the mother's letter. A little later, Shirley brought her mother to see me on a friendly visit which ended in tears on both sides. My presence was largely ignored. After one obviously brutal attack, Shirley burst out, "Mother, you're horrible." The mother turned to me triumphantly: "You see how she talks?"

As teacher, there seemed little I could do about this situation except try to understand it. A woman who could so self-righteously flout ordinary psychological decencies, who was so unaware of the possibility of values other than her own, whose prized social veneer was so patently thin, would certainly not change because of a word of advice from teacher. Shirley's character, however, became more understandable. As a person, she was not very likable— clinging, fawning, truculent by turns, always demanding special attention, just beginning to overcome a very unpleasant snobbishness, tending to substitute a dogmatic "liberalism" for a dogmatic "Republicanism." The problem at the college was how to deal with a girl whose psychological maneuvers seemed deeply related to her pattern of reaction to a neurotic mother, and also how to help her relate the kind of educational values advocated by the college with the educational values of her home.

College and home often present differing interpretations of "important" goals, but students whose personal integration is sound can, despite frequent initial disorientation, usually make some sort of integration of divergent values. It is evidence of the complexity of our time, emphasized by Horney, that, from kindergarten on, most children are required to make a very complicated adjustment to more or less incompatible social requirements and ideals. For Shirley, the problem was especially difficult for two reasons. The first was the sociological fact that the two sets of values confronting her were more flagrantly at odds than usual. Most parents pay at least lip service to the aims of liberal education and democratic attitudes, but hers did not. The college she attended, on the other hand, makes a special effort to combat social prejudice and to awaken genuine feeling for the materials studied in courses.*

The second reason was Shirley's "neurotic character." She was in no condition to develop an independent judgment about anything or a sound integration of divergent values. She *had* to be liked by everybody. Therefore, she was all too prone to sell her intellectual friends down the river whenever she was in a group tending to ridicule them. She prided herself on her breadth of vision because she liked so many kinds of people. She was deeply hurt when she discovered that most people thought her insincere. She was not consciously insincere, but unfortunately her liking for other people was due mainly to her own need to be liked and approved by all of them at all costs. Her liking veered quickly to antagonism the moment she was hurt. And of course she was hurt easily.

In her first year, she was not above deliberate apple-polishing with teachers. At that time, she took being found out in fairly good part—indeed, with admiration for the teacher whom she could not hoodwink. In her second year, a new dynamism developed. She tended to identify herself with her teachers and with intellectual values. She really "loved" the college. Since some sympathy for the labor movement represented a genuine shift in her *emotional* relationships, she was surprised, distressed, and ultimately spiteful when a teacher persisted in considering her convictions and her work superficial. Once she had emotionally adopted the teacher's liberal point of view, such criticism was tantamount to a personal rejection, to which she reacted in the manner she had learned in her relations with her mother.

As Horney would view this situation, the teacher did not literally stand for the mother. Because of the mother's lack of real warmth for the child, Shirley failed to develop an adequate trust in herself, or a capacity for true friendliness, or objectivity in thinking. Her only means of coping with people was to placate them by adapting to their social pattern. She always anticipated hostility. Even friendly criticism of her intellectual performance meant an attack upon her very self (her idealized image of herself), the more bitter to her because adaptation to liberal ideas had come hard, and perhaps because she had sensed in her teachers a more genuine human feeling for her than she had previously experienced from adults. The confusion of ideas and ideals, mores, and precepts factually present during her college years left her personally

---

* Perhaps we should also remark that at the time Shirley was a student, the college was struggling against a reputation as a rich-girls' finishing school. She was not the only victim of misapprehension as to the kind of education offered. Therefore, among her fellow students as well, she encountered extremes of values. Some of her friends concentrated on dates and social prestige; others scorned them with the intransigeance of youth. A young institution with a burning ideal often presents alternatives with special forthrightness—not only in college but in wider affairs.

confused as to her own pattern of behavior. She could not be consistent even in rebellion against her home background, especially since her teachers refused to supply black-and-white diagrams and kept asking her to think for herself.

Shirley was not neurotic in the sense that she obviously required psychiatric treatment. She was "neurotic" in the Horney sense of showing rigid patterns of reaction rooted in her own distorted needs, exacerbated by social complexities. The college felt that she was not profiting enough by her courses to warrant continuing beyond the second year. I heard indirectly a few years later that she had found a properly wealthy husband in her home town and was cutting a swathe as a young matron. Probably she will become as respectable a member of society as her mother. One may hope that her two years at college will somewhat temper her attitude both toward her husband's controversies with the union in his factory and toward her own children, but this can hardly be more than a hope.

The significance of the example is to show how attitudes derived from early family relationships play into the current situation, and how social confusions may operate further to confuse a young person. Any psychoanalytic school would recognize the connection between Shirley's troubles at college and those with her mother. It is probably Horney, however, who would pay most attention to the details of the college scene, who would be more immediately interested in the interplay of attitudes among Shirley, her contemporaries, and her teachers. For Horney, the girl is not eternally re-enacting a family drama or striving for superiority. She reacts to fellow students and teachers and ideas with attitudes obviously strongly influenced by her home background, especially her mother. The example shows one way in which a person develops into a snob. Put the mother in a different social class, give the daughter a different schooling, and you get a different set of "prejudices," differently handled. Change the family-child relationship drastically and the result in college will also be different, but always in relation to the social situation.

The case of Shirley does not give a complete picture of Horney's views of the social complexity of our time. Shirley was in contact with two obviously discrepant social patterns, and she reacted to both in terms of unconscious needs. Horney's observation about our culture is that the ideals taught are often *essentially* discrepant, over and above the problems of the individual who is confronted by the values of different social subgroups. Our culture as a whole simultaneously sets forth the Christian ethic—with emphasis on brotherly love, turning the other cheek, the inheritance of the meek—and the go-getter, the tough, self-reliant philosophy of a pioneer or capitalistic society. The man who takes his religion seriously is sorely put to it in many situations to maintain his self-respect and the respect of his fellows. Honesty as an ideal is difficult to reconcile with the concomitant ideal of business shrewdness. It is wrong to prostitute one's art for money, but it is equally wrong to fail to provide one's family with a car and a television set. Self-interest and competition loom large in our culture, along with admonitions to self-sacrifice, altruism, and teamwork.

In her books, Horney makes many acute observations as to the nature of the opposing values current in our culture. They are not generalized beyond the idea of conflict itself, with especial emphasis on the role of hostility and self-aggrandizement in such a culture. Instead, she tries to show in case after case how the striving of the individual for security, respect, and self-respect is constantly influenced by the discordant social values confronting him. We shall see, in Chapter 11, on dynamics, more of the intricate relationship between personal goals, conscious and unconscious, and the conflicting demands of society.

SUMMARY

Horney is less elaborate than Adler in describing the specific conditions of the family group that are likely to produce certain kinds of character development, although she often uses sibling rivalries and the like for understanding individual cases. The infantile experiences are never wholly without importance, but they are viewed as really "determining" only for the more inflexible and deeply neurotic patients.

The basic evil in the home is lack of warmth and affection, almost always a consequence of the neuroticism of the parents. The child can accept realistic hardships provided that he feels essentially loved, accepted, appreciated.

In the "neurotic" home, the child develops unrealistic expectations in variety. Later on, he does not directly relive the experience of his childhood but he applies attitudes bred in him at that time. He anticipates hostility; his security depends on expedients designed to overcome unconscious anxieties, to build up his sense of worth. This effort becomes "idealized" beyond the scope of realistic endeavor.

Horney is somewhat more systematic than Adler in calling attention to the impact of social structure on the individual. She emphasizes especially the conflicts inherent in social values and mores. Ideals of brotherly love and of personal success, both inculcated in our society, are to a large extent intrinsically incompatible. Any person finds it difficult to make a full integration of these conflicting trends. The neurotic, since he is more dependent in one fashion or another on social approval, on values external to himself, is especially at the mercy of the contradictions regarding what is approved.

Horney remarks vividly from time to time that different societies have different concepts of the good and even the "normal" person. But she does not elaborate on this theme. In practice, her handling of the cultural aspects of psychological development is almost exclusively confined to the problems of middle-class Americans and Europeans.

Critical Comment

DESPITE her emphasis on cultural factors in the development and functioning of the personality, Horney is a clinician, not a sociologist. She makes meager use of the data available from anthropological and sociological studies. Although in theory she discusses our culture as one among many, she does not work out its distinctive features in detail as relatively local phenomena, in contrast to Kardiner, Roheim, and Fromm. Indeed, she is open to the charge of generalizing too far about basic human trends from observation of our own times. Certainly the richness of her clinical observations is very largely dependent on the interplay of systems and ideas characteristic for middle-class American and European society. I have elaborated this idea repeatedly in critique of her concept of the idealized image of the self and shall not go into it further here.

What I like about Horney's approach to the terms of the milieu is the place given to important cultural ideas and ideals in her immediate approach to the psychology of the individual. The other psychoanalytic schools have been so thoroughly concerned with the deep psychological mechanisms underlying the formation of culture and its acceptance or rejection by the individual that they have sometimes failed to see vividly enough the power of the concrete formulations cogently presented by any society. Horney does not attempt to analyze *why* our society has adopted such contradictory slogans for the good life, although I should think it would not be too difficult for a historically minded disciple to find an appropriate explanation. What she does emphasize, almost alone among psychoanalysts, is the effect on the individual of the effort to live up to these contradictory ideals— or even to make a minimal adjustment to conflicting demands.

FROMM

FROMM SHARES the general position of Horney and Adler on the importance of warmth and encouragement in early childhood, though with less radical rejection of the Freudian concern with the fate of specific biological needs. He points out that different kinds of people tend to train their children in characteristic ways as regards weaning, bowel control, and sexual activities. The general attitude of the parent perhaps impinges most vividly on the child in these areas because of the child's own orientation, so that the mouth, the anus, or the genitals may indeed remain a focus of special attitudes. On the whole, however, it is the climate of the home and the over-all direction of feeling, training, and indoctrination that count most in childhood, and hence for personality development.

The child is born with very little sense of distinction between its own self and the outside world. Months elapse before it effectively recognizes other individuals—years, as Piaget has shown, before it ceases to confuse itself with the universe. The infant enjoys *primary* emotional ties with its environment, particularly with its mother. Partly through growth of its own powers for manipulating the objects around it, partly through education, the child gains in self-strength and independence, gradually renouncing the primary ties. Ideally, the process of individuation should keep pace with the normal growth in strength. Fromm writes:

> The child becomes more free *to* develop and express its own individual self unhampered by those ties which were limiting it. But the child also becomes more free *from* a world which gave it security and reassurance. . . . If every step in the direction of separation and individuation were matched by corresponding growth of the self, the development of the child would be harmonious.[2]

Since there is always some lag between the two, some feeling of isolation and helplessness always accompanies the process of growing up. The child then attempts to recapture the primary ties in a variety of ways, all of which have in common *escape from the freedom of the self.*

Unhappily (or happily for the potential dignity and achievement of man), the primary ties cannot be reinstated. Man cannot return to the Garden of Eden once he has set out upon the path of individual choice. Fromm's major contribution is to show how social patterns help the individual toward coping with the problems of living on his own, and how too often they serve to exacerbate and direct his efforts toward escape from productive, rational, and loving independence.

Like Freud, Fromm sees the average family as the "psychic agency" of society. It is "by adjusting himself to his family [that] the child acquires the character which later makes him adjusted to the tasks he has to perform in social life."[3] Fromm points out further, however, that most members of a given society tend to share a common core of character structure—what Kardiner (see pp. 124*ff.*) calls "basic personality." Although mediated primarily by the family, this common core reflects the social or cultural pattern within which the parents live. The personality of the adult is a highly complex resultant of the inborn equipment of the individual (his generic biological demands, native intelligence, temperament, etc.), his early experience in the family, and his later experience in the wider social group. This last factor operates not only on the maturing child directly but on the parent, modifying his action and to some extent his feeling toward the child. The peasant turned factory worker does not change his essential character overnight, much less his superego, which Freud saw as the main preservative of cultural heritage. Nevertheless, some shift in basic parental attitudes does occur, which, together with immediately operating pressures, works toward solidification of the emerging social pattern in dynamic relationship to the perpetually emerging new individual.

Fromm's attitude is holistic. He tries to make clear that the culture pattern should not be seen either as in itself determining or as a factor to be added *quantitatively* to a list of influences involved in character formation.

> The interaction goes much deeper; the whole personality of the average individual is molded by the way people relate to each other, and it is determined by the socioeconomic and political structure of society to such an extent that, in principle, one can infer from the analysis of one individual the totality of the social structure in which he lives.[4]

Before he is himself culture-sensitive, the individual relates to parents, who are in active relationship to their society and who tend to bring him up in the way in which most children are brought up in a given group. The other children and adults whom he meets outside the family circle behave—on the average—in a manner consonant with the group pattern. The moment the child reaches school, he encounters codified mores and rules to which he must adjust. Later on, he experiences both external compulsion to conform to the expected group style via the policeman and the employer and internal compulsion to relate himself to people on the terms prevalent among his neighbors.

Relatedness to the world of things and of people is essential to the process of living. Recognition of one's true self derives from good early relations with others and is itself the premise for a productive orientation toward life. The person who has learned respect for himself, confidence in and love for himself, is the person who is able to cherish other people as well with full appreciation of their independent worth. He can also work productively with things and ideas, holding a rational faith in the orderliness and potential goodness of the world around him.

Too often, however, relatedness to the outside world is not one of independent, loving cooperation but one of "symbiosis," a term borrowed from biology. If the slave needs his master, the master by the same token *needs* the slave. The person who lives by domination, by cruelty, or by the admiration of others is *dependent* on his victims or cannot be comfortable himself without people to offer adulation. Typically, one finds that the tyrannical member of a partnership is as distressed as the weaker member by any threat of dissolution. The word *symbiosis* implies this reciprocal dependence in such human relationships underlying apparent strength. Unable to endure the aloneness and insignificance of his own self, the person strives for external buttressing of his own ego. His attitude, consciously or unconsciously, must be parasitic or exploitative. People are meaningful to him less in their own right than for what they have to offer to him by way of reassurance, self-aggrandizement, and the like. Even abstract ideas cannot be examined objectively, because their major role is defense against inner terror.

Thus far, Fromm's view does not differ radically from Horney's analysis of the neurotic character. The distinctiveness of Fromm's contribution lies in his effort to show more clearly the relationship between such psychological mechanisms and the undoubted independently operating force of economic and other social forces. Some economists, especially the more convinced Marxists and the more ardent defenders of *laissez-faire* capitalism, accuse Fromm of attempting to explain "everything" by psychology. The truth is, they say, that economic forces are so strong that it does not matter very much what the individual thinks, feels, or even does. He is bound to act in certain ways because of the pressure of outside events; his feelings are vapid sentimentality, whether they take the form of appreciation of the fairness of a specific boss or sympathy for the plight of a specific worker; his thinking ought to be directed toward realistic investigation of economic law.

SOCIAL APPLICATIONS

In a book on psychological forces, Fromm is understandably sketchy in his treatment of other aspects of man's social living, but his main point is clearly the intimate interaction and circular relationship between psychological and other forces. A major portion of *Escape from Freedom* is devoted to historical analysis of the *social and economic* forces underlying the psychological development of the modern individual, from the Middle Ages to the present time, with special consideration of the Renaissance and the Reformation, and of Nazism. The fifteenth and sixteenth centuries, he says, not only set the tone for the whole of modern capitalism but in many respects paralleled the conditions of the present day. Then, as now, radical changes in social and economic structure threatened the old way of life. Especially the middle class was threatened by the power of monopolies and the strength of capital, which undermined the sense of individual worth that was characteristic of small industry and trade, with consequent increase in the sense of being alone and insignificant.

Only the bare outline of the historical shift can be reported here, and only as it relates to Fromm's idea of the essential psychosocial process.

> What characterizes medieval in contrast to modern society is its lack of individual freedom. Everybody in the earlier period was chained to his role in the social order. A man had little chance to move socially from one class to another, he was hardly able to move even geographically from one town or from one country to another. He was often not even free to dress as he pleased or to eat what he liked. . . . Personal, economic, and social life was dominated by rules and obligations from which practically no sphere of activity was exempted.
>
> But although a person was not free in the modern sense, neither was he alone and isolated. In having a distinct, unchangeable, and unquestionable place in the social world from the moment of birth, man was rooted in a structuralized whole, and thus life had a meaning which left no place, and no need, for doubt. . . .
>
> There was much suffering and pain, but there was also the Church, which made this suffering more tolerable . . . and offered a way to acquire the conviction of being forgiven and loved by God. . . .
>
> Awareness of one's individual self, of others, and of the world as separate entities had not yet fully developed.[5]

Political, economic, and social changes disrupted this close world. Of the later period Fromm says,

> The individual is freed *from* the bondage of economic and political ties. He also gains in positive freedom by the active and independent role which he has to play in the new system. But simultaneously he is freed from those ties which used to give him security and a feeling of belonging. . . . He is threatened by powerful suprapersonal forces, capital and the market. His relationship to his fellow men, with everyone a potential competitor, has become hostile and estranged; he is free—that is, he is alone, isolated, threatened from all sides.[6]

The new religious doctrines of the Reformation, put forward by Luther and Calvin and rapidly adopted by the growing middle class, served to rationalize and systematize these attitudes. Internal compulsions of conscience were largely substituted for the external compulsions of feudal society, but the type of conscience developed reflected all too closely the anxiety and bitterness of people left alone and powerless. It was taught that

> by fully accepting his powerlessness and the evilness of his nature, by considering his whole life an atonement for his sins, by the utmost self-

humiliation, and also by unceasing effort, [man] could overcome his doubt and his anxiety; that by complete submission he could be loved by God and could at least hope to belong to those whom God had decided to save.[7]

. . . [Calvin's] picture of a despotic God, who wants unrestricted power over men [destining part of mankind to eternal damnation without any justification] and their submission and humiliation, was the projection of the middle class's own hostility and envy.[8]

The dynamics of the authoritarian conscience and the relationship between submission and hostility will be discussed in more detail at a later point. To continue here with the social implications of the psychological changes, we quote further:

The new character structure, resulting from economic and social changes and intensified by religious doctrines, became in its turn an important factor in shaping further social and economic development. Those very qualities which were rooted in this character structure—compulsion to work, passion for thrift, the readiness to make one's life a tool for the purpose of an extra personal power, asceticism, and a compulsive sense of duty—were character traits which became productive forces in capitalistic society and without which modern economic and social development are unthinkable.[9]

The reader should note especially the to-and-fro relationship between economic and psychological factors. Fromm's careful discussion of Nazism, which shows this relationship even more concretely, is especially interesting for its consideration of the *selective* impact of economic conditions after World War I on the various social groupings in Germany.* He gave full weight to the relatively local factor of support from the representatives of big industry and the half-bankrupt Junkers, without which Hitler could never have come into power, and he points out that "their support was rooted in their understanding of their economic interests much more than in psychological factors."[10] On the other hand, the hold of Nazism over a whole people has to be understood on psychological grounds also. *Which* classes more or less passively accepted the new regime up to the point at which resistance became physically almost impossible? And *why*? Above all, *which* classes ardently espoused the new regime, and *why*?

* Fromm wrote this analysis at a time when we were actively struggling with Nazism as a militant force. His analysis is nonetheless acute because our major fears of a militant social organization now have another focus. Fromm would be the last to say that Russian Communism is exactly the same as German Nazism—though he would point to an underlying relationship to external authority as significantly similar in both instances. Such general similarity does *not* warrant considering the practical-psychological problems of an ideal State Department as essentially the same in Germany, Russia, and China, and in respect to disloyalty in America.

I would like to underline Fromm's effort to make the social analysis specific to the operating culture, however general he considers the underlying psychological trends.

Fanatical attachment came largely from the younger members of the middle class—that is, the class most thoroughly imbued with the character traits previously discussed. Economically nearly bankrupt after 1918, its prestige drastically lowered by the rising power and position of the workers, disillusioned in its former leaders and the social rubrics of loyalty, hard work, and thrift, this very large group was an easy prey to the new ideology.

The *older* members were likely to balk at certain points. They did not relish giving up trade advantages because a firm they dealt with was Jewish, for example, and their sense of justice—rooted both in their character structure and in their long background of experience under the old regime—could not easily tolerate the sudden abnegation of legality and the persecutory handling of persons hitherto considered in the ordinary way in terms of conscience and fellow-feeling. On the whole, the *older* members of this class operated to some extent as brakes on the new regime. An occasional martyr was caught in the toils who would die rather than betray his principles. This class *as a class* did not supply either initial strong opposition or the bulk of later underground resistance, although many individuals became heroically involved, usually as a result of especially vivid personal experience or because of atypical features in their previous history.

The younger members retained the characterological need for authority, structure, rules, external prestige; the same capacity for honesty, industry, courage, and self-immolation to the higher power of outside authority: Government, Ruler, Leader, or Principle. They lacked the long experience of their elders with specific forms of authority relationships—political and economic— and of social and moral principles. They could therefore adapt much more flexibly to the new social program offered by Hitler with startlingly frank acknowledgment of his play on the underlying needs of the masses.*

A great merit of Fromm's discussion is his analysis of the way in which Hitler, as a typical example himself of the frustrated younger generation in the lower middle class, could make a very direct emotional appeal to his own kind. His appeal was not really to "the masses," not even in the general terms of "have not" psychology, but with some specificity to a particular susceptible group large enough *at that juncture of history* (with the money of the Junkers

* What they [the masses] want is the victory of the stronger and the annihilation or the unconditional surrender of the weaker" (A. Hitler, *Mein Kampf*, Reynal & Hitchcock, 1940, p. 469). "Like a woman . . . who will submit to the strong man rather than dominate the weakling, thus the masses love the ruler rather than the suppliant, and inwardly they are far more satisfied by a doctrine which tolerates no rival than by the grant of liberal freedom; they often feel at a loss what to do with it, and even easily feel themselves deserted. They neither realize the impudence with which they are spiritually terrorized, nor the outrageous curtailment of their human liberties, for in no way does the delusion of this doctrine dawn on them." (*Ibid.*, p. 56.)

and industrialists, the weakness and uncertainties of other groups, and a complex world situation) to swing the balance of power toward a kind of regime that is very hard to stop once it is under way.

Fromm was under no illusions as to the immediate success of *individual* virtue against a strong, ruthless Gestapo. Groups of people, he states with no originality, react more or less predictably to more or less definable circumstances. Such *group* reactions (importantly "psychologically determined" but *not* generally human as they operate in special groups under special circumstances) inevitably contribute toward the constellation of the potent social forces to which we must ultimately submit. His point is that we can learn to predict and define social developments as we learn to understand better the pressure of special circumstances on special groups, *and also* how people in these groups are likely to take them psychologically. Thus, the middle class was economically very hard-pressed by postwar conditions in Germany and also suffered an especially severe psychological trauma as its savings, its prestige, its productive industry became worthless almost overnight, along with the authority of the Kaiser, the military caste, the stability of money—all the externals which had previously justified its solid virtues. Nazism offered a substitute ideology and leadership of great appeal to the underlying self-doubt, envy, and hostility. It was, according to Fromm, the concomitance of circumstances that enabled Hitler to consolidate through psychological appeal *to this class* the gains made initially with the aid of big business, landed proprietors, and the riffraff or lunatic fringe attracted in any culture by such bright promises of power and outright sadism. There were, of course, conditions in other countries that made it possible for Hitler to manipulate Chamberlain as well as Thyssen.

THE ETHICS OF THE MARKET

Generally appreciative of the democratic ideal and even of many aspects of American achievement toward human freedom and dignity, Fromm is sharply critical of the *ethics of the market* too often prevalent here.* The traditional European criticisms of our lack of culture, our emphasis on money, on size, on speed, are only the beginnings of an evaluation that strikes much deeper. The American, largely freed *from* the authoritarian trammels of despotic government, rigid social and family structure, the privileges of birth, and uncompromising "conscience" based on authoritarian religion, still has not fully won freedom *to* develop his own self. The reasons are the same. In the

* The essential problem is not so much America as the development of capitalist economy.

marketing world, Fromm says, the individual is again alone and insignificant. In fact, the more his primary ties to family, state, church, tradition, social order are broken—without sufficient development of self-strength—the more he is exposed to the painful sense of isolation and helplessness which always underlies the escape from freedom.

Many Americans (and many Europeans), according to Fromm, live in a world of *things*, of commodities, to be bought and sold at market value—that is, at the face value placed upon them at the moment by the trend of demand. In such a world, there is no point in making a good shoe if nobody buys it, in learning Latin if nobody cares about Latin, in being honest in a business generally run not quite honestly, or in being virtuous if you can't get a date when you are too "prudish." The prudery of Puritanism, rooted in a sense of the evilness of man's nature, is well dispensed with. The *apparently* more direct and free behavior of the modern girl is too often set by the conventions of her group rather than arising spontaneously from her own feeling. Freedom as a reaction against restriction is merely the obverse of the same coin. Freedom in overt behavior which is covertly dictated by group mores is almost worse. It involves a progressive devaluation of *all* personal values, even the bad ones, and the person becomes an automaton rather than a self. One's very virtue and wishes become, in Fromm's words, a commodity on the market. One is never one's self but always what one is expected to be in order to find acceptance in business and social life. Since with occupational and social mobility most people are constantly confronting new groups, with different demands, the self becomes a constantly changing garment—laid finally over nothing at all.*

PERSONALITY STRUCTURE AND SOCIAL STRUCTURE

In *Man for Himself,* Fromm offers a tentative hypothesis of the kinds of personality structure likely to be associated with specific kinds of social structure. Since the personality orientations described are not readily understandable without more explanation of his concepts of psychodynamics, their description is postponed (see pp. 467-472). Here I merely mention briefly the usefulness of understanding the general trend of human reaction likely to be found under varying types of social conditions, very broadly considered. It is well to repeat that not every individual in a given group will show the personality orientation described; in fact, very few will show it in pure form. As Adler remarked in connection with *his* types, there is no one-to-one relationship between the personality pattern and any external condition. Both terms

* This material is drawn largely from *Man for Himself* (Rinehart & Co., 1947).

of the relationship are too complex and too flexible. A great variety of problems must be met by every individual, and meeting them always produces a variety of personality trends. In cultures in which a certain kind of experience permeates the life of most individuals, one finds prevalent reaction patterns, the major contours of which may be described with some specificity.

The more complex a society, the less feasible it becomes to assign personality traits to the usual classifications. German, American, Londoner, New Yorker, urban, rural, capitalist, worker, upper middle class, white-collar employee, unskilled worker, even old and young—all these familiar categories must always be seen in relation to the multiplicity of factors operating together in any given situation. A "German" must be further categorized by all the other rubrics. One may find, for example, that the defensive arrogance often considered typical for the "German" is almost totally submerged in the anxiety of the aging worker who cannot get a job, in Germany as elsewhere.

Successful prediction for any given social situation must take into account the many sectors of the population that make up the group under consideration. For the purposes of nation-wide advertising in a country as stable as the United States, a well-selected numerical sample is usually sufficient. For wide governmental planning, the inner *structure* of the society must be understood, the impact of group on group, the *interplay* of special conditions, economic and psychological, which determines the action of any given set of individuals at any given moment. Just as the person may behave more like an old man than like a German if the conditions of his life thrust the problems of age into the foreground, so a country or any group that achieves autonomy may behave differently as different elements in the group gain power, for whatever reason.

Thus, a fruitful application of psychological insight in social situations involves, for Fromm, insight into the specific structure of the group—not only understanding of the deeper levels of individual motivations but also grasp of the external circumstances and the relationship of subgroups to one another. Economic, historical, and psychological processes of some generality may be isolated. Their concrete functioning requires joint analysis in the situation immediately under consideration.

SUMMARY

Fromm focuses upon the tension between the impulse toward free, productive individuation and the security of primary emotional ties experienced by the infant. Ideally, the process of individuation should keep pace with normal growth in strength. In practice, the demands of living frequently outstrip growth in strength, and hence the individual tries to recapture the primary ties in a variety of ways, all of which have in common escape from the freedom of the self.

Since the self is emergent, the experiences of the young child within the family are as paramount for Fromm as for all psychoanalysts. But the parent is part of the child's society while ministering to the child, and the child rather quickly comes to function in a society—to be sure, with the basic attitudes he learned at home. Thus, both indirectly through the parents and directly through his own experience, the child acquires the *character* that enables him to cope with the tasks he must later perform in social living. Most members of a given social group are therefore likely to share a common core of character structure.

Major social events may occur for a variety of reasons, often quite remote from the character structure of the individual. There can be no one-to-one correlation between psychology and sociology. But social events profoundly influence the kind of situation the person has to cope with; and eventually social events (institutions, economic laws, etc.) are maintained, elaborated, and at times drastically changed by the human "character" that comes to predominate. The Calvinist conscience was, in a sense, created by the shift from a feudal to a capitalistic economy, and the reasons for the shift were not primarily psychological. But the capitalistic economy could not have advanced and taken form without this new *consolidation* of attitudes as the psychological response of individuals to a changed situation become institutionalized.

Fromm considers the "marketing" orientation characteristic for modern capitalistic economies, notably America. Discussion of this topic and the personality syndromes predominantly characteristic for other social forms is postponed to Chapter 11, on dynamics.

Critical Comment

THE chief merit of Fromm's approach seems to me not so much his specific formulations of significant historical and socioeconomic patterns as his insight into the *principle* of constant interplay between social and psychological factors, both aspects envisaged as complex interacting units in their own right as well as creatively interacting with each other. Kardiner and Erikson have much the same idea (see Chap. 4), but Kardiner's search for basic trends through cultures widely different from our own makes it difficult to apply his formulations flexibly in observations of our own society at the present time. And Erikson still pays lip service, as it were, to cultural trends as independent systems, although he shows with especial clarity how they function in the lives of his patients when he recognizes them on the basis of well-informed common sense about our own culture. Fromm the sociologist risks a much more detailed analysis of social trends in our culture (including Europe); Fromm the psychoanalyst risks a detailed analysis of psychological trends. In my opinion, he brings the two aspects together more vividly for the people of our time than any of the other authors discussed in this book. This *concrete demonstration of interrelatedness* seems to me of cardinal importance in educating our thinking about sociopsychological events in a direction everyone considers desirable.

Critique of Fromm's delineation of specific historical and social trends is beyond the purview of this book. But if the reader finds inaccuracies or mistaken emphases in these areas, I suggest that he try to see how his corrections would affect Fromm's general thesis rather than reject his approach altogether. Fromm himself sees his work as a provocative beginning rather than a finished product. Accurate sociological analysis, becoming more correct and acute as data accumulate, is the premise for this aspect of his synthesis.

My critique must be confined to the psychological aspects of Fromm's position, and it rests largely on his general affiliation with the non-libido schools, all of which in my opinion neglect too far the specific dynamic foci of the sexual systems. Furthermore, Fromm's own contribution regarding the primary quality of the feeling of being alone and insignificant seems to me hardly different fundamentally from what other psychoanalysts refer to as the feeling of inferiority and the need for security. Calling attention to the evolutionary process of "individuation" overgeneralizes the actual experience of the individual child (see pp. 604f.). No one doubts that feelings of being alone and insignificant are very painful and very common. Doubtless they are less painful in a society in which the individual readily identifies with a large, stable group to which his parents also belong. Something of this sort was indicated in the Freudian chapters of the present book, with the suggestion that a larger place be made in Freudian theory for investigation of the social climate within which the development of the child takes place.

Societies—our own Occidental society as Fromm describes it, from the Middle Ages to the present—which seriously break the relationship between the family and the social structure, which constantly impose upon the adult values and responsibilities radically different from his childhood image, are very likely to foster a sense of oneself as different, as alone, as insignificant, and as quite confused. One can very easily perceive how the psychological aspects Fromm describes may become predominant. One may even feel that these aspects of the personality are *in fact* the most generally determining in our society, and one may feel grateful to Fromm for pointing out so clearly that "freedom" has two faces, one of which is very frightening. One may largely accept his observations of our attempts to escape from this terrifying face, from this view of ourselves as lonely and insignificant individuals up against problems we cannot master.

What I object to in Fromm's basic theory, however, is the same kind of reductionism I have decried throughout this book. Although in practice he deals flexibly with varieties of social and psychological part-systems, he seems to feel as keenly as Freud the need for an underlying psychological universal. He finds it in the process of individuation— an evolutionary event, the corollary of which is the psychological conflict between growing independence and dependence on primary ties. This formulation colors his whole interpretation of group phenomena as well as individual psychology and tends toward a certain monotonous reiteration of the same constellation of psychic events. In practice, the fear of being alone and insignificant becomes in Fromm's writings a sort of primary drive hardly different from the need for security (Horney) and for superiority (Adler). Fromm himself borrows so much from the psychoanalytic schools, including Freud, that the escape mechanisms he describes (see mainly pp. 467ff.) are highly varied. Yet it seems to me that the multidimensionality of his approach appears almost in spite of his underlying philosophy rather than because of it. I think that his main contribution is the one emphasized in this chapter: an extraordinarily vivid approach to integration of social and psychological complexities. The mode of integration can stand, even if one modifies description of the component systems operating on either side. It is an important milestone in the scientific effort to bring together two disciplines which everyone knows *require* unification but which tend to remain stubbornly distinct.

SULLIVAN

DESPITE THE "ENVIRONMENTALIST" phrasing of many of his key concepts and a certain hospitality toward the ideas of those who emphasize the importance of cultural configurations for the development and function of personality, Sullivan himself has comparatively little to say about the effect of specific variations in the cultural scene. Even with reference to the family circle of significant adults, his approach is more similar to those of Horney and Fromm in stressing the general climate of the home than to Adler's effort to understand the special conditions of psychological development set by the child's position in the family through order of birth, etc. Fromm's analysis of how cultural factors affect the attitude of the parent toward the child, and how the individual formulates and expresses deep-lying attitudes in constant to-and-fro relation to the codified attitudes of the group and its factual vicissitudes—this sort of analysis is *compatible with* Sullivan's position.* But Sullivan himself does not discuss these factors systematically.

The topics I shall report in this chapter are generally rather than specifically cultural. Furthermore, they are so closely related to the native propensities of the organism and to its maturation that I could equally well have discussed them in the preceding chapter or in the next one. I treat them here largely because no other psychoanalyst (except Freud, mainly in *The Interpretation of Dreams*, Chap. 7, in arguments followed up mainly by Rapaport) has even attempted to relate the process of acculturation to the "intellectualistic" problem of how we are basically equipped to perceive and integrate the complex materials of our culture. Sullivan talks a good deal about language and semantics, but language is, for him, essentially merely the most

---

* I have mentioned that Fromm teaches at the William Alanson White Foundation, Sullivan's literal "school."

important example of our use of "symbols." A symbol, for Sullivan, is any-thing that stands for something else—a much more inclusive definition than the one generally used in psychoanalysis (see pp. 61*f.* and 549*ff.*). The usual psychoanalytic use of the term *symbol* tends to imply an emotional—indeed, for some analysts a repressive—dynamic, whereas Sullivan's does not. Sullivan inquires insistently as to how we *develop* symbols (or "signals") and how their meanings relate to our experience.

MODES OF EXPERIENCE

Prototaxis. Sullivan distinguishes three modes of experience. The first, which he calls *prototaxic,* is characteristic of infancy and some deep psychotic states. In this mode, the infant hardly distinguishes between himself and the outer world. External events and their internal consequences are perceived dimly, are organized in a primitive manner, and may be reacted to through primitive signals before their actual development is at all sharply compre-hended. The infant "prehends" earlier and later states. These states are much more generalized ("cosmic") than will be the case later on. They are not organized serially in time or related to the yet unformed distinction between the self and the outside world.

Parataxis. Gradually, as the infant's experience becomes more differ-entiated, the *parataxic* mode develops. The infant becomes aware of the essen-tial difference between himself and the world around him (a difference con-stantly accentuated as the self dynamism is built up). He begins to recognize the recurrent figure of his mother, although at first dimly and in close rela-tionship to his inner experience, for she is not yet a person in her own right. He also learns some discrimination among objects. He can spit out a bad taste, and he recognizes that he can in no sense attain the moon. The un-differentiated wholeness of experience is broken in many ways, which the infant comes to recognize in a rather piecemeal fashion, mainly through auditory and visual channels.

At this stage, his experiences with language play a distinctive and impor-tant role. To some extent, language develops directly out of experience as the spontaneously produced "ma" and other vocal efforts magically provoke re-sponses from the adults which allay discomfort and emerging anxiety.* But the young child's experience goes further. He is typically presented with a

---

* Sullivan also relates this process to more general concern with the "oral zone" in a manner especially important for comparison with the Freudian approach. His argument is so complex and so isolated as regards his own operative concepts that I mention it only in footnotes, referring the reader to *Conceptions of Modern Psychiatry* (William Alanson White Founda-tion, 1947). Especially relevant for discussion of "zones of interaction" in a wider sense are pages 31*ff.*

book in which one aspect of the lively kitten he knows directly in many aspects somehow becomes stationary and important and eventually is linked with the letters c-a-t printed below it. At first the kitten and the picture of the kitten are both part of the total experience of the child to which he is learning to re-act in a differentiated manner. The picture of the kitten in the book and the letters c-a-t begin to seem rather special. The child's experiences with the real kitten are highly varied. The picture, and especially the word *cat*, begin to have a different framework. These symbols "always work." The illustration, taken from Sullivan,[11] is intended to show how the child relates to the various types of symbols he develops *and encounters*. The printed word *cat* has a "consensual validation" (see footnote, p. 356) which makes it different in kind from the other types of symbol the child has been developing out of his own experience. "There is nothing like consistent experience to impress one with the validity of an idea. So one comes to a point where printed words, with or without consensually valid meaning, come to be very important in one's growth of acquaintance with the world." And after summarizing the various types of reference involved in building various types of symbols, Sullivan remarks that "the possibilities for confusion in handling the various kinds of symbols naturally remain quite considerable."[12]

Thus far I have presented only the ingredients of the parataxic mode: a *relatively* well-differentiated sense of the self *vs.* the external world of people and things, of different modes of perception, and of the relative amenity of objects perceived to direct handling, and finally what we may call a *perception* of the consensually validated symbol, mainly via language, which easily be-comes a word-symbol valid in its own right, with or without consensual validation.*

It is characteristic of the parataxic mode, however, that the various per-cepts and symbols and more or less differentiated kinds of experience are not yet connected with one another in an orderly way. They exist side by side, without being logically distinguished, without being reflected upon and com-pared. Each symbol has its own referent, which may be entirely disconnected from other symbols that are logically very close for the objectively minded outsider but that remain separate for the child, or for the adult in so far as he is operating in the parataxic mode. (This type of thinking seems very like what Freud called "the primary process.")

* Sullivan deals with the power of words *as such* in a manner actually closer to that of the outright psychological semanticists (Korzybski, Chase, Burke, *et al.*) than to any other psychoanalyst, although he does not fully adopt their position. All analysts recognize the importance of the personal substratum in the meaning of words. In fact, most psychoanalysts tend rather to *over*emphasize the personal-psychological factor in language and to ignore its role as, generally speaking, a consensually validated set of symbols which has a certain "sign" import as such, whatever the distortions of meaning any or all of us introduce.

The parataxic mode in childhood—and often in later life—is further characterized by its *autistic* quality. The child naturally develops rather arbitrary, highly personalized symbols, which are not checked and tested against "reality." Such autism is at first an inevitable consequence of the child's limited experience and capacities. The effect of *anxiety* is to restrict the development of full reality-testing and objectifying of symbol function, as we shall see in the next chapter. Therefore, all adults, and especially neurotic adults, tend to retain some parataxic autistic trends. The dream functions in the parataxic mode par excellence. These phenomena seem very like the unconscious phenomena we reported in Chapter 2 as described by Freud.

Syntaxis. The *syntaxic* mode is characterized by full appreciation of the logical interrelatedness of the various symbols employed. Consensual validation is here fully utilized—and, indeed, corrected where necessary by a still more precise and tested apprehension of "reality." It is the logical-empirical mode of thought, what Freud called the "secondary process" at its highest stage of development.

Obviously, none of us comes to function exclusively at this high level of rationality. Indeed, the full resources of the adult are far too limited to allow truly reality-oriented judgments of all aspects of our lives. We have observed that Sullivan emphasizes that our knowledge is at best a reflection of our interpersonal experience. A point of more immediate importance than the epistemological consideration is that syntaxic and parataxic meanings of the same word often exist side by side without our being aware of the fact. We ourselves and even our interlocutors assume that the syntaxic meaning is the one operating, whereas all too often it is the parataxic, autistic meaning that is actually determining in our behavior. This confusion is a very natural consequence of the initial learning process during which the child must find his way without help among the different categories of symbol offered him by his society as well as by his own experience.

However, although Sullivan gives weight with his customary sly humor to this socially determined confusedness, his real emphasis is on the restrictions imposed by the self dynamism in its pursuit of security. These will be discussed in Chapter 11, on dynamics, but it is well to comment here that, for all his discussion of semantics and modes of learning different kinds of symbols, Sullivan's position is *not* "intellectualistic." I have the impression, rather, that he means to clear away prevalent confusions about the operation of symbols, especially words, in order to make the dynamic determinants stand out more sharply. I think he prefers the terms *parataxic* and *syntaxic* to *primary* and *secondary process* and to the *very* rough equivalents of *affective* and *rational-empirical* because he wishes to clarify the normal, developmental aspects of autistic, nonlogical thinking. He prefers to avoid the dichotomy between conscious and unconscious because both terms of the dichotomy require, nowadays, endless qualification.

STAGES OF DEVELOPMENT

Although Sullivan neglects the stages of *libidinal* development considered so crucial by the Freudians, he lays great weight on the genetic process and carefully codifies its stages up to late adolescence. The more I study his concept of the genetic process, however, the clearer it becomes that it is totally different from that of the Freudians. At no point in Sullivan's description of the "epochs" of childhood does the *inner need of the child,* distinct for his age, play the determining role in the dynamisms governing his behavior—except at adolescence, when the maturation of the genital lust dynamism becomes important as such. At all other stages, it is the maturing *capacities** (abilities) of the child that make him especially aware of particular aspects of his interpersonal environment and able to deal with them.

Descriptively, the epochs of childhood are characterized by preoccupations that other analysts have often considered libidinal—or, at the very least, "emotional"—in origin. Sullivan tries very hard to keep these epochs *descriptive.* They are biologically maturational only in the sense that the child must undergo a certain amount of neuromuscular and "intellectual" development before he is actually equipped to deal with the realistic complexities of social living. Concomitantly, Sullivan emphasizes the fact that the experience which gives real substance and direction to these maturational "capacities" is always interpersonal and always involves the pursuit of security. In other words, the "capacity" as such plays no *internal* role comparable to the successive foci of libidinal development as outlined by the Freudians. What it really does is contribute toward the determination of what aspects of the interpersonal external situation the child can assimilate, and how. (See my critical comment for further discussion of this point.)

I think the reader can understand Sullivan's position about the genetic process only if he sees it in very intimate relation to the terms of the milieu, as fundamentally different from the Freudian position regarding the constellative dynamic force of emergent biological needs, and as essentially closer to the position of the analysts discussed in this Part. For Sullivan, the crux of the matter is the interpersonal situation, which he interprets mainly as the pursuit of security, via such constructs as the person has made in the course

* Essentially what Hartmann calls ego apparatuses, what I have called exterosystems. Note that Sullivan deals sketchily if at all with what I have called nonsexual drive systems.

of his experience as a biological organism, human in capacity, developing in a human society.

The stages of personality development* may be summarized as follows:

1. *Infancy* to the maturation of the capacity for language behavior.
2. *Childhood* to the maturation of the capacity for living with compeers.
3. *Juvenile Era* to the maturation of the capacity for isophilic intimacy (literally, love of one's own kind).
4. *Preadolescence* to the maturation of the genital lust dynamism.
5. *Early Adolescence* to the patterning of lustful behavior.
6. *Late Adolescence* to maturity.

With the background of our previous discussion, let us see how Sullivan relates these successive "capacities" to the dynamic structure of interpersonal relations.

Infancy. We have already noted that Sullivan, like all other analysts and like almost everyone else dealing scientifically with the development of the personality, begins with an infant organism which is helpless and untutored *vis-à-vis* the interpersonal world it will encounter. ("Loneliness" as the obverse of inborn desire for contact with others is the only exception—unless it may be the power motive. [*Cf.* pp. 359*ff.*] Sullivan makes little use of either concept in basic theory.) The infant organism pursues the bodily satisfaction inherent in its physiological make-up—and this satisfaction is seen as release from tension—"euphoria"—best realized in dreamless sleep.

However, in this very early stage, the infant reacts to the significant adults around it with "empathy"—that is, with a direct reflection of the mood of the parent (usually the mother).† When the parent is anxious, the infant becomes uncomfortable automatically. This is one of the very deep reasons why the children of neurotic parents so often become neurotic, even when their parents seem to have handled them admirably according to the best psychological precepts. Sullivan observes (but does not greatly elaborate beyond infancy) the *reciprocal* relations between child and parent. By the process of "empathy," the infant "prehends" the parental mood. If this mood is anxious or hostile, the infant directly prehends it as such, becomes itself uncomfortable quite as if it suffered bodily discomfort—and strives to allay the

* This summary is taken from Mullahy, *Oedipus—Myth and Complex* (Hermitage Press, 1948), p. 301, but is readily identifiable in Sullivan's own text in the early chapters of *Conceptions of Modern Psychiatry*, William Alanson White Foundation, 1947.

† Probably no other analyst would accept the concept of empathy quite so wholeheartedly and with such debonair carelessness as to how it comes about. Yet I think Spitz and most people who have worked closely with infants would go a long way toward Sullivan's position. The infant clearly reacts to the adults who are close to it in a manner that is both more dramatic in an over-all manner than was realized earlier and less easily analyzable into specific response patterns, biological or social in origin.

discomfort by the infantile (bodily) means it has at its disposal. Usually it cries. Often the cry of the infant intensifies the anxiety or annoyance of the mother and, in fact, brings not relief but intensification of the empathic anxiety, no matter what the mother actually does for the child. Thus, an anxious or hostile mother is very likely to have an anxious, whiny infant even though her care is solicitous beyond the average. And the incipient self dynamism of the child takes shape under a heavy burden of anxiety and hostility.

Conversely, the euphoric states of the infant and the small activities that are at first spontaneous expressions of his pursuit of bodily satisfactions and the power motive readily arouse *approval* in the parent. Such approval is at first merely re-experienced by the child, via empathy, as a heightened state of euphoria. In the prototaxic mode, these states of discomfort and euphoria merely succeed each other; the approval and disapproval of the parent are hardly distinguished from purely bodily states. But as his abilities develop, and as he begins to distinguish between himself and varieties of experience with external objects,* the infant's self dynamism begins to take on more definite contours in close relationship to the mother. He begins to grasp the fact that what he does is related to the states he experiences, mainly via the parents. He enters upon the parataxic mode, although the global aspects of the prototaxic mode still largely persist.

The infant or the small child cannot make fine discriminations as to exactly what he does to provoke the parental response, and he cannot evaluate shades of approval and disapproval with any nicety. On the contrary, his experience of the adults and of himself tends to veer between the poles of euphoria and distress. At this point, correspondingly, two interpretations of the mother develop: the *good mother* and the *bad mother,* which readily become incorporated in the simultaneously emerging self system as the *good me* and the *bad me.*

These fundamental concepts tend to persist as basic "personifications" throughout life, both in one's attitude toward others and in one's feelings for oneself. There is a general tendency to personify in a more or less fantastic fashion all the people and even the ideas and causes we encounter in later life.† As a rule, our evaluations of people and ideas are a blend of early and late experience; indeed, the late experience predominates for most of us most

---

* Here the frustration of reaching for the moon works along with strictly interpersonal events to foster the sense of differentiation and helplessness.

† In fact, it is by this mechanism that Sullivan supports his contention that all human activities are essentially interpersonal. This seems to be essentially the mechanism of identification and projection of which we have heard so much in this book.

of the time. Nevertheless, Sullivan introduces a special term for the personifications that are a relatively direct carry-over from the "real" persons of our
infancy. He calls them *eidetic*—that is, an image with a peculiarly imposing
sense of reality about it.

In a more general way, Sullivan observes that as the infant becomes
capable of differentiating *people* and his own bodily limitations out of the
cosmic matrix of early experience, he becomes capable of the need for security
and for the first time experiences "anxiety." For Sullivan, anxiety is neither
the painful flooding of the nervous system cited by Freud as the prototype
of later anxiety reactions nor the unanalyzable distress reaction of a helpless
infant in a hostile world *à la* Horney. It is built upon extreme bodily tension
(somewhat as in Freud's concept), but it develops as the inevitable consequence of the child's relationship with the mother (actually the significant
adults—usually the mother; the cumbersome distinction may be dispensed
with once "mother" is understood in this general way).

Anxiety, for Sullivan, is, then, an interpersonal phenomenon which
develops as the infant "learns" that his comfort and discomfort lie primarily
with the mother, who may be "good" or "bad" in apparently whimsical succession. But the infant makes this generalization and tailors his interpersonal
behavior accordingly, with a gradually emerging sense of himself. Now, if at
this point the infant wants to do something of which the parent disapproves,
the proposed action invites a familiar distress *vis-à-vis* the parent's attitude
and is therefore renounced on much the same basis that the moon is renounced. But there is an important difference. The moon is a fairly discon-
tinuous experience which the infant does not care very much about anyhow.
But "mother" enters into every experience in a continuing and highly potent
manner. It is the person, not the occasional "thing," that is important for the
infant, and it is the disapproval of the *person*, not any abstraction of danger,
that becomes his enduring fear, his anxiety.

Since the attitudes of the adults have a reasonable degree of consistency
in important matters (however inconsistent in details), the self dynamism
emerging as a reflection of these attitudes has a certain coherence. It "comes
into being . . . to preserve the feeling of security" in the face of the restraints
and frustrations of living in an interpersonal world, and it "is built largely
of personal symbolic elements learned in contact with other significant
people."[13] Anxiety is the instrument by which the self dynamism is structured,
and this anxiety is, as we have just noted, *always the fear of disapproval*.
Initially experienced empathically by the infant, it comes—via the self dynamism—to control one's behavior at a more sophisticated level, and even to

control one's openness to experience and one's awareness of his own feelings. However, elaborated discussion of the actual functioning of the self dynamism and anxiety is again postponed to Chapter 11, on dynamics.

The empathic stage of development is thought by Sullivan to be at its height from about the sixth to the twenty-sixth month, although it begins earlier and empathy continues after a fashion throughout life. During this period of infancy, the "abilities" of the infant have been maturing, at first almost reflexly in the service of bodily satisfactions. The skeletal musculature gradually develops as the *tool* of the child in the interests of security. Any voluntary activity may, and typically does, play a role in his interpersonal relations. Sullivan cites the use of sphincter control by the child in his relations to parents who seem to care a great deal about this matter, and the special meanings that become attached to exploratory efforts in the genital zone. As a reflection of adult attitudes, Sullivan is ready to grant, these zones may become quite important in the child's development.

But his main emphasis is on the oral dynamism. The cry as tool gradually becomes *language*. Speech as such retains, he thinks, something of its early direct emotional significance, reflected in the magical overemphasis many adults place upon words and in the subtle uneasiness (verging on a feeling that these people are not quite human) that even sophisticated adults experience toward foreigners who speak in a different language or with a foreign accent.

But the major importance of language is that it is the major tool of acculturation—the means by which complex cultural concepts may be directly taught. We saw earlier that acculturation by language is to some extent illusory—that autistic and parataxic meanings of words tend to persist side by side with consensually validated meanings, that correct grammatical usage is no guarantee of a truly syntaxic mode of thinking. Nevertheless, maturation of the capacity for language behavior is the *sine qua non* for more complex acculturation.

Childhood. Sullivan sees a rather definite shift in the attitude of the parents as the child learns to talk and get about freely. He becomes an object of *education,* and he is more or less deliberately *trained* in a host of matters important to the adult as the carrier of his culture, although these matters are often not of the least importance to the child as a biological organism. Sullivan points to the "biological fact" that "the human being requires the world of culture, cannot live *and be human* except in communal existence with it."[14] It is primarily during the epoch of childhood (roughly from two to six, although Sullivan avoids simple chronological age limits) that the child learns the essential dimensions of his culture. He learns them through his parents while he is still highly sensitive to their immediate personal attitudes and while his self dynamism is still very actively forming itself under their pattern of approval and disapproval.

But new resources develop. Language becomes a means of communication rather than a mere tool for obtaining bodily comfort and adult approval. The child becomes more sophisticated in ways of *manipulating* people toward the end of security instead of merely reacting to their moods with gross effort at conformity. And as the self system takes on more definite shape in the cultural scene, supported by maturing abilities, new personality mechanisms appear, notably *sublimation*. For Sullivan, this means that impulses which collide with the self system (provoke anxiety) are unwittingly combined with socially approved patterns which the child has now learned and may be partially discharged without anxiety. This process allows for a much more complex formulation of dynamic patterns of behavior—which will be discussed further in Chapter 11, on dynamics. The point here is that the *child* becomes capable of a kind of emotional double-talk impossible to the infant. This is not because of his libidinal growth, as the Freudians would have it, but because of the maturation of his abilities within the necessary framework of his culture.

The Juvenile Era. With the *juvenile era*, a new factor appears—or, rather, a new consolidation of attitudes: the child begins to experience his compeers as *like himself*. The self dynamism, instituted in infancy and elaborated in childhood in close relation to the parents and to basic conditions of bodily satisfaction, has reached a point at which the child is able to see himself as a sort of entity distinct from other entities. This identification of self is aided and very strongly influenced by the fact that the child now goes to school. He is factually surrounded by his peers, encounters powerful adult strangers, his teachers, and is on all sides treated as a person. Sullivan suggests, however, that this more unified view of the self and the need for compeers is so far "maturational" that the child who is environmentally deprived of companions creates them in imagination.

During this era, two very important things happen. One is that the child begins to look at himself objectively—to develop a sort of "internal critic" who tests his impulses and sublimations as it were from the outside (cf. the Freudian superego, which is thought to develop at about the same age). This internal critic becomes a suborganization of the self system and tends to be largely compounded of the potent appraisals of the significant adults from whom the self dynamism has been derived.

The second important development is implicit in relations with one's compeers, who now become of very great importance. Psychologically, attitudes of competition and rivalry and more or less realistic compromise appear. The self takes on a much more socialized "personification" for the individual, which one may call *reputation*. One's own reputation becomes extremely precious. Damage to one's reputation is almost as anxiety-producing as infringement of those aspects of the self system very directly related to the judgments of the significant adults of infancy and childhood—that is to say, conscience. Furthermore, this is the era par excellence during which *cultural* stereotypes develop—"the boys," "the girls," "the Catholics," "the Jews." These abstract personifications arise initially as the child naturally attempts to define his own status, his own self dynamism, in the terms appropriate to the wider culture he is now encountering.

Too often, the personality fails to develop beyond the juvenile stage. A great many people remain fixated at this point or regress to it under stress. (Sullivan is more willing than the other analysts in the non-libido group to use the Freudian concepts of fixation and regression, although he attaches quite different meanings to the stages of development.) If the self dynamism is ridden by anxiety, its possibilities for wide, general experience are seriously curtailed. Actually, an enormous number of adaptive maneuvers have been made in the course of growth from the helpless infant, who knows neither himself nor the world around him, to the juvenile, who not only has developed a complex self dynamism but has fairly well identified his social role and categorized the people around him; who has developed the "abilities" implicit in his human organism, at least to the point of being able to handle the major complexities of human environment.

Preadolescence. According to Sullivan, however, the achievements of the personality thus far are essentially "egocentristic." A still further step must be taken toward full development: ". . . the satisfactions and the security . . . experienced by someone else [must become] as significant to the person as are his own satisfactions and security."[15] Sullivan calls this the end state of love. It cannot occur before the stage of *preadolescence*, because the younger child is not equipped to perceive either himself or others with the requisite fullness of appreciation. Expressions of love and acts of devotion, no matter how important the other person seems, no matter how valuable the acts of devotion, cannot be considered *love* so long as they represent essentially the pursuit of one's own security. (*Cf.* the Freudian concept of object love, and the distinction heavily emphasized by Horney and Fromm between various forms of need-determined "love" and genuine love.)

The preadolescent usually tends to develop this genuine love for another person through a "chum" of the same sex, whose general pattern of behavior is somewhat similar to his own. The first love tends to be *isophilic*—that is, love of one's own kind. However, in so far as the preadolescent love is genuine in the sense described, it gives the young person a new expansiveness, not only toward the loved one but toward the world in general and himself. "For the first time one can begin to express oneself freely."[16] And in freely expressing one's inmost thoughts and feelings to one's chum, without fear of rebuff or humiliation, one's sense of consensual validation is greatly heightened (*cf.* p. 356*n.*). One begins to check and compare notes on points previously held anxiously private; one begins to understand the genuinely human values in contrast to values maintained out of expediency or simply "for fun."

For Sullivan, this more expansive humanization tends to take place, if at all, in preadolescence. Moreover, this period of life is peculiarly favorable for the development of generous love. The child usually still lives at home but has developed a fairly realistic attitude toward his parents. He is familiar with the tasks and responsibilities of school. In short, although he has developed most of the capacities and psychological attitudes necessary for adult life, he remains in a relatively protected situation, not yet assailed by the practical pressures of full adulthood or by the inner demands of the lust dynamism.

Adolescence.   *Adolescence* sets in with the maturation of the lust dynamism. This Sullivan considers a physiological event of the first magnitude. He remarks that it is virtually impossible for anyone to attain full psychological maturity without coming to terms with the sex drive. It "is something that can be dissociated only at grave risk to effective living." Although there is no *physiological* reason why its maturation should be upsetting to the personality, attitudes toward sex in our culture are such that trouble arises quite frequently and an extensively new integration of the personality is required all along the line.

The difficulty arises partly from the typically strong disapproval of infantile sex behavior. According to Sullivan, such behavior is initially merely part of the general exploratory behavior of the child (*i.e.*, it does not have the insistence attributed to it by the Freudians), but it quickly takes on a special, anxiety-laden quality because of the condemnatory attitude of the adults— and I would suppose because of the attitude of compeers during the juvenile epoch. Partly, however, the problem is set by the cultural institution of long delay between physiological maturation and any socially sanctioned fulfillment.

Under these cultural conditions, the physiological facts of adolescence present problems in personality integration which are extremely difficult to solve—and which, in fact, are very often not solved in a satisfactory manner. On the contrary, all too often, even the values of the preadolescent period are lost. Most people survive adolescence, to be sure, but only as caricatures of what they might have been. The tendency (if one avoids the deep regression of psychosis, which is especially likely to appear at this age) is toward regression to the juvenile era. The personality remains egocentristic, narrowly bent on its own pursuit of security, prevented by anxiety from genuine love and from free development of its capacity for broad interpersonal experience.

Obviously, in most instances, heterosexual activity is successfully carried through, but too often on the basis of what Sullivan calls "instrumental masturbation." The real—that is, the ideal—goal of sexual union should be the extension of the values of the preadolescent isophilic stage to persons *other* than ourselves. Genuine *intimacy* and care for a member of the opposite sex, in conjunction with a mutually powerful bodily satisfaction, brings the fullest possible maturation of self-respect and appreciation of others. Far from being personally and socially restrictive, such love is the culmination of the complex personality development we have described and itself deepens the capacity for broad human competence and understanding in all areas.[17]

It is interesting that Sullivan, who has placed rather more stress than most psychoanalysts on the cultural situation the child encounters, does not emphasize the peculiarities of the broader *social* requirements of adolescence. After all, it is at this period that one's self-identification in terms of social role becomes realistically acute and that one is called upon for a *vocational* choice very likely to be determining for one's whole future life. At least, this is what most adolescents suppose, with very considerable encouragement from their advisors. Furthermore, the adolescent is expected by his culture to assume "adulthood," in a manner definitely formalized by many cultures, implicit in all. One of the most obvious facts about adolescents is that they press urgently toward the cultural image of adulthood with much underlying anxiety and reversion to earlier attitudes. Erikson's position (see pp. 222*ff.*) on this point is especially interesting.

Perhaps this observation should be reserved for the pages of critical comment, but the omission of any *ad hoc* consideration of this very familiar concept of the *social* problem of the adolescent seems so striking as to require mention as part of an exposition of Sullivan's views on the terms of the milieu. At this point we are in a position to re-examine what this "culturalist," who asks us to renounce all psychological impulses, goals, etc., as implicit in the organism apart from its interpersonal and humanly social environment—what this "culturalist" really means by cultural (interpersonal) experience.

COMPARATIVE SUMMARY

I have remarked that Sullivan makes very little use of *any* codified views regarding the specific conditions set by specific culturally determined patterns —although he uses such variations freely in illustration of points he wishes to make about variations in personality development. I remark again that Sullivan and such Sullivanians as I have read are *hospitable* to the general idea of the importance of variations in the conditions set by different cultures and sub-cultures, including the subcultures established by *age* within a single culture. But I think I am within the realm of simple exposition when I say that Sulli-van no more than Freud uses cultural *variations* in a systematic way in his consideration of the fundamental psychological development of the child. This is the main point of difference between a true psychoanalytically oriented cul-turalist (Kardiner and Fromm are the best examples) and a psychoanalyst who is highly aware of the milieu aspect of human adaptability (*e.g.*, Erikson, Adler, Horney).

Sullivan is primarily concerned with human adaptability. He sees clearly that this adaptability takes place not in some psychobiological empyrean but in relation to people. The individual must be seen in an interpersonal context. In this general formulation he differs hardly at all from Adler and Horney, although he does differ from Freud, who places much more emphasis on the maturing biological *demands* of the organism as highly constellative in their own right.*

Sullivan differs from Adler, Horney, and Fromm, however, in his psy-chological conception of the self. He categorically denies the existence of any "real self" (Horney) prior to experience, or of a self that must by its very nature feel inferior (Adler), or of a self that finds the evolutionary fact of its individuation burdensome and tries to escape back to a primitive belonging-ness (Fromm). As clinical formulations, the views of the non-libido group are much closer to Sullivan's than to any Freudian view, but *he insists upon an essentially developmental-cultural view of the self*—the self dynamism.

---

* In his general discussions, Sullivan almost totally neglects the Freudian position. On pp. 30-33 of *Conceptions of Modern Psychiatry,* he does discuss oral, anal, and genital zones as constellative in their own right, as determining at the biological level. Since he explicitly develops these "dynamisms" mainly in their social or interpersonal import, and himself does not really connect them with Freudian psychology, I have omitted this refinement in a brief summary report on his theories.

I decided, therefore, in *this* chapter to present Sullivan's "stages of personality development." Sullivan's position is atypical for the school dichotomy employed in this book not so much because he tries to integrate biological and social factors (every thinking psychologist attempts such integration after his fashion) as because he seems to define the acculturative process in a distinctive way, which may be expressed as follows:

The basic biological needs of the child, the person, are matters of pure physiology—mainly of the organs or organismic systems essential to life. The pursuit of satisfaction of these needs is primarily determining in very early infancy, is always operative, but is of general psychological import only when the lust dynamism matures with an urgency our culture is not prepared to assimilate.

Sullivan mainly emphasizes, in his discussion of cultural impacts upon the child at various ages, aspects of the child's development that none of the other psychoanalysts has taken very seriously—namely, the child's actual *capacity* to deal with different types of symbolization, and the relation of these *capacities* to his reactions to his environment.

Beginning with his first interpersonal contacts, the child develops a need for security which, along with the pursuit of satisfactions, continues to motivate his behavior fundamentally throughout life. There is no difference *in basic motivation* from infancy onward. From his earliest empathic experience of the pain of disapproval, the child requires a feeling of approval and prestige. When this feeling is threatened, he becomes anxious and strives in various ways to avoid or alleviate anxiety. The methods he adopts, however, depend on the actual growth of his abilities (*capacities*) in relation to the social scene. Obviously, one cannot love one's neighbor as one's self in a meaningful way if one has no clear feeling of one's self as a separate entity or no recognition of one's neighbor as a truly separate human being. One cannot compete with one's peers in any meaningful sense of the word "competition" until one is able to recognize one's peers as such. One cannot communicate with or manipulate people in any really differentiated way until one has discriminated between one's self and others in a rudimentary fashion and has learned something of the tools and values of organized interpersonal living.

Every society provides experience, codified experience, roughly appropriate to the maturing capacities of the child. He is nurtured in infancy, deliberately taught in childhood, given opportunities for cooperative (and competitive) contact with his fellows and training in techniques during the juvenile era. Chums and heterosexual partners are available; preadolescent and adolescent love is expected—although in this area many societies, including our own, place difficult obstacles in the path of maturity. Human society, with its organized opportunities and demands, is as much a part of being human as having a certain kind of central nervous system. Special drives, such as rivalry, for.example, cannot accurately be said to operate in infancy (Adler) because the infant is really incapable of comparative appreciation of himself and others. Rivalry with siblings and parents in early childhood (Freud) must be quite different in quality from juvenile competition because the child is not yet capable of a relatively distinct view of his social entity—and there is no *necessary* continuity between the two types of reaction. Indeed, the child whose self dynamism has been too seriously warped by special experiences in the home may become actually unable to envisage himself and his compeers with enough "objectivity" to develop genuine competition and cooperation with his kind. Furthermore, without the social experience of the juvenile era, the person becomes incapable of full objective interpersonal relations in the form of genuine love and care for others.

It is in this sense of socialized learning that Sullivan states that all the stages of development *must* be successfully negotiated before the person can become a fully mature adult.

Critical Comment

IN MY own summary comment on the views of these four authors, I recapitulate ideas expressed in greater detail earlier. Adler, Horney, and Fromm present vividly the concrete relations between the person and his society as we encounter them in our own experience, with a tendency—in my opinion—to overgeneralize trends easily observable in our own culture. This strength becomes a weakness when important observations and ideas are converted into psychological ultimates which are then reapplied in a reductionist manner to the whole gamut of human life.

In his emphasis on a self dynamism dominated by the pursuit of security essentially oriented toward interpersonal relationships, Sullivan does not seem very different from the other analysts. He is therefore subject to the same criticisms: for failure to give sufficient weight to the significance of the sexual drive systems and aggression, and for failure to evaluate the role of solid *social* configurations as such in their relatively general influence on the structure of interpersonal relationships for members of special groups.*

In my reading of it, Sullivan's basic theory is more *compatible with* extension in these two directions than any of the other "non-Freudian" theories reported in this book, because of the concept of relatively independent subdynamisms which are variously related to the self dynamism in consequence of the special experience of the human biological organism in necessary relationship to its milieu. This is a very general statement, meaningful mainly to the reader who has followed sympathetically the perspective I have called a "view of systems."

These general remarks are a preface

* On this point, Fromm is the exception.

to very positive appreciation of Sullivan's emphasis on the abilities of the growing child in nonsexual areas. Except for Erikson, all the analysts reported in this book have tended to neglect the role of development in these areas as having *primary* significance in the development and function of "personality." Erikson and Sullivan, in different ways, point to the fact that the nonsexual capacities of the child in their gradual maturation are played upon by and play into broader social relationships. Erikson is bolder in stating that "ego" development autonomously goes through definable stages. Sullivan hints at such autonomy, but his major point is the new relationship to people made possible by the maturation of new capacities in the child, *plus reciprocal shifts in attitudes toward the child by his associates.* The point is well taken, whether or not greater stress should be laid on

the native propensity of the child's "ego" to follow a definable course. Sullivan's position *invites* careful cross-cultural study of precisely how the child is inducted into the broader aspects of his society, as I suggested in my comment on Chapter 4.

Brilliantly acute in many ways, Sullivan's account of the process has occasional serious blind spots—for example, his neglect of the role-finding aspect of adolescence. I like his formulation of the stages of development not so much as a factual sequence as for the stimulus it offers toward a broader, more integrated view of the emergent relations between the individual and his society than is presented by classical Freudians; toward a more differentiated view than that presented by Adler, Horney, and, in a way, even by Fromm, who does not elaborate on the genetic aspects of psychosocial patterns.

[1] K. Horney, *The Neurotic Personality of Our Time,* W. W. Norton & Co., 1937, p. 80.
[2] E. Fromm, *Escape from Freedom,* Farrar & Rinehart, 1941, p. 31.
[3] ———, *Man for Himself,* Rinehart & Co., 1947, p. 60.
[4] *Ibid.,* p. 79.
[5] E. Fromm, *Escape from Freedom,* pp. 41ff.
[6] *Ibid.,* p. 62.
[7] *Ibid.,* p. 101.
[8] *Ibid.,* p. 96.
[9] *Ibid.,* pp. 101f.
[10] *Ibid.,* p. 218.
[11] H. S. Sullivan, *Conceptions of Modern Psychiatry,* William Alanson White Foundation, 1947, p. 16.
[12] *Ibid.*
[13] *Ibid.,* p. 21.
[14] *Ibid.,* p. 18.
[15] *Ibid.,* p. 20.
[16] *Ibid.*
[17] *Ibid.,* pp. 28ff.

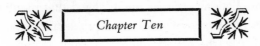

Chapter Ten

THE GENETIC PROCESS

THIS VERY BRIEF CHAPTER stands in clumsy disproportion to every other chapter, but it is a necessary part of the outline of the book, homologous with the very long chapter on the genetic process in Part II. The extreme difference in length reflects the difference in emphasis between the Freudian and the non-libido schools more dramatically than pages of critical comment. I found nothing to report on this topic for the non-libido schools (except Sullivan) beyond summary generalizations of points explained more vividly in other connections, in other chapters.

The reader may decide that the biological details of childhood experience are irrelevant to adult reaction patterns—indeed, that the Freudian description of the role of sexual and aggressive trends in childhood is misleading and *should* be omitted from consideration in general psychological theory. The awkward format of this chapter, however, is likely to provoke reflection on a point too often glossed over by glib generalizations on the one hand and a sort of flexible, common-sense appreciation of the special problems of childhood on the other. Is the new human being so specifically "human" that his special needs as a little animal can be considered of no significance as such in his psychological development? Are there no qualitative differences in childhood experience which must be considered *in their own right* during the formative years?

In this chapter, the four authors heretofore presented separately are discussed as a unit with brief indications of difference. With the exception of Sullivan, they seem so alike in their *neglect* of careful examination of psychological constellations peculiar to childhood that lumping them together on this theoretical point presents no serious problem in exposition.

In a general way, the genetic process is fully as important for the non-libido schools as for the Freudians. But the non-libido schools have very explicitly denied that the biological development of the child plays an important constellative role *as such* in personality development. Their emphasis is rather on the general climate of the home, on the warmth, support, and encouragement to realistic, independent activity offered the child in every area of development as he needs it. Conversely, parental attitudes of hostility and fear, overprotection or lack of help, generally or in specific aspects of the child's experience, and sibling rivalries may have a crippling effect on the growth of the personality. Such attitudes may create a faulty life style, exaggerated safety devices, or escape mechanisms which persist throughout life in the sense that the personality tends to retain the unhappy orientation established in childhood, weaving new experience into the old pattern. The infantile attitudes tend to be self-perpetuating or even to grow worse as partial failure in adjustment intensifies the need for further efforts along the same self-protective lines with increasing distance from reality (Adler) and increasing inner tension (Horney).

This concept of the persistence and exacerbation of attitudes originating in childhood differs from the Freudian position in two ways: (1) the problems faced by the child are differently stated, with far less attention to his *inner* libidinal desires, and (2) there is (for Adler and Horney) no idea that the infantile desires and fears may, through repression, become encysted in the personality and continue a timeless existence *as such,* constantly pressing toward overt expression and requiring constant inhibition.

Fromm considers his position on these points as closer to that of Freud, but his emphasis is placed on the dynamics of the acculturative process conceived more in terms of larger social units than in terms of the specific demands of the growing child. He has not re-examined the genetic process in detail.

Except for Sullivan, none of these analysts differentiates *systematically* among the special needs of the child at various stages of his growth. Doubtless they would all agree that the infant, the toddler, the school-age child and the adolescent offer different need pictures, each appropriate to his age, but they handle such variations on a common-sense basis. Their psychological *generalizations* are not tailored to age-level differences. The concepts of fixation and regression, so important in the Freudian ideology, have no relevance in schools in which the genetic process is not envisaged as involving definable stages or aspects, each with its characteristic dynamics.

I discussed earlier my reasons for reporting Sullivan's description of the epochs of childhood under the heading of "The Terms of the Milieu" rather than here. The reader will find the material presented on pages 404-411. My argument was that Sullivan does not seem to conceive the problem in the Freudian sense of inborn *needs* which in themselves provide successive foci for the organization of the personality patterns. Rather there is a maturation of *abilities* which make the child capable of responding to his environment in new ways, and which provoke the adult to different demands upon him. For example, there does not appear to be a *need to talk*, comparable to the need for oral gratification, which inevitably presses toward fulfillment and causes difficulty if frustrated. But as the child learns to talk, his new ability leads to significant differences in his perception of his environment and to very marked changes in the way in which he is handled. I felt that careful discussion of the epochs of childhood was indispensable to an understanding of Sullivan's concept of *acculturation* and that a cross reference here was preferable to artificial isolation of "childhood" for the sake of my outline.

Sullivan does suggest that language has an *emotional* dimension beyond its practical value and importance in adult interpersonal relations. He connects this dimension of language with an oral dynamism originating in the biological needs of the infant as described by Freud.* Sullivan's discussion of this point is an especially good example of how he uses Freudian concepts *in a very subsidiary way*—far short of the emphasis they are given in Freudian theory. Occasionally Sullivan (and Fromm) make use of the concepts of fixation and regression in relation to rather specific childhood experiences, dissociated or repressed, in a manner which aligns them more with Freud than with Adler and Horney. This problem will be discussed further in the next chapter. Here attention to these refinements of theory would obscure the major emphasis of the two men.

Once due allowance has been made for the difficulties implicit in lumping four authors together, one may suggest that none of them has conceived the genetic process as primarily *dictated from within* by the relatively isolable phases of the child's growth, whereas this is the major emphasis of most Freudians. All the non-libido analysts insist upon the crucial importance of the early years, but they have considered mainly the conditions the child has to meet. In their *theories* the needs of the child tend to be generalized as the

* The reader may be interested in comparing for himself Sullivan's use of such a biological need with Freud's more focal use of it. (See especially H. S. Sullivan, *Conceptions of Modern Psychiatry*, William Alanson White Foundation, 1947, p. 31.)

needs of a person—for superiority, for belongingness and significance, for security. The special developmental aspects of childhood are considered as incidental to or (especially in Sullivan's analysis) instrumental toward the working out of these general needs. They do not themselves set the tune for personality development. They are not even important themes recurrent in the symphony of the adult personality.

My own stance in the matter of the importance of the genetic process as such in personality development and function is perhaps already made too clear by the fact that this chapter is so strikingly brief. It does indeed seem to me astonishing that anyone should assume that the growing body of the child would not present foci of concern very significant for psychological development. I cannot think that the long story of animal evolution would suddenly stop *altogether* with man, that the instinctual needs of this creature should have *no* importance beyond the minimal satisfaction necessary to maintain life, that his socialization is *entirely* a matter of the emotional climate of his home.

I state the argument *ad absurdum,* but I am not very much impressed by casual acknowledgment of bodily needs as "obvious but psychologically unimportant." What does the infant know beyond the bodily needs? On what other basis does he learn than by elaboration and correction of what he already "knows"? Can we say, with Fromm, that the infant has biological needs, and so does the adult, but that human needs start where the biological needs leave off? This is true enough, but specifically human needs originate in infancy when the child *who wants to move his bowels* is already in human relationship with his parents, so that his handling of his anal impulses is "humanized" from the beginning. If these impulses are themselves very important to the child, as the Freudians demonstrate, then surely the process of being human must be strongly influenced by this special *inner* aspect of the child's experience.*

Although it would be a mistake to consider humanity solely in terms of biologically determined impulses, surely it is equally a mistake to deny that such impulses partake intimately in the complex process of attitude formation. In fact there can hardly be any doubt that the infant is interested in the world *as he knows it,* and this is certainly not the world which adults take for granted. The infant's world must be experienced by the infant— *i.e.,* in terms available to an extraordinarily ignorant little creature, equipped

---

* In a way this is precisely Fromm's point, but he so emphasizes the cultural, "humanizing" aspects of the problem that acknowledgment of the "Freudian" material is not made sufficiently clear to the reader.

to suck, eliminate, and experience genital pleasure. (I would add grasping, reaching and locomotion—*i.e.*, "motility" patterns—and other nonsexual drive systems.)

My point in critical comment throughout has been that early classical and especially "popular" Freudianism has been overly reductionist on the matter of libidinal factors in development; that the newer ego psychology has not yet fully recognized the importance of the nonsexual systems in ego development. The non-libido schools offer a very useful contribution in the area of ego psychology, of the development of the self. But the problem cannot be dismissed simply by saying that Freud emphasized sex too exclusively; that other factors are important. Surely emphasis on other factors is itself overly reductionist if it neglects in principle the careful analysis of libidinal development. It seems to me that any sound psychological theory *must* give weight to the constellative power of the "sexual" systems as they mature and affect the organism from within.

One may freely criticize the libido theory of Freud as neglecting half or more than half of the story; one may feel that the actual stages of development in these systems have not been perfectly delineated by Freud and require further close empirical study—in themselves and in their major relationships to the nonsexual systems. One might eventually find that the sexual and instinctual aggressive systems as such do in fact play a relatively minor role in the functioning of the healthy adult in a mature society. (One might hope so, even as a classical Freudian.) The nonsexual systems require renewed investigation in relationship to the sexual systems and to emerging patterns of the "self" via the complex mechanism of identification. Nevertheless, and including all the and's, but's and if's in the dictionary, it seems to me quite simply wrong to make a positive point of ignoring the sexual systems as factors in the development of the human psyche. Any sensitive, unbiased study of the young child prior to gross cultural intervention shows spontaneous concern with "sexual" areas—oral, anal, and genital. The fact that the adults, as exponents of their culture, have quite elaborate ideas about how the child should conduct himself is an extraneous factor which by now the reader ought to be able to envisage in its systematic complexities.

It seems to me clear that the maturation of the nonsexual systems of the organism deserves study in its own right, in the specific relationships of these systems to the sexual systems, and in their relationship to the outside world as mediated first through the family, later through social institutions concerned with the induction of the young child into his culture, and finally the full role of the adult in society. I consider it disappointing that analysts so keenly aware of the relationship between the person and his social world should not have developed a more differentiated child psychology oriented around the child's growing capacities for action and understanding. Again I am excepting Sullivan, but I have already pointed out that Sullivan has not related his own scheme either to the sexual developmental stages of the Freudians or to such recurrent problems in adaptation as may be encountered by individuals because of their *special* nonsexual capacities.

The child's developmental status (as regards the nonsexual systems) must strongly condition his assimilation of various aspects of his environment at different times in a manner roughly corresponding to his age. By virtue of his own locomotion, the toddler creates a new world for himself and requires a different kind of helpfulness from the adults around him. Surely adults (and whole cultures) vary in the ways in which they handle the relatively passive stage of infancy and the relatively active stage of toddling. The general prescription of warm affection and encouragement to enterprise does not adequately cover the importance for personality development of these variations in approach. From the angle of individual predisposition, the active baby who learns to walk early presents his nurses with a problem different from that of the baby who quietly sits until he is old enough to learn the significant hazards and prohibitions of his environment.

And so through later ages. I suggested earlier that the induction of the five- or six-year-old into the wider social group must be determined largely by the simple fact that he becomes physically and mentally able to meet its demands. This is a developmental problem which might well be considered as such. (Sullivan and Erikson have approached it.) If one takes seriously the relationship between the strivings of the "self" and the nature of the social environment, then surely *the mode of induction to the group* must be important in its own right and deserving of special study. Societies and individual families within a society are not homogeneous in this respect. Institutional opportunities vary both in their formal offerings and in the feeling tone toward the young child. Parents who are warm toward the baby may be bewildered and even rejecting toward the young hoyden. Psychologies which emphasize the continuing importance of reality impacts should, it seems to me, be especially alert to these problems as regularly recurrent for every growing child and as subject to useful codification.

Another generally crucial period is adolescence, not only because of its relatively focused sexual demands (Sullivan's lust dynamism) but because the child is now confronted with the problem of establishing his full adult role. Even in our society, in which "training" often continues for many years, essential directions must be established for the self-image in concrete relationship to social opportunities. Again it would seem to me that the psychologies discussed in this section ought to be especially interested in how the social transition to adulthood is accomplished; that they should attempt to codify important variations both in the personality "type" of the adolescent and in the cultural pattern within which he lives. Yet no such codification is offered. Any case study of an individual will, of course, describe the course of the life story, and casual comments on adolescence are made by all the schools. Sullivan (pp. 409*ff.*) has devoted particular attention to the psychological meaning of this age, with strange omission of *social* pressures toward the adult role. But in basic theory these schools* rely firmly on the adage "As the twig is bent, so the branch inclines." The conflicts and maneuvers of the adolescent are seen merely as the working out of the basic personality trends already established, not as importantly directive in themselves, in relation to the opportunities and frustrations of the adolescent and the attitudes toward him characteristic for the culture within which he lives.

Of course the adolescent (and even the school child or the toddler) does not come to the experiences typical for these ages as a *tabula rasa* somehow endowed with a set of impulses and capacities peculiar to the age period. This repudiating statement represents with only slight burlesque the point of view that the non-libido schools have been combating, whether it appears in Freudian guise as recrudescence of repressed infantile conflicts or in the tenets of a general psychology long focused on normative studies of age groups, *e.g.*, "mental age." I do not wish to imply that the very important emphasis on the personality as a whole characteristic for all non-libido schools should be diminished. I do think that they should pay more attention to the conditions under which the personality operates during the formative years. Partly these conditions are determined from within by the biological equipment of the child—Freud's point. I urge that the course of the nonsexual systems be accorded the same serious study by analysts as the Freudians have devoted to the sexual systems. Partly the conditions of development are imposed from without by the *specific* attitudes of individual parents and particular social groups toward the *specific* picture presented by the child in different phases of growth.

---

* A reader of the manuscript has commented that this adage is not confined to the non-libido schools; that in Chapter 2 I made a general point of *Freud's* concern with the genetic process; that the infantile libido is more "infantile" and more permanent than the adaptive changes wrought over the years cited by the non-libido schools. Yet Freud's early position actually required the hypothesis of an adult ego dealing with encysted (repressed) traumata. Freud did *not* envisage the personality as an elaboration of infantile modes. On the contrary, the concept of perduring ego mechanisms (character) was of late development and, in my opinion, is still not adequately integrated with the instinct theory. Freud's analogy would be more with the burl (the healed injury) than with the bent twig, but the analogy is really not applicable to his theory. Freud's theory involves much more complex relations between childhood and adult patterns of behavior.

Attention to subsystems in complex interaction seriously complicates the gratifying unity of a basic theory. For the non-libido schools, such attention requires a painful multidimensionality in the area of personal and interpersonal relationships, to which must be added, I feel, the multidimensionality of the "libidinal" approach. Yet I think the discomfort of multidimensionality must be accepted in the interest of scientific truth. The positive values of the non-libido schools cannot be long maintained unless they accept the need for a more differentiated approach to the genetic process. At present they are using their good ideas in too reductionist a manner, too rebelliously. In consequence they have neglected a whole chapter of the life story which actually demands investigation as to the significant subsystems it presents and the effects of their course upon the general development of the personality.

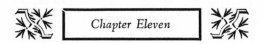

Chapter Eleven

THE DYNAMICS OF THE FUNCTIONING PERSONALITY

ADLER

THE PURPOSE OF THIS CHAPTER is to consider Adler's view of the dynamics of the functioning adult personality. Hitherto we have, following the plan outlined in Chapter 1, considered mainly the ingredients of personality, with such scant and promissory heed to relationships as could not be avoided in an account of essentially integrated dynamic systems. The question now is: How does Adler conceive of the active functioning of the *person*, and how is such functional activity to be recognized?

RECAPITULATION

In all personalities Adler sees a basic inferiority feeling and an urge to overcome it in the reciprocal goal of superiority or perfection. Generally speaking, the greater the feeling of inferiority, the more determined the drive toward "superiority." Where organic imperfections or faulty training in early life predominate, the natural drive toward overcoming inferiority takes on the proportions of a "complex"—i.e., the natural proclivities of the human organism toward "perfection" are systematically distorted by specific needs to compensate for outstanding problems.

The life style emerges from the initial experience of the child in its striving toward superiority. "The condition of the body and the impressions of the external world are the building materials which the child uses for the construction of his personality."[1] These materials are not to be considered objectively, as they may look to outsiders, but rather in terms of the selective process instituted by the life style. The personality functions as a unit. Once its direction is set, it chooses among outside events those that can be assimilated with the life style, and it rejects the rest. Adler was among the first to recognize the individual, creative, goal-directed structuring behind memory, perception, imagination.

The fact remains that the outside world is not infinitely malleable in accordance with the life style of the individual. Adler therefore introduces two further concepts: social feeling and "shock."

The biological origin of *social feeling* was described earlier (see p. 339) as somewhat obscure in Adler's writings. Whatever its origin, its nature and dynamic role seem fairly clear. In his dealings with patients and other people, Adler observes an almost quantitative difference from one person to the next in feeling for others, in common sense, and—more tentatively—in appreciation of the reality of things. People may or may not have "social interest," or rather they may have it in varying degrees, above and beyond the character of their life style.

Adler's position seems to be that in favorable circumstances the human infant "naturally" develops common sense and feeling for his fellows. His personal goal of superiority is thereby "naturally" transmuted into the goal of social welfare, to be obtained rationally, or at least by common sense.

However, if social feeling is inadequate, the life style has relatively full sway without correction. The individual then experiences the requirements of society as external to himself, as a hostile incursion which he must somehow master. He therefore meets society with hostility and protest. Even under cover of extreme helplessness, the life style expresses protest and demands submission of others to the will of the individual. Even suicide typically contains a hostile attack on other persons—in protest against lack of appreciation by others in a life style narrowed down by inadequate social feeling.[2]

Normally, then, according to Adler, the life style incorporates social feeling. Personal superiority is intrinsically related to social welfare. When early experience pushes the life style in a faulty direction for whatever reason, social feeling is not achieved. Social (or common-sense) demands then become an intrusion against which the individual struggles by intensification of his life style. The greater the pressure from outside, the more vigorously the life style is pursued regardless of social feeling.

THE LIFE STYLE, SOCIAL FEELING, AND REALITY

If the life style and social demands are discrepant, if the personality has been badly prepared for cooperation and common sense, active tension develops. Hostility, aggression, sadism are not, for Adler, primary trends. They come into being later on, *when an unprepared personality tries to cope with cogent life situations by means of a limited life style.*

Intrusions from the outside world may precipitate difficulties previously masked by correspondence between the life style and social demands. So long as the child is kingpin in the family, his inadequate preparation for social living may not show itself. The "spoiled" person born to riches and social position may appear active, productive, and generous so long as his personal primacy is not challenged. Such individuals may experience a change in circumstances as "shock." No one takes the affronts of outrageous fortune unmoved. Tragedy, marked change of any sort, provokes reaction in everyone. If adequate social feeling is present, the new requirements are assimilated to the socialized goal. In the absence of social feeling, a limited life style may manifest itself abruptly, and its limitations may become exacerbated as the individual strives for *personal* superiority regardless of external handicaps.

The spoiled child who was generally smiling, active and well-behaved at home may suddenly become sullen and withdrawn, may even appear stupid, when he enters school. Superficially it looks as though the school "caused" the change—an interpretation especially attractive when teachers or classmates have actually been unusually harsh. World events have provided all too many instances of well-born adults who adjusted to refugee status badly, who preferred cadging loans from friends or even dignified starvation to accepting an independent position in a lowered social bracket. Some people in these circumstances act so "uppity" in jobs *almost* commensurate with their background as to earn the frank resentment of American colleagues. The penniless Direktor of a vanished clinic must *earn* respect as attendant physician in a big American hospital. His "habit of command" is anything but endearing to his new associates, who very often accept his appointment in a mood of pity or fair-mindedness. Such instances are, of course, in marked contrast to the number of children who make out well enough in school, and the refugees who adapt themselves to their new lot with admirable flexibility.

Adler's point is that such breaks and poor adaptability to adverse circumstances are not fortuitous. The external shock merely *reveals* the absence of social feeling and poor preparation for life. Examination of the early history will usually show such minor indications of difficulty as night terrors, enuresis, tantrums, crying when the child could not have its own way, or finicky eating habits. Often the doting parents gloss over the annoyance of these common symptoms of childhood maladjustment, remembering only the more charming episodes, refusing to acknowledge any special defect in the cherished youngster. Moreover, it is easier for parents to pick up toys than to train the child to pick them up, to prepare food the child likes than to encourage the development of new tastes, even to rinse out the sheets every morning than to work understandingly with the child toward sphincter control.

So long as the child is able to feel himself master of his environment by these babyish techniques, he actually can afford to be sweetly cooperative much of the time. He can enjoy some freedom of creative activity in fairly good contact with reality. With the shock of actual frustration, however, he is forced toward an *intensification* of his overpersonal life style. Tension mounts. Too often the modicum of social feeling he possesses is swamped by the increasingly insistent demands of the life style which become ever more blatantly self-centered. Thus the problem is not wholly one of the coming to light of difficulties previously masked by a protective environment. The dynamics of the shock situation leads to a real intensification of the initial difficulty. Schooling and other impacts beyond early childhood do not change the fundamental nature of the life style. They may profoundly affect its course: whether it develops in conjunction with social feeling or whether inner patterns of personal superiority develop at odds with social and common-sense requirements in an endless vicious circle.

FANTASY AND DREAMS

The life style shows itself not only in the pattern of overt behavior but also in fantasy and imagination, in dreams, and in artistic production. Because these activities are relatively distant from reality, they can be used with relative freedom by the individual in the elaboration and consolidation of his basic attitudes. If the attitudes are essentially sound, the process is valuable. "Its significance consists in its being a test and a search for a solution."[3] The dream, Adler says, is not merely a combination of the day's residue with repressed infantile wishes, as Freud supposed, but *a purposeful creation, aimed at integration of immediate problems in terms of the enduring life style.*

If social feeling is weak, fantasy and dream further intensify the distance from reality demands. Here, too, they are used for the "strengthening and acceleration of the movement directed by the style of life,"[4] but the direction is erroneous. For this reason daydreams and night dreams may have a deleterious influence. Like Penelope, the patient unweaves at night the progress made during the day toward realistic adaptation, or fortifies himself in fantasy against the "hostile" demands of his actual life situation. Adler's position is not that fantasy and imagination are bad *per se*. On the contrary; they become bad only when the life style is fundamentally inadequate, since they serve to consolidate personality trends with little correction from reality. Like other experiences, they follow the supreme law: that the ego's sense of worth shall not be allowed to diminish.[5] They allow a primitive symbolism which may encourage self-deception at the expense of social feeling and common sense.

DIAGNOSING THE LIFE STYLE

In studying a personality, Adler emphasizes the outlines of the life story, the significant external circumstances with which the person has had to cope, and the attitudes he has adopted toward them. These attitudes are to be seen mainly in the *pattern* of his overt behavior: the nature of his vocation, of his illnesses, of his conscious attitudes and moods, of his relations with his family, friends, and business associates, his love affairs, his habits of eating and sleeping, etc. The life style manifests itself in all these characteristic areas of human activity and constantly determines the ways in which the individual handles his life situation. The skilled observer may see recurrent trends in the behavioral *facts* which serve to explain and predict the peculiarities in the overt functioning of each individual. Thus the main Adlerian data for personality study are the actions of the person in ordinary and in relatively crucial situations.

Art productions, night dreams and day dreams, memories elicited outside the practical requirements of daily living, all have special value for study of the life style, because they are less directly under the control of reality—*i.e.*, of social feeling and common sense. They represent the selective integrative power of the life style quite directly to the observer who knows how to read the language of images uncorrected by reality considerations. The distortions of the dream are, for Adler, merely the consequence of its greater distance from reality. The dynamics are those of the everyday life style in purer culture as it were, less complicated by common sense.

Thus Adler, like Freud, considers the dream and related phenomena interpretable. He lays great weight on individual meanings, but he offers something of a lexicon for typical dreams. For example, the common dreams of falling "indicate that the dreamer is anxious about losing his sense of worth; but at the same time they show by spatial representation that the dreamer is under the delusion that he is 'above.'"[6] To present this dream interpretation as fundamental for Adler would be like presenting Freud's libidinal interpretation of the same dream as fundamental to Freudian dream interpretation. The brief dream lexicon of both men illustrates well their characteristic *direction* in interpretation. In practice both of them see the dream mostly in very intimate and highly individual relationship to the specific problems and experience of the dreamer. Naturally the *direction* of Adlerian interpretation is typically different from the Freudian, corresponding to the direction of their theories. Both try to understand the dream as a relatively direct expression of underlying trends (once one gets the hang of this kind of direct expression). Both emphasize the importance of concrete images and symbols of an infantile and reality-distant character.

In the realm of dreams, fantasies, and art, Adler made no very special contribution, and the task of the present book is fulfilled if we merely recognize that he used them intelligently, with some bias toward his own theoretical considerations.

Adler's emphasis on "the first memory" was unique and deserves special consideration. He routinely asked the patient to report the first thing he could remember from his childhood. Adler believed that such "memory" is not adventitious. In daily life, memory subserves the conscious demands of the moment, with such odd failures as Freud considered in his *Psychopathology of Everyday Life*. If you ask somebody for his earliest recollection, in realistically neutral circumstances, the "first memory" is very revealing of the life style. The apparently random recovery of the past seems actually to be deeply determined, like the dream, like art. A merit of Adler's technique is that everybody has a first memory, whereas most of us are not artistically productive, and our dreams, if we remember them at all, are often relatively transient reactions to current problems.*

* As a clinical psychologist, I have a special interest in diagnosing relatively enduring personality trends from slight but "important" cues. From this point of view, it seems to me that Adler's routine request for a first memory was actually the first approach toward the *projective*-test methodology now so widely used. Adler knew very well that the first memory is realistically

The earliest memory may be supplemented by asking in addition for first memories concerning the parents and siblings.[8] As a rule the very earliest memory appears to give a clue to the life style. The more specific memories often suggest unconscious attitudes underlying the life style, sometimes at variance with it. The tension between the various aspects of development so revealed, often quite different from the superficially apparent character of the person, provides helpful cues for the therapist.

A detailed example may illustrate not only this technique but Adlerian dynamics generally. The earliest memory of a woman who appears somewhat excessively poised, assured, and rather cold concerns her first day in a new neighborhood at about the age of four. There are two pretty little girls with a big dog. One of them says "You don't have to be afraid of Shep. He won't hurt you." The woman remembers being surprised at this remark because she had not thought of being afraid of the *dog*. She had wanted to be friends with the children, had not known how to go about it, and had felt shy because she thought they might not want to be friends. The Adlerian is not surprised to discover in further conversation that this woman's poise is a cover for shyness; that social relations are very important to her and that she typically anticipates rejection. The dog is important too. At forty, as at four, she is courageous in situations which do not involve people.

Such a little scene may occur in the life of any child, and the remembered feelings are in no way peculiar. The distinctive point is really that it was remembered, that it came to mind *first* in all its triviality and with great vividness of detail. The girls had little red hats; Shep is minutely described with the adult summary that he must have been a collie. Most genuine earliest memories have this vividness and triviality. (Some patients give as their earliest memory a dramatic incident often recounted at home which, on careful inquiry, they themselves do not remember at all. Even these "memories" are of some value, but the therapist usually tries tactfully to find out what the patient really remembers from the early years as against later stories about himself.)

---

often incorrect, that its chronology is often suspect. His idea was that the item selected as "first" was *creatively* selected, and could be interpreted in relation to the total personality. Adler's notion of comparing people on the basis of their spontaneous "conscious" reaction to a fairly simple but dynamic question is the very core of contemporary projective techniques. In this field, as in others, no one picked up Adler's ideas. Within the last few years several Freudians have returned to interest in first memories.[7]

Out of concern with "credits," it seems important to emphasize Adler's priority in systematic observations on the significance of a complex *conscious* reaction to a relatively unstructured stimulus. His first-memory technique was not only unique as a quasi-test device but at its inception unique in the theory that loosely governed conscious productions may be used *systematically* to reveal deep personality trends.

This patient's first memory of her *mother* involved being sent to bed alone while the family chatted on the porch below; she cried, and finally was spanked. The mother died when the patient was only seven. Although affectionately cared for by relatives, she grew up with a feeling of unbelongingness. She cherished *consciously* the image of a lost, beneficent mother in considerable contrast to this first memory of being spanked for a protest against loneliness and fright. Again there is nothing remarkable about the episode remembered. It is a very common bedtime incident. The interesting feature is that despite the adult's conscious overidealized image of the mother, her unconscious selection shows a rejecting and punishing figure in her childhood.

One might almost deduce from the material thus far presented why this woman came for treatment. She constantly wants a very close relationship with her intimate friends, male or female, and wants to "belong" in any social group she enters. But somehow her love affairs never work out, and she is admired rather than liked by her acquaintances. Beneath her conscious wish for closeness lies the unconscious fear of rejection and punishment. Her own story, up to the point at which the gloom of her spinsterhood became too apparent to be ignored, was that her ideals were too high. She was *differently* disappointed in every love affair. Sharing an apartment with women friends worked out badly for such a variety of reasons that at first glance she seemed to have no pronounced life style. Her first memory, in conjunction with materials obtained in interview, shows the long-standing pattern of a deep uncertainty in interpersonal relations. Special tension between longing for the ideal and fear of rejection appears in the first memory of the mother.

There is no reason to suppose in this case that the real mother was rejecting beyond the ordinary. In fact, the patient seems to have been actually more spoiled than hated. Every spoiled child tends to react to ordinary discipline with a feeling of being rejected because its expectation of gratification is set too high and—as the Freudians have emphasized—maternal oversolicitude is not infrequently a compensation on the part of the mother for an unconscious hostility ("hatred") toward her child. The premature death of the mother deprived this little girl of the opportunity to work out *gradually* through continuing experience a more realistic appreciation of the mother as partly "good" and partly "bad." Instead, the mother became a fantasy figure onto which she could project all her longings for closeness and support, while her infantile fears and resentments went uncorrected. The patient was certainly wrong in ascribing her difficulties to the fact of being orphaned. The psychoanalyst of any school would date them earlier, although the mother's death would operate to set the infantile pattern more firmly. But her first memory of the mother, obtained as a sort of test-response, would quickly alert the analyst to the deep significance of the dead mother as extremely punishing.

THE UNCONSCIOUS

What does Adler make of the "unconscious," the concept cited in Chapter 2 as one of the fundamental contributions of Freud? The answer is not easy. It must be quite clear from the foregoing discussion that Adler *operates* constantly with the concept. He remarks that "man knows more than he understands." His patients do not deliberately manufacture a migraine in order to dominate their families. The whole process of selectiveness in terms of the life style as it applies to overt behavior, bodily symptoms, dreams, memory and perception is essentially "unconscious."

Nevertheless Adler rarely uses the term; indeed, he explicitly describes the division between conscious and unconscious as an artificial one, having its origin merely in "psychoanalytic fanaticism."[9] His main objection to the psychoanalytic point of view derives from his insistence that the personality always functions as a unit. The erection of the censor, or of superego and ego, as more or less independent provinces of the mind which exert a repressive force on other impulses seems to Adler an unjustifiable theoretical construction in antithesis to unity of function. Psychic events, he says, are always to be interpreted in terms of the movement of the personality as a whole.

Infantile wishes, for Adler, are not actively excluded from consciousness because their recognition would entail intolerable anxiety and guilt. They are simply not understood, because of the tight selectiveness of the life style. No phenomena are to be considered "regressive" or "repetitive." Competition with an older brother may set the life style before the age of five, but only in the sense that the child develops the conviction "I must always strive against odds." Adler's self-diagnosis of his relations with Freud as a "second child" reaction was mentioned earlier. Adler meant not that Freud in any way represented his older brother but rather that early competition with his brother had fostered in him an energetic ambition and intolerance for the role of second fiddle. When the adult under pressure (and lacking social feeling) behaves in an infantile, unrealistic manner or repetitively, the reason is that he seeks a solution in terms of a life style which has become very narrow, not that he is re-enacting the events of childhood.

SEXUALITY

It is hardly necessary to point out again Adler's total repudiation of the Freudian concept of sexuality. For Adler the Oedipus complex arises, if at all, out of the dependency of the pampered child on his mother, fused with the beginnings of sexual feeling. The castration complex is, for him, merely one variety of the feeling of inferiority. It may be of frequent occurrence in a society which places a premium on masculinity, in which childish masturbation is often accompanied by direct threats. Of course the child has sexual impulses and feelings as part of his biological make-up, like hunger and thirst and breathing. But they affect his psychological development only through the role they come to play in his striving for superiority. The masculine protest is only secondarily sexual, the product of life conditions offering special handicaps to the "weaker" sex and the effeminate male.

INTRAPSYCHIC CONFLICT

A corollary of Adler's strict adherence to the concept of the unity of the personality is his repudiation of the idea of intrapsychic conflict which, as we shall see, plays so large a role in Horney's theory as well as in Freud's. For Adler the conflict is between the "exogenous" (external) factor of environmental pressures and the native striving for superiority or perfection, not between intrinsically different—at times incompatible—strivings *within* the personality. Of course, environmental pressures are not to be construed as having the same impact for everyone. Loss of fortune, health, occasionally even of loved people, may be handled well. For some persons such losses may even be positively helpful in releasing socially constructive effort.

During a period of family prosperity, for example, a woman may "keep up with the Jones's"—at considerable emotional cost. She feels inadequate in her role as hostess, perhaps resents her subsidiary position in a man's world. Her protests may take the form of headaches, nagging, or other neurotic symptoms. With the advent of a depression or a war, the ailing wife may suddenly become the bulwark of the family. She may earn money herself, or she may merely dispense with domestic service, an act which entails no small amount of responsible work in a big house with several children. Some women may use their new-found freedom to dominate their husbands in another way, "rubbing in" the husband's failure to provide, dominating overtly where they had previously dominated by illness. Other women may actually become "sweeter" when social catastrophe finally relieves them of the necessity for the distasteful superficiality of conventional social life and allows the expression of social feeling and self-fulfillment along lines for which they are genuinely better fitted.

The at least temporary cure of many ambulatory psychoneuroses of long standing during air bombardment was noted in every European city, whatever the final psychological cost of the periods of stress to the population generally. A major difficulty in psychiatric screening for the armed forces was the disconcerting propensity of *some* young neurotics, even psychotics, to find positive satisfaction in military life or at least to perform excellently as soldiers, whereas other individuals, with unblemished civilian histories, went to pieces.

The problem is clearly not one of the degree of environmental stress as measured on an absolute scale of what most of us would consider stress. The problem centers upon *the relationship of the environmental pressures to the life style of the individual.*

In practice, exogenous factors are, then, very closely related to internal factors in so far as they play an active part in precipitating psychological illness or in determining the everyday function of the "normal" person. Serious constitutional defects, illness, poverty, the whole roster of woe *may* be the focus of successful compensation. Minor—even apparently quite fanciful—outside events *may* precipitate outbreaks of neurotic behavior—depending on how the external events are related to the life style, and upon the amount of social feeling present.

The nature of the conflict with the outside world always depends upon the specific demands of the life style. In one way or another, in Adler's view, however, the struggle is always against *other people* who withhold support and appreciation, or against events which discourage the striving for superiority. Melancholia (*i.e.*, the psychosis) and suicide, despite the attack upon the self by the self so frankly indicated, are resolved by Adler into desperate attacks upon other people psychologically designed to exact support and maintenance of the life style. In theory Adler never admits a house divided against itself as a personality description; instead, he tries to show how every expedient of the neurotic or psychotic is oriented toward a single goal, no matter how inexpedient his devices may appear.*

* I refer readers interested in how an Adlerian handles the problem of conflict in the discussion of clinical material to a case published by Ansbacher.[10]

ANXIETY

Another word familiar to other schools which rarely occurs in Adler's writings is *anxiety*. But Adler uses the concept repeatedly without using the term. It is the fear of confronting a feeling of worthlessness that drives the neurotic into retreat or unrealistic compensation, that makes him resist the solution of his problems in therapy. "So long as he thinks himself in danger of having his worthlessness revealed [the neurotic] cannot be brought to take a single step forward."[11] The pain of self-discovery is worse than the ailments or defeats of the erroneous solution the person has adopted; the closer he is pushed to recognition of failure, the more vigorously the life style asserts itself despite common sense.

Working pragmatically with these facts, Adler does not make the generalization—as does Freud or Horney or Sullivan—that the discomfort of anxiety *per se* is the dynamic factor. It is enough that if a person wants to be superior at all costs, he will struggle mightily, albeit in fantasy and even in the teeth of reality, against any threat to his superiority. The trained observer sees the pattern of the struggle, which the struggling person does not "understand." The patient's understanding is hampered not so much by fear of actual defeat as by fear of having to admit his own inadequacy. By Horney's definition this is anxiety rather than fear, since it is a reaction to a danger which is "hidden and subjective." As usual, the parallel between Adler's position and that of other analytic schools is obscured by his failure to make explicit distinctions which loom large in other constructions—although he uses them in practice.

However, a genuine difference from other schools lies in Adler's conviction that the determining factor is always the fear of feeling inferior, no matter how varied its manifestations. Far from accepting the criticism that this formulation involves a rigidity of interpretation, Adler finds in it freedom from the strait jacket of theoretical constructions. Since the basic striving is always the same, Adler feels that he is at liberty to examine the manifold techniques developed by the life style, unhampered by the codifications put forward in one way or another by other schools. We must reiterate that the skilled Individual Psychology clinician is by no means as stereotyped in his interpretations as Adlerian theory seems to imply. Indeed, his problem may be rather the lack of sufficient guidelines for ready understanding of individual cases, and too heavy demands on his own ingenuity.

RESISTANCE

The familiar Freudian concept of *resistance* is implicit in the paragraphs above. Like reality shocks, therapeutic pressure toward understanding leads to intensification of problems unless the patient's need for security is fully dealt with by the therapist. The patient does not really want to get over his symptoms, because they constitute his main protection against the disaster of facing his inadequacy. The life style therefore puts up a battle to maintain its own solution of the basic problem—a solution which becomes more fiercely defended and more tightly organized as it is threatened by growing understanding. The protest may often be seen in dreams and fantasy with especial clarity because here the life style can express itself with less correction from common sense.

Again the problem in reporting Adler's position is that he does not supply a conceptual label for a phenomenon he describes vividly. Again, too, he prefers to see "resistance" as a natural reaction to a genuine threat to the life style as a whole rather than as an instance of the array of specific defensive forces against specific impulses. As usual, the deeper implications of Adler's repudiation of familiar Freudian formulations proceed from his radically holistic approach.

SUMMARY

Adler insists that the personality be considered as a goal-directed unit. The goal is superiority, or compensation for inferiority. The life style of the individual can be understood as the effort to achieve this goal. The effort is often disguised, and the person is himself unaware of the relation of his acts to this central goal. (Adler deals with unconscious processes in fact, although he avoids using the term.) Conflicts arise when the life style demands superiority without adequate relation to social feeling and common sense. Ideally, or perhaps normally, the child develops social feeling and common sense along with fulfillment of the need for superiority, and hence there is no *necessary* intrapsychic conflict. Indeed Adler considers no conflicts *intrapsychic*. For him the basic conflict is always between the personal goal of superiority and the external (exogenous) forces which prevent fulfillment. Conflict takes the form dictated by the peculiar structure of the individual's inferiorities, organic or social. Its form is infinitely variable, but the basic problem is the same.

Special refinements of Adler's approach will appear in later summaries, related to the positions of other authors in the non-libido group.

Critical Comment

ADLER'S view of dynamics is likely to seem thin to any reader who has grasped the intent behind the various "complications" introduced by other psychoanalytic schools. His position is not *simple* as he tries to work out in practice an explanation of the manifold peculiarities of human behavior, but in the long run his complexities have the forced quality of any radically reductionist system. The apostle of common sense tends to tie himself into quite extraordinary knots in the attempt to explain everything by the free striving of the whole personality toward superiority.

A few examples of his handling of pathological syndromes have been given here to show his approach to such recurrent "peculiarities." They seem so strained and so inadequate to the task of explaining why psychiatrists frequently encounter rather clear clusters of symptoms that I shall not even attempt to deal further with the specialized problem of the dynamics of pathology in Chapter 12. Adler himself made little effort to consider the psychiatric entities as such. His pronouncements on these syndromes have been little regarded by his medical colleagues. In reading his reports of cases, one even feels at times that he has failed to recognize a *psychotic* variation in thought processes—and one is glad to remember that his therapeutic approach emphasizes encouragement and support and therefore was probably more helpful than otherwise, regardless of the failure in diagnosis.

These comments are made here because I think that any sound theoretical statement of basic psychological dynamics ought to encompass without contortionism the special cases presented by pathology. I have already suggested that Adler's special rubrics concerning the milieu have not been applied to cultures with markedly different family constellations as early experience. I could well have added that explanation of cultural differences by the Adlerian reductionism would require a great deal of forcing if anyone took the trouble to attempt it.

A would-be universal view of dynamics which cannot supply workable tools for understanding these rather frequent "exceptional" constellations seems to me suspect no matter how convincing it may seem when we look at our friends and neighbors. Adler goes farther in theoretical reductionism than any other analyst. He rejects *on principle* any dynamically active subsystems of the personality whatsoever, and he considers any psychological event either a direct expression of the will to power (appropriately disguised) or at the very most a not very well delineated reaction between the life style as a sort of psychic unit and common-sense–social feeling.

It seems to me that Adler does *in fact* make plentiful use of the important psychoanalytic concepts discussed in Chapter 2 although he does not call them by name. I believe that his efforts to avoid the separatist structuralization implied in naming a process actually prevented the development of a more soundly differentiated Individual Psychology. He could not deal consistently and enduringly even with such specific dynamic concepts as he himself achieved; instead, he kept throwing them back into the theoretical pot and pulling them out afresh for each new problem.

This point has been emphasized because it is the obverse of Adler's most impressive positive contribution—the insistence on the unified action of the total personality. Criticism of his short-comings should not detract from the historical importance of this insistence against the atomistic approaches of his time, even against Freud's early approach. Adler's insistence on constant reference to the person-as-a-whole is still a valuable corrective against the tendency to view part-systems mechanically in non-creative interaction—a tendency which must be guarded against in every school of thought.

Furthermore, Adler's observations in the field which Freudians call ego-psychology are acute and brilliant. In a footnote (see p. 428), I related his "early memory" technique to the testing techniques now widely used by "psychologists," with rather similar rationale. In Part II mention was made of the "new" emphasis on analysis of the life pattern of the individual. Adler worked out this approach in detail many years earlier, with good insight into its significance. Starting with the problem of the symptom and the concept of the relatively encysted, repressed, timeless infantile unconscious which influenced conscious activity in a rather spotty way, "Freudians" were a long time in fully recognizing the constantly operating deviations in reality appreciation and behavior introduced by the ego mechanisms, and in understanding the role of "character" in psychodynamics. In a way (a rather limited way, to be sure) one may say that the "Freudians" have *caught up* with Adler on two points: a more vivid appreciation of the personality-as-a-whole; the widespread structuring of the personality in a manner which is clearly not fully conscious but

which also cannot be ascribed to the repressed, infantile unconscious.*

Splitting off from Freud so early and with so much hostility, Adler not only did not learn directly from Freud's later revisions of theory, but became over-insistent upon his denial of Freudian views—with consequent blanket rejection of the unconscious as well as the libido theory. Emphasizing the goal-directedness and unity of the personality, he was not able to formulate useful *theoretical* subsystems as an aid to understanding. He worked independently and unsystematically (beyond his reductionist generalization) with ideas the value of which has been widely recognized in recent years.

It seems a pity that ideas of such importance should not have penetrated psychoanalytic thinking earlier and more directly, that Adler's most significant contributions should be generally ignored, that he should be identified scientifically almost exclusively with

* Parenthetically I should like to remark on Adler's comments on the dream, revery, legend, etc. So far as I know, the Freudians still think of these phenomena mostly as revealing unconscious trends but not as in themselves contributing to personality function. Adler's idea that the dream is an active solution of life problems and actually influences the course of life adjustment seems to me a good one. He states that the direction of influence for good or ill depends upon what we may here call the economic aspect of the personality, borrowing Freud's word for the adjustment of forces *quantitatively* preponderant at one time or another. Thus, the healthy person may in dream and fantasy consolidate the inner direction which will enable him to move more vigorously toward a desirable goal; when the balance of the personality economics is on the side of illness, these uncontrolled aspects of the personality may work toward consolidation of the neurotic solution.

It does not require much imagination to apply this idea beyond the Adlerian view of dynamics. Sullivan does so. So does Jung. And although it is peripheral to Adler's theoretical principles, it is a further illustration of his clinical acumen, and the still untapped values of his concrete observations of how the personality-as-a-whole functions.

the least valuable part of his approach —the overinsistence on the drive to superiority. It is possible, however, that his great *popular* vogue played an important role in educating all of us to a more dynamic view of human psychology, to the concept (though not the terminology) of unconscious motivation, to the notion of the coherence of basic character trends beneath the bewildering array of traits, to a greater appreciation of how "heredity and environment" function within the individual. Adler's books seem dated because he valiantly fights battles which are already won, with the overstatements appropriate to battle. One forgets too easily that the victory is recent and that Adler contributed as much as any single person to its achievement.

HORNEY

THE DYNAMICS OF HORNEY resemble those of Adler in that every psychic event is interpreted rather directly in terms of the movement of the personality as a whole. We observed earlier that for Horney the basic need is for security in a potentially hostile world as against the Adlerian drive to superiority. We noted, too, the emphasis of both authors on the "natural" expansiveness of the human organism when not specifically hampered by early difficulties with the environment. They are discussed together mainly because of the explicit rejection of the dynamics of the libido theory. The bulk of this section will concern the points at which Horney is at variance with Adler, but it is worth while to review the significance of their central agreement.

The difference goes deeper than the substitution of a need for superiority or safety for the Freudian emphasis on "sexuality." The essential point is that man is considered as a social being from the very beginning rather than as a biological specimen which learns sociability. Horney writes, "The formulation I have sketched . . . puts the environment and its perplexities into the center. Among the environmental factors, however, that which is most relevant to character formation is the kind of human relationships in which a child grows up."[12] The irresistible quality of neurotic needs, seen by Freud as proof of their instinctual nature, is, according to Horney, "due to the fact that they are the only means for the individual to have some feeling of safety."[13] When the individual is not unduly threatened, his needs have the diffuse—or, better, the *flexible*—quality discussed earlier. They include, to be sure, adequate satisfaction of his biological requirements, but in natural relationship to his role and to his integrity as a person in an essentially social environment.

The term *neurotic trend* is introduced by Horney as "new" in order to designate compelling needs rooted in the search for safety.[14] Occasionally, as in the situational neurosis, a contemporary problem may be so severe as to provoke quite serious difficulties of the kind ordinarily called neurotic. The patient quickly recovers when the contemporary difficulties are resolved or somehow handled. *Neurotic trends,* deriving from basic attitudes usually initiated in childhood, characterize (1) the stubborn, deep neurosis in the pathological field, and (2) the odd expedients adopted by normal individuals and societies in response to the pressures imposed by the imperfections of any human society.

The major divergence in dynamics from the libido theory is that the *neurotic trend* aims primarily and always at the solution of a problem of immediate importance to the person, to what Freud would call the ego. The person is not, for Horney, concerned with handling the repressed fantasy of the Oedipus complex or other infantile difficulties as such. Infantile sexual experience may give a special twist to the developing personality. A boy severely threatened with punishment or disapproval for some sexual activity may, indeed, bear the mark all his life. But the initial fear was not, for Horney, the instinctual fear of damage to his organ but the social fear of retribution or ostracism. If his life story shows a neurotic Don Juanism, it is because he currently needs to overcome a damaged sense of worth, given a specific direction by the early episode. Sexual experiences are often significant in themselves. Horney does not deny the biological importance of the sex drive, or its social importance. Her point is that the neurotic malignancy of sexual difficulties is due to the value placed upon them socially, *not* to their extreme biological urgency.

We have noted the difference between the Adlerian (implicit) concept of the unconscious and the Freudian. According to Adler the person frequently does not understand the significance of the methods he employs in pursuing his goal—indeed, often *appears* to be aiming in the opposite direction. Nevertheless, his behavior, no matter how disguised, is always to be interpreted according to the structure of the life style, not as the repressed unconscious. Horney's position on this point is similar. In a rather polemic book, *New Ways in Psychoanalysis,* she vigorously denies the "timelessness" of the unconscious in the Freudian sense of the preservation through repression of infantile wishes and fears. What is preserved is a certain character trend, and this results from the sum total of childhood experiences. Specific early memories may be usefully recovered during analysis, but their function is to clarify for the patient the origin and meaning of his current reaction patterns. Their purpose is definitely not release from the repression of specific infantile material of continuing dynamic importance as such.

Wishes and fears of an unconscious nature are, of course, created in childhood. They are constantly *reworked* by the personality in its efforts to cope with later events. The pattern of experience usually shows a great deal of continuity, especially in neurotic individuals, because the inner problems remain the same. The child who felt unwanted by his parents carries with him the general expectation of being unwanted. He tries in characteristic ways to handle the inevitable discomfort of such feelings—for example, by being overcompliant or, conversely, by excessive independence or indifference to other people. Bringing to light memories of early rejection will not automatically change his current attitudes. Before he can afford to risk warm relations with people, it is necessary for him to understand how his present philosophy of goodness, detachment, or whatever covers his present fear of rejection.*

The renunciation of the dynamics of the unconscious as the repression of infantile libido entails for Horney the renunciation of the concepts of fixation and regression, and of the repetition compulsion as defined by the Freudian instinct theory. The neurotic child is less free to experiment with new modes of handling situations, because they are always interpreted as severely threatening in the old pattern. Only in this sense is he "fixated" at an early level of development. The adult's excessive compliance toward his boss is due to his *contemporary* fear of self-assertion, not to the infantile fear of going beyond oral pleasure, or to the residuum of the Oedipus complex. Regression means only the natural tendency to have recourse to less expedient techniques in panic states, which may have some resemblance to infantile solutions but are never a literal reinstatement of earlier reactions. People repeat their mistakes irrationally and compulsively because the inner psychic condition which caused them in the first place remains unchanged.

Thus far Horney's position is reminiscent of Adler's. On several closely related points, however, there is a real difference, perhaps we may say an advance. Horney retains, with modification, the Freudian concepts of anxiety, repression, and conflict, and she strongly emphasizes the role of unconscious processes as such, eliminating only their relationship to the infantile libido.†

---

* Freudians call this process of handling present attitudes "working through." Cf. Chapters 7 and 12.

† Some Freudians consider elimination of this relationship so radical that they say that Horney dispenses with the unconscious altogether.

ANXIETY

For Horney, as for Freud, *anxiety is the motive force behind repression.* She characterizes anxiety as the most painful experience a person can have, hence to be avoided at all costs. It is like fear except that its cause is "hidden and subjective." The neurotic is like a person who spends his entire life in a trench under constant shellfire—except that the bombardment is "subjective." Trenches can be made fairly comfortable. The Maginot Line was quite luxurious, allowing freedom of movement and even freedom from fear within its confines. Just so, many neurotics function well and cheerfully within their defense systems. At best, however, their activities are rigidly restricted. They are extremely vulnerable to attack from unguarded quarters. Above all, neither they nor their associates can understand the situation because the danger is unrealistic and unconscious.

Let us examine the case of a schoolteacher cited by Horney[15] who developed a severe depression following a mild criticism from her principal. The realistic cause of her disturbance was out of all proportion to her reaction. Most teachers react to mild criticism with mild resentment, mild hurt, mild guilt, and a realistic consideration of the merits of the situation—in varying proportions. Horney comments: "In a person *whose equilibrium [safety] depends mainly on the illusion of being infallible* and being recognized as such, a slight criticism by a superior may bring about neurotic disturbances" [my italics].[16] With this statement Adler would fully agree. He, too, appreciated the cardinal importance of the meaning of the episode to the life style of the person in contrast to its common-sense reality value. This teacher's view of her own superiority or her own safety is deeply threatened. Her "infallibility" is her Maginot Line. She is, according to Horney's view of her, even more fearful and more resentful than most people. Why, then, does she not become angry or panicky? Why the *depression?*

Adler would see in the depression another device for dominating others through helplessness or for punishing other people who have not lived up to the patient's fantastic demands for support and admiration. Horney sees here the work of anxiety itself, the most painful emotion of all. Probably the teacher is in part directly afraid of losing her job and—more important—her exaggerated image of her own perfections. But what she fears most is the fancied consequences of *her own anger* against the principal. For some people any stirring of resentment awakens terrific anxiety because of the neurotic expectation of retribution. (See pp. 446f. for further dynamic complications.)

The anxiety aroused by the faintest emergence into consciousness of hostile feelings is so intense that the personality will go to any lengths to avoid it. If the woman does nothing at all (a major symptom of depression is retardation in all activities), if she condemns her own self mercilessly (the main danger in depression is suicide in an excess of aggression directed toward the self), then she can feel consciously entirely innocent of those hostile intents which, for her, are sure to bring swift and terrible retaliation. However painful the depression, it is less painful than the mortal anxiety experienced when resentment comes into consciousness.

I have elaborated this discussion somewhat beyond the meager case material offered by Horney about this woman. The case is chosen because Horney herself uses it in contrast to the probable Freudian interpretation along lines of longing-and-guilt feelings attached to the principal as image of the father, and because Adler's discussion of depression[17] also facilitates direct comparison. For Adler, the dynamic event is always construed as the expedient of the person to maintain his life style against *exogenous* (external) factors. He simply fears an attack upon what to him is most important—his feelings of superiority—and organizes his behavior for indirect defense or offense.

INTRAPSYCHIC CONFLICT

For Horney, the dynamic event relates more to safety than to superiority, but the main difference is that the *feeling of anxiety* is the direct cause of the neurotic expedient. Its motive force is typically *intrapsychic,* its connection with external fears relatively remote.

In this analysis Horney is in some respects closer to Adler's view than to Freud's careful inquiry into the meaning of anxiety. Yet the reader recalls how Freud traced anxiety back to a danger signal for a real fear which was not consciously acknowledged. (For him it reflected the terrors of infancy, no longer real except in the timeless unconscious.) Horney comes closer to Freudian doctrine in recognizing anxiety—a hidden and subjective fear—as the intermediary between the actual life situation and the institution of all neurotic devices. Anxiety is so powerful because it represents, in sundry disguises, a threat which is to the person entirely real, however absurd it may seem to others or to the conscious mind of the person himself.

From this point it is an easy step to repression as a dynamic factor beyond Adler's general observation that "man knows more than he understands." Conscious recognition of her resentment toward the principal would immediately arouse intense anxiety in the teacher. Therefore she *actively* does not become conscious of it, but resorts to depression instead. Repression is a positive force for Horney as for Freud.

Also, the teacher inevitably will strenuously *resist* the efforts of the therapist to explain her motivations. Adler made the sound general observation that a patient must be reassured that he is not the lowest of the low before he can take a step out of his neurotic defenses and genuinely examine the defects in his life style. Patients, whatever their protestations, do not want to be told the truth about the really crucial points in their defense systems. Indeed, they are honestly unable to *feel* the emotions which the analyst deduces must be present, except in very special circumstances in which the emotions can be made acceptable to the self-image. According to Horney (and to Freud), the *inner feelings* themselves cause such anxiety that they are eliminated from consciousness, to find expression as best they can in symptoms and character traits.

Let us look at another example. Miss B tells the following story of her first months in a new school at the age of twelve. The old girls presented tightly organized social groupings, snippy toward the few newcomers. A fellow newcomer proposed being "best friends," an offer gratefully accepted by Miss B as a shy little girl. In a short time, however, her family became disturbed by the relationship, urging the girl to stand up for herself against her friend Phil, who seemed extremely domineering and physically rough. Miss B tells how she adored Phil, gladly carried her books, did her homework, and defended her quite sadistic teasing roughhouse as good clean fun, even though it often resulted in black and blue marks.

The dénouement came after about two months, when Phil teased a still smaller child to the point of tears. Our shy, adoring twelve-year-old pleaded with her, shouted at her, and finally attacked her physically with such fury that Phil acquired a fine black eye. The girls had to be separated forcibly by the scandalized by-standers.

"Of course I got a good scolding for behavior unbecoming a lady," Miss B recalls. "My family was relieved that the spell of Phil was broken. I was pretty much of a goody-goody then, but *I* was not ashamed. I felt I had gallantly protected the weak. I didn't care if Phil did those things to *me*—I was her friend, I could take it—but I wouldn't stand for bullying a smaller child." (On inquiry it developed that Phil was fifteen and nearly a head taller than Miss B at the age of twelve.)

In her late twenties this woman is still gentle and tolerant, not to say ingratiating, in her general demeanor. She still defends her superiors and herself when taxed with not standing up for her rights, rationalizing their neglect of her job achievements, disdaining personal rewards, convinced that she is herself not ambitious. She is still capable of bursts of righteous indignation and vigorous action in a good cause, mainly when other people are unfairly treated.

Horney would see in the attachment to Phil the positive effort of the child to find security in a threatening situation by having not only a "best friend," but one stronger and more confident than herself. Miss B's *pride*, her basic self-esteem, demanded exaggeration of Phil's virtues to justify her own subservience. Furthermore, hostile feelings toward Phil were taboo no matter what the provocation because they might bring down wrath or abandonment upon her. The more the child built up the fantasy of an all-powerful protector, the more helpless she became herself, and the less able she was to acknowledge her resentment of the teasing of which she was the hapless victim.

That she was "actually" fully aware of the nature of Phil's behavior and harbored very strong hostility toward her is made abundantly clear by the explosion into fisticuffs—unprecedented for Miss B and distinctly rare for any gently reared girl of twelve. Yet even on this dramatic occasion, resentment *on her own behalf* was explicitly denied. She could accept her own feelings of helpless distress only in the person of the third child, and she could recognize her own hostility only in the guise of chivalry.

It is important to stress Miss B's report that she honestly had not *felt* either subservient or resentful. Her statement gains credence from the fact that she disclaims such emotions in similar situations today. The genuine absence of the condemned feelings is the work of true repression, not to be confused with the conscious or semiconscious bottling up of rage. It serves the purpose, of course, of allowing her to carry people's books for them "gladly," to feel secure instead of anxious in difficult situations.

Analysis of the complex interplay of emotions, conscious and unconscious, within the personality is characteristic of Horney. The pleasure or distress of the feelings themselves is considered a motive force. This position is again in some contrast to Adler's more intellectualistic version of the maneuvers of the person as he seeks expedients for manipulating his environment in the interest of realizing his "external" goal.

CONFLICT *vs.* "INSTINCT"

Horney's view of *intrapsychic conflict* as the mainspring of neurotic trends expresses the cardinal point of difference between herself and Adler. Adler, it will be remembered, because of his extreme insistence on the wholeness of personality, objected to anything that smacked of disunity of function.

Horney protests against the *Freudian* theory of conflict on much the same grounds as Adler. She finds the structure of the id, ego, and superego too rigid and limited a formulation to cope with the complex dynamics of conflict. She criticizes Freud's concept of the ego as confused, and further objects to his considering "weak" an aspect of the personality which for her is the strongest of all—namely, the sense of self in direct relation to other people.

For her, the fundamental error of the Freudian formulation is the derivation of conflict from the pressure of instinctual needs against the inhibitions imposed by society. Hence the inevitable pessimism of the doctrine. Man is, for Freud, born to conflict and can at best only mitigate and sublimate its effects.* Horney believes that man is born a potentially harmonious organism, capable of expanding his own capacities normally, in happy relationship with his surroundings. Conflict appears only as a consequence of social mishandling which institutes exaggerated impulses and fears in contradictory directions. "Normally" the child is confident of help from his parents, because he has experienced it regularly. The neurotic child believes he must fight for everything he wants in a hostile world, because he has experienced deprivation. Yet open aggression in a creature as helpless as the human infant brings swift and overwhelming counteraggression. Thus aggression and the fear of being aggressive *both* develop to an exaggerated degree. "The neurotic person engulfed in a conflict is not free to choose [as is the normal person confronted with two alternatives]. He is driven by equally compelling forces in opposite directions, neither of which he wants to follow. . . . He is stranded, with no way out"[18]—except the way of neurotic trends. Conflict thus becomes for Horney the core of every neurosis. A way out can be found only by working at *both* neurotic trends—or, rather, at *all* of them, since various types of solution have usually gained solidity with advancing years.

Thus polarity between hostility and helplessness appears constantly in the Horney case analysis as basic to the many special safety devices she describes. The overly sweet person invariably turns out to have extreme unconscious hostilities; the overbearing person to be essentially frightened. Horney cites Jung's observation of the contradictory tendencies in human nature (see pp. 562*f.*) but rejects his view that they are necessary complementary aspects of the whole person. Instead, she conceives of both trends as provoked by the effort of the neurotic individual to cope with a threatening environment directly, and with reciprocal dynamic relations between the two trends. Resolution of the conflict cannot come about through therapeutic encouragement of the "hidden" tendency, as in Jung's therapy, but only through analysis of the underlying reasons which make both of them compelling.

* This is *Horney's* summary of the main import of Freudian doctrine.

THE VICIOUS CIRCLE

The dynamic relationship between these familiar opposites is typically a *vicious circle*. The moment anxiety develops in the child and he adopts a fairly consistent neurotic technique for finding safety, the very expedient he chooses leads to an intensification of the neurosis because it tends to exacerbate precisely the condition it is intended to allay. Let us suppose, for example, that the neurotic solution of an excessive feeling of helplessness has taken the form predominantly of an excessive need for affectionate support. The consequence is disappointing in two ways, both leading to increase in the problem and hence to more frantic application of the neurotic formula.

The first consequence is realistic. The person whose neurotic need for affection is too great is actually difficult to live with. He alienates people by the behavior resulting from his need. If he is openly demanding of attention and care, it is easy enough to understand the impatience of associates nakedly exploited to this end. More subtly, however, he may wish for affection without venturing to ask for it, or may try to buy it by constant self-sacrifice and elaborate undemandingness. The timid yearner who scuttles away from every social contact in desperate fear of a possible rebuff naturally does not make many friends. Anyone who has lived with a neurotic martyr even as a house guest knows the actual *burden* of a person who cannot say, "Please pass the butter," who silently and resentfully dries himself with his underwear when the rushed hostess forgot to lay out towels. The behavior of these neurotics is such that they are often *factually* ignored or exploited beyond the average, or arouse increasingly genuine hostility in their more tender-skinned associates. I quote from an article in the *Reader's Digest*: "Celia's ubiquitous selflessness brought us all to the verge of a nervous breakdown"—and very open bitterness.[19]

Thus the behavior motivated by the neurotic need for affection defeats its own end and institutes further need on a basis which becomes increasingly realistic as other people are factually alienated.

Horney, however, lays major stress on the *internal* consequence. She writes:

The vicious circle formed by the various implications of the neurotic need for affection may be roughly schematized as follows: anxiety; excessive need for affection, including demands for exclusive and unconditional love; a feeling of rebuff if these demands are not fulfilled; reaction to the rebuff with intense hostility; need to repress the hostility because of fear of losing the affection; the tension of a diffuse rage; increased anxiety; increased need for reassurance. . . . Thus the very means which serve to reassure against anxiety create in turn new hostility and new anxiety.[20]

The moment the neurotic demand goes beyond realistic possibility of fulfillment, it inevitably meets disappointment, which necessarily creates hostility or fear. These reactions just as inevitably renew in intensified form the original anxiety, which again necessitates even more stringent application of the original defense. The patient tends to blame other people or himself for a condition which becomes increasingly desperate. The truth is, according to Horney, that he is caught in a process which is self-perpetuating and tends to become progressively worse if left to its own momentum.

PERSONALITY TYPES

Faced with the problem of an essentially insecure and hostile attitude toward the world, the individual has three general modes of operation open to him, according to Horney. He can move *toward* people, *against* people, or *away* from them. He can try to get people on his side as friendly protectors, try to dominate and fight them, or try to simply ignore them. These general movements never appear in pure form, of course. Exaggerated movement toward always involves hidden exaggeration of hostility (movement against); conversely, movement against always involves hidden longings for love and protection—as in popular novels in which the ruthless captain of business is putty in the hands of a small child who has naively penetrated his bluster by a spontaneous show of affection—or he may suddenly weep like a child himself in the arms of a previously despised wife after a catastrophic break in his far-flung enterprises.

Movement away, detachment, also shows signs of hidden longings for intimate relations, either affectionate or hostile.

Popular stories, especially those in which the emphasis is on plot, as in the whodunits, frequently present stark examples of the trends and the ambivalences noted by Horney as fundamental. The reader accepts these characterizations as entirely plausible, although he knows that his neighbors are more complicated, and he expects more than a black-and-white ambivalence in his serious reading. He also expects more consistency, often to the point of missing the psychological honesty offered in the crude fictional portraits. In a story we recognize readily the heart of gold beneath the crusty exterior, but we are usually merely annoyed by our crusty neighbors, even though an occasional "unmotivated" act of kindness ought to suggest to us an under-lying softness.

Here is an example. Old Tom had a shack down the road near our country place. He lived by himself, with forty cats. We met him once be-cause we wanted a kitten, which he reluctantly relinquished when we fer-vently promised it a good home. Shortly afterwards, all his cats died in an epidemic. Thereafter for a couple of years we took a longer route to town because Old Tom stood at the roadside glowering at us with rake and broom, ready to repair the damage of our passing. He had adopted the *road* as his love-object! It was a narrow dirt road with only local traffic, and actually most of the neighbors left it to Tom if they possibly could. We all drove care-fully over the 50-foot space he cherished. The third spring following his attachment to the road, Tom took a shot at the road crew going through with a tractor. So Tom is now in the State Hospital. He still has nothing to do with any *people,* patients or doctors. But he has adopted a neglected corner of the grounds which his keepers had the wit to "give" to him. He rakes it carefully, and grows a few flowers. He is reported to be quite happy.

Here again the point is that this person, detached to the point of in-sanity, still expresses his need for affectionate attachment in his devotion to the cats, the road, and now his little patch of garden. The more dangerous he finds human relationships, the more peculiar and violent become the re-pressed longings for contact.

These three general directions of the neurotic personality (toward, against, and away) lead to a rough typology: the compliant (or dependent), the aggressive, and the detached personality. Miss B (cited on pp. 443ff.) could be classed as *compliant,* though not to an extreme degree. Her security lay with people rather than with things or ideas. She seemed capable of intense devotion, loyalty, self-sacrifice, and tolerance, yet we observed how her adora-tion for Phil masked her own helplessness, and how her outbursts of moral indignation expressed in highly rationalized form the hostility which invari-ably accompanies neurotic compliance. Affection and approval are the breath of life to these people—many of whom do not even make the show of inde-pendence Miss B developed in her later life. Hence they are often pleasant, well-behaved, easy to get along with—so long as their needs are supplied. By the same token, any criticism is experienced as devastating.

As Adler pointed out, they tend to dominate through weakness. Their suffering exacts its toll from their loved ones, who must always maintain an uncomfortable position on a pedestal and exhibit reciprocal devotion in no mean degree. Horney is at pains to show that the very "love" of this kind of personality is not the genuine love which enjoys the fulfillment of the partner, but rather demands absorption. Fromm, borrowing Freudian phraseology, uses the term "swallowing" for this type, although he agrees with Horney in emphasizing the totality of experience rather than "orality" as its true origin (see p. 469).

The *aggressive* type tends to demand power and prestige and personal infallibility as its major mode of coping with a hostile world. There is exaggerated independence, ruthlessness, cynical "realism" expressed in a dog-eat-dog philosophy of life. People are considered as exploitable possessions. If sexual prowess has become important to him, the man proves his success by conquering women. Often he wants money or social prestige in his choice of wife and is indifferent—consciously—to "love" and to her personal merits in so far as they fail to contribute to his own status. Ruthless in business himself, he distrusts his business associates. The compliant type typically does not bother to read contracts carefully on the psychologically important assumption that everyone is honorable and nice. The aggressive type typically assumes that he will be imposed upon unless he watches out for his interests. "Outsmarting others" is the principal he uses for his own conduct and in his interpretation of the behavior of others.

The *aggressive* type, like the compliant, may often appear loving, loyal, and honest—replete with cardinal virtues. Yet his family and other associates are likely to suffer from the neurotic defensiveness of his life pattern. Mr. C may serve as example. He was a self-made man from the wrong side of the tracks who had married somewhat above his station. His wife not only helped him socially but worked in his business during their early years together. Her secretarial training and a cultivated flair for art and advertising were definitely useful in his trade in consumer goods. Having made his pile, however, he was quite unwilling to have his wife work. At the time I saw the family, the business was threatened by changed world conditions and income was lowered. The wife wanted to help and felt, probably correctly, that she could. Any gesture she made in this direction, however, met with belligerent rejection.

The children were resentful and baffled. When they wanted a car to keep up with their friends, it was refused on the grounds that (1) they would doubtless kill themselves by drunken driving (neither child "drank") and (2) their father had never had such luxuries. In fact, Mr. C suddenly decided to cut off their allowance and make them work in a factory all summer to "harden" them. On the other hand, he was deeply hurt and scornfully reproachful when his son was eliminated in the tennis semifinals at the country club because he had not had much time to practice. The mother was concealing from Mr. C the fact that she brought the daughter to me because the girl at sixteen was generally unhappy and was acutely afraid of the parties she was supposed to attend. Mother and daughter agreed that father was so rude to the boys who called on her that she feared to have them visit her; at the same time he would not allow her to go out with a boy he had not met, and he ridiculed her unmercifully if she failed to have "dates."

The lot of the psychologist advising in such a situation is not easy. The mother looked like a fairly "aggressive" type on her own account. Both children showed psychological problems which seemed natural enough in the circumstances, but which would doubtless provoke further neurotic reactions in the father. Horney would be fully alert to these family ramifications, and also to the social and economic problems of wider scope which affected Mr. C's business affairs. Horney would be especially interested in the *timing* of a business recession that threw the father back into his major neuroticisms at the moment when the daughter was struggling with the social-sexual problems of adolescence. The C family can thus be used in passing illustration of the deference Horney pays to intrafamily and social factors.

Let us return to Mr. C as an "aggressive" type. Note that he marries above his station and uses his wife's capacities in his youth but cannot tolerate the threat to his ego or his social position if she goes back to work after he has become successful. Note that his children are required to enhance his prestige by being tennis champions and debutante belles, while at the same time he resents their "easy" success, and irrationally denies them the perquisites of money and family status on which this kind of success ordinarily rests. In fact, he demands from them "work" of a nature which makes no sense to the children, which is even positively detrimental to their social and vocational prospects.

In this last demand, and in the probably quite genuine anxiety lest the son kill himself with a car, one sees the "love" of Mr. C for his children. In a life premised on self-interest, these items are "loving" in the sense that they are not directly related to his own external goals. Horney would remark that the demand for "work," irrespective of what the child wants to work at, represents seeing the child as himself. Mr. C would not require of the child of a friend that he take a disagreeable job at laborer's wages. His own son, because his son is "himself," must start at the bottom—and do better. At the same time, Mr. C does not really want his son to succeed, certainly not beyond his own success, and he is envious of the advantages he has himself pridefully created for the boy. The resentments he felt as an underprivileged lad are visited upon his son. In the terms of Mr. C's neurosis, the son is damned from the start. He must succeed to please his father, and he must not succeed to please his father. Mr. C is caught between envy and direct rivalry with the boy, between his need to have his son reflect credit upon him and the "unselfish" desire to live out through his son the areas of success in which he was himself thwarted. He is overanxious partly because he looks to his son for self-fulfillment, partly because of repressed hostility—and partly because of his direct need for the affectionate intimacy of family ties.

In talking with the wife, I asked whether she had considered leaving her husband. The question was put at the height of her recriminations against him and was actually designed to test her feelings in the other direction. She immediately produced evidence of his need for her. One could readily believe her account of an underlying "softness" and dependency in the man. She recounted how he paced the floor sleeplessly when one of the children was overdue at night, and she correctly diagnosed his fury when they arrived as an expression of "love." The wife related with some wryness that he would not let her work officially in the office but that he also could not sleep until he had obtained her judgment on the affairs of the day. One sees here the obverse of his "aggressive" character development. The overt personality pattern is defensive. Far from solving his basic insecurities, it actually increases his *sub rosa* dependency.

Horney's position concerning the family is, I think, that one never deals with a Mr. C in a vacuum, or with a Mr. C reliving his relations with his mother unchanged in his wife. Mr. C is immediately threatened and annoyed by the *actual* neurotic difficulties of his family. But a "neurotic" person almost inevitably marries a "neurotic" wife, and even more inevitably rears "neurotic" children. The problem faced by the daughter in this family was intimated above. On testing and interviewing, Mrs. C and the children showed problems "neurotic" by the Horney definition, but not truly pathological. Presumably Mr. C also was not "neurotic" to a truly pathological degree.

The aggressive type is common enough in a competitive society and is fostered by it. One can hardly hope to haul Mr. C in for treatment because he is an overanxious and blustery father and wishes to keep his wife out of business. Discussion of the C family as a whole illustrates how the aggressive type actually functions in the ordinary family and business relations of our culture.

The *detached* type has already been flagrantly illustrated by Old Tom. A number of accountants, research scientists, even artists are of this type. Indeed, one may find the type in any walk of life, often functioning very usefully. Our society offers rewards to the person who cares deeply for his job, and it can often forgive a dryness in human relationships provided the job is well done. The main defect, in terms of productiveness, is that a compulsive perfectionism may be substituted for flexible adaptation to realistic demands. The accountant may work so long on reporting a single case accurately that he is forced to neglect others which may be even more pressing. He may require even of his employer a meticulous adherence to a prescribed system which becomes intolerable to a more adventurous soul.

Creativeness is rare in this type and, if it appears at all, tends to be highly personalized. The detached individual may invent something nobody wants and may fail to see new possibilities along lines of practical usefulness to his associates. Whatever his abilities, he makes a poor executive, both because he does not grasp quickly the contours of the over-all practical situation (in research, however, he may see over-all contours that have been masked by more immediate concern with a particular common-sense problem) and because he does not have adequate feeling for the resources of his subordinates, or for their attitudes toward innovations.

In more intimate relationships with people he is often difficult, partly because of his aloofness and apparent indifference, partly because his underlying need for warmth is likely to lead him into situations from which he cannot extricate himself without painful repercussions.

Mr. D married an unusually warm sort of woman with compliant trends. Such matches are not uncommon because the woman's warmth can, at a propitious moment, break through the front of detachment to the unconscious longings for closeness, and her compliance allows the man a considerable measure of independence.

Like all such women, Mrs. D suffered somewhat from her husband's lack of demonstrativeness, and perhaps for this reason was especially eager to have a child. After some reluctance, based ostensibly on sound financial reasons, Mr. D consented. It is noteworthy that at this point he developed curious attacks of asthma. Just as he had made up his mind to consult a doctor, his wife had a miscarriage, and in the excitement over her hospitalization his own symptoms subsided. A year later a second pregnancy occurred, this time uneventfully for both partners till close to term. Then the asthmatic attacks recurred with such violence that Mr. D was forced to consult a physician, who—finding nothing organically amiss—referred him to a psychiatrist.

It seemed clear in therapy that Mr. D deeply feared the emotional entanglements of fatherhood. He was literally suffocated by the prospect of family involvements threatening both his detachment and the one emotional relationship he had been able to establish. From his treatment of her, Mrs. D could hardly have suspected how deeply her husband needed her exclusive devotion, yet this seemed to be the case. The man who so casually took marriage and the prospect of fatherhood in his stride with rational coldness, was forced unconsciously to psychosomatic expression of his terror when his Maginot Line was attacked from quarters in which his defenses were inadequate.

MECHANISMS OF THE UNCONSCIOUS

Horney, like Freud, makes use of the unconscious mechanisms described in Chapter 2. The difference is mainly that she interprets the reasons for disguise along the lines just described. In *Our Inner Conflicts,* she lays especial stress on the mechanisms of *rationalization* and *externalization.* Every patient, every human being, rationalizes. Horney emphasizes the social benefits of the process and shows how compliance with the canons of reasonableness set by our society operates to ensure the "safety" of the several personality types. Reasonableness *as such* is the stock-in-trade of the detached type, well beyond the incidental efforts of other types to rationalize whatever impulses they cannot consciously tolerate.* Mr. D was always eminently reasonable, in his initial reluctance to have a child, in his later reactions to his wife's pregnancies. Miss B, it will be remembered, could express her buried hostilities openly—in behalf of a good cause. All along the line rationalization permits partial expression of underlying conflicts (as Freud indicated) and is also construed by the person in our society as a positive good. Mr. D prides himself on his reasonableness. Miss B's *righteous* indignation has behind it the full force of her "reasonable" efforts at adjustment.

Externalization is, for Horney, a broader term for the familiar mechanism of projection. Again the difference lies mainly in the fact that the whole personality may participate in an effort to project *all* motive forces outside the personality, not only those which seem blameworthy or threatening.†

---

* This pattern was mentioned briefly as "overintellectualizing" in the discussion of "Freudian" dynamics (pp. 285 ff.). It is related to the obsessive-compulsive syndrome, although not identical. Horney slices the orange in a different way.

† Horney curiously neglects the phenomenon of "identification," so heavily emphasized by Freud. The word does not even appear in the index to *Our Inner Conflicts.* Apparently this mechanism, along with projection, is subsumed under the rubric of externalization, whereby one's own emotions are experienced through others. Thus when Miss B at the age of twelve defended the helpless child against Phil, Horney would see the process as one whereby self-feelings are externalized, quite naturally along the avenues easiest for the personality to grasp and approve. Feeling helpless in a similar situation, herself, the young Miss B could only *experience* the feeling as presented by the younger child. Horney elides the step whereby Miss B for the moment "is" her little friend.

In critical comment, we may observe that Horney's formulation makes especially clear the purposive dynamics behind the common mechanism of identification. It does not account con-

Good moods and personal success as well as "guilt feelings" are ascribed to outside events: to fate, to luck, to the weather.

The penalty for these mechanisms is, of course, that the person is unable to resolve constructively his own inner conflicts or to appreciate his own capacities and limitations. He does not appraise the external situation correctly but assigns malevolence or benevolence to people and events with little regard to reality. Finally, the distance between his real self and the outside world is continually widened, the person becoming increasingly dependent on external circumstances for his own feelings of satisfaction.

THE SELF

The role of the "self" is discussed very explicitly by Horney. The pain of inner conflict is made especially acute by the "longing for unity within ourselves [which] is no mystical desire but is prompted by the practical necessity of having to function in life—an impossibility when one is continually driven in opposite directions—and by what in consequence amounts to a supreme terror of being split apart."[21] Thus one of the major reasons for the repression of one side of the conflicting tendencies in the personality is the need to maintain a sense of unity.

This process is greatly advanced by the development of an *idealized image* of the self. Everyone constructs a sense of self which supplies integration and positive striving in dealing with the world of people and things. In the neurotic, this sense of self is "idealized" at the expense of true appreciation of one's potentialities, authentic goals, genuine interpersonal relationships. The idealized image becomes a dictator which demands rigid fulfillment of its canons, regardless of the cost in personal satisfaction or to other people. *The real self becomes lost in neurotic effort to preserve the unrealistic exaggerated image of the self.* It is even *hated* for its limitations, and for the vague uneasiness which arise out of its actual strangulation by the idealized image.[22]

Like Adler, Horney emphasizes that the more uncertain a person is of his basic worth, the more likely he is to build up fantastic inner requirements—so fantastic that they cannot actually be fulfilled. The student who could easily get a B with ordinary application can only accept himself as an

---

veniently for the careful aping of the adopted personality even in details irrelevant or even inimical to the prevalent trends observable in the character structure of the individual, or for the deep *feeling-with* another person as oneself. In discussing such a question Horney would undoubtedly point to the selective process in all "identification." Choice of the object for identification always reflects important trends in the individual's own personality and is never complete. Nevertheless, it seems inexpedient to dismiss a concept which usefully includes aspects of the relationship inadequately described by the broader term "externalization."

A student. Fearful of being "shown up" as something less than his ideal for himself, he finds himself unable to study at all, with appropriate excuses.

Laura made a brilliant record in her freshman year at college but unaccountably refused to continue any of the lines of study undertaken with initial enthusiasm, except by direct coercion from the authorities. In her sophomore year, she again did very well along new lines but exasperated her teachers by neglect of more advanced work in fields previously begun. Finally this highly talented girl barely got through college and remained a promising amateur afterwards in the many enterprises she undertook. In a moment of bitterness she remarked, "I do everything so well at first that people expect too much of me, but I haven't any real talents."

This comment was partly true. She did receive excessive admiration as a beginner. The main trouble, however, lay in the excessive demands she made on herself. After a few months' study she could not tolerate the idea that any other student could be superior, even with more training. Mediocrity, or even moderate superiority, was insupportable to her. Her realization that with hard work she might still achieve less than perfection made it easier for her to protect her idealized image of herself by not working rather than to run such a risk. Taxed again, by herself as well as by her mentors, with the criticism that not-working is hardly laudable, she had recourse to conscious self-derogation of her abilities. Laura's behavior is inconsistent, of course, but we have seen that the neurotic is basically inconsistent. Furthermore, the self-derogation shielded her self-image against recognition of an overweening vanity and ambition as unacceptable to her as failure.

The consequence was frustration of her creative potential and an increasing *impoverishment* of her whole personality. In time she became unable to enjoy painting, dancing, singing, writing, even productive reading, gradually closing sources of pleasure quite genuine in her freshman days. Her relations with people became poisoned with a subterranean envy of those who were more successful. She felt that college friends who had once looked up to her would be "bored" by her present incompetence. Her acquaintance became more and more limited to simple souls whose sterling virtues she suddenly began to appreciate, but here again she was tortured by the fancy, not wholly unjustified, that they considered her conceited because of her manifestly greater intelligence and educational background. She quickly terminated a brief venture into psychotherapy because she felt that the doctor cynically reduced her convictions regarding altruistic principles to mere self-seeking, thus depriving her of the only meaning in life left to her.

We may see in this last complaint the unhappy roots of her extreme idealism in her own neurotically exaggerated defenses. The idea that she might prefer the company of a vain shopgirl to that of a vain college graduate because there was less danger to her self-image provoked a violent espousal of "democracy" as the only thing that could give life meaning. That is, only the idealized self-image was left from the vivid, gifted *real self* which originally had found "meaning" in the spontaneous enjoyment of many types of activity and people.

The central neurotic problem of the idealized image is, for Horney, just this progressive alienation from the *real self*. Instituted originally as an effort to bridge the split in the personality resulting from implacably contradictory trends, the idealized image becomes still a third factor to be placated, again something outside the genuinely felt impulses of the person. Whatever the type of idealized image set up, or the mechanisms employed in enhancing it, the consequence is a growing sense of distance from life, of futility, of hopelessness. Laura's self-punishing attitudes are very common in our culture and typically cover a grandiose perfectionism in the idealized image. In her last book, Horney comes to consider tension between the real self and the idealized image of the self as the central conflict in all neurosis.

In many respects the idealized image is similar to Adler's neurotic life style, which also becomes more demanding and more distant from reality as the basic problems of life are handled without social feeling, common sense, and courage. It is also similar to the Freudian superego. As for other concepts which approach those of other schools, the difference lies in Horney's effort to show how the idealized image grows out of the struggle of the personality against its helplessness in a hostile world, and out of the compelling need to find wholeness and direction despite inner conflict.

SUMMARY

Horney's dynamics are similar to Adler's in the attempt to envisage human behavior as a constant and contemporaneous effort at adaptation. The dynamic significance of repressed infantile wishes and fears, operating in the timeless unconscious, is explicitly denied.

However, Horney makes much more use than Adler of the concept of the unconscious as a significant factor in itself. Aspects of the personality are genuinely repressed—*almost* in the Freudian sense of the term—because they awaken intolerable anxiety. Failure to understand one's own motives and the peculiar devices adopted in their pursuit does not necessarily represent the direct effort of the personality to cope with *exogenous* factors in terms of the life style. Typically such devices are mediated by anxiety, the most painful emotion of all, *endogenously* produced. They very often result in behavior which is inexpedient even for the neurotic aims of the personality. Impoverishment and hopelessness are characteristic of people whose need to escape anxiety involves extensive repression, even with the palliatives of rationalization and externalization of their unconscious feelings.

Like Freud, Horney considers *intrapsychic conflict* basic to neurosis, and she agrees with Jung that contradictory trends are invariably present. This characteristic of neurosis is not considered basic to human nature, however, but is the result of the dynamic interplay between techniques adopted by the child who comes to feel helpless in a potentially hostile world. This interplay leads to a *vicious circle*. The individual may seek to obtain safety by moving *toward* people, *against* them, or *away from* them. The corresponding personality types are *compliant* (or dependent), *aggressive,* and *detached*—so far, that is to say, as the *predominant* mode of reaction is concerned. The compliant type develops exaggerated fears of his own assertiveness and of the hostility engendered by constant submission; the aggressive type regularly harbors strong dependency needs which he is unwilling to admit because they suggest to him a weakness threatening to his main strategy for defending himself in a hostile world. The detached type is also prey to undercover longings for closeness, to unconscious dependency and hostility.

The upshot of these strong unconscious impulses in opposite directions is that the neurotic individual is unable to move at all, or can attain only a very restricted freedom of movement and enjoyment within the limited areas of the complex defenses he has gradually built up.

Another feature of the defensive effort is the compelling need to maintain a sense of unity and integration despite the essential rift in the personality. The compulsive need for wholeness is reflected in a neurotically *idealized image of the self*. Because this image is rooted in the attempt to excise all possibly discordant elements, its development entails progressively more desperate repression of increasingly vigorous impulses of the undesired character. Even when the repression is successfully maintained, the personality suffers from a sense of alienation from the self, with distressing feelings of futility, emptiness, unreality, and incapacity for enjoyment. The idealized image offers a major stumbling block to therapy, since recognition of trends in himself which the patient could readily forgive in others means for him a collapse of his own integrity as a person. In her last book, Horney presents the tension between the idealized image of the self and the real self as the *central* conflict in all neurosis.

Critical Comment

I HOPE it will not be offensive to the Horney school if I describe her as the Adler of our decades. Partly I say this because her books are written for the intelligent layman and have been read very widely. She offers concepts which we can all understand, with appropriate effort, and which immediately clarify for us a great many of our own feelings and the odd behavior of our friends. Partly the similarity goes deeper. Horney, like Adler, made a radical split with the "Freudians" in hostile mood. Accepting more of Freud's analysis of unconscious processes than did Adler, Horney has tended to emphasize lines of difference and to restate Freudian theory so radically that it is difficult to see clearly the parallels between her work and that of contemporary Freudians who approach her emphases. Far from acknowledging her significant contributions, the mood of the "Freudians" is to repudiate the Horney approach in toto. "Freudians," mostly under the label of ego psychology, are just beginning to give proper theoretical weight to concepts which Horney has been shouting from the housetops for twenty years. I have acknowledged—and, I hope, supported —a preference for the "Freudian" approach as more substantially multidimensional. This preference in terms of ultimate theory need not prevent a forthright statement of points at which Horney's current emphasis seems especially valuable.

Valuable Aspects of Horney's Position

(1) Emphasis on the current adaptation of the person-as-a-whole is very important. It should not be exclusive, and I shall suggest that Horney oversimplifies the problem, though not to the extent of Adler. Current adaptation plays a far greater role in theory and practice than most Freudians admit at the present time, even if one grants increased attention to the matter in the Freudian camp.

(2) Anxiety is a more widespread determinant of behavior than even Freud realized. It operates not only in reference to the repression of infantile wishes and their derivatives but wherever there is a significant threat to the organism's organized stance. Horney's view seems an advance on Adler's idea that the threat is essentially exogenous. The formulation of protective intrapsychic constellations, so strong that threats peculiar to them are warded off as dangerous, is closer to observational fact than the formulation that every threat must be examined for its immediate danger to self-esteem.

Although Adler continually pointed out that every individual interprets the external threat in his own way, he resisted the abstract concept of a mind at war within itself. Such dividedness is no problem in Horney's view of the holistic functioning of the person. To be sure, the ultimate goal is security (cf. Adler's "superiority"), and the patient fancies that his devices make him more secure. But the most important threat comes from the inner tendency to react out of harmony with one's conscious pattern—indeed, in the opposite direction. Our schoolteacher was more terrified by her own hostilities than by the injury to her self-esteem wrought by the criticism of the principal. Her defense (a depression) was primarily against her own hostilities, not against the unappreciative external world. Deep neurotic anxieties have intrapsychic dynamics.

(3) Conflict, a favorite Freudian concept, is more important than Adler

states, and is more pervasive as a central dynamic factor than appears in Freudian ideology. The safety devices (defense mechanisms) adopted by the personality tend by their very exaggeration to foster their opposite in a vicious circle, so that conflict is actually created and as a rule constantly intensified by the course of the neurotic process itself. Freudians have observed this phenomenon, of course (cf. Fenichel's example [p. 257] of the patient who threw a nickel into the gutter), but only as a sort of by-product to specific defensive maneuvers. I believe that Horney overgeneralizes this process at the expense of a more differentiated view of the systems underlying neurosis. Nevertheless, it is common enough to warrant attention, probably especially in the character disorders and limitations of normal function.

(4) In explaining why conflict is so painful, Horney brings into prominence two concepts which certainly deserve more emphasis than they receive in Freudian ideology: the need for security and the need for self-esteem. In my opinion these concepts cannot, in basic theory, be considered as unanalyzable, self-understood entities. That they play an enormous role in the life adjustment of most of us can hardly be doubted. Classical Freudians have tended to become so absorbed in the infantile origins of anxiety and "narcissism" that they have often neglected the clinical observation that most of us are quite bothered by *any* threat to our existence and *any* threat to our self-respect. Common sense seems to tell us that these threats (or the implicit needs behind them) are absolutely basic. Although one may profitably analyze common sense, one cannot properly ignore impulses which *seem* basic and which seem to function in a well-systematized manner. Too often classical psychoanalytic therapy bogged down in its early stages not because the analyst was wrong about the underlying libidinal conflicts but because the self-esteem of the patient was

so hurt that he could not really absorb any interpretations or he was blindly terrified by any crack in his security system. This problem will be discussed further in the next chapter. One may say, perhaps, that attention to these matters has come in by the back door in Freudian ideology, and that they are still neglected by many Freudians. Horney's vigorous insistence on their crucial importance has been of great value.

(5) Of similar importance clinically is Horney's emphasis on the feelings of *impoverishment* and *hopelessness* so often encountered in neuroses of long standing, especially in the character neuroses, in which the patient often looks so "normal" that he usually passes as such in his society—too often as a dull or unpleasant "normal" whose recurrent difficulties wear thin the patience of his friends. All schools recognize in a way that these feelings are a consequence of the neurosis (I am here using "neurosis" in the broad, Horney sense of the term), but Horney has emphasized the fact that they often come to constitute a problem in themselves which must be handled as such. They easily become a systematized defense in their own right. The person must be brought to see the bright colors of the world he has renounced before he is willing to struggle against his protective limitations. He must be made dissatisfied with his Maginot Line. His hopelessness must be made clear to him as a symptom instead of a rational judgment upon himself before he can actively resume arms in the fight for recovery, for his inner right to the many-faceted happiness available to the human organism.

It seems to me that the most classical Freudian could read Horney's books with profit, and that if he called her approach "study of the defense mechanisms of the ego" (ignoring her theoretical reductionism), he would find little that was essentially incompatible with his own point of view. In Chapter 6 on Freudian dynamics, I quoted Anna Freud to the effect that the Freudian list of defense mechanisms was incomplete and still obscurely related to etiological factors. This list derives mainly from major pathology, and I think represents a rather heterogeneous assortment of relatively limited techniques *and* broadly operative trends. It might be proper to look at Horney's classification of types as a broader grouping of defensive devices: moving toward, against, or away from the tension-creating objects, with their correlated behavior patterns of overt compliance, aggression, and detachment. I urge the reader to think through for himself the relationship between Horney's *modes of operation* and the defense mechanisms of the ego offered by the Freudians.

Sexuality; Identification

The Freudian point that Horney explicitly—indeed, polemically—renounces is the role of the sexual drive systems per se in personality development and later dynamics. I think one may value her contributions and respect many of her criticisms of the Freudian position without accepting this major renunciation. There is every reason to suppose that the biologically determined sexual systems *do* have an autonomous course of development which must profoundly affect the relationship of the young child to his environment during the early months and years of life—and therefore profoundly affect the attitudes he develops along the lines emphasized by Horney herself. In her efforts to combat a theoretical reductionism along lines of the libido theory, Horney developed, I think, a reductionism along lines of ego development which suffers from the same defects, according to the point of view expressed in Chapter 1. If I were asked to choose between a *very narrow* formulation of the libido theory and Horney for an explanation of the psy-

chodynamics we normally encounter in our friends and ourselves, I think I would choose Horney. In our general contacts we encounter mainly ego mechanisms, and these Horney has worked out in a manner which is in many respects superior to the Freudian manner, and more appropriate to most of our daily life problems.

But this is not the choice offered in a book on basic theory, and it is not the choice ultimately offered in practice. A multidimensional approach rooted in the complex interaction of dynamic subsystems (biological and social) takes longer to develop and is never so neatly satisfying as one derived from a few generally operating principles. But I believe it is the only approach that can ultimately lead to sound understanding of the endless intricacies of human behavior, that can provide the theoretical background for empirical investigation of the various facets of human existence without necessitating a totalistic change of venue. For this reason the relatively cumbersome maneuvers of Freudian ego psychology, developed in close relationship to the libido theory, seem to me preferable to the creation of a new school exclusively oriented around what Freudians call the "ego."

Furthermore, Horney does nothing to advance understanding of the development of the nonsexual systems of the organism and their specific relationship to the formation and functioning of the personality. This problem was discussed in comment on the preceding chapter, where the neglect of differentiated study of the genetic process was pointed out.

Thus, although Horney's theory offers a much more sophisticated view of intrapsychic dynamics than Adler's, it suffers from the same defect of over-generalization. The movements of the personality-as-a-whole tend to become dialectical abstracts, which are then used to explain all the multifaceted events of human living. This essentially abstract theoretical oversimplification is obscured by the brilliance of Horney's clinical acumen—especially as regards the neurotic personality of our times—and by the same kind of mental gymnastics involved in uncovering the basic trends in many combinations that we observed in Adler.

The point is illustrated by Horney's substitution of the term *externalization* for a number of Freudian mechanisms, among which identification and projection are the most prominent. I am indebted to Dr. Peter Glauber for further clarification to me of the rather puzzled footnote I had written (p. 453) pointing out Horney's omission of the concept of identification.[23] As a good clinician, Horney does not neglect identification in practice. She would, I think, agree readily enough that Miss B's outburst as a child took the form it did because the small child being teased was like herself. The concept of externalization, however, places the entire burden of the psychodynamics on the *internal* problem of Miss B's conflict, which was handled temporarily, or even characteristically, by "externalization." Dynamically, such outbursts can be put off just as well on the weather—as Horney herself remarks.

Glauber pointed out that this approach misses the dynamic to-and-fro relationship between the special aspects of the external situation to which the child is drawn and the child's inner development. The child's *love* (object attachment, object cathexis) leads him to identify with the object and to take on (introject) aspects of the object well beyond the inner drive state which led to the identification. These introjected aspects are reworked and again projected—again form the basis for new identifications. In this manner highly complex relations with the environment are formed, and highly complex images of the self, which are much more directly influenced by the actual nature of the objects the person encounters than Horney's theory of intrapsychic dynamics suggests. The biological needs of the child (the person) are, of course, also envisaged in a more complex manner by the Freudians, so that the initial impetus toward identification is seen in a more differentiated manner.

Horney's critique of Freud is as oversimplified as her own position. She discusses the instinctual drives and the important generalizations drawn from them as if this basic schema were the whole of Freudian doctrine. Her account omits the multidimensional dynamics described in Chapter 6, and therefore seriously misrepresents Freud's approach.

The Self

The idealized image of the self seems to me one of Horney's most important contributions. In comment on Chapter 8, I strongly suggested the need for study of the self image as an "institution" of enormous power, at least in our culture, which should be distinguished from the superego as defined by Freud and from the overly broad Freudian concept of the ego. In many ways Horney's study of the idealized image seems more adequate than the concepts of any of the other analysts discussed in this book, with the possible exception of Jung (see Chap. 13).

But I liked Horney's concept better in her earlier books than in *Neurosis and Human Growth,* in which it becomes the central conflict. At first it was an important but limited aspect of human adjustment. She observed it sharply in clinical operation as a dynamic system which seemed to cross-cut her view of intrapsychic dynamics oriented around the need for security as experienced "neurotically" by an endamaged "real self." The shadowy concept of the "real self" always seemed to me suspect, for reasons explained earlier (see Critical Comment, Chap. 8), but it did not interfere seriously with clinical observation of very important personality trends, which Horney presented in clinical, common-sense relationship to cultural trends. The later development, placing the tension between the idealized image and the real self at the very center of psychological theory, seems to me an error almost as serious as the reductionist trend of Adler. To my mind it obscures the value of Horney's clinical observations concerning the idealized image by overextending the concept of the self to the point at which it is used as a "general principle," as an abstraction which seems quite unwarranted no matter how well it seems to "work" in our culture.

The growing child may not find it necessary to differentiate himself sharply from his family and social group, and his neurotic problems, if any, may then be set primarily by the frustrations and conflicts typical for his group with comparatively little *self*-conscious elaboration. To be aggressive, or weak, or whatever is directly "bad." Impulses in the "bad" direction are then immediately repressed. On the other hand, if special handicaps or gifts make the child stand out as *different* in his family, if his family is *different* from most families in its social group, if the culture emphasizes the dignity of the self and the need for inner consistency—one could continue with many such "if's"—then it is much more likely that the child will build up a more particularized image of himself. In such circumstances the idealized image may easily become itself a refuge and, unfortunately, a limitation. The *conditions for* the development of an especially vivid or pathological self image could, I suggest, be the subject of focused investigation.

Variations in the structure of the self image and in its relations to other subsystems of the personality, notably to the superego, should be studied clinically. (We shall return to this problem in the Epilogue.) My impression is that Horney's clinical observation is correct mainly for the upper-middle-class intellectual urbanites who come for analysis. One might expect to find different patterns in small towns, among poor people,

in societies with a more rigid caste system, etc., etc. Although some sort of more or less organized image of the self is likely to develop in any culture and to function as a relatively independent psychological system, an ego function so closely related to the social group can hardly be expected to show the kind of universality that Horney posits.

In summary, it seems to me that Horney's dynamics offer many concepts the clinical validity and importance of which cannot be doubted. I have suggested that if the classical Freudian labeled her work as a study of ego defense mechanisms, he could learn a great deal from her books without in the least changing his basic ideology.

In her general theory, I feel, Horney shows the kind of reductionism I have tried to combat in all the schools. I see no reason to reject the constellative power of the sexual systems which are part of man's biological equipment. Furthermore, the tendency to generalize about the movement of the personality-as-a-whole obscures that specific investigation of the actual development of the idea of the self and ego attitudes via the nonsexual systems which seems to me urgently necessary (see my critical comment on Chap. 10). Blanket repudiation of the system dynamics organized around libidinal needs and neglect of the developmental processes in the nonsexual systems make it impossible to study the creative interaction between the general orders of functioning systems or the relationships among small subsystems.

The concept of the idealized image of the self was discussed in some detail partly for its actual merit and partly to show concretely how a system developed primarily out of "ego" reactions need not *replace* its Freudian counterpart, the superego. Rather, both may be seen as dynamically operating systems very likely to develop in some independence of each other, with the possibility of direct conflict with each other. The Freudian formulation of ego-superego conflict too far neglects the organized stance which the ego attains (the self image), and which may reach pathological proportions in its own right. The *substitution* of the idealized image of the self does not accomplish a discriminating limitation of the superego and leaves the relationship of the "self" to the ego still undefined (*i.e.,* within the Freudian framework). I would prefer, as suggested before, the idea of still a fourth institution of the mind, constellated around the person's role in his external world—his self image.

FROMM

IN BOOKS oriented toward the application of psychoanalysis to social and ethical problems, Fromm offers comparatively little explicit discussion of the terms we have previously considered under the heading of "Dynamics." His *use* of the concepts of the unconscious, repression, conflict, and the like seems fairly close to that of Horney. I shall not repeat the description of these concepts given above but shall instead concentrate on the differences between Fromm and Horney, and on the distinctively Frommian formulations.

The most striking difference from Horney, perhaps, is the less systematic emphasis on anxiety and conflict as themselves the core of neurosis almost regardless of their content in the individual case. Fromm seems closer to Adler than to Horney in his contention that the basic problems of humanity can be stated quite concretely and that they apply to everyone, neurotic or not. We have seen that for Fromm the problems result from the evolutionary fact of individuation. Man needs, because of his biological history and nature, to find meaning for his life and to "belong." His basic terror, then, springs from feeling alone and insignificant. His escape mechanisms always involve the escape from the fears attendant upon his emerging freedom (individuation) and are not provoked by anxiety per se as in the Horney doctrine, motivated by the threat to security. Thus the theme of Frommian dynamics is the search for relatedness and significance. The basic conflict, for Fromm, is between the self and the unbearable isolation of selfhood. Once the primary ties of infancy are broken, as they must be, the person tries in a variety of ways to recapture them. But "a basic antagonism [between the individual and the object-ties secondarily developed] remains and with it an impulse, even if it is not conscious at all, to overcome the masochistic dependence [or other escapist trends] and to become free."[24]

Subsidiary conflicts often develop also as the person finds that the mode of escape he mainly adopts provokes exactly the result he is attempting to avoid, as when the power-seeker again finds himself alone and helpless when he is abandoned by his "victim." One mode of escape quite often develops its counterpart, partly along the paths of the vicious circle described in the section on Horney, partly for other reasons to be discussed. Analysis of the functioning personality, therefore, can never rest with a single trend but always involves a number of trends in more or less direct dynamic relationship to one another.

AUTHORITARIANISM

For Fromm the most general category of escapism seems to be *authoritarianism*. Although in his treatment of this topic in *Escape from Freedom* he emphasizes sado-masochistic trends (to be explained in a moment), the most general formulation appears to be *any* escape from the isolation of one's selfhood by recourse to external powers. Such powers may be personal and direct, as exemplified in the leader, whether of a totalitarian state or of a Boy Scout troop, in the father or an all-seeing God who enforces decrees by immediate punishment or tender love. The Authority may be internalized as conscience, like the Freudian superego. It may have the anonymity of "natural law" or the still more concealed power of "the market," as discussed on pages 393*f.* and 471.

All these forms of authoritarianism are characterized by the *extrinsic* nature of the standards set. All serve the purpose, one way or another, of relief from the burden of personal responsibility. All are unsatisfactory for two reasons. The first, a social reason, is that they stultify the creative productivity of man, which resides essentially in the utilization of his own resources for reasonable, satisfying control of himself and his world. Thus, a society rooted in authoritarianism cannot develop fully and tends to rot from within. The second, a psychological reason, is that the drive *toward* free expansion of man's own powers is, however obscurely, in continuous revolt against authoritarianism, with consequent subjective feelings of dissatisfaction, anxiety, frustration, emptiness, and the like.

Obedience to the leader brought to the Nazi follower a measure of relief. He did not have to make decisions himself; he enjoyed the protection and prestige of the state, to which he so deeply "belonged." Typically the virtues and power of the Authority are exaggerated and preserved in the teeth of evidence, because they are so greatly needed. Hitler could not make a mistake. In line with this Authority, edicts for humanly revolting acts were executed far beyond individual conscience. In established religious doctrine, such items as the indiscriminate slaughter of the first-born of the Egyptians, of all male infants contemporaneous with the birth of Jesus, predestination to eternal damnation of unbaptized infants or merely some people irrespective of merit, show immediately the *power* of God the Almighty. This demonstration of power is in itself reassuring but difficult to reconcile with the emerging ethics of humanity. In an enlightened age we are appalled at the practice of taking a sick baby miles to church in freezing weather and dousing it with cold water to save its soul, too often at the expense of its body. Extreme cruelty in the name of religion is an unhappy commonplace. Governmental red tape can seem just as sadistic, with the uncomfortable addition that the unfortunate victim can curse nobody, not even God. The Authority has become anonymous.

The *humanistic* ethics presented by Fromm also requires conscience and social regulation, of course, but the distinction he emphasizes is that the authority behind them resides in man himself. External authority is always limiting and distorting. Fromm remarks that under authoritarian ethics *guilt* is generally defined as *disobedience,* no matter how productive the act involved—e.g., the sin of Adam in eating of the tree of knowledge, the crime of Prometheus in giving fire to men. A good conscience, from the authoritarian point of view, depends upon blind submission, mitigated by trust in the love of the superior. It is a withdrawal from the constructive love of self and from human responsibility for the destiny of the race. Two familiar hymns sung in almost every Protestant church come to mind:

> Content to let the world go by,
> To know no gain nor loss,
> My sinful self my only shame,
> My glory all, the Cross.

> Keep Thou my feet. I do not ask to see
> The distant scene; one step enough for me.

The dynamic consequence of any variety of reliance on external authority or extrinsic values is impoverishment of the very nature of man. Fromm states *"the principle that the power to act creates a need to use this power and that failure to use it results in dysfunction and unhappiness"* [my italics].[25]

Although Horney's approach is less humanistic in the philosophical sense of systematic consideration of the relation of man to the universe, we noted her insistence on a "real" self, "genuine" feeling, and "truly" reasonable behavior. Both authors have the deep conviction that man not only *can* be integrated and productive, to use Fromm's word, but that he *naturally* is so, and further that he somehow *knows,* however obscurely, the dictates of this real self. Fromm speaks occasionally of the "pseudo" self, in many respects reminiscent of Horney's "idealized image." Both concepts involve alienation from genuine satisfactions and loss of the sense of identity as the person becomes more and more dependent on extrinsic values for security. Rather oddly in a system constellated around the self, Fromm pays less attention than Horney to the *dynamics* of the pseudo self—its progressive inner elaboration, idealization, and consolidation until the idealized image itself becomes a sort of unit factor working against the solution of neurotic conflicts.

Somewhat more in the vein of Adler, Fromm seems to lay the main emphasis on the mechanisms of escape from basic human problems as they operate universally, and to be somewhat averse to the anatomization of the personality even along lines as broad as those proposed by Horney. The pseudo self is "essentially a reflex of other people's expectations."[26] Despite the fact that spontaneous integrated selfhood is for Fromm the only successful means of relating the individual anew to his world, he does not make much use of the tendency of the individual to create a *false integration* which then further represses spontaneity. The Freudian superego is broadened by Fromm to mean the process of internalization whereby any external authority is pleased or placated by an act apparently one's own which is in fact pseudo. Like Horney and Adler, Fromm seems to elide the step of "identification" and to move directly to the unconscious purpose served by *internalization*— namely, protection against the feeling of insignificance and aloneness.

PRODUCTIVITY

Fromm's basic premise—a philosophical one, if you like—is that of the relationship between man's emerging individualism and the matrix of nature from which he springs as a species. In more concrete psychological terms, the problem is how he relates himself to the world of people and things around him, and to his own "self." This relatedness *can* be a productive one in so far as man is able to accept his freedom as an individual with inborn capacity for reason and love. In a book largely concerned with ethics, *Man for Himself*, Fromm chooses the term *productivity* as the moral standard and aim of man. He spends many pages describing what he means, with numerous quotations from great writers of the past: Aristotle, Spinoza, Goethe, Ibsen, and others. I quote only the lines Fromm italicizes from the end of the second part of *Faust*: "Though not secure, *yet free to active toil.* . . . / He only earns his freedom and existence, / Who daily conquers them anew." It is in the active use of his powers that man fulfills and constantly creates his destiny.

Such activity obviously does not mean merely running about in a hectic manner, producing a great many things of one sort or another with no sense of their inner relatedness to one's own "self." In fact, such compulsive running about is as neurotic as laziness. Both poles of such activity usually result from some sort of oversensitivity to external standards, whether adherence or defiance, conscious or unconscious. They are both quite different from the productiveness Fromm has in mind, and, indeed, they usually result from neurotic crippling of the true human potential.

True productiveness involves the ability to see things pretty much as they are and to respect them. (The word *things* merges into *people* as in most psychoanalytic thinking. Possibly one may say that Fromm differentiates a little more sharply between the two categories than do other analysts.) But this ability, this approach to the world which Fromm calls objective, even "photographic,"[27] is combined with a subjective, "generative" approach whereby the material is enlivened and re-created through the spontaneous activity of one's own mental powers. Both approaches are necessary, but when they are used one-sidedly, the consequence is a very serious limitation in function if not actual insanity.* The productive attitude springs out of the polarity between the two.

The productive attitude also involves love. Love is an inevitable requirement of the isolated human being who longs for oneness with his world. "Love," in the common meaning of the word, too often demands this oneness at the expense of personal integrity. It becomes merely an expression of the escape from freedom, and it no more represents Fromm's concept of the deeply valid human potential than the production line represents his concept of productivity. Love as part of the productive attitude includes respect for the integrity of the other person and of one's self. It includes a sense of care and responsibility toward the other person in his own right and as a representative of humankind, also recognized in one's self. Falling in love is easy. Real love is the achievement of a lifetime as one comes to *understand* the loved one better and to share progressively in a wider, more realistic understanding of the wider problems of living and to work actively at their solution.

PERSONALITY TYPES

Failing adequate development of the productive attitude, various mechanisms may be adopted by the personality in order to cope with the distress of feeling alone and insignificant. In *Escape from Freedom,* Fromm emphasizes

---

* I should like to draw the reader's attention to the essential similarity of these approaches to Jung's extraversion-introversion dichotomy. Fromm does not build a typology on this dichotomy —but we shall see in Chapter 13 that Jung's own typology is cautious.

the two main alternatives of a *symbiotic* relationship with other people and *withdrawal.* The symbiotic relationship may take the form of masochistic dependence or sadistic domination, or more typically a combination of the two trends in the sado-masochistic character. Withdrawal may take the form of exaggerated indifference or active destructiveness toward the world which makes the person feel isolated and powerless. Instead of reporting in detail the analysis Fromm offers in this book, I shall concentrate my account on the fourfold classification of nonproductive attitudes he develops in *Man for Himself.* The later classification offers more direct parallels with the Freud-Abraham typology mentioned in Chapter 6. Furthermore Fromm accompanies it with a more penetrating discussion of the problem of "types," and with a more direct effort toward relating typical personality configurations to specific social constellations.

Through his analysis of the major *nonproductive* "orientations" (he uses the word with some specialness) in personality, Fromm sees four ways of escaping isolation and powerlessness. In so far as many individuals tend to favor one mechanism as their *predominant* mode of reaction, these rubrics may be considered a typology. It must be emphasized repeatedly, however, that "pure" types are not to be expected. The functioning personality shows a mixture of trends, in more or less dynamic relationship to one another. Fromm calls this mixture a blend. Opposed to all of these orientations is the *productive* one, described above.

No individual, says Fromm, is wholly productive, as none is wholly nonproductive. Indeed, the qualities we shall present as characteristic of the various nonproductive orientations are in essence necessary facets of human experience. They are virtues "to a fault," in the common phrase. *In the setting of a generally productive personality,* they resume their rightful place. Fromm lists a dozen adjectives for each orientation, pairing its negative aspect with the positive one which emerges more clearly "according to the degree of productiveness in the total character structure."[28] A few such pairs are presented here in illustration:

adaptable	unprincipled
idealistic	unrealistic
polite	spineless
tender	sentimental
active	exploitative
proud	conceited
self-confident	arrogant
impulsive	rash
practical	unimaginative
economical	stingy

```
reserved ......................... cold
loyal ......................... possessive
purposeful ................. opportunistic
flexible ..................... inconsistent
youthful ....................... childish
curious ........................ tactless
```

The *receptive* orientation anticipates and deeply requires support from outside—from parents, friends, authorities, God. By themselves, people with this orientation feel helpless and alone. Optimistic, friendly, loving when things go well, they easily become anxious and distraught at any rebuff or equivocation on the part of the authorities on which they depend. The strength of their masters is essential to their security, even if the masters are selfish and cruel. It does not occur to the receptive type that he could attain any success in coping with life by his own efforts; hence it is always better to placate the higher power and make do with what scraps of comfort come his way. This type is very similar to the Freud-Abraham *oral-passive* type. Indeed, Fromm mentions that the "open mouth" tends to be a prominent feature. These people often find consolation in eating and drinking, and they dream of being fed as a sign of being loved. The type is also reminiscent of Adler's pampered child and Horney's compliant character. "The receptive orientation," says Fromm, "is often to be found in societies in which the right of one group to exploit another is firmly established."[29] Feudal societies and the institution of slavery are good examples. Even in contemporary America, however, the need to conform and to please and to succeed without effort persists despite widespread admonition toward initiative and personal responsibility for getting ahead. Get-rich-quick schemes flourish; books are advertised to make us happy and strong and cultured or almost anything in a few minutes; gadgets relieve us of the labor of unscrewing the cap from a fountain pen or winding a watch.

The *exploitative* character has the motto "I take what I need." This orientation is close to the *oral-aggressive* type described by Freud and Abraham, and again Fromm points out the symbolization of the biting mouth. These people also derive their values from outside—they want what other people own and prize. The free gift, so necessary to the receptive (oral-passive) type, is meaningless to them. They assume that it is not wanted by the giver and is therefore worthless. They must always take away from others by force or guile. What they themselves produce is less valuable in their eyes than what they have somehow stolen. Men of this type do not love a woman for herself but because she is loved by another man. Even in the realm of ideas they are plagiarists. Their mood is often one of envy, hostility, and cynicism. They feel powerful and at ease with themselves only when they have brought off a good coup.

Sociologically, these people are the robber barons of feudal times, the pirates, the "adventure capitalists" nourished by the free market of the eighteenth and nineteenth centuries, lately the nakedly exploiting top Nazi clique. The true lord of the manor lived symbiotically with his serfs, under the obligation of nobility. He, too, expected total support, but he was usually psychologically cruel, if at all, out of thoughtlessness, tradition, or actual poverty, not out of positive pleasure in taking from others. The robber barons and the adventure capitalists lacked the framework of support offered by a society firmly rooted in the *right* of one group to exploit another. They were on the make, for what they could grab and steal. Fromm's point is that the inner motivations of these people is such that no reasonable appeasement of superficially rational demands can possibly succeed. We have already discussed the essential escapism and dependency behind the sadistic trends.

In a given society, the "exploiters" may gain control *under certain conditions,* and may then become the Authority so necessary to the "receptive" people (cf. the discussion of Nazism, Chap. 9).

The *hoarding* orientation is close to the *Freudian anal type.* These people measure their security by what they can save and own. Spending is a threat. Men of this type want to "possess" a woman, not love her. Their intellectual approach tends to be pedantic, orderly and sterile, highly conservative. They are withdrawn from other people and from the intrusion of new ideas. Their form of mastery is to have everything in its proper place and time. Their justice says "Mine is mine and yours is yours"—with especial emphasis on "mine."[30]

Sociologically these people flourished in the eighteenth and nineteenth centuries under a relatively stable bourgeois economy. Their ethics were mainly Calvinistic—in America, Puritan. They believed in sound business principles and thrift. Property and family were evidence of the grace of God. We have seen (Chap. 9) that in *Escape from Freedom* Fromm shows carefully how this class came into existence during the shift from the feudalistic to capitalistic economy, and how business principles were related to the shift in religion and the shift in the basis of security offered to the individual.

The *marketing* orientation is, according to Fromm, a definitely modern product. "It is only recently that the package, the label, the brand name have become important, in people as well as in commodities."[31] A consequence of large-scale capitalism has been a loss in person-to-person valuation of the individual. Even the three nonproductive orientations thus far described represent a way of relating oneself to people in terms of one's own self. With the market orientation, *no* personal qualities have value in themselves. They have become commodities for exchange. The "personality" of the salesman, the executive, the worker is part of his stock in trade.

It is not enough to have skill, knowledge, ingenuity, integrity. In almost every walk of life it has become necessary to sell *oneself* as well—not crudely, of course, but by being the kind of person who is in demand for a particular kind of job in a particular organization. There are "fashions" in personality as in handbags, transmitted by various media—among which Fromm cites the motion picture for especial emphasis. With increase in social mobility, individual relations with a given set of neighbors, employers, fellow workers are constantly broken. The common coin becomes the Hollywood version of the successful personality. The young person emulates not so much his parents, his boss, the local bigwigs, as the screen model closest to his ideal.[32]

The marketing orientation leaves modern man increasingly without any deep relatedness either to himself or to his fellows. A prototype is Peer Gynt, who peels off one layer after another of his superficial values in his search of himself, only to find himself finally without any inner core whatever. Love for another individual cannot take the place of personal integrity and love of mankind. Playing a role in the contemporary commercial scene leaves mankind with a feeling of emptiness and growing dissatisfaction—the aloneness and insignificance so often mentioned above.

Even Fromm, the sociologist and philosopher who makes a special effort to describe the positive aspects of man's destiny, does not relate the *productive* orientation very specifically to social factors. He obviously finds the democratic way of life more productive than the authoritarian state, but he is sharply critical of the authoritarian and marketing trends in American culture.* Our enthusiasm for education is to a large extent vitiated, he thinks, by an emphasis on knowledge as a commodity, coupled with impatience "toward the allegedly impractical . . . thinking which is concerned 'only' with the truth."[33] Our dream of a casteless society with equal opportunity for all is not only unrealized for the economically underprivileged but, in the circumstances of modern

---

* The marketing orientation is an American problem only inasmuch as America has the most highly developed type of capitalistic industrial society. It holds true of Europe also to the extent to which the feudal remnants are disappearing.

life, fosters the marketing orientation. The advances of the western world have entailed certain losses as well, mainly the loss of faith in oneself and in mankind.

Fromm has no nostalgia for a past Golden Age, and no complacency about an imperfect present. He offers a "humanistic ethics." The future rests with man. It depends "upon his courage to be himself and to be for himself." He describes man's relations with the world of nature and society, uncovering his essential problems and many of the special problems he confronts in various socioeconomic groups. It would not be fair to characterize Fromm's approach as merely showing what is wrong with society, because his criticism is always related to the *dynamics* of man's relationship to the conditions of his life. Fromm's own faith in the essential productivity of man is explicit. Intrafamily and social conditions are to be desired which encourage intrinsic trust in the self and active respect for people and nature. No positive social prescriptions are offered in Fromm's published writings comparable in specificity to his analysis of forces making for nonproductive orientations. Concrete constructive social programs must be the invention of the productive power of the human race. They cannot be adequately formulated as the ideal prescription of a single writer.

SUMMARY

Fromm, like Adler and Horney, emphasizes the climate of the home, the need of the young child for warmth, affection, respect. Fromm is less rejecting of the Freudian contribution toward analysis of the specific biological orientation of the child, and gives room more explicitly to individual differences in native endowment. He is also more explicit about the positive values of self-love, that is the *development* of a true sense of individuation which fosters a productive relationship of the person to the reality of things and of his fellows. Failing trust in himself, man tries in various ways to recapture the feeling of belongingness and significance by adaptation to external values.

Thus far, Fromm's contribution is *mainly* one of putting into words ideas implicit in other schools, plus an emphasis on the "self" entirely consonant with Adler and Horney, albeit more clearly formulated and related to the evolutionary scheme.

New to psychoanalytic discussion is the effort to relate specific personality types to specific social-economic patterns. In a general way the "authoritarian" approach is contrasted with the "humanistic" approach, and the distinction is emphasized between any sort of reliance on external values somehow imposed on the individual (even if enthusiastically accepted) and the development of values proper to the self. The self always involves relatedness to the world of things and of people. One of the most important conditions for the growth of different types of relatedness (orientations) is the framework of the society in which the person lives.

The *receptive* orientation is typical of societies in which the right of one group to exploit another is firmly established—e.g., feudalism or slavery. The individual does not trust his own initiative and prefers even meager support from an outside power to being left to his own resources (*cf.* Freud's oral-passive type, Horney's moving-toward, compliant type).

The *exploitative* orientation is characteristic of the robber barons, the adventure capitalists of the eighteenth and nineteenth centuries, the Nazi clique. The keynote here, too, is the lack of an inner sense of value, but the solution lies in taking *what other people want* by force or by guile. The free gift and one's own creation are both scorned as worthless (*cf.* Freud's oral-aggressive type, Horney's moving-against, aggressive type).

The *hoarding* orientation was very common under a relatively stable bourgeois economy in which property and family were the outward signs of the grace of God or inner worth. Thrift, caution, orderliness in all things become major virtues. Taking from others is restrained by a niggling sense of justice based on the principle "Mine is mine and yours is yours." Personal (or family) success is the only guarantee of personal security; hence, the success of others becomes a source of envy, and the risk of trying something new in commerce, ideas or human relations is not to be thought of (*cf.* Freud's anal type—*possibly* Horney's moving-away-from, detached type, though the parallel is not very close).

The *marketing* orientation is a recent development of large-scale capitalism. The label becomes more important than the product. Character becomes a commodity for exchange, personality traits an important part of one's stock-in-trade for success in almost any field. People—even one's own self—are equated with things, to be manipulated in terms of their usefulness toward one or another practical end. The consequence is a generalized sense of emptiness and futility.

The *productive* orientation is given no specific social prescription, perhaps because it has not yet become typical for any society. Fromm has faith in man's destiny provided man takes himself seriously. Institutional reforms and better methods of child training should rest upon understanding of man's moral responsibility toward his own integrity as a "self."

Critical Comment

THE merit of Fromm's analysis of psychodynamics stems, I think, from the broad philosophical and social setting he gives to psychoanalytic concepts. He breaks through the absolutism of traditional ethics and of the natural and social sciences in their isolation from ethics and psychology. He provides a way of thinking about man as an evolutionary product whose special proclivities impose special problems, personal and social. His discussion of the burden and promise implicit in man's capacity for flexible adaptation seems to me in general valuable.

But this merit becomes something of a limitation when applied too directly to the concrete problems of psychology and the social sciences. I have tried to explain that most of Fromm's concepts about individual psychodynamics are explicitly derived from other schools of psychoanalysis, mainly from Freud himself, with special affiliations with Abraham and Horney. His more personal emphasis on the profound meaning of feeling alone and insignificant seems to me interesting at the same level as Freud's generalizations concerning Eros and Thanatos—and just as dangerous in so far as a very broad generalization is used to *explain* a specific situation in which more often than not quite limited subsystems provide the major dynamics of the observed event.

Fromm himself does not intend that his philosophical analysis be used directly in psychoanalysis. I dwell on the point because enthusiastic lay readers of his books and critical psychoanalytic colleagues often assume a much more immediate connection between theory and practice than is at all justified. Fromm's special contribution does not lie in the area of refined analysis of the individual. Here, like any good practicing psycho-

analyst, he uses the contributions of other people and would himself consider direct application of his philosophical orientation to treatment of the individual as a travesty upon psychoanalysis.

I have already remarked that, for an analyst who *in theory* lays so much stress on the concept of the "self," Fromm is curiously silent about the genesis and functional role of the self image. He speaks of a "pseudo self" but does not analyze the concept in differentiated functional terms even as far as Horney and Jung. On this point he remains the philosopher and does not undertake investigation of the special clinical problem. In my opinion this is an unfortunate omission. His major original contribution—the struggle toward and away from individuation—remains overgeneralized. Surely the precise contours of our image of ourselves deserve study in relation to the special contours of our culture and need not be left at the vague level of an increasing sense of individuality, of loneliness and responsibility. The self image is much more specific. It is by no means the same thing as the characterological orientation of the personality. (See other critical comment, especially on Horney [pp. 461ff.] and Jung [pp. 570f.].)

In comment following Chapter 9, I expressed appreciation of Fromm's effort to understand psychological trends in their to-and-fro relationship to cultural factors. The more systematically Fromm attempts to outline basic "orientations" in relation to wide social groups, the more suspect his procedure becomes. As he himself observes, most individuals and most modern societies present very complex *blends* of "orientations." Borrowing very extensively from Freud and

Abraham for his basic characterology, he rejects the bio-psychological theory that gives these "types" some sort of intrinsic dynamic basis. And he does not explain in detail how the social structure within which they appear arose and is maintained, as Kardiner tries to do.

Fromm shows this kind of specific to-and-fro relationship in *Escape from Freedom,* but in his later books he becomes increasingly philosophical and "clinical"—to my mind a bad mixture for a sociologist. Classification of character trends, shaky enough as regards the individual, are generalized and identified as characteristic for cultural groups in a manner which may well be sound for the groups mentioned—but which smacks too much of armchair generalization from a few "established" principles. Here we have once again what I have called reductionism.

It is helpful to observe that some social groups, as well as some individuals, may be fruitfully characterized by major psychological trends. It is *not* helpful to supply a list of such trends in such a manner as to suggest a sort of inclusiveness. I do not think Fromm means to do this, and I am here arguing more against what many people have understood from his books (especially *Man for Himself*) than against what Fromm actually says.

I should like to discuss Fromm's "marketing orientation" in some detail. The other "orientations" derive essentially from classical psychoanalysis, but the marketing orientation is original with Fromm and is very closely related to his emphasis on the "self." The reader will recall his formulation: in a capitalistic industrial society, the sense of self tends to be lost altogether. The label is substituted for the product; personality becomes a commodity which must be tailored to the market. The effort toward adaptation under constantly varying circumstances becomes the self—becomes nothing, as Peer Gynt discovered.

Valuable as it is, Fromm's discussion of factors in modern life leading to the marketing orientation seems to me to leave out aspects of our culture which make for a greater *humanization.* True enough the old face-to-face ties in the small community have been broken by social and geographical mobility; the local pattern of meanings has been taken over by the great mass media—the press, the radio, movies and television, national advertising. America is pre-eminent in all these matters.

But I should like to add that America is also pre-eminent in private-car ownership and in the amount of personal correspondence. Actually it is rare, nowadays, for people who move away to lose touch with the family and even with the home town. Through letters and visits quite lively contacts are maintained. Moreover, the home folks are listening to the same programs, seeing the same movies. The old oaken bucket has increasingly become a faucet hardly different from city facilities. Thus there is far less sharp a break between city and country, between one town and another, than there was even a generation or two ago. There is, indeed, much more common coin between old and young. As I think about the families I know in all walks of life instead of about social generalizations, it seems to me that the families actually stick together very well. They quarrel a good deal, perhaps more openly than families quarreled in the past and more superficially. But I think that their quarreling is *more* humane rather than less, rooted in a more vivid sense of intimacy and shared interpersonal values in contrast to mere deference to social patterns of value.

Another aspect of our culture that strikes me very forcibly is the participation of the father in the care of the child, especially the very young child. Any fine Sunday at any public beach shows hundreds of American parents on all fours playing with their offspring in a manner quite different from the past as we see it in old prints and old stories. The games are not always pure fun, of course, as Johnny gets obstreperous and Daddy would rather take a nap or a swim than continue playing pickaback. Johnny may suddenly be cuffed and yelled at; Mother may become terrified or exasperated; a family row may develop openly about whether and how Johnny should be disciplined.

There can be little doubt that American parents nowadays are confused and uncertain about their own values and about their handling of their children; in all probability they give in too much, are too solicitous, make too much of the child. But at least there seems to be a *directness of relationship* that is a new cultural phenomenon. Parents and children no longer *work* together as closely as in the days before the Industrial Revolution, before urbanization and mechanization. But they *play* together much more.

It would be foolhardy even to speculate in a paragraph or two as to the consequence of these shifts for character formation in American society. Certainly it is far more difficult for the American to define his "self" in terms of specific behavior and codified values. He is very likely to *feel* confused, perplexed as to his own direction and his fundamental values. Yet it seems to me very unlikely that the core of the American character would have the *emptiness* Fromm attributes to the marketing orientation. What he loses sight of in his sociological analysis is the positive increment in direct interpersonal relationships consequent upon precisely the same developments that have broken down the communal ties which so greatly influenced the person's view of his role, his behavior, his very self. Daddy playing on the beach does not offer the same cogent image for later social relations as Father behind the plow, Father at the head of the table, respected by the neighbors, reinforced in his dicta by all the fathers

one knows. But Daddy is a very real person, and one keeps on dealing with him as a real person even after one goes away to school and settles down in another town.

If we take a broad sociological view, is the Hollywood version of values really worse than the values which have been proffered by local communities through the ages? It is my impression that the values presented to the populace have quite typically been unrealistic, oversimplified, and in large measure hypocritical. In the movies one at least sees that a great variety of people in all social classes have very similar troubles, and that solid virtue always triumphs. Is it worse to identify with the movie hero than with the glamorous youth glimpsed at the manor? As I listen to talk about specific movies at many family tables, I am mainly impressed with the quite realistic discussion of the problems raised by the plot—discussion in which the young occasionally listen to their elders on important issues, and vice versa. Most of the young people I know talk freely of feeling "dreamy" about this or that star, and share their dreaminess in a manner which robs it of its extreme fantasy quality. Indeed the *shared* fantasy, I suspect, gives most of these youngsters a relatively wholesome boost in the growing-up process.

Thus I do not like to cry Cassandra about social mobility and the influence of mass media. I would rather suggest that the "emptiness" Fromm describes really belongs to the era of Kafka and Ibsen and Fitzgerald, when the old communal values were tottering and the mass media had not yet become part of a new kind of family—where the car and the letter, plus the common mass media, actually create a continuing directness in personal relationships, which begins, I suggest, with the new cultural phenomenon of the parent (especially the father) who *plays* with the child.

I suggest that the major pathology of

this kind of society does involve an enormous emphasis on the sense of one's self as the ultimate criterion, and a very great uncertainty about the self image. But the problem is not one of "emptiness," except as a secondary mode of adaptation. It is the problem of the idealized image of the self, so vividly described by Horney, and the problem of borderline psychosis which has become an overwhelmingly common diagnostic rubric. In this condition the "self" fails in its task of organizing perceived reality in close dynamic relationship to its inner needs—with varying consequences. The patients are not psychotic in the old sense of the word, but they do show profound difficulties in integration of experience.

In the long run, my complaint about Fromm's formulation is the same as that about Adler and Horney: it is reductionist rather than multidimensional. Although Fromm adds the factor of the social setting in an especially vivid and thought-provoking manner, his philosophical and sociological approach tends to oversimplify the problem at the point at which it takes on concrete form: the psychodynamics of the individual.

SULLIVAN

WE MUST HERE mention again the two major classifications of the pursuits of the organism: satisfaction (bodily) and security (interpersonal). We have seen that except for the lust dynamism and occasional bodily crisis situations, the pursuit of satisfaction can rarely be discerned as a separate or even as a preponderant aspect of behavior, although it must be continuous. For Sullivan, human psychology is essentially built on the pursuit of security, which is for him an essentially interpersonal phenomenon.

We have seen how the infant directly empathizes the anxiety and disapproval of the adults close to him, how he gradually "catches on" to the fact that these uncomfortable states have something to do with his own behavior, and gradually begins to organize his behavior in such a manner as to avoid the distressing experience of *anxiety*. Anxiety for Sullivan, we have seen, is always an interpersonal matter. It is, to be sure, built upon the bodily sense of discomfort in earliest infancy, but it very rapidly assumes its special powerful referrants because the human animal is an essentially social being whose psychological experiences are necessarily with its own kind.

We have seen that although the infant is born without any effective discrimination between self and not-self, organization of behavior very early *becomes* oriented in a manner which Sullivan calls the self dynamism. This orientation operates in an integrative manner from its inception, although it can operate only through the capabilities and tools that the child has at his disposal. I hope that it became obvious through the discussion of the epochs of childhood how closely Sullivan relates the maturing capacities of the child for more complex experience with the actual opportunities for experience offered to him—opportunities which are *necessarily* social rather than biological or purely individual. The emergent self dynamism determines the aspects of the total available experience that will be utilized and integrated in the successive moments which make up a person's life. Many aspects of experience are simply not relevant to the self at any given moment. Writing this book excludes from my attention the familiar sights and sounds of my study—although, as I now look around me like the typical armchair philosopher in sudden consciousness of my surroundings, I observe with disfavor a pot of faded flowers which should be thrown out. I should have seen them at once if I had been expecting a patient in my study, or even if I had been functioning in my usual housewifely mode. Absorbed in work, I honestly did not "see" the eyesore before me.

SELECTIVE INATTENTION AND DISSOCIATION

This "oversight" is an example of what Sullivan calls *selective inattention*. I have chosen it because it starts out with the simple narrowing of the field of attention familiar to any psychologist or philosopher discussing concentration—but it can be taken a little further. Many housewives would find it impossible to settle down to work in a room with a pot of faded flowers. For them this particular selective inattention could not occur, or if it did they would somehow try to justify it in the housewifely mode, perhaps even get up and dispose of the offending pot. I handle this problem differently. I am quite willing to have my attention called to the fact that I am only a middling good housewife, either by observing the pot or by listening to friends. I may or may not do something about remedying the shortcomings my friends point out in this respect, but I can at least listen to their comments and consider them more or less realistically.

The situation is quite different for the housewife whose domestic duties are the very warp and woof of her being—or for me in areas of my self dynamism more closely related to my own concept of "security." There are certain truths about ourselves which we simply cannot hear or see no matter how cogently our attention is drawn to them by well-meaning friends or psychoanalysts. At best we can make a verbalistic acknowledgment which leaves our actual behavior and feelings quite untouched. This general phenomenon is familiar to us from the discussion of other schools under the heading of repression, with the continuation of impulses at the unconscious level.

Sullivan's term for the phenomenon is *dissociation* (at times disassociation). Whatever aspects of our experience would lead to anxiety tend to be excluded from our awareness before they can interfere with our peace of mind. Partly this mechanism leads us simply to avoid situations which currently make us (or in the past have made us) feel helpless or "bad" (guilty). Sullivan uses as example the judgment of many people that they are no good at mathematics—a fact they can easily support by poor adult performance on the relatively minor occasions when most of us are called upon to deal with figures. In the great majority of instances, he thinks, this disability has nothing to do with native lack of talent. The explanation very often is that one's initial efforts at coping with arithmetic, perhaps not very keenly motivated in early school years, met with the irony of a harsh teacher and with disapproval at home over a bad report card. Thereafter any encounter with figures awakens this old anxiety. No one can think clearly in a state of anxiety, and everyone tends to avoid its discomfort so far as possible. Thus the small initial difficulty of the scolded pupil is built upon in two ways: by the anxiety itself, and by the lack of that actual practice in dealing with figures which the most gifted and secure would find necessary in developing real competence with advanced mathematical concepts and manipulations.

The example may be examined more narrowly for deeper insight into the meaning of dissociation. Mathematics occupies a special niche in our culture—very highly honored, but not the sort of thing most of us have to cope with beyond counting change. Once school days are over, we can even announce with some pride that we are no good at mathematics and cheerfully forget the whole matter, not observing in the least that our prideful statement actually covers a severe *limitation of experience determined by anxiety*.

Unfortunately no such harmless sleight of hand is possible for many other types of experience. We have seen that the school child must learn a great deal about the social dimensions of his own self in relation to his compeers—or, more correctly, that it is through his experiences at this age that the self dynamism normally acquires these dimensions. If anything goes seriously wrong with the learning process in this broader area of interpersonal relationships, exactly the same *limiting of experience under the whip of anxiety* is bound to occur as in the learning of mathematics. But there is an important difference: the limitation tends to be all-pervasive. We have seen that every stage of childhood development is essential in learning how to be a mature adult. The self dynamism has to be *grown*, and is fully integrating at every moment of its function. We can do well enough without competence in dealing with mathematical symbols. We cannot do well without competence in dealing with people, because our very self is premised upon interpersonal relationships. We can *try* to say pridefully, "Oh, I'm not good at dealing with people," as we do about our mathematical blunders. As a matter of fact, this is just what many of us *do* say with very careful, usually derogatory description of the kind of people we cannot deal with, plus a positive emphasis on the much more valuable people we *do* get on with, even if we have to resort to books and ideas or other fantastic personifications to find our compeers.

THE INTEGRATING "SELF"

It is precisely in this effort to define ourselves pridefully despite the very severe limitations of our actual learning in the all-pervasive area of interpersonal relations that we can see the crux of Sullivanian dynamics. His view is like that of Adler, Horney, and Fromm in the emphasis on the supreme importance of the movements of the "self" as a unit—in some contrast to the emphasis of the libido theory on the specific biological needs of the human organism as major contributors toward its psychological constellation. Sullivan's view is roughly similar to that of the other non-libido authors in the specific emphasis on security (belongingness) and prestige (superiority, self-esteem, significance) as the determining motives isolable in a general way from among the colorful variations to be observed in human behavior. The integrative action of the "self" is considered primary—and since the "self" functions necessarily in human society, its security is a reflection of social values, and its very integrity requires doing well.

In one (rather restricted) way Sullivan and Adler may be paired together in a contrast with Horney and Fromm. The latter make a very positive point of the "real self," the human *potential*, which not only underlies personality development but functions quite concretely in opposition to the limitations imposed more or less drastically in actual living by the pursuit of security or the escape from freedom. Adler and Sullivan take a generally benign view toward the human potential (in contrast to the death instinct) and even call upon a natural tendency in the organism to use its abilities expansively. But they do not envisage a human "self" apart from the empirical self which develops from the actual experience of the organism in its social milieu.

Sullivan's *difference* from Adler is not so much in the nature of the basic drive underlying human behavior (Adler's drive to superiority, Sullivan's pursuit of security—*i.e.*, approval and prestige) as in his conception of how it comes about and how it operates. Both men try to be empirical, but where Adler suggests that because the infant feels inferior, he will try to overcome inferiority as the law of his being, Sullivan asks that we look more carefully at the infant. He could not possibly "feel inferior" in the highly socialized manner Adler presupposes because he has initially no concept either of himself or of other people. He responds much more "biologically," as it were, to the attitudes of the adults around him in the quite simple terms of comfort (euphoria) attendant upon release from tension and discomfort (muscular tension which quickly takes the form of anxiety as the infant responds to the specific discomfort of adult disapproval). But the pattern of adult disapproval is very closely related to the adult's pattern of behavior—first communicated to the child by empathy, later rather directly taught with all the force of the infantile relationship to the parent. In the juvenile era, the child's orientation toward learning is already slanted, but Sullivan's point is that he still *must* learn quite new interpersonal relationships with his compeers and strange authority figures outside the family. It is only the very unfortunate child whose self dynamism and capacity for symbolization is so set by the age of six that he cannot make a fresh integration which *includes* the new learning experience, so important for the development of the self dynamism as an *empirical* integrating concept.

Thus we can see why Sullivan would doubtless have objected very strenuously to any continued bracketing with Adler. I want to throw into clear relief the fact that the essential theoretical difference does *not* lie in subtle variations about the definition of a quite general psychological construct related to prestige, power, superiority, striving toward perfection, mastery, or whatnot. It lies in the description of how this construct comes about via the actual experience of the individual with other people at different levels of his ability to deal with them.

PARATAXIC DISTORTION

It will be remembered that the young child functions mainly in the parataxic mode (see pp. 399ff.), and that he builds up all sorts of personal, autistic symbols out of his specific experiences with the significant adults around him. Concomitantly he begins to learn a great many consensually validated symbols, mainly via the medium of language. These symbols are very often superficially the same as those he has developed privately, so that "the possibilities of confusion are very great." In our dealings with people and in the view of ourselves that we construct in the course of such dealings, the consensually validated symbols naturally predominate and are related to one another so far as possible in the *syntaxic* mode characteristic for reasonable adult communication. Acceptance of the consensually validated symbols, and even quite elaborate manipulation of them by the strictest rules of logic, does not in the least preclude continuation of their concomitant autistic meaning. In fact, it is the more personalized meaning that typically governs the pattern of behavior, usually outside of awareness—that is, outside of the construct of ourselves and others elaborately built from consensually validated symbols in the syntaxic mode.

This kind of falsification due to the predominant action of autistic interpretations Sullivan calls *parataxic distortion*. Naturally such distortion is extremely common in every aspect of human thought, with the exception of those mathematical or scientific symbols which deal with recurrent relationships totally independent of human life. Nevertheless the person reasonably fortunate in his particular experience within his society develops personal meanings in rather close relationship to consensually validated meanings. They may hardly be distorting at all; in fact, they may be considerably more in the syntaxic mode than the consensually validated symbols of his society. By contrast, the child whose personal experience was especially unfortunate because movements toward wider experience created anxiety (and limitation—as we saw in the mathematics example) is especially prone to parataxic distortion no matter how skillful his apparent use of consensually validated symbols.

The concept of parataxic distortion clearly does not in itself define any dynamic pattern. But distortion results from dynamic patterns, and observation of its operation may provide a major clue toward insight into the patterns. The distortion extends beyond mere use of words (although Sullivan pays especial attention to odd verbalisms as revealing of the patient's mind) to any sort of misinterpretation or seemingly inappropriate attitude. Thus if a patient coming for treatment on the recommendation of a trusted family physician reacts to the psychiatrist with suspicion and abuse before much of anything has been said, the chances are that the patient interprets the situation parataxically far beyond anything which has yet transpired. Obviously the situation has a somewhat idiosyncratic meaning for this patient which is different from its meaning for the majority. The task of the psychiatrist is to discover so far as possible what meaning or meanings it actually has for the patient, where the limitation in consensual validation came from, and how it operates in the patient's pursuit of security.

The aim of *dissociation* (roughly, repression) is, as we have seen, to prevent the feeling of anxiety attendant upon experiences which run counter to the powerful reflected appraisals basic to the development of the self dynamism. Caught with his hand in the jam pot, Johnny may say, "*I didn't steal the jam; my hand did it.*" Much the same mechanism may be seen in psychosis, in which dissociation may become quite extreme, with aspects of the personality normally altogether excluded from awareness manifesting themselves vigorously and often hallucinated by the patient as illusory personifications coming from outside. In these hallucinatory states, it is very clear that the dissociated aspects of the personality have undergone a measure of independent development—as the Freudians observed for aspects of the "unconscious."

The process of dissociation is, naturally, very inexpedient in the long run as a *démarche* of the self system. At best it limits the self system unduly. At worst, when the self dynamism attempts dissociation of very powerful subdynamisms, severe crippling or total incapacitation of its integrative function is extremely likely.

Yet dissociation is a universal dynamic process. Every individual simply excludes chunks of impulse and quasi-interpreted experience from awareness and from the socially integrated aspects of the self dynamism. Like Adler, Sullivan points out the *constructive* aspect of dreams, reveries, unconsidered acts (parapraxes) for the normal person. In Sullivan's opinion, they tend to *discharge* impulses which might otherwise become overwhelming. A rather extreme example used by Sullivan is the fantasy of suicide. Faced by a situation which seems impossible of solution, the person resolves to die and in the process of reverie works out in some detail the interpersonal consequences of his act, and "almost incidentally" the situation is resolved and the reverie leads into more constructive ends.* "It is quite possible that *minor* [italics added] integrating tendencies dissociated from the awareness often discharge themselves predominantly during sleep . . . and [this process] helps to maintain adjustment and mental health despite dissociation."[34] Doubtless Sullivan would in his own way support Adler's point (see pp. 426f.) that when a large discrepancy already exists within the personality, these "normal" parapraxic activities actually serve to consolidate the dissociations (the erroneous life style).

Another way by which dissociated impulses may find partial discharge is through the process of *sublimation,* which so far as I can make out in reading Sullivan merges into the process of *substitution,* in which the idiosyncratic, parataxic distortion is more extreme. In sublimation the impulse, whether it proceeds from the pursuit of satisfaction or the child's concept of security, attains a certain amount of direct expression under a convenient

* H. S. Sullivan, *Conceptions of Modern Psychiatry,* William Alanson White Foundation, 1947, p. 12—although this is not Sullivan's main intent with the example.

label and in a socially acceptable manner. This is no mean achievement. In fact, when the adaptive pattern is not *too* constrictive, sublimation may allow very extensive development of consensually validated symbol behavior either in specific areas of personality function or quite generally, despite severe limitation in the self dynamism. A surgeon or a dentist, for example, *may* be in general an impoverished personality who has found in his profession a social pattern which allows highly constructive expression of impulses experienced as disapproved and therefore dissociated. A social reformer *may* find in his work with the underprivileged certain satisfactions of impulses which he could never acknowledge directly.*

Partial Summary

I have tried to show that although Sullivan introduces a host of new terms and is sparing in his use of the terms commonly employed by analysts, his essential concept of psychodynamics is not *radically* different. In a general way the self dynamism is comparable to the "self" of the non-libido group, to the "ego" of the Freudians. Selective inattention is rather like Freud's foreconscious. Items rejected from awareness at the moment may be brought into consciousness without much difficulty. Dissociation is rather like the true unconscious of other analysts. Items are dynamically excluded from awareness (repressed) because they arouse intolerable anxiety. (I here use the word *item* for any more-or-less isolable configuration.) Parataxic distortion is a general term for the autistic, personally determined meanings operating for every individual "unconsciously," as he copes with life situations *apparently* according to consensually validated meanings in the syntaxic mode—that is, by the common sense of his culture and by reason.

Sullivan's vocabulary reflects his effort to suggest that the "self" is not so definite a potential as Horney and Fromm maintain, in such clear contrast to the idealized or pseudo self. Nor is it as feeble a by-product as the Freudian "synthetic function of the ego" sometimes seems. It is wholly emergent but extremely powerful. Hence the term self dynamism. For the same reason he prefers selective inattention and dissociation, plus the general mechanism of parataxic distortion, to the more common varieties of nomenclature for phe-

---

* In these days of overpsychologizing, it is perhaps expedient to remark that Sullivan would not dream of considering surgery, dentistry, and the profession of social work as *social* phenomena to be generally explicable in any such manner. On the contrary, it is the sound social pattern which allows some individuals to express partially impulses which would otherwise be dissociated. Modern social work has been keenly aware of the dangers of just such bias and has tried to deal with it by careful selection of candidates for training and by careful controls in professional function. We are legitimately less concerned about the deeper motives of the surgeon and dentist, so long as they do a good job and can be trusted not to recommend operation for their private gratification in the parataxic mode.

nomena outside the field of awareness. Sullivan's terms derive directly from his central concept of the emerging "self" as the dynamism which integrates— or actively refuses to integrate—the experiences proffered more or less insistently by the human environment within which it develops. Parataxic distortion refers to a developmental period when *all* experience was perceived in this mode, when consensually validated symbols were just beginning to be appreciated as such in close relation to the vivid patterns of symbolization the child is forming for his interpersonal world. The term does not imply a timeless infantile unconscious, but it does suggest a developmental slant toward the peculiarities of the unconscious phenomena. Above all, it attempts to keep the unconscious within the framework of an essentially developmental, empirical psychology.

Through the process of sublimation impulses actively dissociated from the self dynamism may still find partial expression under a socially accepted label. This process merges into substitution as the discrepancy between the inner, dissociated pressure and the socially accepted label becomes more extreme. The sublimatory process may then appear as an intolerable narrowing of the personality, as neurotic symptoms, even as a psychotic break.

PERSONALITY TYPES; SYNDROMES

Like the other authors discussed, Sullivan attempts a sort of typing of people based on their most prevalent interpersonal attitudes, and offers some suggestions as to how these attitudes come about. The list is longer (ten "syndromes") and does not pretend to be comprehensive. I shall not attempt to describe these ten syndromes in detail; instead, I shall select those that seem to me especially revealing of the concrete use to which Sullivan puts the concepts I have up to now reported rather abstractly. The reader is referred to pages 37 to 42 of *Conceptions of Modern Psychiatry* for full presentation.

The first syndrome offered is that of the "so-called psychopathic personality," for which Sullivan prefers the term *non-integrative*. Apart from remarking upon the extraordinary peculiarity of the self dynamism and its "relatively vestigial" nature, Sullivan appears to offer no theory as to how such a condition comes about. (See pp. 291*ff*. for description of the psychopath.)

His second syndrome relates to the *self-absorbed*, or fantastic, person, who is given to "wishful thinking." It was suggested earlier that the infant inevitably tends to bifurcate his interpretation of his world in the direction of the states he can differentiate: euphoria and tension → anxiety; that correspondingly his early prehension of the external world has a powerful bifurcation: the Good Mother and the Bad Mother. Now as the child begins to perceive the real mother a little more clearly, she becomes both less Good and less Bad. Because the loss of the *representative* fantasy of the Good Mother is painful, the child begins a *constructive* fantasy along the lines of his prototaxic experience. He imagines a good mother who will give him all satisfactions, and he attributes all actual hardships to an equally fantastic bad mother. All children must go through this phase, but if anything happens to make differentiated learning in interpersonal relations especially difficult, the child and the adult he becomes may continue this early mode of adjustment. Sullivan calls this a *career-line* which may continue relatively uninterruptedly throughout life (*cf*. Adler's life style). Thus all the associates of this kind of person are either perfectly wonderful or perfectly impossible. They become eidetic personifications of the infantile fantasy mothers. In his general dealings with others, a person of this type is easily disappointed, wounded, "misunderstood." Often enough two of them get together. "By a sustained miracle of accommodating—or ignoring—the individualistic misconceptions of each other, two of these folk can have quite a good time."[35] Actually their life story frequently includes a long series of intense intimacies, often emotionalized devotion to a series of "causes," regularly terminated in profound disillusionment—although the next person, the next cause is adopted with a failure in learning from experience at which we "cannot but marvel."

For this type of character, persons cannot be seen realistically, with generous care for another individual in his own right. We have seen that genuine love is the product of long and intricate development in interpersonal experience. Such persons may have such excellent sublimatory techniques that their profound failure in interpersonal growth is hardly noticeable as more than a character trend—often annoying, often endearing if they happen to envisage us in the Good Mother category without being embarrassingly demanding. When sublimation is inadequate and even substitutive processes come to fail, the basic autistic, almost prototaxic, quality of their career-line becomes all too apparent. Fantastic reconstruction of the Good Mother becomes ever more fantastic, and fears of the Bad Mother more uncontrollable.

A third syndrome, that of the *incorrigible* person, involves "less blandly a cosmic centering of the person." The basic attitude toward others is hostile, unfriendly, morose, or forbidding—with the exception of people whom he can regard as his inferiors. This syndrome makes its clear appearance in the juvenile era, when the child has difficulty in healthy competition and self-satisfying compromise, but it rarely begins there. It seems to have its deeper origin very often in the parent "who just would not be satisfied with the child." A good teacher and friendly classmates may help importantly to undo the restrictive orientation of the personality started with the significant adults of infancy and childhood; harsh teachers and difficult classmates may profoundly confirm an orientation even moderately restrictive, or fail to help the child onward toward a more differentiated picture of himself and others. Nevertheless, in his consideration of these deep "career-line" syndromes, Sullivan, like the other analysts, points primarily to the very early years for his major dynamic etiology.

As a child the incorrigible person felt unable to overcome the dissatisfaction of others with him. Subsequently he continues to experience all authority *eidetically*—that is, as a more or less direct image of the actual significant persons of his childhood. (Naturally he is not aware of this tie-up.) He has no objection to authority as such, or to exercising authority—indeed he can conceive of no other kind of interpersonal relationship. But he complains bitterly and openly about any uncertainty in authority, any irrationality or "stupidity." He is a thorn in the side of his teachers, and in later life puts "stuffed shirts" where they belong.

Sullivan does not discuss this syndrome in detail, but I gather that he means that ineffectual kind of trouble-maker who constantly and indiscriminately attacks every person, institution, and idea which makes the slightest pretense at being authoritative—but who actually shuns office, never publishes any opposing generalizations to the ones he considers so "stupid," will not commit himself even in conversation to a positive program, and is unexpectedly kind in his practical dealings with many people.

Since I had trouble understanding this syndrome myself—possibly because I was bemused by the more comprehensive typological efforts of other authors—I was especially delighted in suddenly identifying a friend of the family who has puzzled me vaguely for years. He is a successful lawyer, very well informed, and full of interesting anecdotes. But it is impossible to carry on with him what most of us call conversation. One's most casual remark on any social topic suddenly provokes a flood of vituperation against the imbeciles and gangsters who run our government, and the abysmal stupidity of all those who comment upon any aspect of the administration of the commonweal.

In my youth I was ready to write him off as "paranoid," but he obviously does not *act* any more paranoid than the rest of us, and I observe that his considered public speech is usually expediently controlled. In fact he does not seem an especially hostile or aggressive person in the Horney-Fromm sense. Although I do not know the intimacies of his close family relationships, I have seen the family together on relatively informal occasions off and on during most of my life. His wife *looks* a bit like the victim in a symbiotic relationship, since she talks relatively little, never contradicts her husband, appears to admire him boundlessly and to provide for his slightest whim. George rarely expresses appreciation of her efforts. Yet if one observes the couple more closely, it is apparent that she has and enjoys a very large autonomy in the way they manage their lives—indeed, that her decision predominates or at least is always jointly considered in some quite curious fashion.

In conversation a typical sequence is as follows: (1) the husband makes a quite reasonable answer to a reasonable question related to his special areas of competence—so clouded by vituperative attack that one is hardly able to follow what he is saying. (2) His wife says, "What George means is that you should do so and so." (3) George then usually merely agrees, muttering another vituperation, or he may quite realistically insist on some aspect of the problem which his wife has ignored or misunderstood in her restatement of his meaning. Noteworthy is the fact that he is never annoyed by this constant wifely interpretation—surely a rare trait among husbands.

It is clear that George considers his wife "inferior," and that she is quite willing to accept this position *vis-à-vis* George. Within this mutually accepted framework, however, he accords her full liberty and openly relies upon her. In his profession he was never able to cooperate with a group of lawyers, even when he held a high position in an important firm. Naturally many clients in private practice do not like him and take their business elsewhere in a huff about something he has said. Since he can usually consider the client as appropriately "inferior," at least in respect to his legal problems, he can usually treat him quite pleasantly and handle the legal problems with admirable competence and integrity. His advice is singularly free from his personal bias toward Authority. He may say to a client (I quote his own anecdotes): "You're dealing with a bunch of gangsters. Better make the best adjustment you can" or "These gangsters ought to be taught a lesson, and if you fight on this point you'll win." His practical judgment is very little influenced by his personal attitudes.

Thus it seems to me that neither in his marriage nor in his profession does George actually live out the sado-masochistic picture suggested at first glance; he cannot without quite considerable amendment be typed according to any of the comprehensive typologies thus far presented. But he fits perfectly Sullivan's description of the person who needs authority and tries to live up to it but is deeply convinced that it can never be satisfied and constantly complains about any actual authority with deep, irrational, and almost consciously futile resentment. The only way one can get George to go against authority is to taunt him with being afraid. He takes up a dare like a little boy, as one may see by the violence of his reaction if one "baits" him a little—and I gather that his withdrawal from various groups in the past often involved moderately outrageous behavior *under provocation,* so frequent that finally the difficulties could not be patched up. On the other hand, the relationship to Authority is such that once the authority issue is settled he can go about the business of living in a reasonable, kindly, and moderately productive fashion; his demands in this area are modest and tend to remain modest—in contrast to the insatiable demands of the personality whose aggression is a total defense against total helplessness.

I have presented George at some length because, if I understand Sullivan correctly, he illustrates an approach to typology which is unlike any we have thus far encountered and which seems to me important. This kind of person is the product of a home in which the major bodily satisfactions and the minimal requirements for healthy interpersonal development are supplied. The child is treated affectionately and goes to school under good auspices. Yet the parents are never satisfied with his performance. There is constant belittling criticism of everything he does, with no appreciation of his actual achievements on his own terms—although he is expected to behave well. Thus a career-line of defiant resentment develops—resentment which is almost consciously envisaged as futile but which appears compulsively against *any* authoritative person or idea. Sullivan comments that treatment of this syndrome is very difficult, although apparently in favorable life circumstances a fair degree of adjustment may be achieved, and in a way the vicious circle of Horney may be avoided by the life-long pattern of inner acceptance of "griping" without serious revolt. And a measure of relatively free, almost friendly development is allowed with "inferiors" and compeers.

The next syndrome Sullivan presents is that of the *negativistic* person. The selves of these people "are organized on the basis of appraisals that make them insignificant—until their constructive fantasy hit upon negation as a device for forcing notice if not approval. . . . Insecurity is met . . . with an assertion of refusal."[36] At first these individuals make this assertion merely by acting as problem children as a means of gaining attention, but as they grow older they often develop very subtle techniques—including the technique of cynical conciliation. They learn how to deal with people and ideas expertly. In treatment, early sessions are difficult, but once the patient gains insight into a few of his own parataxic processes, he may be especially skilled in proceeding to discover others.

The fifth syndrome is the *stammerer*. Sullivan does not elaborate very fully, and I shall not try to condense further his description of a syndrome which most of us have considered a symptom in a variety of personality types. Some of the Freudian analysts too, notably Glauber, have been much interested in the peculiar underlying dynamics characteristic of this speech defect, but it does not seem feasible to discuss this rather special problem here.

The next five syndromes represent distortions which develop after a fairly extensive acculturation has been achieved—that is, after the juvenile era.

The sixth may be called the *ambition-ridden personality*. "These people have to use everyone with whom they are integrated."[37] They are competitive in every situation—including the psychoanalytic session. The mode of reaction characteristic for the insecure school child seems to have become consolidated as their general mode of interpersonal relationship.

The seventh syndrome Sullivan calls the *asocial*. These people typically have a well-formulated sense of values, which often includes a proper sense of their own worth. The difficulty is that "they have not grasped the possibility that they themselves may be valued, cherished, by others."[38] Thus they become detached and lonely, unable to establish and maintain warm interpersonal relationships—although they often behave in a friendly, sensitive manner. In analysis the main problem is that they cannot believe that the psychiatrist is really interested and friendly, and for a very long time will revert to their deep feeling of remoteness and unlovableness. "Even as children [these patients] came to realize that their prehended reality was quite different from the illusions of them that the parents persistently entertained." Therefore they developed a "duplex pattern of what *is* and what is expected." They readily shift from one pattern to the other, and even evaluate "the illusions of others" with relatively little parataxic distortion.[39]

The eighth syndrome includes the *inadequate* people—all those whose integration with others is built upon dependency—the clinging-vine adaptation. The syndrome may result from accepted obedience to a domineering parent, or identification with a helpless parent. The person always requires a strong person to tell him what to do, and under favorable circumstances he may function quite well. Sullivan remarks that he may be for some time a boon to any domineering physician but comes usually to be rather like the albatross around the neck of the Ancient Mariner.

The ninth syndrome is *homosexuality*, which Sullivan considers as an adjustive device rather than as a problem in itself. The tenth involves the *chronically adolescent* person who always pursues the ideal and never finds it.[40] Sullivan comments as follows:

> These are some of the more outstanding diagnostic syndromes which appear in the series of interpersonal relations through which one passes. They tell us of the past and permit shrewd guesses—predictions of high probability—as to the future integrations which the person will show. More significant for the clinical practice of psychiatry, they provide the meaning for otherwise mystifying episodes that occur in the lives of those who experience mental disorder. For the broader aspects of psychiatry, they are reference-frames for understanding what will and what will not work, in connection with a particular person.[41]

Critical Comment

ONCE I became accustomed to Sullivan's odd terminology, I found it quite useful. It allows for a multidimensional approach as complex as one wishes to make it, while still highlighting certain basic concepts. I refer mainly to his use of the term "dynamism" and to the use of grammatical terms—*e.g.*, "parataxic distortion," or terms derived from familiar modes of thought, *e.g.*, "selective inattention," as expressing the *continuity* of normal and abnormal, conscious and unconscious, infantile and adult experience as well as differences which must be observed. Using unambiguous common words and deliberate word-building where no common word will suffice may actually be less confusing than redefinition of familiar technical terms. The word "ego," for example, has many different meanings within Freud's own writings, none of which corresponds to the meaning Jung gives it, or Rank, or the dictionary. The simple word "self" is even worse. It has multiple meanings in everybody's writings, and as "Self" is quite elaborately and quite variously described.

If my comments here seem predominantly negative, it is only because I am taking the values of Sullivan's approach for granted. To make my own position

quite clear, this is the only "non-libido" approach which seems to me at all comparable to Freud's approach in its theoretical potential, and I see no fundamental incompatibility between the two.

Sullivan's self dynamism has the merit, I think, of emphasizing the synthesizing and excluding power of *what the individual becomes* more sharply than the Freudian ego, and without the philosophical romanticism of the other self psychologies. I think Sullivan's self dynamism should be further analyzed in two ways: (1) The special dynamics of the Freudian superego should be recognized as a relatively independent dynamism, very important in our culture and probably in a way universal because it derives from biologically fundamental relations between the helpless child and the ministering adults. (2) One might add what I have called the self image as still another subdynamism, constructed mainly out of the relations between the growing child and his social milieu beyond the very direct quasibiological tie with the parental figures implicit in the superego. In fact, it is very likely that most people have quite a series of self images, variously derived and related to one another, which are more determining in many situations than the over-all self dynamism, or than the underlying bio-psychological processes emphasized by the various schools. Sullivan's position offers an excellent take-off point in theory for these further subdynamisms of the self.

Sullivan does not himself attempt to formulate such subdynamisms. Furthermore, although he makes a place for oral, anal, and genital (lust) dynamisms in basic theory, his practice tends to deny the important role ascribed to them in Freudian theory. They become incidental rather than constellative aspects of development. I have remarked repeatedly that underemphasis on aspects of experience which must be of paramount importance to the infant seems to me a mistake. When infantile sexuality is denied, the Freudian concept of the superego automatically becomes meaningless. Here again it seems to me that very sound generalizations about the course of childhood development are lost sight of. And again it seems to me that they *could* be introduced into the Sullivan scheme with no great dislocation of his basic theory.

In Chapters 9 and 10, I suggested that Sullivan pays more attention to the role of "ego functions" (capacities, abilities—in my vocabulary, the nonsexual systems) than any other analyst here reported, but he leaves them at the level of conditions under which the more complex personality functions develop. He neglects their special dynamic potential as he neglects the dynamic potential of the sexual systems.

In this schematic review we come finally to the emphasis on interpersonal relations. Perhaps I can sharpen my critique by the paradox that I find Sullivan's scheme the most useful in drawing attention to the importance of *non*personal aspects of experience. It would be absurd to credit Sullivan with originality in the observation that people are important to people. The Freudian "object"

is a *person* from the outset—so much so that the perception of objects in the nonpersonal sense and their logical relationships with one another is considered a late and not-well-understood secondary development. It is Sullivan, not Freud or Adler, who stresses the point that the infant learns about the fact that he can in no way manage the moon—that is, about the very stubborn nature of physical "reality." In my opinion Sullivan does not carry through far enough on this point, but the other analytic schools hardly mention the problem. Their emphasis seems even more exclusively *interpersonal* than Sullivan's.

As I read Sullivan, the emphasis does not belong on the fact that persons are of primary significance for personality development. That is the most orthodox Freud. The significant emphasis is on the point that one becomes a person oneself only in relation to other people, not as a consequence of what one *is* by virtue of inborn drives. In so far as Sullivan neglects the role of the biologically determined dynamisms (drive systems, pursuit of satisfaction) in orienting the child's experience with people, his position seems to me one-sided. The concept of the pursuit of security tends to become as reductionist as the theories of the other non-libido authors, because it is not kept in sufficiently close relationship to the pursuit of satisfaction.

This reductionism does not seem to me at all a necessary part of Sullivan's theory. On the contrary, I suspect that it is a relatively temporary phase which comes into prominence as a reaction against unduly reductionist approaches in the older libido theory. The theoretical analysis of drives as existing only in relation to the living complex of an organism in its milieu is a very healthy corrective to the tendency to think of instincts as existing somehow in themselves and as identifiable apart from the environment within which they function. But such analysis should not go so far as to ignore the organismic systems through which the child perceives his environment. Exaggeration of the cultural side of this living complex is quite as objectionable according to Sullivan's own theory as an over-emphasis on the drive-systems ("instincts").

Sullivan's ten personality syndromes illustrate well the actual complexity of his thinking about human development and function. I like the nonsystematic character of his approach to the problem of types. The next chapter will point out that he also deals understandingly with the conventional psychiatric classifications. This empirically derived pluralism of dynamic constellations is reminiscent of the complexity of the Freudian view of dynamics, in contrast to the more neatly organized theories of the other analysts discussed in this Part.

Given the complexity of the human biological equipment and its flexible, creatively adaptive relationship to a complex human society, it seems to me that such pluralism is a theoretical necessity for psychological science. Broad groupings of recurrent phenomena (systems) offer the only means of scientific prediction. Many kinds of groupings are useful for different purposes, but the nature of the grouping used for prediction should be carefully examined.

Systems based on the essential relationship of man to his world, to himself and his fellow men, are always "true" to a large extent. This statement applies to many of the older profound philosophical and ethical systems, as well as to Adler, Horney, and Fromm. In fact the great merit of these analysts seems to me their correction of would-be scientific systems based on abstractions about faculties, instincts, reflexes, etc., in mechanically conceived relationship to social "laws." The Freud they criticize deserves criticism. The only question on this point is whether their target is the real Freud as he actually wrote, and as

he is now widely understood among Freudians, or a straw man who never quite existed except in the minds of some of his followers and enemies.

A true psychological science cannot be based on a theoretically comprehensive abstraction of man's possible relationships to his world. These are orienting concepts, *not* dynamic systems of intrinsic constellative power, rooted in the terms of the organism and of the milieu. Usefully corrective and inspiring for a time, very appealing to our desire to understand the human scene as the orderly working out of trends we can easily identify in ourselves and our friends, these orienting concepts are ultimately sterile and misleading if they are considered as *the* basic dynamic principles.

If one reads them attentively, both Sullivan and Freud avoid this kind of reductionist error. In the foregoing pages I have talked mainly about what Sullivan leaves out, and have suggested what Freud puts in if one reads him carefully and listens to the Freudian ego psychologists. My personal taste runs to the kind of *theorizing* Sullivan offers as basic—a repudiation of all instincts as identifiable abstracts, a radical insistence on the organism-milieu as a fundamental psychological principle. Freud's theory retains the primary quality of the instinctual drives in a more special sense than the one I suggested in comment on Chapter 3; his "institutions" lead easily to overinstitutionalization if their developmental character is lost sight of; the array of ego functions, mechanisms, etc., etc., becomes confusing. I feel that the cultural aspect of the organism-milieu complex is still insufficiently recognized by most Freudians.

Nevertheless at the present time the Freudian doctrine at its best seems to me more richly elaborated. It recognizes fundamental conceptual approaches more clearly, and deals more effectively with the problem of isolating the subsystems inherent in man's bodily structure and consequent orientation toward early experience. I prefer a certain cumbersomeness and confusion (and even the dangers of overinstitutionalization on some topics, in some minds) to the perils of reductionism arising from a streamlined theory. These perils Sullivan has not altogether escaped.

[1] A. Adler, *Social Interest*, Faber & Faber, 1938, p. 161.

[2] *Ibid.*, pp. 132*ff*.

[3] *Ibid.*, p. 256.

[4] *Ibid.*, p. 261.

[5] *Ibid.*, p. 255.

[6] *Ibid.*, p. 263.

[7] V. W. Einstein and R. Ryerson, "Psychodynamic Significance of the First Conscious Memory," *Bulletin of the Menninger Clinic*, 1951, *15*:213-220.

[8] H. L. Ansbacher, "Adler's Place Today in the Psychology of Memory," *Individual Psychology Bulletin*, 1947, 6:32-40.

[9] A. Adler, *op. cit.*, p. 93.

[10] R. Dreikurs, "A Child with Compulsive Neurosis," *Individual Psychology Bulletin*, 1947, 6, 137-141.

[11] A. Adler, *op. cit.*, p. 164.

[12] K. Horney, *New Ways in Psychoanalysis*, W. W. Norton & Co., 1939, p. 78.

[13] *Ibid.*

[14] *Ibid.*, p. 77.

[15] *Ibid.*, p. 150.

[16] *Ibid.*, pp. 150*f*.

[17] A. Adler, *op. cit.*, pp. 132*ff*.

[18] K. Horney, *Our Inner Conflicts*, W. W. Norton & Co., 1945, p. 32.

[19] I. A. R. Wylie, "And I Gave up Everything for You," *Reader's Digest*, October, 1949, 85-87.

[20] K. Horney, *The Neurotic Personality of Our Time*, W. W. Norton & Co., 1937, pp. 137*f*.

[21] ——, *Our Inner Conflicts*, pp. 56*f*.

[22] ——, *Neurosis and Human Growth*, W. W. Norton & Co., 1950.

[23] Personal discussion after reading this manuscript.

[24] E. Fromm, *Escape from Freedom*, Farrar & Rinehart, 1941, p. 157.

[25] ——, *Man for Himself*, Rinehart & Co., 1947, p. 219.

[26] ——, *Escape from Freedom*, p. 206.

[27] ——, *Man for Himself*, p. 88.

[28] *Ibid.*, p. 114.

[29] *Ibid.*, p. 79.

[30] *Ibid.*, p. 67.

[31] *Ibid.*, p. 81.

[32] *Cf.* D. Riesman, N. Glazer, and R. Denney, *The Lonely Crowd*, Yale University Press, 1950.

[33] E. Fromm, *Man for Himself*, p. 76.

[34] H. S. Sullivan, *Conceptions of Modern Psychiatry*, William Alanson White Foundation, 1947, p. 34.

[35] *Ibid.*, p. 39.

[36] *Ibid.*, pp. 39*f*.

[37] *Ibid.*, p. 40.

[38] *Ibid.*, p. 41.

[39] *Ibid.*, pp. 103*f*.

[40] *Ibid.*, p. 42.

[41] *Ibid.*

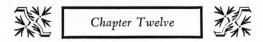

Chapter Twelve

PATHOLOGY AND

TREATMENT

THERAPY IS THE MAJOR CONCERN of analysts reported in this group, as it is among those discussed in Part II. In fact variations in theory have usually originated in variations in therapeutic approach rather than in the abstract points emphasized in a book dealing with schools of thought. Like Freud, these analysts often express indebtedness to their patients for insight into psychodynamics. To some extent the type of patient most commonly treated provides the focus for the theory. Freud began his work with hysterics. Although he modified his position as he worked with other types of mental disorder, his early observations remained crucial for a continued emphasis on repression and the Oedipus complex.

Adler very early extended his interest to more general problems of maladjustment. Horney and Fromm until quite recently treated *mainly* the character neuroses of the upper middle class. It must have been partly the success of psychoanalysis itself that brought to treatment a kind of patient who would merely have been considered "difficult"—or wicked or stupid—in Freud's early years. There seems also to have been an actual change in the type of pathological response to pressure since the days of Charcot → Freud, a change probably attributable to social changes.

These remarks preface the observation that none of the analysts discussed in Part III, except Sullivan, has dealt systematically *in print* with the problem of differential diagnosis among the syndromes of mental disorder recognized in psychiatry, or with the problem of differentiating relatively "normal" personality difficulties from severe mental disease. Indeed, the implication is often that the psychiatric classification operates as a positive handicap to a dynamic understanding of the very sick patient, and that the so-called normal person is often as neurotic as the patient who comes for treatment. We have seen that the environment may protect the neurosis, sheltering or even rewarding trends which the analyst would consider as pathological.

It should be emphasized that this paragraph applies only to the books that Horney and Fromm have written for a rather general public. In their private practice and in their teaching of young psychiatrists, they are alert to problems of differential diagnosis. Psychotic syndromes are identified as such and are *not* handled in the same manner as neurotic reactions. Psychoanalysis is *not* recommended to all comers regardless of the practical situation of the patient, and these analysts are much more wary of disturbing a reasonably good adjustment in the interests of full development of the human potential than many of their enthusiastic lay followers seem to suppose. This is my impression from personal dealings with these schools and from reading the list of courses offered by the teaching branch of the Horney group, the American Institute of Psychoanalysis.

PATHOLOGY

THE IDEAS of *Sullivan* monopolize the discussion of pathology in this section because he has written about it forthrightly. "My impression" is useful for a general statement but cannot be used as a basis for detailed reporting. Probably the other non-libido schools would share most of Sullivan's opinions on the applicability of psychoanalysis and its general relationship to other therapeutic approaches. Probably they will eventually offer in print a reinterpretation of the conventional psychiatric syndromes in terms of their own dynamic concepts. But I cannot here review ideas which I know only by word of mouth.

I shall discuss Sullivan's views under two headings: (1) Interpretation of the conventional psychiatric syndromes in a manner homologous with Chapter 7, on the Freudian interpretation of pathology. (2) Discussion of situations in which psychoanalysis as a therapeutic method cannot be recommended. This latter discussion has no counterpart in the Freudian section. My impression from reading and observation is that most "Freudians" as well as the non-libido analysts would essentially agree with Sullivan's practical formulations on this point.

Sullivan was trained in American psychiatry, with William Alanson White and Adolf Meyer rather than Freud as his early mentors. He remained much more closely involved with hospital work than did most psychoanalysts. Schizophrenia was a sort of specialty for him. He further developed an extensive consultation practice and was deeply concerned with teaching and with the selection of young candidates for training in psychiatry. This background and experience doubtless fostered a more focused interest in the problems discussed in this section than has been typical for psychoanalysts.*

PSYCHIATRIC SYNDROMES

Every psychiatrist recognizes recurrent psychiatric syndromes in approximately the same manner. The question to be discussed is Sullivan's interpretation of their psychological dynamics. Sullivan distinguishes generally between *substitutive processes* (roughly the neuroses) and *disintegrative processes* (roughly the psychoses). The general principle underlying his differentiation is the manner in which the self dynamism maintains—or fails to maintain—itself.

In *hysteria*[1] the major mechanism is amnesia, the technique of actually forgetting aspects of experience which provoke anxiety. This statement is directly reminiscent of the comment in Chapter 7 that the major mechanism is repression. Sullivan does not relate the specific development of this syndrome to difficulties in the phallic stage, of course, but he suggests that the *self-absorbed* individual (see pp. 485f.) is especially prone to this brand of pathology. The early *fantasy* reconstruction of the Good Mother becomes a life pattern

* The situation is changing rapidly as psychoanalysts are now appointed to directorships in hospitals and out-patient clinics, to psychiatric services in the armed forces, to professorships in medical schools, and to a host of other positions in which therapeutic responsibility goes far beyond intensive treatment of the patient on the couch. I think one may expect systematic discussion of these problems from many sources in the near future.

whereby the patient may see the world largely as he needs to for the security of his self system without the trouble of clear recollection and without recognizing the nature of his feelings. Furthermore, the bodily ailments of the hysteric, produced very freely, quite clearly serve his purposes in interpersonal relations in the manner so heavily emphasized by Adler.

In *obsessional states* the process is more complicated. "The trouble arises from a very early, if not a lifelong, condition of profound insecurity. This has been made endurable by the perpetuation and refinement of personal magic, lineally descended from the late infantile and early verbal stages of personality development."[2] (This would correspond roughly with the anal period suggested by the Freudians.) These patients, too, engage in serious parataxic distortion, but never on the simple basis of "forgetting." On the contrary, there is very little dissociated discharge of impulse even in dreams, and their frequent somatic disorders seem to be the unhappy consequence of severe inner tension rather than devices to control others and to maintain the untrammeled security supplied by the fantasized Good Mother. It is profoundly necessary for them to feel in control of themselves and of others at all times and to be "right" in all matters. Making a mistake, being criticized, is intolerable to their fundamentally low self-esteem and must be countered by all sorts of rationalizations in which a ruminative verbal magic or compulsive ritual plays an important role. Because of their need to maintain their own security-giving view of the world, they may quite seriously misinterpret the behavior of other people, but more as a distortion than as an actual forgetting of a reasonably accurate perception such as may be observed in the hysteric.

Psychopathy has already been mentioned (p. 485) as a failure in the integration of the self dynamism for reasons which Sullivan feels are still obscure.

As for *psychosis*, Sullivan retains the old term dementia praecox, simple type, for "an organic, degenerative disease usually of insidious development."[3] The outlook is poor. He thinks that there is a truly distinct, unrelated condition for which he would prefer to reserve the term schizophrenia.* This is a state which he considers primarily a disorder of living. Usually "schizophrenia"

---

* The distinction is not generally maintained by psychiatrists. Usually the terms dementia praecox and schizophrenia are used interchangeably. Many psychiatrists now use the term "process" schizophrenia rather than dementia praecox to refer to the organic, disintegrative disease. Few would disagree with Sullivan in the basic distinction he draws, although many, including Sullivan, would question whether the two conditions are quite so *unrelated* as my sentence implies. It would be more correct to say that the relationship is not understood at present.

is of more or less acute onset and is experienced by the patient as a severe disruption of his world. The outlook for recovery is better, although at times the final dénouement is hardly distinguishable from that of dementia praecox. What happens seems to be a real failure of the self dynamism to maintain its functional unity. Repressed aspects of the personality are released from dissociation. They may be experienced as external to the self in an hallucinatory way. The patient may fall into the profound schizophrenic state of *catatonia,* in which he loses all sense of himself as a personality with limited needs, desires, and responsibilities and becomes the scene of a cosmic struggle between opposing forces. Like Freud, Sullivan considers this state deeply *regressive.* It harks back to the infantile polarization of experience as the Good and the Bad Mother, with whatever coloring the patient may have absorbed through religious teaching. The patient feels that it is terribly necessary—and impossible—to understand this cosmos and to take action. But since he can in no way adequately "understand," his state takes two forms: almost total immobility (stupor) in which he literally inhibits all action, and the wildest, most undirected excitement (catatonic rage).

However dramatic to the onlooker and painful to the patient, this state is the least dangerous of the schizophrenic maneuvers. The patient usually comes out of it, sooner or later, and may return to his old career-line (life style) without any great change. The episode may remain quite isolated. This result is most likely when some actual event has sharply overburdened the self dynamism, and when the patient is able to find a way of life relatively protected from the kind of hazard *his* security mechanism finds intolerable. In some cases, a loving home without responsibility may, for example, reinstate all the old anxieties whereas the patient may make out well in circumstances most of us would consider more harassing. This is a distinctly individual matter, requiring careful study of the personality dynamics behind the psychotic episode. It is not a problem that can be solved by general recommendations for after-care. Too often relapse occurs because the patient and his family joyfully resume life exactly where it was interrupted by the psychosis, too often merely with intensified anxiety about relationships whose anxiety-provoking character *for the patient* led to impossible dissociation and psychotic break originally.

According to Sullivan (and I think most psychiatrists would agree), the most ominous phase of the psychosis sets in when the patient's self system begins a "constructive" resolution of the intolerable problem of disintegration before there has been full restitution of the pre-psychotic state. The patient may reorganize the self system by suppressing all negative or doubt-provoking instances, and by bolstering an inherently inadequate account of experience with rationalizations in the service of building up a new sense of integration.[4] Thus *paranoid* trends appear. Since they offer a kind of solution for his desperate distress, the patient is very likely to maintain and develop them. Therapeutic intervention becomes increasingly difficult, not because the patient is "happy" in his delusions, but because any port in a storm is a good one and the patient is deeply afraid of starting forth again on the open seas.

Another outcome (and one to which the paranoid solutions are likely to come eventually) is *hebephrenic dilapidation*. The storm of catatonia is indeed over, and eventually the patient gives up the effort to interpret life on his own overpersonalized terms. The remnants of the self dynamism continue to function in a manner which seems to the onlooker merely absurd. Silly mannerisms appear which, Sullivan remarks, are not purposive in themselves but are futile, compulsive leftovers from the pre-psychotic state. The patient is not only seclusive but retreats in terror from any *real* invitation to human intercourse. He may like to be with his fellows, but only when the fellowship in no way challenges his personal view of the world, which has become very narrow and very fragmentary.

Sullivan suggests that what happens here is that the organized self dynamism becomes the *repressed* part of the personality, in direct contrast to the state of affairs in normal life and in the substitutive processes of neurosis. It is just as painful for the hebephrenic to become aware of the healthy, socialized meanings of his manneristic behavior as for the normal or neurotic person to become aware of the dissociated significance of his small mannerisms and unconsidered mistakes. In both cases the pursuit of security, the avoidance of anxiety, is paramount. But there has been a radical shift in direction. The hebephrenic is not simply pursuing universal human needs in an odd, regressively infantile fashion. As the psychotic condition becomes firmly established, he pursues more and more the aspects of his living that were previously dissociated. Having made something of an adjustment on this level (albeit one that often requires outside care even to preserve life), he becomes again acutely anxious when any aspects of the highly organized self dynamism are again called into play. Treating him like a well person, interpreting the normal aspects of his behavior, is likely to provoke an anxiety reaction in much the same way as overdirect interpretation of the aims of the dissociated aspects of the neurotic adjustment provokes anxiety.

Sullivan here attempts to interpret the symptoms of deteriorated psychosis in a new way, much as Freud once attempted to explain hysterical symptoms —except that the process goes in reverse, as it were. The oddity of symptoms is to be explained by the repression (not the loss) of highly organized aspects of the personality. The process is not simply one of regression, with adventitious retention of fragments of past experience and massive restitutive effort at a narcissistic level. These theoretical statements (see pp. 290f.) express the final adaptive measures of the personality, but they fail to take account of what happens by the way. It is difficult, perhaps impossible, to penetrate the world of the established hebephrenic, but Sullivan suggests that we may at least understand better the nature of his problem and the meaning of his symptoms if we understand what he is repressing—that is, precisely the self dynamism, which causes so much trouble for the neurotic and which is the main glory of mankind when it matures successfully.

This "self" is never considered a given attribute of the organism regardless of experience but an emergent system which never fully encompasses the personality. The emergent system remains profoundly operative even in its eclipse. The hebephrenic regresses to a state very like early infancy, but he does not learn as an infant does. On the contrary every forward step awakens the *repressed* self dynamism and causes intolerable anxiety. Every human participation which might be understood at a higher level becomes a severe threat. Therapy is not a matter of patiently starting all over again with an infant mind. It is a matter of getting the patient to accept his own self dynamism as a less terrifying thing—in a way, just the obverse of bringing the neurotic patient to awareness of dissociated trends in himself.

Critical Comment

AS a layman writing for laymen, I hesitate to take a critical stance on problems of psychiatric diagnosis, and I urge that the following remarks be envisaged as tentative. With this caution to the reader, I suggest that what is wrong with Sullivan's account of the neuroses is precisely his omission of the important sexual dynamisms, the superego, and perhaps "my" self image dynamism as explained at the end of the preceding chapter. In writing about Sullivan's view of hysteria, I was puzzled about how to relate the fantasy Good Mother of the hysteric, as a person "self-absorbed" from way back, to the fantasies of the schizophrenic. What is the etiological and dynamic difference? Freud does give an answer of sorts—the "Good Mother" of the hysteric is still an infantile construct, but the construct of the Oedipal period, *not* the crib fantasy in its all-pervasiveness, as one encounters it in catatonia. In his discussion of the obsessive-compulsive states, Sullivan comes rather closer to Freud, I would think, with a valid emphasis on general relations with the parents—but I also think with serious neglect of the constellative importance of anal drive-systems per se. The basic psychological mechanisms Sullivan describes are the same as those emphasized by Freud. They seem less adequately interpreted, and in a rather left-handed way, as if he were working out a theory in areas he did not care very much about. As long as it worked pretty well, that was enough.

Sullivan cared about schizophrenia, and it may be that the excellent concept of the self dynamism arose mainly out of his experience with this group, in which disintegration of the self dynamism seems to be the major dynamic feature. It is interesting that the Freudian who has written about the "ego" as an *experience* whose *felt* boundaries must be considered (Federn, see p. 103) also based his approach on the study of psychotics.

The diagnostic term, "schizophrenia," is being used so widely nowadays, and in such different ways, as almost to supersede "neurosis" as a catch-all term for disordered function. A few people are already saying that the other psychoses and the neuroses are merely subdivisions of schizophrenia—a statement which I think means only that all serious illness may be considered as essentially a damage to the self dynamism.

This formulation has great allure. Nevertheless the problem remains as to why and how some people manage to stay essentially normal, or to develop special devices, commonly known as "neuroses," which still somehow preserve the basic relationship of their self dynamism to their outside world. Psychiatry is a long way from possessing the answer to this problem. In my opinion the Freudian view of the structure of the major neuroses is more soundly differentiated than Sullivan's, because it takes into account more effectively the significant subsystems typically developed in childhood in consequence of the biological equipment of the infant and his quasi-necessary relations to the ministering adults.

I suggested earlier that the nonsexual systems might well be studied in their own right and in their relationship to a self image or images probably more directly influenced by broad cultural factors than the superego, and in varying relationship to it. Perhaps such investigation, plus focused study of the *economic* approach which Freud himself calls neglected, would greatly assist in answering the question as to who falls ill to the extent of severe pathology, in what special circumstances; and why one type of illness appears rather than another. Constitutional factors or factors related essentially to the "interosystems" (see p. 112) also require study, but such study requires collaborative effort between specialists in the physiological and the psychological aspects of the human organism.

SITUATIONS IN WHICH PSYCHOANALYSIS
IS NOT RECOMMENDED

In discussing the handling of pathology by means *other than* the very specific method of treatment known as psychoanalysis, I shall quote Sullivan exclusively, but my impression is that most analysts, including the Freudians, would essentially agree with his position.[5] Diagnostic guide lines would, of course, be *stated* differently according to the different basic theories.

After discussing the course of initial interviews with prospective analytic patients, Sullivan writes as follows:

This optimum performance with patients is not always desirable. One encounters some situations in these consultations that forbid the frank expression of certain conclusions as to the mental disorder present. Quite aside from rationalizing his inadequate performances, the psychiatrist realizes that it is futile, fool-hardy, or actually viciously irresponsible to undermine any patient's security when one can offer nothing that will promptly be constructive.[6]

Sullivan discounts the alleged harmful effects of psychoanalysis in the hands of a competent practitioner, but he comments on the high aims and great cost in time (usually correlated with money) of such intensive treatment. Of the great numbers of people who feel there is something wrong with their lives, he remarks: "For most of these patients, the psychiatrist has to compromise with the ideal of cure and proceed along the line of *amelioration*" (my italics).[7]

Sullivan points out the responsibility of the psychiatrist to use his total knowledge for all of the people whom he encounters professionally. An all-too common type of patient is the severely ill person, often borderline psychotic, whose limiting defenses nevertheless allow him fairly adequate function in limited situations. Another type is the almost-normal person whose special aims are neurotically determined and are likely to lead to special difficulties. Sullivan cites here the hypothetical case of a promising young doctor who would like to become a psychiatrist. The position he aspires to will place him in a position in which he can exercise power over other people in a confined interpersonal situation. The elder psychiatrist may feel that the aspirant's personality is not sufficiently mature to allow such potential power with true benefit to prospective patients, that the impulse toward this particular professional aim has its roots in a somewhat exaggerated "pursuit of security" on the part of the prospective psychiatrist. Nevertheless Sullivan urges that it is the business of the elder psychiatrist to discover some other valid orientation of interest in the young doctor and to attempt to phrase his rejection for psychiatry in such a manner as to forward advance in another direction.* [8]

In general Sullivan points out the special delicacy and skill required in cases in which the aim of therapy is *amelioration* rather than cure. There must be a very careful evaluation of the organization of the self system (diagnosis) on the one hand, and on the other a responsible consideration of

---

* This example is already somewhat dated because in recent years the flood of applicants for psychoanalytic training has so very far exceeded facilities for the necessary carefully individualized instruction that group procedures in selection have become necessary—and the rejected candidate can more easily align himself with other rejectees, and himself evaluate his rejection in less devastating personal terms. Institutionalization of these problems makes them more exasperating in many ways, and less accessible to the direct evaluation of interpersonal factors—but in a way easier to bear. The applicant nowadays knows that rejection must be made on limited, comparative grounds. He is therefore not so deeply threatened "personally" by rejection, or so totally dependent on what a specific senior professional has to say. The responsibility of the elder psychiatrist is lessened, but by no means wholly dissolved.

the actual resources available for therapy. Intensive therapy will not be recommended if suitable practitioners are not to be found for the type of problem presented, at the rate the patient could be expected to pay, in his locality, etc., without impossibly severe dislocation of his life situation.

Far from merely attempting to gain and give as much insight as possible in a few interviews, the psychiatrist must recognize that the interview itself has impressive implications for the patient which must be considered therapeutically. "Objective" questioning readily arouses either resentment or sudden insights with which the patient may not be able to cope. Sullivan urges that the psychiatrist consider himself a *participant observer* in a special kind of interpersonal relationship in which by virtue of his training and attitude he is able to observe with greater clarity what the patient makes of the situation parataxically, and to lead the patient adroitly to talk of other situations, past and present, which will clarify the nature of the parataxic distortion. It is the business of the psychiatrist to determine whether it is desirable to help the patient to become aware of dissociated trends in himself, or whether—as part of the *alleviative* approach—it is desirable actually to forestall awareness and direct the patient toward a more expedient type of sublimation.

Often a rather partial awareness may be encouraged, along with energetic encouragement of a new formulation. Thus a patient at the breaking point because hostility toward a loved parent can no longer be adequately dissociated may be encouraged to awareness of the hostility, but may also be told that it is a quite general phenomenon, and definitely aided toward expedient handling of the current relationship with the parent. Often some interpretation of the *parent's* behavior may help him, by allowing the patient a new sense of understanding tolerance instead of a dissociated battle, and may reduce "unnecessary exchanges of hostility."[9]

Apparently Sullivan considers all the old staples of superficial therapy as part of the valid armamentarium of the psychiatrist dealing with the problem of amelioration: partial interpretation, rest, change of scene or occupation, hobbies, even drugs—*provided they are used with insight by the psychiatrist.* The one thing he does not approve of is the generalized "bucking up" approach. His reasons for rejecting this popular approach give the clue to why he does accept the others. "Bucking up" applied to the self dynamism as a whole merely exacerbates problems due to the already excessive efforts of the self dynamism to preserve its unifying function by keeping large areas of the personality dissociated. Pathology arises when one or another dissociated area becomes unduly insistent in its demands, beyond the power of the self system to handle it. Thus "bucking up" as such is like belaboring a tired horse for a final spurt. The other approaches take account of the specific problems of the tired self dynamism and are designed to relieve its specific burdens.

The recommendations must be appropriate to the burden. The general recommendation to relax and play a few rounds of golf to a man whose self dynamism—whose concept of security—is built around a quite special interpersonal focus is as inappropriate as trying to cure an ailing or refractory horse off his feed with silken reins and caviar. But enforced rest via a prescribed vacation, drugs, shock, or certain types of therapy which "enfeeble" the self dynamism may *in some cases* avert a crisis and allow the hard-pressed self time to recover its bearings. A medically prescribed vacation in Florida can hope for success only if the patient *can be prepared for* a fairly radical temporary break with his whole involved self dynamism. Otherwise he merely carries his problems with him and may be further harassed by increased difficulties in his business and financial affairs, plus the possible resentment of his associates who have had to carry on at home under difficulties to make possible the patient's vacation.

Thus Sullivan states that deliberate "enfeeblement" of the self dynamism may at times be a good recourse—or at least the best recourse available. It should always be considered in relation to the interpersonal situation. The quasi-relaxation of the typical prescribed vacation is usually irrelevant to the major problem, as is use of drugs on a continuing basis. The psychiatrist deliberately enfeebles the total self system only when he feels that it will recover its power after a respite—or when limited function seems the only feasible solution of a difficult personal or social problem.

Appropriately selected hobbies and sports may allow for sublimated expression of dissociated trends which are threatening to become so strong as to disrupt the self system. Aspects of the self which are condemned in serious work and close family relationships are socially sanctioned in games and may be *played* out rather openly, thus relieving the self of some of the task of repression.

Critical Comment

ALTHOUGH Sullivan sees no *danger* in the psychoanalysis of any individual by a competent therapist, he points out that the method is often inexpedient. No suitable analyst may be available in the patient's community. The expense in money and time may be greater than the patient or his family can afford without serious dislocation of their lives, with no guarantee of full success in many cases. In point of fact the number of properly trained analysts now available, each able to handle a maximum of eight to ten patients a day, is a drop in the bucket compared to the number of people who need treatment.

It is not within the province of this book to discuss other types of treatment in detail. It has seemed important to suggest, via Sullivan's remarks, how the understanding of the psychoanalyst may be used to *evaluate the patient's needs and resources* in situations in which psychoanalysis is inexpedient. The analyst may then use the technique of giving partial insight with hard-headed reassurance and advice; he may recommend drugs, a vacation, hobbies, at times a new job orientation—almost any of the prescriptions offered by lay advisers in variety. The difference is that the trained analyst may understand more quickly and more deeply than the lay adviser what ails the patient and may therefore make more specific prescriptions.

When one of my friends was in such a jam about his domestic affairs that he was finding it hard to work at his job, I referred him to an analyst—it happened to be Horney—for consultation. He had just had the offer of a more responsible, more remunerative job, which he hesitated to accept when he could not even handle the job he had. After a couple of interviews which my friend describes as just shooting off his mouth about his worries—"I even cried! Me!"—Horney said quietly: "I think you ought to take the new job. You clearly have the ability for it. It's a pity to waste such ability." She added: "You're very close to the people you are working with now. Would you perhaps feel humiliated that they know about your family

problems and are kind to you because of your troubles? You've always handled your work well before, but nobody can work well without self-confidence. The new job will take you away from the part of you that is hurt by the family situation. I think you will like its challenge." He took the job, made out well on it, and managed rather better at home.

I am here summarizing what my friend told me in bits. Horney doubtless told it to him in bits, although she seems to have given him a sort of summary at the end—some good phrases to take away with him. I cite this example partly because it shows an aspect of *Horney's* approach that does not emerge clearly in her writings about psychoanalysis, but mainly to illustrate the importance of deeper knowledge in a superficial, advisory relationship. The key question here was whether to put more "job" burdens on a man already faltering at his job. We all know that it sometimes helps, but sometimes the man goes to pieces altogether. The psychoanalyst is in a better position to discover what the extra work will mean to the person— intolerable burden, refuge, perhaps opportunity for a constructive expansion all along the line. Horney *in this case* gave straightforward advice, coupled with strong reassurance and a dash of insight, enough to keep the man from blathering about his personal affairs in the new situation, enough for him to see his job as a rather separate aspect of his life which he and his family should respect. Other cases require different handling, with all the techniques mentioned by Sullivan and more. The question is when to use them, a question to be decided only by informed evaluation of the deeper trends.

TREATMENT

PSYCHOANALYSIS AS A SPECIFIC THERAPEUTIC METHOD is not to be confused with psychoanalytic theory, or with other types of therapeutic procedure carried out by psychoanalysts as discussed in the preceding pages. All schools make this distinction, including Adler, who is at pains to make clear that his therapy is *not* psychoanalysis. Like the Freudians, Horney, Fromm, Sullivan, and their associates consider psychoanalysis an intensive, time-consuming method of treatment with the high aim of fundamental reorganization of the pathological personality. This aim is recognized as different from curing symptoms or helping the patient to adjust better in his particular life situation on a limited basis (Sullivan's "ameliorative techniques"; the Freudian psycho-analytically oriented psychotherapy). In the following pages I shall discuss Adler's position briefly, and then attempt to report the treatment procedures of the other analysts discussed in Part III.

All good analytic work is actually centered around the patient, not around a theory. The various therapeutic techniques are flexibly applied in accordance with the special requirements of each case and are somewhat modified by each analyst in accordance with his own temperament. Since much the same ground is covered by every "theory," it is inevitable that there should be a great deal of overlapping in practice.

Thus it has seemed preferable to emphasize the wide similarity in thera-peutic approach and to show the differences piecemeal against this general background, than to write discrete accounts which would artificially exag-gerate the importance of variations in theory. While it cannot be entirely accurate, the impression of an observer in fairly close contact with analysts of many schools would seem to offer a truer picture of the actual conduct of treatment than a compilation of theoretical statements.

ADLER'S THERAPY

Adler does not write systematically about his treatment procedures. I know no Adlerians whom I could canvass on the matter. "My impression" is here based on fragmentary published material and the comments of a few knowledgeable friends who had closer contact with Individual Psychology in its heyday. Adler writes as follows:

> Individual psychology considers the essence of therapy to lie in making the patient aware of his lack of co-operative power, and to convince him of the origin of this lack in early childhood maladjustments. What passes during this process is no small matter; his power of co-operation is enhanced by collaboration with the doctor. His "inferiority complex" is revealed as erroneous. Courage and optimism are awakened. And the "meaning of life" dawns upon him as the fact that proper meaning must be given to life.[10]

The keynote of Adler's therapy seems to be (1) helping the patient toward understanding of his life style (the Adlerian equivalent of the "insight" to be discussed later in this chapter as the crux of psychoanalytic therapy), (2) a warmly encouraging attitude on the part of the therapist, and (3) help to the patient in finding concrete ways of reorienting himself toward greater social interest, perhaps by a change of situation, more often by a different attitude toward the situation he is in, plus such outside learning as might help him advance realistically, or such outside hobbies as might give him valid satisfactions.

Understanding (insight) meant for Adler understanding of the special devices the person employs for attaining the goal of superiority. He was well aware of the multifarious forms such devices may take, but he thought of them as variations around this central theme. Furthermore he thought of them primarily in terms of the life style of the patient, as reflected in his actual behavior over his whole span of life. In an appendix to the late book *Social Interest*, Adler offers a detailed questionnaire about the life history of the patient—for the orientation of the therapist. In the same manner as many contemporary "psychologists," but somewhat earlier and quite independently, Adler hit upon the idea of using the questionnaire not so much for the correct answer to a series of questions or for a general "score" on predefined aspects of the personality, as for the significant *patterns of behavior* that become visible to the informed clinician if he can learn enough about many separate small items. The therapist gains understanding—and uses his understanding in helping the patient.

Just how such understanding is to be used is not explained in detail. Adler did not have a naive trust in the immediate goodness of every person who comes along. After all, if Jean Valjean was lucky to meet the priest in *Les Misérables*, the priest was equally lucky to meet a criminal whose deep trends allowed this kind of total reversal. Most criminals and most people with characterological or neurotic problems do not respond so simply to an act of trust. The therapist must temper his *warmth and encouragement* with understanding of the special problems of the patient, and must bring the patient to the same understanding.

A friend, himself a psychoanalyst, tells me about attending a case seminar conducted by Adler years ago in which a delinquent boy was "bedevilled" by Adler into acknowledging with tears that he had done wrong. I am quoting a hostile witness, but on cross-examination it seemed clear that Adler's aim was to cut through the boy's erroneous life style and then invite a new one. I use this example to show that Adler's emphasis on warmth and encouragement was no namby-pamby "bucking up" treatment. His procedure could involve the most painful recognition of one's mistakes and realistic limitations. Indeed, such recognition was stringently required. Furthermore, it reached far back into childhood and extended to the patient's current activities as related to his social life, his vocation, and his love for his intimate associates.

But Adler did not expect cure to follow merely as a result of this new insight. Equally important was the positive experience of love in the relationship with the therapist, and the positive appreciation the patient obtained for any advance toward a more realistic evaluation of himself and toward more genuine social feeling. Adler does not discuss the "transference" as elaborately as the other authors reported in Parts II and III, but he was clearly aware of its importance. The experience of "collaboration" with the doctor is envisaged as therapeutic along with and even beyond the intellectual understanding toward which the patient is guided.

It is not clear how far Adler recommended direct advice to the patient in the conduct of his life. Certainly new endeavor was encouraged, and the patient was actively supported in his efforts toward greater "social interest." In fact an ex-patient (an asthmatic who later went to a Freudian) tells me that the *prescription* of greater social interest became something of a burden to him—an image of what he ought to be considerably beyond what he could achieve at that time. It is very likely that many patients derived much profit from active support by the therapist of their new ventures into more realistic handling of their problems in all spheres: social, work, and love. Some pressure toward such effort is often therapeutically useful.

In summary, although Adler emphasized the importance of understanding in therapy, he also emphasized the importance of the direct experience of love, appreciation, and *collaboration* in the therapeutic situation. The therapist loves and appreciates the patient for what he is, not for his neurotic strivings, and so reassures him during the difficult period of transition from the faulty life style to a life style in which social feeling and common sense hold sway. The therapist supports the patient in new ventures—indeed, holds out new ideals.

Critical Comment

IT seems to me that Adler's therapy has the merits and defects of his theory. The great merit is appreciation of the patient as a *person* who is constantly adjusting to the demands of his own life situation and whose future requires such adjustment. Past, present, and future are clearly aligned, and made a vivid part of the treatment.

The defect is what I prefer to call reductionism rather than over simplification. "Insight" here means insight into the endless complications of the inferiority complex, a limitation already discussed at length. Instead of criticizing Adler myself about the essential relationship between patient and analyst, I refer the reader to the long discussion of analyst-patient relationships (transference) as envisaged by the other analysts discussed in Part III and by Freud. It seems clear that Adler tends to ignore aspects of the therapeutic situation emphasized by all of the other analysts, notably the "neutrality" of the analyst as a person participating in the life problems of the patient, with explicit recognition of the varying roles the analyst plays.

Adler himself wished to separate his approach from "psychoanalysis." The very direct relationship between doctor and patient suggested in his therapy is certainly *often* very helpful. Yet it is premised on a limited view of insight and tends to merge the social values of the therapist, however generally stated, with the emerging values of the patient. My friend felt a therapeutic *prescription* toward a way of life he could not realize at that point. For him the therapist re-inforced an already overactive superego and burdened him with further self-doubts at precisely the points at which he needed help—*i.e.*, his general social relations. The proposed encouragement had the effect of increasing the contempt he already felt for his shyness. With the heightened tension of trying to meet the therapeutic prescription, his psychosomatic symptoms grew more severe as the treatment progressed.

The analyst of any school may use the essential features of Adler's therapy in treating *some* of his patients. Perhaps one may go so far as to say that psychotherapists are only now beginning to understand the value of the mixture of insight, experience-with-the-therapist, encouragement, and direct help which Adler proposed long ago. Social workers and psychologists engaged in psychotherapy require some such orientation toward their task. Too often psychoanalysts have approached problems of brief or superficial therapy with condescension, not realizing the special problems involved when one tries to help the patient without the analytic couch and the long labor of psychoanalysis. Here Adler is again a forerunner.

The difficulty is that Individual Psychology was conceived as a complete therapy, applicable to all conditions, and as achieving the same results as psychoanalysis. The best defense of the other analytic schools is further explanation of what they mean by *analysis as a special method* which cannot be supplanted by good psychotherapy. Sullivan's discussion of ameliorative methods suggests the growing sense of responsibility among analysts for helping many patients by other means. But the more thoroughly this point is recognized, the more sharply the goals and techniques of "psychoanalysis" are defined. The method may be considered inexpedient for any given patient for a variety of reasons. It is subject to considerable variation from school to school, from one analyst to another, from one patient to another. It is difficult to define precisely.

Nevertheless I think the reader will have no trouble in seeing the difference between the kind of treatment problem discussed from here on and the more general problem of helping the patient. The fervent aim of *psychoanalysis* is to help the patient help himself by change at a quite fundamental level. Here direct encouragement and practical help are inadequate, because the deep unconscious layers of the personality are untouched.

PSYCHOANALYSIS AS A THERAPY: HORNEY, FROMM, AND SULLIVAN

In spite of the loudly proclaimed differences in therapeutic approach among the analytic schools, it is difficult to formulate very clear-cut distinctions, once psychoanalysis has been accepted as a specific therapeutic method. The classical Freudians tend to consider the schools now under consideration "superficial" in their neglect of the libidinal roots of behavior and of aggression as an instinctual drive. The non-libido analysts tend to write as though contemporary Freudians worked entirely in terms of the release of infantile repressions and the Oedipus complex, in a mood of pessimistic, cynical defeatism. The later reports of Freud, the very widespread concern with ego psychology, even the work of Alexander, French, and their associates (which seems to approach the position of this group of analysts) are scarcely mentioned. Honor is done to Freud's basic concepts, as described in Chapter 2, but report of "recent developments in psychoanalysis" is confined almost exclusively to the point of view presented in this Part.*

So far as I can see, the only really sharp distinction between the group of analysts presented in this chapter and the analysts I have called "Freudian" is the one that dictated my groupings—that is, the repudiation of the constellative power of the sexual instincts and aggression per se. Even this distinction becomes tenuous in practice because the "Freudian" does not often

---

* Authors creatively presenting their own ideas are entitled to selectivity in reporting the work of others. Such omissions are less understandable in books purporting to survey the development of "psychoanalysis." (Cf. P. Mullahy, *Oedipus—Myth and Complex*, Hermitage Press, 1948, and C. Thompson, *Psychoanalysis: Evolution and Development*, Hermitage House, 1950.) The reader may also wish to consider a compilation of psychoanalytic points of view written with the objectivity of a nonparticipant "psychologist" and supplemented by references to a large number of scientifically controlled studies in the various areas selected as significant by psychoanalysts: G. S. Blum, *Psychoanalytic Theories of Personality*, McGraw-Hill Book Co., 1953.

interpret the patient's problems *to the patient* as orality, anal sadism, etc., however he thinks about them, and however he reports his thinking to colleagues. He is fully aware of the therapeutic assignment of talking to the patient in terms the patient can understand and accept. "Freudian" interpretation mostly follows a common-sense vocabulary hardly different from that of other schools. It often uses the same materials and draws much the same conclusions. It is not necessary to talk about "orality" in discussing dependency needs. Conversely, the non-libido authors have never denied that pregenital and early genital experiences *may* be crucially important for some individuals and are always of interest.

But one can go only so far in minimizing differences. As we have noted earlier, the Freudian finds his *major orientation* to the problems of the patient in the constellation of instinctual drives (sexual and aggressive), and he tries ultimately to bring the patient to constructive awareness of these drives, *as currently operating*, despite distortion and repression. Analyzing the "ego" is so important as to take up most of the time of analysis, but recognition of the basic "id" materials and the basic infantile story is still considered fundamental. Talking to fellow analysts, Freud comments that we analyze "now a fragment of the id and now a fragment of the ego."[11] The schools discussed in this Part more or less radically discount the "id" and consider that the person is treated completely if one handles fully what the Freudians call his "ego functions." Hence the allegation of "superficiality" on the one side, and on the other the feeling that the truly significant aspects of the personality are finally being recognized.

DIFFERENCES IN TECHNIQUE

The *techniques* employed in full psychoanalysis by these schools are roughly similar to those described in Chapter 7 but are probably applied somewhat less rigorously. Like Alexander, these analysts emphasize that the label "psychoanalysis" should rest not upon technicalities of procedure but upon the type of material elicited and the nature of the therapeutic process. So long as a profound restructuring of the personality takes place and the central core of the neurosis is handled, the label is deemed appropriate. As a rule this change is not possible without a very intensive approach, extending over a period of at least a year, usually much longer.

Fromm-Reichmann* positively recommends seeing most patients three times a week instead of five. According to her experience, seeing the patient more often does not hasten the cure, which seems intrinsically to demand

---

* Most of the judgments quoted from Fromm-Reichmann in this chapter are taken from her excellent book, *Principles of Intensive Psychotherapy,* University of Chicago Press, 1950. Page references are not given.

many months or years of collaborative work on the patient's problems. Patients with some talent for introspection, however, appear able to carry on the work outside the office with little guidance from the therapist. A few individuals are apparently able to proceed with genuine psychoanalysis on a once-a-week basis. This is rare. Some patients *require* five sessions.

This is Fromm-Reichmann's judgment. Although other analysts in these schools are less forthright in considering three sessions a week as *optimal* procedure, they seem more willing to accept such a compromise as a practical necessity than the classical Freudians, and to believe that true psychoanalysis *may* be conducted under these conditions.

Fromm-Reichmann also positively recommends that the patient sit up, facing the analyst. Other analysts seem to consider the couch as the method of choice but are probably more willing to permit variations than the "Freudians."

Possibly these analysts are somewhat less rigorous about prohibiting social or professional contact between analyst and patient outside of the office (I believe this statement is especially appropriate for Fromm) but they all recommend against such contact. My impression is that the analyst is encouraged to a more positively friendly, sympathetic approach, and that the taboo against offering practical advice is somewhat less stringent. Probably personality differences among analysts are more determining on this point than school affiliation. The point will be discussed further on pages 521*ff*.

Nevertheless there is strong emphasis on keeping the role of the analyst well structured outside the hubbub of the patient's immediate life problems. Bids for sympathy, tendencies to rely on advice, and all efforts at personal involvement with the analyst are *analyzed* when the patient is ready for it. There is essentially no abatement in the ideal of objectivity but there is more *explicit* acknowledgment of the fact that the patient may interpret objectivity as hostile criticism or whatever and may at times need positive expression of sympathy, appreciation, etc., in order to continue the task of therapy. The doctor himself must fully recognize the difference between the analytic situation and the real-life situation and must ultimately bring the patient to such realization. He cannot, as analyst, play the role of benign father, big brother, or even wise doctor. His essential task is to help the patient confront himself and work out a better personal integration independent of the analyst.

Related to this *controlled* relaxation of the Freudian insistence on the objectivity of the analyst is perhaps a somewhat greater concern with finding the right analyst for the patient. The most orthodox Freudians have always paid common-sense attention to the problem of referring patients to analysts likely to handle their particular illness, personality type, or even cultural background especially well. In recent years some classical Freudians, notably

Oberndorf,[12] have urged the need for more focused recognition of this problem, with practical recommendations for more frequent consultation with colleagues when treatment seems to bog down too long or encounter other difficulties. It is by no means unusual for an analyst of any school to recommend change to another analyst when the patient seems settled in some line of resistance which the analyst cannot break.

Probably one may say that the more the psychoanalytic approach emphasizes examination of the reaction patterns of the patient in the current life situation, the more important it becomes that the analyst be able to understand very directly the patient's value systems, the cultural background of his attitudes, his modes of verbal expression, even his personality make-up. Although the analyst must always be on guard against overidentification with the patient (see Fromm-Reichmann's careful discussion of this point[13]), there can be little doubt that the analytic work proceeds better when the analyst as a person is well equipped to understand the special problems of the patient. I would add that this therapeutic compatibility is not necessarily established along the lines expected by outsiders. The patient who hates women may respond especially well to treatment by the right woman. The patient who ardently and narrowly believes in "America first" may find a Jewish refugee more effective therapeutically than a conventionally accepted Aryan. Initial dislike of the analyst often gives way not only to respect but also to a deep sense of compatibility in later sessions.

Such variations are familiar, but up to now no school has attempted to *codify* judgments as to allocation of patients to specific analysts. The problem remains in the realm of judgment based on the experience of the alert analyst with his colleagues as well as with his patients. Thus far one can say only that the analysts discussed in this Part have formulated the problem more explicitly, but I think in practice not very far beyond the common-sense judgment of any psychoanalyst.

Procedures during the analytic session. Discussion of these relatively external conditions of psychoanalysis merges into *procedures during the analytic hour.* Generally speaking all the avenues of information and the techniques presented in Chapters 2 and 7 are used by psychoanalysts in this group as well as by the Freudians. I should like to repeat that every analyst of whatever school tailors his technical approach to the needs of the patient, and every analyst tends to develop special sensitivity to one or another avenue of information, usually on the basis of his own temperament and experience. What I present in the following pages is the characteristic emphasis of the school rather than a clear-cut distinction. I follow here the outline of techniques used in Chapter 7 for discussion of "Freudian" treatment.

Free association. The technique of free association was presented as a basic method of psychoanalysis, following Freud's initial discoveries. I think most "Freudians" still consider it fundamental, although I attempted in Chapter 7 to suggest how "Freudians" alert themselves to abuse of the technique by some types of patient, by most patients at some stages of their analysis. Probably it plays a subsidiary role in most "Freudian" analyses today. Sullivan became very suspicious of the merits of this technique generally. He felt that patient and therapist tended to indulge in "parallel autistic reveries" which too often did not meet in truly therapeutic contact. He emphasized the need for genuine *communication* between doctor and patient, and he complained that interminable maunderings on the part of the patient, scarcely attended to by the doctor until the patient produced "significant" material, were a sheer waste of time.*

My impression is that all the non-libido analysts use free association as a technique *on occasion.* They object to the highly honorific place it is supposed to occupy in "Freudian" analysis, but when they are baffled by the current reaction of a patient, they may ask for free associations. On the whole, however, the patient is led to talk in a more directed way about significant aspects of his life, present and past, gradually becoming aware of the "parataxic distortions" which pathologically limit his view of other people and himself. He is trained to observe the physical sensations and marginal thoughts which accompany directed activity, and in this manner to come to understand much that has been dissociated from the functioning self dynamism.

Horney and Fromm have not written so forthrightly against the technique of free association, but one gets the impression that they too rely more on relatively focused discussion of the patient's behavior and the nuances of his feelings than upon this formal approach to the unconscious processes.

Dreams. Every school considers the dream an important avenue of information about the unconscious processes, because the dreamer is temporarily relieved of the immediate need for coping with reality in a rationally acceptable manner. Freud's investigation of the language of dreams, as explained in Chapter 2, is generally accepted, although the concept of the latent intent of the dream as the fulfillment of a sexual wish is, of course, vigorously denied

---

* "Freudians" would agree with this complaint, if true. I quote here a "Freudian" analyst discussing his actual use of "free association" in the specialized sense: "Many patients never really get to it, except in snatches. The most I ever get is ten or fifteen minutes in an hour, and that's all you can use anyhow."

by these analysts. The dream *may* be sexually oriented, but it may also express other aspirations and problems. (Incidentally free associations to the dream, or dream parts, are used in arriving at interpretation.)

Fromm-Reichmann comments that patients and analysts vary in the extent to which they work profitably with dream materials and that the degree of attention paid to the dream may be left to the discretion of the analyst. If a patient uses dream interpretation as a means of avoiding discussion of his actual life problems, it thus becomes a form of resistance. Any analyst would agree with this statement, but probably the analysts in this group are especially wary of techniques which may draw attention away from the complex patterns of life adjustment.

Fromm's book on dreams, *The Forgotten Language*,[14] although not specifically concerned with problems of therapy, will give the reader an idea of the criticism that these analysts level against both Freud and Jung and will illustrate the type of interpretation they generally prefer.

Mistakes. All analysts occasionally make use of the variety of small mistakes, unconsidered comments, and the like which Freud described in the *Psychopathology of Everyday Life.* These are especially useful in pointing out the patient's unconscious attitudes toward the doctor. Fromm-Reichmann comments that unless the meaning is rather vivid, little information is gained in this manner that is not more easily obtained in other ways, and the patient may become self-conscious and resentful if his little slips are picked up too often.

Nonverbal behavior. All analysts pay attention to concomitant indexes of emotional tension: timbre of voice, posture and movements, vasomotor reactions, etc. The analysts in this group have not particularly stressed this avenue of information. In fact, Sullivan directly, and Horney and Fromm by implication, remark upon the positive need for *verbal* formulation on the part of both patient and doctor. There is careful attention to clarifying the use of words in genuine communication. The complex patterns of living seem to require this flexible type of symbolization for adequate discussion and eventual consolidation of conscious insight. So far as I know,* none of these analysts or their followers have been much interested in the deliberate use of nonverbal adjuncts to therapy as suggested in Chapter 7 for the practice of *some* contemporary Freudians. Also, there seems to be little conscious effort to manipulate the life situation therapeutically as suggested by Alexander,

* After reading this section, Clara Thompson comments as follows: "I think we do use non-verbal activities in understanding the patients as much as the Freudians. Sullivan was much interested in voice tensions. Fromm has been much interested in body tensions and has made quite a study of the Gindler methods. However, he has not written about it."

although of course every aspect of the patient's actual behavior is very carefully analyzed.

Horney was among the first to emphasize the importance of asking the patient explicitly to report what he is *feeling* during the hour as well as what he is *thinking,* and Sullivan asks him to become alert to his physical sensations, to the small concomitants of action. These recommendations concern essentially nonverbal experience, but they are to be reported verbally by the patient in the ordinary course of his discussion, the purpose being one of greater clarification of unconscious or parataxic trends.

Use of the life situation, the pattern of behavior. The happenings in the real-life situation of the patient and his memories of past situations constitute the main material for the psychoanalytic approach of all of these schools. Among these three analysts it is probably Horney who most heavily emphasizes the current situation, but my impression is that her emphasis is by no means as exclusive as Thompson implies in her critique of Horney's position.[15] I would also like to remind the reader that "Freudians" also devote a great deal of time to analysis of the patient's actual behavior, present and past. We are dealing here with variations in emphasis, not with clear-cut distinctions.

Repudiating in theory the concept of libidinal and aggressive instinctual drives as such and mechanisms of repression which keep them timelessly active "in the infantile unconscious," these schools envisage their full task as observing how the personality operates, and bringing the patient to effective realization of the hampering, unrealistic nature of many of his attitudes. Thus there is no problem of differentiating between drives and defenses, id and ego, as in the Freudian schools. There is only the problem of understanding the "defenses"—that is, the safety devices or security operations of the personality. Even the Freudians would agree that, if this is the task, study of the life pattern is the pre-eminent method.

At this point a sharper distinction must be drawn between Horney and Sullivan. Like Adler, Horney tends to consider the movement of the personality as a whole as the determining factor. She understands that adaptation to special circumstances, primarily in early childhood, has set the direction of the personality trends observable in the adult patient. But her main concern is with how the developed trends interact *now*—as opposites which grow more and more irreconcilable in a vicious circle, as unhappily unified in the pathogenic idealization of the self. For Horney the past is illustrative and explanatory (in a way), and therefore useful to the patient. But the overwhelming emphasis is on the interaction of trends as currently operative, in their dynamic relations to one another.

In some contrast to Horney, Sullivan tends to look for the origin of presenting symptoms (or rather of characteristic syndromes) in specific kinds of childhood experience which—in pathology—have conditioned massive dissociative processes. This point of view often approaches the Freudian formulation of the repressed infantile unconscious, and requires a more *ad hoc* approach to childhood memories. Understanding of the genesis of pathological trends is a *necessary* part of treatment, although it is never sufficient. Partly, as Thompson points out,[16] recognition of the origin of his attitudes in the frustrations of childhood makes it easier for the patient to bear insight into aspects of his personality which his current self dynamism condemns with horror. His sense of guilt is in some measure alleviated by the observation that his underlying hatreds and fears were natural reactions to actual hardship, so that he can face their current consequences more courageously. But the main point seems to be that the old dissociations tend to remain operative as systems in many areas until they are specifically broken down. Fromm-Reichmann discusses this problem under the heading of "working through." A basic shift in attitude is indeed the most significant part of the analytic experience. But to have it confirmed and widely applied seems to require consideration of the many ramifications of the old attitudes in specific situations, past as well as present. (Again I comment that the term "working through" was suggested by Freud, and the process is emphasized by Freudian analysts as well.)

In a personal communication, Fromm remarks that his position on these matters is much closer to Freud's than to Horney's. Since he has not written much about treatment procedures as such, I shall not try to elaborate.

The doctor-patient relationship. Transference. All psychoanalytic schools strongly emphasize the importance of the personal relationship between doctor and patient in the process of cure, and all of them observe that this relationship goes far beyond any realistic interpersonal contact. The patient inevitably converts the analyst, at least partly, into a representation aligned with his own (the patient's) psychological needs.

Freud emphasized the idea that the patient transfers to the analyst the attributes of the significant persons of his childhood (usually the parents) and quite directly repeats his childhood experience.* This concept has been broadened to the point at which, for the schools now under consideration, transference means any relationship to the analyst determined by the basic attitudes of the patient regardless of "reality." Psychoanalysis is the one life

* This formulation is too crude, but it gives the essence of the Freudian position. For this reason I am glad to mention instances cited by Sullivan and Fromm-Reichmann in which even the personal appearance of the analyst is distorted to fit the parental image—*e.g.,* a blue-eyed female analyst was seen for months as a dark, bearded person—the patient's father.

situation in which the patient is asked *not* to react adaptively to the special demands of another person, but to talk about anything without inner censorship and without fear of condemnation. Obviously no patient can fully achieve this nonrealistic, amoral approach—and it would do him no good if he could. What happens is that the patient creates (and recreates) the image of the "person" (personification, in Sullivan's vocabulary) opposing this direct expression, or it may be offering consolation and encouragement, and this "person" is, by transference, the analyst, whose training enables him to clarify the distortions of the patient's image. We shall discuss this problem further in connection with the dynamics of therapy.

Interpretative Comment. As a technique, interpretation is probably no different in these schools from what it is in those that have been labeled Freudian. Sullivan urges that direct interpretation be used sparingly, and only when the analyst is sure of his ground—a recommendation by no means peculiar to Sullivan's school. A loaded question, a significant silence, a parallel anecdote will frequently bring the patient to his own formulation of the "interpretation" the analyst considers important, and the formulation will be more meaningful to the patient because he has evolved it himself. Interpretation should never take the form of a short lecture to the patient, or of joint speculation about his possible mechanisms. Its function is to guide the patient toward greater awareness of the problems and resources of his own psyche, and to help him consolidate fragmentary experiences of greater awareness into more substantial insight. (This usage of the term "insight" follows Fromm-Reichmann, who prefers to reserve it specifically for the integrated grasp of dynamic trends achieved by the patient, in contrast to his increased "understanding" and "awareness" of more special parataxic distortions. All analysts are aware of these important periods of consolidation—Horney is especially emphatic about them—but the term "insight" is not usually specifically reserved for this kind of integrated understanding.)

I have cited Sullivan and Fromm-Reichmann here partly to reaffirm important aspects of the technique of interpretation discussed in Chapter 7. It should be made clear to readers whose acquaintance with psychoanalysis has come mainly from the non-libido authors, that "Freudians" hold very similar views. Too often the somewhat tendentious flavor of books written in the spirit of these schools is extended by the reader beyond the intent of the authors. If I may again call upon personal observation, I may say quite firmly that manner of interpretation is much more closely related to the personality of the analyst than to his school affiliation. Furthermore, all schools recognize that the manner of interpretation must be adapted to the needs of the patient. It may be therapeutically necessary at times to take a highly authoritative stance toward some patients, and to impress them with the almost magical interpretative skill of the analyst. (Note the discussion of the Lindbergh dream, p. 53.) Adopting the role of magician pro tem or using active interpretative thrusts with some types of patient in some phases of their analysis does not mean abrogation of the general attitude toward interpretation described here as valid for all schools. These are special techniques any analyst will use on occasion—and he will always consider them "special."

I have tried to underline that we are here talking about interpretation as a *technique*. The *content* of the interpretation, and even the type of behavior which the analyst considers significant enough to bring into focus for the patient, are very largely determined by the theoretical system of the analyst. Attention to the analysis of ego defenses and to the process of working through on the part of Freudians, to sexual problems and hostility on the part of the non-libido schools, must work in the direction of minimizing even this difference in practice, but it remains significant.

THE DYNAMICS OF THERAPY

The crux of the therapeutic process for these schools as well as for the "Freudians," may be stated as the development of *insight*. This does not mean, of course, mere *intellectual* appreciation of the complex of conscious and unconscious patterns operating in one's personality; it means the actual *experiencing* of aspects of one's personality which have been made defensively unconscious. Fromm-Reichmann has described the process in these words:

> The aim of psychoanalytic therapy is to bring these rejected drives and wishes, together with the patient's individual and environmental moral standards, which are the instruments for his rejections, into consciousness and in this way place them at his free disposal. In doing this the conscious self becomes strengthened, since it is no longer involved in the continuous job of repressing mental content from his own awareness. The patient can then decide independently which desires he wants to accept and which he wishes to reject, his personality no longer being warped or dominated by uncontrollable drives and moral standards. This process permits growth and maturation.[17]

The patient is thought to achieve such insight through his experience with the analyst in the analytic sessions. The techniques described in the foregoing pages are designed to foster expression of the rejected aspects of the personality in a situation in which overt action is not required (is, indeed, discouraged), and in which no attitude is condemned. The patient does not simply deduce that he must have unconscious hostility; he actually feels hostile. His experience may be directed toward the analyst by the mechanism of transference (*i.e.*, the analyst stands for someone else); or he may recognize *in the presence of the analyst* hostility (or any other forbidden feeling) toward real people in real situations in which hostility is to him quite unacceptable. Thus the material of the analysis becomes genuine feelings, not intellectual abstractions—feelings which are usually repressed by the patient. Fromm-Reichmann writes, "Our attitude is to help our patients, in neutrality, to re-experience and re-evaluate emotional reactions."[18]

"Real" and "As-if" Relations with the Analyst. It is recognized that the patient responds to the analyst partly as to a real person, like any other person encountered in life situations, and partly as to a figure who represents pro tem the significant people of the past. The analytic situation is partly completely "real" to the patient, partly a situation in which he is deliberately taught to relax his customary evaluative, self-controlling techniques and recreate other situations, past and current, *as if* they were presently happening, and *as if* the analyst were the person or personification in the original situation now recalled.*

As regards the analyst as a "real" person, I have remarked that the non-libido schools seem to encourage a greater informality and positive friendliness toward the patient, although the difference from the "Freudians" in this respect has probably been exaggerated. The "Freudians" are friendlier than their non-libido critics imply; the "objectivity" recommended by Freud comes close to the "neutrality" urged by Fromm-Reichmann. At most there are technical variations in executing what Freud presented as a major *therapeutic* function of the analyst as a person.

This function is to supply realistic support to the patient in his fearsome task of confronting the repressed aspects of his personality. Such support, Freud says, can be achieved only through the patient's *trust* in the professional competence of the doctor, his absolute integrity, his objectivity in relation to the manifold problems of the patient. Only in this "real" trust can the healthy aspects of the patient's ego find a firm ally which will help him through the storms of the transference relationships, the pains and dangers of growing insight. Freud recommended establishing such trust very solidly before attempting analysis of the "as if" aspects of the relationship, and carefully maintaining it at all times. Hence the rules of conduct for the analyst.

It is probably true, as Fromm-Reichmann suggests, that Freud was rather frightened by the powerful impulses his techniques unleashed, and dis-

---

* In passing, it should be remarked that some types of patient are unable to establish this "as if" relationship, with adequate distinction between the analyst as a person and the analyst as substitute person; between the "real" experience in the analytic hour and the therapeutic re-creation of life experience. This is typically a major problem in the treatment of psychotics and children, requiring special understanding and special techniques on the part of the analyst.

trustful of the wisdom of his disciples in coping with them.* It is probably also true that "the doctor" in Freud's Vienna was generally a more authoritative, even authoritarian figure than he is in contemporary America. Maintaining the usual prestige of "doctor" at that time and place very probably required behavior which strikes us now as pompous and cold. Freud was too much part of his time to interpret it as such, but I think he would deplore any "rules" for doctor behavior which would invite such interpretation from patients. His therapeutic principle was the respectful and even loving trust of the patient in the "real" doctor, plus the patient's feeling of being accepted. At any rate contemporary Freudians seem to interpret the "rules" by the spirit rather than the letter. Freud and Freudians might well feel, however, that any general recommendation toward loosening of "rules" in this area puts too great a strain on both doctor and patient in preserving the *neutrality* which Fromm-Reichmann still considers essential. General adherence to the "rules" makes the rather peculiar "real" interpersonal relationship easier for the patient to understand and may actually permit a more sharply significant use of direct personal response in selected situations.

A corollary of the role of the "real" doctor in treatment is its relationship to handling the more flagrantly "as-if" aspects of the situation—the "transference"—as they occur. Freud recommended that positive transference be allowed to build up and that it should be analyzed only when it interfered with the patient's insight, whereas negative transference should be analyzed at once. In this manner the patient's trust in the analyst was enhanced and could be employed on the side of the angels in giving the patient courage to attack his problems. However, the deliberate "objectivity" of the analyst tends to remove him from the proper reality valuations of the patient. Therefore Freud

---

* A little-known aspect of the famous Anna O. case (see pp. 282*f.*) is that the patient suddenly made a direct sexual advance to Breuer, an event which so frightened the worthy doctor that Freud had great difficulty in persuading him to continue further consideration and publication of the line of thought suggested by her case. The same sort of thing happened in at least one of Freud's early cases (see E. Jones, *The Life and Work of Sigmund Freud*, Vol. I, Basic Books, 1953, p. 250) and is not unknown today.

Very possibly Freud's Vienna was both more prudish and more "lecherous" than our modern day—but it remains true that people who work directly with explosive materials need protection. The privacy of psychoanalysis makes any external protection impossible. The analyst defends himself against the sexual advance primarily by his professional attitude. The patient must not be "shamed" when such advances occur but must be brought to an understanding of their meaning in his (or her) own life. The elaborately *professional* relationship emphasized by Freud as the pattern of reality contacts with the patient makes it easier for the analyst to deal with such explosions constructively—indeed forestalls their development in most cases.

Released aggression may take the form of a pistol pointed at the analyst, or physical attack. Such instances are rare, but in an evening of gossip most analysts can cite one or two hair-raising episodes on the topic of sudden overt aggression. I admire the *sang-froid* of the analyst who looked into a gun and said calmly, "This is what I meant about your murderous feelings toward your father. [Laugh] Do you see it now?" According to the analyst, the patient suddenly laughed also, albeit a bit hysterically, and lay down on the couch—in such a position that the analyst could unobtrusively wipe the sweat off his brow.

suggested a short terminal phase in which the analysand sits up and discusses his experience with the analyst, establishing a full "reality" relationship.*

The analysts discussed in this part recommended analyzing all "as-if" reactions to the analyst, positive as well as negative, from the outset, with the definite intent of keeping the patient clear at all times about the reality relationship to the analyst. Constant analysis of the "me-you" relationship between doctor and patient is considered as a preventive of undue dependency on the doctor, as well as useful for analytic handling of current attitudes—a point to be discussed in a moment.[19]

Again I offer my impression as outsider, and on this point I have actually "quizzed" a number of analysts who are proud to be considered classical Freudians. My impression is that "analysis of the transference" is quite generally considered standard procedure by all analysts *at all stages* of the analysis —subject only to "tact and sensitivity for the right moment."[20] The point that analysis does not fall into neat stages is a good one, but it is the kind of point likely to be developed in *any* mature psychoanalytic approach. The real issue is greater understanding of the therapeutic process in its complex relations to reality and "as-if."

I may add my impression that the Horney group distinguishes less sharply between "reality" and "as-if" attitudes in the doctor-patient relationship than the William Alanson White school and the classical Freudians. This would be consonant with the tendency to work directly with current attitudes of all sorts, no matter how manifested, rather than with more or less specific re-creations of the past. Fromm's position seems more closely aligned to that of Freud and Sullivan.

The Transference

In the following pages the discussion turns to the "as-if" relationships themselves. I have minimized the more technical word "transference" in the foregoing pages, because strictly speaking all relationships involve transference, and purely "realistic" attitudes do not exist. The patient sees all people, including the analyst, at all times through the glasses of his own personality. So does the healthy person, though his image may be somewhat less distorted. This inevitable distortion of a hypothetical reality occurs because we always interpret the present partly in terms of expectations established through our past experience. The "real" analyst is "real" only in so far as he is no more distorted than other associates the patient encounters outside the analyst's office.

In practice when analysts of any school speak of transference they

* Discussion of stages in therapeutic approach is illustrated by one of the elder British analysts, Edward Glover. (*The Technique of Psycho-Analysis*, rev. ed., International Universities Press, 1955.)

usually mean the rather special attitudes toward the doctor which develop in the analytic situation as such—attitudes fostered by its very special conditions. I am indebted to Dr. Bela Mittelmann for the following grouping of transference phenomena, thus broadly conceived. The classification cross-cuts the various schools here reported and would be acceptable to all. Probably Horney has been especially influential in drawing attention to the last four. In less focused manner a host of articles on various technical points of the transference relationship have permeated psychoanalytic literature in the past decade or two.

Repetitive phenomena. This set of events directly supports Freud's early view that the patient actually reinstates in the analytic hour the attitudes he experienced in infancy toward the significant adults of that period. We have seen that Sullivan's emphasis on the interpersonal character of infantile experience and on the importance of dissociation techniques instituted in infancy and early childhood led him to rather similar views. I hope it has been made clear, however, that neither Freud nor Sullivan suggest that *all* of the attitudes of the patient toward the analyst can be immediately interpreted on the basis of sheer repetition. Such interpretation requires at best a long road back, with many detours into firmly established defenses (subdynamisms). Furthermore, established defenses do not crumble at a touch, even if the nuclear problems have been reached and even if they have been effectively handled. Although the analyst of any of these schools may perceive at once the major determinants in early experience of the patient's attitudes toward himself (*i.e.*, the analyst),* he will usually help the patient see what his current attitudes "really" are before he tries to identify them *for the patient* as repetitive.

The word *usually* should be underlined in the last sentence. Some types of patient can stand and may even require a prompt interpretation of the repetitive character of their manifest feeling toward the analyst. Other types find such interpretation totally meaningless for a long time. Still others may find their whole defense structure swept away by an interpretation of a conflict already too close to the surface and not defended in depth.

Expectation of magical support. According to all schools, profound feelings of helplessness, conscious or unconscious, are a general characteristic of

---

* Fromm-Reichmann comments that the analyst nowadays is entitled both to *ex*clude some allegations of the patient about his childhood as "impossible" for his current personality picture and also to *con*clude that some rather specific types of difficulty must have existed. She sees this theoretical inference on the part of the analyst as a means of shortening therapy by discreet guidance of the patient toward recognition of his *actual* childhood experience.

neurosis. We have seen that the roots of these feelings lie deep in infancy, although Horney further stresses their exacerbation by the mechanism of the vicious circle. There is a corresponding yearning for boundless love and support. Furthermore, the patient enters analysis essentially because his independent efforts at managing his own life have in some fashion failed despite more or less frantic expedients. And the analyst deliberately asks him to give up, during the hour, many of his practiced controls—often attitudes which seem to the patient the very essence of his independence.

Fromm-Reichmann points out that for some patients the sheer experience of relaxing comfortably in the presence of another human being has therapeutic value, and that they should not be hurried into a renewed, albeit different, sense of responsibility for themselves. A touch of magic in the patient's "realistic" trust in the doctor is doubtless all to the good in most cases (as indeed Freud suggested in recommending that the positive transference be allowed to develop rather firmly). The danger, obviously, is that the patient will too far relax into an exaggerated attitude of "let George do it," placing the entire burden of his cure on the analyst. Not infrequently the patient makes a positive parade of his helplessness, consciously or unconsciously. I remember a point in my own analysis when I literally fell down three times in one week. Although the circumstances each time made an accident natural enough, it can hardly be accidental for an adult normally steady on her pins to be the victim of accident quite so often. Or there may be a kind of infantile defiance: "Let's see if you can make me well," which is really only the obverse of the demand for total care.

These attitudes are in some measure intrinsic to the analytic situation and can be considered "repetitive" only in the very deep theoretical sense that all basic attitudes are established in infancy. Horney especially has urged that they be recognized in their own right, and analyzed in their own right.

Analysis as a threat. Perhaps one may say that the natural defense of the patient against lapsing into expectations of magical support is to cling to his illness. After all, he has *achieved* his illness as it were, as an active means of coping with his problems and of protecting himself against the "danger" of letting his impulses get out of hand. (For the Freudians this danger typically involves the overwhelming sense of *guilt*, rather than insecurity, but the essential problem is the same.) Even the painful symptoms he so much wants to get rid of are merely relatively focused expressions of much more general conflicts, and are in their way *adaptive*. According to every school, it is the *anxiety* that lies behind the illness, that has dictated its every maneuver.

In his early formulations, while he was dealing mainly with hysterical symptomatology, Freud tended to consider the symptom an ego-alien intrusion. The "secondary gain" of illness was then truly secondary—as though a soldier would get his leg shot off in order to obtain compensation payments. Adler insisted too directly that every aspect of the illness is immediately gainful to the personality (as demonstration of its power). The later Freud and Freudians, and also the analysts discussed in this Part, have all recognized that the person-as-a-whole is deeply involved in every symptom (Adler's point), although not in so simple a manner as Adler suggested. Thus Adler's valuable statement that the patient cannot take one step forward "so long as he thinks himself in danger of having his worthlessness revealed"[21] must be modified in terms of the greater complexity of personality structure now envisaged by all schools.

By definition, however, psychoanalysis attempts to undermine the pathogenic defense systems of the patient in the interest of quite fundamental reorganization of the personality. In so far as the pathology the patient consciously wants to get rid of is intimately interwoven with his total personality (and that is very far indeed, especially for the non-libido schools), *any* effective psychoanalytic insight may be experienced as a threat. Quite apart from the specific resistances the analyst encounters (*cf.* Chapter 7 for Freudian groupings of resistance phenomena), the patient always tends to fear (and therefore resist) *any* attack on his major security systems, and even the idea that he may be changed by the analysis. Clearly this is not a logical position, but it is very profoundly human. One may say, perhaps, that the more the analyst envisages the psyche as a functional unit, and works very directly with current attitudes, the more likely he is to arouse these more generalized fears—although they must be present in any successful analytic procedure.

At any rate it is again Horney who has described most vividly these generalized fears as a universal psychoanalytic problem (they are widely recognized), and who has pointed specifically to a kind of rhythm of partial relapse after major gains in insight have been achieved. These generalized fears, and the fears attendant upon a still shaky, unconfirmed recovery, again should be analyzed in their own right. If the patient in his new confidence is tactfully warned of a probable downgrade in feeling, with analysis of his mood fluctuations as a function of the new insight, he is likely to be less alarmed and discouraged.[22]

Fear of exposure; shame and humiliation. Analytic schools differ in their concept of the origin and underlying significance of fear of exposure, shame, and humiliation, but there can be no doubt of their general operation in the analytic hour. To "tell all" to another person is foreign to our whole social training—a training doubtless heavily laden with fear and guilt as the sexual activities of the young child encounter the overwhelming disapproval of the adult world—perhaps as any of the activities and fantasies deeply meaningful to the child are condemned by the significant people. Again Horney would stress attitudes instead of origins—the current humiliation of telling all to a person who tells the patient nothing about himself in return, the shame and danger of putting oneself in a bad light. At times the patient may also fear putting the analyst in a bad light, either by direct criticism or by quoting criticisms heard outside the hour from other people.

Patients vary in the degree of anxiety caused by the fundamental rule of psychoanalysis (to tell everything that comes into your mind), and in the areas in which obedience to the rule becomes extremely embarrassing if not impossible. The variations must be carefully related to the problems of the individual patient—but *all* patients may be expected to have difficulties quite specifically focused around the problem of *telling*. The *New Yorker* cartoon of the smiling patient on the couch saying enthusiastically, "I just remembered another terrific chapter in my life," suggests to the specialist either a psychopath or a patient whose defenses take the form of a fourflushing egotism. Such total denial of distress about past behavior *is* encountered predominantly in a few individuals, at times in all patients. The cartoon is funny because it presents the obverse of the general attitude I am here describing— the shame, embarrassment, and humiliation widely considered typical for the patient talking on the couch.

This order of attitude, partly intrinsic to the analytic situation, albeit deeply rooted, also requires direct handling by the analyst in its own right. The universally recommended "tact" of the analyst comes into play here for every school—but again it is Horney, perhaps, who has pointed out most sharply that the current, quasi-realistic feelings of the patient in this novel situation should be not only tactfully considered but actively discussed throughout the analysis.

Characterological trends. Although all the attitudes described above are generally encountered in the analytic situation, they vary in intensity and rigidity from one patient to another and merge into the specific *characterological* defense of the personality. We saw in Chapter 7 that some patients have to be *right* all of the time; or it may be that they absolutely require a sense of power in all situations. Such patients resist any interpretation whatsoever which puts them in a bad light according to their own code, which suggests that they may unwittingly have made mistakes in judgment, or even that the analyst may understand some of their problems better than they understand them themselves. Other types of patient tend to distort any interpretation into a confirmation of their total worthlessness, which they gladly accept—because it confirms their demands on the analyst and on their associates for total love and support without any personal effort. Or it may allow them the self-punishment which for them, unconsciously, permits gratification of their forbidden longings. Or (Adler's emphasis) the distortion continues the life style of domination through weakness. Or the patient may superficially accept the interpretation and elaborate upon it intellectually—"really" in order to show his cooperative attitude and tough-minded approach to his own problems. This may be his special characterological line of defense. Often such patients are of the "detached" type, and they are not easy to help. Or the compulsive patient may feel that he has to describe every little incident in great detail in order to comply with the analytic rule.

These are, of course, merely samples of how character trends may show themselves in the analytic hour. We have seen in earlier chapters how the various schools envisage the development of character, its inner dynamics, and its role. We saw in Chapter 7 that the development of ego psychology by Freud and Freudians corrected the early oversimplified view of the patient's behavior as the sexual wish handled by repression, compromise, etc., and now takes into consideration the relatively autonomous character of ego mechanisms which come into being either as organized defenses or as expansion in the conflict-free areas of ego function. Such mechanisms vary in their *inclusiveness* as regards personality function from relatively temporary, shifting, and localized reaction patterns to the at times almost impenetrable "armour-plating of character."

Analysts of all schools recognize, nowadays, that the attitudes toward the analyst rooted in *characterological trends* are not a direct repetition of attitudes toward significant persons of the patient's childhood, although they are thought to derive from the early experience with people. These attitudes, too, must be analyzed in their own right. The patient may be shown through his vivid immediate experience with the analyst the pathological aspects of his attitudes toward his real-life associates. In the analytic transference situation, the complicating factor of the variable behavior of the other person is reduced to a minimum. The patient may be quite correct in feeling that his boss deliberately humiliates him, but if he can be brought to see that he also feels humiliated by the analyst *without adequate cause,* he can begin to understand the pattern of his own reactions better. The analysis will not change the character of the boss, and it may be realistically necessary to put up with a difficult superior. At the very least, however, the excessive, "neurotic" pain of humiliation is relieved. Not infrequently the patient discovers that his boss is really as decent a fellow as the analyst, not "really" dominating at all. Or it may turn out that a subtle truculence or cringing subservience in the patient tended to provoke the boss to genuinely unpleasant behavior, and that the boss readily changes *his* attitude with change in the patient.

Working Through; Stages of the Analysis. The patient does not work out his characterological patterns in the vacuum of the transference relations with the doctor and then automatically apply his new attitudes in his real-life relationships. The process is much more complex. I remind the reader of the Freudian phrase *working through.* A major part of the analyst's task is to help the patient relate the attitudes brought out with especial sharpness in the transference situation to the attitudes the patient shows in his report of real-life situations. Actually, unless he has a sense of their relatedness to situations of "real" moment to him, the patient is hardly likely to consider shades of difference in his attitude toward the analyst interesting enough to examine; hence discussion of the patient's life is necessary for fruitful analysis of the transference. But, also, analysis of the transference does not become really effective, as a rule, until the patient *works through* the corresponding attitudes toward his own associates. Thus there is a constant irregular to-and-fro movement between analysis of the transference to the analyst at the various levels here suggested, of the past as it clarifies the origin of the transference attitudes or as a release of repressed (dissociated) attitudes, and, finally, of the current life of the patient.

If I may again be allowed a personal impression of school differences, I would say that Freud developed his final complex position rather gradually, high-lighting one aspect of the therapeutic situation after another with the insight of his genius. All Freudians distinguish sharply in theory between analysis of the id materials and the defense mechanisms of the ego. Possibly *some* classical Freudians (more than other schools) tend to envisage the analytic process as a series of temporarily distinguishable phases—establishing the transference, analyzing the defenses, getting at the fundamental "id" problems, working through, resolving the transference. To most Freudians, and certainly to Freud himself, this outline would seem a travesty of analysis. These are relatively separable aspects of the therapeutic approach, but they usually operate simultaneously and continuously, with at most successive phases in which one or the other special aspect tends to predominate in approximately the sequence indicated. The duration of any phase naturally depends on the patient, and no aspect of the treatment is ever wholly neglected or dropped as "finished." I need only requote Freud: "Our therapeutic work swings to and fro during the treatment like a pendulum, analysing now a fragment of the id and now a fragment of the ego."[23]

My impression is that the non-libido schools have combatted this "stage" concept of analysis beyond the actual practice of Freudian analysts. Sullivan emphasizes the idea that the initial interviews are already construed by the patient as "therapeutic" and should be used by the analyst not only for fact-finding but for introducing the patient (and analyst) to the essential features of their subsequent relationship—an emphasis not too different from "building up the transference." That the patient is likely to require a relatively gradual induction to consideration of his oldest and deepest problems is hardly more than common sense, but there is not so sharp a difference in kind between the superficial and deep problems for the non-libido schools as for the classical Freudians. Analysis of defenses and working through tend to merge, for the non-libido schools, into the general concept of handling the patient as a human being living his own life outside the analyst's office—i.e., without the temporal distinction between the two phases suggested by the Freudian outline, and probably with less concentration on reactions so deep as to escape direct relatedness to current attitudes. The militant aspects of the non-libido schools as regards therapy seem to revolve around the need for continuous relation of the analysis to the real-life problems of the patient, and continuous analysis of the transference at all levels. There is more emphasis on the "democratic" attitude of respect for the analyst as a participant observer with special training as against authoritarian respect for "the doctor." I have explained above that this distinction does not seem tenable as of "schools," although it may well apply to the personality trends of some analysts in all schools.

The Role of Differences in Theoretical Orientation

School differences in therapy as described by the non-libido analysts have been outlined mainly as differences in emphasis—in fact, mainly as differences in words for therapeutic processes everywhere recognized as important. I explained that I was unwilling to quote these authors in either implied or explicit difference from Freudian analysts whom I knew to be operating in a very similar way, with a rather similar conception of what they were doing. Although I have tried to point out differences in words and in emphasis, my own emphasis has been on similarities. It has not been an unconsidered emphasis.

Actually, especially at the deeper levels of the analytic process, there are profound differences in the content of interpretation and the kind of insight the patient is expected to reach. So long as the task is to make the patient aware of prevailing attitudes which he has repressed and of sundry irrational maneuvers by which he attempts to gain security and satisfaction, the difference in basic theoretical concept plays no great role. "Oral" dependency needs, with their extreme passive expectation of total care or fretful demandingness, are clearly described by the non-libido schools without reference to "orality." Shades of difference in types of competitiveness, ambition, need for power, hostile aggression, and the like are observed and given a dynamic explanation, although they are not related to deep biological functions and their fate in the family drama. Since the patient in psychotherapy and in many aspects of full Freudian analysis is not asked to consider the biological roots of his reaction patterns, it often looks as though there were *no* difference in approach except verbalisms about origins more important to the intellectual comfort of the analyst than to the therapeutic process itself. This formulation is inadequate.

The Freudian believes that the shades of difference between one patient and the next in his handling of the basic trends that *every* analyst considers important can be understood best in terms of the constellative power of his instinctual drives. *In brief psychoanalytically oriented therapy,* he tries to cut through the special manifestations of problem dictated by pressure of circumstances (past as well as present) to an understanding of the basic personality as constellated around the instinctual drives. Although he usually does not attempt to share this formulation with the patient, his own grasp of the kind of pressure the patient cannot stand in real life or in therapy, of the kind of support and gratification the patient most desperately needs, will dictate his brief-therapy approach and his recommendations as regards the environment. In full analysis, however, the Freudian does feel that the patient must share his formulation. Oral dependency needs are directly related to current eating habits and attitudes toward food. Feelings of injury, inadequacy, and guilt are, eventually, directly related to castration fear and the deep rivalry with the father. The effort is not merely historical in intent, showing the patient how he got into his condition; it aims at showing him that here and now, under devious disguises, he still wants "food," a bigger penis than his father's, etc.

It is at this point, I think, that the major difference between Freud and Sullivan appears. Like Freud, Sullivan maintains that the specific early experiences are important *in their specificity,* and his therapy urges that these experiences be recaptured in the analysis. Under the large heading "pursuit of satisfaction," and under subordinate headings of "oral," "anal," and "lust" dynamisms, Sullivan attempts to deal with the major biological determinants so heavily emphasized by Freud. But his main position centers around the "pursuit of security," which is envisaged almost entirely as a problem in interpersonal relations. It is the fear of disapproval by the parents *in a very general sense* that brought about the dissociations and parataxic distortions responsible for the mental illness. Specific instinctual (sexual) needs and the instinct representatives are for him secondary to the need for security and approval. They were not in themselves the main foci of personality organization in infancy; still less do they remain dominantly operative in adult life. The sexual activities of the child often arouse especially sharp disapproval in the parent and thus come to arouse pathogenic anxiety in the child. Hence sexuality typically comes in for frequent discussion in the analysis. The trend, however, is toward interpretation of the interpersonal problems caused by these "pursuits of satisfaction" rather than their significance as such.

Interpretation in the *Horney* vein carries the analysis of the characterological trends in the patient further, with little attention to the "repetitive" aspects of the transference. Horney's greatest contribution seems to me her study of the intrapsychic dynamics of important trends, no matter how they originated. Partly this type of dynamics is expressed by the concept of the vicious circle, suggesting how the major line of defense chosen fosters automatically the covert development of its opposite. In the course of analysis, interpretation may, I gather,[24] be focused for a long time on one aspect of this dynamic dichotomy until the patient has become very clearly aware of his unconscious attitude—for example, the anxiety underlying his compliant or detached behavior, however well rationalized. Far from insisting upon insight into the complementary hostility and aggression, the analyst may tend to discourage glimmers of understanding in the patient for a period, because they are easily used as defenses against the major insight he needs at the moment. ("If I get so mad, I'm not really a door mat.") Eventually the opposite number of the trend must also be interpreted—and integrated with the first.

In some cases an incomplete analysis may have progressed far enough so that a *benign* circle is set up. Lessened neurotic compliance lessens the unconscious resentment → hostility with its further induced protective maneuvers. As a rule, however, it seems necessary to bring all the major aspects of the personality into analysis, and to aim at developing insight into their interrelationships. Although Horney does not use the phrase "working through," she, too, discovers the necessity for very extensive analytic review of all important ramifications of the patient's basic attitudes. Like Alexander, she often points to the fact that the patient makes discoveries on his own, during and after analysis, and emphasizes the idea that these independent discoveries have analytic validity. Nevertheless all analysts have found that problem areas tend to remain potent unless they have been thoroughly canvassed in the analytic hour. From Horney's point of view, it is especially important that the complementary dynamics of any analyzed trend be fully considered before the patient can firmly establish constructive insight.

In her last book, *Neurosis and Human Growth,* Horney focuses attention on the idealized image of the self, which in a way cross-cuts her previous emphasis on the intrapsychic dynamics of special trends. My impression is that interpretation aimed at bringing to awareness the deeply unconscious directive *attitudes* is not abrogated but supplemented by the new emphasis. At all points in the analysis, the attention of the patient may be called to the exaggerated demands he makes upon himself, with their compulsive, self-glorifying idealism and their underlying self-hate. The idealized self becomes the context within which other trends are seen, a context more meaningful and integrating for the patient than his hostilities, fears, or whatever which too often he can learn about analytically as somehow peripheral to the core of his being. Such peripheral learning does not affect the core of the neurosis.

Thus Horney feels that the self system should be directly interpreted to the patient, and frankly calls this aspect of the analysis a "disillusioning process." Partly she feels that a constructive process sets in spontaneously as the strangle-hold of the idealized image on the real self is weakened. She writes: "The therapeutic value of the disillusioning process lies in the possibility that, with the weakening of the obstructive forces, the constructive forces of the real self have a chance to grow."[25]

At first the analyst usually can support the constructive aspects of the personality only by "working with the good will or positive interest in analysis that is available," and the desire of the patient to get rid of whatever he himself considers disturbing. Very soon, however, dreams or minor life episodes reveal a kind of longing to become alive, to cultivate growth. The patient begins to wonder, "Who am I?" and (with the analyst's help) to realize how little he knows about his *real* feelings and wishes. He becomes more aware of his conflicts, at first very often as things that have happened *to* him because of other persons or events, or in some manner peripheral or compartmentalized; but eventually with glimmers of their internal operation within himself.

This phase of the analysis is difficult but liberating. The patient gradually comes to see something good in himself, not defensively as at first, but with genuine appreciation. He has flashes of the exhilarating sense of acting as he really feels, and he intuitively recognizes the difference from his previous feelings. Here the analyst may step in to help the patient fix these flashes in his memory as an earnest of the goal he is to reach, as a spur and direction to further analytic work. As we have noted earlier, it is often well to warn the patient that the victory is not yet won, that he may again experience periods of self-alienation when the whole concept of a free *real self* may again become meaningless to him. Interpretation of the false self system is, then, a major part of Horney's recommended therapeutic approach, together with interpretative support of the liberated real self of the patient.

Although all analysts interpret attitudes toward the self and characterological defenses as *part* of their therapeutic approach, Horney considers such interpretation the main task of analysis. Her positive contribution to technical insight into these aspects of the personality is widely appreciated. The limitations many analysts see in her treatment procedures are part and parcel of their critique of her underlying theory. In comment on Chapter 8, I attempted to explain my own objections to her call upon the "real self" as something of an organized unit available to the patient once he understands how misguided his previous efforts at the solution of his problems have been. Fromm and Sullivan, who have been especially concerned with the dynamic importance of the "self," raise objections to a view of therapy so heavily oriented toward current attitudes, so confident of the effectiveness of a "release" of repressed potentialities.

SUMMARY

Technical approaches to full psychoanalysis were reviewed in this chapter, with the statement that the non-libido schools are probably more "flexible" in all their techniques, although the line of division becomes very thin if one considers the common aim of benign neutrality. Although the non-libido schools emphasize a "democratic" relationship, the analyst cannot allow himself to be drawn into the reality problems of the patient without compromising his therapeutic neutrality. The number of sessions per week is often reduced. The patient is more often permitted to sit facing the analyst.

All psychoanalytic schools emphasize the importance of "insight" in effecting the profound change in the organization of the personality which is considered a true psychoanalytic cure. Such insight does not mean an intellectual, verbalistic understanding, although verbalization seems necessary to a flexible, complex review of the patient's personality patterns and to consolidation of his new approach. Effective insight involves the ability to *feel* differently about the significant aspects of one's experience and about one's self, because the special distortions wrought by repression, dissociation, and the like are corrected. The limitation caused by *unconscious* fears, goals, and attitudes is removed.

Such liberating insight must be achieved by the patient himself, under the facilitating circumstances of the analytic sessions. In a unique interpersonal relationship of benign neutrality, he is encouraged to review the events of his current and past life with as much immediacy of feeling as he can recapture, and with the sense that he can now re-evaluate them without the pressure toward expedient (defensive) action ordinarily required. A point emphasized by Fromm-Reichmann is that nowadays the analyst is sufficiently familiar with the common misinterpretations of patients to be able to help toward sharper insight by discreetly calling the patient's attention to aspects of his story he tends to neglect. This "interpretation" may be no more than a deliberately pointed question. It should never *impose* the analyst's view, however accurate, beyond what the patient can himself experience. Although this point is a welcome addition to Freud's earliest theories of psychoanalytic therapy, it is by no means foreign to his later position, or to the current "Freudian" approach. Nor would Fromm-Reichmann claim such opposition. Throughout this chapter I have been at pains to emphasize the noncontroversial quality of such statements, because the tendentious atmosphere of the books of different "schools" easily leads the lay reader to an assumption of controversy where none exists.

Every analyst has observed that the analytic situation does not remain "neutral" for the patient. On the contrary, the patient typically draws the analyst into his own orbit via "the transference." The analyst becomes, pro tem, the personification of whatever the patient wants or fears—a kind of stick figure used as protagonist in the patient's inner drama for whatever personage or attitude the patient chooses in the course of his analytic reconstruction of his own deep experience. Every analyst is prepared for this phenomenon, and to some extent deliberately lends himself to it. It is usually "via the transference" that the patient can re-experience his actual relations with people, past and present, with sufficient emotional vividness to attain genuine insight rather than a therapeutically meaningless intellectual understanding.

Various types of transference phenomena were discussed in relation to the attitudes the patient brings to the treatment situation.

The main difference among schools involves the type of material selected for interpretation and the type of interpretation offered. This difference corresponds to the theoretical variations presented earlier and is probably less extreme than is commonly believed. All analysts work with current attitudes and childhood memories. Although "sexual" experiences are almost always considered important by the non-libido analysts, they are usually considered as foci of especially vivid interpersonal problems rather than as dynamic foci in their own right, as for the "Freudians." Horney has gone further than the other analysts in an almost exclusive emphasis on the intrapsychic drama of current attitudes, with stress on attitudes toward the self.

Throughout this chapter I have elaborated published statements about therapy from my personal impression of what analysts actually *do,* an impression based on collaborative work and informal conversation, often merely overheard as they talk among themselves. Centered upon the welfare of the individual patient, their attitudes are more flexible and, may I say, more *sensible,* than the layman might suppose in reading the technical literature.

[1] H. S. Sullivan, *Conceptions of Modern Psychiatry,* William Alanson White Foundation, 1947, pp. 54f.

[2] *Ibid.,* p. 56.

[3] *Ibid.,* p. 73.

[4] *Ibid.,* p. 77.

[5] *Cf.* R. P. Knight, "An Evaluation of Psychotherapeutic Techniques," *Bulletin of the Menninger Clinic,* 1952, 16:113-124.

[6] H. S. Sullivan, *op. cit.,* p. 106.

[7] *Ibid.,* p. 107.

[8] *Ibid.,* p. 106n.

[9] *Ibid.,* p. 109 mainly.

[10] A. Adler, "Individual Psychology," in C. Murchison (ed.), *Psychologies of 1930,* Clark University Press, 1930, p. 404.

[11] S. Freud, "Analysis Terminable and Interminable," *Collected Papers,* London: Hogarth Press, 1950, V, 316-357.

[12] C. P. Oberndorf, "Unsatisfactory Results of Psychoanalytic Therapy," *Psychoanalytic Quarterly,* 1950, 19:393-407.

[13] F. Fromm-Reichmann, *Principles of Intensive Psychotherapy,* University of Chicago Press, 1950, pp. 32ff.

[14] E. Fromm, *The Forgotten Language,* Rinehart & Co., 1951.

[15] C. Thompson, *Psychoanalysis: Evolution and Development,* Hermitage House, 1950, pp. 197ff.

[16] *Ibid.,* pp. 201f.

[17] F. Fromm-Reichmann, "Recent Advances in Psychoanalytic Therapy," in P. Mullahy (ed.), *A Study of Interpersonal Relations,* Hermitage Press, 1949, pp. 122f.

[18] *Ibid.,* p. 126.

[19] C. Thompson, *op. cit.,* pp. 233f.

[20] *Ibid.,* p. 234.

[21] A. Adler, *Social Interest,* Faber & Faber, 1938, p. 164.

[22] K. Horney, *Neurosis and Human Growth,* W. W. Norton & Co., 1950, p. 362.

[23] S. Freud, *op. cit.,* p. 341.

[24] See especially K. Horney, *Self-Analysis,* W. W. Norton & Co., 1942.

[25] K. Horney, *Neurosis and Human Growth,* p. 348.

Part Four

JUNG AND RANK

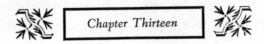
JUNG

THE YOUNG Zurich psychiatrist C. G. Jung, a pupil of Bleuler, was among the first to become interested in the new ideas of Sigmund Freud. For some years, Jung was an enthusiastic and favored participant in the infant psychoanalytic movement, but soon serious ideological and personal differences developed which by 1912 resulted in definite and increasingly embittered cleavage. Like Adler, Jung founded his own school with a distinct name: Analytical Psychology.

Jung's ideas have had an important influence on the development of modern thought, perhaps especially outside the professional discipline of psychiatry. Contemporary studies of cultural history and mythology are profoundly indebted to Jung. Especially in Europe, much careful work is being done with direct acknowledgment of his principles. Many of his concepts have penetrated modern thought even to the level of the popular cliché. "Everybody" knows what an introvert is, just as he knows about the inferiority complex—and usually just as mistakenly.

Jung, the pupil of Bleuler, influenced by the German experimental-psychological trend, first reacted to Freud's new ideas by attempting to incorporate them in an extensive objective, experimental testing program designed both to "prove" Freud's theories and to facilitate short-cuts in treatment. In the early years, Jung was the originator of the word-association test, which is still widely used, in modified form, as an aid to psychodiagnosis. It was Jung who introduced the term *complex* for the cluster of emotionally toned ideas whose dynamic significance had been indicated by Freud. Jung felt initially that if these complexes could be correctly identified, the task of analysis would be greatly shortened—an idea quite consonant with the early Freud-Breuer position.

Actually, as their experience and insight grew, both Jung and Freud had to modify their early position. Jung often seems to attack a "Freudian" concept of sexuality (of sexual *trauma*) which Freud himself corrected quite early as if it were the essence of Freudian doctrine. At the present time I have found intelligent Jungians righteously repudiating "Freudian" attitudes which neither Freud nor Freudians have entertained for thirty years. The main point here is that Jung also changed his early approach. Far from continuing an objective and experimental program, he became the most anti-"scientific" of the analysts. I put "scientific" in quotes to suggest the *narrow* exclusively rational-empirical approach which Jung attacks. Jung does not deny the value of controlled thinking and investigation in their proper place. Many controlled studies have been made of his concepts as observable in contemporary groups—notably the extraversion-introversion dichotomy (see p. 544)—but they have been made mainly by "psychologists" rather than by *Jungians*.

Scientific investigation by Jung and Jungians seems to have taken mainly the form of study of ancient or primitive myths and art forms, a study which is expected to clarify the deep images of the unconscious. Although Jung, like Freud, allows plentiful space for the influence of current social values and special individual experience in his understanding of the individual case, his sense of psychological science plunges deeper into the experience of the human race. The very impressive erudition of the Jungians aims at showing the underlying characteristics of groups at the level of the deep unconscious, to the end of greater understanding of basic psychological truths. As a group, they do not seem much interested in the more inclusive type of social study as envisaged by Kardiner and many contemporary cultural anthropologists (see Chap. 4) in the sociological analysis of the forms of society, or in experimental social psychology.*

* In writing this chapter, I have relied heavily on the books of Frances Wickes, especially *The Inner World of Man* (Henry Holt & Co., 1938). For Jungians, including Mrs. Wickes herself, this is a "practical" book, related to problems of therapy rather than the exposition or advancement of basic theory. By its sympathetic, detailed presentation of the problems of patients and therapist, it helped me toward a better understanding of how Jungian theory applies *concretely* to the kind of problem discussed in this book: the individual in relation to his society, as seen "practically" by the therapist who tries to help him. Among Jung's own writings *Two Essays on Analytical Psychology* (Ballière, Tindall & Cox, 1928; first edition 1916) presents his point of view most vividly to the clinician. His other books are oriented toward theoretical and broadly social problems—at the level of deep psychological analysis.

THE LIBIDO

Jung retains the Freudian term *libido* but gives it a different meaning that is at once more monistic and more pluralistic. He means by the term a life energy underlying all natural phenomena, including the human psyche— apparently rather similar to Bergson's concept of the *élan vital*. Sexuality (genitality) is one manifestation of it. It is essentially creative. Although it takes many forms, it can no more be obliterated than the energy of physics, which Jung often uses in analogy. This position of the indestructibility of energy is reminiscent of important aspects of Freud's theory, as described in Chapter 6. Jung carries the idea even further than Freud. In his later writings the direct analogies to physics give way to a poetic sense of the dark life forces within us, which are also divine—forces which threaten and ennoble us and which may not be denied.

Jung objected early to Freud's denomination of the libido as specifically *sexual—i.e.,* the energies striving for gratification and pleasure contrasted *at that time* by Freud with the ego instincts. The objection was not dictated by prudishness. Sexuality (genitality) and incestuous longings are prominent in Jungian interpretations too. What Jung protested was the grouping to-gether of all forms of pleasure striving and setting them off in contrast to the instinct of self-preservation. Alignment of oral and anal pleasures with genital urges seemed to him gratuitous and unfortunate. For Jung the libido is life itself. As the biological organism matures and as the person has varying reality problems to meet, the libido may follow different channels. Among these channels the sexual (genital) is perhaps the most important—in fact, Jung speculated about the reproductive urges as the primal life urge. He felt, how-ever, that once differentiation has taken place in the human species, it becomes futile to consider all libidinal expression as essentially sexual.

On the contrary, he suggested three stages of development. Up to the third or fourth year the infant is concerned mainly with problems of *nutrition* and growth. This is the epoch of suckling. Rhythmic activities associated with suckling become important in their own right, with the hand as auxiliary organ. This is the epoch of the displaced rhythmic activity, the presexual period, a period comparable to the chrysalis stage in butterflies. It coincides in a general way with the time of the development of the mind and of speech, the turning of the child from the parents to the real world around him. "The gaining of pleasure leaves the mouth zone and turns to other regions. The possibilities are now many."[1] The libido normally proceeds to other zones, arriving at the genital. "In its migration the libido takes more than a little of the function of nutrition with it into the sexual zone."

With the onset of puberty, the child becomes capable of maturity. However, "if, after the occupation of the sexual zone, an obstacle arises against the present form of application of the libido, then there occurs, according to the well-known laws, a regression to the nearest station lying behind."[2] Thus physiological maturity does not guarantee psychological maturity. On the contrary, the "sexual libido" frees itself only very gradually and with difficulty from that which is peculiar to the function of nutrition. For many individuals such freedom is never attained, or is lost in the course of later living. In fact, true maturity requires a kind of Sacrifice of the child-self with all its deep longings by the "hero."* The Sacrifice is followed by Rebirth of the hero as a full man. A book by Joseph Campbell, *The Hero with a Thousand Faces*,[3] describes this aspect of Jung's position very beautifully through a compilation of relevant myths and legends, with some instances from the dreams of contemporary men and women.

This genetic picture leads to an emphasis on incestuous longings which play almost as great a role in Jung's scheme as in Freud's. But they are not, for Jung, primarily and exclusively sexual. Rather the parents are first experienced by the child as protectors, caretakers, suppliers of *nutritive* wants—and also as withholders and punishers. Because the parents are still the chief love objects, this parental image naturally becomes fused with the independently developing focus on the genital zone. Thus Jung accepts the Freudian Oedipus complex as humanly important on a somewhat different basis from Freud's, and readily proposes an analogous Electra complex for women without the complications which Freud found necessary.

For the infant the mother is the major image, regardless of the sex of the child, and the mother remains the symbol of bliss, repose, comfort, and total passivity, the source of life. But a duality is apparent in the definition. Life is not passive. The child must go forth into the real world. So while the man retains a nostalgia for the Eternal Mother and is, indeed, "driven by the eternal thirst to find her again, and to drink renewal from her,"[4] he must also leave the Mother. The Good Mother of his deepest dreams is also the Terrible Mother who has actually punished and denied him in the significant years of infancy and, even more importantly, the Terrible Mother within the per-

* When he made this formulation (1913), Jung was still working within the framework of Freudian ideology. One may already see the different "broader" concept of the libido. In later years he tended to emphasize generally human trends with less interest in their development in childhood. It might have been better had he chosen a term other than libido for "life energy" if he wished to distinguish his position from Freud's. The reader is reminded of the problem involved in the use of technical terms the meaning of which varies with the author.

son's own psyche which tends to paralyze his energies "with the consuming poison of the stealthy, retrospective longing."[5]

Thus the incestuous longings and fears are implicit in the nature of mankind. Since the mother image reflects the "irregular commingling of the elements of nutrition and of sexual functions,"[6] she will have many aspects. She will be the Divine Harlot and the devouring witch, as well as the symbol of eternal compassion and infinite loving care. "Incest prohibition can be understood . . . as a result of regression, and as the result of a libidinous anxiety, which regressively attacks the mother."[7] It has nothing to do with biological damage but is rather a purely psychological matter—the resistance against reversion to the infantile state. Jung sometimes speaks of the return to the womb in a manner suggestive of Rank's position (see Chap. 13). And at times Jung (1913) writes in a manner suggestive of Freud's Eros-Thanatos dichotomy (1920):

> I . . . venture to suggest that it may have been a question of a primitive separation of the pairs of opposites which are hidden in the will of life: the will for life and for death. It remains obscure what adaptation the primitive man tried to evade through introversion and regression to the parents; but, according to the analogy of the soul life in general, it may be assumed that the libido, which disturbed the initial equilibrium of becoming and of ceasing to be, had been stored up in the attempt to make an especially difficult adaptation, and from which it recedes even today.[8]

Having noted the similarity between Jung's position and Freud's in some fundamental respects, let us now examine what Jung felt to be their most essential difference. Jung asserts that Freud's position is essentially reductive, retrospective, and causal in an analytic, mechanical sense. According to Jung, Freud considers present phenomena as "nothing but" the combination of elements which are inborn or determined by infantile experience. Jung's own position, he says, is prospective and functional. Clarification of the past and of special instincts is, to be sure, helpful, "but when exalted into a general explanation of the nature of the soul, whether sick or healthy—*a reductive theory becomes impossible*. . . . Life has also a tomorrow, and today is only understood if we are able to add the indications of tomorrow to our knowledge of what was yesterday."[9]

Beatrice Hinkle expresses the differences for therapy as follows:

> The conflict is produced by some important task or duty which is essential biologically and practically for the fulfilment of the ego of the individual, but before which an obstacle arises from which he shrinks, and thus halted cannot go on. . . . Therefore Jung does not ask from what psychic experience or point of fixation in childhood the patient is

suffering, but what is the present duty or task he is avoiding, or what obstacle in his life's path he is unable to overcome? What is the cause of his regression to past psychic experiences?[10]

Thus the emphasis in therapy is placed on the present adaptation of the patient and aims toward the future. His difficulties are not considered as the changeless persistence in the unconscious of infantile desires and terrors which press toward escape from repression. It is not expected that he will recover automatically if these repressions are released.* The problem is rather one of clearly understanding the present difficulties as they are handled partly by regressive trends and by the unconscious struggle against them.

This emphasis on the present and future in the Jungian scheme should *not* be construed as an injection of "practicality" into psychoanalysis, such as many laymen have wished. On the contrary, Jung distrusts the "practicality" of the modern age as a limitation of the human spirit greatly to be feared. The modern businessman walks with Hiawatha on the eternal quest for and against the mother. The present, for Jung, is not the "practical adjustment" of the individual to the unhappy structure of our contemporary society but the eternally current relationship of the individual to his own self, to his fellows, and to the extra-individual energy of life.

ATTITUDES AND FUNCTIONS; PERSONALITY TYPES

Introversion-Extraversion. As the person relates himself to the world around him, the libido takes two general directions. One direction, which Jung calls introversion, is toward the self; the other, extraversion, is toward the outside world. The one is essentially subjective in its orientation; the other objective.† Clearly both directions are necessary to wholeness of living. Although complementary, they tend to function in opposition. This statement is the first instance in the present report of Jung's recurrent stress on thesis and antithesis, a philosophy of opposites which require reconciliation.

These two directions of the libido are considered as fundamental *attitudes* of the personality, apparently inborn as temperamental differences. Some

* Most "Freudians" would protest this description of their therapeutic approach. The reader is reminded that I am quoting Jung.

† It seems to me that in a general way this dichotomy of Jung's corresponds to Freud's concept of narcissistic libido and object libido. We have seen (Chap. 6) that Freud thought that the libido could take predominantly one or the other direction and could change direction under varying circumstances. Freud did not, however, envisage individual differences in the preponderance of one or the other direction as sufficiently stable to form the basis of a typology. He used his concept in explanation of the genetic process and of some aspects of pathology, not in describing characteristic personality trends of enduring nature.

individuals seem from the very beginning to approach the world subjectively and may be thought of as the introverted type. Jung writes,

> The first [attitude], if normal, is revealed by a hesitating, reflective, reticent disposition, that does not easily give itself away, that shrinks from objects, always assuming the defensive, and preferring to make its cautious observations as from a hiding place. The second type, if normal, is characterized by an accommodating, and apparently open and ready disposition, at ease in any given situation. This type forms attachments quickly, and ventures, unconcerned and confident, into unknown situations, rejecting thoughts of possible contingencies. In the former case, manifestly the subject, in the latter the object, is the decisive factor.[11]

These basic differences in attitude are, Jung believes, decisive for many aspects of interpersonal relations and for the general pattern of our approach to life, even for differences in ideologies. He contrasts Nietzsche's introversive emphasis on the individual with Wagner's outgoingness, explaining on these grounds not only their fundamental difference in philosophy but their personal antipathy to each other. More relevant to this book is Jung's contrast of Adler and Freud. Jung maintains that Adler's concentration on the individual and his intransigeant will to power is essentially introversive. Freud's insistence on relations with the sexual object is essentially extraversive. Both men, Jung says, were in a sense right, but neither could develop a fully satisfactory theory because each too far rejected the opposing attitude in himself and in his theoretical understanding of psychology.[12]

Because these attitudes complement each other, individuals are frequently drawn to those of the opposite type in friendship or marriage. (Nietzsche and Wagner, Adler and Freud were at first friends.) But irreconcilable problems are likely to develop in time, especially under conditions of stress.

A major aspect of Jung's idea, too often neglected by non-Jungians, is that every individual has *within himself* the counterpart of the predominant attitude. The more consciously and exclusively he develops his natural bent, the greater the *un*conscious development of its opposite. Jung's concept of the unconscious will be discussed in detail a little later. Here we shall merely point out the reciprocal relationship, and the fact that the *un*conscious attitude remains relatively undifferentiated. As it gains in power, it may break through in action of relatively crude nature—normally fairly well integrated with the personality, in pathology as a very disturbing element.

Jung uses the illustration of two young men, introvert and extravert, who have been enjoying a walking tour together. They come upon a castle which *both* would like to explore. Here the introvert is extravert enough for curiosity. But he draws back and relies upon his friend's greater enterprise.

Once inside, they find that the castle has been turned into a sort of museum, with a room full of valuable old manuscripts. The introvert is delighted. He becomes absorbed in these "objects" and establishes social relations with their custodian—in short behaves like an extravert. The other lad is disappointed in his fantasy of knightly hospitality, has no interest in musty manuscripts— and behaves like a disgruntled introvert. The friends quarrel. The introvert in his enthusiasm for an object of interest to himself, in his mood of extraversion, loses sight of his friend's boredom; the extravert, in his disillusionment, draws back into subjective ideas and moods and fails to empathize with the pleasure of his friend.[13]

In the later years of life, aspects of the psyche submerged in successful development of one bent not infrequently come to the fore in a manner which affects the personality to the point of neurosis or even psychotic breakdown. For Jung this is not primarily a matter of the special stresses of the climacteric or of environmental changes, including the radical changes brought about by retirement. It is due rather to the developing power of the unconscious antithesis of whichever attitude has been too one-sidedly developed earlier. Jung calls this unconscious antithesis of overt trends the *shadow*. Cure of such conditions cannot consist merely in the release of powerful attitudes toward the parents, repressed in early childhood, as Freud would say (according to Jung). Rather, the patient must become aware of the complementary aspects of his own psyche which he has excluded but which have grown in the unconscious to monstrous proportions.

The problem may arise much earlier if, for some reason, the person goes against his natural bent very early in life. An introvert child in an extravert family has a hard time. He may find *his way of living* through an exaggeration of his own introversive bent because he rebels against coercion—a solution especially likely to lead eventually to the kind of inner rebellion just described. Or he may try to be an extravert in compliance with the family pattern—a solution which often leads to a variety of unconscious protests. (I may remark here on Jung's distinction between modes of treatment for young people who can be helped to find their own bent, with better means of sublimation, and for older people who must face specific unconscious trends built up as the obverse of their long-established way of living.)

The main point here is that both introversion and extraversion are *necessary* directions for the libido in establishing relations between the person and the outside world. Individuals vary in the predominance of one attitude or the other—by native temperament, reinforced or at times contradicted by the circumstances of living. Overly exclusive development in either direction brings about *un*conscious development in the other, which may show itself in relatively brief, isolated shifts of behavior (as in the illustration of the castle) or in deeper disturbances, more global in character (as in many of the neuroses of late adulthood). Although Jung believes that these attitudes may be usefully distinguished from each other in individuals and even in ideologies, he clearly does *not* mean that people and theories can be sufficiently disposed of by labeling them introversive or extraversive. On the contrary, the more "pure" the conscious expression of one type, the more inevitable becomes the unconscious antithesis. For Jung maturity lies in harmonious integration, not in development along a single line, however virtuous it may appear.

The Four Functions.   To the two general attitudes—introversive and extraversive—Jung adds four *functions* of the personality: sensation and intuition (modes of apprehension) and feeling and thinking (modes of judgment). "The functional type describes the way in which the empirical material is specifically grasped and formed, the attitudinal type introversion-extraversion characterizes the general psychological orientation, *i.e.*, the general direction of that general psychological energy which Jung conceives the libido to be."[14] All four functions are necessary to adequate living, just as both introversive and extraversive attitudes are necessary. In the ideal personality they work in harmony, but for Jung the ideal personality is the achievement of the few. Usually two of the functions tend to predominate at the expense of the other two—which then grow in the unconscious in much the way described for the submerged attitude. Sensation and intuition are to some extent incompatible. Where one is overly developed consciously, the other tends to be submerged. So also with feeling and thinking. However, one representative of each pair is usually observable as the *dominant* function in an individual, with a representative of the other pair as an *auxiliary* function. Thus a Jungian may speak of a person as a sensation-thinking type, or as a feeling-intuitive type, or as any combination of the pairs. He will *not* describe a person as a sensation-intuitive type, because in so far as this combination exists, its dynamics involve the kind of war between opposite trends described above for the introversion-extraversion dichotomy. Harmony is a difficult achievement. Disquieting eruptions and stalemates are all too common.

After this overly abstract statement of relationships between the four functions, let us proceed to more concrete description and illustration.

Sensation concerns the present, the *now*. It tells us that a thing *is*, either in the outer world or in ourselves.

Intuition deals with the potential—what the thing will be or has been, not what it *is*.

Feeling gives a sense of values. Is the thing agreeable or disagreeable, to be accepted by the self or rejected? A necessary part of our judgment, it may lead to out-of-hand rejection or blind enthusiasm on no broader base than our personal whim. This is especially true if sensation is the auxiliary function. The person may behave in an infantile or even a psychopathic manner.

Thinking tells us *what the thing is* in an abstract, conceptualized manner. Carried too far without support from other functions, thinking may take us away from reality instead of giving us more control over it. Combined with strong sensation, it leads to pedantic attention to pure fact and to theory divorced from life.

Intuition offers the fructifying "hunch" which allows us to estimate the possibilities of a situation or to reconstruct its dynamic trends by insight into the past. The strongly intuitive person tends to resist the pedantry of facts, the function of sensation. If thinking is his auxiliary function, he may become the creative scientist—whose work requires checking and detailed application to human affairs by other personality types. If feeling is the secondary function, he may become the visionary prophet burning with zeal for the betterment of mankind, distrustful of fact and logic. Obviously I am merely giving easy illustrations, not necessary consequences even for the special combinations chosen for illustration.

All these functions appear within a personality whose temperamental orientation is extraverted or introverted. This orientation, of course, will further determine how the dominant functions operate. The prophet, as extravert, may actively lead a nation, or, as introvert, he may be a spiritual leader whose influence is felt through the example of his living, through quiet writing or preaching to those who seek him out.

Since extraversion and introversion and all the four functions are necessary to wholeness of living, it is obvious that extreme exaggeration in any direction would be pathogenic. "Pure" types cannot be expected, and their closest approximation occurs in pathology. Nevertheless, Jung feels that these temperamental orientations and functions are so much a part of human living that their action and interaction can be used to explain significant patterns of human behavior. They are constantly used by Jungians in therapy. Furthermore Jung feels that Western culture as a whole has concentrated energetically on the world around us, with a consequently dangerous impoverishment of functions connected with the inner world and the stream of life. Thus in *Modern Man in Search of a Soul*, a typology developed from the observation of individuals is extended to the culture.

SYMBOL AND IMAGE

A further conceptual tool is necessary before the major problem of the organization of the personality as Jung sees it may be stated. Because the symbol and image play a much greater role in his theory and in his therapeutic approach than is common in psychoanalytic thought, the somewhat special sense in which Jung uses these terms must be explained.

Like Cassirer and others, Jung makes a distinction between semiotic and truly symbolic terms → images. *Semiotic* terms are *signs* whereby complex ideas are designated by a conventionally accepted shorthand. Jung uses the winged wheel worn as a badge by railroad employees as example of a *sign* (semiotic) which identifies certain personnel. The fact that most Americans are unfamiliar with the winged wheel as an insigne for the railroad and are familiar with "wings" for airmen serves Jung's point. The *semiotic* term merely suggests a prominent aspect of a known "situation" (quotation marks here imply generalization) which is identified by convention. Such convention may be local—like Jung's example of the winged wheel for the railroad employees and the current example of "wings" for airmen. The symbols of mathematics, physics and chemistry are different in that they express "conventionally" relationships among events in the outer world which in a way we all must recognize. These symbols too are semiotic, however, in that they are signs for agreed-upon concepts. They are not intrinsically expressive.

The *symbol* in Jung's definition is something different. It is not merely an analogous or abbreviated expression of a known thing, like the badge of the railway employees or the airforce, or the very careful "signs" employed in the exact sciences. For Jung the term *symbol* should be applied to expression "as the best possible formulation of a relatively unknown thing which cannot conceivably, therefore, be more clearly or characteristically represented."[15] For St. Paul and the early Christian mystics the Cross was "a living symbol which represented the inexpressible *in an unsurpassable way*."[16] In this passage Jung does not attempt to describe the inexpressible for St. Paul more concretely, but one may suppose he had in mind the torture of sacrifice and rebirth as *imaged* in the life and passion of Christ and profoundly re-experienced by the religious mystic in his own soul. For many of the Crusaders the Cross became little more than a secular banner with the relatively limited symbol value of the modern flag. For many people nowadays the Cross is little more than a *sign* that the building it tops is a church. Jung's criterion for the distinction between symbol and sign lies not in the objective characteristics of the symbol but rather in its subjective meaning for the person.

Symbols of deep psychological significance are not simple. Jung writes, "The symbol is always a creation of an extremely complex nature, since data proceeding from every psychic function have entered into its composition."[17]

In part the symbol accords with reason, the function of thinking. One cannot choose just anything for a valid symbol—for a validity beyond a relatively temporary state of one's own psyche. Wickes cites the dream of a patient in which a cheap mug surmounted the waves. Such a mug was the first purchase the patient had made with money she had earned herself. For her in one phase of her analysis, this dime-store item was a reasonable selection. It would not be reasonable for the rest of us. Napoleon's bee represents a similar arbitrary choice on a more grandiose and a more conscious level. By now, however, few people even know that Napoleon tried to make the bee a symbol of empire, his empire.

In still larger part, the importantly valid symbol must accord with the other functions of the mind: sensation, intuition, and feeling. It must express our deep perceptions, our anticipations, our longings and fears. (These words follow, roughly, Jung's definition of the other "functions.") When the thinking function predominates in the conscious life of an individual or a culture, valid (valuable) living symbols do not appear. Modern industrial societies lack great integrating symbols because of the emphasis on the thinking function; they may develop very limited symbolizations in which the shadow of submerged functions may, at times, take the lead, not only against reason but against the conscious collective ideal. The swastika and the "almighty dollar" are examples.

Thus far symbol and image have been merged in discussion. In point of fact, most of the symbols Jung discusses do have the form of a concrete image, whether of an object like the Cross, of a person like the Witch, of abstract forces like the wind, or of an action like crossing a river as the symbol of rebirth. This concretization is similar to that described in Chapter 2 as typical for the dream process. It is not, however, a *necessary* form for the symbol. Words, numbers, relationships, and the like may also serve. The sacred word Om is an example. Yahweh (Jehovah) was originally the God who may not be named, not the bearded patriarch of pictorial representation and childhood fantasy. Some numbers are sacred or lucky, others evil. Higher and lower, larger and smaller have symbolic meaning beyond the specific objects used to express the relationship. Smells may have symbol value.*

* A "psychologist" presented an ambiguous figure to a group, establishing the fact that judgments as to its sex were about equally divided between made and female. Presenting the same

The image in plastic or pictorial form or presented through verbal allusion offers the best medium for complex symbolic expression in the human species. Vision is our most refined distance receptor, the sense modality most directly and elaborately related to concept formation.* At any rate the visual image, understood in its complex ramifications, is the mainstay of Jung's psychology of symbols.

The study of symbols, especially the symbols created by the deep unconscious and found all over the world, becomes for Jung a true and necessary study of human experience. In therapy the symbols created by the patient in dream, fantasy, and art productions, and recognized by him with the help of the analyst, serve to reveal the depths of his soul. They point out to him the dangers incurred by repressing one or another aspect of his being, and by the same token the harmonious, productive freedom to be attained as his antithetical functions become reconciled. The living symbol is not only a matter of dreams and visions. By its very nature it is lived by the person. Any withdrawal from the real world will be reflected in the type of symbol created, which will quietly repeat its statement of the problem beyond the rational will of the patient until the difficulty is finally resolved.

In Wickes' book on therapy, images and symbols seem to play a quasi hortatory role in the patient's life. At crucial periods in real-life situations and in the course of the analysis, submerged aspects of the personality, constructive as well as regressive, make their appearance in dream and fantasy—stating the problem in its deepest terms, pointing the way toward solution. Wickes is careful to make clear that these images are in no sense *deliberately* hortatory. They are possessed of no supernatural foreknowledge, of no power or even intent to guide the fumbling steps of the dreamer. They merely present truly the inner drama of psychic forces, the neglected potentials as well as the monsters and sirens of the past. The images come from the past of the individual

---

figure in a room filled with cigar smoke shifted the judgment of a comparable new group very heavily toward a masculine identification. The association of maleness with cigar smoke is doubtless culturally determined at a relatively superficial level and hence of no great interest to Jungians. The experiment is valuable in demonstrating that modalities other than vision readily develop symbol-sign attributes which operate at the unconscious level.

* Jung is not given to this kind of analysis, but it would seem that emphasis on visual cues may have—along with erect posture and a prehensile thumb—contributed to man's evolution as a concept-forming animal. A visual cue can be communicated and recorded. A gifted dog may make a complex analysis of smells, but his resources for teaching other dogs are limited. Smells, tastes, and sounds are subjective experiences, difficult to reproduce, impossible to record for posterity without the aid of very recent human inventions.

The combination of an emphasis on visual cues plus a bodily structure favoring flexible manipulation of objects probably *began* about a million years ago. It would not be surprising if a predisposition to the formation of images were indeed the heritage of the human species. This footnote may serve as background for discussion of Jung's concept of the collective unconscious, to be presented in a moment.

and of the race (as we shall see in a moment), but the drama they enact is based upon the present conflict. If analyst and patient know how to understand the presentation, the dangers and the promise of the future may be seen, in so far as the psychological future grows from the past—that is, from a past constantly renewed by the present. Thus, although they derive in large part from the remote past, the symbolic productions of the patient are seen as eternally new and prospective in their current structure and meaning.

THE COLLECTIVE UNCONSCIOUS; ARCHETYPES

Thus far we have spoken of symbols as if they were wholly related to the experience of the individual. The vast majority of the symbols we use even in our dreams are of this character, even though they include unconscious aspects of our personality. Jung believes, however, that underlying the experience of the individual is the experience of the human race: the collective unconscious. I quote Jung himself as the best expositor:

> This psychic life is the mind of our ancient ancestors, the way in which they thought and felt, the way in which they conceived of life and the world, of gods and human beings. The existence of these historical layers is presumably the source of the belief in reincarnation and in memories of past lives. As the body is a sort of museum of its phylogenetic history, so is the mind. There is no reason for believing that the psyche, with its peculiar structure, is the only thing in the world that has no history beyond its individual manifestation. Even the conscious mind cannot be denied a history extending over at least five thousand years. It is only individual ego-consciousness that has forever a new beginning and an early end. But the unconscious psyche is not only immensely old, it is also able to grow increasingly into an equally remote future. It forms, and is part of, the human species just as much as the body, which is also individually ephemeral, yet collectively of immeasurable duration.[18]

The collective unconscious is, I quote again, "the all-controlling deposit of ancestral experience from untold millions of years, the echo of prehistoric world events to which each century adds an infinitesimally small amount of variation and differentiation."[19]

The deposit of the racial past provides what Jung calls "a living system of reactions and aptitudes determining the individual life in invisible ways."[20] These ancient systems of reactions show themselves in the form of *archetypes*, or images which express them in the manner of the meaningful symbol described above. The archetypes may thus be distinguished from the more personal symbols, because they belong to the collective unconscious and in this sense transcend the experience of the individual. They do not appear frequently in normal thinking, even the thinking of dreams, since they are in a way antithetical to the development of ego-consciousness.* They may be seen in profound religious thought, in enduring literature and art which draw their universal inspiration from the depths of the human psyche. In these instances the archetypal images are integrated with the development of the individual ego in a valid way. One may also observe the archetypes in psychosis in which the individual ego has been overwhelmed by the archaic collective unconscious. The speech and the art productions of psychotics are deeply revealing, once one tries to understand their basic structure.

The archetypal images are limited in number, corresponding to the relatively limited number of fundamental and typical human situations, rooted in the generalities of our existence. They come into consciousness whenever a personal situation reaches a degree of tension (for good or ill) which stimulates a corresponding archetypal image.† The archetypal images are not inherited as such. They are "not closely circumscribed static figures but rather unconscious inherited predispositions to certain reactions."[21]

Far from being common, the experience of the archetype is "one of the most vivid experiences that man can have."[22] It occurs in the highest manifestations of the creative spirit, in psychosis, and in analytic treatment.‡

What are these archetypes? I have already mentioned the Mother and the various forms she assumes: the life-giver, the all-compassionate, the terrible punisher, the devourer, the divine harlot. Jung also emphasizes the *anima* and the *animus* as principles of the human psyche, so important that I shall discuss them separately a little later. They typically appear in dream and fantasy as images of the opposite sex, whereas the *shadow*, which I shall also discuss later, is likely to appear as an inferior person of the same sex as the dreamer. The four functions described above may appear as part of an image or symbol, either alone or in relation to the *mandala*—the "magic circle"

* This term will be explained later in its full Jungian implications. A good guess at its meaning must suffice the reader here.

† I am here freely using a passage in G. Adler, "A Contribution of Clinical Material," *British Journal of Medical Psychology*, 1949, 22, p. 16.

‡ My impression is that the appearance in treatment is, for Jungians, a complex matter, though I recall no specific discussion of this problem in the Jungian literature I have read. Patients become patients primarily because their modes of effort toward ego integration have in fact too far increased the power of unconscious trends in variety, and typically produce those personal situations of tension which stimulate the corresponding archetypal image. The treatment itself encourages the relatively uncontrolled appearance of the images of the unconscious, so that the patient, with the help of the therapist, may learn better modes of integration.

which in all cultures, even the most primitive, seems to represent a wholeness to which parts contribute in an essentially fourfold manner.*

The archetypes may appear as persons. They may appear as demons or as fabulous animals. They may appear as natural forces and objects. "The star in a dream may be the symbol of a guiding light, the wind a symbol of the breath of the spirit, the rose, of the center of the being and also of the power of growth within the human psyche."[23] Or they may appear as geometrical forms, numbers, and the like, the symbolic meaning of which has been known to esoteric lore throughout the ages in all countries.

The chief evidence for this position is the fact that *highly complex* representations of this nature appear all over the world and may be dreamed or painted by patients who have no conscious knowledge of the ancient symbols. The Jungian analyst studies the arcana of the past for the practical purpose of understanding the meaning of his patient's productions at this level. The deep, universal meanings are interpreted to the patient—with the tact and caution used by all analytic schools and with similar recognition of the need for inner participation by the patient if the interpretation is to have therapeutic value.

The archaic aspects of human life are both beautiful and terrifyingly hideous. On the one hand the deep unconscious is seen as the undifferentiated primitive force which may engulf the life of the individual spirit in darkness and destruction. But it is also the essential source of creative power, necessary to fullness of living. In fact, if the person attempts to deny the deep unconscious instead of relating himself to it, he dooms himself to the half-life of the automaton, and in many cases to mental illness in which the efforts of the conscious self are swamped by archaic forces normally controlled by and subordinated to the individual personality. This problem will be discussed further shortly.

Critical Comment

THE foregoing section has been interlarded with an unusually long series of direct quotations—and I freely confess the reason. I am not able to form a reliable personal opinion about what *Jung* actually means by the collective unconscious and the deep inheritance of mankind. The problem is essentially the same as the one raised in Chapter 4 concerning Freud's view of the phylogenetic origin of the Oedipus complex. At least some of Jung's followers—those I have talked with about my own account of Jung—insist ardently that Jung

---

* Jacobi gives a succinct but well-focused and illustrated discussion of the mandala. (J. Jacobi, *The Psychology of C. G. Jung*, Kegan Paul, Trench, Trubner & Co., 1942, pp. 128 *ff.*)

never intended to imply the inheritance of acquired characteristics. What is inherited is merely a fundamental appreciation of basic problems of human existence, with a predisposition toward certain types of solution embedded in the human psyche, which is immensely old, but still "changing infinitesimally with each century."

According to modern theories of evolution, a century is far too short a span to register the slightest change in the basic biological equipment of man, except as conditions of living may cause special strains in the population to reproduce freely or to die out. Strains of genetic importance are *not* well correlated with cultural achievements along conventional racist or class lines. In so far as Jung is interpreted as suggesting that any important race of man currently known as such (white, black, yellow; Aryan, semitic, negroid, from whatever country of origin) varies from any other race in basic biological equipment, the evidence seems to be against him.* And it is not at all likely that age-old variations in living conditions have at all changed man's inborn nature. The evolution of so complex an organism requires millions of years, and even small changes require thousands.

If, however, Jung's meaning is limited to the statement that evolutionary history has conditioned very deep reaction patterns implicit in man's biological make-up and infantile experience, then I see nothing to quarrel with in the concept of the collective unconscious. But then I also do not see any *fundamental* difference from Freud's position. Jung sometimes writes as if Freud's unconscious were a paltry affair, consisting entirely of rather concrete childhood experiences, subsequently repressed; as if the process of repression took place

* Very isolated cultures may present special genetic problems due to the inbreeding of special strains. This argument does not apply at all to the racial groups commonly cited in "racist" discussions.

as a consequence of difficulties appreciated at a quasi-adult level of sophistication. Something of the sort may have been true of Freud's very early work on hysteria, but it is not true of his later work. The English school especially has emphasized primitive symbolization as occurring long before the phallic stage, and as remaining unconsciously operative, in much more complex relationship to the mechanism of repression. Archaic symbols are used by Freudians as well as Jungians in studies of the deep unconscious but are called universal rather than collective and are usually ascribed to biological structure and infantile experience rather than to living conditions of prehistory. (Freud's concept of the primal horde approaches a "collective" interpretation; in Chapter 4, I remarked that this concept is not much used or is actively repudiated by most Freudians today.)

Jung discusses these archaic symbols in much greater detail than the Freudians, and more in the sense of relatively independent entities. In my final critical comment I shall suggest a general tendency in Jungian theory toward reification of important reaction systems in some contrast to the Freudian genetic approach. Here I offer a few words about the nature of the archetypes Jung proposes. No one will object to his formulations about the Mother. Even Sullivan, who is not much interested in symbol formation at the unconscious level, writes of the Good Mother and the Terrible Mother as personifications of profound significance.

It has occurred to me that the *father* image is far less elaborated in Jung's presentation of archetypes. It seems to appear mainly as power, the Logos principle, benevolent or despotic, usually with abstract or highly personalized symbolism. According to Freud's theory, one might expect *images* representing the Avenger, the Great Rival, and so on. Possibly this relative omission of the father image is a consequence of Jung's rejection of the sexual aspect of Freud's theory and of Freud's undue emphasis on the father. Possibly it is a consequence of the fact that the child comes to appreciation of the specific psychic roles of the father at a somewhat later period, when he already sees the father as a person with individualized characteristics. Hence the personalized symbolism, along with the more generalized sense of benevolent or despotic power. If one assumes a universal primitive-infantile origin for the archetypes, then surely the deepest images should correspond to what the infant can experience. It is the "mother"* who serves the child in the early months when these images are taking form, and so absorbs his emergent attitudes to her feminine person.

Another variety of Jungian archetype is more difficult to explain on the genetic grounds of Freudian theory—the mandala, and other geometrical or arithmetical configurations. It seems incredible to me that Jung's four functions are basic enough to serve in archetypal imagery. I would rather call them a fairly good *descriptive* and *logical* systematization of observable psychic constellations—which, I would think, could be broken down in many other ways. I see nothing intrinsically dynamic about the four functions, nothing deeply related to the human organism as an evolutionary product. In reading dreams reported by Jungian analysts, I have often felt that the patient was dreaming in relation to his analysis (a point discussed in Chapters 2 and 7 as regards "Freudian" dreams) and that the dreams

* I put mother in quotation marks because anyone who cares for the infant is experienced as "mother," even if it happens to be the father. The infant does not make the sexual discrimination, or distinguish between nurse and biological mother. Since women usually do the mothering, the cultural version is feminine, and easily overrides small actual variations in the care accorded the infant.

were more interesting as transference phenomena than as psychic universals.

However, the mandala and the construction on the basis of four are doubtless very common outside of Jungian analysis, in art forms of many origins. I would like to *speculate* on the problem. The circle is the most primitive drawing of little children. In their drawings of people the circular head comes first, later elaborated by legs, then by trunk and arms. The four limbs are very prominent, at first with little attention to body proportions. It seems possible that we are dealing here with a primitive body image, built out of an archaic awareness of the relationship of the nonsexual systems to experience. Certainly the infant appears greatly interested in his hands and feet both as "objects" and increasingly as instruments in his emergent relations with the world around him. Furthermore it seems likely that the infant has a sense of the movement of things in relation to himself as one of his most primitive experiences, and that this sense too may be represented schematically in the essential balances, rhythms, and arrhythms of "universal" art forms.

It would be overbold to insist on the point, but it seems to me possible that archetypes of this more abstract nature are related to those patterns of development in manipulation, locomotion, and the like which have not yet been studied thoroughly in their implications for the growth of personality. Mandalas spontaneously produced by patients have seemed to me to illustrate vividly this "body-image" version of the four poles—obviously limbs, with a central head.

Another set of archetypes seems to be concerned with aspects of the personality which are already crystallized in consequence of interpersonal experience but which attain their special form so early, in relation to conditions so general in human society, that they may fairly be considered universal or collective. The anima and the animus, the guiding spirit, the various views of the self, the persona, and I think even the shadow belong in this category—which is not unlike Freud's "institutions," although more particularized.*

I have usually found that if I translate a Jungian archetype into the dull term "basic trend" or "a dynamic system organized at a deep level of bio-social experience," I have something I can not only understand but may even find an exhilarating extension of familiar ideas about "basic trends."

Jung's emphasis is on the symbol, the image. In Chapter 2 it was pointed out that the unconscious tends to take this concrete form of expression. Any dream illustrates the mechanism. The images of the archetypes follow the same mechanism, but the trends symbolized are older, deeper, less immediately related

* These concepts will be discussed shortly.

to the dreamer's conscious, day-to-day experience.

In brief summary, *if* one may interpret Jung's concept of the collective unconscious as meaning deep trends inherent in the biological equipment of man, and the quasi-necessary experience of his infancy, I see no fundamental discord with Freudian and other views presented in this book. The "image" quality of the expression of the unconscious is well known and may be applied to the special problem of symbolizing basic trends.

If this interpretation of Jung's view of the collective unconscious is correct, the important psychological problem becomes whether the archetypes Jung describes are really basic, and what their relationship is to other aspects of the personality. Jung himself has a great deal to say on this point which must be reported before final comment.

SUBSIDIARY CONCEPTS

Ego-consciousness. Ego-consciousness in Jung's sense is like that of Freud in that it is not thought of as coextensive with the personality or the self. Rather it is one aspect of growth. The emphasis seems to be more upon consciousness than in Freud's mature concept of the ego. A further difference is that many of the functions Freud ascribes to the ego (to sub-organizations of the ego) are handled by Jung in a series of separate concepts: the four functions, the soul-image (anima and animus), the persona, etc. Also ego-consciousness appears to have a more definite focus in the "I" of common parlance. It is, perhaps, similar in this respect to Federn's concept of the ego as something "felt" by the person as himself. We all have a vague sense that "we" are feeling or doing something, that things are happening to "us." Our consciousness of inner and outer events is almost always tacitly related to this sense of "I," even though we cannot formulate clearly exactly what we mean by it. We are, indeed, surprised at times to find ourselves doing certain things which we feel are unlike us; we are often surprised at the picture other people have of us, and at what we can come to recognize about ourselves in analytic treatment.

As I understand Jung's position, ego-consciousness refers to this rather undifferentiated *awareness* of the "I" and the events of living. A more organized sense of self resulting from efforts at social adaptation is called the *persona*. The term *Self* is reserved for the integrative achievement of harmonious function among the various aspects of the personality, conscious and unconscious. It will be discussed at the end of this chapter. Here I may say merely that despite his emphasis on the creative power of the unconscious, Jung's hope for mankind lies in the development of consciousness. His stipulation is that the dark creative forces be accepted and brought into relationship to conscious effort. They become destructive only as they are excluded from control and rich elaboration by a fully developed ego-consciousness.

The Persona. The adaptively organized image of the self which all of us form in the course of living Jung calls the *persona*. The word is taken from the mask worn by the actors of ancient Greece; it represents the face we show to the world. The persona is formed partly consciously as we develop specific personal ideals, goals, and a sense of our social role. Partly the process is unconscious as we identify with persons of importance to us and subtly take over the social values of our environment without being aware of the adoption. The *collective ideals* of specific social groups influence all of their members through the persona to a degree far in excess of conscious conformity or rebellion.*

In essence, the persona is a necessity for social living. Constant baring of the soul in everyday situations with all one's associates would be not only embarrassing but highly inefficient for most of the small transactions required in a complex society. Wickes[24] cites a dream of a young man who tended to wear his heart on his sleeve on all occasions. His ideal was "frankness." At a social gathering people were avoiding an uncouth monster—a turtle without its shell. He considered the turtle disgusting, and after discussion of the dream for the first time began to appreciate the quality of his own behavior.

A much more common difficulty is the obverse of the turtle without its shell. The shell becomes too strong, smothering the life within, preventing genuine contact with people and with life itself. Too often the ego-consciousness becomes almost exclusively identified with the persona. The individual becomes a fine lawyer, a gracious hostess, or whatever, and forgets how to be a human being. In such cases the shadow aspects of the personality tend

---

* It should be noted that the collective ideals of the group are different from the collective unconscious, discussed earlier. They are the specific product of the adaptation of the group to its actual conditions of living in all their contemporary complexity, whereas the collective unconscious refers to the most deeply human problems of existence which are the same through all the ages over the whole world.

to grow to unmanageable proportions, because the life forces cannot really be denied. The consequences are those of any severe repression. They vary from person to person depending on the nature of the shell, the mask, the nature of the forces denied, the nature of the society, which may or may not continue to approve the inflexible shell and which may or may not permit *sub rosa* gratifications. The consequences of identification with a limited persona are always bad and may be disastrous.

Thus far the persona has been described as something of a unit. This is true for some people, mainly for introverts. These people present a single face to the world, and although the face has been developed in large part as a means of adaptation, the person now demands that it be accepted as his genuine self. Or at least he cannot readily change his face to fit the changing circumstances of life. He may be highly regarded in some situations—*e.g.,* on the lecture platform or in his office—but considered awkward, shy, or clumsy elsewhere. Highly introverted persons tend to identify too far with a single persona and to feel uneasy when it does not fit the situation. Or they may feel uneasy with *any* persona, experiencing too consciously the "mask" character of their behavior in all situations. For these people the question "Who am I?" may become a daily torture, different in kind from the sudden question of the person whose accepted persona has been dramatically challenged.

For some people—mainly the extraverts, in Jung's typology—changing the persona is as easy as changing their attire. The pontifical professor adjourns with his students to an informal get-together over a manly glass of beer. He is suave at a cocktail party, easily tactful at the Womens' Club, inspirational in a talk to the young people at the church, tender with his wife, a pal with his children, and so on. Such people are rarely conscious hypocrites. They have become sensitive to the demands of the group and select the proper mask without thinking, without any sense that they are playing a part. They are often rightfully indignant when accused of double-dealing, and they are no more necessarily "show-offs" than people who concentrate on a single persona. Normally, and even ideally, the social front is adapted to current group demands—within limits. Yet the person whose persona veers radically with every group demand may ultimately ask the same question as the introvert: "Who am I?" When one of his major roles has been effectively challenged, the question may come to the extravert like a clap of thunder. Or the question may come insidiously after a series of small failures, or perhaps after experience of a loving relationship which comes in spite of the persona rather than because of it.

Thus the persona takes different forms in different societies and with different people. It may show one face or many faces. It may be a cheerfully minor part of conscious adaptation to social requirements—or it may become pathogenic in its dominance. The role of the persona depends upon the organization of the personality as a whole, and upon the organization of the society, whose collective ideals may be more or less flexible, more or less directly related to the forces of the deep unconscious, more or less accepting of the special persona developed by the individual.

The Soul-image (Anima and Animus). The persona is a construct of relatively late development as the individual encounters the *social* problem of establishing the contours of his own individuality in relation to other people. I described it first because it is closest to what most of us think of as ego-consciousness. It is not fully conscious, and is not the self, in Jung's theory. The *soul-image* lies deeper in the unconscious. Its determinants are sexual, or rather contra-sexual in origin. Every man bears within his psyche an *anima,* which represents the feminine aspects of his being. Every woman has her *animus,* the male component.

Jung writes of a principle which forms and differentiates, which brings order out of chaos, which strives for mastery and competence, the *dynamis.* This is the *Logos.* There is also a principle of relatedness and receptivity, a tendency to love and nurture the potentials of life. For this principle Jung, like Freud, *although in a more specialized sense,* uses the term *Eros.* Jung seems to feel that in a general way the forming, mastering trend is masculine, the receptive, nurturing trend feminine. Both of these trends are necessary, however, to human function, and both sexes are in a way bisexual. Thus the normal development of the boy tends to be in the direction of the *Logos,* but he cannot successfully deny his anima. Conversely for the girl. These trends, implicit in biological difference, take special forms in later development, depending on actual relations with the parents and other significant figures in the person's life.* The anima includes archetypal images of woman: the

---

* I may here summarize the major theories as to sex differences discussed in this book. Adler considers *no* psychological sex differences as inborn. The differences observable between men and women are due solely to differences in the *attitude of the culture* toward the sexes, an attitude which profoundly affects the life style of the little girl or boy from the very beginning. The other analysts discussed in Part III are less intransigent, but the emphasis is on cultural factors.

Freud states that there is no *intrinsic psychological* difference between the male and female infant, basic human trends being bisexual. However, since personality, for Freud, develops mainly out of the relationship between biologically determined needs and possibilities for fulfillment, the course of personality development must be different for the girl because of the nature of her genital organs. (See pp. 216ff.) By this detour, Freud arrives at a description of basic masculine and feminine trends not unlike Jung's description, and with a rather similar sense of the bisexual trends (*Anlage*) inherent in both sexes. Both indicate how these differences may contribute toward neurosis as they come into conflict with cultural stereotypes.

eternal Mother, the Virgin, the Harlot, the Witch, the Temptress, the Spiritual Guide, like Dante's Beatrice. If the man has somehow failed to establish good relations with the real women of his life and with the feminine elements in his own psyche, these archaic forms of the feminine principle tend to dominate the unconscious. In extreme cases of mother fixation, the anima may be completely dominated by the archetypal mother image; in less extreme cases, or as the patient improves in the course of analysis, other forms appear. The man may give himself over so completely to his anima as to destroy his masculine potential. His view of the real women he meets may be distorted by the images of the unconscious in many forms, depending more upon his own mood than upon the actual behavior of the living women. The man may identify with his anima and seek his own masculinity in other men—*i.e.,* homosexual trends may become dominant.

Conversely a man may attempt an overmasculine adaptation, severely rejecting his anima. This happens especially often when the boy identifies with a powerful father image and aspires to a "masculine" career. The consequence may be a pervasive sense of coldness and aridity, or frustration or fear. The anima may appear in the image of a beautiful frail woman being devoured by a masculine monster, as a leprous woman asking alms who is nevertheless powerful, etc., etc. Wickes[25] describes in some detail a young man whose problem was repeated failing in college entrance examinations and in job situations despite an earnest wish to succeed in accordance with the desires of his parents which he had consciously entirely accepted, and despite good native abilities. Invited to do exactly what he pleased, for once, he drew a picture of a huge Oriental male face swallowing a woman—his anima. This picture and others drawn in quick succession allowed the boy, with the analyst's help, to recognize how an early artistic bent had been renounced under the pressures of parental values, reinforced by the conventionally fine prep school to which he had been sent. In this case the anima had to be rescued from the devouring masculinity. Wickes reports that the boy not only did well at the art school he then elected to attend, but was able to support himself by part-time jobs of the type in which he had failed earlier.

Wickes is careful to point out that the boy's problems were not fully

---

I think both have been widely misunderstood as relegating woman's nature to *Kinder, Küche, and Kirche* (children, kitchen, and church). In point of fact, although both emphasize the *depth* of the basic trends in woman's nature, both indicate how they can function productively outside the kitchen and church, although still in good relationship with children. Furthermore the male cannot safely deny the "feminine" aspects of his psyche any more than the female can renounce active "masculine" strivings.

In theory, Jung's position is more direct than Freud's. The sexes are different. He does not theorize about emergent reaction patterns developed via special organs. But his concept of the essential bisexuality of the human spirit leads to conclusions that are at least compatible with Freud's conclusions and are opposed to the radically cultural view of Adler.

solved by the few sessions with the analyst which resulted in a change of professional aspiration. She does suggest that, especially with young people, timely recognition (*by the patient*) of a submerged bent may quite effectively change the direction of his efforts toward a more harmonious integration of the conscious and unconscious aspects of the personality. In this case the anima was being submerged, partly because family and school tacitly condemned artistic pursuits as effeminate. More often the problem cannot be resolved in terms of a change in professional aim. The profession remains the same, but the person comes to accept tender, nurturing attitudes as part of his job. Its "he-man" aspects are tempered by the Eros principle. The image of the anima leads the man to relatedness and love.

In the same way every woman has her animus, the forming, differentiating, mastering side of her personality. The woman can no more deny her animus than the man can deny the anima. Denial leads to infantile helplessness or to all-absorbing "motherhood." To be constructively feminine, receptive, nurturing, the woman must somehow recognize the masculine element within herself in order to recognize the constructive aspects of her husband's and children's lives, and to live out her own potentialities. If she fails to do so, her life may become as sour and as arid as the life of the man who denies his anima. Unrecognized, the animus may come to dictate her behavior. It makes little difference whether she engages in "masculine" pursuits, or forces "obedience" in the home, or demands that her family fulfill rigidly her ideals of prestige, accomplishment, or whatever.

The Shadow. The shadow represents the unconscious, but in a way peculiar to Jung's theory. It is quite literally the shadow, the dark side, the unconscious *obverse* of whatever trends the person has emphasized in his ego-consciousness, in the active trend of his living. It is personalized in the sense that our shadows are intimately related to us as the dark reflection of our conscious efforts. The more sharply delimited these become, the sharper the shadow. In fact, the shadow may become monstrous and actually overwhelm the ego-consciousness.

Jung contrasts the deep unconscious (represented by the archetypes) with lesser images more closely related to individual experience in a specific society. He describes basic attitudes (extraversive-introversive) and basic functions (sensation, intuition; feeling, thinking). But he presents all of his theses with an antithesis—a shadow, which is unconscious and which lengthens with one-sided exaggeration of the conscious modes.

Thus in a sense the shadow is a highly personal creation, the dark side of our specific personality trends. In another sense it is no more personal than Freud's unconscious. It reflects the universals of human experience and

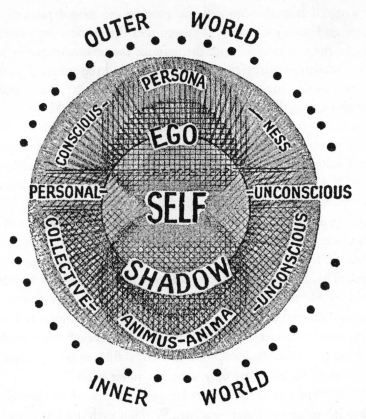

is "personal" only in so far as each individual draws differently upon the primitive human within all personalities. As an empirical concept, it refers primarily to Jung's psychology of opposites, elaborated as described throughout this chapter.

THE INTEGRATION OF THE PERSONALITY; THE SELF

In Jung's vocabulary the term *Self* is reserved for the integration of the various aspects of the personality, conscious and unconscious, thus far discussed. It should be distinguished from ego-consciousness, which is the vague "I" of common parlance, and from the more organized persona, which represents the face or faces we construct in the course of social adaptation. The Self is an achievement rather than a biological given.*

I reproduce above a diagram presented, rather cautiously, by Jacobi in his efforts to explain the relationship among the concepts we have been consider-

---

* The reader may be reminded of several discussions of the semantic problem previously presented. By now variations in the meaning of the same words from school to school must be familiar.

ing. It suggests how the ego and the persona are related primarily to consciousness and the outer world. The ego and the shadow are placed in the same circle, the one involved with the persona, the other with the more deeply unconscious contra-sexual trends of the animus and the anima. The collective unconscious is the fundament of the personality in its inner aspects, in a general way opposed to consciousness and the outer world. Jacobi remarks that "the different parts of the total psyche already discussed are . . . included in the diagram, without any claim being made to represent their real order, positional value, etc., it being impossible to show anything so abstract schematically."[26] Areas of shading suggest especially close connections among these major areas, regardless of the factor of consciousness.

Jacobi puts the Self at the center of the diagram but implies in his text that it is also at the periphery. The ideal Self, for Jung, includes and thoroughly integrates all the various aspects, functions, attitudes, and images thus far described. This Self is not inborn, not even in the sense of a potential as suggested by Horney's concept of the "real self." On the contrary, it is an achievement attained only by the few, the heroes, after arduous endeavor.

Jung writes: "Personality as a complete realization of the fullness of our being is an unattainable ideal. But unattainability is no counterargument against an ideal, for ideals are only signposts, never goals."[27]

The development of the personality proceeds first of all through human need, through inner and outer coercions. Without such need, it would become "mere acrobatics of the will." Secondly, it requires the courage to bear separation from the herd and its conventions, to be isolated. (Cf. the emphasis of Fromm and Rank on this point.) And finally it means fidelity and trust in the law of one's own being,

> a loyal perseverance and trustful hope; in short, such an attitude as a religious man should have to God. And now it becomes apparent that a dilemma heavily weighted with consequences emerges from behind our problem: personality can never develop itself unless the individual chooses his own way consciously and with conscious, moral decision. Not only the causal motive, the need, but a conscious, moral decision must lend its strength to the process of the development of personality.[28]

SUMMARY

Jung envisages the libido as a single energic life principle, which takes many forms. In the growth of the child it normally moves from the nutritive to the genital zone, although there is normally a period of irregular commingling during which rhythmic activities related to one or the other function become important in their own right and are associated with the development of the mind and of speech. The image of the parents, especially the Mother, plays a crucial role in this development. The child seeks the nourishing, compassionate figure of the early phase of infancy, and fuses this figure with his emergent genital libido. He thus tends to be dominated by incestuous longings. These are prohibited not only or even primarily by his realistic biological and social fears. The deepest terror that the Mother holds is fear of the retrospective longing for the passivity of the suckling era, of the Terrible Mother, the Witch who devours the constructive energies of mankind. Human growth requires a sacrifice of the child self, and a rebirth into adulthood—a process which is by no means general. The majority of mankind remains caught in the nursery, as it were.

The libido (life energy) takes two directions, the one extraversive (outgoing, concerned with objects and people), the other introversive (concerned with the inner world, the subject, the "I"). Both directions are necessary, but individuals tend to exhibit one attitude predominantly and so to be subject to typing along these lines. Modes of grasping and forming empirical material are described by Jung as the four functions: sensation and intuition, feeling and thinking. Again all functions are necessary, but again individuals tend to cultivate one or the other in a manner which becomes characteristic. The neglected attitude or function is relegated to the unconscious, where it may gain in power, although it remains relatively undifferentiated. Hence many of the nervous disorders in middle life, when the antithetical aspects of the dominant personality break through or sap the energy of the person.

The special use of symbols by Jung requires discussion. Aspects of living become concretized in a manner which expresses their living role "in an unsurpassable way." As such living symbols appear in dreams, visions, fantasies, and art productions, they may be used as accurate reflections of the current status of the personality, and for indication of its major trends toward the future. The symbols often refer to the remote past of the individual, even of the race (the collective unconscious; archetypes). But their appearance is functionally related to the present. For Jung the distortions of the dream are not merely *semiotic* as for Freud—i.e., indicators of a whole alluded to but not included in the dream or pathological symptom—but tend to be truly *symbolic* in the sense that the current problem is actually expressed, symbolically, in its major dynamic outlines.

Thus Jung considers that his approach is functionally oriented toward the present and future, whereas Freud's is reductive and mechanistic, viewing the present as nothing but a deterministic compromise with the repressed past, essentially devoid of meaning. (It was remarked that Freudians reject this view of their approach.)

The collective unconscious consists of the powerful psychological trends rooted in man's biological equipment—that is, in the ancient experience of the species. Symbols arising at this level are of universal importance—the archetypes. The unconscious obverse of trends emphasized in the life of the individual is called the shadow. The soul-image, anima or animus, is the unconscious contra-sexual counterpart of attitudes deeply connected with the orientation of the two sexes: a masculine forming, mastering principle (Logos) and a feminine receptive, loving, nurturing principle (Eros). Again both principles are necessary to wholeness of living. The man who too far denies his anima or who too far identifies with it is likely to develop neurotic difficulties, as will the man who too far rejects the counterpart of his attitudinal and functional type.

Jung uses the term *ego-consciousness* for awareness, and for the primitive sense of "I" that we feel toward the inner and outer events of which we are aware. He has a special word—the *persona*—for the "I" as a product of efforts at interpersonal adaptation. This construct of the personality varies in format with the personality type as well as the circumstances of living. The extravert often has several personae, each appropriate to the situation within which he is functioning; the introvert tends to concentrate on one. Although the persona is a necessary and very useful development of the personality, it should not be confused with the personality itself. It is only one aspect.

Full development of the personality, of the Self, is—for Jung—an adventure and an achievement of heroic proportions. The mass of mankind lives out its span within the safe confines of convention. We have no reason to be satisfied with our current conventions. The hero springs from common human stuff, experiences the same needs, but he has the courage to go his own way in isolation, to be faithful to the law of his being—which includes the dark forces of the shadow and the collective unconscious. It is only by the painful path of conscious individuation, of integration in consciousness of the archaic and the contemporary, of the natural bent and its shadow, that the hero arrives at the fulfillment of the human potential.

Critical Comment

IT is perhaps well to confess that I began the reading of Jungian material with an antipathy not uncommon among American psychologists, especially those who take their psychoanalytic orientation mainly from Freud. A number of my highly respected colleagues and friends were Jungians, but their allegiance seemed to me merely an amiable foible, essentially unrelated to the almost uncanny insights they sometimes showed. The specifically Jungian concepts I knew seemed to me mainly mystical balderdash.

In these pages I shall remain critical of Jung's basic theoretical position. To my way of thinking he turns important dynamic systems into "universals." He is reductionist, albeit in a more pluralistic manner than the schools discussed in Part III. What I have learned from the study necessary to writing this chapter, however, is the profound importance of the concrete systems he observes. Although to my mind they are not universal, they are so general and reach so deeply into the human psyche as to merit careful attention. I came to see Jung's rubrics as creative syntheses of observable trends which I might explain differently but which I had to respect. Since reading this material, I have developed a few new "uncanny insights" of my own. In trying to get across workable psychological generalizations to students of projective methods, I find myself consciously inhibiting a tendency to use Jungian concepts. I often feel that if they had read Jung I would not have to struggle so hard to convey a sense of *underlying trends* revealed in the test materials instead of the direct *linkage* of test data with behavioral trait or identifiable instinctual drive, role, or diagnostic entity which students trained in academic psychology tend to expect. The trends can usually be explained in other terms, but they lose the vividness and focus of the Jungian formulation. If, nevertheless, I do not espouse Jung's system as a whole, it is because, as I shall try to show in detail, it lacks the fluidity characteristic of a developmental psychology. I hope, therefore, that the following remarks will be read in the perspective of a genuine appreciation of the clinical values of Jung's theory.

The major difference from Freudian theory seems to me the one Jung himself stresses—the repudiation of Freud's idea of the genetic process as "causal."

Indeed, as Jung moved away from Freud, he lost interest even in his own modifications of the Freudian view of childhood development. The comment of Jungian readers on my discussion of the movement of the libido from the nutritive to the genital zone was that it is correct "but not much used nowadays." The emphasis lies almost exclusively on the action and, above all, the interaction of systems whose major outlines have already taken form. Some of these systems belong to the past of the species and are inborn as biologically determined predispositions. Others are the consequence of trends of living for specific individuals or cultures. For example, concentration on the thinking function often leads to neglect of the feeling function to the point at which in late middle age everything seems futile, or there may be untoward eruptions of feeling-dictated behavior from the shadow aspect of the personality. Our extraverted, scientifically oriented culture shows a similar trend.

Jung's critique of Freud's genetic theory seems to me justified *if one interprets Freud's theory as narrowly as did Jung.* Perhaps Jung's interpretation was correct for psychoanalysis in the early 1900's. Certainly his critique is correct for any theory which assumes static biological needs, some of which are repressed and continue active as "the unconscious." A therapy of release on a purely historical basis of recapturing the childhood events leading to the repression is clearly a bad therapy. But this is not Freud's mature theory or his therapy, as I trust was made abundantly clear in Part II.

My own point of view, in most respects essentially Freudian, insists upon a genetic orientation toward the development of significant psychological systems, in creative interaction with systems constellated around other, nonpsychological foci—*i.e.,* events in the natural universe and in organized society. Psychological systems are relatively general *when rooted in the structure of the organism.* Illustrations are Jung's collective unconscious, the archetypes; the deep unconscious of Freud. They are also relatively general *when they represent an early or constant reaction pattern to cogent and enduring external systems.* Examples may be found in much of Jung's analysis of types as regards attitudes and functions, although these are partly inborn; on a somewhat different level the soul-image, the anima and animus; finally the persona which is definitely adaptive in origin. Freud has no convenient generalizing terms for these systems, but uncodified equivalents may be suggested in the structure of the narcissistic and object libido; the concept of bisexuality, with profound differences between male and female psychology as it develops through early sexual experience, conditioned by difference in the anatomical structure of the genital organs; in the growth of the superego and ego ideal; in deeply established defense mechanisms merging into characterological patterns.

There is the further problem of relating the more changeable aspects of living to these deep-lying systems—our immediate selective attention, our interests, our concrete goals. These aspects of living too are to be considered as systems in my view of systems, but they are transient systems which cannot be explained in their full particularity by psychological insight into the more general deep-lying systems. I hold no brief for any psychological system which takes common contingencies of social adaptation as basic psychological principles. (Here I include most of the psychologies evolved by or used by economists and political scientists who want to get on with the study of systems proper to their own disciplines with as little bother from the psychological element as possible.) But a good basic theory of psychology must include detailed insight into *how these flexibly adaptive sys-*

tems of relatively transient nature are achieved.

On this last point, all the psychoanalytic schools are weak. One should not ask of any theory of systems lying deep in the organism that it be *directly* applicable to the transient systems of daily living in diverse societies, under the special conditions every individual encounters in his moment of time. But one *should* ask that the psychological theory be oriented toward understanding the creative interaction of systems at all levels.

In my comment on Chapter 7, I suggested that the *multidimensionality* of the Freudian approach offers an excellent basis for such understanding. Because of its emphasis on the developmental process, it allows for endless growth of insight into the nature of the drive systems and the way in which they become elaborated into later psychological structures of more or less enduring quality. I took issue with Freud's dichotomy of instinctual drives (sexuality and aggression; Eros and Thanatos) in so far as they are used reductively to explain the complex present. However, if we grant a more liberal view of Freud's position than the one Jung attacks, it seems to me that Jung's theory is really more analytic, deductive, and static than Freud's. Jung formulates many *significantly operating systems* in the adult psyche more vividly than Freud—for some purposes more usefully. But he tends to envisage them as primal entities rather than emergent dynamic systems. And he seems even less interested than Freudians in studying the ways in which they are modified and altered.

The danger of Jung's position is *reification* of developmental and adaptive systems to such an extent that they become a pluralism of universals, which are then considered as interacting along complex but essentially mechanistic lines. The various subdivisions of the psyche described in the foregoing chapter become quite stable "things" (often personified), which are then studied in relation to one another and to their own intrinsic antithesis or shadow. Since the psychic entities Jung proposes are systems of profound importance, since he is sensitively alert to their interaction, and since he calls upon intuition to penetrate the disguises they assume, it sounds like a foolish paradox to say that his theory leads toward a static intellectualism. Nevertheless, I think that this is the ultimate fate of any theory that does not find its psychological roots in the genetic process.

Types

For convenience in this discussion, I have divided Jung's theory into two parts —a psychology of types and a psychology of symbols. By *types* I mean the introversive or extraversive *attitudes* and the four *functions* with their intrinsic auxiliary and antithetical relationships. As a specialist in the Rorschach method, I have used the dichotomy of *attitudes* in a very practical way for many years. Hermann Rorschach was a contemporary of Jung's in Zurich, and he guardedly built the dichotomy into his test. As teacher of the Rorschach method I have some difficulty every term in explaining to beginners the essential difference between the predilection of subjects for movement *vs.* color responses—roughly speaking, introversive *vs.* extraversive trends. I have to hammer out of the students a tendency to interpret a ratio between these types of response high on the movement side (introversive) as a safe indication of withdrawn, timid, self-centered *behavior* on the part of the test subject. Not infrequently the subject's *behavior* is quite different, either as a rather constant personality pattern or on special occasions—just as Jung remarks. It is hard to bring students trained in psychologies emphasizing observable behavior to a

feeling for underlying trends whose expression varies both in overt manifestation and in subjective report. Nevertheless, the Rorschach expert will not interpret other test indices in the same way when they occur in an "introversive" setting as when they occur in an "extratensive" setting, and much of his skill depends upon this insight. Even in research with other tests, I have found this basic dichotomy significant and useful.[29]

I am less favorably impressed by Jung's analysis of the four functions, possibly because they do not have the backing of actual use in an important psychological test and because they do not correspond directly with familiar clinical formulations. They seem to me abstractions, logically arrived at, rather than emergent trends basic to the organismic function. After all, the introversion-extraversion dichotomy has a correspondence in Freud's narcissistic-libido and object-libido; perhaps even in the classification I chose as a basis for the outline for this book: the terms of the organism and the terms of the milieu. Sensation and intuition, feeling and thinking seem to me rather arbitrary and intellectualistic subdivisions of psychological function.

In earlier comment (p. 556) I hazarded the guess that the impressive appearance of "four" in the mandala might be related to a primitive body image. It is difficult for me to believe that subdivisions rooted in an analysis of complex, highly socialized functions have the psychological depth and substance attributed to them by Jung. I suggest that they be considered, if at all, as convenient codifications of observable phenomena rather than as intrinsically dynamic systems in their own right.

On somewhat similar grounds, I would myself reject Jung's emphasis on thesis and antithesis—hence also the *theoretical* background of the shadow. Jung's theory seems here an intellectualistic generalization. The phenomenon of the shadow is doubtless very common in our culture but not universal in the sense of being deeply rooted in biological structure and the quasi-necessary experience of the infant. *Some* alternating cycles are so rooted: hunger and satiety, night and day, winter and summer, right and left. What goes up must come down. An exaggeration of action in one direction very often brings a reaction in the opposite direction measurable almost as exactly as the swing of a pendulum. Opposites are profoundly important in our experience, and our experience tends toward a generalization of opposites as a principle even beyond the events that we have directly experienced. This acknowledgment does not give Jung (or Hegel) the right to assume a *general* theory of opposites and to turn a common, important psychological experience into a philosophical law. A *view of systems* can use these dichotomies in many situations, but it cannot be bound by a theoretical abstraction of thesis and antithesis.

In so far as Jung's concept of the shadow offers a *convenient generalizing term* for what Freud calls reaction formation and what Horney calls the vicious circle, it seems to me valuable. A sort of antithesis to any exaggerated defense mechanism *does* tend to occur. But Freud and Horney, by their respective dynamic theoretical systems, try to explain *why*. They are not content with a philosophical generalization, broadly applied to psychological phenomena.

Thus, although the concept of the shadow often expresses very well the dynamic antitheses of the person's unconscious reaction patterns, although it may sometimes offer a needed corrective for the overspecificity of the Freudian concept of reaction formation and the overgeneralization of Horney's vicious circle, I cannot think it a good concept for a flexibly enduring theory of psychological science. It is too far

rooted in a logico-philosophical approach conceived as universal in principle and hence reductionist.

I have remarked that Jung's view of the anima and animus as typical contrasexual patterns in a species that is essentially bisexual—but differentiated along sexual lines—was not unlike that of Freud in its final conclusions. But with Jung we have psychological differences *inborn* with the sex difference, whereas Freud tries to show how they *develop*. In our culture the anima and the animus seem to me quite useful concepts. Again, however, the flat affirmation that these frequently observable sex differences are necessary predispositions of the soul is not justified by available evidence and does not constitute a helpful hypothesis for further investigation. It too far accepts as basic ideas of masculinity and femininity that are probably strongly influenced by our culture pattern, that may require deep revision as the roles of men and women change in a changing world. Although, in my opinion, Freud places too exclusive emphasis on the structure of the external genital organs, his analysis of the problem in terms of emergent systems constellated around aspects, of biological equipment in relation to experience seems to me more sound as an initial approach, more in line with a view of systems. It suggests that sex differences lie deeper in human nature than Adler and culturalists of the feministic persuasion have supposed, but it does not presuppose a particular psychological definition. Freud's view of sex differences can be corrected and elaborated with less change in underlying theory.

We come finally to the persona. This concept of Jung's is frankly developmental—the consequence of the actual adaptive experience of the individual. It escapes the typical Jungian formulation of thesis and antithesis. It is not, therefore, subject to the kind of criticism I have thus far offered. On the contrary, it corresponds remarkably well with my proposal of a "self image" as a construct of some stability arising primarily from the person's pattern of social adaptation. This construct has seemed to me sufficiently important, especially in our culture, to require recognition as something like a fourth institution in the Freudian structural view of the developing personality. It is not inborn, but it comes to function with a kind of cogency and unity in its own right well beyond instinctual drive systems and well beyond the external patterns characteristic of the culture. It is an adaptive integration.

Jung points out that the persona varies not only in content but in structure, so that whereas some people have a single, rather tightly organized persona, others have several personae. Furthermore, the persona may be differently related to ego-consciousness and to the self. This is the kind of variability I have tried to suggest in my discussion of the self image, which might be investigated further as regards both individual differences and the culture patterns affecting the individual in the course of developing and maintaining his self image(s). For example, if the self image is closely related to the superego, and the superego to well-defined social patterns, one might expect extremely powerful adherence to or rebellion against rather specific ego ideals and social codes. (Cf. the importance of knightly honor in the Middle Ages.) If social mobility is great, if childhood discipline is permissive and "reasonable," the self image is likely to be more clearly adaptive at the social level but probably more subject to the pathogenic idealization that Horney has observed. In Erikson's language, the problem of establishing one's *identity* becomes more complex and more troublesome and more compelling. In the language of the social psychologists, role-finding takes on different contours with variations in the deeper personality configurations and in the structure of the social group effective for the individual.

I am, of course, offering only speculations which serve to illustrate the kind of inquiry which might be facilitated by this enlargement of Freudian rubrics in a perspective that uses rather than repudiates the contributions of other schools. I have tried to show that Jung's concept of the persona is not so deeply infused with principles inherent in his theoretical system that it cannot be used rather directly in other systems. To my mind he states the nature of this construct well, and I for one would like to take some of his special generalizations about it as hypotheses for investigation.

An aspect of Jung's work little noticed by outsiders is its explicit concern with the middle and later years of life. Here his critique of Freud and the positive —though to my mind limited—values of his approach come to a focus. Jung justly remarks that trends established over a lifetime cannot be "cured" by release of infantile repressions. They have developed power in their own right. Every analyst, including the "Freudians," would agree, although the ego-psychology aspects of Freud's position took effective form only in the late 1920's. The broader constellations of deep-lying personality trends, solidified in the course of living, are still not so firmly defined as in Jung's system. Indeed, "Freudians" are chary of too much codification of the "defense mechanisms" lest the unique structure of the individual personality be lost. The instinctual drives and their components, the three psychic institutions (id, ego, superego), the four approaches (topographical, structural, genetic, and quantitative) the ego functions, the processes of identification, introjection and projection, etc., etc., present a view of personality dynamics that is much more complex but one that the Freudians consider more sound.

As critic, I share this "Freudian" uneasiness about Jung's system—or Horney's or any system that attempts to derive personality from a relatively limited number of trends, no matter how established, no matter how flexible and complexly interactive. I do feel, however, that significantly recurrent systems neither so broad nor so narrow as the Freudian units are built up in the course of living in any culture, partly through external pressures, partly through intrapsychic dynamics. With proper attention to their developmental and relatively limited nature, they could, I believe, be added to the Freudian scheme, not so much as complications as a needed simplification of *certain important types of event very commonly encountered*. Observations in group psychology and in brief therapy, as well as treatment of older patients, could be better focused if more systematic attention were paid to characteristic trends in adaptation.

Schools less adequate in theory than the mature Freudian approach are clearly successful in many situations, social and therapeutic—I think because they have appreciated these recurrent systems accurately. They fail when the theoretical system is applied generally (reductively) in situations in which it does not fit. Although it would be folly for the Freudians to take over specific formulations from other schools without careful reformulation in terms of their own dynamic system, they would do well, in my opinion, to study these successful formulations for the *substance* they offer in codifying "significantly recurring systems" which are useful in practice.

Symbols

The second aspect of Jung's theory— a psychology of symbols—seems to me worthy of very careful consideration and esteem. The distinction between semiotic items (signs) and the creative transformation involved in living symbols is important. Susanne Langer[30] develops the point well from the philosophical point of view—incidentally, without reference to Jung. The living symbol does not merely *represent* wider experience on the *pars pro toto* principle familiar to early experiments in conditioning, nor is it the agreed-upon sign for highly abstract relationships as in mathematics and the natural sciences. It is creative. Freudian use of the term "symbol" is closer to Jung's in its emphasis on deep personal meaning, but the Freudian emphasis is on the repressed sexual meanings of the "symbol."[31]

This difference could be explained as a matter of theoretical differences as to what constitutes basic meanings in terms of general psychological theory. Such an explanation is true as far as it goes. It ought, I think, to go further. Jung's major point is that the symbols are used *creatively* in dreams, in art, in psychosis, in many social phenomena. Living symbols provide a means of active expression → resolution of the *present* conflict. The dream is not so much a wish (sexual) as a continued effort to work out basic personality problems on the terms available to the organism.

To be sure, much dream content is essentially semiotic, and many dreams are concerned with relatively trivial adaptational problems. The dream approach *may* be repetitious or, as Adler remarked, may actually operate to confirm the personality in a fantasy withdrawal from constructive goals. By the same token, not all art is great art. Religious symbols may become mere signs of social status. Folk symbols become quaint and are manufactured for the tourist trade.

But the great dreams, the art that speaks to men of all ages, the religious and folk symbols that inspire even the casual tourist with a kind of nostalgia for what he has never really known are rooted deep in human nature. In psychosis, another area in which great symbols *live,* they typically reflect the primitivization and disintegration of the personality, sometimes with terrifying beauty. There may be stark conflict, or there may be the unity achieved by giving one's self over to a single trend with something of the global reaction patterns of infancy. In great art, the symbols are basically the same, but they are presented with more balance and integrative relationship, reflecting the greater development of the conscious Self (*i.e.,* the Jungian Self, not the persona developed out of social adaptation).

Jung's concept of symbols is concentrated on the archetypes and what he conceives as universal processes. I would suggest a broader orientation toward investigation. The archetypes seem to me to be mainly personifications of the significant persons and forces experienced by the infant in his initial efforts to relate himself to his world, and of the process of relationship. I have suggested that the body image of the young child and its motility patterns probably contribute toward the formulation of basic symbolizations in a way in which psychologists operating in a visual-verbal culture do not yet clearly understand. Probably many of the experiments of "psychologists" on the creation and transformation of symbols in the laboratory are relevant to insight into the basic processes involved, although work with adults in situations of very mild and artificial stress is not strictly comparable to the overwhelmingly new and drastically serious process of learning in infancy. I suspect, indeed, that the processes revealed in the laboratory can become intelligible only as they are related to the deeper symbolizations each subject developed in infancy. I suspect that the process of symbolization in the Jungian sense is very close to the process of human living—of instituting basic modes of integration between the systems inherent in the bodily structure of

the human organism and the world in which it functions. Symbolic logic and a psychology of symbols will, I think, have to effect a merger at a deeper level of agreement than is now apparent, with a deeper insight into modes of symbol formation.

The foregoing paragraph can merely hint at tie-ups between Jung's position and materials from contemporary experimental psychology and philosophy with which many readers may be unfamiliar. It hardly more than alludes to an aspect of my own thinking which I have found impossible to develop properly in this book, because adequate presentation wrenches the reader too far from its generally clinical orientation. Perhaps I shall find the courage to think it through and write about it in some later publication.

My excuse for including an obscure paragraph is that I consider the study of symbols, semiotic, semantic, and "living," as a major avenue of approach to the study of man. He is a symbol-forming animal. His society is based on commonly held symbols far more immediately than on his animal needs. The two are not unrelated, as most theorizers have observed. What is required is a more dynamic view of their relationships, rooted in what I have called psychosocial integration. We need to get away from most of our current sharp dichotomies, not only of body and mind but also of individual and society. We need to get away from theories which take the extremes of dynamic systematization, biological or social, as universal principles to be applied as such in highly complex but essentially mechanical interaction.

The language of living symbols can, I think, provide a flexible tool for the purpose of discovering lines of systematization *between* the inner and outer world of the person. We must learn better how to understand the basic structure of this language and how it relates to the experience of the individual—as a member of a social group and as a unique person.

How does this structure develop and change? Is the visual image—one may almost say the personification—so heavily stressed by Jung a constant factor? Or can other sense modalities be symbol-forming? And in what relation to the visual? What about words, the great human invention which allows us to communicate with one another and manipulate one another with a flexibility unknown in other animals? The semanticists, logical and psychological, have dealt extensively with the problem of meaning. We know very little about verbalization as such beyond the observable fact that some people express themselves via loquacity, others are rather inarticulate; some are very resourceful

in manipulating words, others are not, although they may be gifted beyond their more talkative brethren in handling spatial and numerical symbols. There appear to be individual variations of some constancy in *ways of symbolizing* as well as in the important symbols themselves. I suspect that predilection for one or another mode of symbolization is more closely related to inborn drive systems and to the nuclear experiences of infancy than is recognized at present. I suspect that greater recognition of these basic modes, in conjunction with greater understanding of the living symbols (images) investigated by the Jungians, will eventually provide a means of discovering the "deep" personality trends of the individual far more accurately and quickly than our present test batteries, and perhaps a means of using far more effectively nonverbal adjuncts to treatment.

[1] C. G. Jung, *Psychology of the Unconscious,* Dodd, Mead & Co., 1949, p. 161.
[2] *Ibid.*
[3] J. Campbell, *The Hero with a Thousand Faces,* Pantheon Books, 1949.
[4] C. G. Jung, *op. cit.,* p. 427.
[5] *Ibid.*
[6] *Ibid.,* p. 162.
[7] *Ibid.,* p. 464.
[8] *Ibid.,* pp. 464f.
[9] C. G. Jung, *Collected Papers on Analytical Psychology,* Ballière, Tindall & Cox, 2nd ed., 1920, pp. 385ff.
[10] ———, *Psychology of the Unconscious,* p. XXXV.
[11] ———, *Two Essays on Analytical Psychology,* Ballière, Tindall & Cox, 1928, pp. 41f.
[12] *Ibid.,* Chap. 4.
[13] *Ibid.,* pp. 55ff.
[14] J. Jacobi, *The Psychology of C. G. Jung,* Kegan Paul, Trench, Trubner & Co., 1942, p. 22.
[15] C. G. Jung, *Psychological Types,* Routledge & Kegan Paul, 1923, p. 601.
[16] *Ibid.,* p. 602.
[17] *Ibid.,* pp. 606f.
[18] C. G. Jung, *The Integration of the Person-*

ality, Farrar & Rinehart, 1939, pp. 24f.
[19] ———, *Contributions to Analytical Psychology,* Kegan Paul, 1928, p. 162.
[20] *Ibid.,* p. 117.
[21] G. Adler, "A Contribution of Clinical Material," *British Journal of Medical Psychology,* 1949, 22, p. 16.
[22] *Ibid.,* p. 17.
[23] F. G. Wickes, *The Inner World of Man,* Henry Holt & Co., 1938, p. 17.
[24] *Ibid.,* p. 67.
[25] *Ibid.,* pp. 137ff.
[26] J. Jacobi, *op. cit.,* p. 121.
[27] C. G. Jung, *The Integration of the Personality,* p. 287.
[28] *Ibid.,* p. 289.
[29] *Cf.* R. L. Munroe, "Rorschach Findings on College Students Showing Different Constellations of Subscores on the A.C.E.," *Journal of Consulting Psychology,* 1946, 10:301-316.
[30] S. Langer, *Philosophy in a New Key,* Harvard University Press, 1942; also Pelican Books, 1948.
[31] *Cf.* L. S. Kubie, "The Distortion of the Symbolic Process in Neurosis and Psychosis," *Journal of the American Psychoanalytic Association,* 1953, 1:59-86.

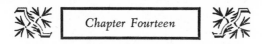

Chapter Fourteen

RANK

OTTO RANK, like Adler and Jung, was a member of Freud's early coterie and a powerful figure in the young psychoanalytic movement. He was not a doctor of medicine. His background and training were in the areas of engineering, philosophy, psychology, history, and art. In the early 1900's, Freud welcomed this difference. There is more than a hint that Freud almost assigned the expansion of analytic theory in the area of "culture" to this brilliant young outsider. Sympathetic relations prevailed for more than twenty years but gradually became strained to the breaking point. In later years Rank preferred to call his technique *psychotherapy* rather than psychoanalysis. He developed severe and fundamental criticism of many Freudian concepts, and his own concepts are in turn criticized by "Freudians."

Rank's major impact on American psychological thinking has been through the field of social work—the "functional" approach. In the late 1920's, his ideas were taking a form which seemed much more adaptable to the problem of bringing deep psychological understanding to the professional task of helping troubled families to better social functioning than were the elaborate theories and practices then characteristic of Freudian psychoanalysis. Rank himself lectured at the important schools of social work in New York and Philadelphia. Under the sponsorship of Jessie Taft and her co-workers in Philadelphia, his views have had a profound influence on the development of psychiatric social work, psychotherapy, counseling, education and other nonmedical fields in which deep psychological insight is required.

THE BIRTH TRAUMA

AMONG the various biological emphases of Freud's early theories, it was the trauma of birth which caught Rank's attention. We have seen (pp. 176*f.*) the important role that Freud *in 1926* ascribed to this event as the prototype of anxiety, as the reality situation on which later signals of danger are built.[1] I do not know how far Freud's earlier position on this point influenced Rank's thinking, or how far Freud was influenced by Rank, who published his major book on this topic (*Das Trauma der Geburt*) in 1924.[2]

Rank felt that the change from the all-encompassing, effortless bliss of the womb to the painful hurlyburly of postnatal conditions requiring initiative from the infant—a change during which the infant experiences mortal fear—was actually determining for life: as a consequence of it, the most normal among us carry a load of *primal anxiety*. The human goal is reinstatement of embryonic bliss—and the greatest human terror is *separation*. The overwhelming trauma of the birth experience is repressed (*primal repression*). The central human conflict thus becomes the wish to return to the womb versus the terrible fear indelibly associated with the womb by virtue of the event of birth.

In the books he wrote within the Freudian ideology, Rank attempted essentially to reinterpret the familiar Freudian concepts in the light of his idea of the basic significance of the birth trauma. He used even more insistently than Freud (and far less critically than contemporary "Freudians") the concept of identification to explain how people manage to work out this basic conflict. Rank's concept of symbolism was even broader than that of the "Freudians"—for example, primitive man "first created a vessel for a receptacle and a protection in imitation of the womb." But these concepts were tools for a reinterpretation of the crucial events of childhood which Freud had considered as directly "sexual"—*i.e.*, the consequence of the fate of the sexual instincts in society. Rank did not interpret weaning as the frustration of a component instinct but as a *separation* to which the child reacts as to the *separation* experienced in its birth. "Orality" is incidental to the fear of abandonment. "Genitality" is interpreted for the male as a re-entrance into the mother's body—the only possible return to the womb. The female is denied such direct return. She may, however, identify with the father and with males to whom she becomes attached later. She may identify with the mother and above all with her own child. Given the basic conflict of existence, *fear* is implicit in these genital relations as well as deep fulfillment. Like Sullivan, Rank considers strictly biological needs, especially "lust," as *facts*. But, again like Sullivan, he was already (1924) denying their psychological importance in their own right and was placing his emphasis on the profound problem arising out of birth—that is, out of *separation*.

I shall not try to report the conclusions about cultural history, neurosis, and therapy which Rank drew from his major hypothesis in the early 1920's. *The Trauma of Birth* has been reprinted. Mullahy offers a good digest.[3] Still written within the Freudian spirit, the ideas are presented in terms of the physiological events of birth, closely related body symbolisms, and the like. At times the description of the child's need to get inside the mother's body, his sadistic curiosity about it, his hatred of and longing for the womb, sound very much like the writings of Melanie Klein. This aspect of Rank's approach is largely given up in his later books in favor of a purely psychological vocabulary, although he continues to stress the fact of birth as the prototype of later separations.

Apparently the rather hostile reception of *The Trauma of Birth* in Freudian circles was something of a surprise to Rank.[4] It was the more painful because the aspects of his theory which he considered the most significant (those which I am tempted to characterize as the forerunners of ego psychology—to use a Freudian vocabulary) were neglected or condemned. After a few years of trying in vain to work things out within the Freudian group, Rank severed connections with Vienna physically as well as theoretically. He lived in Paris and America; his theory was developed further in conscious opposition to Freud and was perhaps needlessly limited on that account.*

Concentration on the birth trauma led Rank more and more toward an emphasis on *the powerful movements of the personality as a whole*. Perhaps one should reverse the sequence: his philosophical background and his clinical observations favored such an approach, so that he selected from the wealth of Freudian theory that fundamental concept which could best support a

---

* The libido theory *at that time* (the mid-1920's) was rather rigidly set in terms of developments in the erogenous zones and the castration complex as the major dynamic forces—set more rigorously for "Freudians" than for Freud. Rank toppled the structure by placing the whole weight of his dynamic system on the birth trauma, on *separation*, with reinterpretation of the sacred canons as mere special incidents. That he should ever have expected "Freudians" to approve is the remarkable thing.

Actually Freud was interested in Rank's development of the birth trauma. Many aspects of Rank's work at this early period are still considered valuable by Freudians who repudiate his later emphasis.

deep sense of the essential unity and creativity of the human spirit and take cognizance of its intrinsic conflicts. Thus although Rank and Adler and Jung are very different in many respects, they have in common an insistence on the primacy of the personality-as-a-whole, the self. This was a necessary insistence, which, like all rebellious insistences, perhaps somewhat overshot its goal.

THE WILL

THE ESSENTIALS of Rank's later position are implicit in *The Trauma of Birth,* but they become explicit in volumes in German dating from 1926.* The name Rank gives to the integrative power of the personality as a whole is the *will.* For him the will is not the rather vague mystical or logical postulate of the philosophers and faculty psychologists. Rather, it is the consequence of being born and of living, a *necessary* development of the human organism. How this development comes about will be discussed later, but it is important to recognize first of all the central position that Rank assigns to the will in his theory of personality and in his therapy. Man is not merely the battleground of impulses at war with one another and with external pressures. Man cannot be explained or therapeutically helped by analysis of the separate biological and social forces operating within him and upon him. The very core of his being is his *active* relationship to himself and his world—his "will."

Therapy must address itself primarily to this active will. Its main instrument is the relationship between patient and therapist, a relationship in which the therapist uses himself as the complement of the patient's will problem. The essential task of therapy is *not* to give the patient insight, or even an

* The volume of Rank's work that I have mainly used in writing this chapter is a compilation of earlier work (1926-1929) entitled *Will Therapy and Truth and Reality* (Alfred A. Knopf, 1945). Frederick H. Allen's *Psychotherapy with Children* (W. W. Norton & Co., 1942) is an excellent presentation of the psychiatric approach to Rank's theory and provides concrete case illustrations.

I have used F. B. Karpf's *The Psychology and Psychotherapy of Otto Rank* (Philosophical Library, 1953) beyond specific acknowledgment of quoted passages. I am even more indebted to a slim volume published by the Family Service Association of America entitled *A Comparison of Diagnostic and Functional Casework Concepts* (1950). This volume contains a succinct statement of the Rankian ideology and presents in detail two cases handled by Rankian case workers, with interpretation of the worker's rationale. Contrasts with the "diagnostic" approach are drawn rather too sharply for continued validity at a time of rapid change toward integration in the theoretical background of social work. The book offers a vivid, appealing picture of the "functional" caseworker in action. I have used freely Jessie Taft's digests of Rank's position: *The Dynamics of Therapy in a Controlled Relationship* (Macmillan Co., 1933), and *Family Casework and Counseling: A Functional Approach* (University of Pennsylvania Press, 1948).

emotional re-education as regards pathological attitudes. Therapy succeeds only in so far as the will orientation of the patient is changed.

ADVANCE SUMMARY OF RANK'S LATER POSITION

Following a review of my manuscript by some Rankians during which certain obscurities and emphases were discussed, one of the group present volunteered to write a clarifying statement. I do not find it desirable to use it merely as an insert on the page for which it was destined. It ranges back into developmental factors and forward into therapy, regardless of the outline set for exposition in this chapter. Rank's theory *should* be seen as a whole. It is inextricably mixed with therapeutic procedures for most of the people who consider themselves as "Rankian." The more detailed concepts may be more comprehensible after one has read the following general orientation prepared by a Rankian practitioner.

The child at birth (or before birth) is completely at one with the mother; they are one entity. Separation, through which individuality (the self) develops, begins as the infant—and later, the child—comes to find out through experience that he and the mother are two different beings. Thus the process of differentiation sets in. The child, and especially the adolescent, feels it necessary to assert himself in a negative way *against* the parent, in order to define his *own* self; it is really for purposes of defining himself to himself rather than fighting against the parent. In this process there is a clash of wills: parent's will, child's "counter-will." Since the child is bound to the parent by still-existing dependence, identification, love, gratitude, etc., his assertion of counter-will stirs up guilt in him. The guilt experienced by the young person, which begins in the framework of child-parent relationship, may be carried over into other interpersonal relationships—with the teacher, the friend, the spouse, and others—that is, if the guilt has not been resolved within the original framework.

Now, if this guilt is the problem, or an important part of the problem, of the individual who comes into therapy, it must be worked through in the course of the therapeutic relationship. The content of the therapy may be mainly focused in the present in the relationship of the patient to the therapist, although some going-back into the past is, of course, inevitable.

Rank looks upon the therapeutic relationship as a releasing one, ideally and essentially, and he believes (to put it in a highly simplified statement) that it is the therapist's responsibility to help the patient separate from him (the therapist), within a certain known time limit—one that has been set by the type of problem or, better still, by the needs of the patient. The working-through of the patient's guilt[5] which he feels toward the therapist—by means of an end-of-therapy set up at its inception—will also serve as the means by which the patient's original guilt (because of his early wish to separate from the parent, with its ambivalence, of course) becomes resolved.

With the disappearance or diminution of his guilt, the person can begin to come together with "the world"—that is, he can begin to achieve relationships with others in a more positive way than was hitherto possible for him. This is to say that essentially he is no longer conflicted because he had wanted to be himself—to be different from the others, to be a separate individual. This "difference," then, has now become acceptable to *him;* and so is the "difference" of the other persons acceptable to him.

Ideally an individual gains self-acceptance in childhood through his love relationships with his parents. They accept him as a separate individual and he, in turn, accepts them as being like him in some ways and different in others. This ideal person does not usually become known to a therapist. The neurotic, on the other hand, has suffered acute difficulties in his interpersonal relations. Nobody seems to love him. He comes to the therapist helpless and abused; it is either his fault entirely or not at all.

The therapeutic process is under way when the patient not only gains some feeling of acceptance by the therapist but has also been enabled to find some way (acceptable to him) of participating with the therapist in working on his problem. By setting a time limit to the relationship, the therapist conveys to the patient his conviction that the patient can eventually come to function independently of him. This endsetting, together with the constant discussion of the "reality" aspects of the therapeutic relationship, helps the patient toward a valid and realistic self-acceptance.

The therapist's acceptance of the patient's own way of working on his problem is in effect an acceptance of the patient's will. Since the patient's problem has been that his "difference" has been unacceptable to him and to others, the therapeutic relationship has been a new and fortifying experience—one which has engaged his positive will and affirmed his right to be different from others, even from that "great accepter" the therapist. Having had his own difference accepted by another (the therapist) he can now accept himself. Thus, in the therapeutic relationship, as in the ideal example cited above, self-acceptance becomes possible through the "love experience" of being accepted by another person.

LIFE FEAR AND DEATH FEAR

Rank's definition of the person is rooted in the experience of birth. The will is ambivalent from the outset. If I understand correctly the current version among Rankians of the birth trauma itself and the later impulse needs, there is less emphasis on the physiological event of passage through the birth canal than formerly, less emphasis on symbolic repetition, and more emphasis on an essentially philosophical antithesis of separation and union, of life and death. Within the womb, the embryo functions as a unit in symbiosis with its surroundings. Birth means the death of this union. It is the prototype not only of anxiety, as Freud saw it, but of the general problem of relinquishing the old integration in adopting a new one: dying in order to be born. On the one hand, the individual strives to reinstate a unity between himself and his environment; he experiences every advance toward independence as a threat. The fear of independence, of giving up the safety of symbiotic relationships analogous to the prenatal state, is given a special name—the *life fear*.

On the other hand, the emergent will is assertive and potentially creative. It strives toward individualization. The symbiotic union is experienced as a sort of death, a regression, a return to the womb, a loss of individuality and "life." Thus, union also becomes a threat, something to be feared. Rank's term for this experience is the *death fear*. It is the death fear which drives the person to vital effort, and the life fear which inhibits effort.

The essential point is the polarity between life and death, between separation (individuation → life-fear) and union (loss of individuality → death-fear). This necessary human conflict (so conceived by Rank) leads to three important further concepts to be discussed later. (1) *Fear* becomes, at least potentially, a constructive force rather than the crippling anxiety emphasized by other schools. (2) *Resistance* becomes, at least potentially, the constructive power of the will—even though it may be maldirected. (3) The major ideal of the human race in general and of psychotherapy in particular should be the *constructive, creative integration* of the trends toward union and separation.

Rank contrasts this theory with Freud's theory of instincts,[6] which assumes certain biological aims as the determinants of personality. As summarized by Rank, the Freudian aims are expressed, inhibited, or modified in the course of integrative experience with the environment. Rank does not deny the importance of *impulses* inherent in biological structure, including the sexual impulses so heavily stressed by Freud. But, if I understand Rank correctly, they function merely as the *arena* for the essential will conflict between separation and union, life and death. They should not be considered as determining in themselves.

The fact that biological growth involves a relationship between union and separation similar to his concept of birth is, for Rank, a further illustration of *a general principle fundamental to all living*. The child must renounce the breast to establish a new unity with the mother. He must stop creeping in order to walk. Rank does not attempt to use the biologically integrative trends *directly* as evidence for a psychological holism, as do some analysts. And he does not see the tendency toward stasis and falling apart as evidence for a "death instinct." Both of these formulations imply a kind of inborn directedness in the biological structure that is foreign to Rank's fundamental idea. The principle of separation and union goes deeper than the instinctual goals of the organism. It is the psychological equivalent of what he considers a general biological principle.

Rank becomes more concrete. For the neonate, the breast is the nearest equivalent to the womb. After birth, hunger is the vividly recurrent pain of separation, relieved by the breast or its equivalent. The breast thus becomes the symbol of reinstatement of the old unity. Weaning becomes the symbol of separation. The problem is only incidentally the problem of hunger and oral pleasure. The main conflict for the child is the pain of a new separation from the precious union with the mother which he has acquired after the trauma of birth.

It is often said that Rank emphasizes the relationship of the child to the mother in contrast to Freud's emphasis on the relationship to the father. This statement is true in that Rank considers problems of *separation* as primary, in contradistinction to the fate of separate instincts, including genital urges. Freud's emphasis on the father is based upon the direction and fate of the genital (phallic) urge, which he considers as a biological given of profound importance in itself. Rank denies this "instinctual" relationship of the emergent will to the father image and prefers to re-examine the Freudian concept of the Oedipus complex in terms of varieties of separation problems. His major *genetic* emphasis is on the mother, in birth, and in weaning. In a general way the father often comes to have the meaning of external authority—a figure which helps and opposes the development of the individual will in a manner which depends far more on the personal and social constellation of the individual than upon his infantile biological needs. I hesitate to speak for "Rankians," but it seems to me a mistake to call Rank's position a "mother" vs. a "father" psychology. This dichotomy implies an interpersonal dynamics which Rank recognized but did not greatly stress; a genetic dynamics which Rank tended to distrust.

PARTIALIZATION

The problem of separation and union is also referred to by Rank as *partialization and totality*. Growth requires the breaking down of the wholeness that the individual has established in order to achieve a new integration. Partialization is the necessary means of adaptation to reality. The embryo as an indivisible whole in total relationship to the environment of the womb offers the prototype of a blissful totality which is obviously impractical in a real world. After birth the person must in a very real sense *create* a new unity for his own being and for his relationship to his surroundings. The neonate does not have an ego-unity apart from his world. Out of his pain and experience of satisfaction by external means (for example, the breast) he learns new totalities which in some measure replace the union he has lost. This learning is selective as regards the outer world. The external totality is broken down along lines significant for the child (partialization). Lines of differentiation come to be recognized "objectively" beyond their immediate reference to his inner state, but Rank has not been much interested in the "objective" aspects of this learning process. His emphasis is on the phrase "significant for the child" as the clue to the psychological dynamics of learning.

THE COUNTER-WILL

Along with this "objective" learning, a new ego-unity develops. In the early postnatal state the infant tries to recreate the intra-uterine state so recently abandoned. As he grows older, the child *comes to experience his own self as a totality*. Once recognized, however dimly, *his* will becomes an active force, which he and his fellows must take very seriously. Rank takes it so seriously as to make it the basis of his theory and of his therapy.

The will emerges, Rank feels, essentially as *counter-will*. The child learns that *he* can say no to adults and to his own impulses. This is already an achievement of moment. It is the beginning of a *conscious* integration of the person as a unit distinct from the womb of the outer world. The integration of the person *vis-à-vis* his environment is, for Rank, the "essential human." It is the ideal implicit in man's special gifts. For this reason the counter-will is *in itself* valuable, more valuable than personal happiness or social adjustment established on the basis of nondifferentiation between the person and the milieu.

The counter-will, developed *against* the parents and later representatives of external forces, against the "other" or "others," is thus wholesomely rooted in the basic human striving toward life and individualization. By itself, however, it tends to destroy the *union* which is equally necessary to the human spirit. Assertion of the counter-will, therefore, tends to arouse feelings of "guilt." The profound distress implicit in the effort to be one's own self at the expense of the precious sense of union and support Rank calls *ethical* guilt. He contrasts this almost universal and potentially creative problem with *moralistic* guilt, which arises when one has committed an act disapproved by one's society or one's own socially developed code of behavior. Ethical guilt goes deeper. It may arise with *any* expression of the own will—and also with *any* compliance which, for the person, has involved an abrogation of such willing, even though correct from a moralistic standpoint. Ethical guilt, if I understand Rank aright, is his term for the tension between the two poles of human experience—separation and union—between the need for partialization (acceptance and development of individuality in many ways) and for wholeness (need for support, for belonging, for reinstatement of the prenatal symbiosis with the environment). There is ethical guilt toward the emerging self if too far denied, as well as toward the parents or later "others" who are alienated by this new self.

Resolution of this guilt becomes, for Rank, the human ideal and the goal of psychotherapy. The person must regain a sense of unity with his world reminiscent of the intra-uterine state, but the unity cannot be effortlessly symbiotic. It must be based on a positive acceptance of the own will and the will of "others" at a new level of integration—indeed at constantly renewed levels of integration as the self expands and as "others" are selected or understood in an enlarging perspective.

This progressive reintegration is accomplished mainly by *love*. The valid love relationship requires acceptance of the self-willing *by* another, and also acceptance of self-willing *in* another. Ideally the parent accepts the counter-will of the child as a lovable part of its effort to establish its own self as an independent being but is equally aware of the child's need for support and belonging, and also of its need for learning the realities of its external world if the child is to make creative reintegrations beyond the nursery. The parent-child relationship must, however, be largely regulated by the need of the child for support. It cannot be established on a basis of equality. Ideally the beloved and loving sexual partner supplies the full mutuality of relationship whereby the own will is accepted in and through the "other" and becomes a positive, constructive force. The own will does not arouse guilt because it is loved by the other. The mature person loves himself in the other, and the other in himself. Awareness of difference, of partialization, enriches the new sense of union. This union is not the effortless bliss of the womb, but a constantly renewed creation.

THE AVERAGE MAN

Rank's term for the person who achieves this pattern of creative reintegration is the *artist*.* Those who fail to achieve it are grouped under two

* Obviously Rank does not mean artist in the conventional sense of an adept in painting, music, writing, acting, or the flying trapeze. The successful painter may be a thoroughly average man or a neurotic; the humble backwoodsman or simple housewife *may* be an artist—although the latter usually do not leave records for careful psychological analysis by professional investigators.

headings—the *average man* and the *neurotic*. Every child develops something of a counter-will through the ordinary pains and frustrations of post-uterine existence. Many children, however, soon find it possible to so identify their own will with the will of their parents as to avoid much of the guilt of separation and the pain of developing the own will further. Adaptation to the will of the parents and later to the dictates of a wider society is the keynote of these characters. Where there is no effort toward individuation, there is also no conflict about conformance. The person's life may be hard or dull, but so long as the person takes its external conditions for granted, so long as they seem really part of himself, he is spared the inner distress of guilt. Rank does not refer here to people who consciously conform for the sake of expediency. The average man is the man who naturally conforms to his society because he has never thought of doing anything else. His relations with his society are reminiscent of the symbiotic relationship between person and environment which prevailed in the womb. They represent the first and easiest solution of the problem set by birth.

In a stable society such a person is automatically well adjusted and is a model of social virtues. This essentially adaptive individual has a relatively harmonious relationship to his society, but only because he has never truly differentiated his own will from the significant surroundings. He is the prey of social change as victim or executioner. His truths are illusory, and his virtues may vanish overnight if the social configuration to which he belongs shifts its values. The average man is a useful creature for society and as a human being is entitled to respect. Rank doesn't like him very much. Having defined him as a person who can live on the terms of his society, Rank seems to forget about him. Or rather the average man becomes a sort of social "norm" whose values should *not* be imposed on the people Rank concerns himself with as individuals: the neurotics and the artists.

THE ARTIST

The "neurotic" and the "artist" have this fundamental point in common: they have committed themselves to the pain of separation from the herd—that is, from unreflective incorporation of the views of their society. The path of the *artist* so committed is not an easy one, and he not infrequently resorts to "neurotic" maneuvers in order to maintain a necessary equilibrium. But the artist is essentially able to achieve an integration of his separate will and his need for union through a creative relationship to "others."

We have seen that this relationship requires an acceptance by the individual of his personal will as valuable—an acceptance begun in the counter-will. But this personal will cannot become truly constructive until it is accepted by another person, human or divine. Until the person can feel that his own willing is *right* (*i.e.*, not guilty), until he can feel that it is accepted by "others," he cannot fully resolve the problem of separation with its counterpart of union. Rank's artist, like Jung's hero and Freud's great man, does not stand alone on a pinnacle of individual worth. On the contrary "he who loseth his life shall find it." The act of separation is not enough, no matter how heroically accomplished. Neither is sacrifice of the self, whether it takes the form of heroic altruism and self-immolation or the unthinking compromise of the average man. These are the poles of experience, neither of which can fully express the human ideal. Rank's choice of the term *artist* for the human ideal is an attempt to convey a sense of creative integration as the highest goal of man—in contrast to more limited ideals of spiritual or material achievement.

By its very nature the *artist* approach reconciles the separation of the individual with his need for union on an essentially *constructive* basis. I italicize constructive because Rank emphasizes the *bringing-together* of opposite trends in his concept of constructive effort, in some theoretical contrast to a great variety of theories which consider man as essentially "good" or essentially "bad," or as in the grip of "instincts" which determine his actions. The constructive attitude by its very nature involves realistic partialization and reintegration. It is not, for Rank, a matter of realization of the human potential, as it is for Horney and even for Fromm, but a *creation* of the human spirit, resolving the opposing principles of its being.

THE NEUROTIC

The neurotic does not win through to this constructive bringing-together of the basic dichotomous trends. Somehow or other the neurotic has achieved or been forced into a sense of his separateness so great that the adjustive quasi-identification with the patterns of his culture characteristic of the average man is no longer possible for him. Unlike the artist, he has not been able to achieve full integration of the opposing trends of life into a constructive positive will. Thus the counter-will of the neurotic is likely to be strong, whatever devices he has developed. He is likely to be profoundly resistant to "being changed" in therapy, and his sense of separateness is likely to be guilt-ridden and basically hostile to others.

Rank considers this hostility and resistance as essentially constructive rather than destructive. Far from attempting to break down resistance as a hindrance to insight, the therapist should, in Rank's opinion, work with it as the major resource the patient brings to the therapeutic situation. The neurotic is not an average man whose "adjustment" has failed because one or another instinctual drive was mishandled. He, too, is an artist, but his effort toward differentiation and integration has been sidetracked or defeated. He is in trouble *because he tried beyond the easy average solution*. His "cure" must respect and build upon this essentially creative effort. The therapist will not have in mind any specific social goals to which the patient should be brought, no matter how sound, how generous, or even how vague. Instead, *the relationship with the therapist should*, Rank feels, *offer the patient that acceptance of his own will which will enable him to accept it himself*, and so to move toward a more complex and constructive kind of willing. It is a kind of love relationship.

Unable to live adaptively, like the average man, the neurotic may handle his problem in two ways. (1) He may throw his whole ego into every experience, no matter how trivial, in order to spare himself the pain of a separating, independent act of willing. He may accept the dictates of "others" with overly consistent compliance or overly consistent rebelliousness. To deviate from such wholeness is, for the neurotic, to invite death through the loss of the own ego with its supporting environmental matrix. The dominating fear is the fear of life—that is, of differentiation and separateness.

If I understand Rank correctly, neurotics in whom the life fear predominates are roughly similar to those whom Horney describes as moving toward or against the outside world, the sado-masochistic or "oral" types suggested by Fromm and Abraham. In a general way this seems to be the "hysterical" orientation, in which a sense of wholeness is preserved by means of an overly direct, totalistic relationship to "others."

(2) The neurotic may endeavor to keep his whole ego apart from life experience. These are the detached people, moving away from the outside world, the Freudian "anal" types, those with an obsessive-compulsive orientation. The dominant fear here, according to Rank, is the death fear, fear of the loss of individuality in any effort toward union and direct experience with others.

I should make clear that this suggestion of a relationship between Rank's description of the life-death fear and the typologies offered by other schools represents my own effort to bring his views into some sort of alignment with schools previously discussed. There is no one-to-one correspondence. Furthermore Rank's major intent is to break down typologies and diagnostic categories, and to insist upon the primary dynamics of the will.

THERAPY

FEAR AND HOSTILITY IN THERAPY

Living, as we have seen, implies for Rank, the need both for separation and union. *Fear* is the obverse of these needs. *Fear*, Rank says, is constructive as well as inhibitory. Where Horney emphasizes the vicious circle which drives the neurotic deeper and deeper into neurosis, Rank points out that exaggeration of adaptation to either the life or the death fear actually frightens the person *toward* a more constructive revision of his willing. He can no more tolerate total separation than total union. Thus his fear tends to act as a corrective, healing agent as well as an inhibiting force. The therapist may work constructively with the patient's fear, but he must recognize its quality at any given moment of the therapeutic relationship.

The most distinctive aspect of Rankian therapy is related to recognition and constructive use of the basic life fear and death fear. Before launching into this topic, however, I must mention what Rank calls the "empirical" death fear and refer back to "moralistic" guilt. The little child does not know death as an empirical fact, nor does it appreciate realistically the dangers which beset its path. The empirical fear of death is learned—and learned in the context of special hazards. Rank does not seem interested in the *discomfort* of the infant, allayed with some regularity by the ministration of its nurses, so much as in the catastrophic fear attendant upon birth and the tendency of the child to equate any hurt with total annihilation. Hurts from the outside thus tend to be assimilated to the primary fears. The moralistic guilt mentioned earlier proceeds from the empirical death fear as the child → person learns that some actions lead to active punishment or such withdrawal of love as means "death." The primary death fear is resistance against the human longing for the repose of the womb. The empirical death fear is resistance against such external forces as might annihilate the self.

Rank stresses the interaction of these fears in therapy, especially as they relate to the patient's attitude toward the therapist. The central problem is usually to help the patient toward acceptance of the own will with less guilt and with more toleration of the pain of separation. Advances in this direction, however, frequently involve the empirical death fear for the patient as well as the primary life fear. He engages in acts of independence which he has previously considered dangerous, giving up the safety devices (to use a Horney term for an aspect of Rank's theory that he has not elaborated) which have previously protected him against the empirical death fear. The neurotic's judgment of danger is often warped, but the danger is very real to him. Furthermore his first essays into independence may be so clumsy as to provoke an objectively real slapping down, or his situation may be impossible to handle with the courageous directness that the patient often sees initially as the corrective to his tortuous neurotic fears.

The very success of therapy in the early phase of growing confidence in the own will, therefore, typically leads to an exaggeration of the empirical death fear and of moralistic guilt. This empirical fear and moralistic guilt must be handled with sympathetic understanding and encouragement. The patient must feel the *support* of the therapist in his new ventures, even though the therapist does not take the position that the patient is always right. The therapist warmly accepts the constructive effort regardless of the immediate result and interprets to the patient his "natural" reactions of fear, guilt, and disappointment.

But the warmly supportive attitude of the therapist, leading to gratitude, trust, and love in the patient, tends to arouse the basic death fear. Furthermore the patient usually comes for treatment in a mood of despair about his own will, actively wishing to submit himself to the higher will of the doctor. This mood also inevitably predisposes him to such exacerbation of the death fear as actually frightens him *toward* renewed effort in the direction of individuation—the potentially benign circle. The therapist must be ready to recognize symptoms of a fear which is actually implicit in the extra measure of trust and love accorded him by the patient. If the therapist can discern *this* death fear early, and show it to the patient as an irrational but valuable part of his growth, then the patient is helped in limiting the pendulum swings between trust and fear, between love and hate.

When the patient is preoccupied with his empirical death fear and moralistic guilt, the therapist is supportive. At all times, however, the therapist must be aware that acceptance of support and feelings of love provoke the primary death fear and resistance against the alluring sense of union with the therapist.

Rank welcomes such resistance as a manifestation of the own will of the patient. It is not, for him, simply a block in the therapeutic release of repressed materials. The hostility is not, in essence, a reaction to the parent transferred to the benign, objective figure of the analyst. It is not even, as Horney suggests, the price of an excessive submission. Instead, it is the counter-will of the patient not only against what he conceives to be the compulsion (force) of the analyst but also against the profound trend in himself which fears death in union (dependence). As such, it is basically life-giving and constructive. It should not be ignored or analyzed away but accepted and used in clarifying for the patient his actual will relationship with the analyst. The therapist does not merely *tolerate* hostility with objective sympathy for a suffering human being but tries to help the patient toward a more constructive experience by discerning the hostile resistance before the patient is aware of it, if possible, and clearly accepting it as a *positive* value in the treatment. The therapist may even find it desirable to encourage the mobilization of hostility toward himself, to encourage the death fear, in order to help the patient toward the courage of separation, toward handling the life fear.

It should be emphasized that this mobilization of fear and hostility, this welcoming of resistance, is only part of the story. Support of the capacity to love and relate to others is also basic in Rankian theory. Current critics of the Rankian approach often talk about this "mobilization of hostility" in a manner which reminds me of the early criticism of Freud's *supposed* view that because sexual inhibitions are important in the etiology of neurosis, the cure of neurosis is free sexual expression. The criticism is premised on misunderstanding. The Rankian no more encourages uninhibited expression of hostility than the Freudian encourages uninhibited sexuality.

TRANSFERENCE AND RELATIONSHIP

In course of treatment the patient often equates the therapist with those aspects of his experience which he finds unduly compelling, with the "force" he fears, with external commands leading to *moralistic* guilt. At such times hostility to the therapist and resistance to interpretations are related to the drama of the life fear. The therapist may *stand for* those persons in his life situation, past or present, in relation to whom the patient has developed the particular structure of his will. To some extent this process is helpful in bringing the real world of the patient vividly into the therapeutic situation. By "relating himself" differently to the various concrete attitudes of the patient thus revealed, the therapist can hope to modify them in the direction of greater constructiveness *vis-à-vis* the actual conditions of the patient's life.

However, this *substitutive* transference relationship (so important for the Freudians) is not the aspect of therapy which Rank considers the most significant. The therapist tries gently and continuously to disassociate himself from the unreal, repetitive role thus assigned him and relies for cure (the Rankian word is "helping") on the direct relationship between himself and the patient. The primary need of the patient is to accept his own will constructively and creatively, going beyond the negative phase of counter-will and guilty compliance. The shattering problem for the neurotic is not so much moralistic guilt as *ethical* guilt—i.e., the blanket fear of his own will, an endless tossing between the extremes of life and death, separation and union. He cannot accept partialization in the blindly adaptive manner of the average man, or yet in the constructive manner of the artist. What he needs is *the acceptance of his will by another so as to justify it to himself*.

We have seen that Rank conceives the will, the constructive will, as by its very nature a relationship with the "other." It is the means of handling the basic problem of separation without renouncement of the necessary separateness of living. The therapist may become that "other" through whom the will of the patient is justified to himself. In a sense the therapist is a *complement* to the patient's will, not the omnipotent God or the objective Authority which in its Olympian detachment delivers the patient over to the terrors of his separation problems. *It is through the will experience with the therapist that the patient can creatively establish his own will*. It is in therapy that the patient can encounter an "other" who accepts his will problem as entirely valid and requires that he face it directly; who *throws back the essential will conflict into the patient's own ego*. This conflict is essentially between the own will as personified *in* another (God, moralistic guilt, the counter-will of the person in whatever habiliments it has adopted), and *through* another (love). The therapist is neither God nor lover, although the patient may tend to envisage him as both. The therapist's task is to bring this basic conflict to the fore and to help the patient handle it directly. Rank writes:[7]

> The therapeutic problem, therefore, is to overcome the personal element more inherent in the analytic situation than in any other experience by leading back to the will conflict at least far enough so that the patient is in a position to separate his inner conflict from the present content, the therapist, and thereby also to separate from earlier contents.

In a general way, then, Rank's idea is that the patient should be helped to accept his own willing in both its negative and positive aspects. Only thus can he achieve a constructive reintegration of the basic conflict of existence, and the *creative* attitude toward life which alone can lead to fullness of living and action.

THE PROBLEM OF REALITY IN THERAPY

But we must return to the problem of partialization in order to understand several significant aspects of the Rankian approach. Just because the neurotic has become separated from his world beyond the average, he fears separation and tries at all costs to reinstate some kind of *total* relationship. We have seen that he tends to interpret events and himself totalistically. He does so the more urgently as the external situation is acutely important to him—notably the therapeutic situation.

In part, therefore, the course of Rankian therapy is aimed at the encouragement of a more *realistic partialization through constant discussion of the actual life situation,* past and present. The purpose of such discussion is not primarily to get the patient to "face facts" or to overcome distortions of feeling and thinking. Such purposes are usually achieved and are, of course, considered valuable. For the Rankian, however, they are incidental to the process of helping the patient tolerate partialization, or rather to use it constructively in the creative integration developed by his own will. The will operates not in a vacuum but on the stuff of living. It is essential to the growth of the patient's will that the relationship with the therapist be in close connection with his everyday reality problems.

Thus the Rankian case-worker, for example, makes a particular point of explaining to the client* the realistic services offered by the agency and of repeatedly working out with him what he may reasonably expect from his therapeutic contact. This procedure itself helps to partialize the unbounded hopes and resentments of the patient (client) and puts him in the position of deliberately accepting a limited and realistic view of the relationship. It works against the totalistic trend of the neurosis from the start. It keeps the patient oriented toward his own life while he works out his basic will conflict with the therapist. The therapist accepts the will of the patient in counter-will and in love, *within tentative limits which enlist the conscious understanding of the patient.*

It is obviously impossible for the patient to adhere to his agreement without very considerable help from the therapist. Indeed, the therapist may at times welcome extra demands and unreasonable protests which reflect the more vivid will experience of the patient, and will not be pedantic about "agency" requirements. At all times, however, the patient is gently brought back to his conscious acceptance of the limited nature of the therapist's services—quite as firmly in periods of exuberant gratitude as in periods of protest. Thus, although the Rankian accepts the patient's will in whatever guise it appears, the therapist himself becomes a reality figure in a manner new to the patient: *accepting, but limited.* While the therapist does not offer direct advice—much less practical support or prohibition—on the conduct of

* The word *patient* is unacceptable in the field of social work. I prefer to use it in this chapter by way of continuity with other chapters, disregarding a distinction properly made in social work.

the patient's affairs—it is understood that he is a real person, helping on a real problem. The nature of the problem is clarified for the patient at the outset, and revised as necessary.

END-SETTING

Similar in underlying philosophy is the well-known Rankian idea of *setting a definite end* to the therapy fairly early in contact. The number of interviews per week and the total duration of treatment varies, of course, according to the needs of each person. Furthermore, the prospective end is set in collaboration with the patient in a rather tentative manner, with full assurance that it can be postponed if he still needs the therapist's help. He is also assured that he can return at a later time if things do not go well with him, and he is given to feel the continuing interest of the therapist in his welfare.

Rank felt that this practice serves two important purposes. First, it works against the building up of an extreme dependence on the therapist, so common in any protracted Freudian analysis, and instead focuses the attention of the patient on his responsibility for getting along by himself. His "cure" is not a remote fantasy but a perfectly real event which may be expected to happen in a quite limited time span—not total perfection, of course, but a sufficient shift in attitude so that he can continue to work out desirable changes by himself.

Secondly, the advance notice of the termination is supposed to make the event less traumatic, less reminiscent of the primal birth trauma. It helps to *partialize* a separation which must be difficult in any well-going treatment. It brings the excessive (totalistic) attitudes of love and resentment toward the therapist vividly to the fore in the therapeutic situation itself, where they can be fruitfully interpreted to the patient over a long period. If I may use a Freudian term, it allows for analysis of the transference and for its resolution.

Freudian criticism of this technique points out that it does not allow the transference to build up with sufficient power to effect any deep-level change in the personality. The patient is so far focused on the limited reality relationship to the therapist and his own current life adjustments that he can in no way recover those deeply repressed conflicts of infancy which still condition the major dynamics of his behavior. To this criticism Rank's reply is that the truly significant factor is the will itself, not content—repressed or conscious, past or present. The therapist is not a divine midwife through whose mediation the patient may recover his true self either by release of repression or discovery of his "real" potential. (Here I present Freud and Horney in burlesque.) In Rank's view, the therapist helps the patient through a *direct* experience of the will relationship between patient and therapist. This is not a more constructive reliving of the parent-child relationship (Ferenczi, more or less) or an emotional re-education of attitudes (Alexander, more or less). It is a radical insistence on the almost Hegelian triad: the thesis and antithesis of separation and union, life fear and death fear, which require synthesis in the constructive will. Because the therapist accepts his will, the patient can accept it himself—acceptance by the other being a necessary part of the creative synthesis. Because the therapist is unconditional in this basic acceptance, but deliberately realistic and "partial" in his concrete relationship to the patient, he can help the patient toward creative, constructively integrated partialization instead of the blind, totalistic reaction to separation fear characteristic of the neurotic.

Critical Comment

I FEEL that I must preface my comments on Rank with a relatively explicit statement of personal background and bias. I have had less direct professional contact with Rankians than with any other psychoanalytic school. Indeed, most of the psychoanalysts, "psychologists," and even social workers whom I know well tend to be definitely opposed to his theories. My experience is not unique. The key identifying phrases of Rank— the birth trauma, the will—are not popular today. Most of us are ill informed as to Rank's own position. We get him at second hand in the capsule form of brief mention in many psychological texts, and in the diffuse form of an on-going perspective in social work currently called "functional." The "social work" aspect of the theory has been well reported in several books and in articles in professional journals. Although such exposition does not pretend to present the depth and subtlety of Rank's thinking, I found it indispensable as an orientation to Ranks' own books.

For Rank's books are difficult to read, even after one becomes accustomed to an involved sentence structure rather too literally translated from the German in the English editions. Rank was an expert clinician himself, and in the late 1920's was able to grasp the problems of the social worker in a much more practical and stimulating manner than were the Freudian analysts of the time. However, this expert clinician almost never mentions a concrete case in illustration of innovations in therapeutic procedures. The will of the patient *vis-à-vis* the will of the therapist is presented in a series of verbally dramatic abstractions which slid off my mind like water off a duck's back until I had read enough about Rankian social work to fill in concrete relations to the problems of patients, therapists, and the task of psychotherapy. Once in possession of this key to Rank's views on therapy, however, I found his abstractions highly meaningful. Indeed, I have occasionally reported Rankian abstractions somewhat beyond those emphasized in the current literature of social work, since they seemed of theoretical interest.

Although Rank's theory is in a way more "social" than Freud's "biological" approach, he is no more concrete about specific social groups than he is about individuals.* A vast amount of "social" material is woven into his writings, but it derives mainly from history and anthropology, with slight reference to his own varied experience in Vienna, Paris, New York, and Philadelphia. The social materials are used to illustrate points about the *will* in a fragmentary manner, torn from their group context. One gets a sense of broad social implications, inadequately related to social *patterns* as they appear in diverse societies and subgroups. Valuable in its time for breaking up Grundyisms and the overly narrow concepts of earlier social sciences, Rank's approach misses the concept of the group—any group—as somehow a functioning system in its own right which must be considered as such. The relationship of the individual to the group is overgeneralized, with insufficient recognition of the factors, social and psychological, which make for cohesiveness or dispersion within particular groups, which make group pressures at times very determining for individual psychology and at times quite peripheral.

It must be admitted that I have not reported enough of Rank's writings on group reactions to allow the reader to form a judgment of his own on this point. Perhaps orienting books by Rankians would have alerted me to his special contribution to psychosocial problems as the writings of social workers helped me understand the significance of his discussion of clinical problems. The reader should take my critical pronouncements about Rank's social theorizing with a grain of salt. They may be biased by

* Allen does discuss "biological" factors (*Psychotherapy with Children*, pp. 18ff.) and treats social factors in a more concrete manner.

the kind of ignorance that comes from reading words in an unfamiliar context, without appreciation of what the author is really trying to say.

For Rank's very *words* are difficult for an American "psychologist." He uses the vocabulary of philosophical and religious tradition. The Will, Truth, Reality, God, etc. He uses them in a way which many of us reared to a contemporary version of the rational-empirical, "materialist" approach find rather offensive as well as confusing. Because his vocabulary is not the vocabulary of science, it becomes hard for us to integrate Rank's ideas, however sound, with the rest of our scientific thinking.

I introduce here a full paragraph of Rank's own writing (the final paragraph of *Will Therapy and Truth and Reality*[8]) partly for its content but mainly as a sample to help the reader decide for himself on the merits of this style versus the more pedantic efforts of the "scientists."

> If the will is affirmed and not negated or denied, there results the life instinct, and happiness, like salvation, is found in life and experience, in the creation and acceptance of both without having to ask how, whither, what and why. Questions which originate from the division of will into guilt consciousness and self consciousness cannot be answered through any psychological or philosophic theory for the answer is the more disillusioning the more correct it is. For happiness can only be found in reality, not in truth, and redemption never in reality and from reality, but only in itself and from itself.

In positive appreciation of Rank's contribution, I mention first his emphasis on the creative movement of the personality as a whole. This emphasis is much in line with the approach reported in Part III, in contrast to reifying trends in Freudian theory. Repeated renewal of faith in the creative potential of the human spirit is a necessary safeguard against the *dangers* of a multidimensional approach and the tendency to chop up the personality into a series of abstract entities instead of flexibly changing systematizations focused around one or another aspect of living. Yet I cannot feel that Rank avoided the danger of reductionism in so far as he tried to build a systematic psychology at all.

Rank's more particular emphasis on the problem of separation and union has great clinical value, especially as a supplement to a view of the genetic process too narrowly related to relatively specific instinctual drives of somatic origin (component instincts). I remarked in Chapter 5 on the growing emphasis among "Freudians" on fear of loss of love, on "separation anxiety." Perhaps they are coming around to a Rankian point of view as they are coming around to an *inclusion* of the fundamental ideas of many dissident schools. This statement does not mean that "Freudians" are becoming "Rankians," or even that this emphasis bespeaks the belated influence of Rank. It is a rare contemporary "Freudian" who has read enough of Rank's writings to know what he was talking about. His influence has come through the indirect, to-and-fro relationships of parallel developments in many separate schools of thought, not through the linear development of a specific idea.

Application of the fundamental, continuing dichotomy between trends toward separation and union is clearly observable in the position of Fromm as the need for significance versus the need for belonging. With a little stretching of the imagination, one may see something of the same dichotomy in Adler's emphasis on the striving for superiority as an inborn goal versus the common sense and social interest which relate the person to others; in Horney's contrast between the real self and the adaptively idealized self-image or between the need

for self assertion and the need for supportive love; in Sullivan's sense of the self dynamism versus dispersive part impulses or the need for prestige and the need for security; in Jung's polarity of introversion and extraversion; in Freud's concept of interchange between narcissistic and object libido, between aggression and love.

In outlining this admittedly rather fanciful set of parallel dichotomies among the various schools, I have mingled two aspects of the problem implicit in Rank's view: first, the fundamental relationship between the inner and outer world, between organism and milieu, and, second, the psychological (subjectively experienced) need for selfhood—self-assertion, prestige, and power strivings—versus the need for security—love, belonging, relief from striving. In a very general way, "separation" may be said to imply the trend toward integration of the inner world, an introversive approach, an emphasis on the real self. But where Adler sees this trend as a linear development of power strivings, Rank, like Jung and Horney, sees it in a much more neutral way. Nevertheless, the will drives the person toward separation from the womb—the matrix of the later environment. Although Rank builds his theory on the interplay of "fears," one of these fears (the death fear) is premised upon the positive need to be one's self—or, more correctly, to create one's self, since Rank does not consider that even the major outlines of the self are prefigured in the organism. Here Rank comes close to Fromm and Sullivan.

I myself prefer Sullivan's formulation of an *emergent* self dynamism as even more scientifically neutral than Rank's formulation of the emergent will, and I have repeatedly suggested that this concept be studied in closer relationship to the development and function of a more concrete image(s) of the self. Apart from the tendency to interpret "everything" by a fundamental dichotomy of separation and union, the Rankian formulation is less cogent than Sullivan's for me mainly on semantic grounds. Partly I share the uneasiness of the scientist confronted with terms alien to the scientific tradition, but partly I share the positive hope that psychological science will *develop* a unifying set of basic terms of a more scientifically neutral character. The process cannot be rushed. Elaborate Sullivanese is about as difficult as the Rankian vocabulary. (As for Munroese, it has been used as a technique for continuing a train of thought throughout a book dealing with many terminologies; it is not designed for permanent use.) The term *self dynamism* is semantically closer to a view of systems than is the *will,* and it is less involved with what seems to me a reductionist dichotomy.

Thus far I have emphasized Rank's dichotomy. It is equally important to emphasize his sense of constructive integration of trends as the significant achievement of the human spirit. The human ideal is not more and more achievement along a single line, but a broader and broader type of integration. Rank's artist achieves and keeps re-achieving a sort of cross-sectional harmony rather than a specific goal. The spiral is not a satisfactory image, because its circles are too smoothly related in an upward and onward direction. Rank rather points out the *breaks* in adaptational patterns which—ideally—lead to reintegration on a more inclusive basis. This view does not *require* that creative expansion take place by leaps and starts, although it easily explains the queer jumps from one pattern to another observable in many people which more "linear" psychologies find difficult to explain. Usually change is itself gradual and harmonious. A small excess of "fear" here is quickly compensated there in such manner that the outlines of the personality remain fairly stable.

This concept of the human ideal as a sort of cross-sectional *expansion* rather than a linear upward development is not unique in Rank. Even Adler in his great emphasis on the aspiring nature of man insisted on social interest as *a necessary part* of this nature and felt very deeply that striving must constantly be integrated with social feeling and common sense. Horney had much the same notion in her concept of the real self. Fromm's analysis of the productive orientation includes the to-and-fro of striving and love in fruitful relationship. Nevertheless, without claiming uniqueness for Rank's position, I may say that I found his emphasis on creative expansion, on the *artist* approach, very sympathetic.

Approaching the end of this long book, I allow myself a value judgment. My creed, like Rank's, would be the creative expansion of the person as the highest goal. I would myself see this expansion with closer reference to specific biological endowment than Rank, and also with closer reference to specific social patterns. I would prefer more *differentiation* of dynamic subsystems of some stability in the person and the groups to which he belongs—subsystems which may be identified with tentative shrewdness from person to person and from group to group. Then the therapist may more quickly understand the special problems of the patient. And then social science may more effectively discern from fragmentary materials the group trends operating toward the achievement of a new harmony in contrast to those which merely strive to preserve the old, or which tend to one-sided development and ultimate confusion. I have remarked that Rank is not a master of the ringing phrase in print. Nevertheless, I came to a deep respect for his analysis of the fundamental purpose of human life, and for his insistence upon it.

[1] S. Freud, *The Problem of Anxiety*, W. W. Norton & Co., 1936.

[2] O. Rank, *The Trauma of Birth*, Harcourt, Brace & Co., 1929.

[3] P. Mullahy, *Oedipus—Myth and Complex*, Hermitage Press, 1948.

[4] F. B. Karpf, *The Psychology and Psychotherapy of Otto Rank*, Philosophical Library, 1953, pp. 8ff.

[5] See F. H. Allen, *Psychotherapy with Children*, W. W. Norton & Co., 1942, pp. 40 and 204-227 *passim*.

[6] O. Rank, *Will Therapy and Truth and Reality*, Alfred A. Knopf, 1945, p. 121.

[7] *Ibid.*, p. 63.

[8] *Ibid.*, p. 305.

Part Five

EPILOGUE

EPILOGUE

IN WRITING THIS BOOK about theories, presenting them as coherent systems so little dependent on one another directly that even the same terms have quite different meanings from school to school, I have come to realize what is meant by the statement "Psychology is a young science," and how close it is still to deductive philosophy, despite the heavy emphasis on observation and experimentation. Each school erects its own basic principles, which are then used to establish the smaller codifications of events necessary for scientific ordering of observational data. Since the principles of all the major schools are derived from important observations and are reapplied with sensitive intelligence, good results are attained by all—up to a point. I have called the process of overextension from basic principles by logical deduction *reductionism,* and I have protested against it even when the practical results obtained are outstanding, even while admiring many specific formulations in all schools and sympathizing with the special broad emphasis implicit in the basic principles of each school.

As fellow theorizer, I have tried to present a *view of systems* as a philosophical solvent for school variations. This view was described briefly in Chapter 1 and has been referred to throughout. In summary, it avers that scientific truth lies in the progressive recognition of dynamic systems of different types and degrees of inclusiveness. No such system is universal in the absolute sense. Many have a quality approaching universality because they are deeply rooted either in the biological equipment of man or in fundamental necessities of social living. The nature of man (born helpless with a unique capacity for flexible learning) is such that integrative systems *between* the organism and its milieu (the individual and his society) are inevitably of supreme importance.

In fact *only* integrative systems are directly observable from the moment of birth, as Sullivan has remarked with especial cogency, although systems determined primarily by biological structure may be inferred from infant behavior, and doubtless continue throughout life *(the terms of the organism)*. Sociologists and economists have studied *the terms of the milieu* in their own right, too often without attention to their necessary integration with "deep" psychological systems—*i.e.*, trends inherent in biological equipment as it encounters, in an integrative way, the early experience of infancy and childhood. Too often psychobiologically oriented theories have paid insufficient attention to the solidity of social institutions as relatively stable systems. To be sure these institutions have been created by human beings and are subject to change by human beings, but only as their systematic character is somehow recognized. No general fiat, whether psychobiological or sociological in origin, will immediately remake a human society closer to our heart's desire, or to what reason tells us would be a better way of living.

The inevitable consequence for *psychology* of the integrative propensity of the human species is that dynamic *sub*systems of very great variety develop in the course of living which cannot profitably be "reduced" to the quasi-universals of biology and sociology. They must be studied *in their own right*, with due regard for their developmental and adaptational quality, their creative dependence on external circumstances. At one extreme lie the reaction patterns primarily constellated around what I have called the drive systems of the organism. At the other extreme lie the transient subsystems established moment by moment in adaptation to the special circumstances of the immediate present. These are unpredictable in their fullness, although, as Lewin has remarked, the past is essentially a long series of present moments. The past is necessary to understanding of the present because every momentary situation is *interpreted* by the individual organism on the basis of its biological endowment as it has encountered previous experience. A succession of "present moments" which are *significantly the same for the adapting organism* tends to confirm its particular interpretation of the freshly present situation and to build up reaction patterns of a relatively stable nature involving the total organism.

Thus, between the quasi-universal systems (deep-lying psychological trends) and the highly contingent systems of the present situation lie a great number of subsystems, developed in the course of living but fairly well organized in a variety of ways, with greater or less autonomy (tightness) as systems, differently related to the drive systems, to various external systems, and to the emergent self. Although these subsystems should not be made into universals, although investigation of their major relationship to quasi-universal systems must be part of scientific endeavor, the nature and function of such subsystems can be studied in *judicious* independence. Indeed I consider such study the major hope of psychology as an empirical science, and I think it has already been in a measure fulfilled by the schools reported or alluded to in this book.

The *view of systems* has no content peculiar to itself. Its value, to my mind, lies in the perspective it offers for criticism of the many discordant theoretical systems discussed in this book—criticism and a means of utilizing those aspects of each approach which bring concrete observation into workable scientific groupings of sufficient stability for cumulative knowledge. In the following pages I shall supplement the critical comments following each chapter with an effort at general review, selecting such aspects of each school as seem to me important with less regard for a well-rounded presentation. The reader should by now be able to correct for the inevitable distortions involved in such selection. Every school tends in practice to compensate for its special shortcomings, and should not be judged by the summary statements made here.

THE EVOLUTIONARY PROCESS

MAN IS A PRODUCT of the evolutionary process, an animal born with special equipment by virtue of this process alone. Although this proposition was presented in effective scientific form only about a hundred years ago (Darwin, *Origin of Species*, 1859), it is taken for granted by all the schools. Indeed, the idea of man as a special creation, different in kind from his ancestry, is nowadays about as tenable as the theory that babies are brought by storks.

Understanding of the evolutionary process has undergone important modification since Tennyson wrote of Nature, red in tooth and claw, and of the far-off, divine event toward which the whole creation moves. The poetic expression, however, is not too distant from the scientific formulations available to Adler and Freud at the turn of the century. Adler tended to equate his idea of striving toward superiority as the major human goal with the evolutionary trend toward the ever higher and better—toward "perfection." Freud found support for his concept of a death instinct in dualistic evolutionary trends toward creative elaboration (Eros) and toward stasis → disintegration (Thanatos), and finally in a dualism of love and aggression. Although neither Adler nor Freud made very much use of these concepts in their clinical formulations, the concepts remain on the books and are likely to be confusing to thoughtful people whose acquaintance with analytic theories comes from books rather than clinical participation. The "evolutionary" tie-up seems to justify specific conclusions as to the nature of man beyond the cogent empirical data adduced by both Freud and Adler. It leads to pseudo-problems and it supports theoretical contortionism in the effort to explain fundamentally diverse phenomena by the same principle—a principle considered profound because it is thought to operate throughout the animal kingdom. The term *reductionism* is applicable here—a reductionism especially dangerous because biological evolution has about it the flavor of an alien and respected science.

Rank and Fromm also call upon the evolutionary process to buttress their psychological generalizations. They consider the trend toward *individuation* as a universal principle with intrinsic dynamics of its own—the positive urge toward separation and selfhood *vs.* the pain and fear attendant upon leaving the matrix of the womb or the security of instinct-determined behavior. Individuation seems at first glance a more scientifically neutral principle than the striving toward "perfection" or the dichotomy of life and death, of love and hate. Yet it is no more acceptable to modern evolutionary science. Trends toward individuation occur in many animal groups—and at times lead to extinction of the species. They are the result-cause of very complex reaction patterns in animal groups as seen in the perspective of many millions of years. Individuation often took the form of modifications which were hampering to the individual in intragroup relationships (so he did not reproduce freely), or of a group adaptation to the outer world so special that the group died when external conditions changed. The animal groups which have survived longest (some hundred millions of years) are those which were *not* individuated but achieved a "kind" structure adaptable to many circumstances. The oyster, one of the oldest forms of life, is a good example of how one may live in one's own shell to all eternity, presumably without severe inner tension.

In *human society*, perhaps in the human species, the conflict between separation and union, between significance and belonging, is indeed important. But it is the consequence of the peculiar attributes of the human animal and the way of living it has developed. "Separation anxiety" is not intrinsic to the evolutionary process as such. It is a pardonable bias on the part of the human race to consider itself a "higher" form of life than the oyster and to be especially interested in the genetic* and environmental factors which have

---

* I here use the term in the sense of the science of genetics, not the sense, familiar to psychological science, of growth, especially growth in the early years—another example of semantic problems in science.

led toward a more flexible relationship with the environment on the part of individual members of the species. This is the limb the human race has gone out on, *one* branch among many, *one* possible direction in which living organisms could develop. Only with hindsight, however, is this "direction" of evolution discernible.

The hindsight of modern evolutionary theory does not imply belated recognition of a plan, whether of God or any sort of vitalist force, *élan vital*, entelechy, or whatever. On the contrary, the living organism merely did what it could under the varying conditions of its life. It was also subject to genetic change, partly by the process of bisexuality, whereby genes from two parents are mixed, apparently at random, in the offspring, and partly by mutation, *i.e.*, apparently random changes in the germ plasm which suddenly introduce a new *heritable* factor.

Individuals and species survive by the processes of natural selection, by the survival of the fittest, as Darwin suggested. The special development of modern evolutionary theory, however, concerns the definition of fitness. The "struggle for existence" (Nature, red in tooth and claw) is now seen as an over-all principle of *adaptation*. Striving aggression is a relatively incidental part of the process. (After all, the oyster is not a fighter!) The emphasis is thrown on the great variety of forms which organisms may take, and their relationship to the external conditions under which they live. The dusty science of old bones and fossils (paleontology), combined with geological study of the earth's crust and genetic study of such ephemeral creatures as the fruit fly and other organisms whose short span of life allows experimental study of genetic change, presents a picture of *adaptation* very important to psychological science.

The concept of adaptation in evolutionary theory is essentially multi-dimensional. The oyster adapts in its way. We adapt in our way. A multitude of organisms have, over the millennia, adapted or failed to adapt in innumerable ways. Survival and growth in the evolutionary sense require the fortunate concomitance of a great many factors, genetic and environmental, some of which are so common as to serve admirably as general principles for the maintenance or effulgence of living organisms. They are not, however, considered as "universal laws" in the old sense.* Although psychological theory must still guard against taking over principles from evolution too directly, its new approaches offer us a good model for scientific thought.

* Evolutionary science is fortunate in having several sound scholars who write well for the general public. I give here three references which have been especially important for me: G. G. Simpson, *The Meaning of Evolution*, Yale University Press, 1949; J. S. Huxley, *Evolution. The Modern Synthesis*, Harper, 1942; T. Dobzhansky, *Genetics and the Origin of Species*, 2d ed., Columbia University Press, 1941.

THE TOTAL PERSONALITY;
THE SELF

ALL THE ANALYSTS discussed in Parts III and IV have emphasized the self, in more or less active rejection of what I have called loosely the Freudian libido theory. Although I do not agree with the basic repudiation of the libido theory, it does seem to me that the "total personality" has not been given sufficient emphasis by Freudians as an underlying integrative, adaptational system. It is always *implicit* in the basic concepts of constant functional inter-action among the various institutions and mechanisms, of the mobility of the libido, of the importance of the quantitative distribution of energies at any given time. More explicit recognition of the basic integrative trend nec-essary to maintenance of the essentially individual unit, the living organism, might help, however, to guard against the tendency toward static reification of important subsystems. Freudians are so afraid of reification of the self on unduly global terms that their theory easily lends itself to misinterpretation, even by the more pedantically minded in the Freudian school itself. More-over, some broadly integrative trends, usefully observed by other schools, are vehemently rejected by the Freudians. This guarded agreement with Freud's critics does not, of course, imply acceptance of the position they substitute.

The difficulty with most of the "self" theories is that the dynamically very *loose* system of the total personality is construed as a rather *tight* system which can be taken as the basic unit of psychological study. Rank calls the power of this unit the *will* and derives his theory from the movements of the *will* in relation to the realities of living. His emphasis is on positive and negative directions of the will, on totality versus partialization. Adler defines the total personality as constellated around the will to power. Horney contrasts a potential real self with an idealized image built out of the attempt to har-monize discordant trends in the inexpedient efforts of the neurotic to establish modes of coping with the circumstances of living. Fromm is a little like Rank in his strong emphasis on the essential conflict between the fear of individu-ation and the need to attain it.

All these theories tend toward the error of *reductionism*. The basic fact that all psychological events take place within a single organism which must perforce maintain a viable integration is too *directly* translated into cogent psychological systems construed as universal. A sense of self which *develops* in the course of living is too far confused with the truly necessary organismic self. Although these theories have led to important advances in the understanding of patients in our culture, and of broad trends in our culture, although they have been useful correctives to tendencies toward extra-individual generalization about instinct and institutions in Freudian doctrine, they tend to obscure important theoretical problems. Furthermore, they are not helpful in understanding cultures and subgroups of our own culture in which the sense of self (I have called it the self image) takes a form markedly different from the one most people interested in modern psychology take for granted. We psychologists are much more special in this respect than we realize, and we should guard against taking our own intuitive sense of self as a valid premise for generalization about basic human drives.

Among the analysts discussed in the latter half of this book, Sullivan and Jung are exceptions to the present generalization. Both consider the *self* of enormous importance, far more explicitly than Freud. But they do not identify it with the total personality. For them, as for Freud, the total personality remains a quite vague entity, whereas the *self* is given more careful definition as a developmental product. For Sullivan it is a dynamism of very profound importance which integrates experience from birth. For Jung it seems to be an *ideal* integrative achievement. It is not inborn in any usefully definable way, nor can it be used as *the* basic psychological unit. Thus on this point, Sullivan and Jung avoid the reductionism of the other authors in the non-libido group.

I have suggested the term "organismic self" for the fundamental *fact* that any psychological science must take the individual organism as its unit. As a substitute for "total personality" my term is perhaps overly biological. We never encounter a purely organismic self from the moment the neonate is cared for by another person, just as we never encounter the Freudian "id" directly. Perhaps my term differs from the id only in greater emphasis on the deeply integrative trends built into the biological equipment of man. Selye[1] and others have demonstrated that widespread neurochemical connections exist between organ systems which until recently have been considered relatively independent of one another. Eventually theories about the content of the "id" may be profoundly modified by extension of knowledge about human physiology. Nevertheless, the undeniable fact that the individual perishes when integrative functions fail does *not* imply a positive organismic or psychological urge toward integration *as such*.

The distinction is overly subtle if the major point is attention to integrative trends in psychology versus universal "laws" conceived as operating independently of the individual. It becomes of crucial importance when *de facto* integrative phenomena observable in the organism and in cultural history are turned into tight dynamic systems by the sleight of hand of theory, and when the theoretically derived system is applied reductively to concrete events. It cannot be too strongly emphasized that recognizing a measure of integration as the *sine qua non* of survival is *not* the same as taking integration as a biological goal, or as a need for wholeness in the Rankian sense, or as a "real self" in Horney's theory.

Too often the holistic approach to the total personality has led to a neglect of the truly dynamic subsystems inherent in the organism and its milieu, and—as a corollary—to the erection of subsystems on the basis of logic. Thus, for example, Horney's grouping of neurotic personality trends as involving movement toward, away from, or against objects has the very dubious merit of being logically inclusive. Sullivan's less neat listing of nine personality syndromes as "frequently encountered" seems to me preferable because it proceeds from analysis of powerful concrete dynamisms (subsystems) in creative interaction and elaboration. And although I think that the Freudians should pay more attention to the problem of observing relatively stable postnatal trends and syndromes of a complex nature related to the "self," the insistence on making clear their relationship to fundamental biological systems (needs) seems to me wise. A *tentativeness* about the elaboration of relatively stable complex units is valuable. However, it should not clamp down on efforts toward elaboration, and should not substitute a rational deductiveness based on biological systems for a deductiveness based on the "total personality."

An aspect of Sullivan's concept of the self dynamism which deserves special consideration is its fundamentally interpersonal character. The significant experience of the infant is with the *people* who care for it; the child grows in a *social* world. There can be no "real" self, even no identifiable "organismic" self, apart from the dynamism developed through living with people. Sullivan goes so far as to call the self the reflected appraisals of others, but he so constantly traces the *effective* social appraisal back to infancy and childhood that in practice his position differs from Freud's less drastically than might be supposed. He has shown little systematic concern with the consequences of specific social patterns for the development of the self dynamism, although investigation of the culturally determined systems to which the person must adapt would seem entirely compatible with his point of view. It is here that Kardiner's concept of action systems cross-cutting the dynamisms established genetically for the individual and the patterns of his society could become relevant.

THE SELF IMAGE

Returning to the discussion of the total personality as a dynamic system, I call attention again to a concept of the *self image* for which I must accept a large measure of personal responsibility, although the term is loosely used by many schools. Jung's concept of the *persona* seems very similar to the sub-system I had evolved as a means of explaining the cogent data of many schools.* The self image is not coextensive with the total personality. It is not inborn, nor is it *necessarily* a subsystem which becomes very importantly constellative in its own right. Doubtless there is always a loose sense of self, roughly corresponding on the psychological level to the organismic self—a crudely adaptive "total personality." The self image is a much "tighter" sub-system which emerges out of the experience of this loosely organized organis-mic self with the milieu. Where *relations with parental figures* are strong and markedly syntonic or dystonic with the general culture pattern within which the child develops, the self image may be very closely related to—in fact, almost identical with—Freud's superego. Where *the pattern of the culture* is very strong and unified but child-parent relations are diffuse, the self image may be very closely related to the *social role* which the individual learns early and strives to maintain as his very self with relatively slight or highly complex relationship to the superego.

Freud's concept of the superego as inheritor of the Oedipus complex requires a fairly developed sense of the self, as well as a sense of the parents as separate selves of some distinctness. Otherwise the process of identification with and introjection of the parental image could not occur. There could be no such image, and no self to receive it as a powerful institution within a larger unit.

The *theoretical* conflicts about the superego between many Freudians and the English school could be resolved, I think, if Melanie Klein did not

---

* Freud's concept of the ego-ideal should also be mentioned in so far as it differs from the superego. In his early writings Freud stressed the narcissistic elements in the ego-ideal— the love of the person for himself as object. Once he had fully developed the concept of the superego, this aspect of the problem of the self was neglected. Freud himself did not clarify the difference in his later writings. A few recent articles and conversation with some Freudians suggest a growing interest in the ego-ideal as distinct from the superego. Until the ego-ideal plays a more substantial part in Freudian thinking, I shall not elaborate upon it, although I may prophesy that this is a point in my account of Freudians that will require revision in a few years.

At present neither the narcissistic components of the ego-ideal nor the powerful Oedipal components of Freud's superego seem to take account adequately of the *psychosocial* deter-minants I would like to emphasize in the term *self image*.

label her observations about projection and introjection in infancy "superego," and if Freudians understood these phenomena as something more than precursors of the superego. I would prefer to limit the term superego to Freud's own definition, even though this means a limitation of his description of "conscience" to cultures which have, roughly, our kind of family organization and early training for selfhood. This limitation frankly acknowledges that Freud here mistook our culture pattern for a "universal." That the child in any culture tends to develop supra-individual controls through identifications with some sort of external figure or pattern seems incontrovertible—and is perhaps the essence of Freud's contribution in his time. But it becomes merely confusing when experts writing for one another in technical journals use the same term in a variety of ways.

I have found Klein's material and ideas about basic infantile mechanisms of great interest. I think they would be more usable by other Freudians if she emphasized the development of a self and an image of others which then may (and in our culture typically does) undergo the special experience of the phallic stage observed by Freud in his formulation of the superego. Her tendency to equate very primitive mechanisms of projection and introjection with the superego leads to blurring or actual misunderstanding of aspects of Freudian doctrine and therapy which depend on a sharp perception of the development and function of *Freud's* superego.

After these somewhat digressive remarks about the Freudian concept of the superego, I return to the aspect of the problem more directly related to the culture pattern, to the *role* of the self image in different societies. Each society prescribes the details of the self image to some extent. Societies differ very markedly, however, not only in role specification but in mobility of role and in the valuation put on being one's *self*. I suggested in comment on Chapter 4 that cross-cultural studies of the juvenile period would contribute importantly to better understanding of how the child's sense of self, begun in the family circle, becomes related to social opportunities and demands. I have also suggested repeatedly that the widespread emphasis on the self image as a highly individualized subsystem, flexibly adapted to changing cultural conditions, may be a characteristically modern process, specific to our type of culture. Horney's emphasis on the pathologically idealized self image offers a very important insight into the dynamics of this subsystem in the social group from which most of her analytic patients come. Such dynamics are probably not universally human in the form she describes, and her concept of a submerged "real self" seems to me untenable.

Valuable in many ways, Fromm's emphasis on the loss of selfhood in the "marketing orientation" seems to neglect what one may almost call the *exacerbation* of the sense of self in a society in which role identity is highly mobile, in which there is little role continuity between father and son, in which individual merit → demonstrable success is supported by a vigorous philosophy of the worth of the individual as such. The bane of our modern parenthood is its uncertainty in its relations with the child, its uneasy abnegation of authority, its fear of imposing the "wrong" rules in training the child for a changing society, its *self-consciousness*.

In comment on Chapter 9, I suggested that this approach, increasingly typical, is not altogether bad. At any rate we shall probably have to live with it, since "society" is rapidly becoming mobile all over the world. The positive factor in this social change is—it seems to me—an increase in affectional and communicative relations between father and son, between parents and the children who moved away. Self-conscious parents make for children conscious of the "self" in a manner new to social history.*

I have thus far spoken as though the self image were a single entity. This may be predominantly true for some individuals. (*Cf.* Jung's observation that pronounced introverts tend to develop a single persona.) Typically there are important sub-images, which may have a high degree of autonomy. Most of us have several pictures of ourselves, not always logically compatible with one another, which serve as a dynamic focus under varying circumstances. An impressive example in a society which supported such divergence is the loving respectable family man who was something of a cutthroat and a libertine in his business and away-from-home pleasures—with little or no sense of guilt because the discordant images were both sanctioned by his society and were not *brought together* in the uneasy manner of today. Our Victorian forebears may have been far less hypocritical to themselves than they seem to us. Some individuals seem to live almost entirely through a variety of social adaptations: the many personae of the pronounced extravert in Jung's vocabulary. The frankly adaptive self image may be subjectively experienced as a sort of mask covering a deeper image, more or less clearly delineated at some level of the personality. Or, as Jung remarks, the person may profoundly identify himself with his persona, his socially adaptive "mask." I use quotation marks here because, to my way of thinking, such profound identifications

* I *suspect* that this consciousness is an important factor in the observed increase in schizophrenia and its relatively benign course in comparison with the flagrant symptom neuroses and psychoses of the past. Perhaps Horney should have called her book *The* Psychotic *Personality of Our Times*, since the typical minor disturbances she discusses mainly concern the sense of self in relation to reality (psychosis) rather than id impulses in relation to ego structure (neurosis).

become genuine in their psychodynamics, and I feel that the professional psychologist is sometimes covertly applying his own liberal value system when he considers an essentially social adaptation as essentially neurotic.

I have emphasized in the foregoing pages the socially adaptive aspects of the self image or images. I do not wish to *exclude* self images constellated around organs of the body. The person may feel himself vividly in his mouth, his eyes, his penis, etc., and may overextend the biological role of such organ systems in a purely psychological way. In some instances the problem is not merely that the organ becomes unduly important in the general psychic economy but that it actually becomes "me." Glauber discusses this problem cogently in a paper on the dynamics of stuttering.[2]

UNDERLYING DYNAMICS OF THE SELF IMAGE IN OUR CULTURE

If it is to be very convincing, this descriptive discussion of the self image requires analysis of its underlying dynamics. I cannot here go into detail. It seems to me that the Freudian concept of identification, with the to-and-fro action of the mechanisms of introjection and projection, most adequately explains its early development and the sources of its "energy." I would like only to suggest that further attention be paid to aspects of the child's experience leading toward the formation of his sense of "me," and the parallel sense of other people as substantial independent entities. Freud and Sullivan offer important groundwork for such attention. Several points seem to me underemphasized in most psychoanalytic theory, and therefore important for discussion here.

(1) The "reflected appraisal" of the adults may be considered from the rather subtle angle of their *taking the child as a responsible unit,* rather than simply calling specific acts good or bad. "Modern" child training has perhaps overemphasized this point, with benign intent, before the little child was ready for so complex an attitude toward himself. "Calvinist" training (cf. Fromm's discussion, pp. 390f.) also made the child prematurely aware of his own soul, but with much more definite directives as to good and bad action. Hence, perhaps, the diffuse but powerfully organized self image in our times observed by Horney, in some contrast to the severe conscience related to relatively specific impulses and actions characteristic for patients of puritanical background. Some cultures, including many groups or families in our own culture, are less concerned with the problem of the individual as such. The child is trained to his social role with less emphasis on what he is in himself,

with less individualized parental models for identification, with less exhortation to individual achievement and high social valuation of personal merit. Observation of the subtle ways in which the little child is brought to awareness of his selfhood would add an important dimension to the developmental process. (See the discussion of "negativism," pp. 624ff.)

(2) Psychoanalytic theory tends to limit itself too closely to consideration of the immediate family. The little child does not clearly experience its parents as individuals. What other people do is often ascribed to the parent, just as attributes of the parents are assigned to other people. By this process of non-differentiation, other persons, even casual strangers, tend to enter into the formulation of the powerful parent image and reflected self image. Furthermore, people are evaluated by the young child in terms of their interaction with him, not on objective terms, which have not yet been learned. In this sense it is the *situation* which must be considered rather than the "personality" of the adult as observed by adult outsiders. The "personality" of the parents is important because the fundamental attitudes of the significant adults around the child create the *situations* most meaningful to him. Recognition of this latter point has too often obscured the essential complexity of the genetic process within the family and led to an almost mystical overemphasis on purely psychological connections between the child and his parents and siblings. Scientific observation could well include more careful study of the precise role of "other people" in the life of the little child, and of the total *situation* which may dictate special emphases in the *approach of the parent to the child* which are not predictable from insight into the general personality of the parent.

(3) However the early images of the self and the parental images are built up, a next stage in what Sullivan calls the juvenile era involves the relationship between these early images and the later *social* images the child encounters. In most societies the social images tend to specify rather clearly what a child and his parents should be like. When these images correspond fairly well with the early formulations, there is likely to be a rather continuous development for good or ill. If the "young prince," spoiled at home by family, servants, and friends, is equally spoiled at school, he is very likely to show an uncomplicated syndrome of the pampered child as described by Adler. Very often there is an important discrepancy between the earlier images and the "school" images (*identities* in Erikson's vocabulary), such that a more or less thorough revamping is necessary. This revamping cannot be considered apart from the structure of the early images. It is absurd to say that school is school and to erect an educational psychology apart from the "deep" psychology of the nursery. Going to school late, after the Oedipal crisis has been lived

through in the family setting, must have a different dynamic effect from going to nursery school and kindergarten, where teachers and the school situation participate much more in the formation of the early images. This may be primarily a matter of timing. Equally important is the relationship between the ideals and opportunities of the school situation and the early family setting, partly on the basis of already formulated images (these images largely determine expectation and action), partly on the basis of the social judgment of his family which the child now becomes able to recognize.

Nothing in the preceding paragraph is foreign to psychoanalytic thinking, but the analysts have usually left the problem at the level of insight into the individual case, with common-sense appreciation of what the child is up against. Since the dynamics of the individual case depend on so many factors, it is dangerous to codify the effect of a particular *late* factor. Nevertheless, careful statistical studies of pupil populations in relation to achievement, measurable capacity, and background should help toward a better under-standing of factors of widespread influence, provided they are coupled with studies of how these factors operate within the individual. It is only by such concomitant studies that we can begin to extend our understanding of how "social" factors affect the individual.

(4) The role of the self image must be studied in relation to the ideals and opportunities offered by the society to its adult members. Partly this is a matter of finding one's own "self" and matching it to one's "role." (*Cf.* Erikson.) Instances are fairly common of an awkward, unhappy, disagreeable, irresponsible, even stupid-appearing young person who changes dramatically when he gets into a line of work—or it may be a new community—to which he is somehow especially suited. Jung has emphasized the *inward* changes which gradually take place as character trends become more pronounced and rigid with long living in a particular role, so that the middle-aged personality may be invaded by aspects of himself previously repressed and starved. Kardiner has investigated with especial cogency the relationship of social opportunities to individual needs, among which one may surely number the self image.

I cannot here go into detail about the complex relations between the individual and his society (see Chaps. 4 and 9). I believe, however, that focus on the nature of the self image or images as they develop in dynamic relationship to biological systems and external systems in widening circles from the immediate family to society would be a healthy addition to all the schools. This formulation does not presuppose an inborn self system with drives, needs, goals proper to itself, not even the need for security and prestige. The relation to the drive systems emphasized by Freud is perhaps theoretically understandable (see pp. 89-104)—although much more information is needed for understanding of the different ways in which the self images develop and operate. With due caution, it seems to me possible to use a great many of the concepts of the various analytic schools as offering excellent insights into deep relationships *operating under certain conditions* (for example Freud's superego and Horney's idealized image).

Although I have not been able to discuss "psychologists" in a book on psychoanalysis, it seems to me that this formulation relates itself easily to the emphasis of Murphy on the power of a self which *develops* in complex creative interaction with the surrounding social "field," and to the emphasis of Newcomb, Hartley and other social psychologists on the development and dynamic significance of the person's sense of his "role" in the constant interpersonal situations he encounters.[3]

INSTINCTUAL DRIVES

THE STATEMENT of relationship between the foregoing discussion of the total personality and Freud's instinct theory has thus far been more promissory than real. I have hardly more than intimated my feeling that the *biological* aspects of personality development are of enormous importance, and that Freud has studied them well, whereas the other schools have too far neglected them. If the next several pages sound mainly critical of Freud's position, it is only because I take its essential outlines for granted. The problem is how to reconcile the established data of the Freudian approach with cogent observations from other schools in a manner which encourages cooperative inquiry. It must be apparent from earlier discussions that the *view of systems* rejects any interpretation of the role of biologically determined systems as operating in a vacuum, or as "instinctual drives" in complex mechanical relationship to ill-defined environmental situations. In so far as Freud's theory is interpreted in this manner, I cannot accept it. To my mind, Freud's libido theory is a brilliant description of important dynamic connections among systems constellated around the emergent biologically focused trends of the maturing organism. It offers a view of *creative but generally expectable relationships* among systems at a very deep level of human function.

Probably no Freudian would accept this definition of the libido theory as fully descriptive. Although Freud suggests a somatic source for all instinctual drives, he also remarks that present-day physiology cannot define such sources adequately. He therefore urges provisional definition in terms of psychological generalizations from psychologically observable phenomena. He often writes as though the major instinctual drives were "forces" in themselves, as though the libido were a psychic energy of given amount which could be considered as a sort of unit, analogous to the energy of the physics of his time, subject to similar laws of conservation. This was a natural hypothesis in his generation (Jung's theory of the libido is similar in this respect), especially alluring because it seemed to offer a means of establishing psychological "universals" in the manner required of Science until very recently.

I think it greatly to his credit that Freud was never entirely consistent on this point. "A foolish consistency," says Emerson, "is the hobgoblin of little minds." As a very great mind, Freud was able to observe freshly and to integrate his observations at many levels. He was never as reductive in approach as many of his followers and opponents. Thus, if I firmly reject a naively "energic" view of instinctual drives and the libido, I do not feel that I am going *against* Freud. Instead I am assuming he meant very earnestly the modest caution with which he presented such generalizations. The contemporary Freudians who have stressed aspects of Freud's writings dealing with ego psychology, have usually discounted this bogey of instinctual "forces" and the libido as a fixed quantum of psychic energy which is merely disposed in various ways.

In my efforts toward a theoretical framework, I have tried to use the hobgoblin of consistency constructively in an attempt to extend Freud's generalizations about somatic sources in such a manner as to integrate them with other phenomena. Freud isolated the oral, anal, and genital systems as of especial importance for psychological development. The libido theory (here considered strictly in its energic aspects), with the concept of cathexis to account for object relations, is introduced as a means of expressing the dynamic to-and-fro relationships among these aspects of our biological equipment. Theoretically, Freud writes, the libido includes the whole body, but the erogenous zones are the ones we know most about.[4]

Throughout this book I have urged that "nonsexual" systems inherent in the human organism be considered in something of the same manner as the "sexual" systems investigated by Freud. The proposal involves the danger of erecting again the concept of "ego instincts" which Freud initially proposed and abandoned for good reason. Furthermore, much of the careful work done by "psychologists" on the nonsexual systems is difficult to use because it was done without control of the concomitantly operating sexual systems, often with little control even of the context *for the subject* of the situation chosen for experimentation or controlled observation.

TYPES OF SYSTEMATIZATION

In comment on Chapter 3, I attempted an analysis of the problem at a level of basic theory which to my mind offers a useful perspective. Although the organism must function "as a whole" if it is to survive as an organism, its holism operates through the integration of a series of subsystems, all to some degree autonomous, all creatively interlocking. It is equally true that no organism exists without a milieu, to the special nature of which it must adapt, but the nature of the milieu is not our primary concern just now.

I suggested that instead of thinking in terms of instincts, or even instinctual drives or needs, we think in terms of the major *systematizations* of the organism as a biological unit. Some of these *systematizations* are so profoundly necessary to animal survival as to have been built into the human species as an evolutionary product over a period measurable in hundreds of thousands of years. They antedate by far any of the special terms of the milieu introduced by the more distinctively human evolutionary development—especially those introduced by human society as we know it. They are profoundly similar to the systems observable in most mammals.*

I called the essential maintenance systems of the body *interosystems.* They are concerned with the deep, vegetative functions of the organism, are mainly outside the sphere of conscious control and even of awareness, and are connected only indirectly with events in the outer world. Nevertheless, they are highly organized as systems, and intricately interconnected in a manner which physiology is probably just beginning to appreciate. Although I am not able to evaluate the correctness of Selye's specific conclusions, his general hypothesis of inclusive adaptational systems of the body seems valid.[5] Indeed, evolutionary theory requires some such *functional* cross-cutting if the extraordinarily complex morphology of the various organ systems is to be explained without the hypothesis of a deity or a mysterious entelechy.

I found it convenient to label as *exterosystems* those systems of the body which are concerned very directly with registering impressions from the outer

---

* I am reluctant to range further in phylogenetic developments, because although all living organisms on our planet have many basic problems of existence in common, the basic systematizations of their modes of coping with these problems are so different that analogies are often more dangerous than helpful in psychological science. The societies of ants and bees are marvelous in many respects but their structure is totally foreign to the basic equipment of the human species.

world and with executing action. Freud calls these systems ego functions but includes under this term so many other functions of the ego that the term has no sharpness of reference. Hartmann's concept of ego functions of primary autonomy is very close to what I have in mind, although I think there is some merit in reserving the label *exterosystems* more specifically for those functions which *in themselves* operate only (or almost only) in response to external stimuli. Many bodily systems build up inner tensions which require some sort of discharge, regardless of external experience, or sometimes *beyond* the external event, as when we have to "calm down" after an experience involving rage or fear. By contrast the visual system is very highly organized as such but apparently does not have an inner rhythm or need *in itself* and reacts beyond experience only in a transitory, mechanical way (*e.g.*, the afterimage).

Psychologists of all schools have rightly considered the details of the radically intero- and exterosystems as beyond their province, although acquaintance with their nature is required in every training program. The almost wholly nonconscious interosystems are beginning to impinge on psychological science via psychosomatic medicine, partly in connection with conditions in which the pathology involves the interosystems very specifically (allergies, ulcers, etc.), partly because more general interaction among established patterns within the "total personality" has received scientific recognition. Some psychological schools—for example, the classical Gestalt schools—have devoted much attention to the exterosystems, notably visual perception. I think the contribution of these schools is often limited by an overly exclusive concentration on the exterosystems, with insufficient appreciation of their predominantly instrumental character in relation to other body systems, especially the drive systems.

DRIVE SYSTEMS

Now I come to the pre-eminent domain of modern psychological science: the *drive systems*. I have suggested that some body systems, fairly well-structured in the long course of evolutionary development, are essentially intermediary. They are sufficiently *inward* to develop tensions within the organism itself regardless of external stimuli. *But they require an external object for their fulfillment as systems.*

In some species the nature of the external object is narrowly prescribed, and the means of attaining it is built into the organism. In other species sexual *behavior* (the Freudian "aim"?) seems set by inner rhythms in minute detail, but the sexual *object* is not exactly prefigured. Under normal conditions, of course, the inborn sexual behavior is complemented by the behavior of the mate. In the absence of an appropriate mate, however, the creature may "fall in love with" (become sexually fixated upon) any object which somehow corresponds to its stimulus need. *In species which tend toward monogamous relations with the mate*, this early fixation may become very strong. An esthetically charming example is the white peacock mentioned by Lorenz[6] who fell in love with a tortoise—because he happened to be housed, during a cold spell, in the warm reptile house of the zoo at the time of his sexual maturation. Presumably something about the tortoise related more closely to the bird's sexual instinct pattern ("aim"?) than the behavior of the other reptiles and humans he encountered, and the monogamous trend of the species resulted in inappropriate fidelity to the first object incorporated into the drive system.

In man the nature of the object is extremely vague at birth—if, indeed, it is prefigured at all. The instinctual systems are relatively diffuse and malleable, even in comparison with those of the higher mammals. Nevertheless, these systems build up strong inner tensions like the interosystems, which continue operating until the *object* aspect of the system is introduced in a satisfactory manner. Sensations of unpleasure (*Unlust*) and motor restlessness normally appear until the tension is reduced by what the Gestaltists call closure of the system—here the introduction of the object aspect with appropriate response.

I have deliberately kept this statement as abstract and nontelic as possible in order to emphasize the theoretical continuity of the drive systems with the intero- and exterosystems. This continuity seems to me very important in integrating psychological phenomena with physiological phenomena—negatively stated, in avoiding the age-old philosophical problem of psychic "forces," however defined, in relation to physiological and physical events: soul and body; mind and matter; instinct and reality; drive, goal, or need as intrinsically *special* attributes of the organism.

Having thus far emphasized the theoretical continuity of the drive systems with other systems, I may freely point out their special goal-directed quality. I have already said that these systems are the province of psychology. *Within our province*, the goal is, or quickly becomes, the focus of these systems. By the definition here offered they require an external object for closure. One may emphasize the goal or the need aspect as one pleases, nevertheless one must keep in mind the essential point that drive systems are not basically different from the other bodily systematizations except in respect of this inclusion of sensory-motor patterns involving an external component.

For some of the most important drive systems, notably the sexual systems,

Freud's analysis of the source, aim, and object aspects of "instinct" seems to me valid and brilliantly implemented. It seems to me possible to retain all of the Freudian work and thought on these systems, including the integrating concept of the libido—save only the exclusiveness and tendency toward theoretical reductionism based on these particular systems, considered either as *the* systems of psychology or as disposing of a fixed quantum of "energy."

NONSEXUAL DRIVE SYSTEMS

I have suggested the term *nonsexual* for all the other drive systems—that is, for systems which tend to build up tensions within the organism spontaneously, although relations with the outside world are implicit in the very structure of the system. Since these systems have not been adequately investigated from the point of view of personality dynamics within the individual, I have chosen a term that is merely the obverse of Freud's. I must be vague and tentative about which systems should be included and how.

"Hunger" is doubtless the outstanding example, but it is not a very instructive example for several reasons. The first is that it has acquired so many and such various theoretical connotations that it is hard to view the problem freshly. The second is that although "hunger" seems simple, it is in fact highly complex in the pattern of body subsystems involved, and in relation to external phenomena. The third reason is that viable cultures have so far solved the problem of feeding the people, especially the very young, that "hunger" is never encountered in "pure" form, and in most cultures it becomes quite incidental to *social forms* which indirectly supply food. Looting for food is a surprisingly rare phenomenon. In modern cultures black markets are the usual answer in a country short of food—and the black market is always organized along the lines of the culture.

Thus, although hunger is in one sense the most insistent and direct of the drive systems, in another sense it is among the most highly acculturated under reasonably normal situations from earliest infancy, and in human society rarely provides a continuing focus of systematized activity in its own right. I quoted Freud earlier (p. 78) to the effect that *because* the satisfaction of hunger cannot be long delayed, the individual learns moderate postponement and expedient action (*i.e.*, ego action) earlier in this area than in the more malleable sexual systems.*

Presumably, neural and chemical reaction patterns are inborn as direct,

---

* Indeed, the basic patterns, including the capacity for postponement, must be inborn. For once I am more impressed with the phylogenetic aspects of the problem than Freud.

though rather fragmentary, connections between aspects of the interosystems involved in "hunger" and the exterosystems. Thus the familiar hand-mouth pattern of early infancy may well be part of this "nonsexual" systematization *as well as* related to the sexual (pleasure-seeking) aspects of the oral zone. But this small inborn subsystem so quickly becomes incorporated into the integrative systems which the infant *develops* that its inborn functional relations to the major inborn drive systems seem irrelevant to psychological science.

There is nothing remarkable in the fact that the same subsystems may be incorporated in different, even in antagonistic, drive systems. The adult puts his hand to his mouth for many reasons. So does the infant. The infant's "reasons" are much more closely related to the evolutionary patterns of the species. It is the adult onlooker who infers the reason for putting things to the mouth, and the tendency of the scientific onlooker is to see *the* reason for the bit of inborn activity. It seems clear that this inborn subsystem and others like it are what Freud called "overdetermined." The evolutionary process did not take the costly form of developing new organs and specific connections for all the functions necessary to maintenance of life. It was much less planful and much more efficient. Part-systems developed in one connection were taken over by other wider systems in intricate variety with different types of innervation. The point is that they form an integral part of several inborn systems stable enough to be called drive systems, and *also* have some autonomy of their own. The same process continues with the learned systems developing out of experience.

The difficulty with Freud's *early* formulation of sexual and ego instincts lay in his overemphasis on the broad telic organization of these subsystems around the life problems of reproduction and self-preservation, with reductionist dichotomizing of observable behavior patterns as serving one or the other set of instincts—a very pardonable error in view of the general ideology of his time, and one which he tried to correct. But his correction too far neglected the autonomous dynamics of the nonsexual systems (roughly his early ego instincts), whereas his further development of the libido theory beyond the pleasure principle tends to retain the telic flavor of the earlier concept of a fairly unitary and goal-directed complex of instincts for Eros. And Thanatos, I think, becomes artificially goal-directed as the opposite of Eros.

I shall come in a moment to the instinct of aggression, Thanatos, which Freud proposed when he gave up the concept of ego instincts, but first I should like to discuss somewhat further the nonsexual drive systems other than "hunger"—roughly what Freud called "ego functions." Although many of my ideas are the same as or even derived from those of Freudians who have been especially interested in ego psychology, the implications drawn by Freudians are so various and complex that it seems well to assume personal responsibility for them here. (See Chap. 3 for further discussion.)

Some of these "ego functions" appear to have an inner-tension pattern intrinsic to the organism, albeit readily modifiable. Mittelmann has suggested a native urge toward "motility," somewhat comparable to the sexual drive systems in its inward urgency, its positive seeking for expression regardless of external stimulation. Any infant allowed freedom of movement *moves*. In fact, this is so striking a feature of infancy that it may have been ignored in psychoanalytic theory because of its very obviousness. Movement is almost equivalent to living. Subpatterns related to the drive systems and the exterosystems develop very early—indeed are doubtless present in rudimentary form from the outset. The relationship between the *external* stimulating situation and inner tensions within the other bodily systems is apparently closer for these "nonsexual" systems than for the systems Freud offers as instinctual drives. They readily become *instrumental*. Nevertheless I should prefer to formulate the problem as a difference in the intrinsic constellating trend of this broad system type rather than envisage it as basically different in kind.

Freud's grouping of sexual and aggressive trends as "the" instinctual drives rather misses the point I am trying to make, no matter how much weight one gives to ego mechanisms and apparatuses of primary autonomy. Hendrick's instinct of "mastery"[7] is a useful concept in that it emphasizes the drive character of some of the nonsexual systems, but it also has a telic flavor which I should like to avoid in basic theorizing. It smacks of purism—and perhaps even of the "mechanistic" approach I heartily dislike—to insist on the "system" quality of the impressive struggles of the healthy infant to achieve the successive stages of locomotor and manipulatory development long observed by "psychologists"—not to mention the increasing interpersonal awareness of the little child and his growing sense that "I" do it, and his sense that the significant adults around him differ and must be approached differently. Yet it is very important that these complex integrative events should not be obscured by a lumping together as a single process, an instinctual drive, which is then recombined as such with the sexual systems which Freud called libido. I come again to the points made in the earlier pages of this epilogue.

Even more than is the case with the sexual drive systems, the nonsexual systems are involved with the outer world. It is difficult for us to think of inborn involvement without inborn direction, but we must, I believe, make the effort to preserve this distinction. Although the locomotor and perceptual patterns of man's inborn equipment were doubtless developed in terms broadly adaptational as regards the viability of the species, their distinctively human feature is the absence of *specific* inborn external goals, together with a high degree of flexibility and potential interconnectedness via the cortex among the subsystems of the body. It is this fact which enables the inner tensions of these systems (their "drive" aspect) to function *instrumentally* as regards adaptation to the social world within which the child perforce matures, and as regards the sexual systems.

Freud saw clearly this *instrumentality* and the fact that it was mediated by the *nature of the ego apparatuses*. What he missed, at least in emphasis, was (1) the autonomous dynamics of the instruments, whether primary or secondary (*cf.* discussion of Hartmann and Anna Freud, pp. 89*ff.* and 95*ff.*) and (2) the drive aspect of the nonsexual systems (Mittelmann, Hendrick with modification).

AGGRESSION

WE COME NOW to the problem of *aggression,* which I have not discussed earlier in critical comment because I wanted the full background of the psycho-analytic schools and full presentation of my own view of systems before attacking this difficult topic. Freud and Freudians talk of an instinctual aggressive drive, but it is an awkward concept for them. They are not able to point to a clear somatic source and aim in the manner which makes their discussion of the sexual instincts so cogent. Freud attempts to handle the problem by the general biological concept of a death instinct (Thanatos). I have already indicated (pp. 108*f.*) why this position seems to me untenable as a means of explaining the observable facts of human cruelty. Many *Freudians* reject the concept of Thanatos, calling it a metaphysical speculation, but most of them retain the clinical concept of an instinctual drive, called aggression, which is different in kind from the libidinal drives.

Since I am here primarily concerned with *Freudian* theory, I merely mention in passing the fact that all psychoanalytic schools are fully cognizant of hostility as an extremely potent factor in human psychology. No one can look honestly at the delightful baby who bites, hits, and scratches, and smirks as he deliberately "hurts," or at a human race whose record of cruelty appalls us even in our "civilized" times, without drawing the conclusion that sadism, aggression, hostility, whatever you want to call it, is a prominent feature of the human psyche.

My own feeling is that many aspects of "aggression" do belong among the inborn systems. Thus, in a limited way I align myself with the Freudians against the analysts who consider hostility as purely reactive to understandable social frustrations. It seems to me, however, that what is currently called "aggression" is not a *unitary* drive system, and that much confusion in Freudian theory could be avoided if the concept of *an* instinctual drive opposed to Eros were given up. The analysis of the problem I shall offer is complex and necessarily somewhat speculative because I shall suggest possible somatic sources beyond secure knowledge of basic physiological patterns.

Freud himself was impressed by the fact that the skeletal musculature seemed intimately involved in the instinct of aggression. Many contemporary Freudians point to the *constructive* aspects of aggression, via the musculature, and often seem to equate it, in part, with an urge to mastery and growth which is neither reactive or purely instrumental. Since they retain the concept of a single drive toward hate and destruction, I find this position needlessly confusing. I would prefer to subsume these constructive aspects of "aggression" under the neutral heading of nonsexual drive systems just discussed, with emphasis on the inborn motility patterns. These patterns may *in fact* be "destructive," because the baby does not properly distinguish between valuable *objets d'art* and the objects he is permitted to bang around in baby fashion. Furthermore, these systems by their very nature readily become instrumental in relationship to other systems. Finally, the degree of motility in the infant is by no means an indifferent factor in the development of parent-child relations. I have repeatedly urged more attention to the extra-vivid frustration experiences encountered by the active child who is "into everything." I might have added the "neglect" which is often the lot of the placid baby. Detailed discussion is inappropriate here, but it seems clear how drive-systems in themselves neutral as regards the problem of aggression easily become integrated with other patterns, inborn or of early development, which can be called "aggressive" or "destructive" from a social viewpoint, and may come to express "hostility."

A comment on one stage of early development which has often been considered as essentially "aggressive" may be in order—the *negativistic* stage almost regularly encountered in the toddler. The comment should not be considered inclusive; in fact I point in passing to the significance of the anal stage as presented by Freudians (see pp. 194*ff.*). The present comment relates to the development of the sense of self, which I feel has not received sufficient attention.

The *infant* tends to be dominated by whatever drive system is prepotent at the moment, other systems swinging into supportive alignment. The first inhibitory control is probably rather directly related to the operating system with some specificity: mustn't touch, mustn't hit or bite, mustn't wet, "because" this particular activity leads to direful consequences. The totalistic adaptive personality follows the drive system. The *toddler* is in process of learning a more complex type of control through the increased stability of the self system. Such increase in the stable dynamics of a quite new system does not "just happen" with the advancing months. The child is talked to and handled as a unit, and he apparently begins (sometimes rather suddenly) to think of himself as such. He learns that "he" can say no. He can say it to his own impulses, and he can say it to his parents. This is a very important discovery. A period of saying no to almost everything is a familiar phenomenon in the most normal childhood, often occurring along with the phrase "Me do it." *In some part* (perhaps enough to make it stand out from the more continuing aggressions of the human psyche), the negativistic phase is part of learning to be a person—a way of testing out the potentials of this early glimpse of a new dimension.* However trying to parents, many of these primitive, defiant no's do not seem in themselves destructive or hostile, although they easily acquire a hostile flavor if badly handled.

To recapitulate, the nonsexual systems discussed thus far do not seem to me "aggressive" in their own right, although they often look aggressive to the adult. Furthermore, they often provoke adult behavior which the child interprets as frustrating or terrifying, and they readily become instrumental in reactive hostility. I discussed the negativism and defiance so often encountered in the toddler as a complex matter, where *one component* is learning the veto powers of an emergent "self."

INBORN PATTERNS OF AGGRESSION

This analysis does *not*, to my mind, cover all of the evidence for an instinct of aggression. The nonsexual drives thus far discussed are only part of the story, but a part which should be disentangled as regards basic dynamics from the deep pattern I am about to discuss. This pattern comes much closer to the Freudian concept of an inborn drive, and has, I believe, somatic sources which are rather clearly recognizable once one considers them independently of the complex, constructive aspects of aggression.

The pattern I refer to is *rage*. I am using the term in the sense proposed by Cannon.[8] His early description (1915) stands, with such modification as

---

* *In some part* the equally familiar rebellious "Me do it" phases of middle childhood, adolescence, the climacteric, and senescence are doubtless also closely related to the self system.

might be expected after some forty years of careful physiological research. Among the psychoanalysts, it is Rado who has pointed most clearly to the significance of this *affectomotor* pattern for psychological development.[9] Probably Darwin was essentially correct in his attempt to relate basic modes of affective expression[10] to the experience of the human species under conditions of *animal* "struggle for survival." Darwin rode his theory too hard at times as regards specific motor acts, and little was known in his time about the extensive neurochemical patterns underlying the rage phenomena. With these corrections, however, it does seem as though Darwin was justified in supposing that the rage pattern had the evolutionary function of mobilizing the organism for active combat. Active combat involves "the musculature," but rage also involves *changes in the interosystems* which seem in a general way functional as supporting the combat or escape status of the animal organism. It would be absurd to confine the rage pattern to hitting, biting, and other motor patterns. Increase in blood sugar, adrenalin, heart rate, etc., etc., inhibition of the digestive and at times the reproductive systems, etc., etc., under strain are familiar phenomena.

One may easily understand the very close relations, physiologically, between fear and rage: it is the appreciation of danger that provokes the reaction of combat—danger or frustration. This pattern (doubtless patterns would be preferable) is indeed built into the organism, and therefore has a dynamic "drive" quality rooted in inner tensions.*

---

* Since writing these paragraphs I have become aware of a new *ordered* type of observation and experiment which warrants a specialty label—*ethology*. Invented by physiologists, this discipline concerns itself with the comparative study of animal *behavior* under conditions which preserve, in so far as possible the natural environment of the animal, with such controlled variation as makes sense to the animal. The creature is not thrust into a humanly constructed maze or puzzle box and expected to reveal itself under conditions about as fair to the animal as setting down a group of successful businessmen in an Eskimo village, keeping them separated, starving them a bit, and observing how ingenious they are in figuring out how to catch a fish. This would be an interesting experiment, but not really very revealing of the complex human patterns the men would show if studied in their natural habitat. The anthropomorphizing of animal behavior has come quite as much from scientists who set the animals to tasks determined by quite *human* concepts of significant problems as from the sentimentalizers.

Careful observation of the behavior of the animal in its own world, *long* observation under natural conditions (and by "long" these scientists may mean years of sitting with binoculars day after day on a lonely beach in all weathers to study the life of the herring gull, etc., etc.), is used to suggest the crucial experiments which reveal more sharply the cues the animal uses in its adaptational behavior, *which* patterns seem inborn, *when* they may appear nonfunctionally, the range and manner of developing new adaptational patterns.

The immediate value of these studies for psychological science is the demonstration of the enormous variability in instinctual behavior from one species to another, even though all species must cope with the same major problems of existence on this planet. It becomes clear that no bits of behavior can be considered as "instinctive" throughout the animal kingdom with the same relationship to the functional "drive." The bits are functional only if seen within the general adaptational pattern of the species.

Furthermore they *may* be related to each other in a manner which looks nonadaptational, even mechanistic. The herring gulls (also some other birds, the stickleback and several other fish carefully studied) have a species pattern of building nests and defending their sanctity

It should be emphasized, however, that these "inner tensions" do not have *an inner rhythm* of their own, like the sexual systems, like hunger and in a way motility. They arise in response to an *external* danger or frustration and are oriented toward motor expression. Although the degree and nature of involvement of the interosystems in patterned response gives "rage" an inborn quality far beyond appropriate reaction to most actual dangers, and far beyond what is encountered in the "exterosystems" per se, it seems to me mistaken to speak of an "instinct" of aggression in the sense of spontaneously generated "energy" inherent in man.

In practice this distinction may well seem an unnecessary quibble. Every infant is frightened and frustrated by external stimuli, and he builds up signals for danger and frustration which continue to arouse this inborn pattern, very often outside of awareness. Probably aggression *operates* very much like the primary drive systems we have been discussing, in that once the inner tension system is aroused it tends to press toward closure as a system, toward expression or reduction of tension, to use terms more familiar to Freudian theory. My formulation hardly affects current Freudian interpretation of clinical observation, but perhaps it helps guard against such interpretation of Freud's position as assumes a measure of evil in the human breast which must somehow be worked off as such.

The main value of the formulation, to me, is an orientation toward the problem of aggression which can more easily lead to fruitful integration with current studies of the interosystems (broadly speaking, physiology) and also with studies in the area roughly called "psychology"—educational psychology, group psychology, many aspects of so-called general and experimental psychology which are concerned with how people act in more or less specifiable situations. The concept of the "energies" of the sexual systems and their summary as libido is not easily accepted by these related disciplines, although my impression is that the importance of the erogenous zones in personality development is rather generally recognized. The "instinct of aggression," with no definable somatic source and no very clear description of its aim and object,

---

over a fairly wide area. Patterns of aggression and defense related to these areas are easily observable. An interesting point is that at the moment when the animal is in severe conflict as to fight or flight, it often goes into the behavior characteristic for nest-building—totally irrelevant to the current conflict, and quite abortive. This behavior is interpreted as a spill-over, a displacement of the instinctual energies mobilized in the combat situation to a closely related instinctual pattern. I am not entirely sure that this interpretation is correct, and I shall return to the problem in a later footnote. The point of emphasis here is the recognizable patterning of instinctual *behavior* in varying relationship to its adaptive purpose.

For bibliography in this field, I refer the reader to *King Solomon's Ring* by Konrad Lorenz (Crowell, 1952), an utterly charming book written for the layman. Lorenz has also written for his colleagues. Perhaps the best over-all scientific presentation of ethology is *A Study of Instincts* by N. Tinbergen (Oxford University Press, 1951).

is even less acceptable and even less easy to work with conceptually outside of the complex Freudian formulation. "Psychology" has so far recovered from its own tendency toward establishing separate faculties, instincts, drives, and the like as to be very suspicious of anything in Freudian doctrine that seems like a carry-over from this earlier position. Contemporary "field" theories and the rather general emphasis on patterns of response versus instincts, no matter how broadly defined, are closer, I think, to my formulation than to the concept of aggression as an instinctual drive. A theoretical quibble seems valuable if it encourages more direct integration of the powerful methodological skills and interest in normal problems characteristic of "psychology" with psychoanalytic insights derived from close study of the individual patient.

THE ASPECT OF PERCEPTION

The formulation that the "rage pattern" (or patterns) of the interosystems is oriented around perception of danger or frustration and toward motor expression invites investigation of how this orientation takes place. *On the side of perception,* we must call to mind again the extreme lack of specificity in the native equipment of the human infant as regards cognizance of objects in the outer world, and the capacity of the human mind to build up complex signals and symbols on the basis of experience—to develop substitute signals → activity. The process of *learning* discussed throughout this book is applicable here, including the emphasis on its unconscious aspects characteristic of the psychoanalytic schools. In fact it is the *unconscious* (infantile) evaluation of a situation as dangerous or frustrating which makes many reactions of rage, aggression, and hostility so general and so inappropriate to the actual situation as to seem "instinctive." This is because they are rooted in experiences of terror and frustration against which the child cannot be wholly protected, which tend to be repressed and so dissociated from conscious learning.

Since I have so heavily stressed the *external* nature of the stimulus situation, it is important to remark that I consider Freud's analysis of how an external danger may become internalized one of his most brilliant achievements. Partly this is a matter of response to the current external situation on the basis of interpretation via signals learned by the individual. We can easily train a subject to react with fear to an innocent buzzer signal by following it repeatedly with an electric shock. But Freud showed also how the person becomes afraid of *his own* impulses. After the important experiences of the early years, it can happen all too easily that quite natural *inner* feelings of sexual excitement or hate become *themselves* signals for further anxiety → rage. Such reactions may—indeed, typically do—happen outside of clear awareness. In my theoretical concern with the inward rage pattern as a system *which requires a stimulus,* I do not wish to take issue with Freud's profound clinical insight as to the complex relationships between inner and outer stimuli, especially at the unconscious level. Freud's discussion of *anxiety* (after 1926) supplies almost all the subsidiary concepts necessary to my position concerning the "rage" pattern, and I shall come to focused discussion of similarities and differences a little later.

Horney's concept of hostility as not inborn but as a natural reaction against frustration may be mentioned. The child fears retribution for his hostile acts, but then the problem becomes self-perpetuating or increased as the person comes to fear *his own* hostility—a stimulus from within (the vicious circle). This position is an improvement on positions which consider hostility as purely a reaction to exogenous factors (*e.g.,* Adler) and closer to Freud's insight. In critique of Horney's theoretical position, I repeat earlier comments to the effect that Horney merges inborn systems and learned adaptational systems with an insouciance which cannot stand the test of careful inquiry by other disciplines, which unduly limits interpretation of many clinical phenomena. This limitation in clinical understanding is less striking as regards aggression than as regards the sexual drive systems (which she largely ignores), because of the very important role she assigns to hostility. In practice, indeed, it has often seemed to me that Horney's "reactive hostility" becomes a more universal and undifferentiated concept than the Freudian instinctual aggressive drive. Everybody has it, in rather stereotyped relationship to fears of self-assertion ⟷ dependency.

My formulation of the problem seems useful in explaining how "aggression" is normally overcome by realistic learning and by the insights won in therapy. The child kicks at the chair which gets in his way (frustration or danger). The adult moves the chair or goes around it, usually without rage, aggression, or hostility. Easy understanding of the problem and our ability to handle it makes a difficulty emotionally indifferent—vexatious perhaps, or at times pleasurable if it engages just the right amount of internal secretions etc. appropriate to the effort with perhaps a *little* over. The anger of the child is dissipated by his progressive learning. *In so far as his anger was provoked by the chair,* it simply no longer exists once he learns about chairs. In our psychologizing about personality trends, we too often overlook altogether the enormous modifications in rage reactions which take place on the principle of realistic learning and which truly *dissolve* the rage reaction.

I have italicized the clause that profoundly qualifies these remarks. Once the offending "chair" comes to *stand for a significant person* (unconsciously) whom the child is learning to evaluate, or once the *expressive gesture of kicking* is condemned as such by the emerging self, rage reactions cannot be dissolved by a conscious, realistic understanding of the nature of a "chair." The reason is simple: the "chair" is not the significant focus of the child's interpretation, of his actual experience in the complex "field" of the present moment when he kicks the chair. If he is angry at Daddy, the little child easily interprets such aspects of the external situation as part of "Daddy." Parents object to primitive expressions of rage in a manner which is usually very useful in training the child to his culture but which cannot *as such* make much sense to the young human animal.

The "perceptual side" of the rage patterns, therefore, has components far beyond what is usually called perception. "Understanding" for psychoanalysts does not mean objective appreciation of this hypothetical "chair" in relation to the actual ability of the person to move it or walk around it. *Psychoanalytic* understanding, insight, involves a full grasp of the signal or symbol aspects of the disturbing situation as a psychological whole. It is only as the patient becomes aware of the interpretation he unconsciously makes that the old stimulus to rage can be properly evaluated, and often dissipated as effectively as is the case in ordinary realistic learning.

THE MOTOR ASPECT

The problem is further complicated on *the motor side of the rage pattern.* Our evolutionary heritage seems to be functionally oriented around an increase in physical activity *which is inappropriate in most of the situations of danger or frustration encountered by civilized man.* This problem has often been recognized. Indeed a popular cure for recognized anger is working it off by vigorous physical exercise. The great popularity of rough sports for *spectators* is often seen as a means of working off aggression vicariously by identification with the athletes. I think there is some measure of truth in these ideas, but they require cautious examination.

Exercise or excitement about something else often provides a healthy fatigue or distraction which may abate a temporary rage crisis and thus allow *more enduring personality patterns to regain ascendancy.* Sedation may achieve the same end. These techniques are very useful in essentially normal personalities under stress and in some pathological conditions (*cf.* the discussion of what Sullivan calls "ameliorative methods," pp. 504*ff.* This "cooling off" period, however, is not dynamically related to the problem of aggression and is mentioned merely to avoid confusion.

The implication of cure by exercise, especially of "hostile" exercise, such as wood chopping, usually contains the further idea that the physical expression of the anger pattern will relieve the inner tensions produced by *any* rage-provoking situation. It assumes a quantum of energy that has no special aim. The motor component of the rage pattern is merely *released* in a nonspecific manner. This is almost like prescribing arm exercises for the paralytic who needs to exercise his legs. The motor component of the rage pattern is probably almost as undetermined at birth as the perceptual component, but *it is never unrelated to the stimulus*. To suppose such nonspecificity in adult response is to mistake altogether the nature of inborn psychobiological systems and everything we know about how such systems are developed after birth. An *inner* psychological relationship must obtain before any physical expression of rage can have an effect beyond the temporary distraction suggested in the preceding paragraph.

The question arises as to whether *some sort of motor expression* is absolutely necessary to adequate discharge of the inner tensions mobilized by a rage-provoking situation, as might be theoretically expected from the phylogenetic origin of the rage patterns, or whether expression through verbal or physically limited devices will serve. The problem is a complex one both from the physiological and the psychological point of view. I shall not attempt a full answer to a question involving so many unknowns but shall merely discuss some points relevant to an answer.

(1) The increased incidence of hypertension, ulcers, etc. in modern society suggests that constant bodily "preparation for combat" without adequate discharge *may* have secondary consequences throughout the interosystems. These conditions often have a psychogenic basis in that the excessive stimulation of the "preparatory" inner rage pattern derives from psychological situations whose rage-provoking aspects are not consciously recognized or responded to appropriately. The organic changes are genuine and may become irreversible.

(2) The motor component not infrequently takes the form of restlessness or muscular tension shown in fatigue, clumsiness, and at times specific "odd" motor behavior. It is not yet clear why this explicitly "motor" form appears instead of involvement of the interosystems as in (1), although numerous hypotheses are available to the psychoanalyst—among which I may suggest further attention to the course of development in the nonsexual drive systems as discussed earlier, notably motility patterns.

(3) By luck, good judgment, or the nature of his neurotic defense mech-

anisms, the individual may manage to *avoid* rage-provoking situations. If he can steer clear of competition, dominating employers, a difficult family situation, or whatever else he finds disturbing, his life may be limited, but the inner tensions of the rage pattern will not be aroused.

(4) The individual may be so convinced of the efficacy of his method of handling the situations that they no longer require the inner mobilization of the rage pattern. Thus, there is a shift *in perception of the stimulus situation*. This approach was discussed earlier as the *normal* reduction of anger with understanding—moving the chair instead of kicking at it. It is difficult for the layman to understand that an absurd compulsive ritual, which the patient himself considers nonsensical, may serve at the unconscious level to bolster his sense of mastery to the point at which the rage is unnecessary. The neurotic ritual is a "defense," but the defense begins with a distortion of the situation *on the perceptual side* such that the ritual can handle it without the development of the excessive rage-fear pattern. It is known that ritualistic defenses *may* ultimately shift toward somatization (*e.g.*, the ulcer) or toward psychosis if the patient too far exaggerates his distortions on the perceptual-evaluative side.

(5) A Freudian has suggested adding the concept of *neutralization* to this list. I do not altogether like the term because it derives semantically from the Freudian concept of "psychic energies," which I have not so much denied as tried to reinterpret through the view of systems. Like the other "energic" terms of the libido theory, however, it has the merit of important generalization. My listing tends to separate the perceptual and motor aspects of the rage pattern too radically. For most of us, most of the time, it is a complex sensory-motor patterning that develops autonomy as such. The pattern is flexible as regards both aspects and is flexibly integrated—as when a good driver perceives the minor hazards of the road and adjusts his motor response to them with second-by-second exactitude. Our lives are fraught with such systems from the relatively simple act of driving a car to the routine behavior of a business executive or a physicist "on the job."

It seems likely that systems of this easy flexibility develop under conditions of relatively mild "drive" involvement and plentiful opportunity for learning. If we are supported by the similar interests of our fellows and by a general sense of confidence in ourselves, our inherent capacity for flexible learning leads to expansion. A strong *interest*, oriented but not determined by our drive systems, develops ramifications which are essentially integrated, step by step, as regards perceptual and motor aspects. It is this step-by-step, bit-by-bit kind of integration which, I think, can be called "neutralization."

(6) I have not reported Rado's views in this book, but his generalized

term "emergency behavior" seems especially apt in this construction. *In emergencies,* behavior is typically either drive-connected or dominated by intense emotion. The infant, child, or adolescent who has been too severely threatened cannot "learn" in neutrality. He interprets every external stimulus as a threat, as an emergency. Such persons sometimes cannot learn at all because every experience is construed as demanding an immediate response without the delay and relative neutrality necessary for the development of more elaborated systems. These persons are the pseudo feebleminded, who often show brilliant advances in I.Q. under psychotherapy or appropriate change of milieu. More commonly in neurosis a general development takes place with special areas interpreted as "emergency." Or the person may feel that *in some area* he is really master of the problem and is thus enabled to learn with maximal efficiency by a kind of personally induced *neutralization* in this sphere. He may then be able to use this *area* of competent learning as a sort of tool in his general adjustment. The valued specialist in any field is not always a person we admire *as a person.* The tool of his competence may, indeed, become a weapon. Its sharpness may become so narrow as to provide only a cutting edge in situations which require a gentle buffing.

In my opinion the terms "neutralization" and "emergency behavior" represent very important generalizations. They offer, I think, a valid correction to the acknowledged artificiality of my own emphasis on the perceptual and motor aspects of systems which are essentially adaptational and which necessarily include both aspects.

The view of systems recommends, however, a very careful consideration of the aspects of a situation which are determining for the situation under consideration. To use Hartmann's terminology, many systems show an important autonomy as such, whether primary or secondary. Secondary systems developed under conditions favoring "neutralization" may be used as systems in "emergency"—to use Rado's term.

Before concluding this discussion, I recapitulate my position. I have not attempted an inclusive listing of the ways in which the "rage pattern" may be interpreted. Instead I have suggested some interpretations of rather typical psychological constellations as involving one or the other aspect of the pattern: the perceptual or the motor aspect. I accept the concepts of "neutralization" and "emergency behavior" as important principles, even as correctives to any implication that perceptual and motor aspects of behavior should be isolated as such in a routine manner. Hartmann and Rado slice the pie differently when they consider the important subdivisions of psychological science. I think, however, that the principle of neutralization *and* the principle of emergency behavior may both contribute toward understanding of the development and dynamic role of significant subsystems within the functioning personality.

AGGRESSION AND ANXIETY

Had I called the inner pattern discussed in the foregoing pages "anxiety," much of what I have been writing would be acceptable to most contemporary schools, especially to the Freudians. I remind the reader of Freud's effort to derive the prototype of anxiety from the experience of the infant during birth. So far so good. *I suggest that the infant shows this syndrome at birth because it is part of a broad evolutionary patterning which appears spontaneously under a variety of threatening conditions.* Where the "combat" aspect of the pattern is predominant, we may fairly call it "rage"—and "aggression" if we wish to emphasize its motor phase and the self-confident feeling of the organism *vis-à-vis* its enemies. The type of behavior resulting looks aggressive and often has a kind of spontaneous cruelty beyond justifiable defensive reaction.

These are relatively uncontrolled "combat" situations. The relation to "fear" is clear. It is a rare bully who is not a coward underneath. The rage-combat aspects of the pattern may be built up secondarily in their own right and become predominant in most situations, but they are very closely related to the fear-withdrawal patterns. These patterns have a good deal of similarity both in the underlying biological structure and in the kind of external situation which provokes them. We all know how easily fear turns into rage and vice versa—in fact, how often it is difficult to determine whether the person is angry or frightened. This statement holds whether we speak of the physical manifestations of changes in the interosystems or of the psychological manifestations. The psychoanalyst frequently believes that the patient is essentially afraid when he feels angry, or that he masks his aggression under the feeling of fear.*

* I return to the problem of aggression as reported by the ethologists. The wolf has very striking patterns of aggression. This species also has patterns of submission and patterns which may be called chivalry toward the vanquished. The wolf worsted in combat may stop the battle by formally presenting his throat undefended to the victor—and the victor does not take advantage of this "give-up" signal to finish off his enemy. On the contrary, the instinctive pattern in many of the "aggressive" species of animal seems as firmly set toward submission and respect for submission as toward aggression.

In contrast, Lorenz cites the example of a female dove who quietly pecks to death a mate who does not appeal to her. The birds were in a cage. Lorenz makes the point that under normal conditions the unaccepted mate flies away. The species has developed no pattern for the inhibition of aggression by a "give-up" signal. The gentle deer may become dangerous if its "enemy" (for example, an unwary tourist) stands his ground or falls, whereas it would not pursue an enemy in flight. For these species "flight" is the accepted signal of submission.

In summary of the discussion of aggression, it seems to me a mistake to lump all of the phenomena commonly called aggression (mainly by Freudians) under the single heading of a single instinctual drive. Many of these phenomena result from the operation of what I have called the nonsexual drive systems, with special emphasis on motility. "Aggression" in any hostile sense of the term is here a matter of social interpretation of essentially neutral behavior, or a reactive hostility to situations created by the essentially neutral behavior, or a by-product of the effort to establish an effective idea of the self. Doubtless more "or's" could be added.

I further suggested an aspect of "aggression" which goes beyond the systems thus far discussed. I suggested that man inherits patterns of response to situations of danger or frustration which may conveniently be called rage.[11] The nature of these patterns as regards the interosystems must be left essentially to physiological research, although intimate collaboration with experts in psychological science is indispensable. In order to be brought into action, these patterns require an external situation interpreted as dangerous or frustrating, but once aroused they tend to operate like drive systems with their own inner tensions. Although "rage" is not spontaneously generated, as are the tensions of the sexual systems, hunger, motility, etc., experiences of danger and frustration are so universal in infancy that it becomes almost a theoretical quibble to deny the drive quality of aggression.

Stress was laid on the very great modifiability of the *perception* of danger or frustration in the human species and on the development of *unconscious* signals → symbols. The subjective feeling of "rage" may itself become a danger signal (instinctual conflict; the vicious circle). The *expression* of "rage" is also highly modifiable. It seems likely that the evolutionary function of the patterned responses of the interosystems was to prepare the animal for physical combat. The import of this circumstance for societies in which gross motor expression is usually inappropriate was discussed at some length—inconclusively. I did, however, try to suggest how some types of pathology might be understood as the consequence of inhibition or distorted expression of the motor component, and others as means of avoiding or "mastering" rage-provoking situations.

Finally I remarked that most of my discussion of the rage pattern is familiar to psychoanalytic theory under the heading of *anxiety*, and I pointed

---

The moral is that aggression, submission, and chivalry are *all* adaptational patterns built into the biological heritage of the species. Their form varies widely, and I surely overgeneralize in presenting only these three aspects of the adaptational problem. I have wondered, however, whether the herring gull or the stickleback who starts building a nest in a fight-flight conflict is not presenting a species type of "submission" pattern, like the wolf who presents his throat, rather than giving vent to aggressive energies through displacement.

to the very close relationship between fear and rage in clinical observation. Instead of positing a quite vague concept of anxiety and an independently instinctual aggressive drive, I think it is preferable to assume *inborn reaction patterns to stress* at the very deep level of integrated mobilization of the intero- systems. Even at the physiological level the patterns of rage and fear seem to be partly overlapping, partly antagonistic—but so closely related that the fleeing animal *at bay* suddenly becomes a powerful fighter. At the psychological level the problem becomes infinitely more complex, partly because the signals arousing interosystem patterns are learned in an intricate manner, partly because stable integrating systems are developed in the course of living which very profoundly influence modes of perception and response.

PSYCHOSOCIAL INTEGRATION

THIS BOOK has been focused on psychological science as formulated by psy- choanalysts. All the analysts recognize that the individual lives in a society, and all have interested themselves to some extent in the nature of society. But their primary concern, and mine, has been with the individual, not the society. In my opinion, some psychoanalysts have tended to interpret social trends too exclusively and, above all, too *directly* in terms of the psychobio- logical drives of the individual. Others have talked a great deal about "culture" and its influence on the individual, but their evaluation of the independent structure of "cultures" remains surprisingly limited. These analysts often understand variations in our own culture well as their patients are affected, and offer alluring generalizations about social determinants—but without rigorous inquiry on this point. On the contrary they propose as fundamental psychological trends types of social adaptation and maladaptation which are, I suspect, characteristic for *our* culture only.

It is impossible for me to offer here any detailed discussion of organized social rubrics. I have, however, frequently permitted myself small speculations as to the role of this or that *social* pattern in the development of phenomena usually considered as *psychological*. The speculations must often be only half-right. Their purpose has been to present vividly the kind of integrated approach to the basic problems of *man* which seems to me essential. Speculations of this order can be checked empirically. The effort to check sharpens the problem, poses more valid questions. Initial results lead to better research methods, more clearly focused—to an accumulation of information and technique which will perhaps allow an effective genius to discern and implement a new direction. I feel that I and the colleagues whose point of view in this area I most approve are still John the Baptists—harbingers of new insights more direct and integrated than our own heated espousals of special methods and ideas.

My prophecy is that a new direction will come in the area of psychosocial integration. At present we have a good deal of information about societies as as units and about social trends as rather generally operative. We have outgrown the idea of society as an organism analogous to the human body. But a social group must have a certain inherent cohesiveness if it is to continue as a group—what Kardiner calls social homeostasis. I hope that we may outgrow the idea of "universal" social trends or cycles, such as Spengler's concept of the decline of Western civilization or Toynbee's ebb and flow, or a *crude* dialectical materialism. The structure of each society must be studied in its own right *and* in its relations to other social groups. Nevertheless, sociological generalizations of wide import can be made which take our thinking far beyond the apparent necessities of the local scene. These generalizations are necessary. They are the general province of the social sciences. They become dangerous only when they too far neglect the individuals who make up the social group, or when they make unwarranted assumptions about their needs and probable behavior.

For us psychologists, it is extremely important to recognize the relative autonomy of the social groups and social trends *within which the individual functions.* Such recognition is essential to the development of a psychological science genuinely useful to social science. Until very recently our science has complained (often with justification) that the sociologists use implicitly a psychology that is ridiculously oversimplified. But our efforts have been toward supplying a set of universal *psychological* laws, which the sociologist could then apply to his special problems. There has been a tendency among us to consider the psychological laws basic, the group as a transient phenomenon which merely illustrates the basically human. *We have often used a naively oversimplified sociology,* about as valid as the oversimplified psychology of classical economics.

My most earnest hope is that the psychological science I have tried to suggest in this Epilogue provides a way of looking at the fundamental problem more fruitful than the determined effort to find psychological universals. In the view of systems, such "universals" may be found in the biological structure of the human species—*but* these structures operate from the start through "signals" (signs → symbols), flexibly learned, and learned mainly through other people. One cannot neglect the biological focus of deeply personal systems. Neither can one neglect the way in which "signals" are formed in relationship to these deep systems *and* the social meanings they acquire simultaneously. Ideally the highly personal "signals" developed by the infant and young child would be gradually modified through wider experience in close integration with the social meanings (words and values, signs and symbols) he is learning. The primitive, relatively global reaction systems of the infant would *gradually become more differentiated* in respect to the external (mainly social) situation and to one another—*i.e.*, the burned child would not fear *all* fires; absorption in one activity of prepotent biological concern would not exclude or drastically subordinate all other concerns.

This ideal is, of course, never realized. Some bodily systems remain more global than others; the personal "signal" is less well integrated with social meanings. Probably sex and aggression are examples of systems that are *intrinsically* rather global. Certainly they are the systems in which fully differentiated learning is most hampered by "society"—in which there is most discrepancy between the child's actual experience and the social formulations he is taught. But the problem is not essentially the opposition of instinctual drives to "society." The truly dynamic problem is how quite special social structures (systems) affect the process of differentiated learning in the various relatively independent body systems and their relationship to one another. Granted a necessary minimum, it is not so much the *expression* of primitive sex and aggression that matters as whether and how these body systems are brought under the control of an emergent self in a flexibly integrated way, in some inwardly felt harmony with the wider requirements of the social group. The fundamentals of this learning process are laid in the family—that is, with the first people the child knows—by their personal relationship to him.

But here we come back to the social group. (1) The parents are part of it and transmit its basic systems to the child. (2) The child must be fitted to live in this group—not in absolute harmony but well enough to participate in maintaining and constructively changing its systems. (3) The group systems have an independent autonomy which impose more or less drastic reality conditions upon the individual. Although every individual reacts creatively to his life situation, group trends cannot be changed at his whim or even at his very reasonable wish. They must be understood in their own right as historically determined, as supplying the necessary organization for coping with the necessities of living (*e.g.,* food and shelter, basic "psychological" satisfactions), and finally as subject to *conscious control* by our individual efforts as we learn more about the dynamic structure of the powerful group systematizations mankind produces.

SUMMARY

I HAVE TRIED to present a view of systems as a sort of philosophical solvent for the varying schools of thought reported in this book. This view has no content peculiar to itself, no universal principles in competition with those presented by the schools or electing among them. I have urged, rather, that we renounce the concept of "universal laws," generally operative, and devote our attention instead to the intrinsic dynamics of different types of system and their different modes of interaction.

In psychology some of these systems are so deeply rooted in the structure of the human body as to be quasi-universal for all human beings. If a person inhales, we may be entirely certain that he will exhale, provided he stays alive. The fact that plants "breathe" differently from human beings may modify quite interesting theoretical over-generalizations about the intrinsic rhythms of the external universe—but it does not in the least modify the fact that *a man* is so structured that this essential function of *his* respiratory system is "universal" *for him* in no uncertain terms.

The example is, of course, extreme. Most biological structures of interest to psychology are not so immediately necessitous, but they do operate systematically in their own right. They give an *orientation* (Kardiner calls it polarization) to the experience of the person, especially to the infant learning about the world he is born into. This orientation is of very great importance. Generalizations may be made about it fruitfully beyond the special modifications these systems undergo in consequence of the special complex experience of the person.

The nature of these biological structures is the consequence of an evolutionary process covering millions of years, not the paltry span of socialized man. I objected to any telic version of the evolutionary process, but I referred to the present view of experts in the field that evolutionary changes must be *broadly* adaptational if they are to survive.

Survival for any living organism requires by definition the maintenance of its organization as an individual. This simple fact has needed re-emphasis after the efforts of much science and philosophy to discover the abstract universal laws or "forces" which cross-cut the individual instance. The concept of the "total personality," in this book represented by the non-libido or psychoanalytic "self" theories, is valuable in making explicit the recognition of a factor *implicit* in Freud's approach which he neglected in his theorizing. The libido theory plus the defense mechanisms of the ego do not adequately *focus attention* on the person-as-a-whole. This seems to me clearly a defect in the "classical" Freudian theoretical scheme, no matter how astute the practicing analyst, no matter how fully contemporary ego psychologists substantiate their position with quotations from the master.*

I have suggested the term "organismic self" for this basic organization of the living unit, and I have remarked on the probability of much broader integrational subsystems inherent in our bodily structure than are currently known. But many of the self psychologies appear to equate this necessary "organismic self" and its inborn integrational systems with a psychological self to an extent which seems to me unjustifiable. Human behavior, especially in our highly *self*-conscious culture, tends very strongly to be purposive and integrative, for reasons we are beginning to understand. This observational fact, however, does not justify a telic version of the "total personality" any more than a selective observation of progressive advance in flexible mastery of the environment from the ameba to man justifies the concept of entelechy, of an intrinsic purposiveness in the evolutionary process. Although Adler, Horney, Fromm, and Rank have called attention to very important psychological trends and to methods of handling them in treatment, their theoretical premises, to my way of thinking, confuse psychological developments of the individual-functioning-in-a-culture with inborn, biologically determined trends. They are perhaps even more "reductionist" than the libido theorists in taking limited clinical observations as universal principles.

* Belatedly for this book, I can now refer to the special "scientific" influences impinging on the young Freud—*i.e.*, Freud up to the age of 35 to 40, when he began his radical personal contribution. In 1890 *"Naturphilosophie,"* which might have led to greater theoretical appreciation of the individual—as in the case of Rank—was for Freud almost the opposite of the Science in which he participated for at least 15 years. Although his findings were new and essentially "intuitive," Freud never got over the need to relate them to Science—concretely to the scientific ideas he had considered the very essence of Science during the formative years of his creative work. The reader may now trace these ideas in detail as formulated by Helmholtz, as operating in Bruecke's laboratory of physiology, where Freud worked for the longest and happiest years of his "apprenticeship." The reference is to Jones' biography of Freud. My vague references to "nineteenth-century philosophy of science" here come alive in rich detail. (E. Jones, *The Life and Work of Sigmund Freud,* Vol. I, Basic Books, 1954.)

Jung and Sullivan and Freud's ego psychology represent a more cautious approach. The integrating "self" is a complex development, not a given. Its vicissitudes are dependent on a *variety* of factors, biological and social, rather than on individuation versus belonging, separation and union, the will to power, the real self. In a general way Sullivan's concept of the self dynamism seems to me the most satisfactory statement of an emergent, actively integrating systematization. No one will deny the importance of interpersonal relations in the development of the self; yet I think that Sullivan has emphasized them too exclusively, with insufficient attention to important subdynamisms (systems) which his basic theory *could* assimilate. I refer in part to the dynamisms primarily constellated around the biological structures of the organism. For convenience they may be labeled as Freud's instinctual drives and component instincts, although I postpone discussion to later pages, where I modify the drive concept beyond the point at which it can strictly be called Freudian. In part I refer to the various classifications of "ego-development" observed by other schools. (I choose the *Freudian* term *ego* as the most generally useful and perhaps the most neutral in discussion of the self psychologies.) The self dynamism developed out of interpersonal experience has subsystems of its own, differently constituted, differently related to one another, to the "total personality," and to the culture within which it develops.

I urged that Freud's concept of the superego be retained but limited to Freud's own description of it as the inheritor of the Oedipus complex, rather than extended as in the theories of Klein and Roheim. I suggested *adding* the concept of a self image (or images) more generally interpersonal, even "social," in origin. This concept is similar to Jung's *persona*. Preparation of the self image begins at birth or before and is doubtless deeply influenced by the events of the first two years of life as the infant first learns to discriminate between himself and the outside world. Dating essentially fluid concepts is a thankless business, but probably it is toward the end of the second year of life that the infant normally begins to establish his notion of "self" as an active, integrational system. At any rate, the sense of self begins at the pregenital level and cannot be considered as merely an adjunct or precursor of the superego. On the contrary, to come into being at all, *Freud's* superego requires a sophisticated sense of self and the self of others.

I have speculated that a close relationship between the superego and the ego-ideal was fairly characteristic of Freud's Vienna. In a relatively stable, relatively caste-bound society, there would be little distinction between the ego-ideal derived from the superego and the ego-image derived from the sense of self *vis-à-vis* "society." The content of the narcissistic component would be similar. It seems probable that in societies with high social mobility and great emphasis on individual enterprise, the self image might easily develop more coherence in its own right, different from the superego, and in uneasy relationship to it. Horney's concept of the idealized image of the self seems to me an excellent clinical observation for many people in our culture, although one may wish that she did not use it for a theoretical reductionism which neglects other dynamic subsystems. Feudal and primitive societies, subgroups* of our own society, or even specific families doubtless encourage the development of other versions of the self image.

My own comments on the self image(s) are necessarily scanty and speculative. I have indulged myself in mentioning a number of observations about people and societies in the hope of provoking thought about a dimension of the human psyche so obvious that it has often been either neglected or overgeneralized.

The next topic of discussion was *instinctual drives—i.e.*, the dynamic systems focused around inborn biological structures. I have accepted practically the whole of Freudian theory on this point as *descriptively* correct in its essentials and again remarked that the self psychologies largely ignore systems of demonstrated constellating power. Concretely, I refer to the constellating power of the erogenous zones, to their summary as libido, and to "aggression."

I have suggested, however, that these biological drives be considered as a type of bodily system rather than as forces essentially different in kind from other systems. It seemed convenient to label as *interosystems* those which function primarily (not exclusively, of course) within the body; whose connections with the outside world are indirect; which are mainly unconscious. I refer to the cardiovascular system, the gastrointestinal system, etc., in whatever complication physiologists may discover. At the other extreme are the *exterosystems*, highly organized in themselves but essentially requiring an external stimulus to be brought into function; for example, the visual and auditory systems.

Between these extremes lie the drive systems, whose function is essentially intermediary. They are internal in that tensions arise within the organism which demand relief via the outside world. The distinguishing feature of the human species is that the external object is very dimly prefigured, if at all, but these systems are premised on an object. They are intrinsically goal-directed in that the inner tension cannot be relieved without the external component. Yet the human infant does not know his goals (his "objects") as well as the young of other species. He learns them from his parents and other people in all the complexity of human society. Although he is usually

* It should be kept in mind that scientists and "cultured" people generally represent a kind of subgroup, however inclusive of many national, economic, and social groups.

born fairly well equipped with exterosystems, he has to learn how to use them. They come into function largely as his maturing drive systems develop, and in relationship to them.*

In my opinion, the body-mind problems of philosophy and the organic-psychogenic dichotomies of modern psychological science and medicine simply dissolve as *theoretical* issues if one considers the "drives" as a special kind of biological system, structurally related to other bodily systems in a manner we can at least imagine nowadays in its general outlines. The problem becomes one of empirical investigation. Lines of systematization, both inborn and learned, will be discovered more accurately as physiological, psychological, and social research progresses in closer relationship. At the present time one may point with some security to *aspects* of sexuality (Freud's definition), hunger, and motility as having this quality of inner tension rather directly related to the outside world. Present definitions will surely be revised with further knowledge of physiological systematizations and of the ways in which they are developed through experience, including the conditions imposed by the broad systematizations of his culture which no individual can avoid.

A long section was devoted to the problem of *aggression*, considered by Freudians as a unitary instinctual drive. The non-libido schools object to this formulation very strongly. I suggested that many phenomena currently called aggressive in children and in societies are in fact neutral expressions of the systems we have been discussing. The "aggression" is often a social valuation, not a biological one, although the individual easily develops a true psychological aggression in reaction to social condemnation of his behavior. He interprets the condemnation as frustrating or frightening, and his activity does not remain neutral. The negativism of the toddler was discussed as *partly* a problem in the development of the sense of self; learning the boundaries of the ego;

---

* Two qualifications are important. (1) The exterosystems must have developed in relation to the drive systems as part of the long-term adaptational process of animal evolution. They are largely autonomous in their present structure, but it is *probable* that there are more direct physiological connections between some aspects of the exterosystems and the drive systems than are currently recognized. Psychological-philosophical emphasis on the role of signal → symbol formation in our reactions to external stimuli has corrected many early misconceptions about such connections. I have come to suspect, however, that an emphasis which I have shared throughout this book may ultimately appear unduly limited. Very probably there are *some* inborn connections the nature of which is not fully understood by any of our current scientific disciplines. I repeat my statement that the orders of systematization here offered (intero-extero-drive systems) are *convenient labels*. They are not intended as theoretical ultimates. (2) Individual endowment, including variations in the exterosystems, must play a role in the type of stimulus the infant reacts to and most easily incorporates into the emergent systematization of his "drives." This is an area still unexplored by psychoanalysts, although it has been of interest to "psychologists." I think it will soon come into prominence as "psychologists" learn a better appreciation of the "psychoanalytic" concern with drive systems—and as analysts learn a better appreciation of the significance of the exterosystems and nonsexual drive systems in psychodynamics.

learning how to say no to one's own impulses and to "others" because of the *self* rather than the special drive system prepotent at the moment.

I do not think, however, that this analysis fully covers the phenomena of "aggression." Like Rado, I would accept Cannon's view of an inborn pattern of *rage*—a complex pattern or series of patterns involving widespread changes in the interosystems which seem functionally designed to prepare the organism for fight or flight. This was essentially Darwin's idea about the expression of emotions. Darwin's specific descriptions of emotional states and their functional origin in the living conditions of primitive man require correction and elaboration after nearly a hundred years of research. (Attention was called in the footnote on page 626 to the contributions of *ethology* to this problem.)

Nevertheless, it does seem probable that no significant evolutionary change in the biological structure of the human species has occurred within historical times. In historical times the adaptive process has been mainly *cultural,* and we must firmly recognize that the biological equipment we inherit was functionally designed for a very different way of life. The rage pattern admirably prepares the organism for physical combat. It is very close to the fear pattern, and to the disintegration characteristic of panic. Psychologically and sociologically oriented schools, once beyond an initial burst of enthusiasm which led to a Darwinian reductionism rather worse than anything I have described in this book, have tended to resist this way of thinking as outmoded teleology. I think, however, that many of the phenomena of aggression are best understood if they are seen as part of evolutionary patterns which were once broadly adaptational. The patterns involve the interosystems and powerful motor components. In many ways they function like the drive systems—*i.e.*, inner tensions develop which are rather directly related to the outside world and which demand relief. The essential difference is that the tensions do not develop *spontaneously* as in sexuality and hunger but require a stimulus interpreted as frustration or danger. Strictly speaking, therefore, aggression cannot be called an instinctual drive by my definition of drive systems.

In conclusion I restated a psychosocial orientation which has run through this book. Man is a socializable animal by his birthright of helplessness and his capacity for learning. He becomes socialized as his biological needs develop within a social framework. I have tried to emphasize throughout the to-and-fro relationship between the individual and his society from the close, empathic relation of the infant to his nurse to the role of the adult in varieties of societal organizations. Psychoanalytic theory has mainly concerned itself with the individual. Even within this sphere of interest, however, I have been bold enough to predict that significant reformulations will appear in the area of psychosocial integration.

[1] H. Selye, *The Physiology and Pathology of Exposure to Stress*, Acta, Inc., Montreal, Canada, 1950.

[2] I. P. Glauber, "Dynamic Therapy for the Stutterer," in G. Bychowski and J. L. Despert (eds.), *Specialized Techniques in Psychotherapy*, Basic Books, 1952, pp. 216*ff*.

[3] G. Murphy, *Personality: A Biosocial Approach to Origins and Structure*, Harper & Bros., 1947; T. M. Newcomb, *Social Psychology*, The Dryden Press, 1950; E. L. Hartley and R. E. Hartley, *Fundamentals of Social Psychology*, Alfred A. Knopf, 1952.

[4] S. Freud, *An Outline of Psychoanalysis*, W. W. Norton & Co., 1949, p. 24.

[5] H. Selye, *op. cit.*

[6] K. Lorenz, *King Solomon's Ring*, Crowell, 1952.

[7] I. Hendrick, "Instinct and the Ego During Infancy," *Psychoanalytic Quarterly*, 1942, 11: 33-58.

[8] W. B. Cannon, *Bodily Changes in Pain, Hunger, Fear and Rage*, Appleton-Century, 2nd ed., 1936.

[9] S. Rado, "Emergency Behavior, with an Introduction to the Dynamics of Conscience," in P. H. Hoch and J. Zubin (eds.), *Anxiety*, Grune & Stratton, 1950, pp. 150-175.

[10] C. Darwin, *Expression of the Emotions*, 1872.

[11] W. B. Cannon, *op. cit.*

BIBLIOGRAPHY

BIBLIOGRAPHY

THE PURPOSE OF this book has been the sympathetic presentation and discussion of ideas rather than documentary research or such systematic collation of references on a specific topic as might provide a basic bibliography for further reading. Acknowledgments of direct quotations and fairly close paraphrases appear in the notes at the end of each chapter and are referred to by superior numbers. Often the reference is not to a page but to a book or to a series of articles to which I am indebted for more than a limited direct quotation. When the reference to an author is closely related to the text, full bibliographical data are given on the page in a footnote.

Bibliographic material for authors discussed in the text may be located by reference to the index, where the pages carrying references are listed separately under each author.

A special problem in bibliography arises for most of the major authors discussed. Most of them wrote in German, and their works appear in a variety of translations. I have supplied the date of the first German publication in the text whenever it seemed important, but my page references relate to whatever edition I had available. Thus in references to Freud's *Interpretation of Dreams* I have used the pagination of the Modern Library text of his *Basic Writings—* a text which I have rarely had to correct for special omissions or distortions and which I found convenient because several important books appear in a single volume, easily carried about. In fact, I have used a popular edition whenever I could in preference to a more scholarly text not easily available to the reader.

Readers wishing to build up their own libraries will probably prefer recent editions, when available, to those I have used. Recent editions are usually more accurate and easier to read, and many are helpfully annotated. Above all, they are easier to buy at the present time.

The following bibliography of the major works of the authors discussed has been compiled from standard bibliographical sources; thus the editions listed may not always be identical with those cited in the notes. I have included listings of the major journals and yearbooks concerned with the publication of psychoanalytic materials relating to the various schools. In addition there should be mentioned the eclectic journal *Psychoanalytic Review*.

SIGMUND FREUD

WRITINGS

Collected Papers. Translated by Joan Riviere and Alix and James Strachey. Hogarth Press. Vol. I, 1924; Vol. II, 1924; Vol. III, 1925; Vol. IV, 1925; Vol. V, 1950.

The Standard Edition of the Complete Psychological Works of Sigmund Freud. Translated and edited by James Strachey. Hogarth Press.
This is a new edition, currently being issued, of all the published works of Freud, including articles as well as books. Several volumes have already been published. Editions of those of Freud's books which have not yet appeared in this edition are listed below.

The Basic Writings of Sigmund Freud. Translated and edited by A. A. Brill. Modern Library, 1938.

Beyond the Pleasure Principle. Translated by C. J. M. Hubback. Boni & Liveright, n.d.

Civilization and Its Discontents. Translated by Joan Riviere. Hogarth Press, 1930.

The Ego and the Id. Translated by Joan Riviere. Hogarth Press, 1927.

A General Introduction to Psycho-Analysis. Translated and edited by Joan Riviere. Liveright Publishing Corp., 1935.

Group Psychology and the Analysis of the Ego. Translated by James Strachey. Boni & Liveright, n.d.

Moses and Monotheism. Translated by Katherine Jones. Alfred A. Knopf, 1939.

New Introductory Lectures on Psycho-Analysis. W. W. Norton & Co., 1933.

The Origins of Psychoanalysis: Letters to Wilhelm Fliess, Drafts and Notes: 1887–1902. Translated by Eric Mosbacher and James Strachey. Basic Books, 1954.

An Outline of Psychoanalysis. Translated by James Strachey. W. W. Norton & Co., 1949.

The Problem of Anxiety. Translated by Henry Alden Bunker. W. W. Norton & Co., 1936.

JOURNALS

Imago (official organ of the Internationalen Psychoanalytischen Vereinigung).

International Journal of Psycho-Analysis (official organ of the International Psycho-Analytical Association). Formerly Internationale Zeitschrift für Psychoanalyse.

Journal of the American Psychoanalytic Association (official organ of the American Psychoanalytic Association).

Psychoanalytic Quarterly.

ANNUALS

Annual Survey of Psychoanalysis. International Universities Press.

Psychoanalysis and the Social Sciences. International Universities Press.

Psychoanalytic Study of the Child. International Universities Press.

Yearbook of Psychoanalysis. International Universities Press.

ALFRED ADLER

WRITINGS

The Case of Miss R. Translated by Eleanore and Friedrich Jensen. Greenberg, 1929.

The Case of Mrs. A. C. W. Daniel, 1931.

The Education of Children. Translated by Eleanore and Friedrich Jensen. Greenberg, 1930.

Guiding the Child on the Principles of Individual Psychology. Translated by Benjamin Ginzburg. Greenberg, 1930.

The Neurotic Constitution. Translated by Bernard Glueck and John Lind. Moffat, Yard & Co., 1917.

The Pattern of Life. Translated by W. Beran Wolfe. Cosmopolitan Book Co., 1931.

The Practice and Theory of Individual Psychology. Translated by P. Radin. Humanities Press, 1951.

The Problems of Neurosis. Edited by F. G. Crookshank. Cosmopolitan Book Co., 1939.

The Science of Living. Greenberg, 1929.

Social Interest. Translated by John Linton and Richard Vaughan. G. P. Putnam's Sons, 1939.

Understanding Human Nature. Translated by W. Beran Wolfe. Greenberg, 1946.

What Life Should Mean to You. Edited by Alan Porter. Blue Ribbon Books, 1937.

JOURNALS

American Journal of Individual Psychology.
International Journal of Individual Psychology.

KAREN HORNEY

WRITINGS

Neurosis and Human Growth. W. W. Norton & Co., 1950.

The Neurotic Personality of Our Time. W. W. Norton & Co., 1937.

New Ways in Psychoanalysis. W. W. Norton & Co., 1939.

Our Inner Conflicts. W. W. Norton & Co., 1945.

Self Analysis. W. W. Norton & Co., 1942.

JOURNAL

American Journal of Psychoanalysis (official organ of the Association for the Advancement of Psychoanalysis).

ERICH FROMM

WRITINGS

Escape from Freedom. Farrar & Rinehart, 1941.

The Forgotten Language. Rinehart & Co., 1951.

Man for Himself. Rinehart & Co., 1947.

Psychoanalysis and Religion. Yale University Press, 1950.

Sane Society. Rinehart & Co., in press.

HARRY STACK SULLIVAN

WRITINGS

Conceptions of Modern Psychiatry. William Alanson White Foundation, 1947.

The Interpersonal Theory of Psychiatry. W. W. Norton & Co., 1953.

The Psychiatric Interview. Edited by Helen Swick Perry and Mary Ladd Gawel. W. W. Norton & Co., 1954.

Readers interested in Sullivan's published articles are referred to the bibliography given on pages 231-238 of Patrick Mullahy (ed.), *The Contributions of Harry Stack Sullivan* (Hermitage House, 1952).

JOURNAL

Psychiatry (official organ of the William Alanson White Psychiatric Foundation).

CARL G. JUNG

WRITINGS

Collected Works. Edited by Herbert Read, Michael Fordham, and Gerhard Adler. Bollingen Series, Pantheon Books.

This is a new edition, currently being issued, of all the published works of Jung, including articles as well as books. Several volumes have already been published. Those of his books which have not yet appeared in this edition are listed below.

Answer to Job. Translated by R. F. C. Hull. Routledge & Kegan Paul, 1954.

Collected Papers on Analytical Psychology. Translated by Constance E. Long. Moffat, Yard & Co., 1917.

Contributions to Analytical Psychology. Translated by H. G. and Cary F. Baynes. Kegan Paul, Trench, Trubner, 1928.

Essays on Contemporary Events. Translated by Elizabeth Welsh, Barbara Hannah, and Mary Brian. Kegan Paul, 1947.

Essays on a Science of Mythology (with C. Kerenyi). Translated by R. F. C. Hull. Pantheon Books, 1949.

The Integration of the Personality. Translated by Stanley M. Dell. Farrar & Rinehart, 1939.

Modern Man in Search of a Soul. Translated by W. S. Dell and Cary F. Baynes. Harcourt, Brace & Co., 1950.

On the Psychology of Eastern Meditation. Translated by Carol Baumann. Analytical Psychology Club, 1949.

On the Psychology of the Spirit. Translated by Hildegard Nagel. Analytical Psychology Club, 1948.

Psychological Reflections. Selected and edited by Jolande Jacobi. Pantheon Books, 1953.

Psychological Types. Translated by H. Godwin Baynes. Harcourt, Brace & Co., 1923.

Psychology and Religion. Yale University Press, 1946.

The Psychology of Dementia Praecox. Translated by Abraham Brill. Nervous & Mental Disease Publishing Co., 1936.

The Psychology of the Unconscious. Translated by Beatrice M. Hinkle. Moffat, Yard & Co., 1916.

Studies in Word Association. Translated by M. D. Eder. W. Heinemann, 1918.

The Theory of Psychoanalysis. Journal. of Nervous & Mental Disease Publishing Co., 1915.

JOURNALS

Guild Lectures (official organ of the Guild of Pastoral Psychology, London).

Spring (official organ of the Analytical Psychology Club of New York).

OTTO RANK

WRITINGS

Art and Artist. Translated by Charles Francis Atkinson. Alfred A. Knopf, 1932.

Beyond Psychology. Haddon Craftsmen, 1941.

Modern Education. Translated by Mabel E. Moxon. Alfred A. Knopf, 1932.

The Myth of the Birth of the Hero. Translated by F. Robbins and Smith E. Jollife. Robert Brunner, 1952.

Psychology and the Soul. Translated by William D. Turner. University of Pennsylvania Press, 1950.

The Significance of Psychoanalysis for the Mental Sciences (with Hanns Sachs). Translated by Charles R. Payne. Nervous & Mental Disease Publishing Co., 1916.

The Trauma of Birth. Robert Brunner, 1952.

Truth and Reality. Translated by Julia Taft. Alfred A. Knopf, 1929.

Will Therapy. Translated by Julia Taft. Alfred A. Knopf, 1945.

INDEX

INDEX